DEFENDING GLOBALIZATION

Facts and
Myths about
the Global
Economy *and*
Its Fundamental
Humanity

DEFENDING GLOBALIZATION

Edited by Scott Lincicome and Clark Packard

Paperback ISBN: 978-1-964524-67-2
Digital ISBN: 978-1-964524-72-6

Cover design by Jon Meyers.

Printed in the United States of America.

1000 Massachusetts Ave. NW
Washington, DC 20001

www.cato.org

Contents

Introduction

Scott Lincicome

The pandemic, war in Ukraine, simmering US-China tensions, and rising global populism have led many politicians and pundits to announce a new era of protectionism and global disintegration. Factories are "reshoring," economies are "decoupling," and everyone has abandoned "neoliberal" free trade. Some even have ominously suggested that we are witnessing the "end of globalization" altogether.[1]

Fortunately for the United States and the world, the naysayers are being proved wrong once again. While the last few years have indeed stressed the global economy, evidence shows that the relatively free movement of objects, people, capital, and ideas across national borders—that is, "globalization"—is not dying but evolving in response to economic and geopolitical events. In fact, in many respects globalization has expanded and deepened during our new era of supposed "de-globalization," in the process reflecting a broad misunderstanding of not only globalization's details and effects, but of what it actually is.

That misunderstanding motivated the Cato Institute's 2023 launch of *Defending Globalization*, a multiyear project aimed at educating the public on the past, present, and future of globalization. Among the project's many parts is a collection of essays from Cato scholars and outside experts on the economics, law, politics, history, and cultural impact of globalization. This book provides 25 of the project's most salient essays, divided into three sections:

- **The Globalization Basics** covers the history, law, economics, and institutions underlying the modern global economy. Readers will learn how and why people have engaged in international trade from the Bronze Age to today. They will grapple with core concepts such as comparative advantage and specialization as well as common trade policy mechanisms like trade agreements, tariffs, and the World Trade Organization (WTO). And they'll consider the trade and economic policy of the world's two largest economies today—the United States and China. The section can serve as a "one-stop shop" for understanding the global economy's inner workings.
- **The Globalization Debate** rebuts the most common arguments against globalization today. In the United States and abroad, international trade and migration have become hot-button issues because of their supposed harms to the US economy and manufacturing sector, the global poor, the environment, and national security. Often, globalization is blamed for destroying a once-prosperous American middle class and criticized as immoral, a tool of global government, or contrary to either conservative or progressive ideals. Readers will learn about each of these debates—and why the claims of today's globalization critics are misguided, incomplete, or just plain wrong.
- **Globalization in Our Lives** will educate readers on how globalization intersects with our societies and cultures—from where we live to the films we watch, the clothes we wear, the gods we worship, and the food we eat. Too often "globalization" is discussed only in terms of economics, geopolitics, and certain politically sensitive goods like steel or soybeans. But there may be no better symbols of *real* globalization than a local restaurant or your favorite T-shirt or TV show. Readers will come away from these chapters with a deeper understanding of the many unseen or underappreciated benefits of globalization—ones that make our lives richer, more prosperous, more tolerant, and more fun.

We hope readers find that these essays not only are educational and entertaining but also demonstrate the essential *humanity* of trade and migration that just happens to cross political borders—and why we need more of it in the years ahead.

Before we get to the essays, however, it is important to first understand where "globalization" is today and why trendy claims of "de-globalization" have thus far proved empty.

Global Trade in Goods Is Doing Fine

The primary datapoint used to announce the "death of globalization" is the slowing share of both goods trade and total trade as a percentage of global gross domestic product (GDP) since the Great Recession. However, this is a poor indicator of the state of globalization for several reasons. First, goods trade as a share of world GDP was just below its record high in 2022 and thus remained well above levels seen during the "hyperglobalization" heyday of the 1990s. This trend is therefore best described as "slowbalization," not "de-globalization."

Second, trade in goods was bound to moderate eventually, thanks to practical constraints on shipping, evolving consumer tastes, and new technological developments that naturally make local or nearby production more financially attractive.[2] Some of the moderation also reflects that countries increasingly produce and consume services as they develop—signifying an ascent from poverty to middle class that more than one billion people have achieved since 2001, often thanks to globalization. As a result of this development, world manufacturing output and agriculture output can increase in nominal, inflation-adjusted terms but decline as a share of global economic output because nations are simply shifting more of their economic activity to less-tradeable services.[3]

Finally, there is ample evidence that global trade in goods rebounded strongly after the COVID-19 pandemic and remains quite healthy. In the United States, inflation-adjusted merchandise trade (imports plus exports) reached record levels in 2022 and was largely maintained in 2023 (Figure I.1).[4]

The *DHL Global Connectedness Index 2022* report adds that, "As of mid-2022, the volume of world trade in goods was 10% higher than it

FIGURE I.1

Inflation-adjusted US trade in goods (imports and exports) set a record in 2022

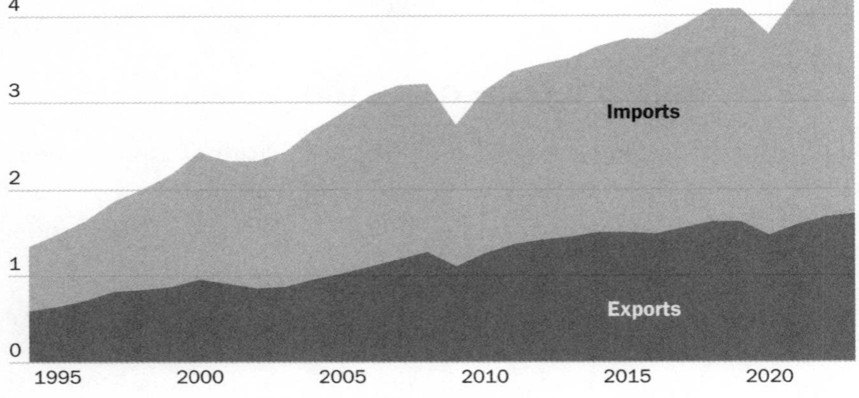

Source: "Real Exports, Imports, and Balance of Goods, Petroleum and Non-Petroleum End-Use Commodity Category Totals," US Census Bureau, updated June 28, 2023.
Note: "Chained dollars" is a method for adjusting nominal dollar amounts for inflation that better accounts for price-induced changes in consumption and production patterns over time.

was at the end of 2019."[5] The 2024 DHL report shows that goods trade remains at a high level and notes that "assuming globalization has ended is misguided."[6]

In short, there are numerous signs that global goods trade *is* still increasing—just not as fast as the rest of the global economy. This is hardly the "death of globalization."

The Other Aspects of Globalization Are Thriving

Just as important, the many non-goods aspects of globalization show little sign of long-term stagnation. For starters, global trade in services was surging before the pandemic (Figure I.2), which cratered all trade (especially travel and many in-person services),[7] and then rebounded strongly after 2022.

FIGURE I.2

Before the pandemic, services trade had been rising as a share of world GDP

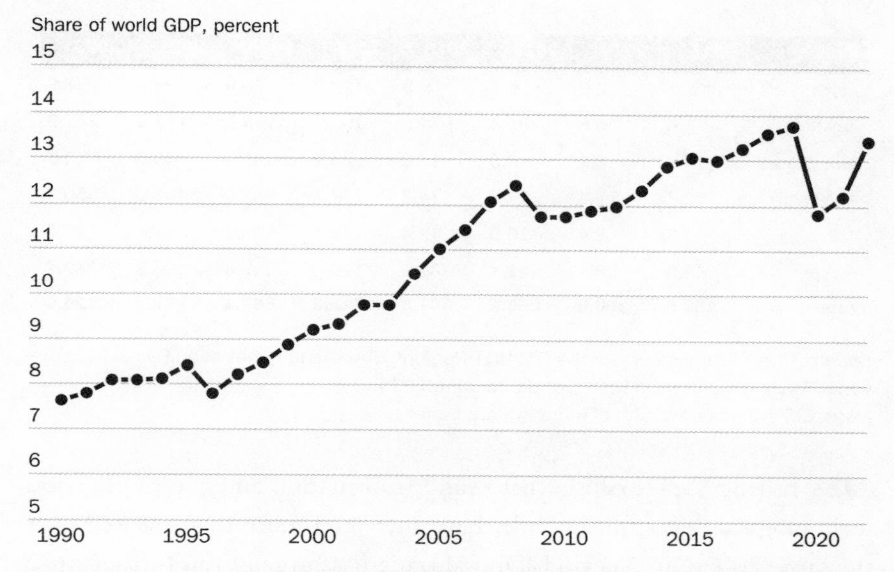

Source: "Trade in Service (% of GDP)," World Development Indicators, World Bank, updated June 26, 2024.

Note: GDP = gross domestic product.

In fact, trade in many services had already exceeded pre-pandemic levels by 2021, including computer services, audiovisual services, insurance and pension services, financial services, business services, and charges for use of intellectual property.[8] Many of these service industries, the WTO reports, avoided large declines in 2020 because of "the widespread adoption of technologies allowing remote work."[9] And the catchall category of "other commercial services," which covers approximately 60 percent of all services trade, has seen its global export growth rapidly outpace that of goods.[10]

These data get to the hottest area of globalization today: digital trade, which includes the cross-border delivery and consumption of both information and communication technology products. As detailed in Gary Winslett's chapter (see Chapter 9, "Digital Trade in Services: Globalization's Exciting New Frontier"), the WTO estimates global exports of digitally delivered services increased almost fourfold between 2005 and

TABLE I.1

Total used capacity of international internet bandwidth (measured in terabits per second) has increased rapidly

Region	2015	2016	2017	2018	2019	2020	2021	2022
Africa	1.7	2.0	5.2	6.8	10.3	20.6	28.2	37.9
Americas	38.8	46.8	51.8	70.9	100.8	134.5	171.5	221.9
Arab States	5.8	8.1	13.0	17.8	23.9	31.9	40.9	50.7
Asia-Pacific	52.4	79.4	124.3	174.8	247.6	311.0	443.9	550.3
CIS	4.9	8.4	10.5	11.4	12.7	16.7	19.4	22.0
Europe	48.9	56.1	61.4	85.6	120.0	152.4	195.8	242.7
Total	**152.5**	**200.8**	**266.2**	**367.3**	**515.3**	**667.1**	**899.7**	**1,125.5**

Source: "Key ICT Indicators for the ITU/BDT Regions (Totals and Penetration Rates)," International Telecommunication Union, updated June 2024.
Note: CIS = Commonwealth of Independent States.

2022, hitting $3.82 trillion that year.[11] Information and communication technology services, meanwhile, have increased more than fivefold over the same 2005–2022 period. Digital trade has surged even further since that time.[12] As Winslett notes, much of this digital trade is traditional services like law or accounting, but an increasing share is novel—what he calls "Peloton globalization," in which leisure activities can now be broadcast abroad and consumed from home.

Global internet traffic and bandwidth capacity (Table I.1) show that digital service trade is poised to grow even more in the years ahead—with big economic benefits for the United States and others. For example, a McKinsey Global Institute report calculated that global data flows in 2014 alone generated $2.8 trillion in economic output and were "exerting a larger impact on growth than traditional goods flows."[13] Digital transactions are much higher today, as are their economic benefits, yet trade statistics still fail to fully capture them. Consequently, actual cross-border trade and economic activity—and thus *actual globalization*—are likely being underestimated by a significant amount.

Other aspects of globalization also show little reason for alarm. For example, the estimated number of international migrants—enticed by opportunity in countries with growing economies—increased from 153

FIGURE I.3
Global connectedness continues to rise

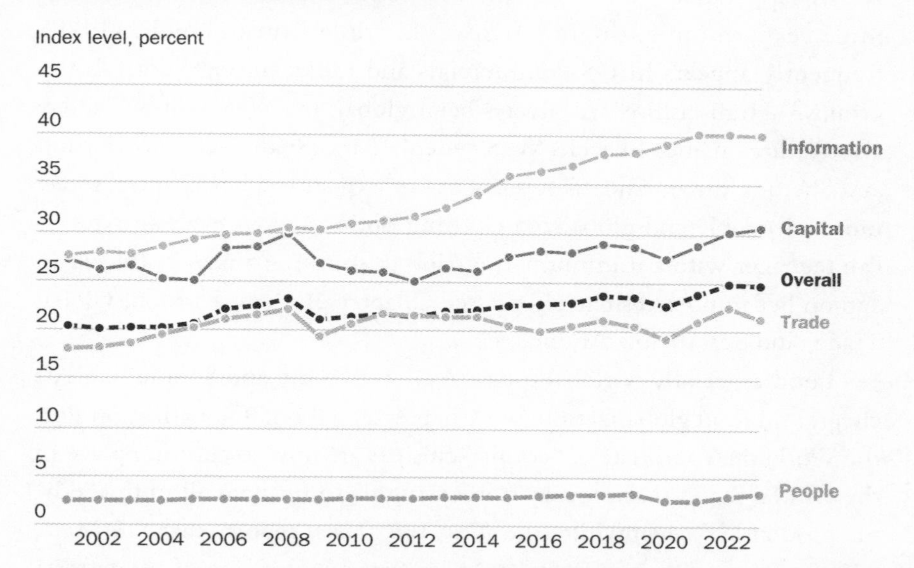

Source: Steven A. Altman and Caroline R. Bastain, *DHL Global Connectedness Report 2024* (Bonn, Germany: DHL Group, Headquarters, 2024).
Note: 0% indicates a world of completely separate countries while 100% indicates a completely globalized, frictionless world.

million in 1990 (2.9 percent of the world's population) to 281 million in 2020 (3.6 percent).[14] And even in the face of the Great Recession, the pandemic, and rising geopolitical tensions, global capital flows have continued flowing. The United Nations reports, for example, that 2023 global foreign direct investment inflows exceeded $1.3 trillion—down from previous records but still far above levels seen in the 1990s and mid-2000s.[15]

DHL's Global Connectedness Index combines data on trade, capital flows, information, and migration into a single snapshot of globalization.[16] According to the latest report, globalization achieved a record high in 2022 and remained near that level in 2023 (Figure I.3). The authors thus conclude that, despite assertions to the contrary, "there has been no retreat from international to domestic business activity, and . . . [t]he resilience of global flows in the face of such formidable threats sends a strong message about the value of a connected world."[17]

Finally, "cultural globalization" continues apace. In music, Puerto Rican rapper Bad Bunny was the most streamed artist on Spotify for three years running, singing in Spanish, while Korean boy band BTS frequently appears in US commercials and ranks among Spotify's top groups.[18] High fashion has always been global, but "fast fashion" today also features names like H&M (Sweden), Zara (Spain), Uniqlo (Japan), and Shein (China). And, as Joy Buchanan explains in her chapter, today more affordable and globalized clothing options allow even an American teenager with a minimum-wage job to summon a new outfit via an app on her imported smartphone (see Chapter 21, "Fast Fashion, Global Trade, and Sustainable Abundance").

Food especially is global today. As noted in my and Sophia Bagley's chapter on food globalization (see Chapter 22, "Food Globalization Puts the World on Your Plate"), "ethnic" cuisines are now so commonplace in the United States that grocery stores struggle to fit them all in the "ethnic food aisle." Meanwhile, the *New York Times* reports that "H Mart, a Korean American supermarket chain, has become one of the fastest-growing retailers by specializing in foods from around the world."[19] And the American restaurant scene has gone from hosting only a handful of foreign cuisines to one with almost every food from every major country on the planet—more than 300 total, almost double the number of categories that were listed just five years ago.

Perhaps the most telling is US streaming media giant Netflix.[20] Of the American company's 200-plus million subscribers, fewer than half are in the United States and Canada. Netflix also streams and produces numerous "foreign" (non-US) shows and movies, and several of the most-watched Netflix shows—including *Squid Game* at number one—are in languages other than English.[21] Lucas Shaw and Yasufumi Saito at Bloomberg add, "People actually spend more time watching foreign-language TV in the [Netflix] top 10 than shows in English."[22] Even American viewers are increasingly consuming foreign-language content, as the record 18 Emmys for Japanese-subtitled *Shogun* just reiterated.[23]

American politicians might be souring on globalization, but American consumers most definitely are not.

FIGURE I.4
CPTPP and RCEP countries

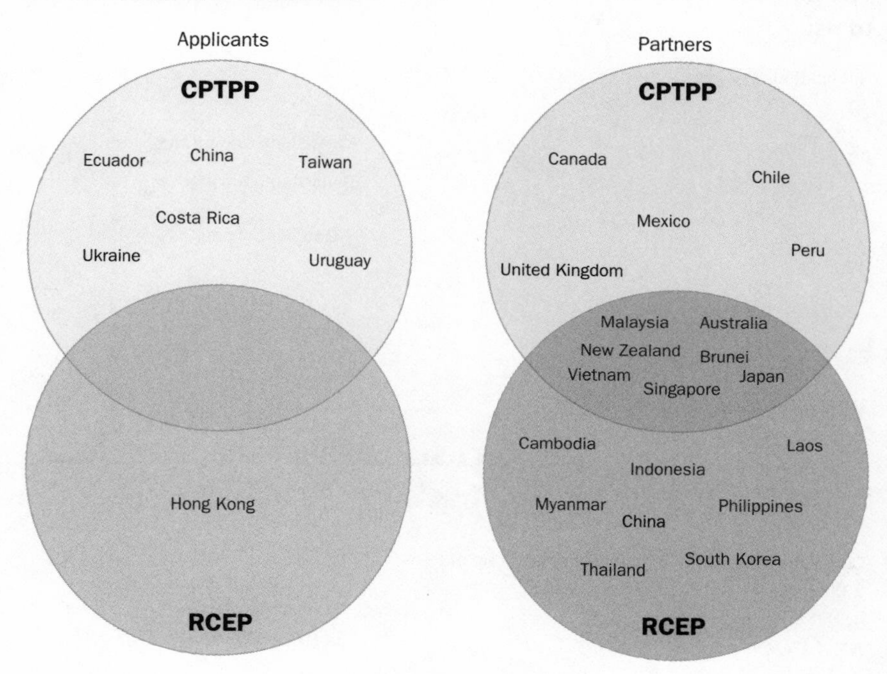

Source: Jeffrey J. Schott, "Which Countries Are in the CPTPP and RCEP Trade Agreements and Which Want In?," Peterson Institute for International Economics, July 27, 2023; "CPTPP Accession," New Zealand Ministry of Foreign Affairs and Trade; and "Hong Kong Applies to Join RCEP Trade Agreement," *Nikkei Asia*, February 23, 2022.
Note: CPTPP = Comprehensive and Progressive Agreement for Trans-Pacific Partnership; RCEP = Regional Comprehensive Economic Partnership. South Korea and Thailand have publicly indicated their interest in applying to join CPTPP, but they have not initiated the process yet. Bangladesh is reportedly considering applying to join RCEP.

Are Governments Abandoning Globalization?

Politicians outside the United States aren't turning their backs on globalization either. Significant agreements like the Comprehensive and Progressive Agreement for Trans-Pacific Partnership (CPTPP), which consists of 12 nations constituting around 14 percent of global GDP, and the even larger Regional Comprehensive Economic Partnership (RCEP), led by China and accounting for more than 30 percent of world GDP, have been completed in recent years (Figure I.4).[24] Africa

FIGURE I.5
The number of regional trade agreements (RTAs) in force continues to rise

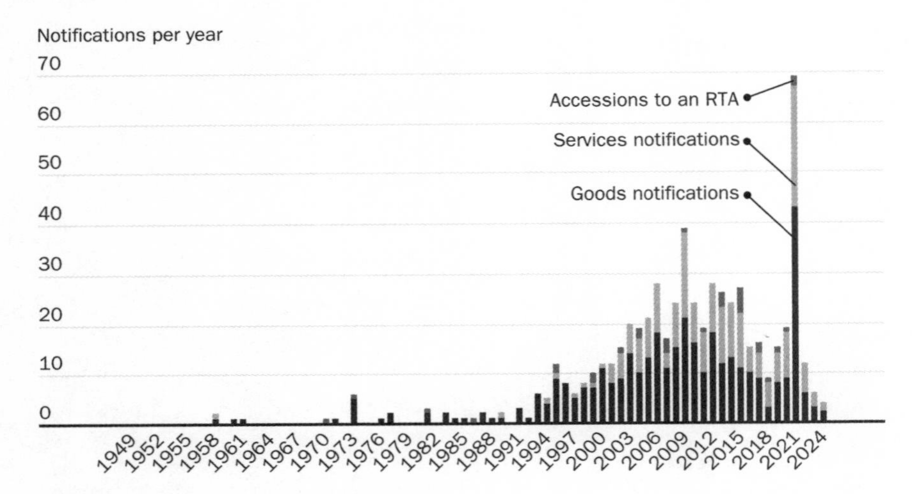

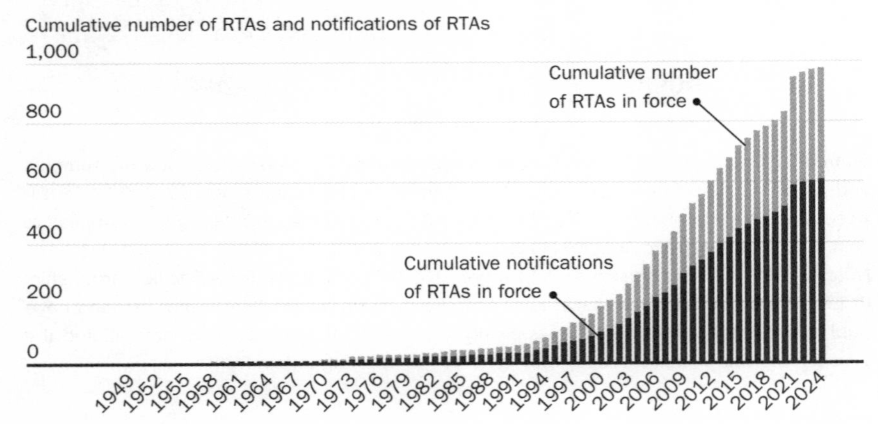

Source: "RTAs Currently in Force (by Year of Entry into Force), 1948–2024," World Trade Organization, updated June 29, 2024.
Note: World Trade Organization (WTO) members notify the WTO Secretariat of any RTAs to which they are parties. The WTO Secretariat reports notifications of RTAs on the basis of the trade flows that these agreements liberalize—goods or services. When an agreement liberalizes both (e.g., the United States-Mexico-Canada Agreement, or the Comprehensive and Progressive Agreement for Trans-Pacific Partnership), the WTO Secretariat reports a goods notification and a services notification for that agreement. For this reason, the cumulative number of notifications of RTAs in force is higher than the cumulative number of RTAs in force.

saw the launch of the African Continental Free Trade Area in January 2021, becoming the largest new free trade area since 1994.[25] The European Union (EU) has signed numerous trade agreements in recent years and is actively negotiating with Australia, China, India, Indonesia, and the Philippines.[26] European external trade, meanwhile, has increased dramatically from 18 percent of GDP in 1980 to 51 percent in 2022.[27]

Even traditionally trade-skeptical nations are signing trade agreements. India implemented one with Australia in 2022 and another with numerous EU countries in 2024.[28] China finalized agreements with Ecuador, Nicaragua, and Serbia in 2023, bringing its total trade agreement count to 22.[29] Although the United States abandoned the Trans-Pacific Partnership (TPP)/CPTPP in 2017, it signed the United States-Mexico-Canada Agreement (USMCA) with Canada and Mexico and a tariff deal with Japan, and it initiated talks with Kenya and the United Kingdom.[30] Last, the UK successfully joined the CPTPP in July 2023.[31]

Overall, data from the WTO show that regional trade agreements continue to proliferate, with 369 in force as of mid-2024 and—importantly—no clear sign of a forthcoming reversal (Figure I.5).[32]

If Not De-Globalizing, What *Are* Supply Chains Doing?

The pandemic and geopolitics have surely caused multinational corporations to rethink their supply chains, but this trend has thus far been a story of *re*-globalization, not *de*-globalization.[33] Many American companies, for example, have shifted some operations out of China but mainly to Southeast Asia or Mexico, not back home. Declines in Russian or Ukrainian commodities, meanwhile, have pushed international buyers to turn not inward but to Canada, South Africa, Latin America, the United States, India, and elsewhere. Inventory, sourcing, and related systems were overhauled, and the market boomed for supply chain and logistics technologies that let multinationals better track shipments and processes.[34]

Thanks to these and other corporate efforts and moderating global demand, 2023 saw US ports mostly clear, global shipping costs back to pre-pandemic levels, remaining supply chain problems manageable, and multinational manufacturers better prepared for future problems.[35]

New issues have emerged in 2024, but they are also surmountable—in part thanks to effective industry responses to previous crises.[36] A 2023 Brookings Institution study even found that "global trade was remarkably resilient during the pandemic"—not simply because of friendshoring but because, contrary to the conventional wisdom that trade necessarily undermines national security and inflames diplomatic tensions, "non-friendly countries *alleviated* rather than *caused* critical bottlenecks."[37] Thus, even after two massive, consecutive, and worldwide economic shocks and several smaller ones too, global business today is still very much global.

Conclusion

Tariffs, managed trade agreements, capital controls, visas, and other government restrictions on commerce and movement are part of globalization's story too, of course.[38] But they are artificial constraints on natural, human interactions that have occurred since the dawn of recorded history. As Adam Smith noted in *The Wealth of Nations*, "man is an animal that bargains"; humans are unique in our ability to peacefully exchange goods and services to meet our needs and improve our lives.[39] Globalization, therefore, is primarily a story about *humanity*, not soulless multinational corporations or faceless political regimes.

Globalization critics revel in the mess and disruption that open trade and migration can produce yet ignore its fundamental humanity. They also ignore that the only alternative to our modern globalized world is a more fragmented and static system that has been repeatedly shown to have more conflict, less freedom, and more poverty. Indeed, despite all of global capitalism's foibles and missteps, its long-term direction and effects are undeniably positive for the human race.[40] Since the famous 1999 anti-globalization protests in Seattle, in fact, the world has seen more than a billion people escape extreme poverty (Figure I.6), important improvements in child labor and environmental conditions, *and* rising US wages and employment—thanks in no small part to what those protesters sought to dismantle.[41]

The critics were wrong back then, and they're wrong today. Globalization isn't going anywhere—and thank goodness for that.

FIGURE I.6

More than 1 billion people have escaped extreme poverty in the past three decades

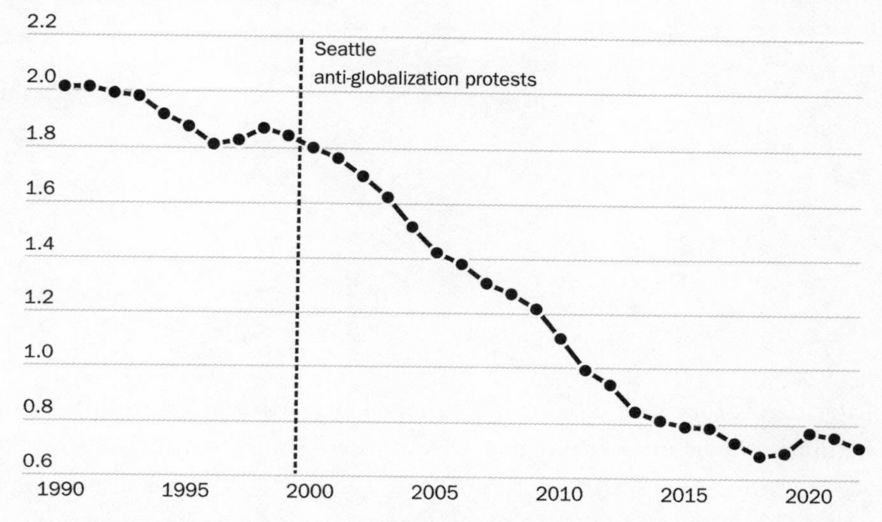

Source: World Bank Poverty and Inequality Platform, “Share of Population Living in Extreme Poverty, 1963 to 2022,” Our World in Data.

Note: Extreme poverty is defined as living below the international poverty line of $2.15 per day, adjusted for inflation and differences in cost of living between countries.

SECTION ONE

Globalization Basics

Chapter 1

Globalization Creates a Global Neighborhood, Benefiting All

Deirdre N. McCloskey

- "Globalization" is a common term that's commonly misunderstood. It is the gradual convergence of prices and markets that results from humans freely doing what they have done throughout history—work, innovate, and transact for mutual benefit.
- The first globalization was part of a wider liberal movement yet only lasted until the beginning of the First World War. The present and second globalization began after the end of the Second World War, aided greatly by new technologies and the reversal of government barriers, and has freed billions from dire poverty.
- Popular worries about globalization are misguided: global inequality has declined; innovation has benefited the environment; manufacturing productivity in rich countries has increased; local cultures and arts are celebrated, not suppressed; and human liberty has expanded, allowing unprecedented creativity and invention to flourish.
- Globalization is elementary liberty. It has been the great teacher and, through efficiency and innovation, the great enricher. Long, *long* may it reign.

The word "globalization" delights some and terrifies others. But it's merely the gradual emergence in our world of a single economy.

It's a natural and beneficial result of humans doing what humans have done since the beginning, making their families better off by working hard, inventing new stuff, keeping alert, looking around, making little deals, etc. The result of all this human liberty of choice has been globalization. At various scales of time, it's been happening from the caves to the modern world, or from 1350 to 1800, or from 1776 to 2024.

Your neighborhood is a "single economy." Most people in Manhattan don't own cars, so the economic neighborhood in effect is smallish. A grocery store at the corner of Broadway and West 143rd Street can't get away with charging $10 for a loaf of bread when another store two blocks away is charging $2. Within 10 blocks or so, the prices of the same brand of bread and the wages of the same quality dentist and the interest charged on a bank loan for the same credit rating will be pretty much the same.

On Long Island, everyone has a car, or two, or three, and the approximate sameness of prices extends for miles. And the overlap of neighborhoods means that anything that can move or can be offered easily to people who do move—bread, cars, dentists, bank loans (not so much for houses, which are usually immovable by nature, and not so much across restricted borders, which are basically immovable by law)—is pretty much the same, as Woody Guthrie's song "This Land Is Your Land" goes, from the redwood forest to the Gulf Stream waters. And the overlap of the overlaps, if not restricted by legal interventions by the state in the prices permitted, means that even globally, from the Amazon forest to the North Atlantic Current waters, the prices of wheat and iron and AK-47s are pretty much the same. Globalization.

The rough sameness of prices is not caused by a gracious state official enforcing a just price or by an evil monopolist imposing an unjust price. It's caused by moderately alert customers making the sameness happen by exercising their liberty to shift from this to that purveyor of cars or dentistry or bread. No one will pay $10 for a loaf when she knows that a couple of blocks away she can pay $2. And the $2 grocery store will make sure she is alert to the difference. In Miami, which has a large population of retired people on fixed incomes, the prices of milk and toilet paper differ very little from store to store, within extraordinarily tight limits (a cent or two). The older people spend their days comparison shopping and sharply buying. Fool me once, shame on you; fool me twice, shame on me. If you thrill to economic jargon, you can call this "arbitrage."

Globalization puts everyone whose government permits it into a global neighborhood in which the price of a Samsung TV at a Best Buy in Washington is pretty much the same as in Beijing or New Delhi. Big price differences in the same neighborhood would mean that you could easily do better. For example, as a low-price buyer, you could resell to a high-price buyer. Or as a low-price seller, you could advertise. Or as a high-price buyer, you could get smarter and look around for a better deal. The deals are voluntary and therefore must benefit both buyer and seller, a little or a lot. If permitted widely in a society, gross domestic product (GDP) per head goes up, a little or a lot. It happens by arbitrage, globalization, and common sense—the natural result of people liberated to better themselves while bettering others.

If the price of TVs is higher in Beijing, then suppliers will send TVs there, instead of to Washington. Ordinary prudence recommends "buy low, sell high" until the arbitrage of suppliers and demanders makes the price difference come down to a level at which no more deals are profitable. Economists call the result of such a mutual exhaustion of deals and the uniform prices that signal its achievement "Pareto efficiency."

Arbitrage also applies, though often at a slower pace, to the labor, capital, materials, and especially to the technical know-how that goes into a Samsung TV. Again, it's all about liberty. China opened economically after 1978, permitting exports and imports, permitting people to move to new jobs, and permitting people to start new businesses. In the largest migration in human history, hundreds of millions of Chinese from the interior moved one by one to the coast to work in the new factories at higher wages than at home. And the Communist Party let wages and prices be set by business suppliers and citizen demanders instead of by the state. Arbitrage ruled, and China waxed pretty prosperous.

Contrary to what you might have heard, however, there's no "Chinese model" to be seen as an intriguing if authoritarian alternative to

Western economic liberalism. The Communist Party of China would like you to believe there is. Nope. After 1978, the party merely started to permit an economic liberalism of the sort partially implemented in the West in the 19th century—though of course the party did not permit anything like a corresponding liberalism in politics. The "Chinese model" is merely "the capitalist road."

The economic result of liberty in China's economy? China's income per head in 1978 was then lower than Sudan's. It's now about 12 times higher, about the same as Mexico's (after adjusting for purchasing power parity), which is in turn about the global average. That's still less than a third of US income per head. But if Premier Xi Jinping fails in reverting to economic anti-liberalism with central planning and controls in prices, China's on the way to parity in one to two generations. India likewise after 1991 opened to global prices, and as a result, if Premier Modi in India like Xi in China does not leave liberalism behind, India can expect parity with Europe and the United States in two or three long generations. Latin America and Africa cannot be far behind. Globalization, which is to say the force of arbitrage exercised by liberated people in the economy, spreads prosperity.

New Transport Creates Globalization; Blocking by States Undoes It

Globalization has gone forward, and occasionally backward, from two sources.

The big source for going forward has been innovation in transport, and the resulting fall in the price of moving goods and people. It came again from individual choice, not by state action. The voyageurs in New France adopted the birchbark canoe from the First Nations, driving down the price differential on furs between the supply in the interior of Canada and the demand in Montreal. The shipping container invented in North Carolina in 1955 drove down the price differential of soybeans between the supply in Iowa and the demand in Shanghai.

An original monopoly in a neighborhood—such as a country store in town in 1800 or the sole purchaser of wheat in a local county in

1850 or Peabody Coal in a company town in 1900—could search out high prices for its selling or buying. But transport costs steadily fell—especially in the last two centuries of frenetic innovation suddenly permitted by liberalism—as people permitted new entrants to break the monopolies.

Enterprise monopoly has steadily declined, because of better roads, longer canals, the railway, the telegraph, riverboats, ocean steamships, bicycles, streetcars, subways, downtown department stores, mail-order companies, telephones, automobiles, longer hours of business, airplanes, superhighways, strip malls, containerization, the internet, Amazon.com, and much more. Prices converged. Prosperity spread, because at the same prices faced by all, there were no more reallocations for additional arbitrage to make both sides of a deal better off. Buying low and selling high had done its job. Economic activity was doing as well for people as it could. The economist's "efficiency" was achieved.

The other significant source of globalization has been the reversal, intended or not, of state-supported monopolies *against* the trade in goods or the flows of financial capital or the migration of people who are poor. Globalization, that is, came from allowing more arbitrage, by dropping instead of raising the taxes on imports on foreign goods—the jargon for the taxes is "tariffs"—and dropping the restrictions on where you can invest, and dropping the legal rules keeping retail prices up, and dropping the laws against selling on Sundays, and especially dropping the numerous state-supported monopolies such as telephones and taxis and citizenship itself. Drop, drop, drop, and you get more arbitrage and more globalization and more income. We all end up trading in the same global neighborhood. We get richer, because we all get the best deals available. The right people specialize in making TVs, and the right people specialize in buying them. (Yes, there's jargon for that too: "following comparative advantage to achieve global efficiency.")

Globalization has occasionally gone backward, because of fresh, brilliant, coerced schemes for state laws to block the arbitrage of prices of goods and people and ideas, globally or locally. "Trading blocs" such as the Council for Mutual Economic Assistance (Comecon) in Eastern Europe until the fall of Russian-imposed communism blocked trade with the West and, administered by bureaucrats, blocked trading within the bloc in a way that prevented complete arbitrage between, say, Poland and Romania. Block, block, block, and globalization stops or reverses. And you get poorer when you could so easily be richer. The Comecon did. Its fall after 1989 made Eastern Europe much richer.

Exactly where, say, melons are grown and where they are eaten matters only if globalization has *not* happened. If everyone under globalization pays pretty much the same price, melons will come from where they are best grown, and they will go to where they are most eagerly eaten. It's all for betterment in a globalized world with decent prosperity. No drama, no corrupt "protection" for Paul at the expense of Peter. But Japan once protected its small group of melon growers. They were incompetent compared with its Toyota employees, speaking relative to US melon growers compared with Detroit automakers, and therefore Japan was violating its comparative advantage in autos as against melons. Japan imposed heavy tariffs on importation of melons from the Philippines or the United States. Melons costing $1.40 in Manila or Los Angeles cost $20 in Tokyo, wrapped in lovely tissue paper and elegantly boxed as wedding gifts. Japanese GDP per head was a little lower than it could have been with thorough globalization.

If people are allowed to buy and sell where they want, geography gradually stops mattering much. We've come to live in one big economic neighborhood. Marketed income is higher, because the trades that constitute it are accomplished as efficiently as can be. During the 1950s, an American could basically buy from just three Detroit auto manufacturers. Then the tariffs and quotas on foreign cars, imposed when US policymakers were still hostile to free trade, were eliminated, slowly, with much anger in Detroit about the evils of Volkswagens and Toyotas. Now American consumers of cars have the choice of 20 companies competing (even Chinese) and hundreds of models. Look at the frenetic car-company advertisements on TV.

To consume much, when you come right down to it, we *must* trade. Cooking and childcare in homes is a true and significant part of a properly defined national product. But as the centuries marched down to the present, we've more and more traded away our own work in farm and factory and office to get the benefit of the work of others. A hunter-gatherer band, true, gets most of its consumption inside the band. Yet Aboriginal Australians traded gemstones and boomerangs over hundreds of miles, and prices converged. A medieval village was not averse to trading butter for blacksmithing within the village. But the self-sufficiency of a European medieval village is exaggerated in imagination. It imported iron from other neighborhoods and sold its grain into the little urban markets.

Anciently, a massive trade in grain from Egypt supported bread and circuses in Rome. As commerce revived in medieval Europe (much earlier than was once believed), wheat prices between the lowest European level, Poland as a supplier, and the highest, Venice as a consumer, converged (Figure 1.1). The same was true inside China and inside vast swaths of the rest of the world. In central Mexico from 1000 BCE to the Spanish conquest, the Teotihuacan, the Toltec, and the Aztec mined obsidian, an extremely sharp volcanic glass used for knives. As it was shipped north on the backs of men from the neighborhood of present-day Mexico City, it of course became more and more expensive and was sliced finer and finer. In what is now New Mexico, archaeological sites show it sliced very fine indeed. The Spaniards with their horses caused the price differential to fall. The transport cost had put a big wedge between prices, and innovation caused the wedge to become smaller. It was arbitrage and rising income from the more efficient trade in obsidian.

As late as 1900, a third of Americans still lived on farms. At about the same time, only 15 percent of the global population lived in substantial cities. Today, it's about 60 percent globally. But in 1900, even urban households—even in the relatively rich United States—were little factories of "autarchy." (In Greek, it means "self-rule"; in this economic context, it means not trading at all or self-sufficiency.) A mother would typically spend 40 hours a week on food preparation alone, would make most of the clothing for herself or the children, would store in glass jars the vegetables from her garden for consumption in winter, and before innovation in antibiotics made purchased medical doctoring a good idea, would work as the sole doctor/nurse for most diseases. "Man works from sun to sun," the proverb goes, "but woman's work is never done."

FIGURE 1.1

Wheat prices in Europe converged between 1450 and 1750

Wheat prices in grams of silver

1000

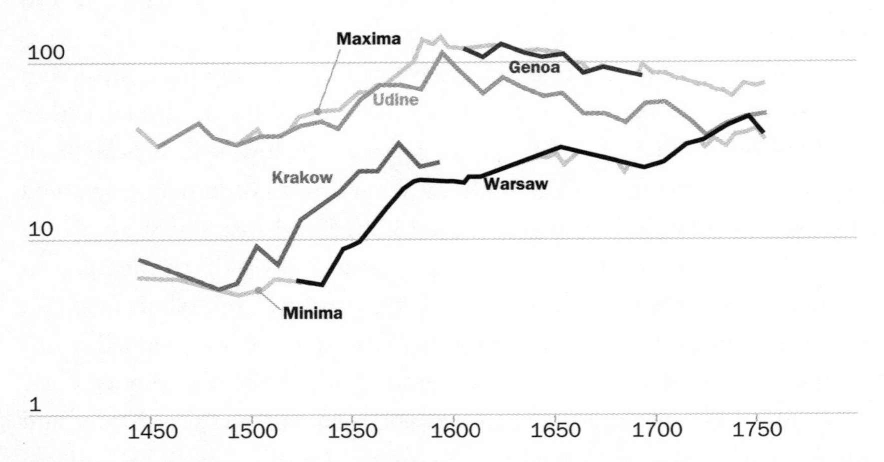

Source: F. P. Braudel and Frank Spooner, "Prices in Europe from 1450 to 1750," in *The Cambridge Economic History of Europe from the Decline of the Roman Empire*, vol. 4, *The Economy of Expanding Europe in the Sixteenth and Seventeenth Centuries*, eds. E. E. Rich and C. H. Wilson (Cambridge: Cambridge University Press, 1967), pp. 470–71.

A hermit could refuse to take advantage of globalization and achieve self-sufficiency in his own little hut. It sounds lovely and brave. Grow your own wheat. Make your own accordion. But it's been calculated that nowadays a hamburger made *wholly* self-sufficiently would cost about $83. Perhaps it would be better to work a little in a market and then take the earnings to spend at the neighborhood McDonald's. When Henry David Thoreau went to be self-sufficient for two years from 1845 to 1847 on the banks of Walden Pond in Concord, Massachusetts, he still bought nails in town for his hut, and hoes for his crops, and books to read. Every Sunday, he went into town for dinner. Towns and trade are mighty tempting, with their low prices in production achieved by specialization and their low prices in marketing achieved by arbitrage.

Self-sufficiency, true, charms people. But it also serves the self-interest of monopolies sitting inside the sufficient place. Medieval market towns run by monopolizing guildsmen arranged to keep the indwellers from buying anywhere else. During the early modern period, the same policy at the level of the entire nation was called "mercantilism." The accumulation of gold in the nation, a "positive balance of payments," was achieved by making exports large and making imports small. Getting gold was seen as just the ticket. Wait a minute. It's like saying that it's good for you as a little nation to work to earn money but bad for you to spend the money on groceries. Keep money stashed away, like Scrooge McDuck.

Modern mercantilism has the same illogical logic. After 2016, both the Trump and Biden administrations in the United States tried to raise exports of airplanes and reduce imports of steel. Negotiation over "trade agreements" have the same rhetorical structure. "I'll let your exports into the United States only if you let US exports into your country." Exports are good, the rhetoric in the negotiation says; imports are bad. Working is good; eating is bad.

Such talk is, of course, lunacy, though still the basis of public policy worldwide, as it was anciently. You have, after all, a balance of payments deficit with your grocer. The grocer accumulates the money. Has the deficit kept you up at night worrying? Not likely. Yet the stop-go policy of the British state during the 1950s and 1960s was based on such mercantilist lunacy and crippled real growth. Words matter. Words like "self-sufficiency" and "protection" and "balance-of-payments deficit" lead us far astray and make us poor. Better to get the economic rhetoric right, and achieve prosperity, by speaking of "arbitrage," "efficiency," and "globalization."

Globalization Flowed and Ebbed, 1848–1948

The first globalization came to its height in the 1890s. An economics-driven ideology in the United Kingdom had inspired in the mid-19th century a brief flurry of "free trade" (i.e., allowing international trade to happen free of let or hindrance). Buy what and where you will. The state will not obstruct you. Reject mercantilist rhetoric.

Free trade was part of a wider liberalization. It began in theorizing by A. R. J. Turgot and Adam Smith and Thomas Paine and Mary Wollstonecraft in the late 18th century, to be applied massively in the 19th century by governments now increasingly of, by, and for the people. Liberalism rejected for the first time a rule of, by, and for the masters. It ended slavery and serfdom, broke down city guilds, and inspired free international trade in goods, people, and investments. A country like Sweden was in 1800 clotted with blocked opportunity for arbitrage, and its people were among the poorest in Europe. In the mid-19th century, it began to liberalize and began its long rise, by the 1930s, to a position among the richest.

The first globalization, then, was notably British. Britain after the 1840s essentially let anyone trade with it free of state-imposed restrictions and became the central market of the world. With few exceptions, the result by the 1890s globally was startlingly free trade in wheat and wine, free migration of people to the New World or the Colonies, and unhindered liberty to invest in Argentinian and Indian railways.

Notice that the liberalization of the first globalization was in goods, yes, but also in migrants and in investments. A deep economic point is that any one of the three liberalizations is a substitute for the other two. You can trade internationally with Juan Valdez in far Colombia by buying his product and letting it be shipped to you, in this case the coffee that he grows. Or Juan can move to your town and trade domestically with you, as a worker in a local restaurant, say. Except for Juan's location, the results in the prices of goods, workers, or capital tend to be similar whether he stays in Colombia and is permitted to trade goods with you or comes to your town and is permitted to trade labor with you. Prices and wages and interest rates tend to converge internationally whether people trade internationally in goods or migrate internationally in person or invest their capital abroad. Capital flowing into new factories and extended railways abroad is, again, a substitute for goods, imports, and human migration. To get around a US tariff, for example, a foreign company opens a factory in Tennessee. Eventually, the economist predicts, and the history of globalization shows, all the world will have the same prices and wages and interest rates and so forth, and much greater prosperity. For example, if present barriers to migration were removed, it has been plausibly calculated that GDP per head worldwide would increase 50 percent.

Until the 1960s, the German and American and most other governments never did sign on to free trade with anything like the 19th-century British enthusiasm. Germans long protected farmers from Ukrainian and American wheat, and the Americans protected steelmakers from German and British steel. Yet so large did Britain, as the first industrial nation, weigh in the world's economy that such corrupt and foolish machinations mattered little to the making of a global neighborhood.

Down to the coming of the income tax in 1913, the US federal government depended on revenues from tariffs on foreign trade. The word "tariffs" sounded scientific and obscured that they were simply taxes on imports. Yet a tariff was a tax that, unlike a tax on domestic beer or incomes, could be claimed to be imposed on the "damned foreigners." The economic claim was silly, because prices of wheat and steel and the rest were by the 19th century largely determined in global markets (Figure 1.1), over which even an increasingly bulky US economy had little influence. A tariff on steel merely raised the price of, say, rails in the United States, to the world price *plus* the tariff. It's still true. A tariff on steel imports means that Americans themselves pay for cutting off their noses to spite their faces. They lose the low price of foreign goods, on the false premise that doing so makes Americans in general better off. It is why countries should adopt free trade even if other countries don't. Keep your own nose, and the lower price of steel, even if others adopt the mercantilist fashion of cutting off theirs.

But especially in the 19th century, such corruptions and foolishness didn't matter much to prosperity in the United States, and not much more in the German Empire, so large were both internally. Wide trade from Chicago to Boston in meat made domestic markets into one big neighborhood. The pressure of domestically arbitraged prices bore great fruit. By Article I, Section 9, Clause 5 of the US Constitution, the individual American states were forbidden from the outset to impose tariffs on one another. Such tariffs still happen between modern Indian states and happened among European nations before the formation of the

European Union. In 1960, trucks crossing from Switzerland to Italy lined up for miles to pay tariffs, and on passenger trains everyone's passport was checked when crossing from the Netherlands to Belgium. Bettering deals were evidently available. But they weren't taken up. Result? Lower income.

A widespread retreat from globalization happened worldwide during and after World War I, a Great Deglobalization. New walls were erected at national borders on the arbitrage of goods, migrants, and capital. Until well after World War II, the economic world had reverted to economic autarchy, nation by nation. The disastrous interlude of retreat from the first globalization began during the 1920s and especially the 1930s. Hard cases make bad law, and hard recessions make bad economic and political policy. The Great Depression of the 1930s, presaged in Britain by a slump in the 1920s, radically undermined earlier liberalism, in both the economy and politics. In the Great Deglobalization, even the British abandoned free trade. Fascist and communist parties flourished worldwide. The three major political ideas dreamed by intellectuals during the past couple of centuries have been, in sequence, liberalism after 1776, nationalism after 1789, and socialism after 1848. The liberation and consequent Great Enrichment of the globe has come from the first one. But if you think you like the other two, maybe you'll like Germany's "national socialism," 1933–1945, or its recent rebirth in white nationalism. I hope not.

Then We Recovered Our Economic Senses

But then our present, second globalization happened, and the second political liberalization. Yet understand that blocking and blocking and blocking arbitrage to benefit this or that special interest never completely stops, even now, well into the second globalization, even with approximately liberal politics.

For example, new schemes have been implemented recently making the Uber taxi service illegal in Germany and imposing a tax on cheap Chinese solar panels imported into the United States. They are always justified as "protecting" Hans the taxi driver in Hamburg or Harriet the stockholder of Hanwha Q CELLS in Dalton, Georgia. A journalist covering home improvement for the business magazine *Forbes* writes that the tariffs imposed by the Trump administration on imported solar panels "result in financial benefit for solar customers."[1] Never mind the rest of us. Uber customers in Hamburg, you see, get financial benefit from paying higher prices for blocked rides. Uh huh. A most ingenious paradox. Just like homeowners in the United States benefit from paying higher wages to their lawn services with blocked immigration from Central America. Sure. And British people benefited from the £50 block imposed in 1966 on the number of pounds sterling allowed to be taken on holidays abroad. Go to Calais, buy a nice if not too expensive French dinner, stay one night in a French hotel, and the next afternoon, board the ferry back to Dover. Financial benefit. Ha, ha.

The second globalization commenced only after fascism had been defeated in World War II and communism was being resisted in the Cold War. The various economic nationalisms started to recede. A crux was the so-called Kennedy Round in 1964–1967 of tariff reductions under the new General Agreement on Tariffs and Trade (GATT). Its surviving offspring is the World Trade Organization (WTO), administered in Geneva. The United States, once addicted to tariffs, began after the Second World War to take adult responsibility as the dominant economy in the world. Suddenly—through something of a political and rhetorical accident—it began enthusiastically free trading. In 1962, Congress passed the Trade Expansion Act, which authorized the government to negotiate tariff cuts of up to 50 percent.

If the neo-mercantilism of the 1930s, or for that matter the long-running opposition on the left of politics to "neoliberalism," as the left calls it, and now also on the right in the "new economic nationalism," was a good idea, then the Kennedy Round and the GATT/WTO and the second globalization would have been a global disaster. It would have impoverished the poor of the world. One could buy bumper stickers declaring, "Milton Friedman, Father of Global Poverty." But in 1960, four billion out of the five billion people in the world lived at an appalling $2 a day in present-day prices, cooking over cow-dung fires, hauling water two miles for drinking, and dying young and illiterate. It was how

FIGURE 1.2

Real GDP per capita has skyrocketed worldwide since the 19th century

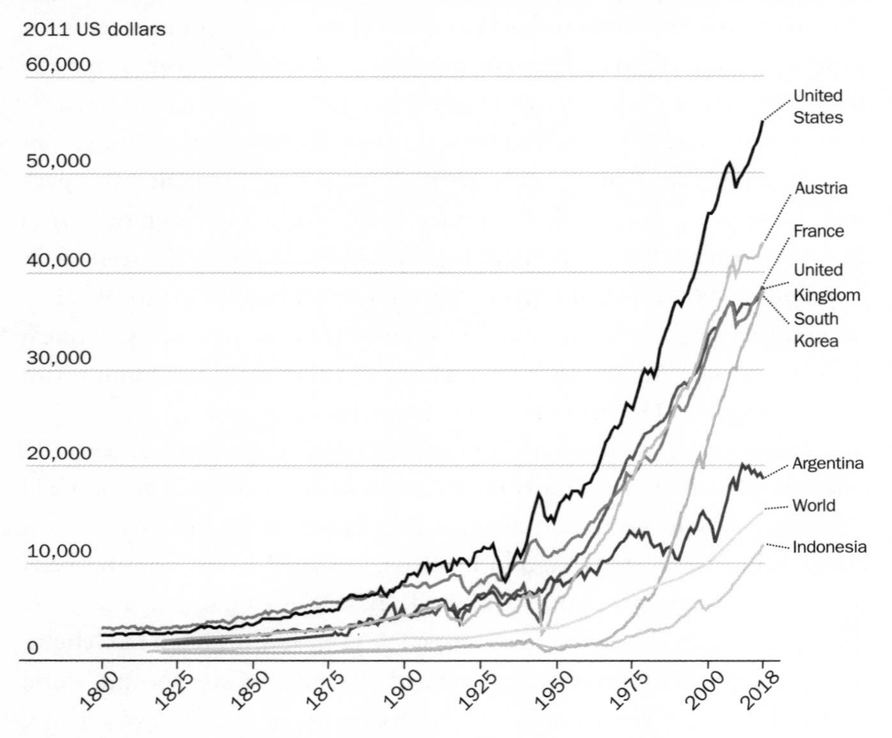

Source: "GDP Per Capita, 1 to 2018," Our World in Data.
Note: GDP = gross domestic product; data in constant 2011 US dollars.

almost all humans had lived from the beginning. By now, one billion of the present eight billion people still live in such misery. But the other seven billion have leapt forward, many to the "superabundance" that Marian Tupy and Gale Pooley have recently chronicled.[2] It happened in the face of gloomy predictions that rising population would starve us all, that our best days were behind us. Real income per head on the globe has risen during the second globalization from a little over $2 a head per day to about $50 a day (Figure 1.2).

The World Bank reckons that it will keep rising at about 2 percent per year into the indefinite future—if we don't kill it with bloody war or policy panic of the sort that caused the Great Deglobalization in

1914–1945. Two percent doesn't sound like much. But at such rates, the average person on the planet, more globalized and urbanized and educated and cured over the next century, will come to earn in real, inflation-adjusted terms three or four times more than a present-day Swiss or American person.

The Doubts Don't Make a Lot of Sense

But wait. Surely the anxieties about globalization have *some* economic and historical justification. Surely, it's not all rosy.

One reason people say so is that pessimistic histories and predictions are popular. You are cooler—if that is what you worry about being—to predict disaster even though it doesn't happen and to paint the past in dark colors though they are false than to adopt the optimistic bet on the century to come and the optimistic history of the two centuries past.

From 1776 to the present, though, the optimistic bet and history have been much the wiser. One important instance, contrary to what you hear about the rich getting richer and the poor getting poorer, is that globalization has radically reduced inequality of incomes. For one thing, the enrichment of the globe brought a great many of the wretched of the earth to a pretty good standard of comfort, the $50 a day. In 1901, the American economist John Bates Clark predicted that "the typical laborer will increase his wages [in real terms, allowing for inflation] from one dollar a day to two, from two to four and from four to eight.[3] Such gains will mean infinitely more to him than any possible increase of capital can mean to the rich. . . . This very change will bring with it a continual approach to equality of genuine comfort." His prediction was spot on.

And in any case, envy of the rich is not a sound basis for social policy, being insatiable. You can envy almost anyone, as Shakespeare put it, "wishing me like to one more rich in hope, / Featured like him, like him with friends possessed, / Desiring this man's art and that man's scope." The football star or rock musician or entrepreneur might inspire envy, but after all, they achieved their wealth by making you better off. You pay to get their services, voluntarily, and you gain. If you don't think so, please give me your season tickets to the Washington Nationals. Better: give me your access to Walmart or Amazon.com. Oh, wait, I already have my own access. Liberty of trade.

Furthermore, the force of arbitrage works to erode pools of great wealth. The Nobel economist William Nordhaus has calculated that the gain from all the innovations in the United States since World War II went overwhelmingly to us, the customers, American and foreign, when competitors to General Motors, General Electric, and General Foods rushed in. Once upon a time we faced the terrible "monopolies" of Kodak, Nokia, IBM, Toys "R" Us, Tower Records, and Blockbuster. They are all now one with Nineveh and Tyre. Eighty-five percent of the *Fortune* 500 firms in 1955 are gone. That's good, not bad. New ideas replace the old ones, and then new investment replaces the old, and new jobs replace the old, which is to our benefit.

The result is that during the second globalization, contrary again to what you may have heard on TV, the inequality of income worldwide has dramatically fallen (Figure 1.3). As China and India have enriched, their large shares of global population have risen from utter misery. Other successes such as Botswana and Ireland have added to the result that individuals worldwide are much more equal than ever. Want to see enormous inequality? Go back to 1800 and compare the Duchess of Norfolk with the average English peasant.

Another worry, especially from the left, is that globalization seems a terrible "minotaur," as the one-time finance minister of Greece Yanis Varoufakis calls it, a beast eating Athenian maidens. Varoufakis's case—that there is something sinister about investors moving investments around the globe in response to opportunities for arbitrage in returns on capital—would have at least a surface plausibility if it had not corresponded to the largest enrichment of the poor in human history.

Another is that the very enrichment from globalization is destroying the planet environmentally. But the invention of the automobile ended horrible pollution from horse poop in cities. Imposition of rules against soft-coal burning, and the replacement in heating by electricity, stopped life-shortening smog. And so forth. Want to save the environment? First get rich by globalization, and then watch the many millions of new engineers and entrepreneurs do it.

FIGURE 1.3

Global inequality declined significantly between 1950 and 2018

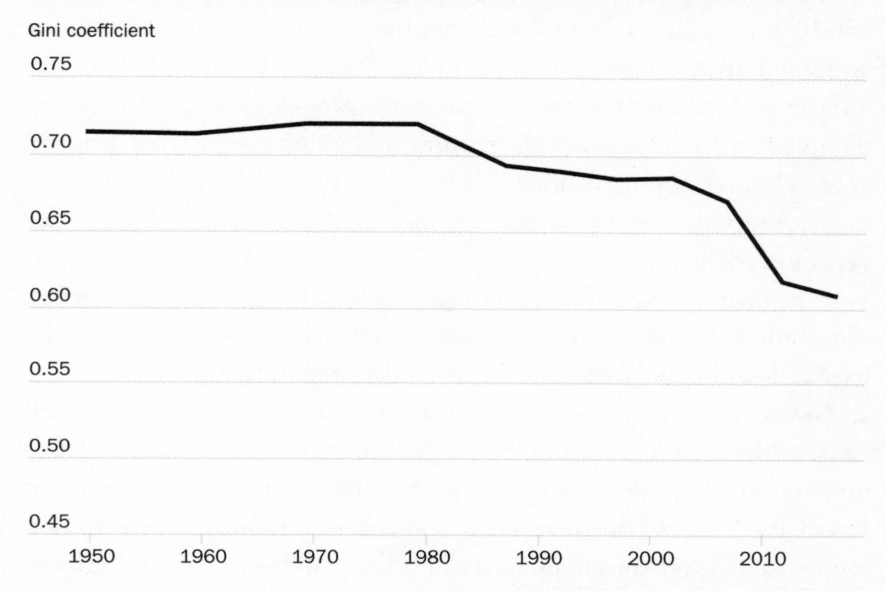

Source: Branko Milanovic, "The Three Eras of Global Inequality, 1820–2020, with the Focus on the Past Thirty Years," Stone Center on Socio-economic Inequality Working Paper no. 59, November 2022.

Note: GDP = gross domestic product; Gini coefficient of GDP per capita among countries, weighted according to population.

Fearful myths proliferate. For example, the decline in the United States, and every other rich country, in the share of the labor force making things such as cars and drill presses inspires fears of "deindustrialization." What the fearful folk mean is that the share of manufacturing *employment* has fallen. But the share of its output has not fallen as fast. That's good, not bad. American and British and French manufacturing is getting more productive per person. Rising productivity is the only way that real income per head can rise. If we don't have a bigger pie, the slices to everyone can't get larger.

Yet left and right and middle cry, "Bring back manufacturing to the United States, and establish self-sufficiency in the making of physical things." The local versions of the cry are: "Keep money in the neighborhood."

"Buy American." "Buy local." But if these are such fine ideas, why not bring manufacturing back to your own house? Make everything yourself. It's crazy. The crazy notion comes from the conviction that genuine output is a material good, an apple or an auto or an airplane, not "mere" services such as banking and insurance. It's part of the prejudice against the middleman dating back to Aristotle and Confucius. It's not sensible, as St. Thomas Aquinas among others noted. We need middlemen to do the necessary middle job of arbitrage, buying low and selling high to our benefit in efficiency.

The master myth haunting the fearful folk is that trade is war, or at best zero sum. They believe that what the United States gains, other countries have to lose. British writers in the 1890s declared imports from Germany an "invasion." Such a way of talking about peaceful trade was not a small cause of the shooting war in 1914. According to the war metaphor, an immigrant, too, "invades"—a Juan Valdez giving you a good, cheap meal in Iowa City. It echoes the mercantilist and Calvinist feeling that production is good, a win, yet consumption is bad, a loss. But we produce in order to consume, not consume in order to produce. You would want your labor to be less and your consumption to be more, yes? Of course.

In the 17th century, the English raised similar fears against the commercial Dutch, erecting protectionist policies against them and fighting three Anglo-Dutch wars. Nowadays, similar "invasion" by enriching East Asian nations arouses fears that would not now be applied to trade with the same Dutch, or the British. In the 1980s, the Japanese were feared by the fearful folk, and now the Chinese are. East Asians both. Is a little racism involved? Of course it is. China today might well be a military threat to the liberal order. Taiwan is a liberal country. But giving Americans TV sets in exchange for some soybeans and a few airplanes is not war.

Yet even if you can persuade the fearful that imports are not warfare and that globalization raises the goods and services available to us all, many folk fear *cultural* "invasions." Globalization is widely viewed as making world culture drearily uniform, "McDonaldization." But globalization has opened a cultural trade, as for instance in the explosion of world cuisine, using tastes and techniques from abroad. Keeping out foreign food, music, ideas, or science clearly makes no sense. The old Soviet Union tried to keep out American jazz and blue jeans, because they were from "capitalist" America and especially because they carried a message of liberal spontaneity. The Soviet masters favored authoritarian, top-down music, like a symphony under a conductor or a ballet under a choreographer, and favored conventional pants from centrally planned factories. They hated improvisation. Plan, plan, plan, and impose the plan coercively.

Local arts are commonly encouraged, not suppressed, by what the economist Tyler Cowen praises as "commercial culture." Soapstone sculptures and woven cloth by First Nations in Canada and the indigenous people of Guatemala end up in fashionable shops on Michigan Avenue, and the makers back in the villages prosper. The fear of cultural globalization causing cultural uniformity is overblown. South Asians learned the game of cricket from the British Raj. But now they play it their own way, the "great *tamasha*." As the anthropologists tell us, goods and procedures are reshaped by other cultures for their own purposes.

Quit being fearful about globalization.

And Globalization Is Ethical

The ethical case for globalization is not simply that it enriches us all, though it does. It's also that permitting arbitrage is an implication of allowing you to buy and sell with anyone you wish. It's elementary liberty. And liberty is liberty is liberty. The liberty to trade is among the liberties to speak and read and vote and live and love.

The left and the right, and often enough the center, disagree. They want to stop you from buying marijuana or buying a Toyota or buying a book with gay characters, even in the land of the free. The economic historian J. R. T. Hughes pointed out long ago that Americans have two contradictory positions, "Don't tread on me" and "Don't do *that*." That "*that*" consists of things like dressing as you want or loving whom you want or buying where you want. Globalization is part of liberty.

Such individual liberties are, well, individual. Not collective. A collective "general will" justifies "Don't do *that*." The only even approximately just notion of a general will is the economist's GDP per head.

Leaving people alone to work and trade, in line with the notion new in the 18th century of "Don't tread on me," led in fact to a Great Enrichment, that rise from $2 to $50 and beyond. Globalization by arbitrage was innovation's necessary environment, without which it wouldn't have happened.

But there's a crucial caveat. The Great Enrichment from 1776 to the present corrected for inflation was on the order of a 3,000 percent rise of income per head. But compared with such an astonishing order of magnitude, greater efficiency by itself accounts only for modest increases. Improvements in the English constitution in 1689, or the free migrations of the first globalization, or the dropping of tariffs in the Kennedy Round, were all to the good, to be sure. But their good was nothing like 3,000 percent. They resulted in economic enrichments on the order of, say, 10 percent, or even 100 percent. But not 3,000 percent, even if you add up all the merely efficiency-yielding arbitrages. Doing the same old routines a little better is, of course, a good idea, and liberal arbitrage makes it happen in both production and consumption. Get the marginal opportunity cost lined up with the marginal utility. Fine and dandy. But the really big developments, as the economist Israel Kirzner puts it in *The Foundation of Modern Austrian Economics*, come from "the incentive . . . to try to get something for nothing, if only one can see what it is that can be done."[4] Creativity is permitted to more and more humans. Massive invention therefore occurs. Innovation with arbitrage in markets makes it happen. The outcome has been the modern world, the bulk of the Great Enrichment, 3,000 percent and more.

That is, wholly new ideas, such as the steam engine and AC electricity and the modern corporation and careers for married women eventually permitted by the new liberalism of the 18th-century theorists like Adam Smith and Mary Wollstonecraft, are mainly what made us rich. Yet these, too, depended upon globalization. If governmental protectionism in goods or migrants was such a good idea, why not exclusively Russian science in Russia or Austrian music in Austria or US technology in the United States? Confining, say, the sonata form in classical music to Italy by strict law would in fact be advantageous only to a few Italian musicians and disadvantageous to everyone else. Ideas flow too. But they follow material trade. National systems of patents and copyrights attempt to obstruct the flow of ideas. Fortunately, they usually fail, even in the short run, and always have since 1776 in the long run. The notion of "intellectual property" raises incomes for lawyers and reduces the incomes of everyone else. Let's stop saying it and implementing it.

"Material" globalization, as it might be called, puts pressure on the more consequential globalization of ideas to take place. India protected its breakfast cereal industry by preventing Kellogg from entering India. Indian cold breakfast cereal was awful until the tariff was dropped after the liberalization from 1991. When auto tariffs into the United States were dropped, US automakers were forced to achieve Toyota standards of excellence. They learned new ideas, such as having one key for ignition, entry, and the trunk.

Conclusion

Globalization, in short, has been the great teacher, both at doing a good old job at old jobs and in creating massively new ideas for new jobs—efficiency and innovation.

Long, long may it reign.

Chapter 2

The Problem of the Tariff in American Economic History, 1787–1934

Philip W. Magness

- James Madison viewed tariffs as necessary to raise revenue but was caught off guard by early attempts to enact tariffs for industry protection.
- Alexander Hamilton and Henry Clay supported the use of tariffs to stimulate infant industries. However, there's little evidence the American System of tariffs and industrial subsidies was responsible for American economic growth in the 19th century.
- Contrary to the "national conservative" narrative, many of the leading figures of the American Founding opposed the protectionist arguments of Hamilton and Clay.
- From 1789 to 1934, tariff-seeking industries were notorious for diverting resources into rent seeking, or the lobbying of Congress for preferential rates with bribes and backroom deals.
- Corruption associated with protectionist tariff policy of the late 19th century directly led to adoption of the 16th Amendment and the federal income tax as an alternative revenue system.
- Modern American trade policy was restructured in 1934 to bypass the disastrous Smoot–Hawley Tariff Act of 1930, which exacerbated the Great Depression and illustrated the tendency of protectionist tariffs to serve corrupt interest groups.

Economists from across the political spectrum have long agreed on one area of policy: the removal of barriers to international trade. This consensus has guided the global embrace of trade liberalization between World War II and the present, coinciding with historically unprecedented levels of economic growth.

In recent years, free trade has gained numerous detractors who denounce the postwar period as an aberration from an alternative American economic history.[1] From Pat Buchanan in the early 1990s to former US Trade Representative Robert Lighthizer today, the United States became an economic powerhouse by strategically cultivating an industrial base through a system of protectionist tariffs, infrastructure improvements, and subsidies—the American System of the 19th century developed by politician Henry Clay.[2] Proponents of this view often depict free trade as a foreign doctrine originating in Britain and present themselves as revivalists of a lost historical record in which the United States industrialized under the active encouragement of government policies.

National conservatives extend their historical account to the present, calling for the use of tariff-based protectionism to reverse the United States' trade deficit between imports and exports. Their reasoning mistakes an accounting tool for a prescriptive policy while further neglecting that import restrictions impose symmetrical harms on exporters.[3] They nonetheless propose leveraging tariffs and other restrictive measures against allegedly unfair foreign actors. China has now taken the place of Britain, yet as the national conservative narrative makes abundantly clear, it is the precursors of the American System where they find their inspiration.

While Clay undoubtedly gave rise to a protectionist or "neo-mercantilist" strain of economic arguments in the United States, his position was heavily contested from the moment he announced it on the Senate floor in 1824. Protectionism certainly aided beneficiary industries, but it also spread the burden of higher prices to consumers at large and to the political system through widespread public corruption. Contrary to national conservatives' claims, the empirical link between tariffs and 19th-century economic development is weak—a case of post hoc, ergo propter hoc reasoning augmented by bad statistics and tendentious historical narratives. Their account also overlooks the numerous instances in which tariff protectionism fomented diplomatic and constitutional crises, triggered international retaliation, and hindered American economic development.

This essay investigates the historical development of tariff policy between the Founding era and the end of World War II. These events illustrate a multicentury contest between protection and free trade, culminating in the disastrous Smoot–Hawley Tariff Act of 1930 and instigating a shift in tariff-setting authority from Congress to the executive branch. The United States abandoned the American System approach with good reason after it produced a global economic quagmire at the outset of the Great Depression, and present trade policy is still conducted under the shadows of that mistake.

Prelude to American Trade Policy

The pursuit of free trade as national policy in the United States predates the Constitution. Responding to a Spanish government inquiry in 1780, John Jay expressed the fledgling nation's commitment to a principle of unimpeded exchange: "every man being then at liberty, by the law, to cultivate the earth as he pleased, to raise what he pleased, to manufacture as he pleased, and to sell the produce of his labor to whom he pleased, and for the best prices, without any duties or impositions whatsoever."[4] Jay's sentiments captured the Founding generation's unease with Britain's habit of manipulating its colonies' trading patterns through political interventions—a stated grievance of the Declaration of Independence some four years prior.

At the same time, tariffs were far from foreign in the Founding era. Owing to their relative ease of collection, they provided a source of tax revenue. The drafters of the Constitution envisioned this role when establishing the "Power To lay and collect Taxes, Duties, Imposts and Excises, to pay the Debts and provide for the common Defence and general Welfare of the United States." James Madison's notes from the convention reflect the primacy of this purpose, noting that the "reiterated and elaborate efforts of Cong. to procure from the States a more adequate power to raise the means of payment had failed."[5] His comments alluded to the failed attempts of the Confederation Congress to establish a low and uniform "impost" of 5 percent on imported goods in 1781 and 1783.

The 1787 Constitution aimed to rectify this obstacle with a system of indirect revenue tools. As convention delegates explained, imposts included a category of taxes that "are appropriated to commerce" whereas domestic goods could be taxed by excises against their value, or by specific "duties" such as a stamp on paper goods.[6] The document further restricted tax power by stipulating that "No Capitation, or other direct, Tax shall be laid, unless in Proportion to the Census." This second clause effectively removed direct taxation from the table, as enacting a levy on property or income would trigger a cumbersome apportionment formula based on the population of the taxed person's state. To raise revenue, the new federal government would either need to tax domestic production or international trade.

The new nation's first foray into tariff policy began innocently enough on April 9, 1789, when Madison introduced a bill to the House of Representatives proposing specific duties on alcohol and applying a tax "on all other articles ___ per cent. on their value at the time and place of import." Most expected a short debate, as indicated by Rep. Elias Boudinot of New Jersey, who followed Madison in suggesting "that the blanks be filled up in the manner they were recommended to be charged by Congress in 1783."[7] Rep. Thomas Fitzsimmons of Pennsylvania derailed the plan with a hastily drawn amendment to "encourage the productions of our country, and protect our infant manufactures."[8] The proposal caught Madison, and most of Congress, off guard. "If the duties should be raised too high," Madison warned in a letter, "the error will proceed as much from the popular ardor to throw the burden of revenue on trade as from the premature policy of stimulating manufactures."[9] And yet the allure of specialized rates swept through Congress, prompting requests from a succession of amendments seeking differentiated rates for favored goods from their home district or state. In his first major congressional action, Madison had unwittingly awakened the very same brand of factional politics he so eloquently diagnosed in *The Federalist Papers*. Except for slavery, tariffs became the most contentious federal policy issue of the 19th century and remained a source of continuous discord until the Great Depression.

Tariffs under the early constitutional system differed substantially from their use today. As Madison's 1798 bill illustrated, they were bound by the competing political objectives of revenue and protection. The government needed revenue, and tariffs on imported goods provided the lion's share for the next 125 years. This required a stable stream of goods crossing the border, with a modest tax attached to each. However, a strategy of protection only works if it discourages consumers from buying foreign goods by raising the price through a tax levy. The aim is to induce consumers to purchase American-made products at a higher price—but at the direct expense of revenue, because tariffs cause imports to decline under the weight of taxation. If Congress catered too heavily to infant industries, the government could unintentionally undermine its own tax base. Most tariff schedules in the following century accordingly strove to balance (a) maximizing revenue under low impost-style rates on heavily imported goods and (b) affording "incidental" protection to specific industries through differentiated rates.[10]

Formalizing Protectionism

Among the major figures of America's Founding, Alexander Hamilton stands alone for his dogged espousal of trade restrictions. As early as 1774, he suggested the colonies could adopt a policy of self-sufficient autarky:

> Those hands which may be deprived of business by the cessation of commerce, may be occupied in various kinds of manufactures and other internal improvements. If, by the necessity of the thing, manufactures should once be established, and take root among us, they will pave the way still more to the future grandeur and glory of America; and, by lessening its need of external commerce, will render it still securer against the encroachments of tyranny.[11]

Hamilton maintained in 1782 that "preserv[ing] the balance of trade in favor of a nation ought to be a leading aim of its policy" and continued to espouse a theoretical case for protectionism for most of his life.[12] His most famous foray into trade theorizing was an elaborate articulation of the "infant industry" argument in his 1791 *Report on Manufactures*.[13] Alluding to Britain's adoption of restrictive commerce and navigation policies against its colonies, the secretary of the treasury argued that considerations of fairness and self-sufficiency trumped theoretical ideals of free and open commerce with the world. Despite the rhetorical allure of his arguments, Hamilton also softened his specific policy prescriptions in the report. He proposed differentiated tariff rates, but they were only modestly protective in order to sustain a stable stream of revenue.

Hamilton's more sweeping prescription—a system of bounties to support industries and infrastructure—failed to gain acceptance in his lifetime. In no small irony given his origins, he spent his final years pushing for restrictions on immigration, believing that they tilted the electorate to his great rival Thomas Jefferson.[14] At the time of his death in a duel in 1804, the former secretary of the treasury left a more ambiguous tariff legacy than his later claimants acknowledge. In rhetoric, he laid out the arguments for heavy protection. In practice, though, he settled for the political realities and revenue needs of the government, acquiescing to a relatively moderate tariff schedule.

The case for high tariff protectionism in the United States fell to the next generation of political figures. The War of 1812 and its preceding embargoes on British goods unintentionally imposed a degree of industrial self-sufficiency on the fledgling nation. With the resumption of peace in 1816, former tariff detractors, including President Madison, acquiesced to higher rates that sustained some "incidental" protection to the same industries. The watershed moment for high protection came in 1824 in a speech by Sen. Henry Clay of Kentucky. Alluding to the boon to industry during and after the war, Clay outlined the tenets of the American System and aggressively called for a national policy of high tariff protection, "internal improvements" to infrastructure, and a robust national bank to sustain federal expenditures through debt finance where necessary.

Clay's speech remains central to the tariff mythology of today's national conservatives, as it allegedly fostered a century-long protectionist consensus in the United States. This version of history ignores the substantial opposition that mobilized against Clay's scheme and the decades of internal contestation that followed.

The American System provoked James Madison to respond to Clay that "I can not concur in the extent to which the pending Bill carries the tariff, nor in some of the reasoning by which it is advocated."[15] Jefferson went even further. Writing to Madison, he denounced the tariff internal improvement components alike and suggested that they exceeded the enumerated powers of the Constitution. In one of his last political acts before his death in 1826, Jefferson drafted a proposed resolution for the Virginia General Assembly, condemning Clay's measures as unconstitutional.[16] These statements marked a sharp turn from each figure's equivocal acceptance of the Tariff of 1816. The American System, in their minds, pushed protective doctrine far beyond its reasonable constitutional limits, which bound any assessment to the purpose of raising revenue.

Clay's proposal became a major dividing line in American politics for the next four decades. Tariffs offer lucrative benefits to recipient industries, allowing them to sell their goods at higher prices than under foreign competition. In a typical legislative setting, this means resources are happily diverted into rent seeking, the process whereby private actors lobby government for favorable laws and regulations that rewards them with private benefits.[17] With protective rates on the table, the tariff issue gave rise to the original lobbying establishment in Washington, DC. The pattern repeated itself every time Congress revised the tariff schedule.[18] Industry representatives flooded the body with requests for preferential rates. Backroom deals were cut to support parallel rates for industries in other districts and states, and bribes changed hands on committee floors. Although Clay packaged his scheme as a strategic and finely tuned economic program, its practical reality turned into a free-for-all of public graft.

Early 19th-century tariffs also depended on the nation's unpredictable sectional rifts. Southern agricultural exporters who faced price-taker status on a global market generally opposed high tariffs. Industrial mid-Atlantic states became the locus of protectionist doctrine, led by the electoral powerhouse of Pennsylvania. New England sundered into protection-seeking textile mills, a merchant sector that was at times more disposed toward trade, and producers of raw materials such as wool that faced import competition. The western states often functioned as a swing block on tariff issues, making them ripe for legislative logrolling to secure their votes.[19]

For Clay, a slaveowner with reservations about the institution, this caused a conundrum. The underlying economics of the American System involved a strategy of import substitution wherein southern cash crops would be redirected from Europe to the textile mills of the northeast in exchange for domestically made manufactured goods. By "harmonizing" these chains of production and ensuring a domestic buyer with subsidized transport improvements, Clay aimed to placate the South into the tariff coalition. In doing so, he risked further entrenching slavery. As a solution, Clay appended the American System with a proposed program of compensated emancipation and colonization of freed slaves abroad in locations such as Liberia—an impractical and racially paternalistic scheme that nonetheless continued to influence national policy until the Civil War.[20]

The period between 1824 and 1846 saw a succession of competing tariff policy regimes, vacillating between protection and free trade as legislative coalitions shifted. In 1828, protectionists gained the advantage after a legislative ploy backfired on the free traders. The latter group attempted to load the revised schedule with so many amendments and carve-outs for industry that it would alienate New England's mercantile businesses and kill the bill. Instead, the "Tariff of Abominations" narrowly passed, raising the average rate on dutiable imports to over 60 percent.

The protectionists' victory in 1828 and a slightly moderated replacement schedule in 1832 precipitated a political crisis that played out in stages over the next five years. Enraged by the new tariff schedule and looking to deflect national attention away from slavery, South Carolina passed a nullification ordinance against the measure in 1832. The fallout from this measure pitted President Andrew Jackson against his own vice president, John C. Calhoun, prompting the latter to resign his position to take a seat in the Senate. With threats of disunion and a counteracting Force Bill authorizing the president to compel tariff collection with military action if necessary, Calhoun and Clay negotiated a détente. The Compromise Tariff of 1833 gradually reduced rates to their 1816 level over the next decade.

Clay's Whig Party resumed the upper hand and briefly imposed higher protectionist rates under the Tariff of 1842, only to see their fortunes reversed by the comprehensive overhauls of the Walker Tariff of 1846. This final iteration of the antebellum tariff system established a standardized schedule of ad valorem rates, intended to streamline the complex and cluttered schedules that preceded it. The Walker act also drastically reduced rates in a free trade direction, although it preserved some "incidental protection" by classifying certain industries on the highest rate schedule. Offered as a reform measure, the tariff reduction intentionally coincided with Britain's near-simultaneous repeal of the protectionist Corn Laws, leading to another decade and a half of relatively free trade on both sides of the Atlantic.[21]

The Civil War upended trade liberalization under the Walker rates. Tariffs did not cause the war, as some Confederates later alleged in attempts to downplay the central role of slavery.[22] Economic recession in 1857 breathed life into protectionism, making tariffs a regional campaign issue in 1860. The withdrawal of southern states from Congress in the 1860–1861 "secession winter" session unexpectedly enabled protectionists to remove a procedural block on the Morrill Tariff bill and secure its passage on the eve of Abraham Lincoln's inauguration.

National conservatives often celebrate this law because it ushered in a period of high tariff protectionism that lasted until 1913. Their enthusiasm fundamentally misunderstands the measure, which economist William Stanley Jevons denounced as "the most retrograde piece of legislation" to ever emerge from the United States.[23] Like its predecessors, the Morrill Tariff emerged from corrupt bargaining of beneficiary interest groups.[24] Its shortsighted favors to recipient industries infuriated Great Britain, one of the country's largest trading partners. All else equal, British anti-slavery sentiments should have made them a natural sympathizer with the Union cause during the Civil War. Instead, tariff irritation became a diplomatic blunder that helped push Britain into an uneasy neutrality.

Enjoying the upper hand provided by the Morrill schedule, protectionist interests entrenched themselves in the postbellum period, particularly after fending off a challenge from the free trade wing of the Liberal Republican movement in 1872. National conservatives often point to the high economic growth of the late 19th-century tariff era as "proof" of the American System's success; however, this position relies on a misreading of evidence.

As economist Douglas Irwin notes, "tariffs coincid[ing] with rapid growth in the late nineteenth century does not imply a causal relationship." American System proponents failed to articulate the mechanism whereby tariffs contributed to this pattern, amid other complications. For example, many "infant" US manufacturing industries they credit to tariffs began in the comparatively low-tariff late antebellum era. Non-traded economic sectors such as utilities also saw faster growth rates and capital accumulation than import-competing manufactured goods in the late 19th century, defying the pattern that the protectionists would predict. Irwin summarily notes that hypothesized "links between tariffs and productivity are elusive."[25] The claimed correlation with growth is both exaggerated and likely spurious. There's also evidence that the harms of late 19th-century protectionism outweighed the isolated benefits to selected industries on net. Economist Bradford DeLong identifies two such harms: (1) the loss of agricultural exports to Europe through symmetry effects, effectively harming farmers in order to prop up northeastern industries, and (2) higher prices on imported machinery and other capital goods, which likely impaired the pace at which America industrialized.[26]

At the same time, high tariff protectionism continued to attract rent-seeking interest groups. The sheer extravagance of the public corruption around tariff schedule revisions came to a head in the late 19th century, eventually leading reformers to call for the abandonment of a tariff-based revenue system. Since tariffs were ostensibly a revenue device under the

Constitution, swapping a different federal tax system would obviate the need for their continuation and thereby break the protectionist interest group coalition. This was the primary argument behind the federal income tax movement that eventually carried the day in 1913.

Tariff reformers had a plan to effect a swap, but they also faced a constitutional obstacle. In the 1895 decision of *Pollock v. Farmers Loan and Trust*, the Supreme Court struck down a federal income tax provision. It violated the Constitution's population apportionment requirement for direct taxation, meaning that the case would either have to be reversed or that the Constitution would have to be amended. The latter outcome emerged from a legislative standoff during the Payne-Aldrich tariff schedule revisions of 1909. When Republican senator Nelson Aldrich opened the revision process to tariff-seeking interest groups, a segment of his party threatened to revolt against the overreach. The combination of these Republican "insurgents" and free trade-aligned Democratic minority cast the chamber into chaos. As a negotiated solution that kept his tariff in place, Aldrich agreed to permit a constitutional amendment authorizing a future income tax. The plan backfired in 1913 after voters swept the Republicans out of office and the newly ratified 16th Amendment authorized the long-sought tax swap.

Protectionism in the Income Tax Era

For a fleeting moment, the tax swap strategy worked. The average tariff rate on dutiable goods had hovered between 40 percent and 50 percent since the Civil War. The Underwood Tariff of 1913 reduced it to less than 20 percent by the end of the decade and compensated for lost revenue by imposing a modest income tax with a top marginal rate of 7 percent on earnings over $500,000 (about $13 million in 2020). The revenue yield from the income tax far exceeded the expectations of its original backers in 1909. Revenue measures prompted by the US entry into World War I hiked the top marginal rate to an astounding 77 percent in 1918, and peacetime measures held it above 50 percent until 1924.

The 16th Amendment completely decoupled tariffs from their function as a revenue source and fundamentally altered the political economy of trade policy. As Frank Chodorov astutely observed in *The Income Tax: The Root of All Evil*, the new "income tax so enriched the Treasury that the revenue from tariffs became unimportant, and the government could afford to give more and more protection to the manufacturers."[27] Before 1913, the government revenue needs imposed an informal upper boundary on tariff rates, lest Congress "protect" itself into autarky and out of a revenue stream. As the tax swappers discovered to their chagrin in 1922, an alternative revenue source meant all bets were off. That year, the new Republican Congress restored rates to their pre-Underwood levels through the Fordney-McCumber Tariff, framing its provisions as economic stimulus to manufacturing as the economy transitioned away from wartime production.

A relatively strong domestic economy absorbed the resulting price increases, but policymakers took the wrong lessons from Fordney-McCumber. When the stock market crashed in 1929, congressional Republicans already had a second tariff schedule hike on the legislative agenda under the Smoot–Hawley Act. At the introduction of the bill in early 1929, Representative Hamilton Fish of New York appealed to the principles "laid down by Henry Clay—the principle of protecting the home market." "The question," Fish continued, "is simply whether you prefer to conserve the home market and protect American wage earners or let the products of low-paid foreign labor destroy the home market for the American producer."[28]

The emerging recession accelerated the adoption of Smoot–Hawley. Its supporters framed the measure as a stimulus package to insulate American industry from the downturn. In practice, it became a legislative free-for-all of corruption. Almost overnight, the measure raised average tariff rates to nearly 60 percent, a level unseen since the "Tariff of Abominations" a century prior. Special interests flooded committee rooms, exchanging cash under the table for favorable rates to insulate themselves from foreign competitors amid the unfolding downturn. Smoot–Hawley backfired catastrophically. Instead of boosting American industry, it precipitated a trade war of retaliatory measures worldwide. American agriculture bore the brunt of it, as crop exports declined, accelerating the insolvency crisis on farm mortgages. The total volume of world trade (measured in 1934 dollars) declined from almost $3 billion in January 1929 to just $992 million in January 1933.

Despite growing recognition of its error, Congress soon found that it had little recourse to repeal Smoot–Hawley, which remains the official US tariff schedule to this day. Game theory explains the conundrum. Universally high rates had killed off international trade, yet if any individual industry succeeded in retaining beneficial rates for itself while all other rates were lowered, it might find itself reaping high concentrated rewards under isolated protection vis-à-vis the rest of the economy. Although most observers agreed that Smoot–Hawley needed to go, no individual industry would voluntarily relinquish its rates. "The very tendencies that have made the legislation bad," wrote political scientist E. E. Schattschneider, "have . . . made it politically invincible."[29]

The solution to the Smoot–Hawley stalemate came through an innovative flanking move. Designed by Secretary of State Cordell Hull, the Reciprocal Trade Agreements Act of 1934 (RTAA) shifted the locus of trade policy to the executive branch. While Congress still retained the constitutional power to set the tariff schedule by law, the RTAA codified presidential power to negotiate bilateral trade agreements with other countries. It also established a congressional ratification procedure requiring only a simple majority, as opposed to the supermajority required for a treaty. Since the presidency draws upon a larger national constituency for electoral support, it enjoys comparatively greater insulation from local interest groups that dominate congressional tariff schedule adjustments. The State Department could consequently negotiate more favorable rates than those specified by Smoot–Hawley, effectively bypassing the congressional impasse one nation at a time.

The RTAA's approach ushered in an unprecedented period of near-continuous trade liberalization. By the end of World War II, the average US tariff rate on dutiable goods dropped from almost 60 percent under Smoot–Hawley to less than 30 percent, without formally changing the tariff schedule. In 1947, its underlying structure provided a model for multilateral trade liberalization under the General Agreement on Tariffs and

FIGURE 2.1

The Reciprocal Trade Agreements Act and the General Agreement on Tariffs and Trade ushered in an unprecedented lowering of US tariffs

Average tariff rate on dutiable imports, percentage

Source: Bureau of the Census, "Series U 207–212. Value of Merchandise Imports and Duties: 1821 to 1970," in *Historical Statistics of the United States: Colonial Times to 1970, Part II* (Washington: US Department of Commerce, 1975), p. 288; and "Table 1 US Imports for Consumption, Duties Collected, and Ratio of Duties Collected to Value, 1891–2021 (Thousand $)," US International Trade Commission.

Note: Only covers goods imports. Dutiable imports are imports that are subject to tariffs (i.e., did not enter duty-free).

Trade (GATT), the precursor to today's World Trade Organization. The RTAA/GATT model is far from free of interest group manipulation—indeed, the GATT created numerous antidumping and emergency "escape clause" exceptions taken directly from Smoot–Hawley and Fordney-McCumber. At the same time, its effects are plainly visible in Figure 2.1. It is noteworthy that over the same period, gross domestic product per capita dramatically rose in the United States (Figure 2.2). While this growth cannot be exclusively attributed to trade liberalization, it belies

FIGURE 2.2
US real GDP per capita rose dramatically over the period when trade was liberalized post–World War II

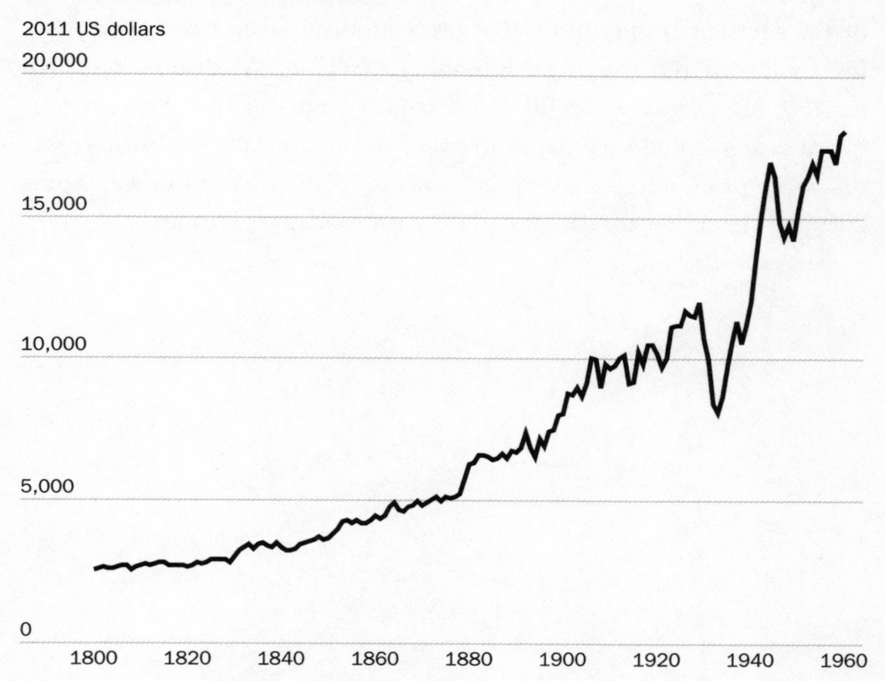

Source: "GDP Per Capita, 1 to 2018," Our World in Data.
Note: GDP = gross domestic product; data in constant 2011 US dollars.

the claims of protectionists who erroneously associate the postwar period with American economic decline.

Conclusion

At its heart, the national conservative charge to revive tariffs is an attempt to reverse this pattern and return the United States to the Smoot–Hawley model of congressional primacy in trade policy. They present this objective as part of a historical narrative that appeals to Hamilton and especially Clay and assert an unsubstantiated link between 19th-century economic growth and tariffs. Concurrently, they conspicuously omit any hint of the rampant corruption of tariff schedules in the congressional era, of the many times that tariff hikes backfired from Civil War diplomacy to the economic ruination of the Great Depression, and of the substantial opposition that protectionism faced from other leading figures of the American Founding. As James Madison discovered in 1789, not even the careful checks and balances of the new constitutional system could keep the problem of the faction at bay. Nowhere was this more pronounced than in the new government's tariff power. Some 230 years later, we are still grappling with Madison's lessons.

Chapter 3

Comparative Advantage

Donald J. Boudreaux

- Superior technical proficiency at producing a particular good is not the same as superior economic efficiency at producing that good.
- The key to understanding comparative advantage is opportunity costs: determining whether to produce something yourself or to purchase it from another producer requires comparing the cost of producing that good yourself to the cost that you'd incur to purchase it. Because of comparative advantage, another producer who is less technically proficient at producing the good might nevertheless be able to profitably sell you that good at a price lower than your cost of making the good yourself. That other producer can do so if it has a comparative advantage at producing that good.
- When one person or productive unit, such as a firm, improves its comparative advantage at some task, it thereby improves its trading partners' comparative advantages at other tasks.
- While government export subsidies harm citizens of the countries that use them, they benefit citizens of countries that purchase the subsidized exports. The use by foreign governments of export subsidies does not justify the home government doing the same or otherwise interfering with trade.

Comparative advantage, like language, is ubiquitous. No one who interacts with anyone can escape its operation, which occurs every moment of every day to everyone everywhere. Also like language, comparative advantage was not invented; it arises naturally whenever humans interact with each other. Nor can its array of vast details be reengineered at will to achieve some visionary's dream. And each of us uses comparative advantage to our benefit without being aware that we're doing so. Except for a handful of economists, almost no one knows about comparative advantage, and therefore, almost no one can describe it or articulate its logic.

So what exactly is this profound economic force?

This essay answers that question and several related others. In the process, it demonstrates how specialization and trade guided by comparative advantage improve our daily lives—*and* that despite being a relatively easy or even trivial concept to grasp, comparative advantage is full of surprising implications.

What Is Comparative Advantage?

Most simply, comparative advantage refers to a person's ability and willingness to supply other people with a good or service that these other people cannot otherwise acquire at a lower cost. Described this way, comparative advantage appears trite: to say that Ann has a comparative advantage at supplying fish to Bob is to say only that, at least for Bob, the lowest-cost supplier of fish is Ann. If, therefore, Bob wants to acquire fish and have as much income remaining as possible to buy other things, he'd best buy fish from Ann. Nothing about such a relationship is remarkable or even interesting.

Yet while the previous paragraph is accurate, it's the tip of an iceberg. The great bulk of the reality and significance of comparative advantage lies beneath the surface, with unseen surprises.

The chief nontrivial insight gained from understanding comparative advantage is this: an economic entity's technical ability to produce a product is, by itself, irrelevant for determining if that entity should produce that product itself or acquire that product by first producing something else and then trading that something else for the desired product.

A simple example: You want a new deck and are willing to pay up to $21,000 for it, but you're also an excellent carpenter. If you work full time to build the deck yourself, you can build it in one month. Your neighbor Jones, however, offers to build you a deck of identical quality, but because his carpentry skills are not as good as yours, it will take Jones two months to complete the job. Clearly, if technical ability were all that mattered, you should build your own deck.

But an understanding of comparative advantage reveals that this reality is insufficient to economically justify your building the deck. Your building the deck would be worthwhile only if your *cost* of doing so were less than the cost of having someone else, such as Jones, build it for you.

How can it be that Jones could build the deck for you at a lower cost? According to comparative advantage, your being a better carpenter than Jones tells us nothing about whether you are economically a more efficient deck builder than Jones. What matters economically is the opportunity cost to you to personally build your deck *compared to* the opportunity cost to you of having Jones build the deck for you. That you possess better skills for building decks than Jones doesn't guarantee that the cost to you of building the deck is less than the cost to Jones.

If you work as a radiologist and earn an annual salary of $240,000, taking one month off work to build your deck would cost you a month's worth of income, or $20,000. Because you value the deck at $21,000, if the only way for you to acquire the deck would be for you to build it yourself, you'd find it worthwhile to spend your time building the deck.

Fortunately, you have a better option. Your neighbor Jones works as a bookkeeper. His annual salary is $84,000, or $7,000 per month. If Jones were to take *two* months off his job to build your deck, he'd forgo an income of $14,000. Clearly Jones can build the deck at a cost $6,000 lower than the cost you'd incur to build it yourself. So you hire Jones for two months at the competitive wage, paying him $14,001 to build your deck.

Had you personally built your deck, you'd have denied yourself $20,000 of income and $20,000 worth of radiology services for others.

TABLE 3.1

While you are better at building a deck than Jones, paying him to build it benefits you and the economy

Scenario A: You build the deck yourself

	$ Value
Your earnings from building the deck	$0
Your opportunity cost of building it*	$20,000
Jones's income at his job (because he is not building)**	$14,000
Net outcome: You lose by building yourself rather than employing Jones for $14,001	**-$5,999**

Scenario B: You hire Jones to build the deck

	$ Value
Jones's earnings from building the deck (i.e., what you pay him)	$14,001
Jones's opportunity cost of building it**	$14,000
Total income you earn at your job (because you hired Jones)*	$20,000
Cost to you of hiring Jones	$14,001
Net outcome: Your savings from employing Jones to build	**$5,999**

*Your opportunity cost is the income you earn at your regular job as a radiologist over the course of a month (i.e., the amount of time it would take you to build the deck).
**Jones's opportunity cost is the income he earns at his regular job as a bookkeeper over the course of two months (i.e., the amount of time it would take him to build the deck).

In contrast, by employing Jones to build your deck, the value of the services denied others is only $14,000.

You're technically a more proficient deck builder than Jones, but economically this is irrelevant. What's relevant are opportunity costs. Because Jones's opportunity cost of building the deck is lower than yours, Jones is economically a better deck builder than you—by $6,000. Jones has a *comparative* advantage over you at building decks. Table 3.1 summarizes this example.

The lesson is that if the goal is maximum possible economic gain, the determination of what an economic entity should or shouldn't produce cannot be made according to that entity's technical proficiency. What matters economically is the cost to the entity of acquiring the desired output by producing the output itself compared to the cost of producing something else, earning income from the sale of that something else and then using that income to buy the desired output from another producer—that is, compared to the cost of trading for the desired output.

This reality is not affected by the political jurisdiction in which the different parties live. You and Jones might be neighbors in the United States, or Jones might live across the border in Canada. Either way, it's worthwhile for Jones to build your deck. And it's better for the economy: If you build the deck, you would deny the economy $20,000 worth of economic output from your regular job; if Jones builds it, the economy loses only $14,000 from his regular job. Nothing—not even government subsidies—alters this conclusion, at least not for citizens of the home country.

What Are Some Comparative Advantage Surprises?

The scholar, financier, and statesman David Ricardo (1772–1823) is credited with first clearly identifying comparative advantage. He did so in Chapter 7 ("On Foreign Trade") of his 1817 treatise, *On the Principles of Political Economy and Taxation*. Ricardo used a simple example to show that under reasonable assumptions, even if the Portuguese were technically superior to the English at producing both wine and cloth, if the Portuguese's superiority over the English at producing wine was greater than their superiority over the English at producing cloth, both the English and the Portuguese would gain if the English specialized at producing cloth, the Portuguese specialized at producing wine, and then each country freely traded with the other.

Ever since Ricardo offered his explanation of what still appears to many people to be a surprising conclusion, the case for free trade has regularly been said to rest on comparative advantage. While correct, the common interpretation of this fact misses an important reality. This common interpretation holds that a pattern of comparative advantage exists and *then* gives rise to the pattern of specialization and trade that reflects the preexisting comparative advantages. This sequence often happens in the real world but not always.

Adam Smith (1723–1790), whose 1776 *Inquiry into the Nature and Causes of the Wealth of Nations* was published 41 years before Ricardo's treatise, demonstrated that specialization is advantageous even *without* a preexisting pattern of comparative advantage. For Smith, specialization improves workers' or businesses' technical proficiency at producing the goods and services in which they specialize. By concentrating on doing a particular task, each producer over time becomes better at performing that task. That is, by specializing, each producer creates for itself a comparative advantage. For Smith, specialization is the *source* of comparative advantage (although Smith was unaware of this principle's full reality); for Ricardo, specialization is the *result* of comparative advantage.

Both Smith and Ricardo are correct. Taken together, their analyses identify a virtuous cycle of improvement in economic productivity. Specialization begets greater comparative advantages, while greater comparative advantages increase the benefits of specialization. This is one surprise; combining Smith's analysis with Ricardo's reveals others.

By concentrating his or her productive efforts on a particular task, a specialized producer further improves his or her skills at doing the task for which that person has a comparative advantage, thereby becoming an economically *worse* performer of other tasks.

Consider the deck-building example. Despite your being technically better at carpentry than Jones, it pays to employ Jones to build your deck. Suppose, as Adam Smith predicts, your concentrating your time working as a radiologist improves your radiology skills and causes your annual salary to rise to $252,000. At your higher salary, building the deck yourself would cost you $21,000 rather than $20,000. Your becoming a better radiologist makes you, economically, a worse—that is, a more costly—deck builder even though your proficiency at carpentry hasn't declined.

More surprisingly, your becoming a better radiologist makes Jones, compared to you, an economically better deck builder—even if Jones's technical proficiency at carpentry remains unchanged. His cost of building the deck ($14,000) was 70 percent of your cost of doing so ($20,000) at your previous wages. Now that your radiology skills have improved and your wages are higher, however, Jones's cost of building the deck is only 66.7 percent of your new cost of doing so ($21,000). Your improved radiology skills economically improves Jones's carpentry skills *in comparison to yours*. Put differently, the improvement in your comparative advantage at radiology improved Jones's comparative advantage at building decks.

You're obviously made better off by becoming a better radiologist. But is Jones made better off by the resulting improvement of his comparative advantage at building decks? Possibly, but not necessarily. If the amount that you pay Jones to build your deck isn't increased by your improved skills at radiology, Jones reaps no benefit from your improved radiology skills (unless he finds himself in need of the services of a radiologist, but that's a different story). But two facts here are worth noting. First, Jones isn't harmed by your becoming a better radiologist. Second, Jones is *potentially* made better off by your becoming a better radiologist.

Before the improvement in your radiology skills, you would have been willing to pay Jones up to $20,000 to build the deck, but not a cent more. Had Jones earlier demanded to be paid, say, $20,500, you would have refused, and he would have had no hope of changing your mind. The reason, of course, is that earlier you could have built the deck yourself for $20,000. But since your radiology skills have improved, you're now willing to pay him as much as $21,000 to build the deck.

Obviously, you want to pay Jones as little as possible. Whether or not your improved comparative advantage at radiology—meaning also Jones's improved comparative advantage at building decks—redounds to Jones's benefit depends on how many people are competing for Jones's services as a producer. The more intense this competition, the more likely it is that market forces will drive you to share with Jones some of the benefits you reap from your improved radiology skills.

The question of whether and by how much you would be driven by market forces to share with Jones the benefits of your enhanced comparative advantage at radiology can be answered only by investigating the structure and competitiveness of markets—chiefly, the number of buyers and suppliers of deck-building services. Such an investigation is beyond this essay's scope. It's enough here to demonstrate the surprising and important fact that when the comparative advantage of party A improves, the comparative advantage of party A's trading partner—party B—also improves, thus at least *potentially* increasing party B's welfare in addition to the certain improvement of party A's welfare.

How Does Comparative Advantage Apply to International Trade?

Comparative advantage ultimately exists at the level of individuals and firms: No country *as such* has comparative advantages or disadvantages. Nevertheless, patterns of international trade reflect the international pattern of comparative advantage. If, for example, producers in the United States have a comparative advantage over producers in Mexico and Sweden at producing pharmaceutical products, the United States would export pharmaceutical products to Mexico and Sweden and import goods from these countries that they produce at a comparative advantage over the United States. If, say, Mexico has a comparative advantage at producing prefabricated buildings while Sweden's comparative advantage is producing fish, Americans would export pharmaceutical products and import prefabricated buildings from Mexico and fish from Sweden. And Mexico and Sweden would similarly produce and trade based on their comparative advantages.

Talking of countries trading with each other can be a useful shorthand as long as it's kept in mind that individuals and firms, not countries, trade and that comparative advantages and disadvantages exist only at the level of the specific producer units, meaning individuals and firms. Observed patterns of international trade reflect the patterns of comparative advantages that exist across the different producer units in each country.

Do Subsidies Obviate Comparative Advantage?

What happens if we introduce subsidies? Let's return to our deck-building example. What would happen if a Canadian producer were to be subsidized by its government to build decks in the United States?

Suppose that you and Jones live in America while Schwartz lives in Canada and is a neurosurgeon whose annual earnings are $360,000. Like Jones, Schwartz is technically a worse carpenter than you are and would require two months to build your deck. Unlike Jones, however, if Schwartz took two months off work, she would sacrifice more income ($60,000) than you'd sacrifice by taking off one month ($21,000). Clearly, among you, Jones, and Schwartz, the comparative advantage at building the deck remains with Jones, so you prepare to hire Jones to do the job.

But before finalizing the contract with Jones, Canada's government announces that it will pay Schwartz $50,000 if she lets herself be hired to build your deck. In this case, were Schwartz to build your deck, her net loss of income from taking time off from the hospital would be only $10,000. If you then offer to pay Schwartz $10,001 to spend two months to build your deck, she'd happily do it.

Because hiring Jones requires that you pay him at least $14,001, you now find it attractive to employ Schwartz at any price less than $14,001. So you employ Schwartz to build your deck for $10,001. She'll accept because her total income over the two months she spends building your deck would be slightly more than $60,000—the $50,000 subsidy paid to her by the Canadian government plus the $10,001 paid to her by you.

Schwartz is slightly better off with this arrangement, as she earns for those two months $1 more than she would by working as a neurosurgeon. Jones is slightly worse off, missing out on the opportunity to earn the extra $1 that he'd have made had you hired him. You, however, are made better off by this subsidy by $4,000.

Canada's subsidy makes the *American* economy better off by $4,000. With your deck being built by the Canadian Schwartz instead of by the American Jones, the US economy doesn't lose the $14,000 in Jones's bookkeeping services. Instead, the cost to the US economy of building your deck under Canada's subsidy scheme is only the $10,001 that you pay to the Canadian Schwartz, a sum $4,000 less than you'd have paid to employ Jones.

Schwartz doesn't have a "real" comparative advantage over Jones at building your deck. Schwartz is employed to build the deck in the United States only because her government subsidizes her. For Canadians, the subsidy only makes it *appear* that Schwartz has the comparative advantage at deck building. Canadians' taxes are raised by $50,000 to entice Schwartz to work at a job at which she would otherwise not work—a job at which she doesn't really have a comparative advantage.

Yet for Americans—whose taxes *aren't* raised to pay for this subsidy—this appearance of Schwartz's comparative advantage at deck building is an economic reality. For Americans, her deck-building services are indeed available at a cost lower than what you or Jones would incur. For Americans, Canada's subsidies are a gift that enriches us no less than we'd be enriched had an unsubsidized Canadian entrepreneur invented a process for lowering the cost of building decks to $10,001, thus enabling you to purchase one of these lower-cost decks at that price.

From Americans' perspective, the *source* of lower-cost options abroad is irrelevant. If these lower-cost options arise naturally—say, because there is discovered abroad more deposits of some raw material—we Americans would gain by taking advantage of the foreigners' improved comparative advantage. If instead these lower-cost options arise artificially—say, because foreign governments subsidize exports—we Americans still would gain, and we would gain no less than when foreigners actually improve their comparative advantage. In both cases we get more exports in exchange for any given amount of our imports.

Any economic downsides, such as some Americans' losing particular jobs, that arise in America from our purchase of foreign outputs made artificially less pricey by subsidies arise no less from our purchase of foreign outputs made naturally less pricey by foreigners' improved real comparative advantage. In both cases we should welcome the increased bounty to which we have access through trade. Artificial advantages might raise *political* concerns (e.g., Jones demanding import protection or his own subsidies), but they do not raise economic ones.

Is Government Intervention Needed to Improve an Economy's Comparative Advantages?

An understandable objection to this conclusion is that governments don't dispense subsidies willy-nilly. At least in some cases, governments use subsidies as tools to transform industries in which their countries don't currently have a comparative advantage into industries that will in the future have a comparative advantage. Subsidies, often combined with protective tariffs, are in these cases designed by each government to ensure that its country hopefully will have a better set of comparative advantages than it would have under a policy of free trade.

This essay's task isn't to assess this so-called industrial policy. Excellent assessments are available from many sources, including Charles Schultze, Don Lavoie, Deirdre McCloskey and Alberto Mingardi, Scott Lincicome, Samuel Gregg, and Linda Cohen and Roger Noll.[1] It's sufficient to note here that industrial policy's historical record offers no reason for optimism that government attempts to artificially improve a nation's pattern of comparative advantage will enhance the wealth of the nation.

Fortunately, to ensure vigorous economic growth, we don't have to rely on the state to engineer improved comparative advantages. Not only does the state have little prospect of succeeding at this task, but individuals have strong incentives and abilities to change their comparative advantages from worse to better.

Indeed, almost no individual goes through life with same comparative advantage that he or she was born with. People get educated. People acquire job skills. Businesses change their product lines, hiring new workers who bring skills that existing employees don't possess. Entrepreneurs innovate with new outputs and techniques of production and distribution—efforts that, when successful, create new comparative advantages for workers and firms.

These individual- and firm-level efforts to change their comparative advantages are, unlike industrial-policy efforts, guided by market prices. When the wages paid to workers with particulars skills rise, other workers are incited to acquire those skills—that is, to change their comparative advantages. When the prices of some outputs rise relative to the prices of other outputs, entrepreneurs shift their efforts into the production of the now-higher-priced outputs, thus often altering their comparative advantages.

Also, unlike industrial-policy efforts, private efforts to explore and pursue different comparative advantages are disciplined by the prospect of loss. Not spending other people's money, private workers and firms abandon failed projects as soon as the likelihood of failure appears sufficiently high. Government officials, in contrast, are too likely to throw (other people's) good money after bad, promising that the vision earlier sold to the public will be realized if only the government shovels yet more resources into the pet projects.

In short, the comparative advantage at pursuing better comparative advantages is had by individuals operating in competitive markets—not by pundits and politicians pursuing their hunches and visions with other people's money and in contradiction to market prices.

Conclusion

The nature of comparative advantage is such that it will exist as long as humanity exists. And as long as comparative advantage exists, there will also exist possibilities for mutually advantageous trade. This reality is unaffected by political borders. Gains from specialization and trade inspired by comparative advantage are not one jot fewer if the trading parties are citizens of different countries than if they're citizens of the same country. Therefore, obstructing international trade with the goal of improving citizens' economic welfare in fact worsens that welfare as it prevents citizens from taking full advantage of the opportunities to specialize and trade according to their comparative advantages.

This conclusion holds even if (as is almost always the case) foreign governments interfere with their citizens' freedom to trade. When a government grants special privileges, such as tariff protection or subsidies, to particular producers within its country's borders, the bulk of the burden of these privileges falls on that government's citizens. As a result, that country is made poorer, not richer. And the home country only worsens its own economic performance if it retaliates with tariffs and subsidies[2] of its own. Further, in the case of export subsidies, there is also an unambiguous *gain* for citizens of the countries that purchase those exports. From the perspective of citizens of the home country, export subsidies paid by foreign governments are sources of benefits identical to those that would be enjoyed if producers in foreign countries had improved their comparative advantages.

Comparative advantage does indeed supply a solid economic justification for a policy of unilateral free trade.

Chapter 4

The Trade Balance and Winning at Trade

Andreas Freytag and Phil Levy

- It would be very convenient if trade balances served as a score-card for winning or losing at trade. The problem is that the data don't support such an interpretation.
- The trade balance does not describe how many jobs will be gained or lost through exports and imports.
- In reality, the trade balance mirrors international borrowing and lending. Those don't clearly indicate whether a country is winning or losing at trade.
- Reducing the US trade deficit would require promoting a higher domestic rate of savings, especially by the heavily indebted US government—not restricting trade.

Are We "Winning" at Trade?

How do we know if the United States is "winning" at international trade?

If we ask that question about economic growth, the answer is pretty easy to find: You can look and see how much US gross domestic product (GDP) has increased. If we ask the same question about the labor market, we can look at the unemployment rate.

So what is the equivalent scorecard for trade?

Here's where economists part ways from most other people. Economists will answer the question by mumbling about national welfare functions and terms of trade gains. It will not be something that comes out in a monthly statistical release.

Most noneconomists answer, "The trade deficit!" By their reasoning, if a country sells more than it buys (that is, exports more than it imports), that country is winning; similarly, a country that buys more than it sells is losing. So trade surpluses are good, and trade deficits are bad.

As it turns out, the trade balance is a particularly bad measure of national well-being. That's not just because of problematic reasoning behind the argument but because it's not usually what shows up in the numbers. We'll start with the numbers and then work to understand them.

Empirical Evidence

We can start by examining two popular hypotheses surrounding the trade balance and the US economy. First, let's see whether higher trade balances correlate with higher economic growth. To do this, we look at 50 years of quarterly data. For the trade balance, we take net exports (exports – imports) as a percentage of GDP and plot that against GDP growth (Figure 4.1).

If that hypothesis were correct, these two series would be rising and falling together. If that isn't apparent in the graph, you have a discerning eye. The correlation between the two series is 0.01, which is statistically indistinguishable from being uncorrelated.[1] Put simply, there is no evidence that higher trade surpluses (or smaller deficits) accompany higher GDP growth.

Second, we can examine the trade balance and US unemployment. Here, the hypothesis would be that larger trade deficits accompany higher unemployment rates—a version of the assertion that imports cost jobs. So, we flip our trade balance measure and look at net imports (imports – exports) as a percentage of GDP. We compare that with a quarterly average of monthly unemployment rates (Figure 4.2).

Again, if this hypothesis were right, the two series would rise and fall together. Here the two series do seem to have something to do with each other, but the movement is the opposite of what is predicted by the hypothesis. The correlation is 0.31 and statistically significant. In other words, when the trade deficit goes up, the unemployment rate goes down.

FIGURE 4.1
Higher trade surpluses do not correlate with higher GDP growth

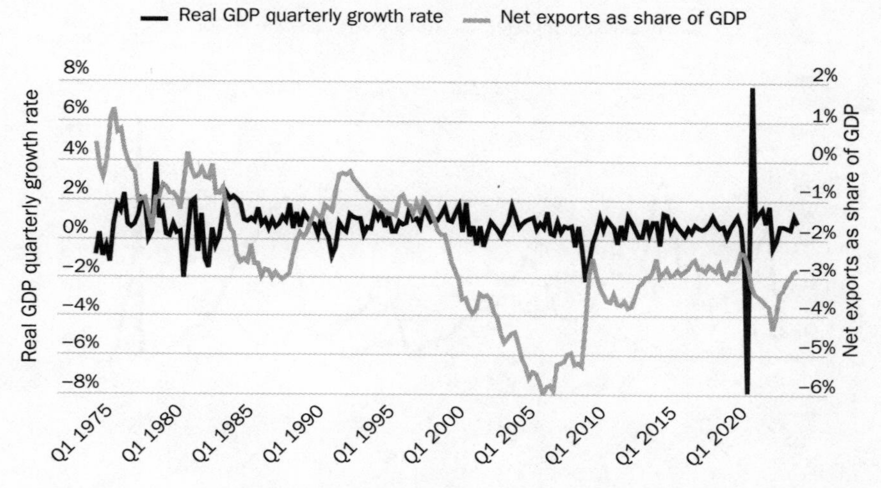

Source: "Net Exports of Goods and Services," Federal Reserve Economic Data, Federal Reserve Bank of St. Louis, updated July 25, 2024; "Gross Domestic Product," Federal Reserve Economic Data, Federal Reserve Bank of St. Louis, updated July 25, 2024; and "Real Gross Domestic Product," Federal Reserve Economic Data, Federal Reserve Bank of St. Louis, updated July 25, 2024.
Note: GDP = gross domestic product.

This does not mean, of course, that a higher US trade deficit *causes* lower US unemployment. Nevertheless, the relationship here is a clear point against the common argument that trade deficits cost jobs. More proof of that claim is needed but rarely offered.

As we'll discuss next, there are good economic reasons for the omission.

Where Did Popular Reasoning Go Wrong?

How could popular intuition differ so sharply from the data? Beyond the yearning for simplicity, two more subtle missteps often play into trade balance reasoning.

First, when we look at what goes into the GDP calculation, the accounting is as follows:

$$GDP = C + I + G + (X - M)$$

FIGURE 4.2
Higher trade deficits do not correlate with higher unemployment

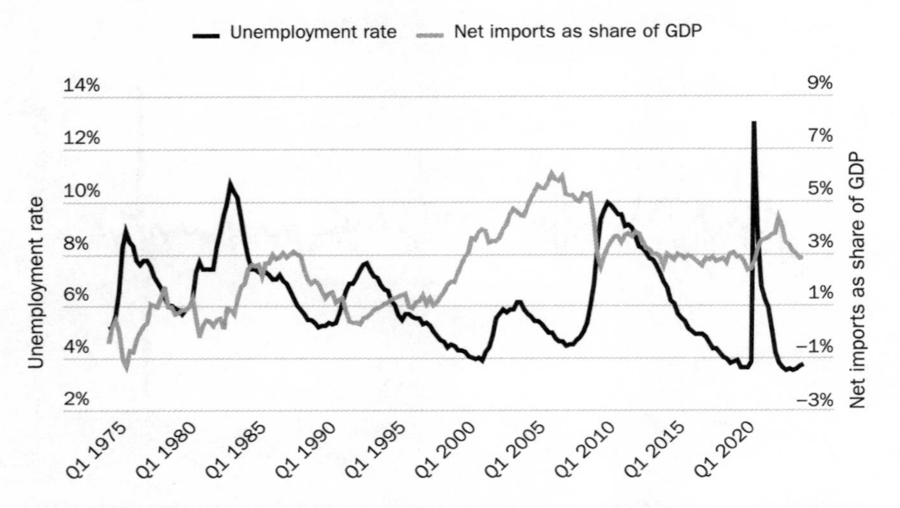

Source: "Net Exports of Goods and Services," Federal Reserve Economic Data, Federal Reserve Bank of St. Louis, updated July 25, 2024; "Gross Domestic Product," Federal Reserve Economic Data, Federal Reserve Bank of St. Louis, updated July 25, 2024; and "Unemployment Rate," Federal Reserve Economic Data, Federal Reserve Bank of St. Louis, updated August 2, 2024.
Note: Net imports (imports − exports) is the flip side of net exports (exports − imports); GDP = gross domestic product.

In this formula, C is consumption, I is investment, G is government spending, and $(X-M)$ is exports minus imports (that is, net exports). Setting aside questions about levels versus changes, this accounting identity is commonly understood to indicate that a decrease in net exports results in a reduction in GDP.[2] It seems obvious, right? But there's a trap in the interpretation.

Imagine if the United States were to import 100 additional cars from abroad. This would increase M by the value of 100 autos and decrease $(X-M)$ by a corresponding amount. If nothing else happened, GDP would have to go down. But something else *does* happen. Those cars were imported to be consumed. So C goes up by the value of 100 autos, exactly offsetting the move in M and leaving GDP unchanged. If the imports were not subtracted from the GDP figure, it would wrongly attribute goods made abroad to those made at home.

Furthermore, this basic math does not reveal the economic activity associated with the imports at issue. For example, imports often complement rather than replace domestic production. In fact, more than half of US imports are intermediate goods, raw materials, and capital equipment, which American companies use to make their final products. Even imported consumer goods can complement domestic output by reducing retail prices and thus freeing consumer dollars for spending on domestic goods and services, boosting their output.

Thus, the common characterization of imports and the trade deficit as a "drag on growth" reflects a misunderstanding of the accounting identity.[3] Net exports are indeed subtracted from the nominal GDP figure, but they tell us *nothing* about how trade (imports and exports) actually affects US economic growth in the real world.

Second, the conventional wisdom about imports and unemployment is driven by a popular computation that aims to determine how many jobs we gain for a certain dollar amount of exports.[4] Such figures often stem from a strong desire by elected officials to quantify the benefits of a trade agreement in terms of jobs gained. That figure doesn't usually pop out of trade models, which generally show that trade will affect the *composition* (type) of jobs, not the total number. However, the economic models often *do* predict the change in trade flows that will result from an agreement. So eager staff accommodate elected officials with a dubious bit of math:

1. Determine how much the country exported in a given year ($1.694 trillion in 2008).
2. Determine how many jobs were supported by exports in that year (10.293 million).
3. Divide the answer in step 1 by the answer in step 2 to calculate that roughly 6,000 jobs were gained per every $1 billion of exports.
4. Finally, multiply the jobs figured in step 3 by the predicted increase in exports, and—voilà!—you have (again, dubiously) calculated the jobs gained by trade.

This math is problematic for several reasons (often detailed and ignored in the reports that generated the number). Here, we can focus on just one: There is a difference between *marginal* and *average*. The ratio described above was an average number. Now, suppose we were to increase exports by 5 percent. Do we need to increase the number of lawyers, accountants, janitorial staff, production line workers, and executives all by 5 percent? No. Maybe some of them, but at the *margin*, the same people could probably make more just by increasing their input orders.[5] So the marginal number need not equal the average number.

However, once one adopts this faulty "exports equal jobs" logic, someone *else* can apply it to imports and thus predict jobs "lost" to imports in an equally flawed way. And this person *also* has a ratio that can say how many jobs supposedly come or go from a change in the trade balance.

One can see the flaw in this logic from a different angle too. At this writing, the United States is at 3.8 percent unemployment—a historically low figure that usually indicates full employment. Now, imagine if exports were to increase significantly and imports were to decrease significantly from here. How much lower would the unemployment rate go?

You don't need to know the ratios to answer this one. If the unemployment rate were to push much below 3.8 percent, the Federal Reserve would grow even more concerned about inflation and raise interest rates to slow the economy down. If anything, the unemployment rate would likely *rise* (given the tighter monetary policy) because of all those exports.

If it seems like cheating to bring in another argument—monetary policy—when we were happily considering just trade balances and unemployment, this is exactly the problem. GDP and unemployment are predominantly determined by factors other than the trade balance.

Bilateral versus Global

Before turning from what the trade balance *isn't* to what it *is*, we have one more distinction to draw. Until now, all our examples of trade balances (net exports) have been for the United States in its trade with the rest of the world. These are global figures.

But some of the most prominent trade balances in popular discourse are *bilateral*, such as the US trade imbalance with China. These data bring

FIGURE 4.3

The share of US imports sourced from China has grown significantly since 1990, yet the share of US imports sourced from Asia as a whole has not grown as much

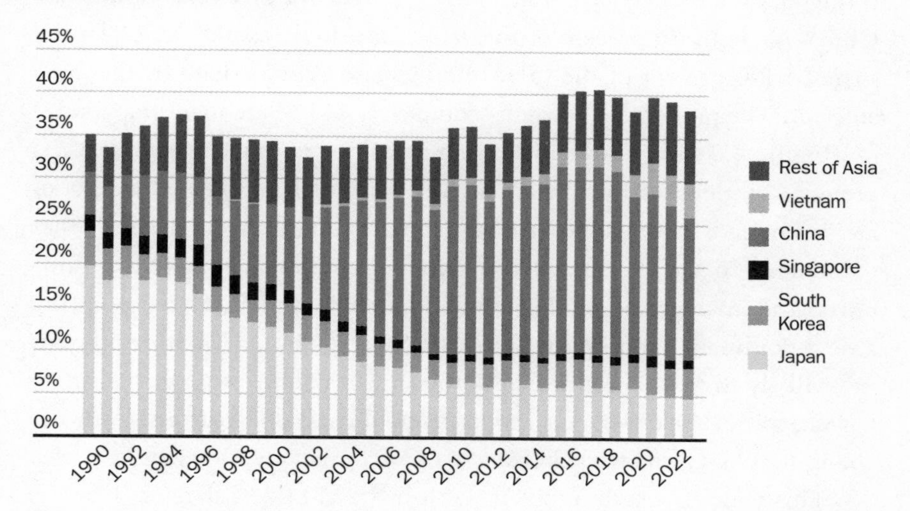

Source: "Exports and Imports by Area and Countries," International Monetary Fund, updated July 26, 2024.

Note: The data for China include the mainland, Hong Kong, and Macao.

all the problems of interpreting trade balances discussed above plus an important additional problem. To explain this problem, we will once again start with the data.

To make it simple, we will look only at the share of US imports. Figure 4.3 shows the share of US imports coming from several Asian countries (also a collection of countries). They sum to the total share of US imports from Asia.

Look at China's rise as a trading partner. In 1989, it accounted for 4.83 percent of US imports. By 2008, it accounted for 16.80 percent, a dramatic increase. Yet over that same period, Asia's percentage of US imports barely budged, moving from 34.92 percent to just 32.57 percent.

This exercise demonstrates one big problem with bilateral trade figures: They are not for *value-added* but rather for the value of finished goods. Thus, suppose a US import product was 100 percent made in Japan in the early 1990s. Suppose the final stage of production then shifted to China in the late 1990s, so the product is now made 70 percent in Japan and 30 percent in China. In trade statistics, such as those shown above, this would not reduce Japan's share by 30 percent of that value or increase China's share by 30 percent of the value. Instead, it would reduce Japan's share by 100 percent of the value and increase China's share by the same amount. The product now counts completely as a Made in China good.

Figure 4.3 shows how misleading it would be—given the increasing presence of global supply chains in Asia and other regions, where goods are assembled in one country but contain inputs from several other countries—to see the long-term increase in China's share of US imports, and an increase in the US-China trade deficit, as representing a new dominance of imports from Asia overall. Instead, Chinese goods most likely displaced goods from other Asian countries in the US market *and* probably contained inputs from those same nations. And the changing US-China trade balance would completely hide this fact.

This is not the only problem with bilateral trade balances. There is also the problem of *triangular trade*. To oversimplify, let us imagine that the United States sells $100 billion of wheat to Saudi Arabia. Saudi Arabia sells $100 billion of oil to China. China sells $100 billion of consumer manufactures to the United States. If this is all the trade they do, each country will have balanced trade ($100 billion in exports and $100 billion in imports). But the United States will run a $100 billion trade deficit with China. Even if you're worried about how trade balances might affect the US economy, that US-China trade deficit tells you nothing.

It's thus difficult to find any economic meaning in the *bilateral trade balance*, even if it causes a great deal of political excitement.[6] Next, we will discuss what a country's *global trade balance* might mean.

What Is the Trade Balance?

Understanding the trade balance requires us to revisit accounting identities. In accounting for international transactions, the trade balance is part of the balance of payments, which summarizes a nation's international transactions in exports and imports of goods and services, foreign direct investments (FDIs) and portfolio investments (i.e., noncontrolling shares of public companies), transfer payments, and the change in foreign reserves of the central bank.

From this accounting emerges the following math, shown in Box 4.1:

- National income (mostly expressed as GDP) is created by producing a range of different products (including services): consumption goods (*C*), government spending (*G*), investment goods (*I*), and export goods (*X*). Each category is produced by using imports (*M*) as inputs, which—as previously discussed—must then be subtracted to avoid double counting (hence, the minus in Equation 1 in Box 4.1).
- That income is then spent on either private consumption (*C*), government consumption (*G*), or savings (*S*), as shown in Equation 2.
- From these two equations emerges the relationship expressed in Equation 3. For every nation engaged in international commerce:[7]
    - exports (goods and services) − imports (of goods and services) = savings minus investment,
- which alternatively can be expressed as
    - current account = capital account + the change in foreign exchange reserves.

This relationship holds for all trading nations because it is based on fundamental equations of national accounting that capture how national income is created (Equation 1 in Box 4.1) and how it is spent (Equation 2).

Consequently, there are two measures of international transactions that must be equal: the capital account ($S-I$) and the current account ($X-M$). If domestic savings do not satisfy the domestic investment appetite, investors (or their banks) must borrow capital from abroad. If they can do so, it means that foreign savers (or their banks) trust the host country—in this case, the United States—to be a safe and profitable haven for their investment. Note that the mechanism by which these two measures equate in the US case is the value of the dollar. For the most part, exchange rates are set in global markets, where savers, investors,

BOX 4.1

The fundamental and irreversible logic of the balance of payments

$$\text{GDP} = C + I + G + X - M \quad (1)$$

$$\text{GDP} = C + G + S \quad (2)$$

By equalizing (1) and (2), we get (3):

$$X - M = S - I \quad (3)$$

exporters, and importers all meet. For investors, factors such as expected exchange rate appreciation play into expected returns. For traders, exchange rate movements determine whether domestic goods appear cheap or expensive compared with those produced abroad.

The United States is a net borrower of foreign capital, meaning that foreigners invest more in the United States than people here invest abroad. According to Equation 3 in Box 1, this net capital inflow must equal the net outflow of payments for goods, services, investment income, and unilateral transfers (i.e., the current account deficit). In other words, a US current account deficit is matched by a US capital account surplus (i.e., a net inflow of foreign capital into the country).

Because net capital inflows (e.g., foreign direct investment, portfolio investment, etc.) can fund US businesses and create or support US jobs, they can partly explain the negative correlation between a trade deficit and unemployment in Figure 4.2. And if the foreign capital is invested well, it can even lead to new jobs or better ones than those potentially displaced by imported goods or services.

Usually, when another country invests in the United States, it demands a return, such as dividends on stock, interest rates on loans, and so on. However, there is an instance in which other countries provide loans for free—when they wish to hold dollars as their reserve currency. While there is an obvious upside to free loans, these dollar holdings add to the demand for dollars and, thus, the capital account surplus that the current account deficit must offset. Many economists have therefore

BOX 4.2
The components of the balance of payments

Current account
- Merchandise trade balance
- Services trade balance
- Primary income balance
- Secondary income balance

Capital account
- FDI account
- Financial assets account
- Other capital transfers
- Changes in foreign currency reserves

Errors and omissions

concluded that as long as the US dollar maintains its long-standing role as the world's main reserve currency, the United States will run perpetual trade deficits irrespective of other factors.

How Exactly Is the Trade Deficit Related to the Balance of Payments?

Understanding the balance of payments helps us see how the trade balance works in practice. First, the balance of payments is not comparable to a company's or a bank's balance sheet as it does not measure stocks of assets and liabilities but flows: specifically, trade flows, remittances to friends or family abroad, official development aid, FDIs, portfolio investments, income generated by past investment flows, and changes in national currency reserves. Second, and equally important, the national balance of payments is the aggregate of transactions between individuals.[8] It is not fundamentally about one nation trading with another but about individuals and firms within those countries engaging in mutually agreeable transactions. Thus, the trade balance has a microeconomic foundation.

There are several sub-balances that form the balance of payments, with the current account and the capital account being its main components (Box 4.2).

The *current account* consists of the *merchandise (or goods) trade balance*, the *services trade balance*, the *primary income balance* (generated through income payments from foreign assets), and the *secondary income balance*, which primarily consists of transfers. The current account should equal the *capital account* plus the *changes in foreign currency reserves*. In total, the national balance of payments should be zero. If this is not the case, the difference is booked under *errors and omissions*. Typically, the difference is small, and the current account and capital account are effectively mirror images of each other.

What Causes a Trade Deficit?

As we now see, these technical definitions and accounting identities can help explain what drives a nation's current account balance—not trade policy (e.g., tariffs) but savings and investment.

Particularly, a nation's current account balance ($X - M$) must be equal to its capital account balance ($S - I$), meaning any change in the trade deficit must be accompanied by a change in the capital account balance. Thus, any real attempt by policymakers to fundamentally change the trade balance must somehow alter the balance between national savings and investment. This further implies that a nation's trade balance has little to do with trade policy and instead is caused by underlying macroeconomic factors affecting levels of national savings and investment. Because different factors can cause changes in the trade balance, one cannot judge the desirability of a trade surplus or trade deficit without fully considering its underlying macroeconomic causes.

The first step to understanding a country's balance of payments is to view it as the sum of the individual transactions its citizens make with partners abroad. To be sure, it is not the United States that runs the deficit; rather, it is American citizens and firms that trade and invest with foreign partners. The one exception is the Treasury Department, which sells government-issued bonds to investors abroad. However, as it is only one of many actors in determining a macroeconomic balance, we can conclude that the balance of payments and its sub-balances are fundamentally based on an individual—economists call it a microeconomic—foundation.

This microeconomic foundation of the balance of payments is also determined by the intertemporal calculus of citizens and firms making decisions about their savings and investments (at home or abroad).

These decisions occur mostly simultaneously with their other decisions to buy or sell goods and services. However, common sense suggests that financial decisions precede the real transactions of the trade account.[9]

This logic implies that in a country with a relatively low savings rate on the one hand and a relatively high level of investment and public consumption on the other hand, there will be a net capital inflow (and a resulting trade deficit).

The question of why savings are low can often be answered by examining an economy's demographic structure (Box 4.3).

Net inflows or outflows of capital then lead to an international movement of purchasing power as well as movements of real and nominal exchange rates. A country with net capital inflows will experience an increase in demand for its currency, which causes a real appreciation of its currency. The appreciation encourages imports and discourages exports (everything else being equal). The opposite happens in a country with net capital outflows.

How, Then, Should We Judge a Trade Deficit?

Here, the typical economist's answer is correct: It depends. A nation's imbalance in the current account cannot be judged without a closer look at the underlying *macroeconomic* drivers. Consider two scenarios:

- A country with many young people (and a relatively low savings rate) and a good investment climate will attract foreign capital, expanding productive capacity while creating more productive and better-paying jobs. The resulting current account deficit would thus be sustainable.
- On the other hand, a country with high social spending and low investment may also attract capital (e.g., through government bonds with the promise of high interest rates). No productive capacity is built, and only consumption goods are imported on net. In this case, the current account deficit would be less sustainable.

BOX 4.3

Demographic trends and savings

The individual savings rate tends to be a function of age. Most people are net savers during their years in employment or self-employment (i.e., between 15 and 64 years). During their early, formative years before joining the workforce, they live on other people's savings (e.g., parents, grandparents, or credit institutions) to pay for education. Once their working years are over, they dis-save to finance their retirement. This implies that a younger population will save less than an aging population.

In the United States, which has a relatively younger population than other Western nations, people tend to save a smaller share of their income. On the same token, a young and growing population needs capital. Thus, the business sector tends to invest at a higher level. **The resulting shortage of savings relative to investment demand drives the current account deficit.**

Germany, in contrast, is more of an aging society. The supply of labor and human capital is in relative decline, while the savings rate remains high, at least as long as most people remain below retirement age. As members of an aging society, Germans invest a larger part of their savings abroad, creating net capital outflows and a trade surplus. The differing trade balances between the United States and Germany, therefore, have nothing to do with competitiveness or unfair trade practices.

Like the regular US current account deficit, the German current account surplus is the rational result of underlying economic and demographic factors.

Thus, whether a current account deficit is good or bad strongly depends on how a nation's capital inflows are used. If the inflows are invested productively and in a way that produces positive economic returns, the deficit will tend to be benign. However, if the current account deficit is primarily financing increased consumption due to higher indebtedness, the current account deficit will be more of a concern.

This framework requires us to judge a nation's trade deficit by examining the structure of its foreign net capital inflows.

- Private investment flows, especially FDIs, as well as investments in stocks or long-term private debt, are typically productive.[10] Foreign capital inflows not only entail new debt but also create new jobs and income, generating tax revenues. If it is an investment (and not a loan), it adds to the domestic capital stock.
- Assessing government-issued foreign debt is more complex. If the US Treasury sells its bonds abroad, they reflect public debt. Nevertheless, public debt can be spent in ways that create real returns for the economy (for example, by investing in better infrastructure or national security) or in ways that create no real returns and are thus unsustainable (such as hiring more public staff without investing or increasing subsidies in election years). The United States' public debt can also satisfy global demand for safe assets. In this case, the repayment of such debt may not even be desirable: If savings rise, domestic savers may purchase treasuries from foreigners, thereby formally exporting capital (and reducing the current account deficit).

In summary, countries with a relatively young population and a need for domestic investment capital should expect net capital inflows, thus producing a trade deficit. That situation only becomes a problem if these capital inflows are not well-invested; for example, when Greece borrowed money after joining the eurozone, it was mainly spent on government salaries and not investments. Aging societies should invest part of their savings abroad to generate a net capital outflow and automatically achieve a trade surplus. Needless to say, an aging society with significant unemployment should still invest the bulk of its savings at home, but it can still potentially export capital. The trade surplus of such a country is caused by neither unfair behavior nor the country's export competitiveness—instead, it is caused by the intertemporal decisions of its aging population.

What Are the Consequences of a Trade Deficit?

The next question concerns the consequences of a trade deficit and whether governments should seek to combat a deficit or even strive for a surplus. We will use the US example to demonstrate that the answer to this question depends on several factors and that the United States has generally benefited from its trade deficit because it has used the capital inflows wisely.

The outcome of a trade deficit can vary because it is determined by the use of capital inflow, which, at first glance, is an increase in negative net wealth. If a country with a current account deficit does not invest its net capital inflow productively, the deficit is unsustainable and leads to long-term problems. It should soon be reversed. If a country with high unemployment has a high net capital outflow, its current account surplus is problematic as it signals poor investment conditions (and not any form of competitiveness).

However, if capital allocation is efficient, neither a net capital outflow (i.e., a current account surplus) nor a net capital inflow (i.e., a current account deficit) is a problem. That said, it is essential to analyze the underlying causes of current account imbalances before making a judgment.

How Should the US Trade Balance Be Judged?

We will now use this logic to examine the US balance of payments more closely since the end of the Bretton Woods system. During the Bretton Woods system, capital flows were highly restricted; disparities in the balance of payments were limited, and a change in foreign currency reserves typically offset any trade surplus. In such a setting, the intertemporal logic does not apply; a nation's investment is mainly financed through its domestic savings. International lending and borrowing are the exception rather than the rule.

However, as soon as international capital flows are possible, the intertemporal calculus—which entails borrowing from the future to finance current investment opportunities—drives the balance of payments. The United States is an example of this economic logic. Since the early 1980s, the US current account has been almost permanently in deficit. This is mostly explained by intertemporal decisions about savings and investments.

As seen in the figures below, the ebb and flow of the US current account deficit in recent decades has been exactly mirrored by the net inflow of foreign capital (Figure 4.4) into the United States.[11] When net capital inflows rise, as they did in the early 1980s and again from the mid-1990s to the mid-2000s, the current account deficit increases in tandem. When net investment declines, the current account deficit contracts. This inverse relationship between net investment inflows and current account deficits is driven by the inescapable logic of the national income account (Box 4.1).

In the early 1980s, the US government started a deregulation program and pursued tax reforms that reduced rates and, at least in the short run, also revenues. Both measures encouraged private investment. Since the US government did not reduce public spending but increased it mainly due to heightened national defense spending, the public budget went into deficit. Both of those developments—the attractive investment conditions and the government's thirst for savings—led to an increased inflow of foreign capital.

This capital inflow caused the US dollar to appreciate compared with leading currencies such as the German mark. The stronger dollar contributed to a surge in imports and a slower increase in exports than possible without the capital inflows or the subsequent appreciation of the dollar, causing a large increase in the current account deficit. The United States experienced so-called twin deficits: Both the federal budget and the current account balance were in deficit.

The US production structure changed as it became clear that the capital inflows would be lasting. Many sectors of manufacturing faced increased international competition, while services sectors grew—these developments benefited the US economy even if specific industries were

FIGURE 4.4
The annual size of the US current account deficit is mirrored by the annual net inflow of foreign investment

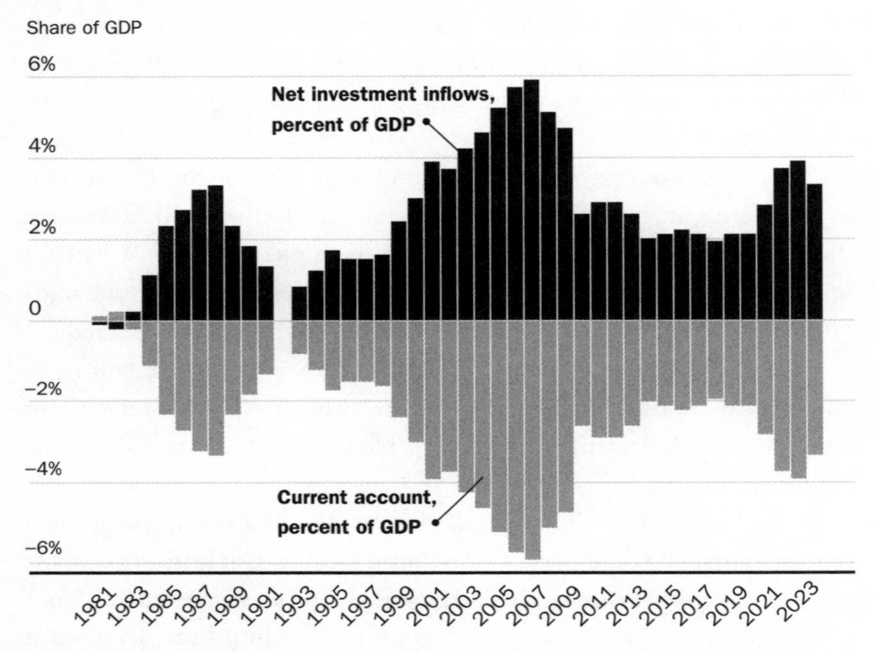

Source: "Table 1.1. US International Transactions," International Data, US Bureau of Economic Analysis, updated June 20, 2024; and "Table 1.1.5. Gross Domestic Product," National Data, US Bureau of Economic Analysis, updated July 25, 2024.
Note: Net foreign investment includes direct investment, portfolio investment, and other investment assets. In 1991, the current account balance was a positive $2.9 billion, or 0.05 percent of GDP; GDP = gross domestic product.

forced to undergo painful transitions.[12] Once this quite substantial structural change was mastered, future capital inflows did not need a strong dollar appreciation to maintain the current account deficit.

Although most observers pay attention to trade in goods and its balance, this episode already shows that it is not enough to focus only on goods. To fully understand the current account, we must add the balance of services trade as well as the primary income balance, which includes interest and dividend payments on foreign investments. For years now, the United States has run a trade surplus in services, where its economy has a strong competitive advantage. Focusing on trade in goods alone is thus misleading.[13]

Similarly, from the 1990s until the global financial crisis in 2008–2009, the United States experienced large net capital inflows and enormous investment, partly in services industries and partly in housing. When the housing boom ended, international capital flows became much smaller—and the so-called global imbalances decreased significantly. Nevertheless, the United States has remained a haven for foreign capital. Public debt rose sharply between 1990 and 2022, from $3.25 trillion to almost $31 trillion.

Meanwhile, the US population grew from 230 million inhabitants in 1980 to more than 335 million in 2020, an increase by nearly half in 40 years. Such a growing population has stimulated demands for both private and public investment to create jobs and secure education, health care, infrastructure, and housing.

The United States' continued role as a haven for foreign investment also plays a role. Figure 4.5 shows net income from US investments abroad and foreign investments in the United States. It shows that American investors who invest overseas earn significantly more than their foreign counterparts who invest in the United States. This is true even though the United States has a high negative balance of net foreign assets, which has been accumulated through the enormous net capital inflows since the 1980s by US citizens, firms, and the government. The strong primary income surplus is good news for the sustainability of the US current account.

If the return on all assets were equal, the US primary income balance would be in deficit. What the figure tells us is that US investors are much more successful in securing higher returns on their investments abroad than their foreign counterparts are in the United States. This in turn implies that foreign investors trust the US capital market and are willing to accept lower interest and dividend payments for that security, whereas US investors can collect much higher returns (interest and dividends) for their investments in foreign destinations. It shows the strength and desirability of the United States as an investment location as well as the success of US investors abroad.[14]

FIGURE 4.5

The US primary income balance shows that US investors abroad earn more from their investments outside the United States than foreigners do from their investments in the United States

Source: "Table 1.1. US International Transactions," International Data, US Bureau of Economic Analysis, updated June 20, 2024.

What Do We Learn? A Concluding Illustration of Germany and the United States

If analyzed through the lenses of economic theory, trade deficits are much less of a problem than many observers and policymakers think. That, however, does not imply that every balance of payments outcome is equally welcome. There may well be problems with a trade deficit or trade surplus, but these are different from the problems the conventional wisdom usually portrays.

Germany and the United States illustrate the misunderstood aspects of the balance of payments. It has often been rightly stated that Germany has underinvested in its domestic economy and that investment abroad, in combination with high domestic savings (in an aging society), drives the German current account and accompanying trade surplus.[15] Indeed, although Germany should have a moderate surplus, it is far too high—but not because of beggar-thy-neighbor trade and industrial policies or the high competitiveness of German firms. Instead, the country urgently needs more private and public investments.

In the United States, which has a relatively younger population, people save a smaller share of GDP than people in Germany, large federal deficits further reduce national savings, and business investment remains high. These factors drive the United States' large current account deficit (and trade deficit). Again, the US trade deficit may be judged too high—but not because of other countries' unfair trade practices or US trade policy but because of low government and private savings in the United States. The chief policy goal should not be to restrict trade but to promote a higher domestic rate of savings, especially by the heavily indebted US government.

In summary, the US trade deficit is caused by the savings and investment decisions of American consumers and firms and by high federal government debt. The answer to whether the US trade deficit is bad greatly depends on whether the United States is borrowing and investing wisely.

The findings, interpretations, and conclusions expressed in this chapter do not necessarily reflect the views of the World Bank, its executive directors, or the governments they represent.

Chapter 5

Separating Tariff Facts from Tariff Fictions

Erica York

- A tariff is a tax on foreign goods that raises revenue for the imposing government. Motivations for imposing tariffs range from revitalizing local industries to addressing unfair trade.
- Importers legally pay US tariffs, but their economic burden (i.e., who *really* pays) depends: it can be borne by American consumers, businesses, and exporters; by foreigners exporting to the United States; or by some combination of these groups.
- Economists use a variety of methods to analyze how tariffs affect protected companies, consumers, importing firms, exporters, and our economy overall. They generally find that tariffs benefit some but hurt far more others, thus lowering overall living standards and economic growth. Tariff-protected industries also rarely (if ever) become stronger.
- Recent empirical evidence indicates the new US tariffs imposed in 2018 and 2019 were almost entirely passed on to US consumers, resulting in higher prices and reduced export growth.
- Tariffs often lead to cascading protectionism and create a fertile ground for corruption. The 2018–2019 tariffs on China led to a complex process of exclusion requests, lobbying, and retaliatory tariffs, demonstrating the multifaceted harms of protectionist measures.

A tariff is a form of tax. And like any other tax, tariffs impose economic costs that reduce our standard of living. But some talk of tariffs as though these taxes can magically raise revenue for the government while making trade fairer, citizens more prosperous, and business endeavors more productive.[1] Do tariffs defy the laws of supply and demand and lift our standard of living?

This essay sets out to answer that question, exploring how the United States has used tariffs, reviewing theoretical and empirical research on who pays and who benefits under tariffs, and demonstrating what else happens when tariffs are imposed. It is dubious to claim that tariffs can be imposed with no economic tradeoffs, and economists generally consider them to be poor tools for achieving various policy objectives. Tariffs repeatedly fail to achieve goals like increasing the number of things we produce, creating more jobs, or fostering healthy and innovative companies. Instead, tariffs tend to raise prices, reduce economic activity and efficiency, and invite foreign retaliation and domestic political dysfunction.

What Is a Tariff, and What Does It Do?

A tariff is a type of tax imposed on the purchase of foreign goods. It may be figured as a percentage of a good's price, called an ad valorem tariff, or as a fixed dollar amount per good. As any tax does, a tariff raises revenue for the levying government, about $100 billion for the US government in 2022.[2]

Tariffs are imposed to shield domestic companies and workers from foreign import competition or to generate revenue for the government. Protectionist motivations for imposing a tariff include revitalizing local industries, creating jobs, offsetting allegedly "unfair" trading practices of other nations, promoting national security, or affecting the balance of trade. Tariffs attempt to achieve these objectives by making imports cost as much or more than similar, higher-priced goods made domestically. (If domestic goods were already priced less than imports in the absence of a tariff, a new tax would be unnecessary.) Thus, a tariff discourages US consumers from purchasing imports and encourages them to buy from domestic producers instead, boosting the producers' sales and profits.

This is not, however, the end of the story. Consumers and other businesses forced to pay tariffs or buy higher-priced domestic goods suffer from lower incomes and profits than they would have without the tariffs. This, in turn, means reduced consumer spending on other goods and services or, for companies, on worker salaries or investments. Tariffs can also lead to increased currency values, placing exporters at a disadvantage in foreign markets and thus reducing their sales and profits. Like any tax, a tariff generally leads to deadweight loss (an excess loss or burden above the amount actually paid in tax) because it decreases aggregate economic activity and incomes.

Finally, tariffs' protectionist objectives and revenue objectives are often in tension because tariffs are only paid (and thus collected) on imports that enter the country. Raise tariffs high enough to reduce or eliminate imports (and thus benefit higher-priced domestic producers), and tariff revenue also is reduced or eliminated. Keeping tariffs low can maintain import levels and thus generate revenue but result in little protection for domestic firms. In fact, revenue considerations once limited the scope and magnitude of US tariffs (and thus of US protectionism).

How Has the United States Used Tariffs?

The US Constitution grants Congress the power to "lay and collect" duties and to "regulate commerce with foreign nations." The economist Douglas A. Irwin describes the US experience with tariffs in three phases: revenue, restriction, and reciprocity.[3] From the Founding era through the Civil War, tariffs were the main source of revenue for the federal government and thus not so broad and high as to discourage imports altogether. As Irwin explains regarding tariff proposals in Alexander Hamilton's 1791 "Report on Manufactures," they "were not highly protectionist because Hamilton feared discouraging imports, which were the critical tax base on which he planned to fund the public debt."[4] Instead, "most of Hamilton's proposals involved changes in tariff rates—raising some duties on imported manufactures and lowering some duties on imported raw materials," and Hamilton's Federalist party actually lost support among domestic manufacturers to more protectionist Republicans.

After the Civil War and especially after the income tax was introduced in 1913, however, the revenue check on US tariffs dissipated, and federal lawmakers gave way to protectionist inclinations (see Chapter 2, "The Problem of the Tariff in American Economic History, 1787–1934"). The Tariff Act of 1930, known as the Smoot–Hawley Act, significantly raised tariffs, which invited retaliation, collapsed world trade, and worsened the Great Depression.[5] It was the last tariff act that Congress enacted and led to a fundamental shift of trade policy away from restriction and toward reciprocity.

In the aftermath of Smoot–Hawley, Congress delegated trade negotiation powers and tariff-setting authority to the president. Since 1934, the general policy of Congress and the president has been to gradually liberalize trade, including reducing and eliminating many tariffs. Accordingly, the average tariff rate across all imports fell from 19.8 percent in 1933 to below 2 percent from 2000 to 2019, as Figure 5.1 shows.[6]

Though average tariff rates fell, US trade has not been unfettered. The United States still maintains high tariffs on politically sensitive products like textiles and pickup trucks, and Washington has continued to impose tariffs through administrative action. Congress has empowered the executive branch to impose tariffs under certain instances:

- if imports threaten to impair US national security (Section 232 of the Trade Expansion Act of 1962);
- if a sudden import surge has caused or threatened serious injury to a US industry or in response to foreign trade barriers or violations (Section 201 and Section 301 of the Trade Act of 1974); or
- to offset a foreign government subsidy (countervailing duties) or a foreign producer selling in the United States below certain price or cost levels (antidumping) when US industries and workers are "materially injured" by "unfairly traded" goods.

FIGURE 5.1

Since 1934, the general policy of Congress and the president has been to liberalize trade

Average US tariff rate applied to dutiable and total imports from 1821–2021, percent

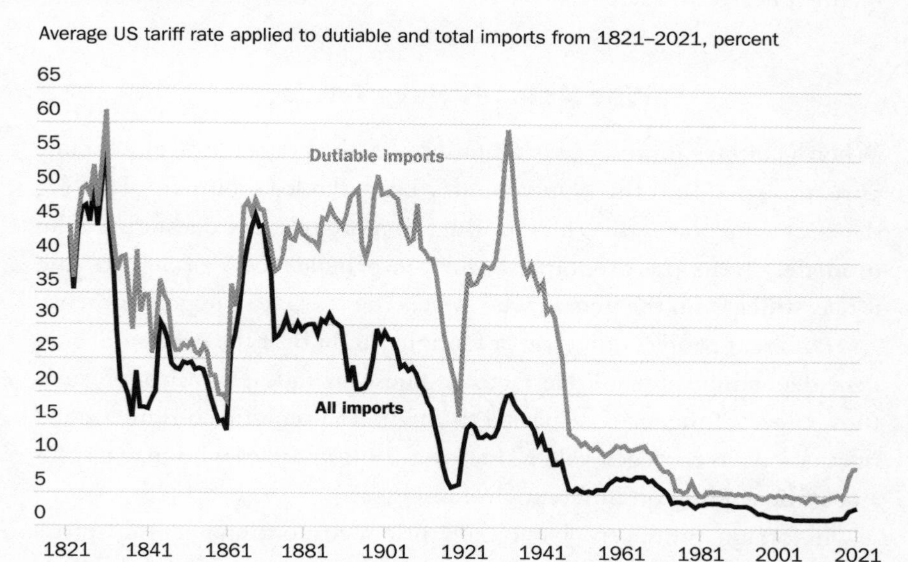

Source: Bureau of the Census, "Series U 207–212. Value of Merchandise Imports and Duties: 1821 to 1970," in *Historical Statistics of the United States: Colonial Times to 1970, Part II* (Washington: Department of Commerce, 1975), p. 288; and "Table 1. US Imports for Consumption, Duties Collected, and Ratio of Duties Collected to Value, 1891–2021 (Thousand $)," US International Trade Commission.

Note: Only covers goods imports. Dutiable imports are imports that are subject to tariffs (i.e., did not enter duty-free).

As Adam Posen, president of the Peterson Institute for International Economics, explains, over the past two decades, the American government has been increasingly insulating the economy from foreign competition and withdrawing from global trade, including through higher tariffs.[7]

The Trump administration accelerated that trend with extensive use of delegated powers to impose new tariffs.[8] The administration imposed Section 201 tariffs on solar panels and washing machines, Section 232 tariffs on steel and aluminum, and Section 301 tariffs on Chinese products (henceforth, 2018–2019 tariffs). Tariffs doubled to 2 percent of federal revenues, while the average tariff rate on all imports increased from 1.4 percent in 2017 to 2.8 percent in 2020. The Biden administration has retained nearly all these new tariffs.

Who *Actually* Pays Tariffs?

When a country imposes a tariff on imports, the person or firm who imports the good into the home country bears the legal burden of paying the tax to the home government. But the more relevant question is who ultimately bears the economic burden (or "incidence") of a tariff, and it may differ from the person who writes the check to the government.

Different people, domestic or foreign, might bear the economic burden, depending on multiple factors. Those include pass-through rates (how much of the tariff is "passed through" to domestic consumers) and fluctuations in currency values. Figure 5.2 summarizes who may pay for a tariff depending on different circumstances.

If foreign producers lower their prices to continue selling into a country after tariffs are imposed, they bear some part of the tariff via lower profits. In that case, the tariff does not pass completely through to the importing economy. But if foreign producers do not lower their prices to offset a tariff, it passes through to the importing economy in two ways: (1) the tax itself, which is paid by importers of the tariffed product to the government; and/or (2) higher prices paid by domestic consumers to sellers of alternative (nontariffed) goods. Importers, then, face the choice of accepting lower profits or passing the higher costs on to domestic consumers through higher prices. For instance, Ford and General Motors both faced more than $1 billion in higher costs from steel and aluminum tariffs in 2018, or about $700 per vehicle produced in North America, and warned that they might be forced to pass on these higher costs to consumers via price increases on their vehicles.[9]

Recent empirical evidence, using a variety of methods, indicates near complete pass-through of the 2018–2019 tariffs to US consumers. Mary Amiti, Stephen J. Redding, and David Weinstein found that the full burden passed through, costing US consumers and the firms that import foreign goods an additional $3 billion per month in added tax

FIGURE 5.2

Who actually pays for a tariff depends on several factors

Setting the stage

A country ("Home") imports foreign widgets that cost $100 each and compete with domestically produced widgets that cost $115 each.

The Home government can levy a tariff on imported widgets to **A) raise revenue or B) protect domestic producers.**

Raise revenue

To raise revenue, tariff levels can't be so high as to block imports, because tariffs are only paid when goods enter Home. Thus, revenue-raising tariffs must be relatively low and let imports keep flowing into Home. **This means revenue-raising tariffs don't offer much (if any) protection for domestic producers.**

Protect domestic industry

To protect industry, the government must impose a tariff that raises an import's price above the price of a domestic alternative. This discourages consumers from buying imports, but that means **the tariff won't raise much revenue.**

But that's not the end of the story. Let's assume a 25% tariff and see what happens . . .

WHO PAYS THE TARIFF?
By law, the importer located in Home must pay the widget tariff, but who actually pays—people in Home or people in a foreign country—depends on whether a foreign widget seller lowers his price.

Foreign seller doesn't lower his price

If the foreign seller (i.e., the exporter) doesn't lower his price, a buyer in Home can **A) continue buying the tariffed widget or B) switch to the $115 widget made in Home.**

Continue buying the foreign widget

Thanks to the tariff, the total cost of the imported widget is now $125 ($100 price + 25% tariff). The government gets the $25 in tariff revenue, but . . .

Switch to a Home widget

Thanks to the tariff, the $115 domestic widget is now $10 cheaper than the imported widget. But, the government sees no tariff revenue.

What happens next depends on **how tariffs affect the value of the Home currency (aka, exchange rates).**

Home currency's value is NOT affected

Home currency's value is affected

Foreign seller lowers his price

If a foreign seller really wants to stay in the Home market, **he can lower the price of his widgets to keep their total unit cost (price + tariff) below the price offered by his competitors in Home. Example: $80 price + 25% tariff (paid by importer) = $100 total**

The protectionist tariff raises revenue and lowers foreign seller's profits but **isn't actually protecting anybody.**

THE END

(*continued*)

FIGURE 5.2 (*continued*)

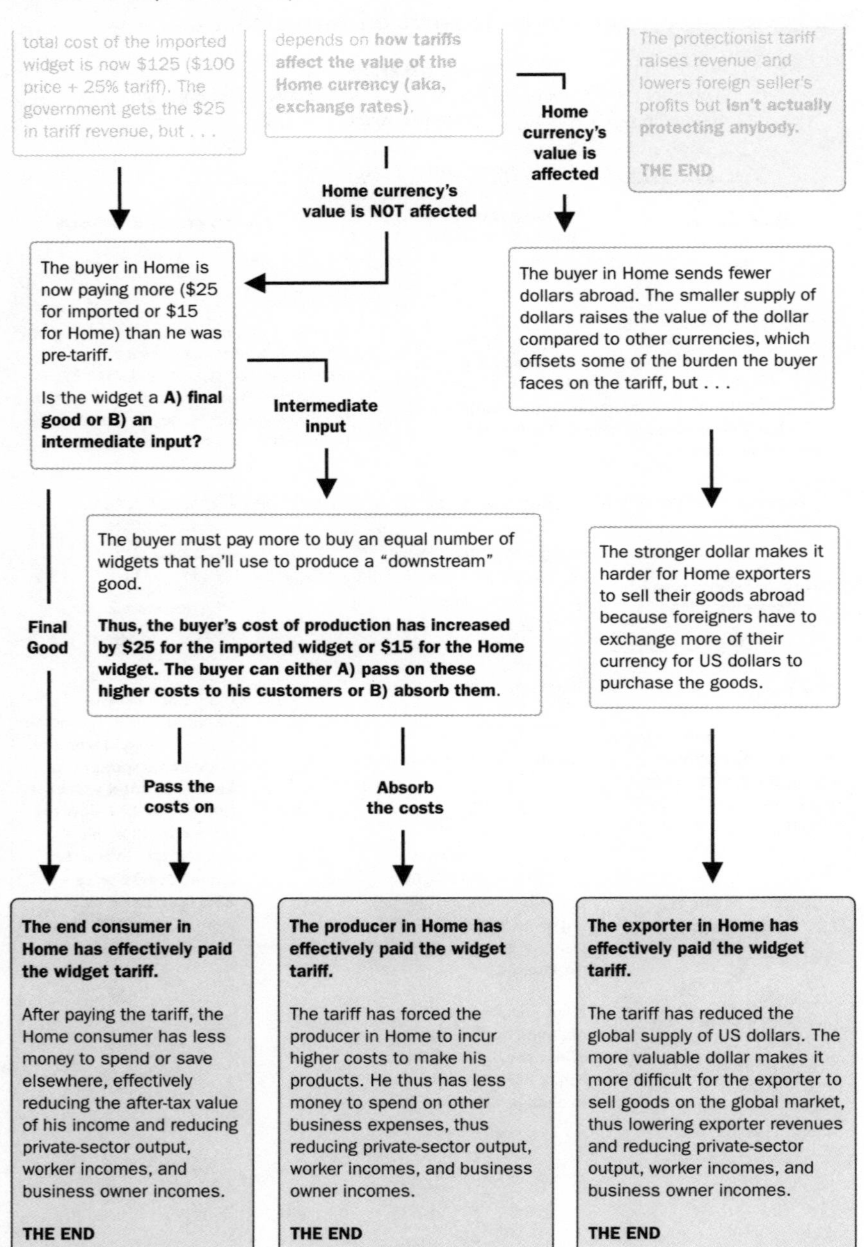

FIGURE 5.3

The 2018 tariffs cost US consumers up to over $4 billion per month in additional taxes and deadweight loss (or lost income)

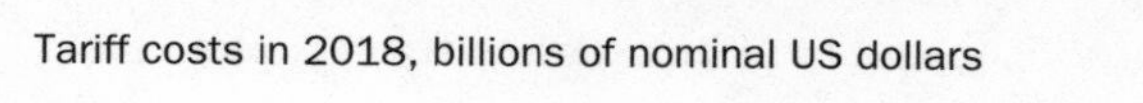

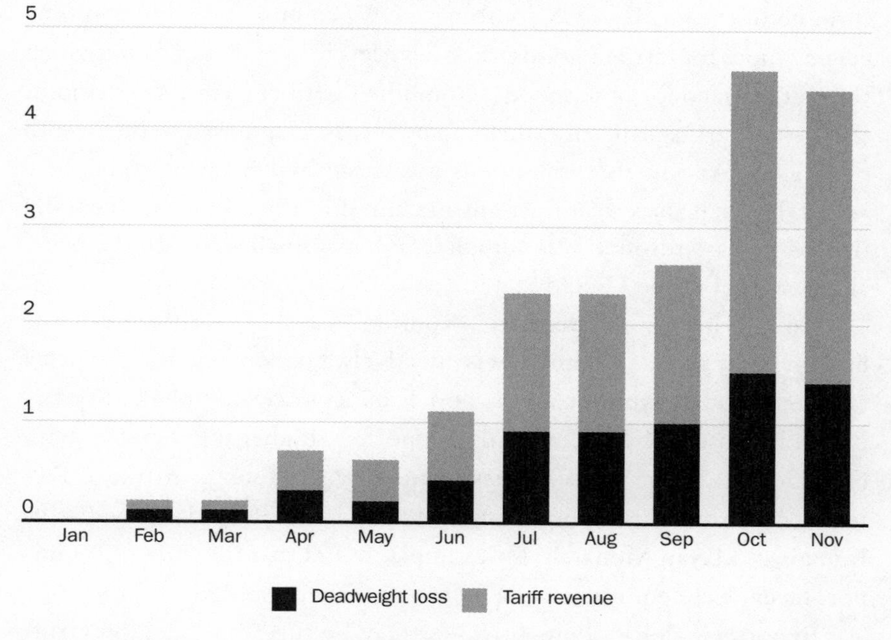

Source: Mary Amiti, Stephen J. Redding, and David Weinstein, "The Impact of the 2018 Trade War on US Prices and Welfare," National Bureau of Economic Research Working Paper no. 25672, March 2019, p. 34.

costs and $1.4 billion in deadweight loss (or lost income) as depicted in Figure 5.3.[10]

For example, after the Trump administration imposed tariffs on washing machines, the price of washers increased by $86 per unit, and so did the price of dryers, by $92 per unit, because they are sold as a package.[11] Overall, the tariffs on washing machines resulted in an aggregate increase in consumer costs of more than $1.5 billion.

Pablo Fajgelbaum and others similarly found that the tariffs were completely passed through to prices paid by US importers.[12] Alberto Cavallo and coauthors found that tariffs on imports from China were almost fully passed through to US import prices but only partially to retail consumers, implying a reduction in retail margins as some businesses absorbed the higher tariff costs rather than passing them on.[13] Likewise, a review from the US International Trade Commission of tariffs on steel, aluminum, and Chinese goods found evidence for nearly complete pass-through of the tariffs to US consumers.[14] When businesses and consumers pay more for tariffed goods, they have less to spend elsewhere, which reduces demand for other goods. Combined with currency fluctuations, that means tariffs primarily affect *relative* prices, as opposed to the overall price level. And further, the goods that faced higher tariffs comprise a relatively small share of the goods measured in price indexes, meaning that while pass-through was complete, it had a small effect on the overall price level in the United States.[15]

Counterintuitively, domestic exporters also share tariffs' economic burden because a tax on imports is effectively a tax on exports.[16] When a tariff is imposed, exporters in the home country may face retaliatory tariffs or, because many are often also importers, higher input costs—both of which make the exporter less competitive in foreign markets. Research confirms that import tariffs harm exporters: Kyle Handley, Fariha Kamal, and Ryan Monarch, for example, found that the 2018–2019 import tariffs were equivalent to a 2 percent tariff on all US exports.[17]

Exporters' global competitiveness may be further eroded by tariff-induced currency changes. When the United States imposes a tariff on goods from China, for example, imports fall as does the sale of US dollars in exchange for Chinese yuan. A lower global supply of US dollars pushes up the value of the dollar, which makes US exports relatively more expensive on the world market. (To take an extreme and simple example, suppose a bushel of grain sells for $10, and a buyer in China who wishes to purchase it must exchange 10 yuan for $10. Now suppose the dollar doubles in value. The buyer would have to exchange 20 yuan for $10 to purchase the same bushel of grain, making it much more expensive. Or for the bushel of grain to stay the same price in yuan in China, the US exporter would have to cut its price in half to $5.) As a result of these dynamics, tariffs can cause exports to fall, with exporters thus bearing a portion of the tariff burden.

One possible counter to the studies on the harms of tariffs is that the costs, while real, are justified by the benefits that tariffs provide to protected companies or American workers. Yet corporate success stories are few and far between. A January 2024 study by David Autor, for example, concludes that the 2018–2019 tariffs failed to provide economic help to the heartland, finding that import tariffs had "neither a sizable nor significant effect on US employment in regions with newly-protected sectors" and foreign retaliation "by contrast had clear negative employment impacts particularly in agriculture."[18]

Furthermore, American jobs supposedly saved by import protection have come at an extremely high cost to consumers, ranging from an annual average of $256,000 per job in the 1980s to more than $800,000 per job in the 1990s (all in 2017 dollars).[19] More recently, tire tariffs and steel tariffs have both annually cost US consumers more than $900,000 per job.[20]

Adding insult to injury, the distributional effect of tariffs (i.e., how tariffs affect people of different income levels) tends to be regressive, meaning that tariffs impose higher burdens on people with lower incomes.[21] In general, tariffs create a larger burden on poorer households because poorer households generally spend more money on traded goods as a share of their income than wealthier households.[22] Exacerbating this regressive impact is the design of existing tariffs, which are systematically higher for lower-end versions of goods than higher-end versions; according to estimates from economists at the Federal Reserve Board and Harvard, within consumer goods, rates are on average 1.2 percentage points higher for lower-end versions (Table 5.1).[23] Both current design and general effect cause lower- and middle-income households to bear a disproportionately larger share of the tariff burden than higher-income households.

Across the different data sources and methodologies, the main takeaway from recent empirical work is that US consumers, including business consumers and particularly poorer consumers, have shouldered the burden of US tariffs through higher prices and reduced export growth, and this burden far outweighs any economic benefits of tariffs.[24]

TABLE 5.1
Tariffs are higher on lower-end versions of goods than higher-end versions

Product	Higher-end good	Medium-end good	Lower-end good
Shoes	8.5% (men's leather dress shoes)	20.0% (running shoes)	48.0% (valued at $3 or less)
Sweaters	4.0% (cashmere)	16.0% (wool)	32.0% (acrylic)
Men's shirts	0.9% (silk)	19.7% (cotton)	32.0% (polyester)
Handbags	5.3% (snakeskin)	10.0% (leather valued at $20 or less)	16.0% (canvas)
Pillowcases	4.5% (silk)	11.9% (cotton)	14.9% (polyester)
Necklaces	5.0% (gold)	6.3% (silver)	13.5% (silver jewelry valued at $1.50 or less)
Scarves	1.5% (silk)	9.6% (wool)	11.3% (polyester)
Blankets	0.0% (wool)	8.4% (cotton)	8.5% (polyester)

Source: US International Trade Commission Tariff Database, https://dataweb.usitc.gov/tariff/database.
Note: The tariff codes for these products are 64035960, 64029142, 64029160, 61101210, 61101100, 61103030, 61059040, 61051000, 61052020, 42022130, 42022160, 42022215, 63022900, 63022130, 63022210, 71131921, 71131110, 71131120, 61171040, 61171010, 61171020, 63012000, 63013000, and 63014000.

How Do Economists Measure the Impact of Tariffs?

Tariffs allow domestic producers to raise prices and increase profits and, in turn, potentially increase production and stem employment losses. However, the gains to domestic producers come at the expense of others in the economy.

To quantify the effects, economists use a range of models with stylized assumptions that simplify the complexity of tariffs, trade, and human nature compared to reality. In some areas within economics, the range of models and variety of assumptions can lead to inconclusive results. But when it comes to the question of whether higher tariffs improve Americans' welfare, economists are uniquely unified against the idea (Figure 5.4).

FIGURE 5.4

Economists strongly agree that "tariffs and import quotas usually reduce general economic welfare"

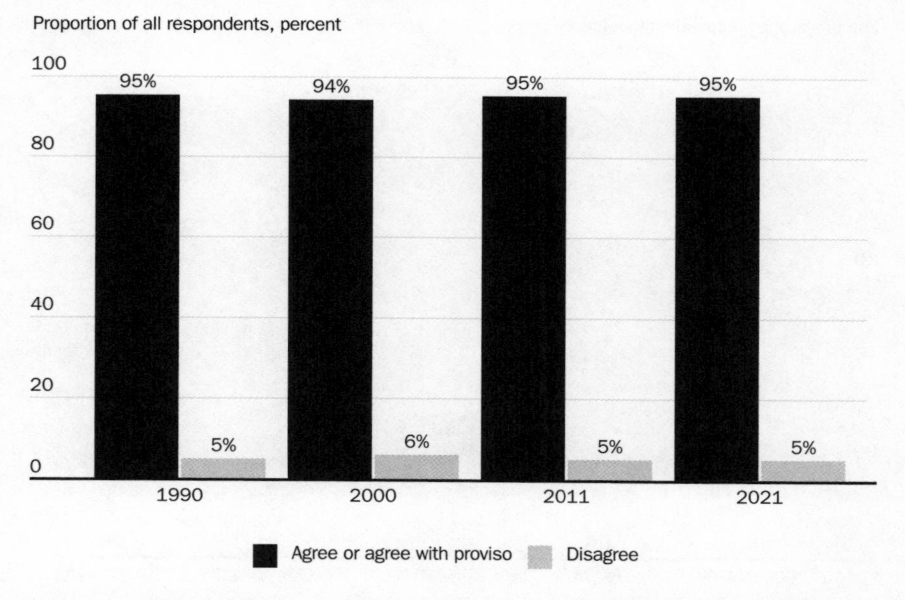

Source: Doris Geide-Stevenson and Alvaro La Parra Perez, "Consensus among Economists 2020—a Sharpening of the Picture," Weber State University, December 2021. The most recent survey (2021) was based on 1,436 responses among the American Economics Association's 8,100 members.

From 1930, when 1,028 economists urged President Herbert Hoover to veto the Smoot–Hawley tariff bill, to 2018, when 0 percent of surveyed US economic experts answered that they agreed that US tariffs on steel and aluminum would improve Americans' welfare (Figure 5.5), economic theory and empirical evidence both confirm the harms of tariffs.[25]

Some economists look at microeconomic effects of tariffs, or how tariffs impact specific sectors of the economy. For example, looking at the manufacturing sector overall, Aaron Flaaen and Justin Pierce examined the short-run effects of the tariffs imposed in 2018.[26] They explicitly measured and estimated how the tariffs impacted manufacturing through three channels: protecting industry output, raising prices for

FIGURE 5.5
All surveyed economists disagreed that "new US tariffs on steel and aluminum would improve American's welfare"

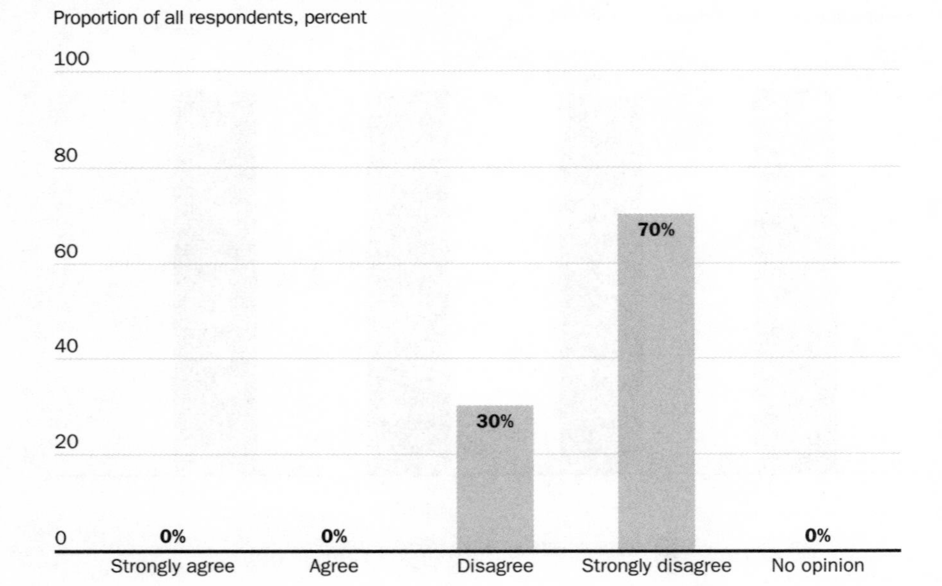

Source: "Steel and Aluminum Tariffs," Kent A. Clark Center for Global Markets, Booth School of Business, University of Chicago, March 12, 2018. The survey collected responses from 40 US economic experts (3 surveyed experts did not answer).

inputs, and subjecting exports to retaliatory tariffs. They found that even though the tariffs provided a small boost to protected firms, that was more than offset by larger drags as input costs rose and retaliatory tariffs took effect. Their findings show that the traditional channel through which tariffs are intended to boost manufacturing employment is completely offset by reduced competitiveness from retaliation and higher costs in downstream industries.

Other economists use general equilibrium models to look beyond the effect on a specific sector to answer the question of how tariffs affect the economy overall. This type of analysis captures how households, governments, private businesses, and foreign economies interact and estimates how factors like output, trade flows, and employment across the whole economy would change in response to a given policy.

International Monetary Fund researchers used a range of different general equilibrium models to estimate what would happen after a 25–percentage point increase in tariffs on all trade between China and the United States. Each model they used emphasizes different channels, but each model estimates that under the higher tariffs, China and the United States would suffer large economic losses.[27] A 2017 US International Trade Commission report used the US Applied General Equilibrium model to estimate what would happen after removing tariffs that the United States still maintains in certain sectors, including food and agriculture, textiles and apparel, and other high-tariff manufacturing and found that while protected firms would be harmed by tariff removal, the policy would on net generate an annual average increase in economic welfare of $3.3 billion from 2015 through 2020.[28] The Tax Foundation's general equilibrium model estimates that a new, across-the-board 10 percent tariff on all imports, as proposed by candidate Donald Trump, would reduce the level of US gross domestic product by 0.7 percent by reducing incentives to work and invest.[29]

Empirical research from David Furceri and others examined 151 countries from 1963 through 2014 and found that tariff increases lead to economically and statistically significant declines in domestic output and productivity, as well as increases in unemployment and inequality.[30] Fajgelbaum and others estimated that US consumers and firms that buy imports lost $51 billion while US producers gained $9.4 billion, implying substantial redistribution from importers to the US government and protected industries.

What Do Tariffs Do, and Who Really Benefits from Tariffs?

While domestic consumers pay, tariffs are supposed to benefit other sectors of the domestic economy. Tariffs may be imposed to "generate jobs," "revitalize industries," or "boost production."[31] Their success on these grounds, however, is questionable at best.

In a survey of literature related to US trade protection from America's Founding to the present day, covering tariffs on a wide range of industries and goods, author Scott Lincicome concludes, "In no case can it confidently be said that American protectionism was a substantial cause of American prosperity or the flourishing of protected US industries. Most often, import restrictions have been abject failures, imposing massive costs on US consumers, workers, and companies without achieving their intended objectives."[32] The United States has famously tried, and failed, to revive several industries with tariff protection, including shoes, softwood lumber, sugar, steel, tires, motorcycles, certain manufacturing goods, apparel, and textiles.

Import restrictions for the steel industry exemplify the failure in promoting overall production and employment. Since the 1970s, the US government has imposed hundreds of restrictions to protect steel producers, with 304 antidumping and countervailing duty orders in place as of March 2024.[33]

Protection from the 1980s to today has consistently generated higher domestic steel prices that benefit domestic producers but cost domestic consumers. For instance, in 1984, the Foreign Trade Council estimated that additional protections under consideration would result in $1.10 billion in annual costs to US consumers at the time, $428 million of which would be gains to US producers.[34] The implied cost-benefit ratio of higher consumer costs to potential steel jobs temporarily retained from the restrictions was $113,622 per job in 1984. University of California, Los Angeles economist Aaron Tornell analyzed how from 1970 to 1989 rising steel prices coincided with falling production and employment coupled with failure to adopt new technologies.[35] Further, even though workers didn't produce more, they were paid more, showing how higher prices and revenues were squandered.

And perhaps worse, protectionism encourages rent-seeking behavior and discourages innovation and research and development. Analyzing protectionist steel policies from the 1980s, economists Stefanie Lenway, Randall Morck, and Bernard Yeung found that steel protection boosted lobbying efforts for less innovative firms and discouraged productive firms from engaging in research and development.[36] They concluded that protection "confers private benefits upon lobbyers' shareholders, senior workers, and top managers . . . [and] appears to reduce returns to true innovation and encourage innovative firms to exit. These dynamic costs of protection . . . are potentially much more serious than the distortions shown in standard trade theory diagrams."

Steel tariffs continued in the 2000s, leading to price increases that again benefited steel producers but cost domestic steel consumers. A May 2023 research brief from James Lake and Ding Liu found that the 2001 steel tariffs under President Bush had large, negative effects on local steel-consuming employment that grew as tariffs remained in place and that persisted even five years after the tariffs were lifted.[37] While the tariffs had a negative impact on local labor markets that used steel, the research found no notable positive effects on local steel-producing employment. The authors note that their results "emphasize the negative employment effects of tariffs in steel-consuming industries and downplay any potential positive effects for the steel-producing industry."

The effects could be even more prominent now. A study by Harvard University and University of California, Davis economists Kadee Russ and Lydia Cox found that steel-consuming jobs outnumber steel-producing jobs 80 to 1.[38] Estimates indeed indicate that steel consumers lose more jobs to higher steel costs than steel producers gain.[39] In a similar vein, an empirical review of the 2018–2019 tariffs by the US International Trade Commission (USITC) estimated that while the tariffs boosted the value of domestic steel production, they reduced production in downstream industries by a larger amount.[40]

Steel is certainly not alone in this regard. Import protection may deliver higher profits for protected industries, but it creates disadvantages for other sectors, has a broadly contractionary effect, and thwarts important competitive forces that would benefit protected industries in the longer term. Thus, while proponents of tariffs may claim the goal is increasing production or employment, tariffs in practice are never about accomplishing that for the economy overall—their purpose is to enrich protected firms at an exorbitant price to others.[41] In the end, even protected firms go bankrupt or are acquired by a foreign competitor (as US Steel's possible purchase by Japan's Nippon Steel again demonstrates), and the clearest beneficiary of tariffs are government officials who enjoy higher tax revenue and who curry votes by funneling benefits to politically favored industries.[42]

Can Tariffs Change the Balance of Trade?

Another common motivation for increasing tariffs is to reduce the trade (technically, the "current account") deficit. While tariffs can certainly reduce imports, their effect on the trade balance is more complicated. In fact, both theory and practice show that because tariffs also decrease exports (and thus the overall level of trade), the measures do not fundamentally alter the current account balance in the long run.

This outcome may be counterintuitive but makes perfect sense to economists, almost all of whom understand that a nation's overall balance of trade is driven not by trade policy measures like tariffs or free trade agreements but by deeper macroeconomic factors, including national saving, national investment, currency values, fiscal policy, demographics, and international capital flows.[43] Given US and global savings and investment patterns, along with the status of the US dollar as the global reserve currency, the United States has run trade deficits for decades, regardless of tariff levels or other trade policy changes (which do not fundamentally alter the macroeconomic factors within or outside the United States).

For this reason, New York Federal Reserve economists warned in 2018 that Trump administration proposals to impose tariffs to narrow the trade deficit would reduce imports *and* US exports, resulting in little to no improvement in the trade deficit.[44] In doing so, the economists cited an equal but opposite experience in China: when China *lowered* its import taxes, it was accompanied by *higher export growth*. Many other trade experts agreed with the economists' conclusions.[45]

The experts' predictions proved correct. As Daniel Griswold and Andreas Freytag documented in a 2023 research paper and as Figure 5.6 shows, the 2018–2019 tariffs imposed by the Trump administration and since maintained by the Biden administration "had no discernible impact on the relative size of the trade deficit"; if anything, the deficit actually increased slightly versus where it was at the end of the Obama

FIGURE 5.6

The US trade deficit in goods as a share of GDP did not change significantly from the first quarter 2016 to the third quarter 2023, despite the Trump-Biden tariffs

US trade deficit in goods as a share of GDP, percent

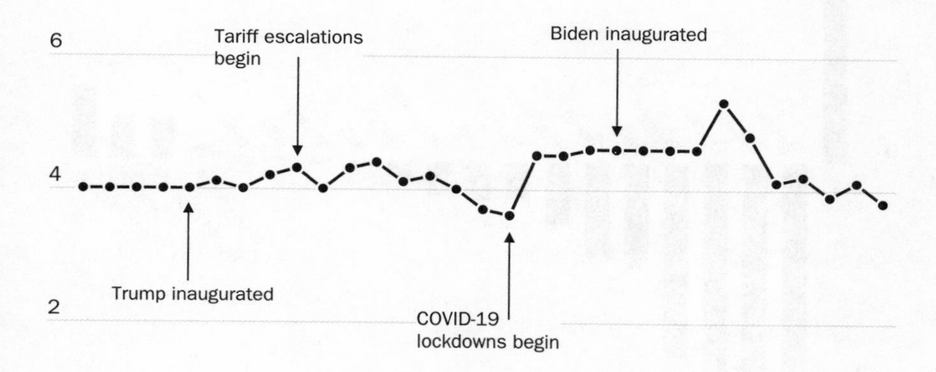

Source: "Table 2.1. US International Trade in Goods," International Data, US Bureau of Economic Analysis, updated December 20, 2023; "Table 1.1.5. Gross Domestic Product," National Data, US Bureau of Economic Analysis, updated January 25, 2024; and Chad P. Bown and Melina Kolb, "Trump's Trade War Timeline: An Up-to-Date Guide," Peterson Institute for International Economics, updated December 31, 2023.

Note: GDP = gross domestic product.

administration.[46] Citing some of the aforementioned studies on the tariffs' other effects, Griswold and Freytag thus conclude that "higher tariffs did exactly what the economics literature predicted they would do: impose net economic harm without changing the current account balance."

One reason why the trade balance was unaffected was "trade diversion," which often occurs when tariffs on imports from one trading partner lead importers in the home country to substitute toward foreign

FIGURE 5.7

During the Trump administration, the decrease in the bilateral trade deficit with China was more than offset by increases in bilateral trade deficits with other countries

Change in the bilateral goods trade balance, 2016–2020, billions of nominal US dollars

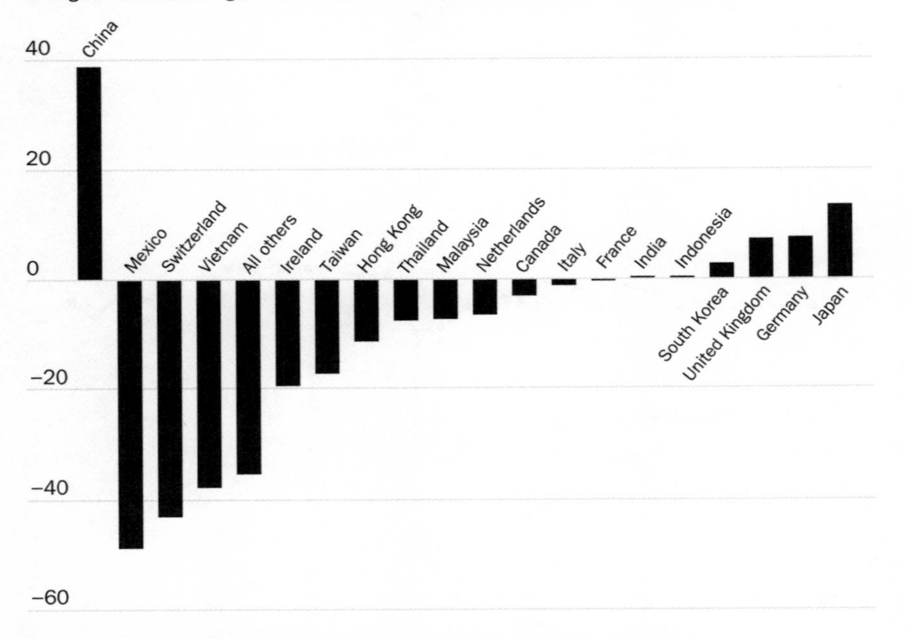

Source: "US Trade in Goods by Country," US Census Bureau, October 5, 2022.

goods that don't face tariffs. When President Trump imposed tariffs on nearly two-thirds of imports from China, for example, trade with China fell, but US companies increased purchases from other foreign suppliers, thus increasing bilateral trade deficits elsewhere and leaving the overall trade balance mostly unchanged (Figure 5.7).

A 2017 USITC paper analyzed the question of whether tariffs can reduce trade imbalances by modeling a 10 percent tariff on imports from China and a 10 percent tariff on imports from all countries.[47] The paper estimated a small, temporary decrease in the trade deficit as initially imports fell by a greater amount than exports, but over time, that effect reversed, and the trade deficit increased slightly in the long run (after

13 years). The USITC also estimated that the tariffs caused an overall decrease in investment, saving, and welfare in the United States. Similarly, a January 2024 International Monetary Fund paper found that unexpected tariff shocks tend to reduce imports more than exports, leading to slight decreases in the trade deficit at the expense of persistent gross domestic product losses—for example, the authors estimate reversing the 2018–2019 tariffs would increase US output by 4 percent over three years.[48]

Overall, empirical research demonstrates that countries maintaining higher tariffs actually tend to have *larger* trade deficits and that tariffs have little if any direct effect on the balance of trade.[49] Research from the International Monetary Fund examining 63 countries over 20 years and across 34 sectors provides further support: "a tariff-induced change in a specific trade balance between two countries tends to be offset by changes in bilateral balances with other partners through trade diversion, with little or no impact on the aggregate trade balance."[50] The Furceri and others empirical study of 151 countries similarly found that tariff increases had no significant, long-term effect on trade balances and, as theory predicts, led to real exchange rate appreciation.[51] The authors thus conclude that "the net effects of higher tariffs on the trade balance are small and insignificant; absent shifts in saving or investment, commercial policy has little effect on the trade balance."

In short, regardless of whether the US trade deficit is a problem, tariffs are not a valid solution.

What *Else* Happens When Tariffs Are Imposed?

If the hundreds of import restrictions granted to the politically powerful steel industry are any indication of US tariff history (and, as Lincicome shows in his 2017 review, they are), one drink from the protectionist trough is rarely enough.[52] Granting tariff protection to one industry mushrooms into requests for tariff protection from additional industries, extensions when initial protections expire, and exclusions for specific firms. More recent empirical research finds, in fact, that US companies facing heightened import competition between 1999 and 2017 responded not by redoubling their commercial efforts (e.g., investing more in research and development) but by substantially increasing their lobbying for government help—a trend concentrated among less-innovative American firms.[53] Tariffs also beget retaliatory actions from foreign countries, creating the potential for offsetting government aid. And it all creates an environment ripe for corruption and geopolitical tension.

The 2018–2019 tariffs are again instructive here. First, there was the inevitable retaliation. Governments of China, the European Union, Canada, and Mexico, as well as nations with smaller levels of trade with the United States, quickly responded with tariffs on American products. Research shows, moreover, that the retaliatory tariffs were politically motivated, targeting products that would disproportionately impact counties that supported Donald Trump in the 2016 election.[54] And in contrast to the near-complete pass-through of US tariffs to US consumers, US exporters bore an estimated 50 percent of retaliatory tariffs because they lowered their export prices to stay competitive in the markets at issue.[55] (They were mainly exporting agricultural commodities that would be easy for foreign importers to source elsewhere.)

This retaliation was costly—for American exporters *and* taxpayers. The Department of Agriculture estimated that direct export losses from the retaliatory tariffs totaled $27 billion during 2018 through the end of 2019.[56] US market share of China's total agricultural imports fell from 20 percent in 2017 to 12 percent in 2018, remained significantly depressed in 2019 at 10 percent, and had not recovered by February 2021. Then, to compensate politically influential US farmers for the damages, the US government gave them nearly $28 billion in direct subsidy payments (in addition to the usual US farm subsidies).[57]

Second, the 2018–2019 tariffs raised multiple political concerns. For the tariffs on Chinese imports, for example, the Office of the US Trade Representative created a process by which domestic companies could request a special exclusion for specific products. The office reviewed exclusion requests on a case-by-case basis that, in turn, led to a flurry of lobbying as businesses sought to make their case for exclusions.[58] Even lawmakers questioned the agency's ability to "pick winners and losers" through granting or denying exclusion requests.[59] As Scott Lincicome and

Inu Manak documented in a 2021 research paper, the exclusion process for the US steel and aluminum tariffs was similarly problematic: it was "arbitrary, erratic, and lacking in transparency" (a conclusion confirmed by the US Department of Commerce's Office of the Inspector General), and it raised "concerns of abuse and crony capitalism."[60]

Third, the 2018–2019 tariffs show how one round of tariffs never satisfies. As already noted, the US steel industry has long benefited from tariff protection, yet it fiercely lobbied for more when Trump took office. After he imposed the metals tariffs, moreover, imports of downstream "derivative goods," such as nails and wire increased, and the administration responded by expanding the scope of the tariffs to cover downstream goods, in what's called "cascading protectionism."[61] American producers of other steel- or aluminum-intensive products, such as beer kegs, oil pipes, and tin cans, have also requested protection because the metals tariffs have made their goods uncompetitive versus foreign companies not facing such taxes.[62]

Overall, trade-related lobbying has boomed since the 2018–2019 tariffs were first imposed.[63] That should come as no surprise given the long history of tariff-related political dysfunction in the United States.[64]

Conclusion

American history provides an abundance of examples of politicians using tariffs to protect domestic industry. Taken together, the examples show that tariffs do not generate higher levels of employment or production for the economy overall; they do not ensure the long-term health of the industries being protected or fundamentally alter the trade balance; and they serve not the strategic interests of the nation but the parochial interests of politicians who get to enrich preferred companies and workers by imposing diffuse and mostly hidden costs on the rest of the US economy.

Chapter 6

Why Do We Need Trade Agreements at All?

Simon Lester

- Corporations and other interest groups, along with flawed economic thinking, create strong demand for protectionism, and therefore the ideal of unilateral free trade is difficult to achieve.
- Free trade is simple in theory but complicated in practice, and trade agreements are necessary to flesh out the details.
- While corporations and interest groups have had success in getting some of their demands inserted into trade agreements, on balance, trade agreements promote liberalization and competition through commitments to lower protectionist trade barriers.
- Trade agreements promote the rule of law in international affairs and act as a check on unilateralism and trade wars.

Imagine a world with two countries in which the people and the political leaders believe in free trade: Cobdenia and Friedmania. Neither country would impose tariffs on imports from the other, and products that could legally be sold in one could also be sold in the other. There would be no need for a trade agreement in this situation, although just to emphasize their point of view, the two countries could sign a one-page agreement that said something along the lines of "the current state of free trade between the two countries shall continue."

The real world, of course, is messier. Many domestic corporations and labor unions object to the competition with foreign companies that free trade would bring. And some people and politicians genuinely do not believe that free trade is good policy, arguing that protectionism is the way to wealth and prosperity. The result has been a trading system characterized by continued protectionism, with trade agreements used as a second-best way to liberalize trade and constrain protectionism. These agreements achieve some liberalization but do not come close to full free trade. And in recent years, interest groups have used them to push for policies outside of the core free trade versus protectionism debate, some of which may restrict trade more than they promote it.

For these reasons, trade agreements are not a perfect way to achieve their goals. And as a result, they have been subject to criticism from some free traders, who say something along the lines of, "why can't we just have a one-page free trade agreement?"[1] These agreements have also been criticized as corporate rent-seeking tools. In this view, trade agreements are simply tools for powerful corporations to receive special treatment that will increase their profits.

The criticisms are mostly misguided. Over the past few decades, trade agreements have reduced protectionism and have created a rules-based system that keeps trade wars in check. And on balance, albeit with some exceptions, they have helped keep corporate demands for government favors at bay. The thousands of pages of trade agreements have helped shift the world in the direction of free trade and have reduced corporate influence over government policymaking.

This chapter explains the key aspects of trade agreements as follows. The free trade part of trade agreements has three components: commitments to keep protectionism within agreed upon levels; clarifications related to how to identify protectionism in domestic laws and regulations; and an enforcement mechanism to help ensure compliance with these commitments and rules. The non–free trade part includes international obligations in a wide range of policy areas, mostly related to corporate demands or social policy advocated by civil society groups. Each of these aspects of trade agreements is elaborated in the following sections.

Trade Agreements Bring Us Freer Trade

As Nobel laureate Paul Krugman observed decades ago, trade agreements would be unnecessary in a world run by economists because national governments would eliminate their trade barriers without regard to what other nations did:

> The economist's case for free trade is essentially a unilateral case—that is, it says that a country serves its own interests by pursuing free trade regardless of what other countries may do. Or as Frederic Bastiat put it, it makes no more sense to be protectionist because other countries have tariffs than it would to block up our harbors because other countries have rocky coasts. So if our theories really held sway, there would be no need for trade treaties: global free trade would emerge spontaneously from the unrestricted pursuit of national interest.[2]

However, Krugman added, "the world is not ruled by economists"; it is run by politicians—ones who, in practice, will usually pursue beneficial market-opening "in return for comparable market-opening on the part of their trading partners." Reciprocal trade agreements have therefore become the primary means by which democratic governments liberalize trade across their national borders.

The mercantilist framing of trade agreements' reciprocity model—where market access (e.g., tariff reduction) is a "concession" only to be traded for another nation's liberalization—supports the fallacy that exports are good, imports are bad, and the trade balance is the "scorecard." That fallacy lies at the root of public skepticism about free trade and allows trade skeptics to paint a free trade agreement as a "failure" if imports increase more than exports following the agreement's implementation. The diplomatic origins of the reciprocity model also have ensured that trade liberalization is treated as a foreign, rather than domestic, policy area in which negotiations take on a zero-sum, warlike mentality where benefits are "won" or "lost," instead of mutually achieved. Thus, free trade agreements can, over the long term, sow the ideological seeds of their own destruction. Nevertheless, as explained in the following sections, trade agreements are a practical way forward on trade liberalization given existing political constraints. Trade agreements promote trade liberalization in three main ways (beyond convincing politicians to get on board): (1) they include mutually agreed upon commitments to limit discrimination and protectionism; (2) they define what free trade means in the context of specific categories of government policies; and (3) they have an enforcement mechanism that provides for adjudication of disagreements about governments' protectionist measures, which helps avoid unilateral action and trade wars.

Specific Commitments to Reduce Discrimination and Protectionism

One of the most important functions of trade agreements is to set limits on the use of protectionism, via reciprocal, market-opening commitments (or "concessions"). While this mercantilist approach falls short of economists' unilateral free trade ideal, it is a practical, incremental approach that moves trade policy in the direction of trade liberalization by balancing the interests of one politically influential group—the farmers, manufacturers, and service providers who want access to foreign markets—against those of the politically influential entities that want government protection from import competition.

Trade agreement commitments apply to several types of measures: ordinary tariffs on trade in goods, restrictions on trade in services, government procurement requirements, and agriculture subsidies. For each, governments commit, in trade agreement "schedules," to limit how much protectionism each will employ.

Tariffs are the easiest to understand. Except for Chile, which has a uniform tariff that applies to all products, governments have complicated domestic tariff schedules that apply different tariff rates to specific products.[3] This approach lets governments generally liberalize trade while still protecting certain politically sensitive products sold domestically by influential companies or individuals (e.g., Florida sugar farmers). As a result, trade agreements contain long schedules that set out maximum tariff rates for each product, at a detailed level. For example, the maximum tariff rate for one kind of steel product might be 10 percent, while the maximum rate for another steel product would be 5 percent.

These scheduled tariff commitments are established through negotiations. Country X might want to sell cars to Country Y, and Country Y might want to sell beer to Country X. In the negotiation, there are a series of requests and offers, the result of which is that each one agrees to lower the tariff on the product the other wants to sell. Importantly, in a multilateral negotiation at the World Trade Organization (WTO), the lower tariff would be granted to all 166 countries on a nondiscriminatory basis, thus amplifying multilateral deals' trade liberalizing effects versus bilateral or regional ones.

Though this approach is complicated and unsatisfying to purists, it has nevertheless been successful: tariffs have declined considerably over the years. For example, economists estimate that the WTO's predecessor agreement, the General Agreement on Tariffs and Trade, reduced average tariffs on the world's industrial goods to less than 5 percent in 1993 from between 22 percent and 40 percent when the agreement took effect in 1947.[4] The North American Free Trade Agreement (NAFTA), meanwhile, brought ordinary tariffs on trade between Canada, Mexico, and the United States to zero. Figure 6.1 shows a steep decline in US tariff levels in the trade agreement era that began after World War II.

For services, trade rules are more complicated because services are supplied via four different "modes": (1) cross-border supply, (2) consumption abroad, (3) commercial presence, and (4) presence of natural persons. For example, an American might go abroad to Thailand for cheaper medical treatment (mode 2), or a Canadian bank might open a branch in the United States to serve American customers (mode 3). Unlike goods, border measures imposed on services at customs entry points are not much of an issue. Rather, trade talks focus on domestic regulations that affect foreign services, and trade agreement services schedules involve detailed commitments for the trade in a particular type of service (e.g., medical services, financial services), with commitments that vary by mode of supply.

On procurement, governments make commitments in trade agreements to open the procurement of specific domestic government agencies to foreign competition. "Buy national" programs such as Buy America are common and show that government contracting still involves a good

FIGURE 6.1

The average US tariff has declined precipitously since the end of World War II

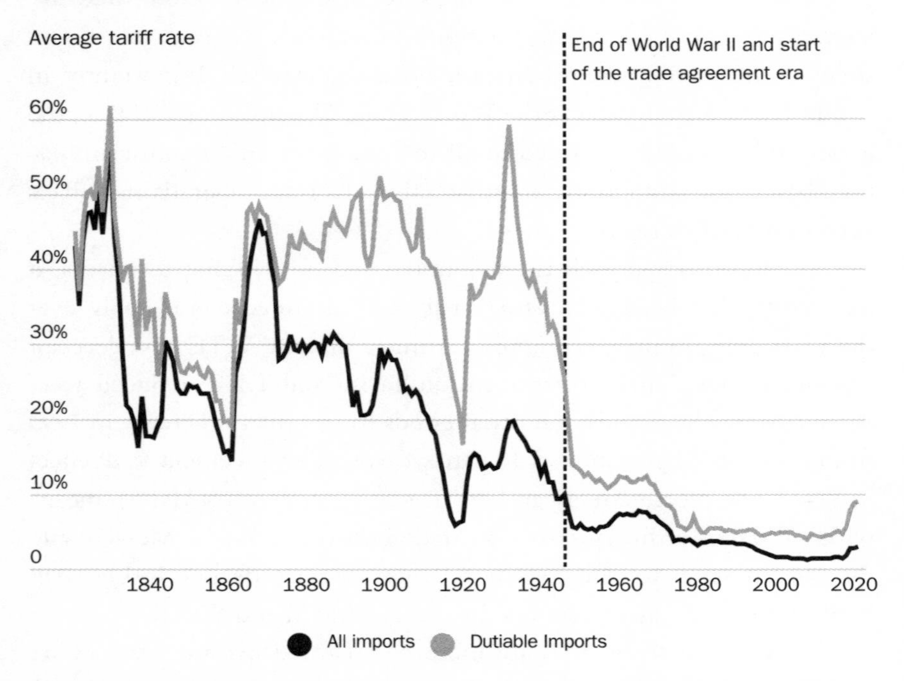

Source: Bureau of the Census, "Series U 207–212. Value of Merchandise Imports and Duties: 1821 to 1970," in *Historical Statistics of the United States: Colonial Times to 1970, Part II* (Washington: US Department of Commerce, 1975), p. 288; and "Table 1 US Imports for Consumption, Duties Collected, and Ratio of Duties Collected to Value, 1891–2021 (Thousand $)," US International Trade Commission.

Note: Only covers goods imports. Dutiable imports are imports that are subject to tariffs (i.e., did not enter duty-free).

deal of protectionism. However, governments do make commitments to open the bidding on certain government contracts to foreign competition, and trade agreements promote free trade in the goods and services that covered agencies buy.

Finally, in the WTO's Uruguay Round of trade negotiations, governments made specific commitments on agriculture subsidies, thus agreeing to limit the amount of financial assistance they would provide to their domestic farmers. Subsidies can distort trade by giving an advantage to domestic companies over their foreign competitors, both in the domestic market and sales abroad. They also can undermine support for trade liberalization among companies and individuals who compete against subsidized foreign counterparts. In the Uruguay Round, governments agreed to limit subsidies considered to be particularly trade distorting. Some limits were set at high levels, but establishing a cap nevertheless prevented governments from substantially increasing subsidies even further.

Because these commitments are so detailed, in terms of specific goods, services, procurement entities, and agricultural subsidies, trade agreements take up thousands of pages to achieve their trade-liberalizing objectives. Their length has led some to criticize trade agreements and suspect that they contain hidden special-interest favors. Some of this cronyism doubtless exists, but make no mistake: the agreements' scheduled commitments shift national trade policies toward freer trade and actually *check* special interest demands for government protection from foreign competition.

Defining Free Trade

"Free trade" sounds simple but can be quite complicated in practice. For starters, domestic regulations may have nonprotectionist policy objectives yet still disproportionally affect foreign goods, thus raising trade concerns. To address this issue, numerous trade agreement provisions define and clarify the boundaries of what agreements require for domestic regulations that affect foreign goods and services.

Most notably, the core WTO principle of "national treatment" sets out the boundaries for when taxes and regulations on goods constitute "disguised" protectionism, as well as for trade in services where commitments have been made. And for specific subcategories of measures, such as product regulations and food safety measures, there are more detailed definitions. And finally, there are exceptions that provide that measures taken for specific social policy reasons can be justified even if they would otherwise violate the rules. These basic rules establish when domestic laws and regulations are contrary to free trade principles.

These rules also help clarify the use of regulatory standards that differ across countries. Regulatory differences can burden trade, but regulatory experimentation can be a good thing, and governments have a general "right to regulate." Some would argue that if a product can legally be sold in one country, it should be legal to sell it in another. But if you think of the example of marijuana, it is easy to see why someone might object to this high level of economic integration. Different values and levels of risk tolerance, among other things, could lead governments to diverge in their regulations and want to apply those differences to imports as well as their own domestic products. Trade agreements thus recognize governments' regulatory autonomy and diversity but also establish rules for when domestic regulations cross the line into costly, "disguised" protectionism.

Second, the relatively recent proliferation of bilateral and regional "free trade" agreements (Figure 6.2) has created a spaghetti bowl trading system full of agreements that connect individual nations.

At the WTO, multilateral rules govern these agreements, defining when and how a small number of the 166 member governments may carve out a deeper, more integrated free trade area within the larger trading system. While called "free trade agreements," bilateral and regional deals can actually be trade distorting rather than trade creating. WTO rules thus govern how these trade agreements operate to ensure that they create trade more than they distort it. Without rules in this area, these "free trade" agreements could do more harm than good.

Beyond these general principles, trade agreements also have some detailed rules that address how parties may apply specific types of trade measures to ensure that they are not being abused for protectionist purposes. For example, trade agreements do the following:

- They discipline how governments can collect tariffs. In calculating the tariffs to be collected for a specific shipment of imported goods, governments must take actions such as determining the country of origin, the customs category of the good, and the good's value. Trade agreements contain detailed rules that guide this process and ensure that governments do not impose more tariffs than they should.

FIGURE 6.2

The number of regional trade agreements (RTAs) in force continues to rise

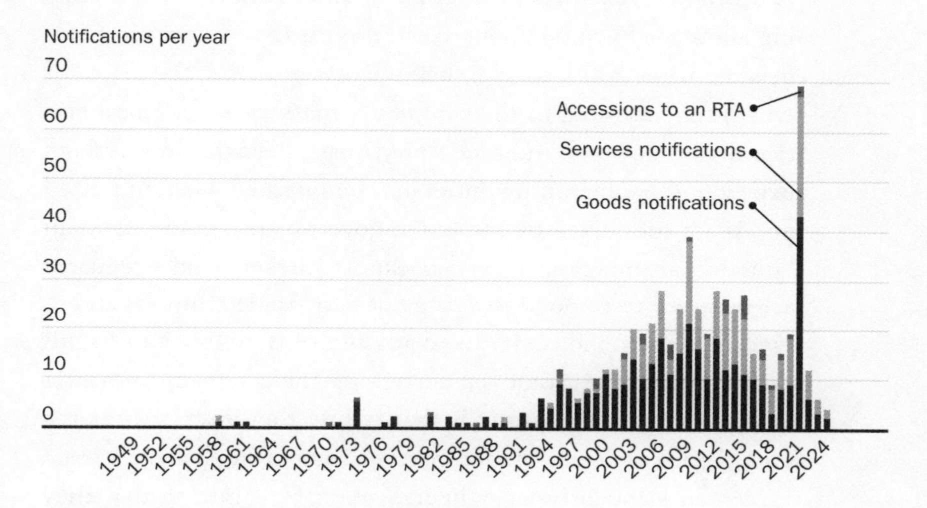

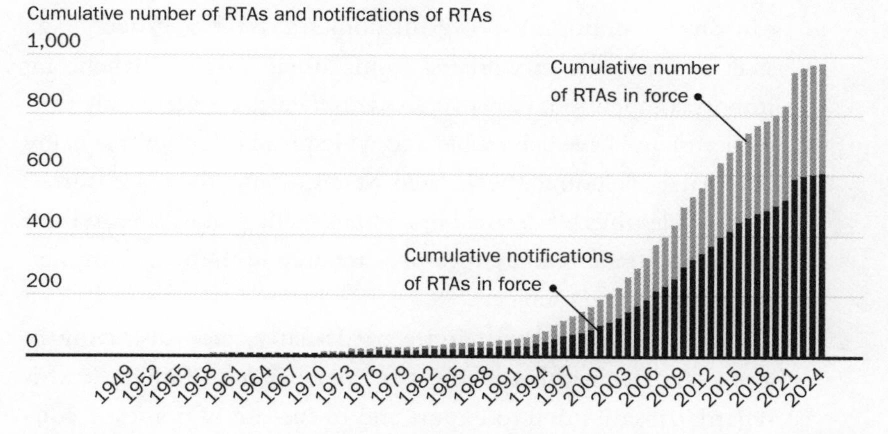

Source: "RTAs Currently in Force (by Year of Entry into Force), 1948–2024," World Trade Organization, updated June 29, 2024.

Note: World Trade Organization (WTO) members notify the WTO Secretariat of any RTAs to which they are parties. The WTO Secretariat reports notifications of RTAs on the basis of the trade flows that these agreements liberalize—goods or services. When an agreement liberalizes both (e.g., the United States-Mexico-Canada Agreement, or the Comprehensive and Progressive Agreement for Trans-Pacific Partnership), the WTO Secretariat reports a goods notification and a services notification for that agreement. For this reason, the cumulative number of notifications of RTAs in force is higher than the cumulative number of RTAs in force.

- They discipline special tariffs called "trade remedies"—antidumping duties, countervailing duties, and safeguards (safeguards also can be implemented through quotas). Rules on antidumping allow tariffs to be imposed on imports that are sold at prices deemed to be too low (e.g., below costs or below the price for which they are sold in their domestic market)—a pricing practice that some argue indicates "predatory" behavior by a foreign exporter. Countervailing duties may be imposed when imported goods are subsidized by the home government, giving them an "unfair" advantage in a certain export market. And safeguards are designed to respond to a surge of fairly traded imports and to give a domestic industry a fixed amount of time to adjust to this new competition. Some supporters of trade remedy measures justify them on the grounds that, while they restrict imports, they are necessary to induce governments to implement a trade agreement's much broader liberalization by ensuring that they can protect politically powerful domestic interest groups (e.g., steel companies and workers) from "unfair" or overwhelming import competition. However, trade remedies are manifestly protectionist and have been subject to widespread criticism that many countries, including the United States, abuse these measures.[5] WTO rules thus set detailed disciplines on these measures to limit abuse, and trade remedy measures are among the most common dispute settlement subjects.
- They classify subsidies that are particularly trade distorting in a special category that is subject to harsher punishment. In this regard, subsidies tied to export and to the use of domestic content are deemed "prohibited." The WTO's Agreement on Subsidies and Countervailing Measures has detailed definitions of the measures that fall into this category.

Through the definitions and obligations described here (and others), trade agreements establish the boundaries of what measures are protectionist and try to prevent certain measures from being abused for protectionist or discriminatory ends.

Enforcement

Trade agreement rules would be of little value if they could not be enforced. In many areas of international law, when one government complains about another's behavior, there are no effective remedies. But international trade agreements have well-developed procedures that have been at the forefront of international dispute settlement, and they have "teeth" in the form of penalties—the loss of certain trade benefits that the agreement confers—in case of noncompliance. Governments file complaints under a dispute settlement mechanism that relies on impartial tribunals, whose decisions have been relatively effective at inducing the losing government to reform an offending trade measure, usually without the imposition of any actual penalties (e.g., new tariffs on a losing government's exports to the winning government's markets). This compliance is voluntary, in that the WTO (or other trade agreement body) cannot force a member government to remove an offending trade measure; it can only authorize a winning government to suspend certain trade benefits that membership in an agreement guarantees a losing member. Nevertheless, governments usually comply because of the potential impact of this suspension, as well as the value governments place on the overall trading system (which would be undermined by frequent noncompliance) or, at least, the public *perception* of them supporting it.

While governments have refused to comply with a handful of adverse decisions, and in recent years the US government has taken actions that have undermined the WTO's dispute settlement system, the system still stands out as one of the most effective in international law (see Chapter 7, "The World Trade Organization: Myths versus Reality").

The WTO system acts as an important check on unilateral protectionism and reduces the chances of a full-blown trade war. Prior to the WTO's creation in 1995, the US government frequently invoked Section 301 of the Trade Act of 1974 to investigate, prosecute, and judge whether a foreign government was doing something "unfair" and then impose tariffs or other measures to address any "unfair" trade practice. This approach could lead to retaliation by the foreign government, and in practice, the approach has rarely induced governments to change their policies.

By contrast, modern trade agreements rely on neutral adjudication to resolve trade disputes among member governments. The agreements contain detailed obligations, require a member government to bring a complaint instead of acting unilaterally, and authorize independent adjudicators to hear those complaints, apply the rules, and authorize retaliation in the event of noncompliance. This approach reduces the possibility of retaliation because the adjudicators' decision is seen as a neutral and objective one, unlike the unilateral determinations of governments. A government's trade retaliation can be used to induce compliance, but the level of retaliation is set by independent arbitrators rather than the complaining governments. And, as noted earlier, actual trade retaliation is rare—in part because it harms the retaliating nation too. This approach reduces the role of politics in trade disputes and brings rule and order to trade conflicts that arise.

In such a system, it is important that obligations be spelled out precisely, or else governments will think they have the flexibility to make creative arguments that they are in compliance with those rules. Vague rules can thus lead to more trade conflict, as governments may decide it is worth seeing if they can convince adjudicators that their policies are not in violation. They also can put adjudicators in a difficult position of filling gaps in the rules or letting member governments get away with obvious violations of the spirit. More specific and detailed trade agreement rules, which take up more pages, can help prevent these scenarios, which can undermine the agreement and the trade that it facilitates.

Some Trade Agreement Provisions Can Actually Discourage Trade

Although the core aspects of trade agreements described here are not true "free trade" but are still generally trade liberalizing, two aspects of these agreements are not about trade liberalization at all and could actually discourage trade: (1) efforts by corporations to lobby for special rules that benefit them and (2) efforts by civil society groups to lobby for social policy regulations.

As an example of pro-business lobbying, in the Trans-Pacific Partnership talks, one controversial issue was the promotion of a long term of data exclusivity after the approval of biologic drugs.[6] The United States already has a long term for this in domestic law, and the idea was to push other governments to change their own domestic policies in this direction by having an international agreement require it.

Some interest groups have pushed successfully for regulations on labor rights and environmental protection. These rules were first included in the NAFTA through a side agreement but were later brought into the main text of trade agreements and were made subject to the regular dispute provisions. Over time, the substantive protections were broadened as well. The initial rules in this area made clear that only labor and environmental measures that affected trade were covered. For example, the Dominican Republic-Central American Free Trade Agreement (CAFTA-DR), signed in 2006, uses the following language: "A Party shall not fail to effectively enforce its labor laws, through a sustained or recurring course of action or inaction, in a manner affecting trade between the Parties, after the date of entry into force of this Agreement." However, after a CAFTA-DR panel rejected a US claim that Guatemala was not acting consistently with its obligations under the labor chapter, the language was tweaked in the United States-Mexico-Canada Agreement (USMCA) to loosen this requirement in a number of ways, including the establishment of a presumption that a failure to comply with the USMCA's labor obligations affects trade or investment.[7]

Do these policies belong in trade agreements?[8] Are the trade agreement provisions in these areas effective at achieving the policy goals? For each issue, there is a debate on the merits of the policy and how best to pursue it, but this debate looks very different from the free trade versus protectionism debate, and it is not clear how well these rules fit into trade policy.

Conclusion

One of the complaints about trade agreements is that they are corporate-dominated exercises that ignore ordinary workers. In reality, however, the core anti-protectionism aspect of trade agreements acts as a check on corporate power. Companies lobby governments to protect them from foreign competition, asking for tariffs, subsidies, Buy National procurement requirements, and other government interventions to limit competition and increase profits above market levels. Trade agreements constrain governments' ability to do these political favors for corporations and in this way should be seen mainly as an anti-corporate power exercise.

At the same time, it is true that corporations and other interest groups have found ways to insert their demands into trade negotiations, just as they do in domestic legislation. When interest groups see that law is being made through a particular method, they look for ways to take advantage of it.

This feature of trade agreements means that they are not perfect, but compromise and incremental gains are the way the world works in practice. In all policy areas, there is a debate over how idealist or practical to be. Should we go for everything we want? Or should we compromise and take what we can get? In trade policy, trade agreements are a compromise. They move policy a bit toward the free trade side by reining in protectionism to some extent.

To get to a state of affairs where free trade can be set out in one-page trade agreements, supporters need to win hearts and minds first. They have the majority of economists, but that's not enough. They need to convince the voters and find a way to beat back the special interests. Until that happens, we are stuck with the second-best solution of long, complex, and sometimes convoluted trade agreements that make progress but, admittedly, leave room for improvement.

Chapter 7

The World Trade Organization: Myths versus Reality

James Bacchus

- Started in 1995 as the successor to the General Agreement on Tariffs and Trade, the now-166-member World Trade Organization (WTO) consists of a baseline set of trade rules (agreements), a negotiating venue for member states, a system for adjudicating member-initiated trade disputes, and a repository for related data and analysis.
- The WTO itself has a small full-time staff and no decision-making powers; its rules, priorities, and activities (including disputes) are determined by member governments alone.
- The WTO is imperfect and faces real challenges. But most trade experts have long considered it to be a highly effective international organization, free from many of the problems that plague other multilateral institutions such as the United Nations.
- The WTO remains the subject of many false or misleading claims about its rules, objectives, operations, and biases. The organization is *not* an aspiring "world government" or "free trade" organization committed to a "neoliberal" agenda; biased against the United States *or* the developing world; routinely acting outside its mandate; or able to impose its will on member states.

- WTO rules do *not* undermine national sovereignty; deny member states "policy space" to address domestic priorities; cause or demand a global "race to the bottom"; or fail to discipline unfair Chinese trade practices or other unfair trade practices in the modern world economy.
- A proper understanding of these myths and realities is essential to understanding today's global economy and the real challenges that we face.

In much of the world, the WTO is believed to be a creation of the United States, imposed on other countries—especially poorer ones—through a calculated exercise of the considerable economic leverage intended to force the world to pursue US economic and geopolitical priorities. In this telling, WTO rules are mainly American rules, even though each has been agreed upon by all WTO members in successive rounds of multilateral trade negotiations. These are myths.

The myths in Washington, DC, are much the opposite. There, the WTO is at best a mistake by naive American diplomats and at worst a "globalist" conspiracy to dictate government policy and reduce US economic might and global influence. A bipartisan majority of lawmakers today see the WTO as bent on undermining US trade laws and unable to discipline China's hybrid of communism and state capitalism. These claims are also incorrect—but still powerful: the organization has been marginalized in Washington and its rules and rulings ignored, harming the WTO and the member states facing new US trade discrimination, fomenting copycat policies around the world, and in the process, harming the United States itself.

It is therefore imperative that the many myths about the WTO—about it as an institution, about its rules and who makes them, and about how it initiates, adjudicates, and enforces disputes—be once again debunked. This essay begins this process with the most prevalent and damaging WTO myths.

Answering Common Questions about the WTO

Is the WTO Part of a Global Plot to Create a World Government, and Does the United States Have No Choice but to Be a Member of the WTO?

Entirely separate from the United Nations, the WTO is an international economic organization consisting of 166 *governments*, accounting for about 98 percent of all world commerce and established by an international agreement *among those governments*. It is a forum for governments to agree by consensus to establish rules that apply to international trade among them and to ensure compliance with those rules when disputes arise between them.

The WTO is a *voluntary* organization: every member government is a member by choice, and every member can withdraw from the organization with six months of notice. Members of the US Congress have introduced WTO withdrawal legislation—and former president Donald Trump threatened to withdraw—but it never happened.[1] That no member has ever withdrawn—and that 21 other governments are still trying to join—strongly indicates the economic and geopolitical benefits of WTO membership.[2] Without the shelter and benefits of binding WTO rules and without a neutral venue for peaceful discussion and dispute resolution, the result would be a worldwide return to the pre–World War II free-for-all of discrimination, high trade barriers, retaliation, and opaqueness that decades of WTO multilateral negotiations and agreements have greatly reduced.

Is the WTO a "Free Trade" Organization, and Does It Aim to Fulfill a "Neoliberal" Agenda of Laissez Faire and "Free Market Fundamentalism" That Mandates the Removal of All International Barriers to Trade, Mass Deregulation, and a "Race to the Bottom"?

There is nothing in the WTO agreements that requires countries to lower their tariffs and other trade barriers unless they have freely chosen and agreed to do so. Members can decide to lower or eliminate tariffs and other obstacles to trade, or they can decide to keep them. The WTO has long been a multilateral means for achieving freer trade; but this has been because WTO members have long wanted it to serve that purpose. The WTO agreement leaves it to individual countries to set their own trade and other economic policies. As the WTO website explains, "The WTO's founding Marrakesh Agreement recognizes that trade should be conducted with a view to raising standards of living, ensuring full employment, increasing real income and expanding global trade in goods and services while allowing for the optimal use of the world's resources."[3] Very often, achieving this goal means freeing trade; but, in many cases, it can also mean erecting tariffs and other barriers against unfair trade where there is dumping by private companies (basically, selling in the target market at below the cost of production in the home market, with injurious results) or subsidies to private companies or industries by governments that cause injury by distorting the marketplace.

There also is nothing in the WTO agreements that requires the implementation of a worldwide "neoliberal" agenda to eliminate government regulations and social safety nets in service of "free-market fundamentalism." Critics of the WTO talk much about the need for "policy space" reserved for domestic law beyond the reach of international economic rules and often fear that the WTO will overrule local regulations that exceed global standards or promote vital, noncommercial societal values.[4] They warn of tainted "Frankenfoods," toxic products, diminished labor protections, shrinking public services, and a litany of other public health, safety, and environmental risks.

None of this is true. In fact, the WTO agreements are replete with provisions that assume there will be domestic health, safety, environmental, and other regulations and allow considerably more local policy space than many WTO critics admit. The rules do not address *whether* national measures—domestic laws, regulations, and practices—are imposed or their stringency but rather *how they affect trade*. If a measure does not affect trade, then WTO rules are not relevant. If the measure does affect trade, it will be consistent with WTO rules if it provides an equal competitive opportunity in the domestic marketplace for all like foreign and domestic products. Rules on trade in goods generally implicate the sovereign "right to regulate" only where the measure at issue discriminates between and among like traded products, either in favor of domestic over foreign products or in favor of some foreign products over others. Much the same is true in the reservation of policy space under the WTO rules on trade in services.

Similarly, WTO rules require members to protect intellectual property rights but grant considerable latitude to provide such protection "in a manner conducive to social and economic welfare" and "to promote the public interest" through domestic measures that "protect public health and nutrition" and promote "socioeconomic and technological development." Also, WTO rules on technical regulations generally limit local regulations only if they discriminate between and among like traded products, or if they create unnecessary obstacles to international trade or are more trade-restrictive than necessary to fulfill a legitimate objective. Rules on "sanitary and phytosanitary" measures permit members to implement measures necessary for the protection of human, animal, or plant life or health, subject to similar conditions and ones regarding the regulations' scientific basis and the sufficiency of the scientific evidence supporting them.

Given these realities, WTO rules have unsurprisingly *not* encouraged members to engage in a regulatory "race to the bottom" to attract multinational investment or boost domestic firms' international competitiveness.[5] In fact, economists have mostly concluded that international trade generally benefits the environment by boosting economic growth, productivity, and innovation and by generating new tax revenues for environmental protection. As economist Jagdish Bhagwati has said, "Efficient policies, such as freer trade, should generally help the environment, not hurt it," and empirical evidence shows that—over the long term—rising national income results in rising environmental protection."[6] (Economists call this the "Environmental Kuznets Curve.") Bhagwati has added, "Eventually environmental degradation peaks. It then begins a steep descent as economy and incomes continue to grow." There also is "little evidence that polluting industries relocate to jurisdictions with lower environmental standards in order to reduce compliance costs."[7] The empirical research thus far, as distilled in a study done for the World Bank, "has found little or no evidence that pollution intensive industry is systematically migrating to jurisdictions with weak environmental policy; hence maintaining a weak environmental policy regime appears to have little effect on a country's comparative advantage.[8] Other factors such as labor productivity, capital abundance, and proximity to markets are much more important in determining firm location and output." (The World Bank does note that there is more evidence thus far from developed than from developing countries.)

A similar conclusion can be drawn for labor standards over the long term. As American political scientist Daniel Drezner has explained, "There is no indication that the reduction of controls on trade and capital flows has forced a generalized downgrading in labor or environmental conditions. If anything, the opposite has occurred."[9]

Does the WTO Undermine US Sovereignty or the American Economy?

The WTO does not undermine the sovereignty of the United States or any other member of the WTO. The WTO is frequently called a "member-driven" organization because (in contrast to some other international institutions) its rules and activities are dictated by its member governments alone. The WTO has a legal identity in international law only for the practical purposes of providing office space; retaining employees; purchasing pens, paper, and computers; and keeping the cafeteria open and the windows clean. The WTO has a relatively tiny annual budget of about $220 million, contributed by members based on their proportion of international trade each year. Because the United States has the largest proportion of international trade and thus contributes the most to the WTO budget, it chairs the WTO budget committee, which makes all financial decisions for the organization.[10] Still, the United States contributes a paltry $23.6 million to the WTO's annual operations, and it does so voluntarily.[11]

About 620 people—mostly economists, lawyers, translators, and administrative staff—work for the WTO members in Geneva, Switzerland; but none of these people can take any action that binds the organization or engage in work other than basic ministerial and administrative tasks. Only the members of the WTO acting together—usually by consensus—can take actions that affect international trade and their government's obligations under the WTO rules to which they or their predecessors have affirmatively agreed. This compliance is not an undermining of their sovereignty. This is an exercise of their sovereignty; for each of the 166 WTO members has made a sovereign choice that participating in the WTO is in their interest.

The WTO does adjudicate disputes among members but cannot initiate them—complaints must be filed by member governments. The WTO also has no power to enforce its rules or dispute settlement decisions; there is no WTO "police force." Furthermore, all WTO members—including the United States—can choose to ignore WTO rules and WTO rulings if they wish. That is their sovereign right. As a matter of principle, and consistently with their collective interest in the success of the organization and its rules, no country should exercise this right. However, WTO members—for whatever reason they choose—remain free to ignore WTO rules and rulings, as long as they are willing to accept the loss of previously granted trade concessions as the agreed price for making that choice. This price can sometimes total billions of dollars of lost trade benefits annually, which—along with a desire to maintain the multilateral system and their government's status therein—has usually proven a strong incentive for WTO members to comply with the rules and the rulings. Noncompliance of the United States has thus, until the recent recalcitrance by first the Trump administration and now the Biden administration, been rare.

It is convenient for politicians to pretend, when complying with a WTO obligation or ruling, that "the WTO" has compelled such action, but this is simply false.

Leaving aside that WTO rules affecting US trade and economic performance have been agreed (and often written) by the US government, or that the US can (and occasionally does) disregard these rules, there is little evidence that they have harmed the US—in fact, it's much the opposite. According to a study by the Bertelsmann Foundation in Germany, for example, WTO membership boosted US gross domestic product (GDP) by about $87 billion since the organization began in 1995—*which is far more than any other country.*[12] Every WTO member from the multilateral trading system has benefited since then; but the

United States has benefited more than all the rest. A study commissioned by the US-based Business Roundtable found that international trade supports nearly 41 million American jobs in both goods- and services-producing industries.[13] One in every five American jobs is linked to imports and exports of goods and services. In the first 25 years following the WTO's establishment, trade-dependent jobs grew more than four times as fast as US jobs generally. Every one of the 50 US states realized net job gains that can be directly attributed to trade. And almost half of all dollars spent on imported goods and services go to American, rather than foreign, workers.[14]

Economists at the Peterson Institute for International Economics have estimated "that the payoff to the United States from trade expansion—stemming from policy liberalization and links to the global economy and improved transportation and communications technology—from 1950 to 2016 [was] roughly $2.1 trillion . . . [and] that US GDP per capita and GDP per household accordingly increased by $7,014 and $18,131, respectively."[15] Further, "disproportionate gains probably accrue[d] to poorer households." One can legitimately debate whether US policy has sufficiently distributed the nation's considerable gains from WTO membership (and trade), but the gains remain considerable, and the WTO cannot and does not dictate how sovereign governments redistribute them.

Is the WTO Biased against the United States and Other Developed Countries?

Because the WTO is member-driven, the WTO cannot be biased against any member, including the United States. There is no evidence that new WTO rules or rulings systematically or disproportionately target US policies; but even if there were, this would mean that *other countries*, not the WTO, are biased against the United States—*and* that Washington has agreed to accept this bias. The United States is not universally popular with all other countries and has its own biases against certain countries (some justified). Yet, 166 countries of all geopolitical views have agreed to cooperate on trade matters by signing the WTO agreement. The United States has long agreed that such cooperation is necessary. The WTO members can make trade rules that bind all members only by consensus. The United States can, if it wishes, block that consensus; but it can only be bound legally by rules with which it has agreed.

WTO critics allege that the United States and other developed countries suffer because WTO rules are biased against all developed countries and are tilted toward developing countries. Former president Trump voiced this sentiment on Twitter: "The WTO is BROKEN when the world's RICHEST countries claim to be developing countries to avoid WTO rules and get special treatment. No more!!!"[16] The assumption in this statement is that developing countries are profiting from being in the WTO while developed countries are not.

The aforementioned economic analyses refute this conclusion, as does even a rudimentary understanding of the WTO rules applicable to developing countries. The 45 countries with less than $1,025 in per capita income—"least-developed countries"—are generally given "special and differential treatment" that can excuse them from certain WTO rules.[17] Economists know that these exceptions are not in the least-developed countries' own economic interest, but because their economies are relatively small, little economic harm befalls the United States because of them. Meanwhile, developing countries at higher stages of development—including large economies such as China, Brazil, and India—still claim to be entitled to certain special and differential treatment provisions, but they derive little benefit from such treatment.[18] For one thing, the exceptions themselves are relatively minor in terms of their legal and economic significance. More important, and as Inu Manak and I concluded in *The Development Dimension*, special and differential treatment "is based on the premise that the growth of developing countries will be hastened if they postpone opening their markets to freer trade for as long as they can."[19] The opposite is true.

Does the WTO Offer No Remedies for the Trade and Other Commercial Abuses of the "State Capitalism" of China and for Unfair Trade Practices in Many Areas of the New "21st-Century" Economy?

China's economic rise poses a unique challenge to the world trading system, but WTO dispute settlement has more potential to address China's practices than most US politicians and pundits understand.[20] Indeed, the United States could today file a lengthy list of legal challenges to an array of Chinese trade practices *under existing WTO rules*, including on intellectual property protection and enforcement, trade secrets protection, forced technology transfer, and subsidies. The unfortunate reality is that, for the most part, the United States and like-minded members have not filed these challenges. Furthermore, the WTO—as a member-driven organization—cannot unilaterally initiate or adjudicate them. The failure to bring these potential legal claims against China is particularly disappointing, given that China does not—also contrary to myth—routinely ignore adverse WTO rulings; in fact, given recent US foot-dragging, China may have a better record of complying with adverse WTO rulings than the United States.

This is not to say that current WTO rules should not be improved or that new WTO rules should not be negotiated and agreed to help counter the unique challenge posed by China to the multilateral trading system. They should be. But the means of accomplishing this (admittedly difficult) end is not by ignoring the WTO and WTO rules; it is by employing those rules in dispute settlement and by giving priority to negotiating new and improved rules within the WTO.

Does WTO Dispute Settlement Discriminate against the United States?

According to President Trump, "We lose . . . almost all the lawsuits in the WTO," and US policymakers often agree with him that WTO jurists are biased against the United States.[21] In reality, however, the United States has *won* the vast majority of the cases it has brought as a complainant in WTO dispute settlement (including the overwhelming majority of the cases it has brought against China) and has the best

FIGURE 7.1

Like most WTO members, the United States has prevailed in most of its dispute settlement cases as a complainant and lost in most of its cases as a respondent

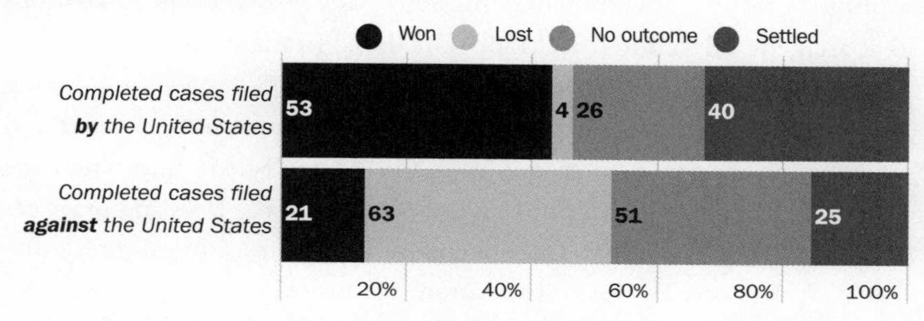

Source: "Snapshot of WTO Cases Involving the United States," Office of the US Trade Representative, September 17, 2021.

Note: Does not include cases that were in consultations, panel, or appellate stages as of September 2021. Where multiple complaints focused on the same measure, the US Trade Representative's list consolidated them into a single case. "Settled" includes cases for which formal requests for consultations were filed but there was no subsequent request for the establishment of a panel because the dispute was resolved through consultations and cases that proceeded to the panel, appellate, or compliance (Article 21.5 of the Dispute Settlement Understanding) stages but were either terminated or withdrawn because a mutually acceptable solution was agreed upon by the parties or otherwise ended before litigation was completed (i.e., because litigation was suspended for a period exceeding 12 months and thus the authority for the establishment of a panel lapsed).

success record of any complainant.[22] By contrast, the United States has lost most of the cases that have been brought against it in WTO dispute settlement, including a series of cases relating to the use of trade remedies in which the United States has lost mainly because it has been recalcitrant in complying with previous adverse rulings on the same or similar legal issues. Figure 7.1 displays these facts.

Much of this reflects institutional dynamics: Out of more than 600 international trade disputes so far, complaining countries have won about 90 percent of the cases they have taken to WTO dispute settlement. Countries tend not to undertake the laborious task of filing a complaint against another country in WTO dispute settlement, with all the costs and geopolitical consequences that sometimes result, unless they believe they have a strong legal case that can be made.

However, some of the United States' record in dispute settlement is of its own choosing. Many of the cases the United States has lost have involved the expansive American use of antidumping duties, countervailing duties to governmental subsidies, and other trade retaliations that are generally known as "trade remedies." In these cases, the United States pushed beyond the legal boundaries of WTO rules for applying such trade restrictions—rules that the US government negotiated and with which it agreed when the WTO was established. And when the United States lost these disputes, it did not reform the laws and practices at fault (an exercise of national sovereignty), thus resulting in more disputes on the same legal issues and more US losses.

There also is no evidence of WTO jurists—many of whom are American—being biased against the United States, regardless of their nationality. Jurists do not serve any one country; they serve the multilateral trading system. Toward this end, they shed their nationality when they become WTO jurists. According to the WTO Rules of Conduct, WTO jurists "shall be independent and impartial" and "shall avoid direct or indirect conflicts of interest," among other requirements designed to safeguard "the integrity and impartiality" of the dispute settlement system.[23] In the more than a quarter of a century since the establishment of the WTO and the adoption of these rules of conduct, the United States has brought not one claim contending that a WTO jurist is not "independent and impartial" or has a "direct or indirect conflict of interest." Allegations of jurist bias—often after losing a dispute—are politics and nothing more.

Do WTO Jurists Routinely Exceed Their Authority under the WTO Agreement?

No. The Trump and Biden administrations have blocked the seating of new members of the WTO Appellate Body, which handles appeals of lower dispute panel decisions, on the grounds that Appellate Body members have routinely exceeded their authority under the WTO agreement. The Appellate Body members are said to have frequently engaged in "overreaching" and in "gap-filling" that have altered the obligations in the WTO agreement, which is in direct violation of their own obligations in that agreement.

This claim, however, is simply not true. Like any tribunal, the Appellate Body is comprised of imperfect jurists who can occasionally get discrete points wrong. So can the Supreme Court of the United States. But, contrary to the US portrayal, the Appellate Body is actually doing its job properly as mandated in the WTO agreement. In particular, WTO members—including the United States—have instructed WTO jurists to "clarify the existing provisions" of the various trade agreements that altogether comprise the WTO agreement "in accordance with customary rules of interpretation of public international law." Those customary rules require that a treaty shall be interpreted in good faith in accordance with the ordinary meaning to be given to the terms of the treaty in their context and in the light of its object and purpose. (These customary rules of treaty interpretation are expressed in Article 31 and Article 32 of the Vienna Convention on the Law of Treaties; however, as customary rules, they exist independently of that convention as international law.[24]) Thus, the members of the Appellate Body are tasked with clarifying the meaning of the provisions in the WTO agreement in accordance with these rules. This is not "overreaching" or "gap-filling." It is simply the Appellate Body doing what the members of the WTO have told it to do in the WTO agreement.

If, in fulfilling its mandate, the Appellate Body makes a mistake in doing its job by reaching the wrong result in its clarification, then there is a ready remedy. The members can overrule the Appellate Body's ruling by adopting their own legal interpretation, which will be binding on all WTO jurists. This would take a vote of a "three-fourths majority of the Members." So far, the United States has not sought to invoke this provision to overturn a single Appellate Body ruling. This inaction is, again, telling.

Conclusion

For the sake of brevity, this essay addresses only the most pervasive myths about the WTO. There are more, and new myths seem to emerge almost daily. Such fallacies may help those who wish to promote their own political or economic agendas at the expense of the continued functioning of the WTO as a global public good, but they imperil reforms that would help improve the multilateral trading system and accomplish its long-standing goals of peace and prosperity through trade. Dispelling them can help to restore the WTO to its rightful place at the center of world trade and of world trade policy and decisionmaking. It is long past time, in the United States especially, to tell the truth about the WTO.

Chapter 8

Technology and Innovation, Not Just Policy, Help Drive Globalization

Colin Grabow

- Discussions of globalization typically focus on the role of government policy in facilitating cross-border trade and investment, yet private-sector innovation has also driven these same trends.
- Containerization has been a key contributor to these lowered costs. By offering vastly more efficient loading and unloading of goods as well as greater protection against pilferage and damage, containers have significantly expanded international trade.
- Efficiency gains in air freight resulting from technological improvements have similarly produced significant cost reductions. Although air freight moves only a small percentage of international trade by weight, it plays a critical role in the transportation of high-value goods.
- Advances in computers and telecommunications have also encouraged international economic linkages, allowing businesses and customers to connect more easily across distances and borders and providing the data processing heft necessary to track and organize shipments across increasingly complex supply chains.

Private Initiatives Help Drive Cross-Border Trade

Discussions around globalization may create the impression that expanded cross-border economic ties have been solely a policy choice or the result of coordinated efforts by governments around the world. That's not surprising, as governments have used both unilateral and coordinated multilateral efforts to significantly reduce obstacles to cross-border trade in the post–World War II era. As a result, the average value of tariffs in force around the world has declined by 85 percent since 1947, and many nontariff barriers have been reduced or eliminated.[1] This policy liberalization correlates with international trade as a percentage of world gross domestic product more than doubling from 25 percent in 1970 to 63 percent in 2022.[2]

Often overlooked, however, is the role of private initiatives that have encouraged cross-border trade. Although engendering far less acrimony—there have been no protests against more efficient shipping or plunging costs in information technology—their impact has been undeniably significant. Indeed, the reduction in transportation and communication costs resulting from private innovation have been of such magnitude that supply chains can now be weaved among specialized firms in numerous countries.

The numbers speak for themselves. According to a 2023 paper, transport costs by weight declined by 33–39 percent from 1970 to 2014, while transport costs by value declined 48–62 percent.[3] Other measures indicate that ocean shipping, which carries around 80 percent of international goods trade by volume, saw costs decline by just over 50 percent from 1974 to 2016, while air cargo costs fell 78 percent from 1970 to 2019.[4]

These advances have made the world dramatically smaller and more prosperous than what many perhaps believed possible. This paper will take a closer look at some of the technological drivers that have advanced globalization by making trade cheaper and easier than ever before.

Containerization Has Significantly Reduced the Cost of Transporting Goods

Perhaps no innovation has done more to promote international trade and globalization in the modern era than the humble shipping container, which is responsible for roughly 35 percent of global merchandise trade by volume and over 60 percent by value.[5] Typically constructed in lengths of 20 or 40 feet, containers greatly ease the loading and unloading of ships, as giant cranes transfer the boxes from ship to shore (or the reverse) in about two minutes. From there they can be either trucked to local warehouses to be unpacked, transferred to smaller vessels for transshipment to other ports, or placed on trucks and railroads to be transported closer to their final destinations.

Although the concept of placing items in containers for easier transport has been around since at least the 18th century, such efforts did not spread beyond niche applications.[6] Succeeding where others failed and ushering in the modern era of containerization was Malcom McLean, the owner of a large trucking company. Although accounts of McLean's foray into container shipping differ—some cite his desire to bypass traffic, while others emphasize his desire to avoid government meddling in interstate trucking—the trucking industry veteran originally conceived of using ships to transport truck chassis and containers together.[7] He soon realized, however, that loading the containers alone would be a more efficient means of transport that allowed for stacking.

McLean's vision was realized on April 26, 1956, when a World War II–built tanker called the SS *Ideal X* departed Port Newark, New Jersey, for Houston.[8] Cheaply acquired thanks to a government maritime promotion program, the vessel had been modified to transport 58 containers on a spar deck above the tanker piping. Although a visual oddity, the ship made clear containerization's compelling economics. While the loading of cargo in piecemeal fashion prior to the advent of containers was estimated to cost $5.83 per ton in 1956, the *Ideal X* was able to reduce that figure to $0.16 per ton—a 97 percent decrease.[9] In *Box Boats: How Container Ships Changed the World*, author Brian J. Cudahy calculates that the cost to unload a conventional cargo ship was at least $15,000, whereas the *Gateway City*, another container ship operated by McLean, could be unloaded for $1,600—an 89 percent decline.[10]

To encourage its adoption, McLean allowed others access to his patented standardized container designs through a royalty-free lease to the International Organization for Standardization. The shipping industry was forever changed.

Containerization's dramatic reduction in cargo handling costs reflected a vast increase in port productivity: From 1965 to 1970, the amount of cargo that could be moved by stevedores onto a ship increased from 1.7 tons per hour to 30 tons per hour. According to *Box Boats*, whereas previously a cargo ship required 150 stevedores working at least four *days* to load and unload, a crew of 14 could do the same task on the *Gateway City* in just over eight *hours*.

Less time loading and unloading meant that ships could spend more time sailing, boosting their own productivity and more quickly speeding goods to market. A 1985 comparison between the container ship *Liverpool Bay* and the cargo ship *Priam*, which was not specially designed to transport containers, found that the former spent 17 percent of its time in port compared with 40 percent for the latter.[11] Cudahy writes that, prior to containerization, it was "not uncommon for a vessel assigned to the busy transatlantic trade route between New York and the channel ports of Europe to spend as much time in port loading and unloading cargo, over its lifetime, as it did steaming across the ocean."

Containers also provided other benefits, such as deterring pilferage, by making the cargo less accessible. (Recalling his stint on a merchant ship prior to widespread containerization, author Christopher Buckley noted that "you knew what cargoes you were carrying because you could see them, smell them, touch them, and on occasion, help yourself to them," while the wages of New York dockworkers were jokingly said to be "twenty dollars a day and all the Scotch you could carry home.")[12] Increased ease of cargo handling also meant fewer damaged goods, which, along with reduced thievery, resulted in reduced insurance costs. As one example, shipping between Australia and Europe saw insurance costs fall from an average of $0.24 per ton to $0.04 per ton from 1965 to 1971.

Containerization had profound implications not only for ships but for transportation more broadly, as cargo could now be easily transferred among various modes, including trucking and rail. The modern era of intermodal freight transport was born and the entire transportation system revolutionized.

Efficiency Gains in Shipping Have Also Contributed to Lower Transportation Costs

Beyond containerization, another contributor to the lower transportation costs that have helped make globalization possible is the increased efficiency of the ships transporting these containers. The scale of their increase in size is almost mind-boggling. While the SS *Ideal X* carried 58 containers that were each 35 feet long, specialized container ships today regularly transport *thousands* of containers. The largest of these oceangoing behemoths, a ship called the *MSC Irina*, can carry 24,346 units that are each the size of one 20-foot container—enough to transport over 12,000 boxes that are 40 feet each.[13] For perspective, the smaller *MSC Oscar*'s capacity of 19,224 units that are 20 feet each is sufficient to carry 39,000 cars, 117 million pairs of sneakers, or over 900 million cans of dog food.[14]

More boxes per ship leads to lower shipping costs, as fixed costs are spread across more containers. Although there is a debate over the optimal size of container ships, particularly given the extra money that must be spent on port facilities to accommodate these oceangoing giants, there is little question that today's container ships are more efficient than those of decades past.[15]

This trend toward larger vessels goes beyond container ships. In 1950, the *Bulkpetrol* was launched as one of the world's largest tankers capable of transporting over 50,000 tons.[16] Nine years after that, a tanker of over 100,000 deadweight tons was launched, and by 1966, the first very large crude carrier was launched at over 200,000 deadweight tons.[17] The year 1968, meanwhile, saw the launch of a tanker whose capacity exceeded 325,000 deadweight tons.[18] Bulk carriers used to transport dry cargo, such as large amounts of grains or coal, have also seen considerable growth in size (Figure 8.1).

FIGURE 8.1

The size of container ships has increased significantly over the past few decades

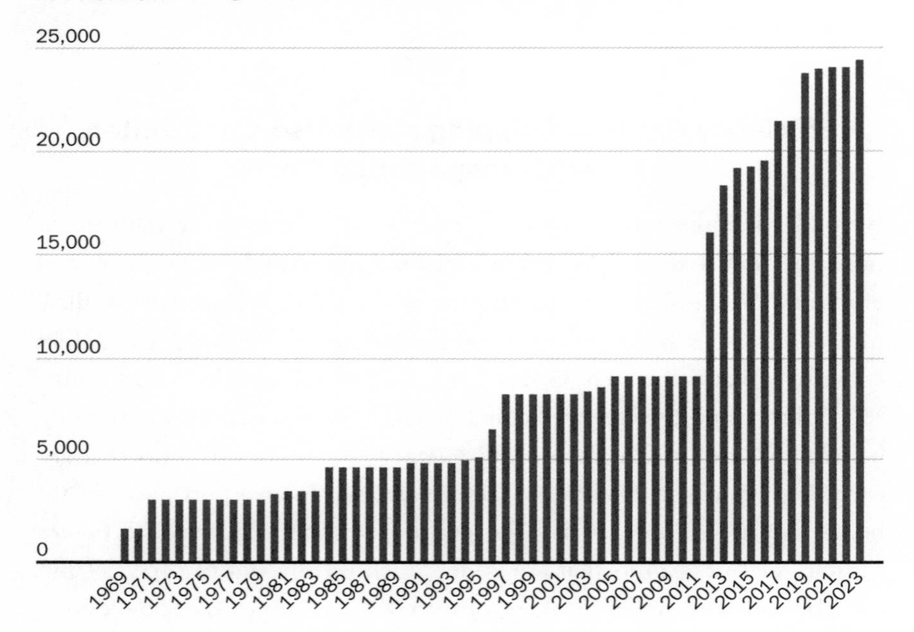

Source: "Largest Container Ships by Year," Logistics eLearning, Allyn International; and Jasmina Ovcina Mandra, "MSC Shatters Records with Delivery of 24,346 TEU MSC Irina," Offshore Energy, March 13, 2023.

Note: TEU = twenty-foot-equivalent unit. This unit of measurement represents a 20-foot container.

But the ships have become not only larger but also more efficient, using automation to significantly reduce the number of crew members. The *Priam*, for example, launched in 1966, featured a crew of 43, while the crew size of modern container ships averages around 22.[19] Some large cargo ships today feature as few as 13 crew members.[20]

Other developments have produced efficiency gains as well. Shipping giant Maersk's introduction of its Triple-E (economy of scale, energy efficiency, and environmental impact improvement) class of ships, for example, relied on a combination of factors, including size, technological refinements, and the use of more efficient slow steaming to reduce its shipping costs by $300–$400 per container.[21]

Beyond technological factors, new means of managing and operating the ships have also contributed to lower costs. Open registries, for example, allow ships to sail under the flag of a country even when there is no link between the vessel—such as the owner or citizenship of the crew—and the country whose flag it flies. Such flexible arrangements allow for ships to be crewed with highly trained mariners from countries such as the Philippines and India that have lower wage demands than mariners from the United States or other highly developed countries.

Countries operating these open registries also typically have lower taxes than elsewhere, further contributing to lower costs. Such arrangements increased the percentage of the global fleet flagged in open registries from 21.6 percent in 1970 to 71.3 percent in 2015.[22] Notably, a number of the leading open registries are also known for their quality, with countries such as Liberia and the Marshall Islands enjoying a better ranking than the United States.[23]

Efficiencies and lowered costs beget more trade, which leads to further efficiencies. Expanded cargo volumes allow for the use of larger ships as well as increased competition as more firms enter the market, both of which serve to restrain costs. Growing trade also promotes the development and utilization of more efficient and specialized vessels, such as the *Toyota Maru* No. 10, which in 1970 became the first vessel developed solely to transport cars.[24] There are also ships specialized for transporting vast quantities of fruit juice.[25] Specialized ships have even been built for moving other vessels, such as the *Blue Marlin*, which was once used to transport 22 barges from South Korea to the Netherlands.[26]

All these factors have combined to produce significant drops in the cost of ocean transportation (Figure 8.2).[27] While in 1890 it cost nearly $200 per ton (2020 dollars) to ship goods from California to Europe, that figure had declined to less than $2 per ton using a standard bulk ship a century later. Today, T-shirts can be transported from China to the Netherlands for $0.025 per garment, and Nike shoes can be shipped over similar distances for just $0.35 per pair.[28]

FIGURE 8.2
Shipping prices have dropped precipitously over time

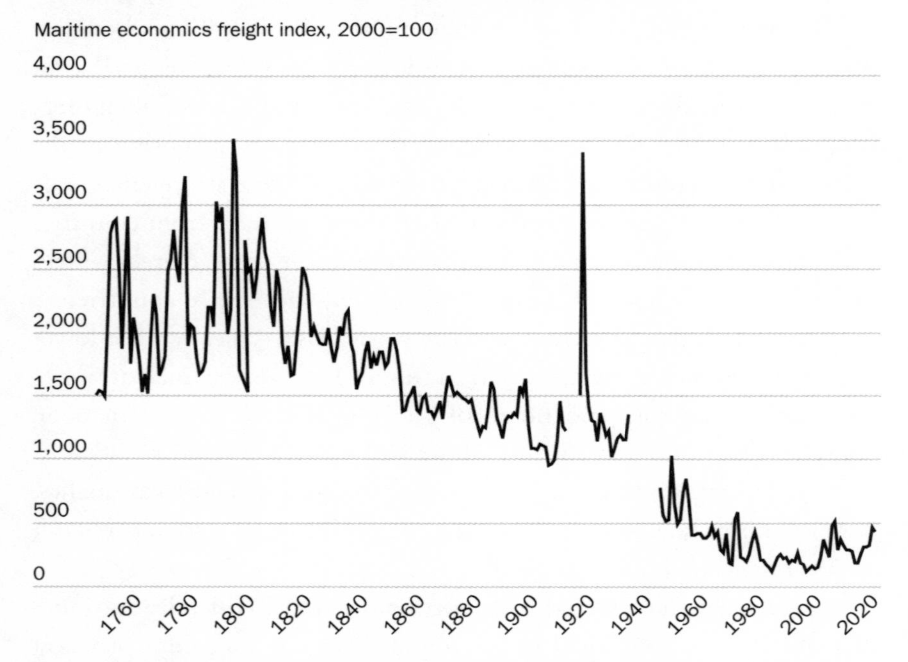

Source: Martin Stopford, "Defining the Future of Shipping Markets," ITC Forum 2000, October 2, 2000, direct communication with author.

More-Efficient Airplanes Have Reduced the Cost of Moving Goods and People

Like sea transport, air cargo has experienced dramatic cost reductions that have contributed to the growth of international trade. Air cargo's increased efficiency, however, is less the story of a single key innovation, such as the shipping container, and more the result of numerous smaller improvements that had a large cumulative impact. However, the jet engine's thrust and fuel costs—as well as fewer moving parts—were one of the more significant contributions. Since its introduction, such engines have been steadily refined to become even more efficient.

In addition to engine enhancements, airplanes have also seen improved designs and the use of lighter composite materials that lower operating costs. Their collective impact has been impressive: from 1968

FIGURE 8.3

The share of total US trade (excluding North America) that was transported via air increased steadily throughout the 20th century

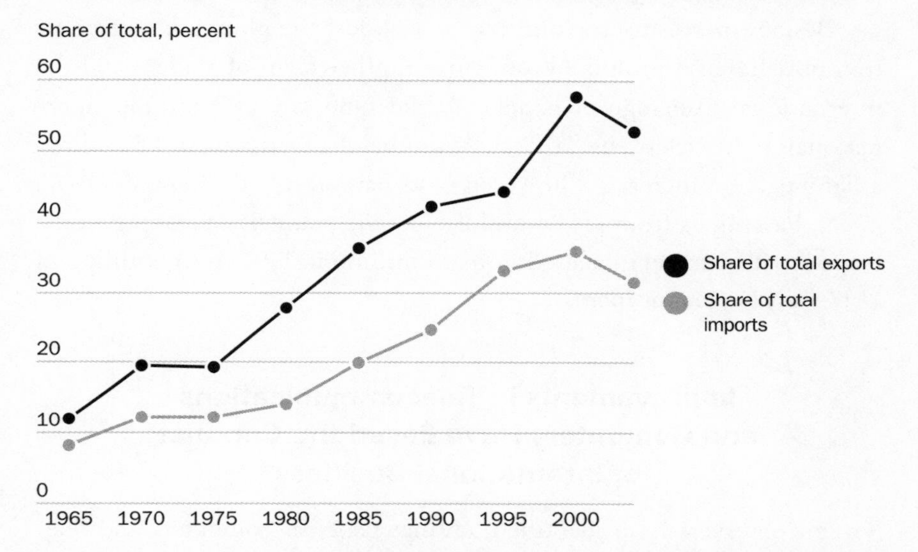

Source: Paul Masson, "Globalization: Facts and Figures," International Monetary Fund Policy Discussion Paper, PDP/01/4, October 2001.

to 2014, the average fuel usage of new aircraft declined by approximately 45 percent.[29] Such cost reductions have contributed to a dramatic increase in air transport's role in international trade.[30] Having once accounted for only 8.1 percent of US imports and 11.9 percent of US exports as measured by value in 1965, air cargo had surged to 31.5 percent of imports and 52.8 percent of exports by 2004 (Figure 8.3).

Beyond increasing quantity, lowered costs also allow air cargo to travel farther. While air-shipped cargo averaged 2,600 miles in 1975, by 2004 that number had increased to 3,383 miles.

The iPhone provides an example of air freight's compelling economics and the distances many goods now travel.[31] In 2013, it cost approximately $242,000 to charter a Boeing 777 to transport 450,000 iPhones from China to the main US distribution facility, or less than $2 per phone. For context, that amounts to approximately 0.3 percent of the $649 starting price for the iPhone 5S released that same year.[32]

Notably, increased air freight efficiency has contributed to supply chain resiliency. During the COVID-19 pandemic, numerous firms used aircraft to avoid congested ports and speed their products to market.[33]

Besides increasing trade in physical goods, the plunging cost of air transport has also promoted tourism—another form of trade—and the international exchange of people. While 1980 saw 200 million international air travelers, by 2019 that number had surged to 4.6 billion, an 850 percent increase.[34] Lowered costs have also had a democratizing effect. Passengers from lower-middle-income countries engaging in international air travel increased from 29 million in 1995 to 138 million in 2017—a 376 percent increase.

Improvements in Telecommunications and Computers Have Eased the Conduct of International Business

Several observers have identified advancements in computers and telecommunications as also playing a key role in the rise of globalization. The decline in cost of such services has been nothing less than astonishing. While the price of a three-minute phone call between New York and London was $75 in 1927—$469 in 2023 dollars—that number had shrunk to $2.77 by 1982 ($8.93 in 2023 dollars) and today essentially has no cost beyond the necessary hardware and monthly price of internet service (Figure 8.4).[35] Computing, meanwhile, has been subject to Moore's law, in which the information-processing capacity of microprocessors doubles every 18 months while cost falls at a similar pace. This combination of cheap computing and communication means that billions of phone calls, emails, video calls, and text messages are made or sent every day.

Besides the benefits that this connectivity brings to our everyday lives, it also helps smooth trade and ease the conduct of international business. According to historian and economist Marc Levinson, these technological leaps—along with efficient transportation over long distances—have provided large companies with the necessary tools to disperse production processes to those locations where they are best suited instead of keeping them in closer geographical proximity for ease of management.[36]

FIGURE 8.4

The cost of a three-minute telephone call from New York to London declined by more than 99 percent between 1960 and 2000

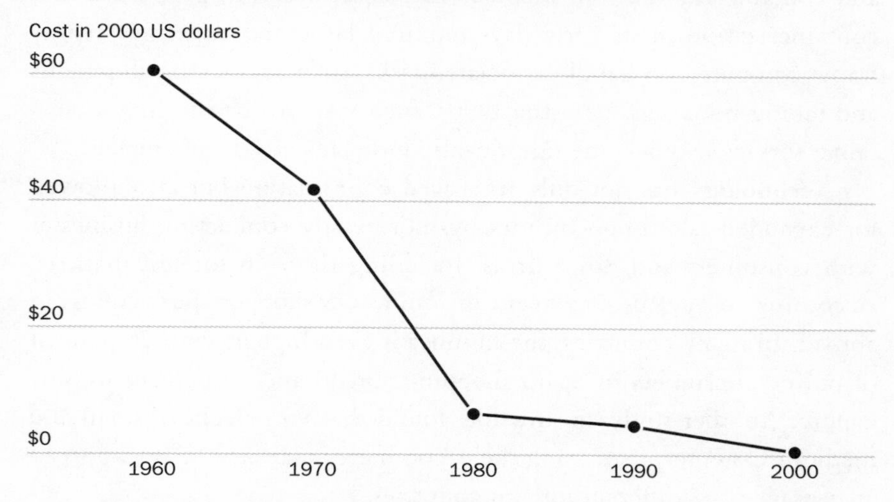

Source: Paul Masson, "Globalization: Facts and Figures," International Monetary Fund Policy Discussion Paper, PDP/01/4, October 2001.

In other words, factories can be set up where production is most efficient rather than being tethered closer to where company executives are located. Geoffrey Garrett, currently dean of the University of Southern California's Marshall School of Business, described a similar phenomenon in a 2000 essay:

> The internet has radically reduced the costs of coordinating complex supply, production, and distribution networks that are geographically decentralized. The automobile industry is a classic example. It may long have been efficient for Volkswagen to buy gear boxes in the United States, build engines in Germany, assemble cars in Brazil, and sell the finished product cars all over the world. But the challenges of coordinating all this activity are immense, especially if Volkswagen wants to pursue just-in-time production/low inventory best practices. Being able to coordinate all elements of the supply and distribution chains on the World Wide Web has been a boon for firms that have incentives to decentralize their activities.[37]

Economist and maritime transportation expert Martin Stopford, meanwhile, sees a connection between the advent of modern computing and containerization.[38] In *Maritime Economics*, Stopford points out that containerization in its early days required large and expensive mainframe computers to handle associated tasks, such as tracking shipments and taking bookings.[39] By the 1990s, such systems for running a container service had become significantly more advanced and efficient.

Technology has not only improved coordination but also allowed for expanded sales opportunities by more easily connecting businesses with consumers and other firms, including those in foreign markets. According to PayPal, 41 percent of online US shoppers purchase from abroad. In many countries, the number is even higher, with 76 percent of online consumers in Spain shopping abroad and 79 percent in Singapore. Another study, meanwhile, found that 96 percent of small and medium US enterprises using the e-commerce platform eBay export to an average of 17 different foreign countries.[40]

Being able to shop internationally and engage with suppliers at the mere click of a button has undoubtedly been yet another contributing factor to expanded economic interconnectedness.

Numerous Factors Help Drive Globalization Forward

Trade is the foundation of prosperity, allowing for greater levels of productivity as workers and firms become ever more specialized. A key factor in enabling this trade is efficient transportation and technologies that help overcome the distances that separate potential trading partners.

Such advancements are fundamental to today's complex supply chains optimized for utilizing the comparative advantages of firms spread across the globe. Apple is a poster child of this phenomenon, relying on hundreds of parts from scores of suppliers spread across over 20 countries in fiscal year 2022.[41] In 2019, Boeing relied on suppliers from 58 countries for the vastly complex aircraft it produces.[42]

These companies are hardly alone in their use of cross-border trade to efficiently produce their products. Automotive firms have noted that vehicle parts and components may cross borders as many as eight times before reaching final assembly as they ping between those places with a unique specialization in each step of the process.[43] It's difficult to imagine this could take place without many of the innovations in transportation and technology developed over the past 50 years.

Cheaper transportation, powerful computing, and inexpensive access to world-spanning telecommunications services, however, hardly constitute the total sum of forces outside policy levers that have helped drive globalization forward. Indeed, they don't even constitute the total sum of *technological* forces, with numerous other technologies helping to spur globalization, such as Universal Product Codes.[44]

Interestingly, many of the forces that contribute to globalization outside the policy realm are in many ways outgrowths of globalization itself. The prosperity generated by increased trade, for example, leads to additional cross-border flows as consumers demand imported goods that were previously unaffordable. Consumers' palates, for example, may evolve toward a taste for Italian prosciutto, cashmere from Mongolia, or high-end consumer electronics assembled in China (using inputs from numerous other countries). Globalization also creates more pathways to the types of employment that provide the disposable incomes for such purchases.[45]

Notably, a 2001 paper calculated that income growth explains about 67 percent of the increase in world trade among several Organisation for Economic Co-operation and Development countries between the late 1950s and the late 1980s, while tariff-rate reductions are responsible for about 25 percent and transport cost declines thought to account for approximately 8 percent.[46]

Globalization's self-reinforcing nature may also apply to the way companies operate. As one paper notes, a "substantial fraction" of companies engaged in importing or exporting do both.[47] This appears to suggest that companies develop a greater appetite for foreign markets as they become more familiar with global trade rules and more adept at navigating the red tape of importing and exporting after dipping their toes into international supply chains. Globalization, in other words, is in many ways a self-reinforcing cycle in which international trade creates yet more demand for the cross-border provision of goods and services.

But technology and innovation haven't stopped, and even more new innovations could be on the way. Experiments with autonomous shipping are already taking place in Japan and Norway, and port automation projects in China, Singapore, and the Netherlands promise to bring a new era of efficiency to cargo handling.[48] Such efforts could bring new efficiencies that further reduce the cost of transportation.

Advancements in telecommunications could also lead to new innovations and opportunities for trade. Ubiquitous internet connectivity, for example, has already ushered in the era of telemedicine, and technological leaps may be able to push the boundaries of such interactions still further to potentially include telesurgery.[49] As technology advances and distances recede, exciting new possibilities await.

Innovators and the Technologies They Have Unleashed Have Helped Drive Globalization

Since the earliest days of trade—which is to say, since the dawn of mankind—the ability to exchange goods has been limited by the proximity and visibility of potential trading partners. As new forms of technology—everything from the wheel to the caravel to the modern shipping container—have emerged to overcome these distances, trade has flourished, expanding the size of the market and enabling increasing levels of scale and specialization. The process of globalization is a long one and continues today as new innovations make it faster and easier for the world's population to engage with one another. And humanity is all the better for it.

The path forward has, of course, been smoothed by wise policy changes of governments around the world. The reduction or outright elimination of tariffs and regulatory barriers to trade is a significant part of the globalization story. And, of course, there is still much more left to do, including policy reforms that would better allow Americans to take advantage of some of the technological advancements described in this essay. Cabotage restrictions in the US maritime and aviation markets result in increased costs and reduced connectivity that harm trade.[50] Similarly, trade is hindered by underperforming US ports whose efficiency levels should be raised through targeted policy measures to match those of international peers.

But policy levers and changes are not the whole story—far from it. As impactful as the actions of lawmakers have been in driving cross-border exchanges, the work of innovators, such as Malcom McLean and myriad other engineers and businesspeople, has produced incremental, steady improvements to various technologies and has led to giant leaps in our ability to efficiently trade goods and services over vast distances. Globalization isn't simply the choice of government officials but the realized aspiration of untold numbers of people whose work has steadily shrunk the world, expanded markets, and brought us closer together.

Chapter 9

Digital Trade in Services: Globalization's Exciting New Frontier

Gary Winslett

- Digital trade in services is larger than most people realize and is set to become even more important as technology continues to advance.
- Increasing digital trade delivers big wins to US consumers, workers, shareholders, and citizens.
- To facilitate these digital services, trade rules like those in the Comprehensive and Progressive Trans-Pacific Partnership and the United States-Mexico-Canada Agreement (USMCA) serve as a strong starting point.

The Pakistani Zoom Tutor

In March 2023, a father in Dallas said on Twitter that his 12-year-old was struggling with his algebra homework. He said he posted an advertisement for tutoring work on Upwork (a freelancing platform) and that 10 minutes later, they were on Zoom with a professor in Pakistan who was able to quickly and effectively help his son and continued to tutor the student for five hours a week thereafter.[1]

Students have been struggling with math homework since the dawn of math homework. And until very recently, the idea of having someone on the other side of the world assist over a real-time video call would have been unthinkable—especially for anyone who wasn't rich. However, this is an example of the next frontier in globalization: digital trade in services.

Digitalization is allowing more services than ever to be traded internationally. I've termed this new globalization "Peloton Globalization."[2] Not so long ago, if you wanted to take a spin class, you had to do it at a local gym or spin studio. Now, if you have the Peloton app and any stationary bike, you can, from anywhere in the world, be led through a spin class by Peloton instructor Ben Alldis, who coaches from the Peloton London studio.

Digitalization has reduced what political economists call the "proximity burden."[3] With goods, the seller and the buyer do not normally need to be near each other. A pair of shoes can be made in Vietnam and purchased in Spain. Traditionally, that has not been the case with services. To provide a service, the seller and the buyer needed to be in the same room. Some services still work that way. If you want a haircut, you must physically go to a barber or stylist, and traveling too far to get that service easily overwhelms the value of the service, which means that the service has to be provided locally. Granted, many services continue to operate this way, but as the Zoom tutor and Peloton examples suggest, an increasing number of services do not, thanks to digitalization.

A variety of services—including content creation, engineering, legal assistance, and customer service—can now be traded internationally. This will continue to grow over time as technology progresses. Advances in augmented and virtual reality could make delivering services internationally even easier and more effective. Imagine being able to take an immersive, virtual cooking class from someone in Thailand or violin lessons from a musician in Poland, who could use augmented or virtual reality to help you better understand how to position your arms.

If you ask the average person what they think of when they think of international trade, they almost always think of goods in containers on ships. Trade in goods is easier for people to grasp and often involves industries such as automobiles that are symbolically powerful and have a lot of lobbying power, which means that trade in services typically is underappreciated.[4]

FIGURE 9.1
Total used capacity of international internet bandwidth has increased rapidly

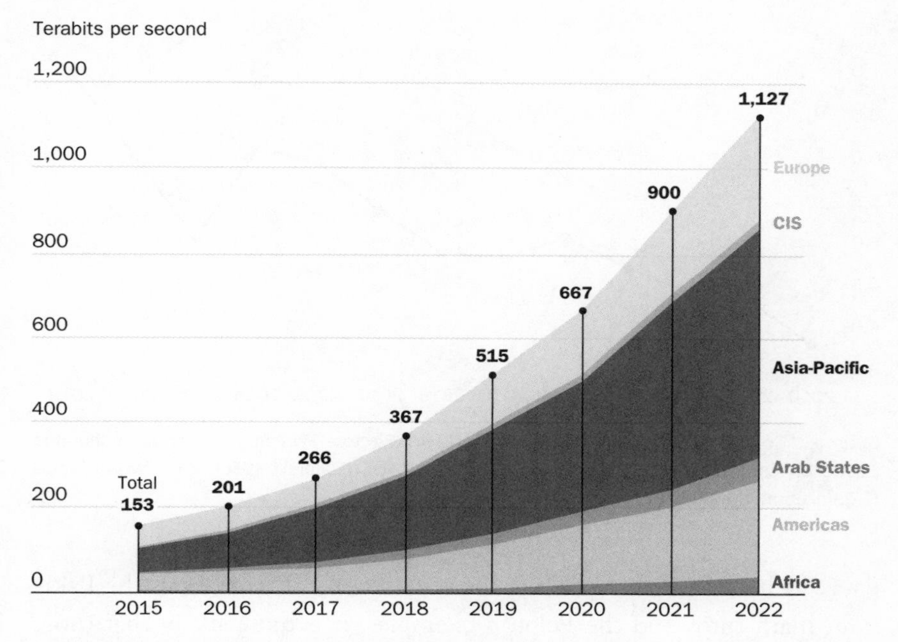

Source: "Key ICT Indicators for the ITU/BDT Regions (Totals and Penetration Rates)," International Telecommunication Union, updated November 2022.
Note: CIS = Commonwealth of Independent States.

Still, despite this underappreciation, the international trade in services is increasingly important. As Scott Lincicome points out, the trade in services as a share of the global economy nearly doubled from less than 8 percent in 1991 to nearly 14 percent in 2019, and digital services were particularly important to this.[5] From 2005 to 2021, trade in digitally delivered services more than tripled, and information and communication technology services increased more than fivefold. As you can see in Figure 9.1, international internet bandwidth is rapidly increasing; that infrastructure is capable of carrying more and more digitally delivered services.

It is also important to understand that digital trade in services is almost certainly understated significantly because traditional statistics and

FIGURE 9.2
Global trade in commercial services has nearly doubled since 2010

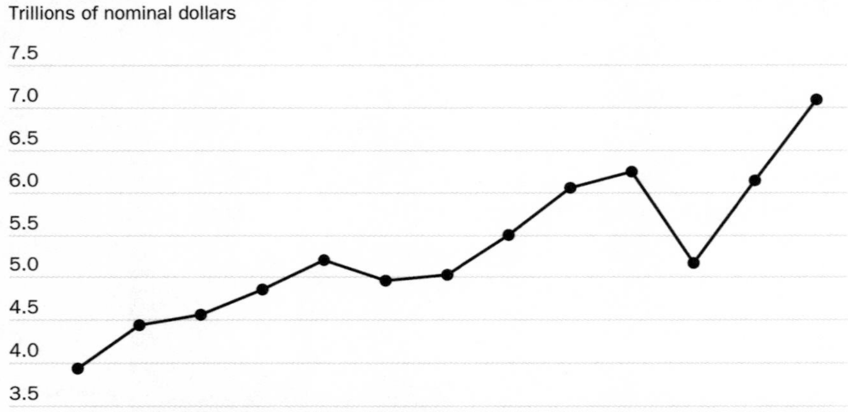

Source: "Commercial Services Exports by Main Sector—Preliminary Annual Estimates Based on Quarterly Statistics (2005–2022) (Million US Dollars)," WTO Stats, World Trade Organization, updated April 5, 2023.

data sets have trouble capturing the transactions. Think about the Pakistani math tutor and the Peloton examples; it is quite likely that those don't make it into any traditional trade flow measures. As impressive as many of the growth numbers in this area are, they are not even capturing all of what is going on. As Shawn Donnan, senior writer for Bloomberg, explains,

> When a player in Asia or Germany buys something in Fortnite, they are effectively buying a digital good, something potentially made by one of the designers at Epic Games' North Carolina headquarters. There is both revenue and a good job tied to it. The thing is, that sort of digital transaction doesn't always show up in the economic data. More often, it ends up being lost in the mix, and given the explosive growth we've seen of digital trade, which includes everything from simple e-commerce to gaming to using software in the cloud, that actually matters.[6]

Globally, the trade in commercial services, digital and analog, has nearly doubled since 2010, from $3.9 trillion to $7.1 trillion in 2022 (Figure 9.2). This trend is likely to continue. By 2026, the market for telemedicine alone is expected to be worth more than $175 billion.[7] Even if the popular image of international trade remains as goods- and ships-based for some time, services and digital tools are going to be an increasingly large part of the picture.

Digital Services Help People Be More Mobile

Reducing the proximity burden makes it easier for people to escape constraints on their mobility. Digital services have helped facilitate working from home. The COVID-19 pandemic made this especially clear. During the pandemic, because of digital services, many people were able to keep working. Even when these digitally enabled interactions felt local (i.e., meeting a physically nearby colleague on Zoom), the providers of those services are based in multiple countries and often rely on cross-border data flows, so those interactions are still very much a part of globalization. Not only is working from home good for many workers, but it could also help bridge America's urban-rural divide.

Being able to sell labor digitally means that people can live wherever they want. Many people will still want to live in Manhattan, but a lot of people, for several reasons—whether it's cost or family connections or proximity to outdoor activities—may instead want to live in smaller places. Digital services and working from home let them do that and could help rural areas. Because rural areas have thinner markets, all kinds of services can be difficult to access, which is inconvenient for people who live in those areas but also can discourage people from moving to them. If, however, it is easy to access some services digitally, such as a spin class or a doctor's visit, that shifts some of the calculus in the cost-benefit analysis of whether to move to a rural area. That's especially heartening given the extent to which many rural areas have been seeing declining working-age populations (Figure 9.3).[8]

Additionally, the increasing trade in digital services is an alternative way to capitalize on Global South talents should we not find a way to increase immigration.[9] It would be better to allow people to immigrate to the United States if they want to. Here, they could not only work in their professions but would also contribute as colleagues, friends, fellow

FIGURE 9.3
Many rural counties have been seeing declining working-age populations

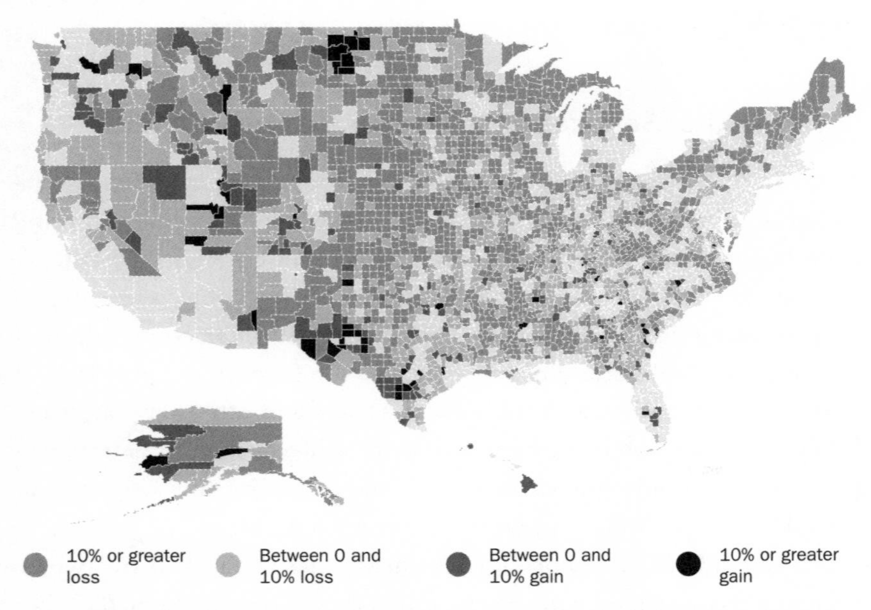

Source: Kennedy O'Dell, "Redefining Rural: Towards a Better Understanding of Geography, Demography, and Economy in America's Rural Places," Economic Innovation Group, March 9, 2021.

citizens, and neighbors. The United States would be stronger for having them. Alas, xenophobia and nativism have made liberalizing immigration significantly harder. If, despite immigrants' obvious merit, policymakers cannot find the political will to more easily allow people to immigrate here, then digital services are the next best option. This is why economist Richard Baldwin terms digital trade services "telemigration."[10] This telemigration may end up being very important as global population skews toward the Global South. In a world where nativists want to build walls, digital trade in services can, at least in part, make those walls irrelevant.[11]

This is not the only way in which digital services bring people together. Many people play *Fortnite* in the United States, China, and around the world. They buy and sell digital goods within the game, and they rarely think about nationality. Another way that *Fortnite* is emblematic of this kind of international cooperation is that Tencent, one of the biggest technology firms in China, owns 40 percent of Epic Games, the North Carolina–based maker of *Fortnite*. The more that digital services can help intertwine the United States and China economically, the more those two countries will have at least some common interests that can make their relationship less conflictual and less dangerous. Just as digital services can help marginalize nativists, it can go around nationalists and hardliners arguing for decoupling.

Another way in which digital trade in services has broad benefits is that it boosts innovation. During the COVID-19 pandemic, researchers in many different countries were able to use digital tools to collaborate on their research. That helped accelerate the creation and rollout of highly effective COVID-19 vaccines that saved millions of lives. Cloud computing has been hugely helpful in cancer research.[12] Digital tools can help multinational firms crowdsource ideas from their customers and business partners around the world and are becoming essential to some companies' innovation.[13]

Digital Trade in Services Is Good for America

The United States is a powerhouse in services and especially digital-friendly services. US services exports grew from $563 billion in 2010 to $897 billion in 2022, a 59 percent increase. A lot of that growth either is or could be connected to digital technology. More than 80 percent of US services exports could, at least in principle, be delivered digitally.[14] In 2020, US exports of information and communication technology–adjacent services totaled $520 billion.[15] Export growth has been especially strong in cloud computing and data services ($397 million in 2010 to $6.9 billion in 2021), computer services ($10.1 billion to $45.2 billion), research and development ($22.2 billion to $47.2 billion), and professional services ($48.7 billion to $132.5 billion). As Figure 9.4 and Figure 9.5 show, US exports of services, and particularly information and community technology services, have grown significantly since 2010.

FIGURE 9.4
US services exports have increased substantially

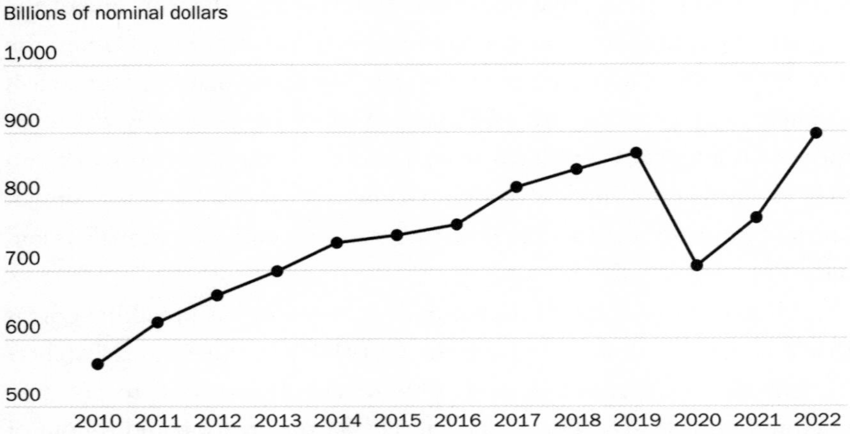

Billions of nominal dollars

1,000
900
800
700
600
500

2010 2011 2012 2013 2014 2015 2016 2017 2018 2019 2020 2021 2022

Source: "Commercial Services Exports by Main Sector—Preliminary Annual Estimates Based on Quarterly Statistics (2005–2022) (Million US Dollars)," WTO Stats, World Trade Organization, updated April 5, 2023.

FIGURE 9.5
Digital technology has powered the growth of US information and communication technology services exports

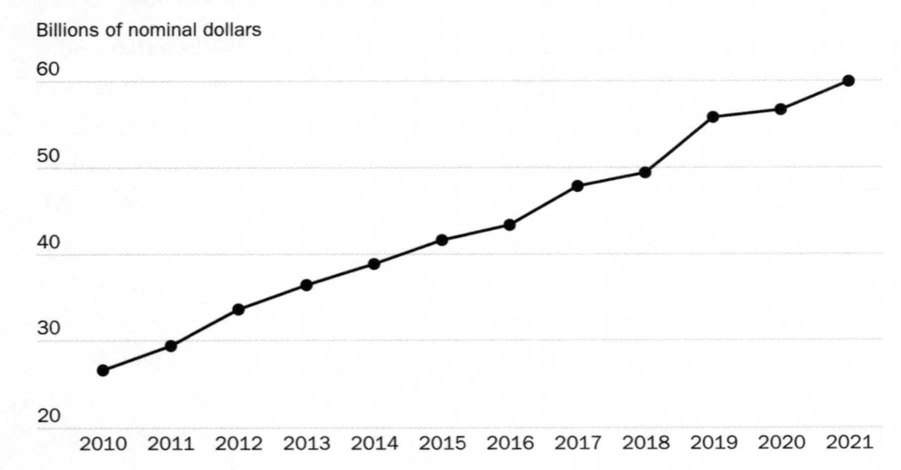

Source: "Commercial Services Exports by Sector and Partner—Annual (Million US Dolllars)," WTO Stats, World Trade Organization, updated April 5, 2023.

The other things to keep in mind are that the digital economy is large and growing and that services are a much larger portion of the overall economy than goods. In 2019, the digital economy was roughly a tenth of American gross domestic product, and from 2005 to 2019, it grew at more than double the rate of the nondigital economy. Roughly two-thirds of the global economy and more than three-quarters of the American economy are services, not goods.[16] The growth potential for digital trade in services is enormous. The more that services can be traded internationally, the more customers American service firms have access to.

Some of the most high-profile American businesses that benefit from this are the Big Tech firms: Apple, Microsoft, Amazon, Google, and Meta. These are five of the most important companies in the American economy—and arguably the world. The more of their services that they can sell abroad (e.g., Microsoft's and Amazon's cloud computing, Google's search and advertising, Apple's media content, and Meta's social media and WhatsApp), the better it is for those firms' workers and shareholders, most of whom are American. Those benefits then spread to the wider economy; one technology sector job supports, on average, five other jobs in the economy.[17] A worker at one of these businesses, or any other business that can better sell its services globally, has more disposable income that they can then spend on local goods and services. Moreover, millions of Americans' retirement savings plans, such as a 401(k), include one or more of these companies' stocks. These firms contribute significantly to the US tax base, and they provide services that delight consumers, often for free. There are a lot of ways in which the success of these companies strengthen America. To the extent that US policy encourages more globally liberalized trade in services and thus helps these companies succeed, those policies make America better.

Moreover, the benefits of digital services do not merely accrue to this small handful of firms but are instead (and encouragingly) widely dispersed throughout the economy. In 2022, Apple's App Store facilitated over $1 trillion in commerce, more than double what it did in 2019.[18] Cloud computing is another good example. As the Congressional Research Service notes, "One driver of the diffusion of the benefits of the internet and digitization has been cloud computing. Cloud services have been called the great equalizer, since they generally allow small companies access to the same information and the same computing power as large firms using a flexible, scalable, and on-demand model."[19] Not only that, but digital services increasingly undergird the movement of physical goods. For example, in 2018, Walmart partnered with IBM to create a blockchain-enabled food traceability system that helps prevent foodborne illness outbreaks.[20] Manufacturing increasingly comes packaged with services, many of which are digital in nature, that add considerable value. So, for example, a manufacturing firm might hire another firm to do product design or supply chain optimization; those services end up embedded in the value of the product, but the design expertise and supply chain expertise are communicated across borders digitally. These services add value to the manufactured product while also reducing costs. Service exports also support jobs (e.g., 71,020 jobs in Michigan, 54,480 jobs in Missouri, 19,380 jobs in Kentucky, 36,320 jobs in Utah, and 97,200 jobs in Ohio).[21] All told, service exports support 4.1 million American jobs.[22]

American consumers also benefit. In 2021, the Korean show *Squid Game* spent nearly a month as the top show on Netflix, which also offers its subscribers popular content from other countries, including *Babylon Berlin* (Germany), *Money Heist* (Spain), *The Great British Baking Show* (UK), *The Magnificent Century* (Turkey), *Borgen* (Denmark), and *The Glory* (South Korea).[23] And the selection keeps growing. As Figure 9.6 shows, annual US imports of audiovisual services have exploded from $3.7 billion in 2010 to more than $25 billion in 2021 and seem likely to continue increasing. In these and many other ways, the increasing digital trade in services benefits Americans as workers, taxpayers, consumers, shareholders, and citizens.

Challenges Moving Forward

To fully realize the benefits of digital globalization, two main challenges need to be effectively dealt with: barriers to the free flow of data and underdeveloped rules on digital services at both the World Trade

FIGURE 9.6
US imports of audiovisual services have exploded since 2010

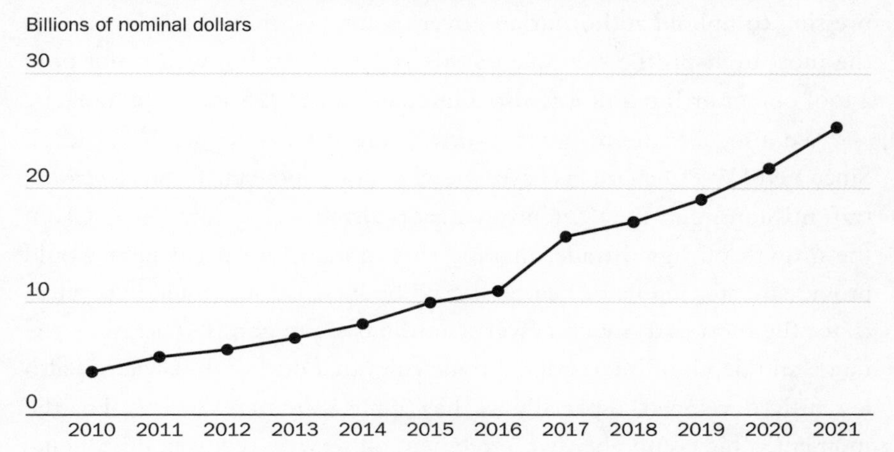

Source: "Commercial Services Imports by Sector and Partner—Annual (Million US Dolllars)," WTO Stats, World Trade Organization, updated April 5, 2023.

Organization (WTO) level and in terms of US free trade agreements. Much of the international trade in services is directly predicated upon enormous cross-border data flows. This, however, has become a major friction point between the United States, the European Union, and China, with China especially insisting that its citizens' privacy can only be properly protected if those citizens' data are kept in-country and stored according to very specific requirements. These mandates hinder US service exporters' access to new markets.[24] Likewise, several countries also have policies that place onerous requirements on cloud computing providers. Vietnam, Korea, France, Indonesia, Malaysia, and China all have protectionist restrictions on cloud computing services. Though this is an important policy challenge, there is some room for optimism. The Safe Harbour Principles, Privacy Shield program, and now the Trans-Atlantic Data Privacy Framework have helped to smooth over US-EU differences with regard to privacy and data transfers.[25] There may also be technological advances that help. Microsoft's Azure cloud computing service is fully capable of localizing data while still providing the service, so it may end up being the case that data localization is not as large a hindrance to commerce as it may seem. What is more worrisome are barriers to data flow imposed to block the spread of ideas and expression to uphold authoritarian governments. China's Great Firewall is the most high-profile example of this.[26] The Great Firewall is not only a tool of censorship, but it is also a huge barrier to US service exporters.

We also need more progress on digital services at the WTO level. Since 1998, WTO members have agreed to not impose tariffs on electronic transmissions, and they extend that moratorium every few years. Given the growth of digital trade, making that moratorium permanent would provide greater regulatory certainty.[27] The international trade in services is, for the most part, much newer than the trade in goods. Therefore, the range and depth of international trade rules that deal with services is also less fully developed, especially as they apply to digital services. For the moment, a big comprehensive agreement on services seems politically infeasible, but WTO members could start taking smaller steps toward curtailing digital protectionism. One area they could take an immediate step on is discriminatory treatment of electronic signatures. That may sound like a tiny thing, but it helps to illustrate the necessity and usefulness of new digital trade rules.

Let's imagine that a government wanted to discriminate against services being provided from abroad via digital means but that it had no legitimate basis on which it could claim that the service provider was causing some kind of social or policy problem. If a government wanted to discriminate against the foreign provider, it could require physical in-person signatures rather than electronic signatures, and that would reimpose all of those proximity burdens even though doing so would achieve no clear public policy objective. It would be protectionism, plain and simple, to the detriment of the provider and often to the detriment of the consumer.

Another area where well-balanced international trade rules could be helpful is in source code access. Businesses want assurances that they will not have to divulge their source code (which is often the very heart of their software and a major part of their trade secrets) as a condition of providing their services in that country. The service provider often has a very credible fear that, once divulged, that source code will be passed on to a domestic competitor. In effect, the national government of that country has conditioned access to that market on expropriating some of that business's most valuable assets. Knowing this, the business cannot enter that market, so its ability to participate in that digital trade in services has been snuffed out from the beginning. On the other hand, there are several completely legitimate reasons why a government might want to review a business's source code. If it has reason to believe that the way a service provider is doing business violates the country's laws—and that could be anything from data protection to anti-discrimination law—to investigate whether that is actually happening, it needs access to the source code. If the states involved were not allowed to do that, they might not want to allow a foreign firm to provide that service in the first place. So, allowing this kind of access for governments both protects their right to engage in legitimate regulation and promotes digital trade in services. Here the language in the USMCA could be a model.[28] The USMCA bars states from forcing firms to divulge their source code simply as a condition of entry to the market but allows governments to require access to the code as part of "a specific investigation, inspection, examination, enforcement action, or judicial proceeding, subject to safeguards against unauthorized disclosure."

International cooperation on clearly discriminatory digital service taxes, whether under the WTO or the Organisation for Economic Co-operation and Development, would be another useful step. However, some countries have instituted digital service taxes in ways that are clearly and obviously designed to target American businesses but not their own businesses. French politicians were open about the fact that their country's digital service taxes were aimed at American companies and even branded the tax the "GAFA tax" for targeting Google, Amazon, Facebook, and Apple. Digital service taxes, when applied to all digital service providers, are one thing; digital service taxes that are blatantly discriminatory are quite another.[29]

Free trade agreements that the United States is part of already have some of these provisions. For example, the USMCA already prohibits data localization and the discriminatory treatment of electronic signatures. The United States should go even further. One way the United States and its most important trading partners could promote the international trade in services while respecting states' ability to engage in legitimate regulation is through mutual recognition agreements (MRAs). MRAs pioneered the trade in goods in the European Union. In an MRA, instead of states changing their domestic regulations, they agree to mutually recognize each other's regulations as equivalent. Perhaps appropriately the Comprehensive Economic and Trade Agreement between the European Union and Canada includes a proposed dialogue on creating MRAs in digital services.[30] With this kind of MRA, if it were to come to fruition, a service provider in the agreed-upon field who was licensed to operate in the EU would also be allowed to provide that service in Canada and vice versa. A particularly ambitious option would be to use MRAs with a negative list. In other words, the parties would say that any professional license issued in one state is valid in the other except for in those areas specifically carved out by each party. This would echo the negative-list approach used by the General Agreement on Trade in Services, the main agreement that structures the trade in services under the WTO. Just as an MRA undergirds trade within the EU, an MRA in services could facilitate greater trade in services among the USMCA countries in at least some industries.

Conclusion

Digital trade in services benefits American businesses, American citizens, rural areas struggling with population decline, and many more. It is simply wrong to say that the benefits of globalization and technology only accrue to the few and not the many. They benefit all of us. Consumers get more choices, workers get more options, shareholders get more value, and citizens get more of all the benefits of internationalism.

Greater digital trade in services isn't just about helping with math homework, flexibility for workers, easier telemedicine, increased exports, television shows or movies, 3D printing, and Zoom calls, as great as all those things are. It's about building a more open, freer, richer world. That's the promise of American-led globalization: material prosperity and ever-greater individual liberty.

Chapter 10

The Rise and Decline of Liberalism in China

James A. Dorn and Clark Packard

- From 1978 and for three decades afterward, China moved from central planning and autarky to a market-oriented economy. The growth of the nonstate sector has been the driving force in China's development. Despite recent backsliding, it remains the world's largest trading nation.
- Marketization and opening to the outside world—not industrial policy or protectionism—allowed China to make better use of its resources and widened the range of choices open to people.
- The post-1978 economic reform was a spontaneous, evolutionary process in which individuals lifted themselves out of poverty as opportunities for trade and entrepreneurship emerged.
- China's desire to enter the World Trade Organization (WTO), which was realized in December 2001, was instrumental in invigorating the nonstate sector and laying the foundation for institutional reforms that increased competition and helped spur economic growth.
- Although China has greatly benefited from marketization and trade liberalization, the country still lacks a free market for ideas and a genuine rule of law to protect persons and property. Under Xi Jinping, there has been a rise in state power, putting a drag on development and freedom.

- In addition, Beijing faces several short-term and long-term headwinds that will almost certainly limit its economic potential—and the supposed threat it poses to the United States.

Today there is a bipartisan consensus emerging in Congress that China is an economic juggernaut, inexorably poised to overtake the United States. Proponents of this consensus argue that the United States naively welcomed Beijing into the WTO to pad the profits of multinational corporations at the expense of average American workers—all on a Panglossian belief about the ability of freer markets to facilitate democracy and peace. That development, critics allege, allowed China to dramatically increase its wealth at Western nations' expense—wealth it is today leveraging to strengthen its military and adopt a revisionist foreign policy.

This line of argument is rife with problems. As we explain, China's rise has a lot more to do with its abandonment of central planning decades ago than it does with today's reembrace of protectionism, industrial policy, and Maoist socialism under Xi Jinping.[1] Indeed, China faces several headwinds that will constrain future growth.

China's journey from central planning under Mao Zedong to market-led development under Deng Xiaoping and beyond is complex. Yet one thing is clear: China could not have become the world's second-largest economy without allowing the market to play a decisive role in allocating resources and without integrating itself into the global trading system.

This chapter examines China's transition from plan to market, especially the early reforms, and then highlights a number of headwinds currently facing Beijing in the Xi era. It carefully examines the spread of marketization in China using the marketization index developed by Fan Gang and others. We show that, in addition to internal reforms that widened the use of markets, China's rapid development was driven by its opening to the outside world. It met strict conditions for joining the WTO and benefited from globalization, as did its trading partners.

China had no blueprint for its spectacular development but found that moving from plan to market, and taking into account the principle of comparative advantage, was a win-win situation.[2] (Contrary to conventional wisdom, the oft-derided "China Shock" generated significant economic *benefits* for the United States on net.[3]) Yet there are many weaknesses in China's institutional architecture, especially the Chinese Communist Party's (CCP) monopoly on power, the lack of an independent judiciary, and the absence of a genuine rule of law to safeguard fundamental rights, all of which will constrain economic growth in the years to come. In 2015, Premier Li Keqiang argued that if China is to reach its full potential, it must "get the relationship right between the government and the market." He recognized that doing so would mean boosting the "vitality of [the] market."[4] The political problem, however, is that allowing a greater scope for the market means reducing the scope of government and diminishing the power of the CCP.

Markets are based on consent, not coercion. Under Mao Zedong, there was little freedom. Deng expanded freedom by allowing legal markets and nonstate enterprises to emerge along with more secure property rights. Today, China is far richer and freer than under Mao, but it is now turning back to some of the old ways under Xi Jinping.

From Plan to Market: An Overview

China's rapid economic growth following its shift from state-led development (central planning) to marketization in 1978 and its drive to join the WTO are testaments to the idea that widening the range of choices open to people—via internal and external trade—is a winning strategy. Under Mao Zedong, protectionism and top-down planning led to a focus on developing heavy industry rather than improving people's lives by using the market price system to guide economic decisions. In 1970, Chinese real gross domestic product (GDP) stood at only $232 billion (measured in 2015 US dollars). However, once widespread marketization took place and individuals had more opportunities to get rich, real GDP grew to more than $16 trillion by 2022 (Figure 10.1).

Mao's Attack on Private Property and Free Markets

Under Mao Zedong, private property was outlawed, private entrepreneurs and landlords were treated as criminals, and Soviet-style central planning dominated economic life. In other words, the state monopolized the market.

FIGURE 10.1
China's shift from state-led development to marketization led to rapid economic growth

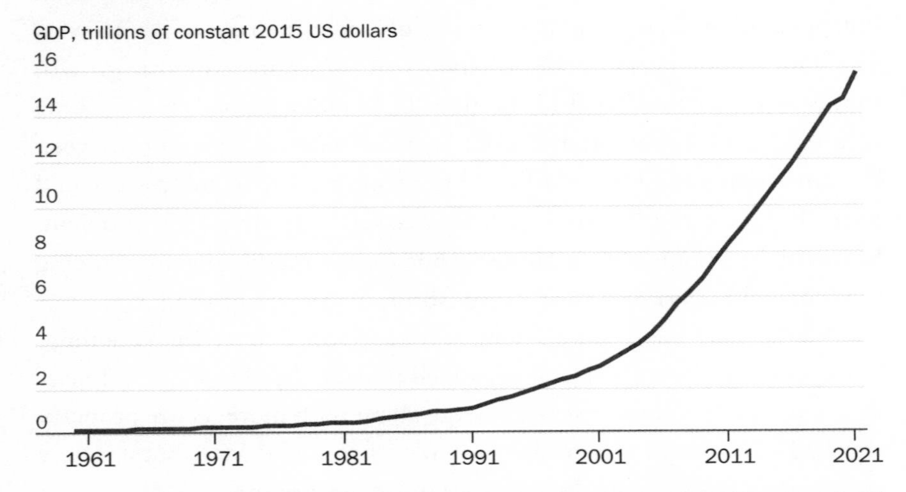

Source: "GDP (Constant 2015 US$)," World Development Indicators, World Bank, updated May 10, 2023.
Note: GDP = gross domestic product.

China's second five-year plan, which launched Mao's Great Leap Forward (1958–1962), was designed to make China an industrial power. Instead, it destroyed agriculture and led to mass starvation as people's communes were established and resources were forcibly shifted from farming to heavy industry. In 1966, Mao initiated the "Cultural Revolution," a period of mass purges that lasted until his death in 1976.

During the Cultural Revolution, Red Guards randomly attacked anyone who might be seen as a "capitalist roader." Intellectuals were sent to the countryside along with all those who might pose a threat to the CCP's monopoly on power. Any deviation from party orthodoxy was deemed a thoughtcrime that could lead to imprisonment or worse. Children turned parents in to the thought police, and people were instructed to "strike hard against the slightest sign of private ownership."[5]

Deng Xiaoping's Quiet Revolution

The death of Mao in September 1976 paved the way for the rise of Deng Xiaoping as China's paramount leader in December 1978. Deng and his allies then began to open the door for a transition to a more market-oriented economic system. The CCP's primary focus became economic development rather than class struggle.

There was no blueprint for economic liberalization. As Cyril Zhiren Lin notes, "The most distinctive aspect of the Chinese reforms is that they have proceeded without a detailed reform blueprint. . . . The result has been a process of open-ended reform unique among the centrally planned economies."[6]

Deng Xiaoping took a pragmatic approach to reform. If open markets could help improve life for the Chinese people, then it made sense to try that option—even in a socialist state. His mindset was that "it doesn't matter if a cat is black or white, as long as it catches mice."

Central planning could not be eliminated overnight. There would be no flag-waving revolution, only a quiet step-by-step movement from plan to market. Experimentation and innovation led the way to rural development, with the emergence of the household responsibility system and the creation of township and village enterprises (TVEs), which in the 1980s were an important component of the emerging private sector. The establishment of special economic zones (SEZs) in the coastal areas and the growth of the nonstate sector paved the way for China to become a major player in global trade. The entrepreneurial spirit of the Chinese people, which had been suppressed under Mao, came to life.

Marketization and Private-Sector Development

The impetus for marketization came from those who were harmed the most under Mao's disastrous policies—namely, people in rural households who had been forced into communes and suffered from the Great Famine. Some farmers began to contract with local authorities to gain rights to lease land from the collective and sell produce in private markets once official quotas were met. As the informal contracting system gained popularity, it was eventually sanctioned by officials. In 1982, Deng recognized the new institutional arrangement and labeled it "the household production responsibility system."[7]

The essence of the household responsibility system is that it arose spontaneously as farmers sought to gain autonomy in their everyday life and improve their standard of living. When farmers became richer, they began to create TVEs. While some of the TVEs were associated with collectives, the most dynamic ones were de facto privately owned.

According to Kate Xiao Zhou,

> The farmers took advantage of the corruptibility of the cadres rather than revolutionary action. Without anyone organizing a revolution, assuming leadership, or inventing an ideology, the farmers gained autonomy in farm planning, revived rural nonagricultural production, expanded old markets, and initiated new markets and migration to the city. . . . These spontaneous and apolitical efforts—rather than state ideology and in spite of Communist organization—formed the primary basis for China's current success in economic development.[8]

The dramatic increase in the role of *private* TVEs, and the important part they played in spurring economic development in China, is clearly examined by Yasheng Huang. In 1978, at the beginning of the reform movement, there were no legally registered private TVEs, but by 1985, there were 10 million. Moreover, Huang notes that, in poorer provinces, "it was private entrepreneurship, not government-run township and village enterprises, that contributed to the bulk of output production."[9]

Deng and other officials did not anticipate the success of TVEs. According to Deng:

> They were like a new force that just came into being spontaneously. . . . If the central Committee made any contribution in this respect, it was only by laying down the correct policy of invigorating the domestic economy. The fact that this policy has had such a favorable result shows that we made a good decision. But this result was not anything that I or any of the other comrades had foreseen; it just came out of the blue.[10]

Under the dual-track price system, planned and market prices existed side by side.[11] However, as individuals "jumped into the sea of private enterprise," the nonstate sector grew and market pricing spread. In October 1987, the CCP approved private enterprises at its 13th Party Congress, and the following year, the Constitution of the People's Republic of China (PRC) was amended to give private businesses legal status.[12]

Growing Out of the Plan

Top-down privatization was not the path to marketization in China. Rather, as Barry Naughton pointed out, China grew out of the plan by allowing development of the nonstate sector.[13] In 1984, top officials agreed to keep planned output targets fixed along with resources allocated to the planned sector of the economy. Thus, as productivity in the market-oriented sector grew, the contribution of the plan to national output declined. In effect, the dual-track price system was seen as transitory.

If we look solely at the industrial sector, it is striking that in 1978, state-owned enterprises (SOEs) accounted for nearly 80 percent of gross industrial output, but by 2016, their share had declined to 20 percent (Figure 10.2). Nicholas Lardy attributed that relative change to "the opening of the economic space available to private firms, the superior financial performance of private firms and the increased access of these firms to funds from banks and the domestic stock markets."[14] However, he noted that SOEs continued to grow in absolute terms.

With rising inflation in 1988 and widespread discontent over corruption and the slow pace of political reform, mass protests erupted in Tiananmen Square during the spring of 1989. The authorities brutally ended the protests and placed Zhao Ziyang, a leading reformer and general secretary of the CCP, under house arrest. During his captivity, Zhao secretly recorded his memoirs, which were published abroad after his death. In *Prisoner of the State*, he expressed what he could never say openly in China: "If a country wishes to modernize, not only should it implement a market economy, it must also adopt a parliamentary democracy as its political system." That means allowing "other political parties and a free press to exist." He recognized that China needed a genuine rule of law if it was to establish a normal market economy.[15]

After Tiananmen, the reform movement stalled, and economic growth slowed until 1992, when Deng took his famous southern tour of the SEZs, which he helped establish in the early 1980s. During his visit to Shenzhen, he stated:

> We should be bolder than before in conducting reform and opening to the outside and have the courage to experiment. We must not act

FIGURE 10.2
State-owned enterprises' share of Chinese gross industrial output declined sharply between the late 1970s and the mid-2010s

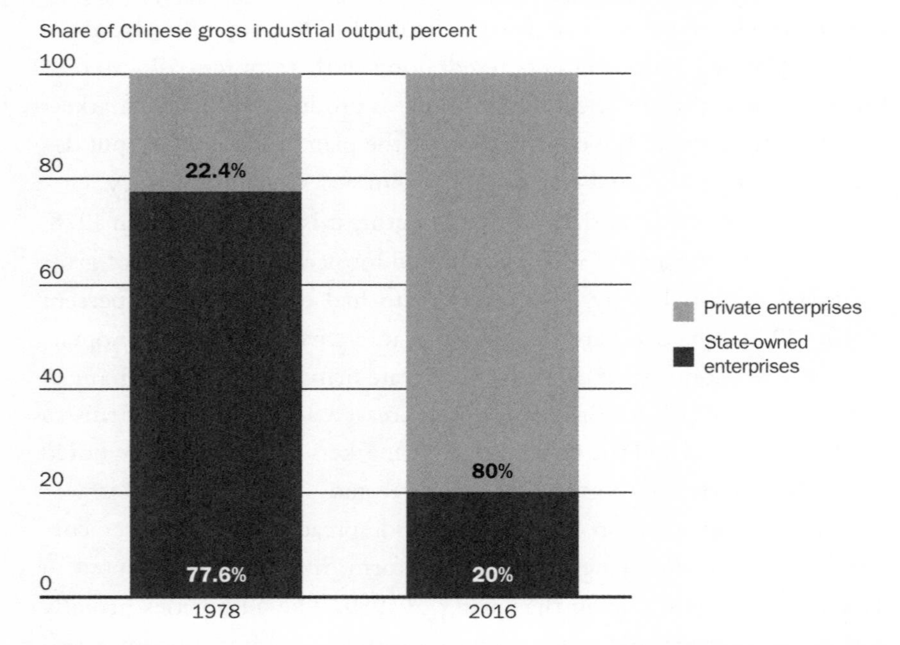

Source: Nicholas Lardy, "Private Sector Development," in Ross Garnaut, Ligang Song, and Cai Fang, eds., *China's 40 Years of Reform and Development: 1978–2018* (Acton, Australia: ANU Press, 2018), p. 333.

> like women with bound feet. Once we are sure that something should be done, we should dare to experiment and break a new path. That is the important lesson to be learned from Shenzhen. If we don't have the pioneering spirit, if we're afraid to take risks, if we have no energy and drive, we cannot break a new path, a good path, or accomplish anything new.[16]

Deng's main message on his tour was that "it doesn't matter if policies are labeled socialist or capitalist, so long as they foster development," according to Barry Naughton.[17] Of course, Deng and his comrades never intended to create what Milton Friedman, in his 1980 visit to China, called "free private markets."[18] The goal of the CCP has been to create a system of market socialism, not market liberalism. As Deng reminded people on his southern tour, "It is essential to adhere to the principle of 'one central task and two basic points.'" Building socialism is the central task, while the two basic points are implementing "the policies of reform" and "opening to the outside world."[19]

A Socialist Market Economy

Deng's message was repeated more than 20 years later at the Third Plenum of the CCP's 18th Central Committee in November 2013. In its "Decision on Some Major Issues Concerning Comprehensively Deepening the Reform," the committee stated:

> The overall goal of deepening the reform comprehensively is to improve and develop socialism with Chinese characteristics, and to promote the modernization of the national governance system and capacity. We must pay more attention to implementing systematic, integrated and coordinated reforms, promoting the development of [a] socialist market economy.

The committee advocated "centering on the decisive role of the market in allocating resources" and the importance of an "open economic system." Accordingly, it proclaimed:

> We must actively and in an orderly manner promote market-oriented reform in width and in depth, greatly reducing the government's role in the direct allocation of resources, and promote resources allocation according to market rules, market prices and market competition.[20]

Unfortunately, under Xi Jinping, China has failed to carry out the deepening of reforms and marketization goals of the Third Plenum.[21] That should not be surprising, given the CCP's adherence to socialist principles and its desire to maintain its monopoly on power.

The following passages from the Constitution of the People's Republic of China make it clear that socialism remains the kingpin of the Chinese state:

> **Article 1:** The socialist system is the basic system of the People's Republic of China. Disruption of the socialist system by any organization or individual is prohibited.

> **Article 7:** The State-owned economy, namely, the socialist economy under ownership by the whole people, is the leading force in the national economy. The State ensures the consolidation and growth of the State-owned economy.
>
> **Article 51:** Citizens of the People's Republic of China, in exercising their freedoms and rights, may not infringe upon the interests of the State, of society or of the collective, or upon the lawful freedoms and rights of other citizens.[22]

Even though the PRC's Constitution recognizes private property and other human rights, Article 51 makes it clear that fundamental human rights, which underpin a true market economy, are not inalienable, as they are under the US Constitution. In China, all rights must be predicated to come from the state if the CCP is to retain its power and authority. In such a system, there will always be tension between state and market.[23]

The Marketization Index

At the beginning of 1978, prior to the development of a market economy, most prices were either guided or fixed by the state. However, by 1999, 95 percent of retail commodity prices, 83 percent of agricultural commodity prices, and 86 percent of producer goods prices were set by the market, not the plan.[24]

To measure the degree of marketization over time, the National Economic Research Institute has developed a marketization index based on five broad categories: (1) government-market relations; (2) development of the nonstate enterprise sector; (3) development of the commodity market; (4) development of factor markets; and (5) intermediate legal framework. Various indicators are then used to rank each of China's 31 provinces (including five autonomous regions and three municipalities under central administration).[25] The province with the most progress toward marketization receives a score of 10, while the province with the least amount of marketization receives a 0. Coastal areas, such as Shanghai, Guangdong, and Zhejiang, are highly marketized relative to less-developed areas.

Figure 10.3 shows that the trend of marketization has been positive, with the *average* score for marketization going from 3.78 in 1997 to 4.48 in

FIGURE 10.3
China's economy has made significant progress toward moving from central planning to market orientation, though much remains to be done

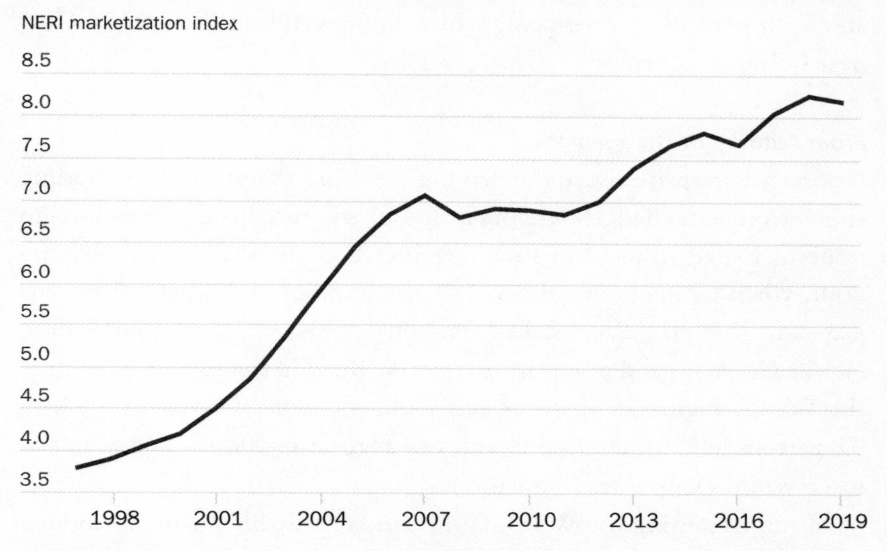

Source: "Total Market Index," China Market Index Database, National Economic Research Institute (NERI).

2001 and 7.06 in 2007. The 2008 global financial crisis reduced progress on marketization, and the index did not exceed 7.06 until 2013. In 2019, the index stood slightly higher at 8.19. What this tells us is that on a number of fronts China has made significant steps toward a market-oriented economy. However, one should not view the marketization index as telling us how close China is to achieving some ideal free-market system. Rather, it is a relative measure that gives us some idea of how well marketization is progressing.[26]

In sum, since China's opening and reform movement began in 1978, there has been significant progress toward moving to a market-oriented economy. Marketization and economic growth went hand in hand. While China has developed a socialist market system, it has allowed a variety of nonstate ownership forms to evolve, including private enterprises, foreign-funded enterprises, and shareholding companies. Indeed, the private/nonstate sector has been the dynamic element in providing individuals with a chance to break the chains of poverty and become more prosperous. Between 1980 and 2016, China's national poverty rate, as judged by the World Bank's poverty line, fell from about 90 percent to 4 percent, which implies 800 million fewer Chinese living in poverty.[27]

From Autarky to Engagement

Nonstate enterprises were the driving force in foreign trade. As trading rights were extended, the number of domestic firms engaged in foreign trade increased from 12 in 1978 to more than 5,000 a decade later. By 2001, when China joined the WTO, the number of domestic firms engaged in foreign trade reached 35,000.[28] China's trade-to-GDP ratio climbed as tariffs and nontariff barriers declined in the run-up to joining the WTO (Figure 10.4). After accession, the general tariff level fell to 9.8 percent in 2007, compared with 16.4 percent in 2000.[29] Today, China is the world's largest trading nation.

Prior to joining the WTO, China unilaterally liberalized its foreign trade sector.[30] Domestic prices became more market oriented as firms were subject to foreign competition and the international price system. Resources were more efficiently allocated, and more open markets meant the Chinese people could benefit from both greater consumption opportunities and the exchange of knowledge.

Those benefits were a far cry from the autarky that existed during Mao's reign. Under central planning, the principle of comparative advantage was ignored in favor of imposing planners' preference for developing heavy industry at a very high opportunity cost.[31] As Zhao Ziyang noted:

> The result of doing everything ourselves was that we were not doing what we did best. We suffered tremendous losses because of this. I now realize more and more that if a nation is closed, is not integrated into the international market, or does not take advantage of international trade, then it will fall behind and modernization will be impossible.[32]

It was China's opening to the outside world (see Figure 10.5)—not protectionism and industrial policy—that propelled economic development. As the editor of this volume, Scott Lincicome, has noted, studies

FIGURE 10.4

China's trade-to-GDP ratio rose as more nonstate enterprises engaged in foreign trade and trade barriers were lowered

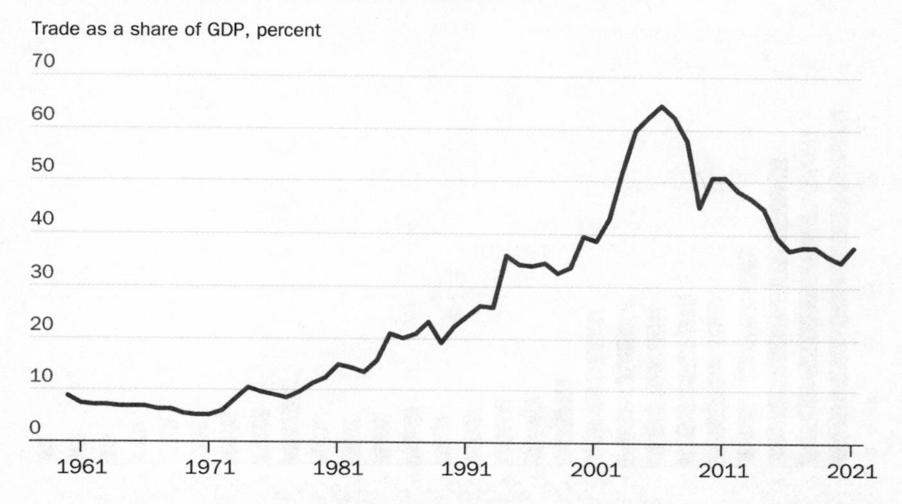

Source: "Trade (% of GDP)," World Development Indicators, World Bank, updated May 10, 2023.
Note: GDP = gross domestic product.

show the overwhelming majority of China's export competitiveness is due to its own market-oriented reforms.[33]

As Lardy points out, it was only in 2003 that China formally established the State-Owned Assets Supervision and Administration Commission (SASAC) and tasked it with overseeing about 200 of China's largest firms and turning them into "national champions." In 2006, SASAC identified a number of "strategic and pillar industries" in the manufacturing sector and hoped industrial policy would spur their growth. However, success was limited: the SOE share of manufacturing output and investment fell, while that of private firms continued to increase. Thus, according to Lardy, although "the state has sought a more direct role in promoting economic development, it almost certainly should be judged a failure."[34]

Premier Zhu Rongji supported China's accession to the WTO. His chief negotiator, Long Yongtu, made a strong case in the *People's Daily* (July 2000) for trade liberalization as a key factor for promoting China's

FIGURE 10.5

China's opening to the outside world laid the groundwork for its economic development

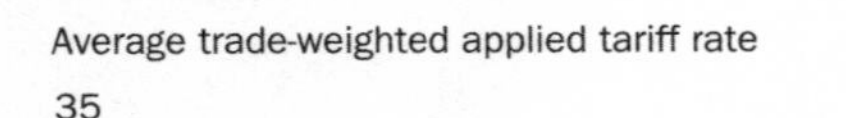

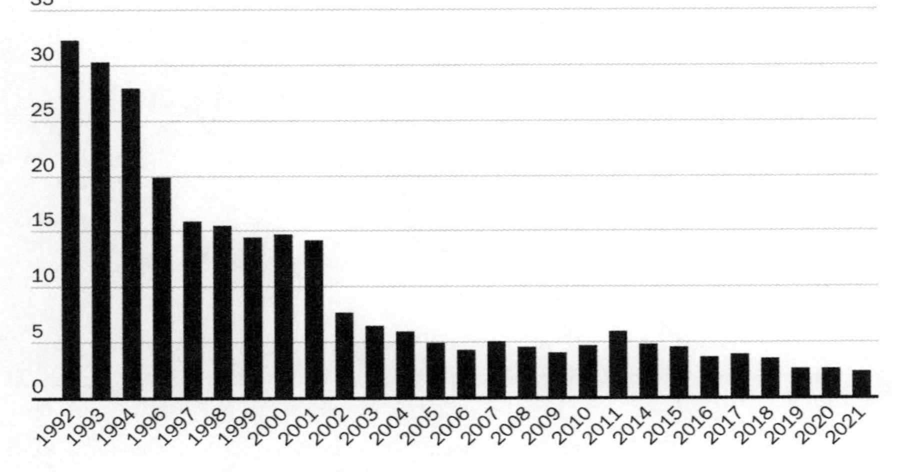

Source: "Tariff Rate, Applied, Weighted Mean, All Products (%) - China," World Development Indicators, World Bank, updated June 28, 2024.

future development. According to Long, "Countries with planned economies have never been part of economic globalization. China's economy must become a market economy in order to become part of the global economic system, as well as the economic globalization process."[35]

China's internal price liberalization and its relaxation of foreign trade restrictions, which began in the 1990s, paved the way for domestic prices of tradable goods to reflect global prices. Indeed, as Lardy notes, by 1992, "the domestic market prices of more than 95 percent of all imported goods were based on international prices."[36]

Although progress has been made in integrating China into the global economy, much remains to be done. The lack of an independent judiciary, overreliance on SOEs (which are about 20 percent less productive than private-sector actors), financial repression, and abusive practices (such as cyberhacking into commercial networks and repression of free speech) threaten future progress.[37]

China's Economic Headwinds

Despite some undeniable economic successes, policymakers in Beijing, particularly under the leadership of Xi Jinping, have moved in an illiberal direction. As a result, China faces several short-term concerns that will likely weigh on growth in the coming years.

The tech sector, once a dynamic and thriving industry, has been paralyzed by Xi's reembrace of Maoist socialism.[38] Likewise, Beijing's crackdown on education platforms and its general antipathy toward private-sector firms continues to fuel youth unemployment. *The Economist* recently noted that China's urban youth unemployment rate is above 20 percent.[39]

China's open embrace of industrial policy in the late 2000s has generated backlash in the global business community and developed country governments, heightening geopolitical tensions and fomenting trade conflicts (or, at the very least, giving Western politicians an excuse to favor their own national industries). Thus, for example, the United States imposed expansive export controls on semiconductors and semiconductor manufacturing equipment to China in late 2022, followed by Japan and the Netherlands, two major players in the semiconductor production supply chain, shortly thereafter. Given the ubiquity of semiconductors in virtually everything produced today, these efforts will hurt China's technology and manufacturing capacities in the short and intermediate term.

The real estate sector is increasingly overinflated while property developers fail to deliver on promised residential units leading to a large middle-class boycott of mortgage payments in 2022.[40] Evergrande, a major Chinese property developer, defaulted on its debt in late 2021.[41] Investment in property development fell by nearly 6 percent in the first quarter of 2023.[42] As a result of real estate struggles, local government coffers, largely reliant on land sales to fund public services, are drying up.

A *Wall Street Journal* story about the Guizhou province is illustrative of this problem. For a while, the southwestern province was one of the fastest-growing regions in China owing to debt-fueled infrastructure development that was financed by local banks that lent heavily to local governments.[43] As the *Wall Street Journal* notes, "Chinese authorities largely stood aside over the past two years as the country's largest property developers slid into financial distress, causing losses for investors and many businesses and depressing the land sales that were a big source of revenue for many local governments," including Guizhou. As Tianlei Huang, a research fellow at the Peterson Institute for International Economics told the newspaper, "It is channeling the problems in the real economy to the financial sector and eventually could pose a threat to financial stability."[44] Indeed, two-thirds of local governments in China are "now in danger of breaching unofficial debt thresholds set by Beijing to signify severe funding stress."[45]

It's not just economic policies that increasingly make China a less desirable country in which to invest and with which to trade. The country recently began cracking down on economic consulting firms, which is drawing criticism.[46] Moreover, China is increasingly relying on forced labor and repression toward Uyghur Muslims in the Xinjiang region. Likewise, Beijing has turned its back on the "One Country, Two Systems"—meaning a great deal of autonomy and self-governance—promise to Hong Kong, which was effectively annexed with the passage of the national security law in 2020. Beijing's hostility to inquiries into the origins of COVID-19 has increasingly alienated countries in the Indo-Pacific region, such as Australia, which led to a simmering trade war between the two countries.[47]

In other words, Beijing's belligerence is adding to growing geopolitical risk and uncertainty. Foreign direct investment (FDI) into China fell 82 percent between 2022 and 2023, and the $32 billion in inward FDI represented the lowest figure since 1993.[48] All told, growth is suffering and will continue to suffer unless these policies are reversed or at least mitigated.[49]

China's short-term problems may be surmountable, but its long-term headwinds pose a much bigger challenge for Chinese economic growth and global influence.

China's Demographic Problems

China's rapidly aging population and a shrinking workforce will weigh on economic output, suppress innovation, and stress government services.

The United Nations recently announced that India will overtake China as the world's largest population in 2023.[50] An essay in *Foreign Affairs* noted, "In 1978, the median age of a Chinese citizen was 21.5 years. By 2021, it had risen to 38.4, surpassing that of the United States."[51] In the 30-year period between 1949 and 1979, China's population grew from 540 million to nearly 970 million. Beginning in the 1970s, however, China began a series of policies aimed at curbing population growth, and fertility rates began to drop precipitously—"from 5.8 births per woman in 1970 to 2.7 in 1978."[52] Today, China's fertility continues to fall; in 2020, for example, the fertility rate of 1.3 births per woman is below the replacement rate of 2.1 births per woman.[53] Data from China's National Bureau of Statistics in 2021 show that the birth rate in the country fell for the fifth consecutive year with a fertility rate of 1.15 births per woman, one of the lowest percentages in the world (Figure 10.6).[54]

In 2016, Beijing reversed course and lifted its brutal One Child Policy. As of May 2021, the limit is three children.[55] Despite this about-face, what explains China's demographic headwinds? For starters, women have seen increased educational and employment opportunities, which has been linked to lower birth rates in other countries, including the United States.[56] Likewise, China has a severe imbalance in the ratio of men to women owing to the One Child Policy that favored males. In most of the world, the sex at birth ratio is 1.06 males for every 1 girl, but in China, it is 1.2 males for every 1 female, and in some provinces, the ratio is 1.3 males for every 1 female.[57] Other possible drivers include the fact that the population has gotten used to having smaller families, rising costs associated with having a child, and a decrease in marriage rates.

Given the significant downturn in the Chinese economy in 2022, early indications are that the birth rate will drop again. Indeed, marriages in 2021 were down to their lowest levels since the mid-1980s, when Beijing began keeping records of annual registrations, and initial data suggest a further decline in 2022.[58] Yi Fuxian, a scientist in obstetrics and gynecology at the University of Wisconsin-Madison and author of *Big Country with an Empty Nest*, a book on China's demographic troubles, projected that China's Zero-COVID policies would lead to a significant drop in marriages in 2020 and 2021 and would lead to a drop of

FIGURE 10.6

The decline in China's fertility rate has outpaced that of other major economies since 2017

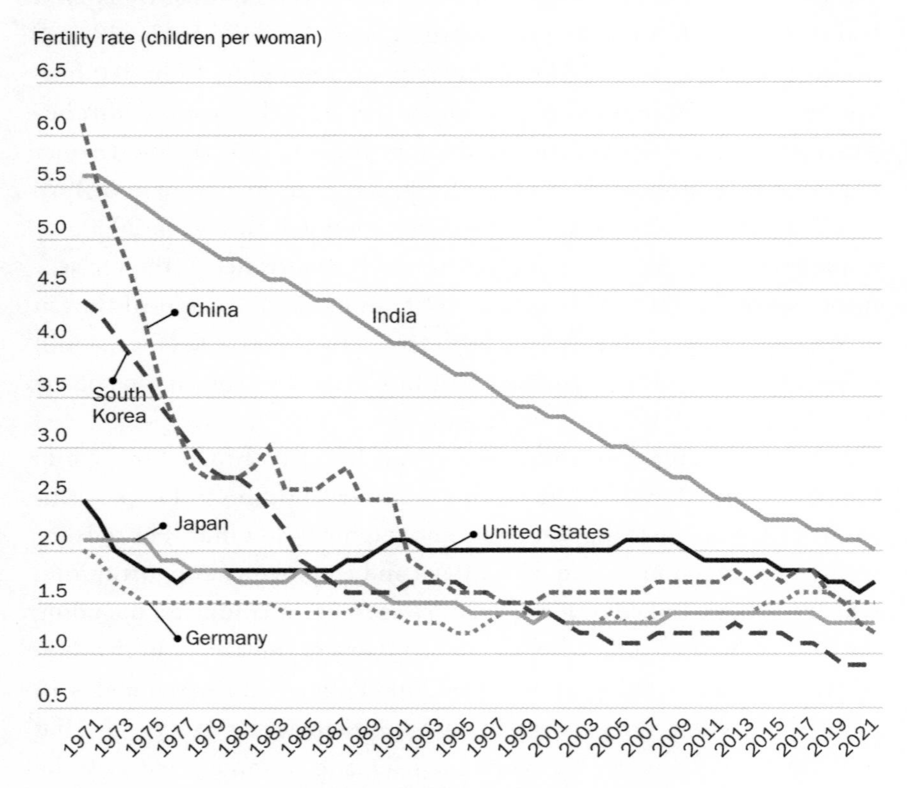

Source: United Nations, "Fertility Rate: Children per Woman," Our World in Data.
Note: Total fertility rate defined as "the number of children that would be born to a woman if she were to live to the end of her childbearing years and give birth to children at the current age-specific fertility rates."

about a million births in 2021 and 2022.[59] Though there are legitimate questions about the veracity of Chinese demographic data, government officials are now acknowledging publicly that the country faces serious challenges. In August 2022, China's National Health Commission wrote in an essay for the Communist Party's journal, "Low births and aging amid negative population will become the norm."[60]

Low birth rates, a rapidly aging population, and a shrinking workforce will almost certainly inhibit China's future GDP growth, but it will also inhibit productivity, dynamism, innovation, and risk-taking, all leading to a weaker social safety net. Yet China's long-term structural problems do not end there.

Talent Is Fleeing China

In theory, China should be leading the way in the high-growth sectors of the global economy. Yet on top of low birth rates and a rapidly aging population, China also faces a serious exodus of young, talented, highly educated citizens.

China now awards "more science and engineering undergraduate degrees than the US, Britain, France, Germany, Japan and South Korea combined."[61] Between 2000 and 2015, "the number of science and engineering undergraduate degrees granted per year in China more than quadrupled"—from about 360,000 annually to more than 1.7 million.[62]

These smart, talented individuals, however, aren't staying in China. Take artificial intelligence (AI). Of the top-tier AI researchers globally, nearly one-third received their undergraduate degree from a university in China, yet the overwhelming majority do not stay in China. In fact, 56 percent come to the United States, and about one-third stay in China.[63] As MacroPolo, a project of the Paulson Institute at the University of Chicago, notes, "After completing graduate studies in the United States, a full 88 percent of those Chinese researchers chose to stay and work in the country, while only 10 percent headed back to China. (This sample includes a combination of recent graduates, mid-career researchers, and veteran researchers to reflect average stay-rates across all these groups.)"[64]

Generally, about 70 percent of international science, technology, engineering, and math (STEM) graduates from US PhD programs stay in the country, but among Chinese graduates, the rate is significantly higher—about 85 percent.[65]

Not only is China failing to keep a large quantity of its highly talented AI researchers, but it also struggles to attract foreign advanced STEM talent. An October 2021 study from the Center on Strategic and International Studies notes, "Only about 10 percent of international scientists and engineers seemed open to moving to China, compared to nearly

60 percent for the United States."[66] This is despite China's decades-long global recruitment efforts.[67]

So why does China struggle to retain and attract talent? As a February 2022 report from Peking University Institute of International and Strategic Studies argues, this is largely due to the "relatively relaxed and innovative scientific research environment" in the United States compared to China.[68] Other reasons include China's "authoritarian political system and restricted freedom" and "language barriers, pervasive internet censorship, and environmental quality."[69] Indeed, *Nikkei* recently reported that China saw the world's largest outflow of wealthy individuals in 2023 and will likely see a record exodus again in 2024.[70]

China's Declining Business Dynamism and Slowing Productivity

A nation's economic growth and global influence generally stem from two things: the size of its population and the productivity of its workforce.[71] China could thus increase global power by, theoretically, offsetting a declining population with strong productivity growth. In reality, however, productivity is a significant challenge for China's economy that will increasingly hamper growth unless policies are radically transformed.

Beginning in the late 1970s and early 1980s—shortly after Deng's market-oriented reforms—China experienced a rapid increase in productivity growth, but much of this was due to catch-up growth given that the country had a very low starting point. Indeed, China's annual productivity growth averaged about 4 percent during this period.[72] Today, however, there is mounting evidence that productivity growth is slowing in China—an even sharper decline than worldwide productivity trends (Figure 10.7).[73]

What are the primary causes of China's productivity slowdown? The aforementioned demographic challenges and brain drain are certainly contributors. China's increasing reliance on top-down economic planning (industrial policy) and state-owned enterprises also play major roles.[74]

It is estimated that about 70 percent of China's subsidies flow to less productive SOEs, and the government increasingly subsidizes

FIGURE 10.7
After decades of growth, China's productivity appears to be stalling

Source: Penn World Table, "Productivity: Output per Hour Worked," Our World in Data.
Note: GDP = gross domestic product; PPP = purchasing power parity.

non-SOEs—to their detriment.[75] A December 2022 paper found, for example, that between 2007 and 2018, direct government subsidies to companies listed on China's stock exchange increased by about sevenfold—from about $4 billion to $29 billion. Examining firm-level data about the relationship between firm productivity and government subsidies, authors of the study found that the latter tended to undermine the former:

> We find little evidence that the Chinese government picks winners—if anything, the evidence suggests that direct subsidies tend to flow to less productive firms rather than more productive firms. In addition, we find that, overall, the receipt of direct government subsidies is negatively correlated with subsequent firm productivity growth over the course of our data window, 2007 to 2018. Even subsidies given out

> by the government in the name of R&D and innovation promotion or industrial and equipment upgrading do not show any statistically significant evidence of positive effects on subsequent firm productivity growth.[76]

Likewise, a November 2022 National Bureau of Economic Research (NBER) paper found "little statistical evidence of productivity improvement or increases in R&D expenditure, patenting and profitability" of China's major industrial policy program known as Made in China 2025, which is the crown jewel for Beijing's goal of indigenous innovation and technological supremacy as a bulwark for future economic and military strength.[77] Finally, another NBER paper found that beginning in 2008, China's industrial policy began heavily subsidizing local firms with many patents. As a result, more patents were awarded, but the quality declined and led to less innovative firms buying patents to receive subsidies. In total, it was a large welfare loss once accounting for the subsidy cost.[78]

Debt continues to plague both the corporate and government sectors, which hurts growth. As the International Monetary Fund noted, "Government and household debt-to-GDP ratios are estimated to have increased to new highs of 108 and 62 percent in the second quarter of 2022, respectively, while corporate debt is hovering around a very elevated 125 percent."[79] The *Wall Street Journal* reported that by June 2022, debt in China reached about $52 trillion, "dwarfing outstanding debt in all other emerging markets combined."[80] The same story reported that between 2012 and 2022, debt in China grew by $37 trillion—nearly one and a half times the amount in the United States, a larger economy. Much of this debt is the result of the massive subsidies China provides on industrial policy projects, the overwhelming majority of which did not create leading-edge companies. In short, Chinese "state capitalism" may have generated a few notable successes in industries like electric vehicles. But as long as Beijing pursues its economic goals through government-influenced SOEs and costly industrial policy, surging debt and sagging productivity will combine with demographic decline to severely hamstring the country's economic growth—and its global influence.

China's Lack of a Free Market for Ideas

After more than 40 years of uneven opening up to the outside world, China still ranks near the bottom in terms of freedom of the press. In the 2023 World Press Freedom Index, China ranked 179th out of 180 countries; only North Korea is lower.[81] The value of free speech is that it allows people to improve institutions by pointing out weaknesses, which can then lead to improvements. As Eswar Prasad notes, "Transparency of public institutions, the right to free expression, and an unfettered media are all necessary for building confidence. They do this not by emphasizing strengths, but by making weaknesses and faults in the system obvious."[82]

The main lesson for China's future development is clear, according to Ronald Coase and Ning Wang: "When the market for goods and the market for ideas are together in full swing, each supporting, augmenting and strengthening the other, human creativity and happiness stand the best chance to prevail."[83]

Conclusion

Industrial policy and central planning under Mao Zedong proved to be a massive failure: they did not bring about sustainable economic growth or widespread prosperity. In 1978, Deng Xiaoping recognized the failure of state-led development and gradually reversed course in making the transition from plan to market.[84]

The reform movement began with actions by farmers to gain rights to collectively owned land and to sell excess produce in the private markets. TVEs emerged spontaneously as farmers sought to increase their wealth by starting small businesses.

The foreign trade sector expanded as China opened to the outside world and established SEZs in coastal areas. Nonstate enterprises, especially private firms, became the dynamic force in promoting economic growth. While there was no blueprint for the household responsibility system or TVEs, the government had a more visible hand in the creation of SEZs.

China became an economic powerhouse by opening its markets, recognizing the nonstate sector, and allowing individuals more economic and personal freedom.

Today, however, the CCP under Xi Jinping is reversing course, and the Chinese economy faces serious headwinds. Talent is fleeing; foreign direct investment is falling; consumer sentiment is sour; and dynamism is stalling out.

The future of the Chinese people will depend on getting back on the path of marketization and liberalization, not reverting to destructive state control, protectionism, and repression. China can learn from its own history as well as from the West that economic and social harmony cannot be imposed from above. The challenge is to allow a free market for ideas, as well as for trade in goods and services, by instituting reforms that protect both economic and personal freedom.

SECTION TWO

The Globalization Debate

Chapter 11

The Misplaced Nostalgia for a Less Globalized Past

Daniel Griswold

- Many critics of free trade argue that American workers and families were better off in the less globalized 1970s and even earlier decades.
- While the US economy is more deeply integrated into the global economy today than 50 years ago, Americans today are undoubtedly better off by numerous measures of economic well-being.
- When we more accurately account for price changes, Americans today enjoy much higher real wages and household incomes than 50 years ago. Thanks in part to globalization, Americans work fewer hours to acquire a wider variety of goods and services.
- Rising living standards in our more globalized era have not come at the expense of the poor, here or abroad. Properly accounting for inflation and government transfers, the poverty rate today is lower than in the 1970s, and inequality is no higher.
- US manufacturing employment has fallen since its peak in 1979, but the main driver is rising productivity, not imports. The US manufacturing sector remains strong, and lost manufacturing jobs have been more than offset by safer and better-paying services jobs.

When we consider the progress that has been made in the past 50 years—in living standards, equality in household consumption, worker safety, and opportunities for women and minorities—the nostalgia for a less globalized past is difficult to understand.

Americans have traditionally been optimistic about the future, but a strain of thinking across the political spectrum today seeks to recapture a time when life was supposedly better for most Americans. Concerns about the present state of the nation often focus on the increased globalization of recent decades and the harm it has allegedly inflicted on American households and workers. Proponents of this view—as disparate as US Rep. Ro Khanna (D-CA) and Sen. Josh Hawley (R-MO)—mourn the loss of manufacturing jobs, the decline of union membership, "stagnant" real wages, and an alleged rise in income inequality since the 1970s or even earlier.[1] They advocate higher barriers to international trade and investment as an obvious remedy to this supposed decline.

This "nostalgianomics" is misplaced. The American economy is certainly more globalized today than it was decades ago, and just as certainly, most Americans are better off today by any real measure of economic well-being than their counterparts were a half century ago. In fact, increased globalization is one of the main reasons why Americans today have higher living standards than they did in the overidealized past.

The US Economy Has Opened and Liberalized in Recent Decades

The world has certainly changed in the past half century. Along with technological and scientific advancements, the US economy has become far more deeply integrated with the rest of the world. This integration has been driven both by new technologies that have facilitated the movement of goods, services, and people around the world—such as containerization and the internet—and by major trading nations' concerted efforts to reduce tariffs and other legal restrictions on those same movements.

Those changes have deepened America's integration into the global economy in recent decades. As Figure 11.1 shows, US imports and exports

FIGURE 11.1

US imports and exports have significantly grown as a share of GDP since the 1970s

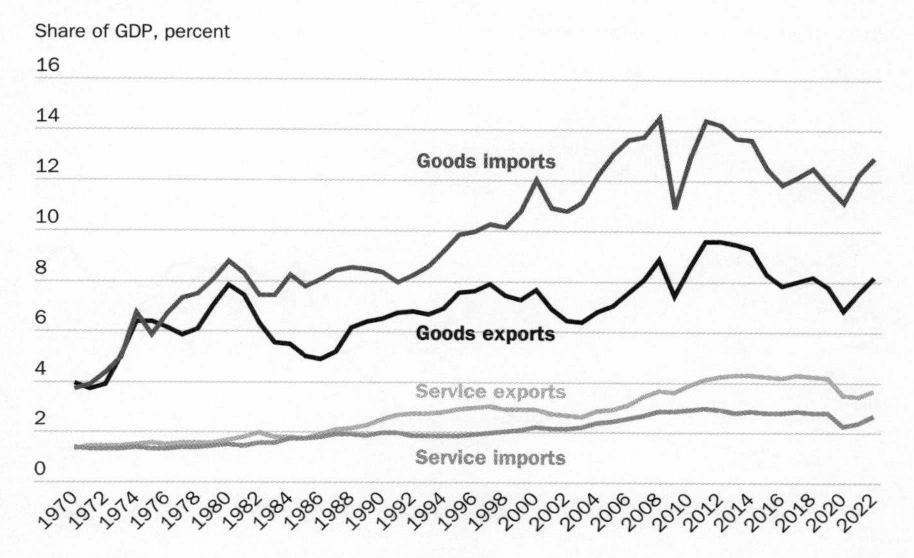

Source: "Table 1.1. US International Transactions," International Data, US Bureau of Economic Analysis, March 23, 2023; "Table 1.1.5. Gross Domestic Product," National Data, US Bureau of Economic Analysis, last revised May 25, 2023; and author's calculations.
Note: GDP = gross domestic product.

of goods and services have increased substantially since the 1970s: the average value of US goods exports increased from 5.4 percent of gross domestic product (GDP) in the 1970s to 8.7 percent in the 2010s, while goods imports increased even more (from 5.9 percent, on average, to 12.9 percent). Over the same period, services exports more than tripled (from 1.2 percent to 4.2 percent), and services imports more than doubled (from 1.3 percent to 2.8 percent).[2]

The United States' international investment position has exhibited similar trends (see Figure 11.2). At the end of the 1970s (1976–79), American-owned assets abroad averaged 22 percent of US GDP; by the most recent five years (2017–2021), the figure hit 150 percent of GDP. Foreign-owned assets in the United States grew even faster: from an average of 16 percent of GDP in the late 1970s to 198 percent in the past five years.[3]

FIGURE 11.2

Both American investment abroad and foreign investment in the United States have increased

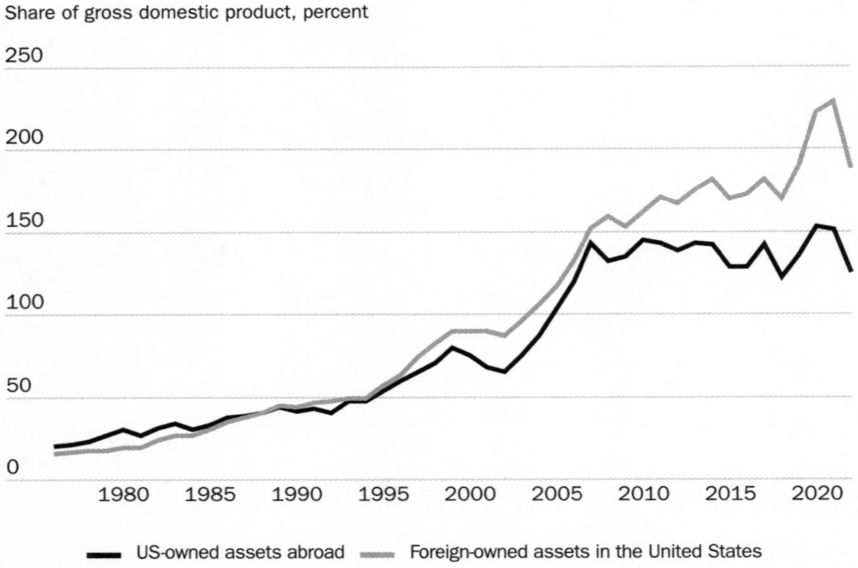

Share of gross domestic product, percent

250
200
150
100
50
0

1980 1985 1990 1995 2000 2005 2010 2015 2020

US-owned assets abroad   Foreign-owned assets in the United States

Source: "Table 1.2. US Net International Investment Position at the End of the Period, Expanded Detail," International Data, US Bureau of Economic Analysis, March 29, 2023; "Table 1.1.5. Gross Domestic Product," National Data, US Bureau of Economic Analysis, May 29, 2023; and author's calculations.

The United States has also become more open and globalized through immigration. The share of the nation's foreign-born population rose from 5.4 percent in 1960 to 6.2 percent in 1980 and then 13.6 percent by 2021.[4]

The United States' international economic liberalization was accompanied by significant domestic liberalization over the same period. Beginning in the 1970s, for example, the US government deregulated domestic trucking; air passenger service; freight rail; oil and natural gas prices; and telephone, cable, and satellite TV services.[5]

These trends, of course, do not mean that the United States today is some sort of free-market paradise or even that the US economy is more globally integrated than its peers abroad. (It isn't.[6]) Nevertheless, it remains undeniably true that the United States has experienced significant domestic and international liberalization in recent decades—liberalization that has produced a more open and competitive US economy that has delivered greater and more widespread benefits to American workers and families.

Americans Are Better Off Today in Many Ways

Globalization has contributed to increased prosperity for most American households over the past half century. Liberalization of markets here and abroad has increased competition among producers, opened new markets for US exporters, increased the productivity of American firms and workers, and lowered the real price of goods and services for American families—resulting in higher real incomes for most Americans.

The Real Story of Hourly Earnings and Household Incomes

Nostalgianomics' depiction of American "wage stagnation" since the 1970s is fundamentally flawed in several key ways. First, the most typical indicator of such stagnation—US production and nonsupervisory workers' average inflation-adjusted hourly earnings—relies on an overstated measure of US inflation that makes Americans' real-wage gains seem smaller over time.[7] As authors Phil Gramm, Robert Ekelund, and John Early explain in *The Myth of American Inequality*, properly accounting for inflation turns American wage "stagnation" into significant gains:

> If the inflation adjustment for real average hourly earnings for production and nonsupervisory employees were to incorporate both the Chained [Consumer Price Index for All Urban Consumers] to remove the substitution bias and more accurate adjustments for new and improved products, real average hourly earnings would have risen 74.0 percent over the last fifty years rather than the official reported number of 8.7 percent. That is an additional $7.50 per hour.[8]

Second, examining only wages excludes nonwage benefits—bonus pay, health insurance, paid leave, contributions to retirement savings, and so forth—that have made up an increasing share of total compensation

FIGURE 11.3

Inflation-adjusted compensation for workers has increased since the 1950s

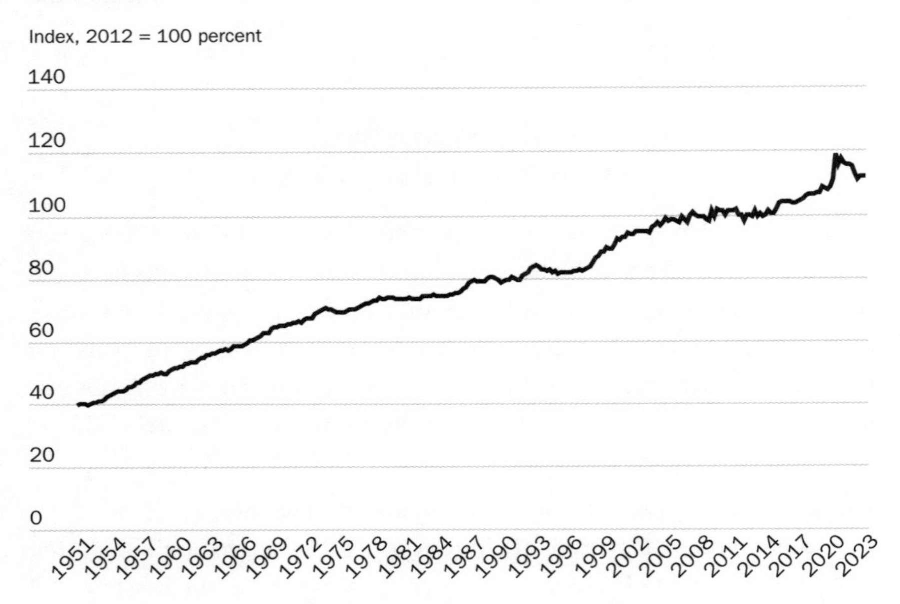

Source: US Bureau of Labor Statistics, "Nonfarm Business Sector: Real Hourly Compensation for All Workers," Federal Reserve Economic Data, Federal Reserve Bank of St. Louis Economic Data, updated June 1, 2023.

in recent decades. As Figure 11.3 shows, including these benefits and more, properly accounting for inflation shows substantial upward progress in workers' total compensation since the 1950s or 1970s.[9]

Other measures of income show similar gains during recent decades of US globalization. William Cline of the Peterson Institute for International Economics, for example, calculates that real median household income rose by 50 percent from 1967 to 2017—almost 30 percentage points more than what US Census Bureau data report—after applying a more accurate inflation measure and normalizing household size across time periods.[10] In their analysis, Gramm, Ekelund, and Early made a similar estimate.[11]

FIGURE 11.4

Adjusting for inflation, the share of poor and middle-class US households has declined since the 1970s, while the share of wealthy households has increased

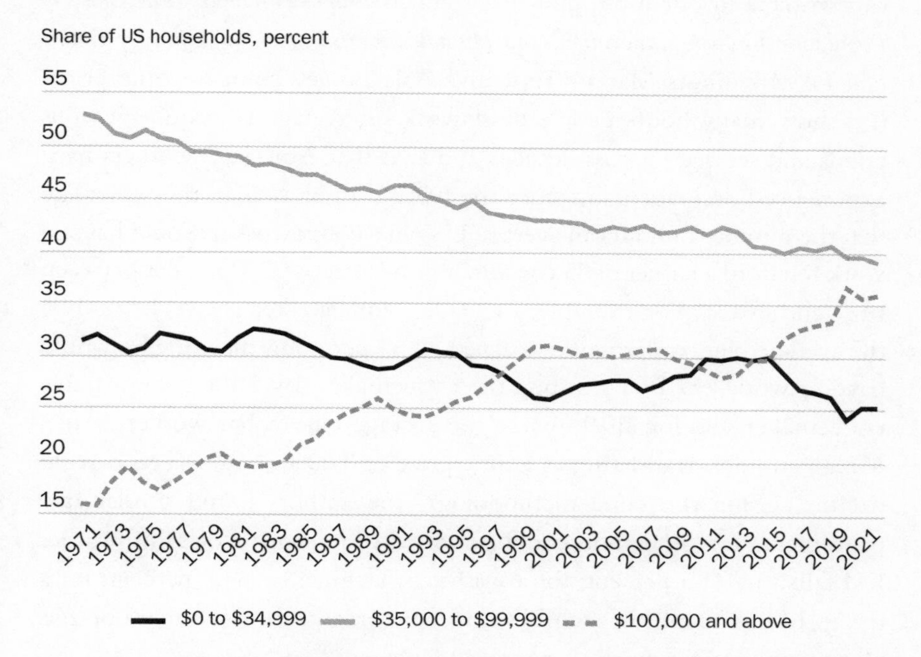

Source: Jessica Semega and Melissa Kollar, "Income in the United States: 2021," US Census Bureau, September 2022, p. 16, Table A-2.

Census data also correct the myth that our more globalized economy has impoverished—and thus "hollowed out"—the American middle class. As Figure 11.4 shows, the share of US households earning a middle-class annual income of $35,000 to $99,999 (in 2021 dollars) did indeed shrink since 1979, from 49.1 percent to 39 percent, but so did the share of households earning below $35,000 (from 30.3 percent to 25.2 percent). By contrast, the share of households annually earning $100,000 or more increased from 20.6 percent to 35.8 percent.[12] Thus, the American middle class has shrunk in recent decades—but only due to *households getting richer.*

Working Less for More: The Plunging Time Price of Consumer Goods

Even these adjusted income data understate the gains enjoyed by American workers in our more globalized era. In *Superabundance: The Story of Population Growth, Innovation, and Human Flourishing on an Infinitely Bountiful Planet*, authors Marian Tupy and Gale Pooley compare time prices (i.e., how many hours people must work on average to acquire various goods and services) across decades and find that American workers have experienced dramatic gains since the 1970s.[13] In particular, they calculate that the number of hours an average US blue-collar worker would have to work to afford a basket of 35 consumer goods fell by 72.3 percent between 1979 and 2019.[14] For example, in 1979, a coffeemaker cost $14.79 while the average blue-collar worker earned $8.34 per hour, meaning he would have to work 1.77 hours to buy the coffeemaker. By 2019, a comparable coffeemaker sold for $19.99 while the average blue-collar worker earned $32.36 an hour, translating to a time price of 0.62 an hour—a 65 percent decline. Using the same methodology, the authors found similar improvements for other household goods: the time price of a dishwasher had fallen by 61.5 percent; for a washing machine, by 64.6 percent; for a dryer, 61.8 percent; for a child's crib, 90 percent; for a women's blazer, 69 percent; and for women's pants, 44.6 percent.[15]

American workers are better off than in decades past not only because familiar goods have become more affordable but also because new types of products have come on the market and spread rapidly. Figure 11.5 shows that a range of products and services became ubiquitous in US households—including automobiles and refrigerators in the first half of the 20th century, color TVs and air conditioning in the second half, and internet access and smartphones at the beginning of the 21st century.[16]

Those who are nostalgic about life in the 1970s would likely have lived without microwaves, personal computers, and the internet. Those looking back to the 1950s forget or ignore the fact that most homes not only lacked air conditioning and color TV but also lacked dishwashers and clothes washers and dryers.

FIGURE 11.5

Household necessities quickly become ubiquitous in the United States

Adoption of technologies in US homes, percent

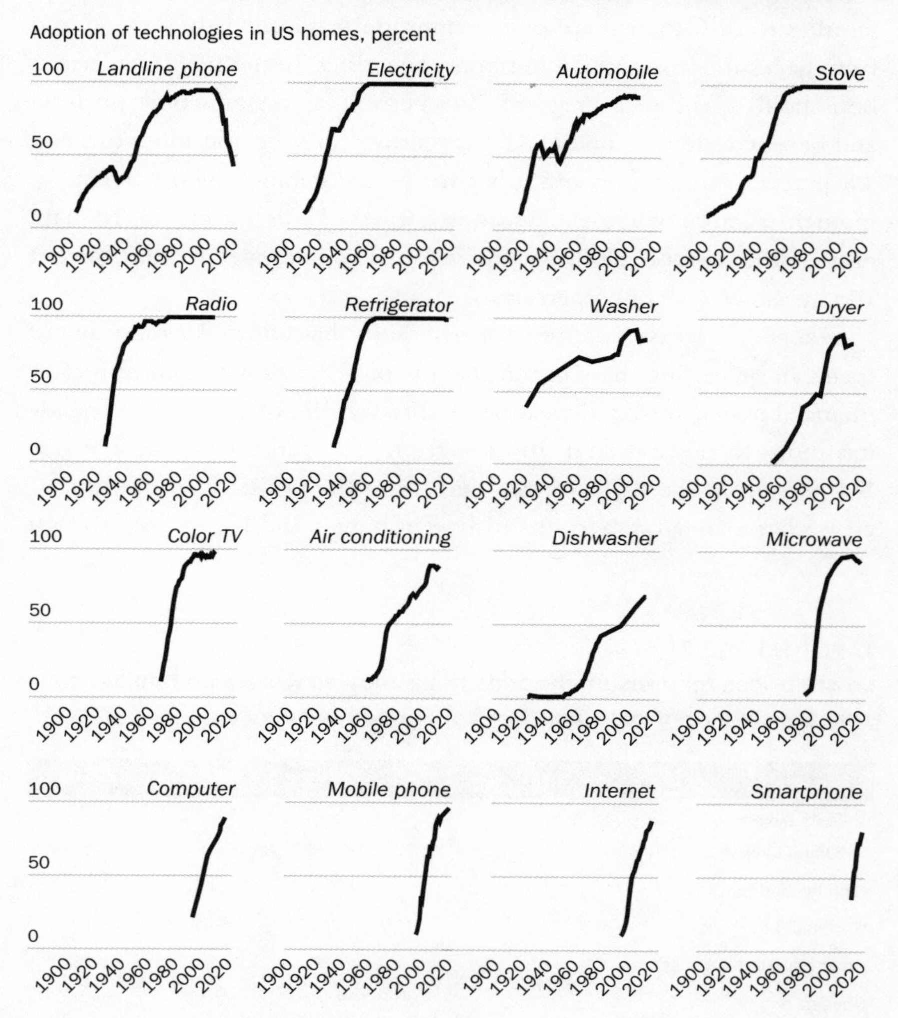

Source: "Share of United States Households Using Specific Technologies," Our World in Data, 2019.

Spending Less of Our Budget on Necessities

The lower relative price of consumer goods has allowed American families to shift their share of consumption from goods to services and from necessities to more discretionary spending. In the 1950s, American households spent an average of 20.8 percent of their income on food and beverages for the home, 8.9 percent on clothing and footwear, and 4.8 percent on gasoline and other fuels—a combined 34.5 percent, or more than a third of household spending. By the 1970s, the combined share of spending on food, clothing, and gasoline had dropped to 25.8 percent and by the 2010s to 13.5 percent (see Table 11.1).

Increased access to affordable necessities has allowed Americans to spend an increasing share of our income on services such as health care, financial management, recreation, and travel. We've also shifted spending more to housing and utilities, from 15.2 percent in the 1950s to 17.1 percent in the 1970s to 18.2 percent in the 2010s. That modest increase has enabled Americans to live in bigger and better houses with

TABLE 11.1

Lower prices for consumer goods have allowed American families to shift their share of consumption from goods to services

	1950s	1970s	2010s
Durable goods	14.8%	14.6%	10.5%
Food and beverages for home	20.8%	14.8%	7.5%
Clothing and footwear	8.9%	6.6%	3.0%
Gasoline, other energy	4.8%	4.4%	3.0%
Other nondurable goods	7.9%	7.6%	8.2%
Housing and utilities	15.2%	17.1%	18.2%
Health care	3.9%	8.4%	16.7%
Food services and accommodations	6.7%	6.6%	6.6%
Financial services and insurance	3.4%	4.9%	7.8%
Other services	13.6%	15.0%	18.6%
Total	**100.0%**	**100.0%**	**100.0%**

Source: "Table 2.3.5. Personal Consumption Expenditures by Major Type of Product," National Data, US Bureau of Economic Analysis, last revised May 25, 2023.

more amenities. According to the Census Bureau, the median size of new homes sold in the United States increased from 1,645 square feet in 1979 to 2,273 square feet in 2021.[17] The rate of homeownership has risen from 55 percent in 1950 to nearly 66 percent today.[18]

Populists on the left and right claim to champion the interests of blue-collar workers, yet they criticize the increased competition and lower barriers to trade since 1980 that have delivered a greater abundance of goods and services to those same people. A lower time price for popular goods means that American workers today need to work fewer hours to bring home a dishwasher, crib, TV set, or new outfit. That means more of their time and money can be devoted to acquiring other goods or services that further enhance their quality of life.

The Rising Tide of Globalization Has Lifted All Sizes of Boats

Critics of globalization may acknowledge that millions of Americans have indeed benefited in recent decades, but they say it has come at the expense of rising inequality and the stubborn persistence of poverty. But here too the past four decades of rising globalization have witnessed real progress against poverty and no overall increase in inequality in living standards among Americans.

In *The Myth of American Inequality*, Gramm, Ekelund, and Early show that the official poverty rate understates the gains of lower-income households because it suffers from the same inflation mismeasurement that taints the official wage and income data and because it omits major government transfers.[19] After properly accounting for inflation and federal, state, and local transfer payments, they found that the real poverty rate in America fell from 7.2 percent in 1979 to 2.5 percent by 2017.[20] Meanwhile, research from economist Bruce Sacerdote found incredible consumption gains for poorer families between 1960 and 2015.[21] In particular, he found that American households with below-median incomes not only have more cars and bigger houses than their earlier-era counterparts but that their *overall consumption* (adjusted for inflation) increased between 62 percent and 164 percent over that period. Thus, poorer

Americans today can consume about *twice* as many goods and services as their 1960s counterparts—thanks in no small part to globalization.

Official inequality figures, reflecting the widely used Gini coefficient, suffer from similar problems. After adjusting for taxes paid and transfer benefits received, Gramm, Ekelund, and Early found that the Gini coefficient has actually declined slightly (i.e., US society has been becoming modestly more equal in our era of expanded globalization) since the 1950s or 1970s. The adjusted Gini coefficient was on average 0.3443 in 1950–1959, 0.3412 in 1970–1979, and 0.3384 in 2010–2017 (the most recent period available).[22] As the authors conclude, "Over that entire postwar period, greater transfers to lower-income households, combined with steeper taxes taken from higher-income households, have more than offset the rising inequality of earned income."[23]

The US Manufacturing Sector Has Changed, Not Died

When they are not dismissing the real gains of US workers and households in recent decades, or bemoaning the alleged rise in inequality, the critics of globalization lament the loss of manufacturing and other goods-producing jobs. They claim that manufacturing jobs have traditionally provided a pathway for less-educated and lower-skilled US workers to enter the middle class. This interpretation misses the changing nature of the US manufacturing sector as well as the continued growth of well-paying jobs in the services sector.

The story of manufacturing in our more globalized era is not that "Americans don't make things anymore" but that US manufacturing workers have become so much more specialized and productive. In particular, fewer Americans are employed in manufacturing today compared to the 1970s, but inflation-adjusted US manufacturing *output* has increased dramatically over that same period, and the United States remains the world's second-largest manufacturing nation. From 2000 to 2021, real manufacturing value-added in the United States rose by 36 percent to a record $2.56 trillion.[24] The US economy has been able to create more manufacturing value-added with fewer workers because of dramatically rising worker productivity, driven by more sophisticated equipment, more efficient production methods, a more skilled workforce, and a shift to the production of more capital-intensive goods. Today, US manufacturing productivity (value-added per worker) exceeds that of Germany, Japan, and South Korea and dwarfs that of China and Mexico.[25]

Trade and globalization undoubtedly play a role in shaping the size and composition of the US manufacturing sector, but their effects should not be oversold. As Figure 11.6 shows, for example, the decline in manufacturing jobs as a share of the US workforce has been remarkably

FIGURE 11.6

The decline in manufacturing jobs as a share of the US workforce has been linear and began long before the wave of trade liberalization of the 1990s and early 2000s

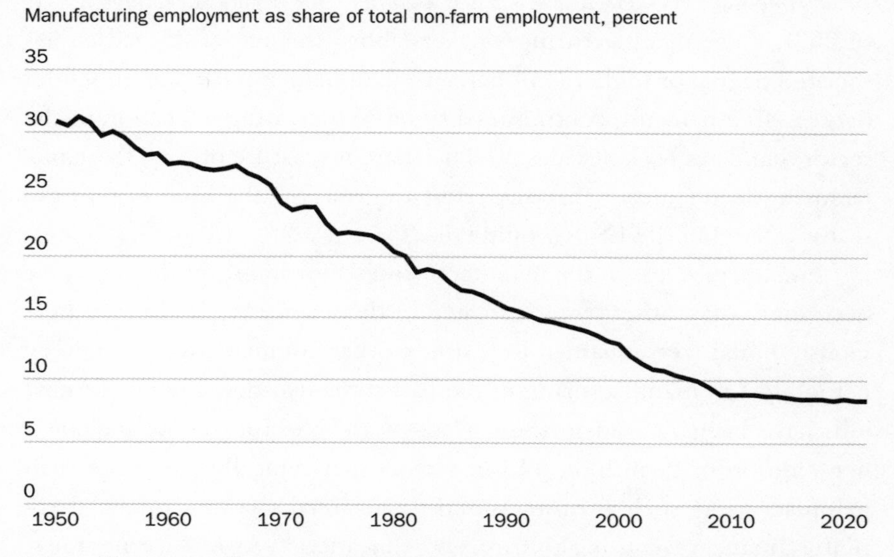

Source: US Bureau of Labor Statistics, "All Employees, Manufacturing/All Employees, Total Nonfarm," Federal Reserve Economic Data, Federal Reserve Bank of St. Louis Economic Data.

linear and occurred throughout the supposed golden age of 1950 to 1980 and long before the United States had entered the North American Free Trade Agreement (1994), joined the World Trade Organization (1995), or granted the status of permanent normal trade relations to China (2001).[26] This same trend has been underway with all our major trading partners, with manufacturing as a share of total employment falling over that same period in Germany, France, and Japan.

American manufacturing workers today are indeed producing less commodity steel, furniture, clothing, and footwear than they once produced, but the sector produces *more* aerospace products, computers, communications equipment, advanced processing chips, and chemicals.[27] To produce those higher value-added products, the typical manufacturing workers today are better educated and more specialized in their skills than their counterparts in the 1970s or 1950s.

Many of the semiskilled workers who filled manufacturing jobs in 1979 would not be qualified for the jobs being created in the manufacturing workplace today. As Scott Lincicome noted in *Empowering the New American Worker: Market-Based Solutions for Today's Workforce*, "As of 2021, more manufacturing workers above the age of 25 had an associate's degree or higher (45.1 percent) than had, at most, a high school degree (40.2 percent), continuing a trend of increasing education in the sector that dates back decades."[28] The changing nature of the US manufacturing sector means that any effort to "restore" the kind of jobs the sector offered in the 1970s would fail.

Finally, jobs lost in the manufacturing sector in recent decades have been more than offset by jobs created in the services sector and, as previously noted, accompanied by rising worker compensation. For every net job lost in manufacturing in the past three decades, a net eight new jobs have been created in the private services sector. Those include a net addition of 19 million jobs in sectors that typically pay more than manufacturing, such as business and professional services, financial activities, management, health care, and education.[29] As Lincicome notes, however, the modern US workforce also includes plenty of services jobs for working-class men: "in 2021, the number of blue-collar, male-dominated (60 percent or more) nonmanufacturing jobs in the United

States outnumbered nonsupervisory manufacturing jobs by a nearly four-to-one margin."[30]

America's More Liberalized Economy Delivers in Other Important Ways

Americans are also better off today in ways that are not directly captured by wage, income, and consumption data. For example:

- Workplace safety has steadily improved in recent decades, with the rate of workplace deaths down 30 percent between 1992 and 2017 and the rate of workplace injury and illness down 69 percent over the same period.[31] A safer work environment has been driven not only by safety improvements within specific workplaces but also by a broader shift in work from heavy industry to more services-sector jobs that are inherently less dangerous.
- Women have joined the workforce by the millions since the 1950s and fill a much wider range of occupations, not only because they are better educated (see Figure 11.7) and find less discrimination in the workplace but also because they have been freed from time-consuming tasks at home by all those modern appliances that have become available and dramatically more affordable in our modern, more globalized economy.
- Life for racial minorities also has significantly improved since the 1950s. As shown in Figure 11.8, for example, the poverty rate for black Americans declined from approximately 55.1 percent to 19 percent between 1959 and 2021.[32] (After accounting for consumption and transfers, of course, this improvement would be even better.) The share of low-income black households fell from about 55 percent in 1967 to 37 percent in 2021, while the share of higher-income black households increased from 4.1 percent to about 22 percent over the same period.[33] Hispanics have made similar progress since the 1970s. And while only 4 percent of Americans surveyed by Gallup in 1958 approved of interracial marriage, 94 percent do today.[34]

FIGURE 11.7

The share of postsecondary degrees earned by US women has risen sharply since the 1950s

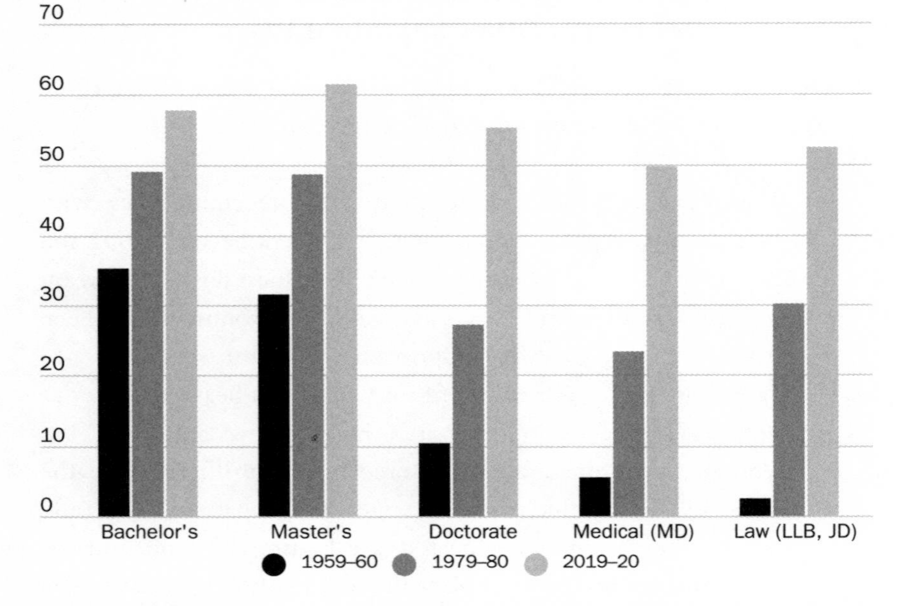

Source: "Table 318.10. Degrees Conferred by Postsecondary Institutions, by Level of Degree and Sex of Student: Selected Years, 1869–70 through 2030–31," Digest of Education Statistics 2021, National Center for Education Statistics, Institute of Education Sciences, Department of Education, October 2021; and "Table 324.40. Number of Postsecondary Institutions Conferring Doctor's Degrees in Dentistry, Medicine, and Law, and Number of Such Degrees Conferred, by Sex of Student: Selected Years, 1949–50 through 2019–20," Digest of Education Statistics 2021, National Center for Education Statistics, Institute of Education Sciences, Department of Education, February 2022.

Note: Doctorate degrees include PhD, EdD, and other comparable degrees, as well as most degrees that the US Department of Education classified as "first-professional" prior to 2010–2011, including MD, DDS, and law degrees.

- As the website Human Progress documents, an American born in the mid-1970s has over his lifetime experienced significant, long-term improvements in life expectancy, infant mortality, food supply, education, and environmental quality.[35] Gains since the 1950s are even larger.[36] Death rates from cancer in the United

FIGURE 11.8

Though much work remains, there has been undeniable progress in American minorities escaping poverty

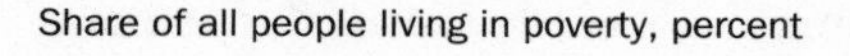

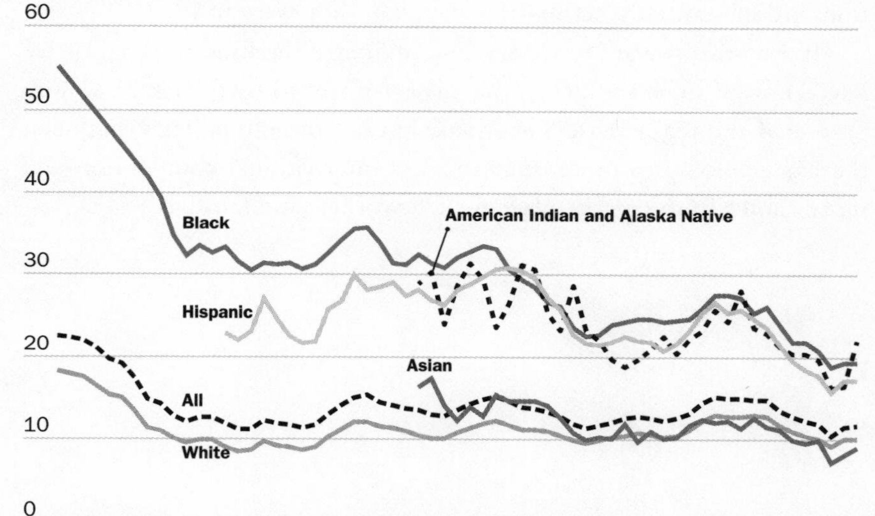

Source: John Creamer et al., "Poverty in the United States: 2021," US Census Bureau, September 2022.

Note: Figures for all minorities (except Hispanic) after 2021 are based on the US Census Bureau's figures for the "alone or in combination" category, which includes individuals reporting multiple races, including the race group of interest. For more information about the US Census's poverty thresholds, see "Poverty Thresholds," US Census Bureau, last revised April 21, 2023.

States fell by 32 percent between 1991 to 2019, saving 3.5 million lives.[37] The United States has also experienced substantial gains in both air quality and water quality since 1970.[38]

Conclusion

When we consider the progress that has been made in the past 50 years—in living standards, equality in household consumption, worker safety, and opportunities for women—the nostalgia for a less globalized past is difficult to understand. As Gramm, Ekelund, and Early summarized in their book, "In short, by virtually any physical definition of economic well-being, working Americans across all income levels, racial classifications, education levels, and other commonly used statistical classifications are substantially better off today than they were in 1972."[39]

If Americans want to extend and revitalize the kind of progress we have enjoyed since the 1970s, the answer is not to turn back to a more protected and regulated US economy but to promote policies that open the US economy to more domestic and international competition and more choice in the marketplace for US workers and families.

Chapter 12

The Reality of American "Deindustrialization"

Colin Grabow

- Despite rhetoric from some politicians that decades of unfettered globalization have hollowed out the US industrial base, the United States remains a manufacturing powerhouse, accounting for a larger share of global output than Japan, Germany, and South Korea combined. In key industries such as autos and aerospace, the United States ranks among the global leaders and is the second-largest manufacturing economy overall.
- That manufacturing employs fewer Americans and accounts for a lower percentage of gross domestic product than in decades past is not cause for serious concern, unique to the United States, or primarily owed to globalization. These trends have instead been largely driven by productivity gains and shifting consumer preferences in favor of services.
- The premium placed by policymakers on manufacturing employment is misplaced. Unlike most of the post–World War II era, jobs in this sector now provide lower compensation than similar roles elsewhere in the economy, while the diversified nature of the US economy is a source of economic resiliency, not weakness.

An unfortunate perception among many commentators and political leaders is that the United States "doesn't make anything anymore."

According to this narrative, the country is a former manufacturing titan brought low by the forces of globalization that have left the rusting hulks of once-humming factories in its wake. Instead of producing their wares in locations such as Pittsburgh and Peoria, some globalization critics claim US corporations have shifted their operations to take advantage of vastly lower wages in China, Mexico, and elsewhere. Factory closures, these critics insist, have forced American workers to trade well-paid work on the assembly line for less financially rewarding jobs in the service sector. In this telling, trade liberalization's legacy is one of industrial decline, wrecked lives, and ruined communities.

Reports of American manufacturing's death, however, are greatly exaggerated. While it is undeniably true that certain manufacturing industries—particularly labor-intensive, low-tech ones—are no longer primarily located in the United States, many other, more advanced ones have flourished. Thus, factories producing consumer staples such as textiles and furniture, for example, have made way for facilities that produce products less often found in retail stores, such as chemicals and machinery. At the same time, productivity gains unleashed by automation and other technologies have enabled manufacturing output to remain near record highs even as direct manufacturing employment has declined. Many other Americans, meanwhile, still work in manufacturing or are involved in the manufacturing process through the design of new products, even if their employers don't operate actual factories.

In short, manufacturing in the United States has not disappeared but has been transformed and very much remains a vital part of the country's economic fabric.

Deindustrialization Worries Are Nothing New

Politicians have sought to advance and capitalize on worries of industrial decline for decades. During his 1984 presidential campaign, Walter Mondale told steelworkers in Cleveland that President Ronald Reagan's policies were "turning our industrial Midwest into a 'rust bowl'"—a turn of phrase soon modified and popularized by the media as "Rust

Belt."[1] This region's misfortunes—and the broader alleged plight of American manufacturing—have been an enduring feature of the political discourse ever since.[2]

Some of this focus is the natural result of politicians' and the media's long-standing attraction to bad news and nostalgia: factory closures make news (or even movies); factory expansions don't. And the industrial Midwest's long-standing importance to the US presidential election means that the region will always receive outsized political attention, regardless of economic realities elsewhere in the country.

Yet certain statistics also lend a superficial plausibility to claims of domestic manufacturing's dire state. US manufacturing employment peaked in 1979 at 19.5 million employees, stood at just over 17 million in 2000, and has since dropped to approximately 13 million as of January 2023.[3] In relative terms, the percentage of workers employed in manufacturing has more than halved since 1980 as did its share of gross domestic product (GDP) from 1978 to 2018.[4]

Such declines also correlate with a growing embrace of trade liberalization over this period via such initiatives as the North American Free Trade Agreement, conclusion of the Uruguay Round of trade negotiations and agreement to establish the World Trade Organization (WTO), and China's accession to the WTO (although the decline was already underway when each of these took place).

No great effort is therefore required to grasp why many Americans believe that the country's industrial sector—and the well-paying jobs that go with it—has received a hammer blow at the hand of globalized commerce more generally and China in particular. But that doesn't mean it's true. A fuller and more accurate picture reveals a sector in remarkably good health whose indications of decline are far less worrisome when placed in proper context.

What Is Manufacturing?

Before delving into the state of US manufacturing, it is worth examining what the industry entails. Although the term may conjure images of glowing hot steel or new automobiles rolling off the assembly line, manufacturing runs a wide gamut of activities. According to the Bureau of Labor Statistics, manufacturers are "establishments engaged in the mechanical, physical, or chemical transformation of materials, substances, or components into new products."[5] These include not only the production of heavy machinery and sophisticated devices but also other items, such as fruit and vegetable preserves, stationery, and beverages. By this definition, Coca-Cola is every bit the manufacturer as Boeing, General Motors, or US Steel.

But the dividing line can sometimes be ambiguous. US-headquartered Nike, for example, engages in the design and marketing—key parts of the manufacturing process—of footwear, apparel, and sports equipment.[6] The actual production of these items, however, is outsourced to independent contractors. Global semiconductor leader Nvidia follows much the same approach.[7] Should these "factoryless goods producers" be considered manufacturers?[8] So far, the government's answer is no. Nevertheless, such firms are key contributors to the manufacturing process and generate considerable value, jobs, and innovations.

The United States Remains a Manufacturing Powerhouse

Regardless of how one defines manufacturing, the United States is clearly one of its heavy hitters. In 2021, it ranked second in the share of global manufacturing output at 15.92 percent—greater than Japan, Germany, and South Korea combined—and the sector by itself would constitute the world's eighth-largest economy.[9] The United States was the world's fourth-largest steel producer in 2020, second-largest automaker in 2021, and largest aerospace exporter in 2021.[10]

That the United States has achieved these rankings with a relatively small industrial workforce is a testament to its world-beating productivity: the country ranks number one in real manufacturing value-added per worker by a large margin. With value-added of over $141,000 per worker in 2019, the United States bested second-ranked South Korea by over $44,000. The gap with China was *over $120,000* per worker (Figure 12.1).

FIGURE 12.1
The United States is the global leader in manufacturing value-added per worker

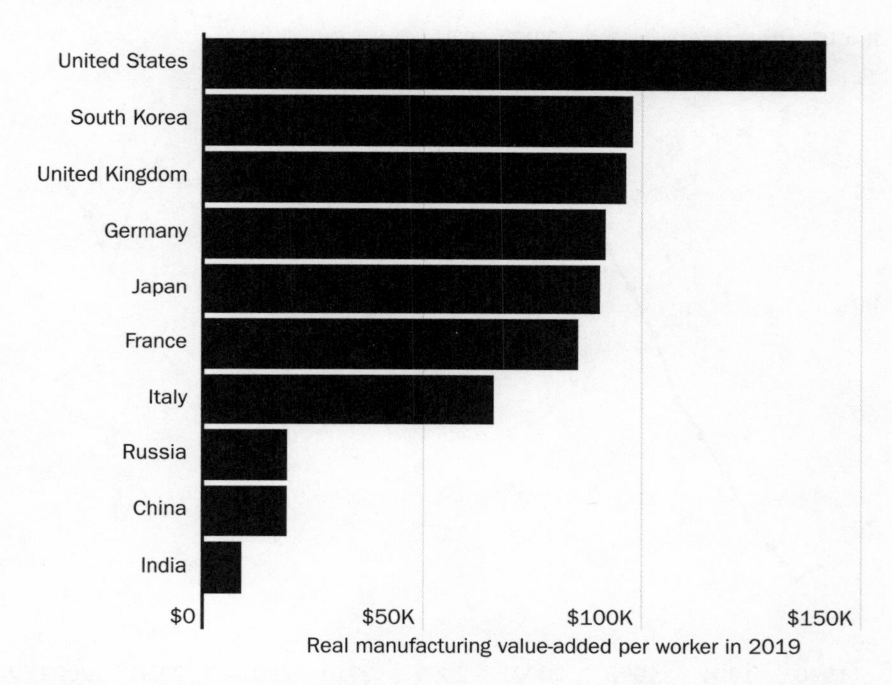

Source: Data on manufacturing value-added (constant 2015 dollars) from "National Accounts Database," United Nations Industrial Development Organization; and data on manufacturing employment from "Employment by Sex and Economic Activity (Thousands)—Annual," International Labour Organization; and author's calculations.

Manufacturing output has also remained strong in historical terms, at only 5 percent lower than its all-time high achieved in the final quarter of 2007 (Figure 12.2).[11] Measured by real value-added, the sector reached its highest level in 2022 (Figure 12.3).[12]

The country's industrial prowess is also evidenced by foreigners' appetite for investment in US manufacturing. As of 2021, the stock of foreign direct investment (FDI) in the sector stood at over $2.1 trillion, while 2021 also saw $121.3 billion of new FDI flow into domestic manufacturing—an amount greater than any other industry.[13]

FIGURE 12.2

Real US manufacturing output is only 5 percent lower than its all-time high

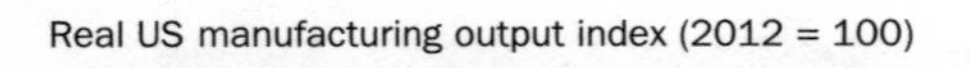

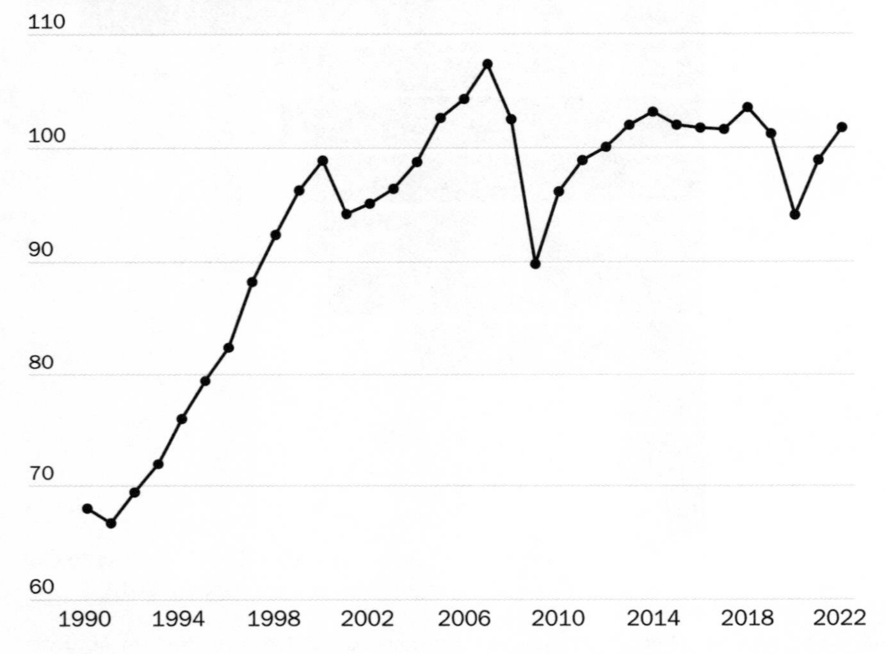

Source: US Bureau of Labor Statistics, "Manufacturing Sector: Real Sectoral Output for All Workers," Federal Reserve Economic Data, Federal Reserve Bank of St. Louis, updated June 1, 2023.

Beyond their direct investment in the sector, foreigners are also eager consumers of US manufactured products. In 2018, the United States ranked second in the world in merchandise exports and third for exports of "manufactures," and from 2002 to 2021, the country's manufacturing exports more than doubled.[14] In 2019, US firms exported over $1.3 trillion in manufactured goods, including aerospace and aircraft parts ($60.1 billion), integrated circuits ($41.2 billion), and medical instruments ($29.4 billion).[15] According to the World Bank, approximately 20 percent of all US manufactured goods exports in 2021—totaling more than $169 billion—were "high technology" products (i.e., "products with high [research and development] intensity, such as in aero-

FIGURE 12.3

Real US manufacturing value-added reached its highest recorded level in 2022

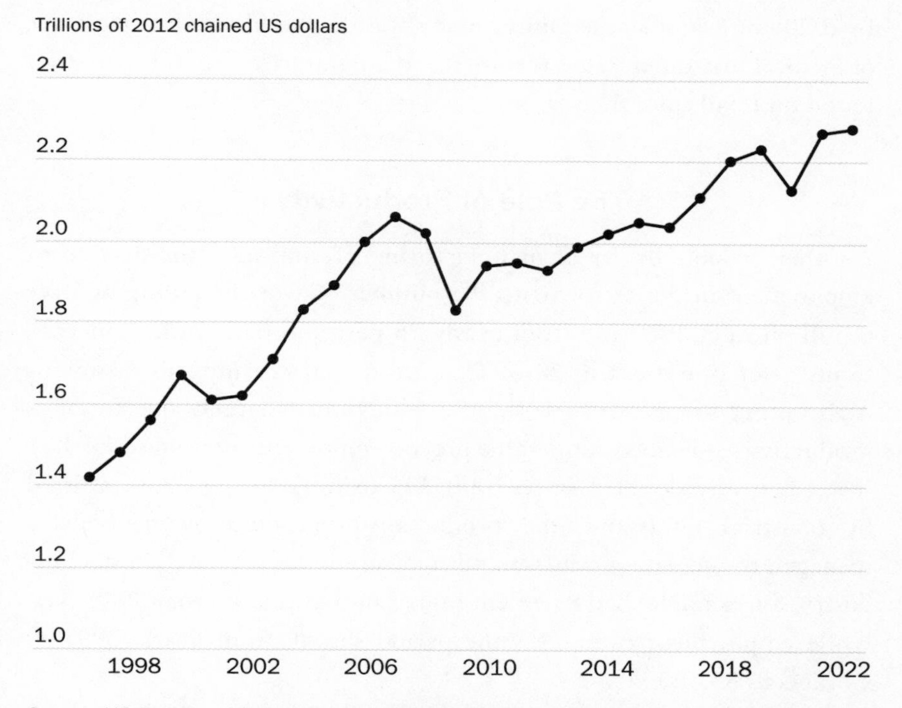

Source: US Bureau of Economic Analysis, "Real Value Added by Industry: Manufacturing," Federal Reserve Economic Data, Federal Reserve Bank of St. Louis, updated June 29, 2023. *Note*: "Chained dollars" is a method for adjusting nominal dollar amounts for inflation that better accounts for price-induced changes in consumption and production patterns over time.

space, computers, pharmaceuticals, scientific instruments, and electrical machinery").[16]

Among the destinations for these goods are other leading manufacturing countries. In 2020, for example, the United States exported $17 billion worth of electrical machinery to China, $6.6 billion in optical and medical instruments to Japan, and $16 billion worth of transportation equipment to Germany.[17] The previous year, the European Union alone imported $35.7 billion worth of aircrafts from the United States.[18]

That so many Americans fail to appreciate the vast size and scale of US manufacturing is perhaps at least partially explained by the fact that many retail purchases by consumers are for products imported from abroad. But much of what US manufacturers make are items whose production requires advanced know-how that consumers rarely encounter. In 2020, for example, the United States was the world's leading exporter of medical instruments, gas turbines, and aircraft parts—goods not often found on retail store shelves.[19]

The Role of Productivity

Another possible driver of manufacturing pessimism is the decline in employment in the sector, with the number of workers falling by over 6 million since 1979 and from nearly 25 percent of all workers in 1973 to just over 10 percent in 2016. That US manufacturing still maintains high output despite such workforce reductions is largely due to labor productivity—robots, computers, process improvements, and so forth—that has nearly doubled since 2000. US manufacturing firms, assisted by industrial robots and other production process improvements, have managed to increase production with fewer workers.[20] The US steel industry, for example, had 8 percent higher output in 2017 than 1980 even while employment over the same period shrank from nearly 399,000 workers to 83,000.[21]

In fact, a 2015 study found that 88 percent of manufacturing job losses from 2000 to 2010 can be attributed to improved productivity.[22] Although other studies assign a larger role to trade and the advent of China as an efficient manufacturing hub, there are few who deny the role of productivity improvements as a significant, if not main, factor behind the long-term decline in manufacturing employment.[23] Supporting this conclusion is the fact that the United States *added* 1.3 million manufacturing jobs between 2009 and 2019 amid stagnating manufacturing productivity (Figure 12.4).

Further confirmation is provided by similar data from other advanced economies—including ones with persistent trade surpluses and active labor and industrial policies. Manufacturing's share of employment nearly halved in Germany from 1973 to 2016 while Australia witnessed a two-thirds reduction over the same period. Manufacturing's

FIGURE 12.4
US manufacturing labor productivity and employment tend to run in opposite directions

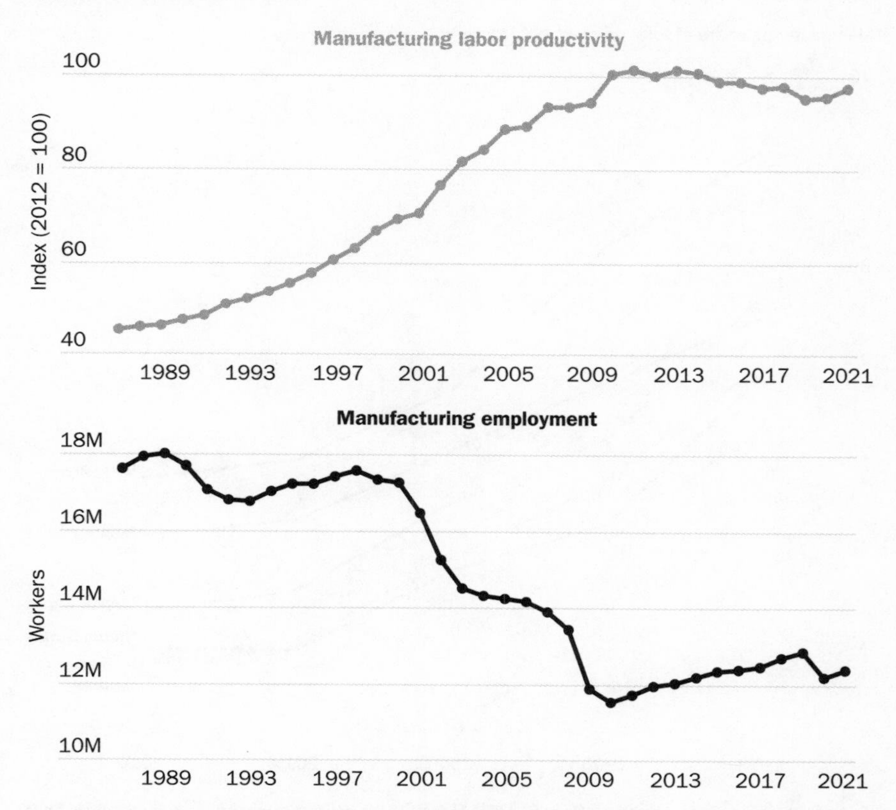

Source: US Bureau of Labor Statistics, "Manufacturing Sector: Labor Productivity," Federal Reserve Economic Data, Federal Reserve Bank of St. Louis, updated March 24, 2023; US Bureau of Labor Statistics, "All Employees, Manufacturing," Federal Reserve Economic Data, Federal Reserve Bank of St. Louis, updated June 2, 2023.

reduced share of employment isn't particular to the United States but rather reflects a broader international phenomenon (Figure 12.5).

Noting this trend over 25 years ago, a 1997 International Monetary Fund paper described the trend away from manufacturing as "simply the natural outcome of successful economic development" and "generally associated with rising living standards."[24]

FIGURE 12.5
Across advanced economies, a lower share of workers are employed in manufacturing

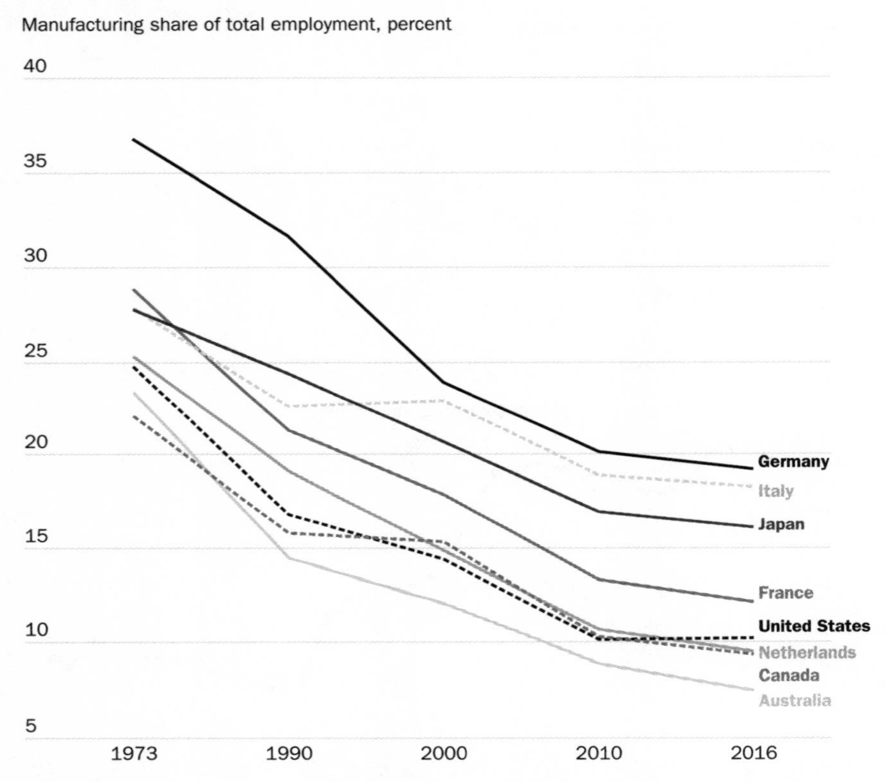

Source: Robert Z. Lawrence, "Recent US Manufacturing Employment: The Exception That Proves the Rule," Peterson Institute for International Economics Working Paper no. 17-12, November 2017.

Manufacturing's Relative Decline Also Reflects Shifting Consumption Patterns

Manufacturing's declining share of employment and GDP can also be explained by shifting US consumption patterns in favor of services over goods. In short, as Americans have become richer, more of their income—nearly twice as much—has been spent on services instead of stuff.[25] This trend was underscored during the COVID-19 pandemic when, faced with greatly restricted entertainment, dining, and vacation options, Americans' consumption of durable goods surged.[26] A possible accelerant of this trend is that some traditionally manufactured products such as maps, notepads, compact discs, and DVDs have been "dematerialized" into streaming services or software applications.

As with automation, the American experience has been replicated in other wealthy economies *as well as global GDP as a whole* where services account for a growing share of consumer spending and where manufacturing's share of both GDP and employment has declined (Figure 12.6).[27]

FIGURE 12.6

Across advanced economies, manufacturing accounts for a lower share of gross domestic product (GDP)

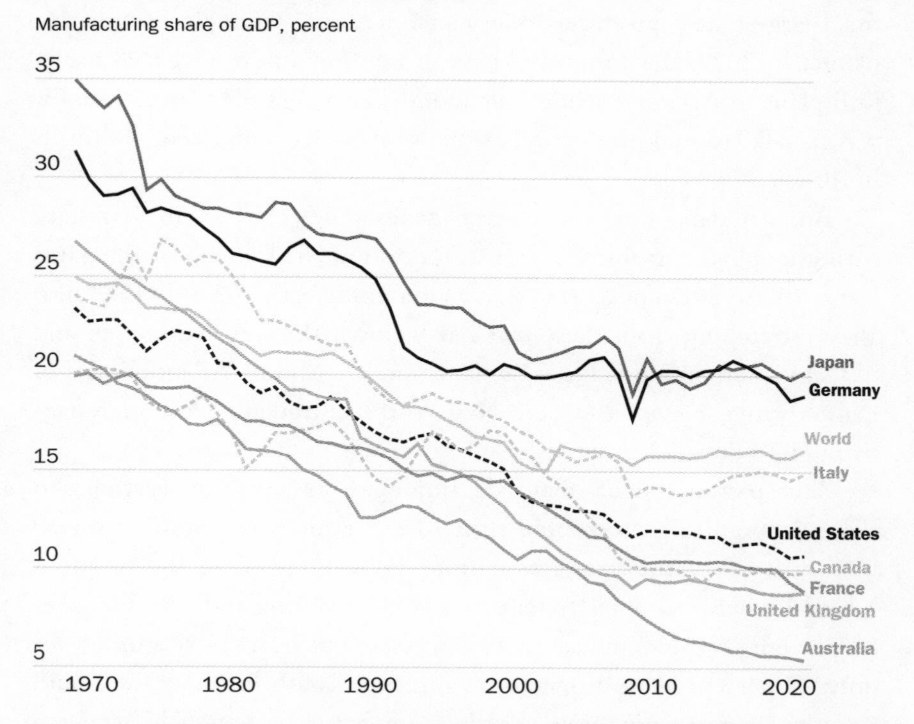

Source: "GDP/Breakdown at Current Prices in US Dollars (All Countries)," National Accounts Section, United Nations Statistics Division, updated January 2023.

"Domestic Outsourcing" Plays a Large Role in Regional Declines

While countries such as China and Mexico are often blamed for the shift of factory work away from the Rust Belt, in many cases the relocation of such work has been not to other countries but to other states. From 2001 to 2018, for example, the South saw a 17 percent increase in the number of automotive manufacturing jobs while other regions experienced declines ranging from 21 percent to 47 percent.[28]

A similar example can be found in the domestic steel industry, which has seen a shift away from large, integrated steel mills in favor of "mini-mills" that employ electric arc furnaces to melt steel scrap or direct reduced iron.[29] While most integrated mills are in Indiana, Michigan, Ohio, and Pennsylvania—Rust Belt states synonymous with industrial decline—many mini-mills are in the South. US Steel, the country's third-largest steel producer, offers an interesting example of this dynamic. In 2022, the company broke ground on a new advanced mini-mill plant in Arkansas while four months later, US Steel announced it was in talks to end production at one of its older integrated steel mills in Illinois.[30]

Broader data show the uneven geographic recovery in manufacturing employment since the Great Recession, with much of the gains from 2010 to 2017 concentrated in Mountain states along with the "auto alley" stretching from the Great Lakes down through Mississippi and Alabama.[31] In contrast, New England and the Middle Atlantic states of Pennsylvania, New Jersey, and New York continued to lose manufacturing jobs during this period.

This pattern of US firms decamping from northern latitudes to more economically hospitable climes farther south is a familiar one.[32] The shift of textile production from New England to the South is a well-known example. As late as 1925, New England was home to 80 percent of the domestic textile industry but by 1954 accounted for only 20 percent as mill operations migrated south.[33] Today the South remains home to numerous textile manufacturers, but such firms account for far less employment than in the past with production having shifted to highly automated facilities.[34] A similar dynamic can be seen among furnituremakers. Domestic employment shifted to the South and then overseas, but several firms maintain a US presence by emphasizing customization and niche markets.[35]

Manufacturing Jobs Aren't Necessarily Better Jobs

Concerns over the relative decline of manufacturing employment often reflects a sense that compensation in the sector is superior to that of services jobs. The United States, some may believe, is losing "good jobs" and replacing them with relatively low-paying ones (aka "McJobs"). More recent data, however, suggest otherwise.[36]

First, not all manufacturing jobs are particularly well paid.[37] In 2016, for example, production workers at US sawmills received average hourly pay of $18.60 while the comparable figure in aircraft manufacturing was over $40 (for reference, the average hourly earnings for all private-sector employees in 2016 was approximately $25).[38]

Perhaps more importantly, compensation levels for manufacturing jobs in some instances may be *inferior* when compared to jobs in other industries after controlling for various factors. As the Congressional Research Service observed in a 2018 report:

> Contrary to the popular perception, production and nonsupervisory workers in manufacturing, on average, earn significantly less per hour than nonsupervisory workers in industries that do not employ large numbers of teenagers, that have average workweeks of similar length, and that have similar levels of worker education. For example, nonsupervisory workers in manufacturing earned an average hourly wage of $21.29 in 2017, compared with $26.73 for nonsupervisory construction workers and $36.21 for nonsupervisory workers in the electric utility industry.[39]

A senior economist at the Federal Reserve Bank of St. Louis pointed out that, while the average manufacturing worker earned $0.50 *more* per hour than the average private-sector worker in 2010, by 2022 the average manufacturing worker was earning $1.12 *less*.[40] This finding comports with a 2019 Bureau of Labor Statistics report noting that in 1990, production workers in manufacturing had hourly earnings approximately 6 percent greater than those of production or nonsupervisory workers in the total private sector ($10.78 versus $10.20) but that by 2018, such workers were earning about 5 percent less ($21.54 versus $22.71).[41] In addition, a 2022 paper found that the wage premium for manufacturing jobs has disappeared and noted that manufacturing wages rank in the *bottom half* of all jobs in the United States.[42]

Such data perhaps explain manufacturers' concerns over labor shortages that have been described as the sector's greatest long-term obstacle to growth.[43] Through most of 2021 and 2022, for example, the number of unfilled US manufacturing jobs never dropped below 800,000, and it remained historically elevated in 2023 even as the industry struggled.[44] Far from a lack of employment opportunities, the apparent greater threat to US manufacturing prosperity is a lack of workers to fill such positions.[45]

Beyond wages, there are also other reasons to discount the premium that is sometimes placed on manufacturing jobs. Research released by the International Monetary Fund in 2018, for example, found that manufacturing does not play a unique role in productivity growth *and* that "some service industries [exhibit] productivity growth rates as high as the top-performing manufacturing industries."[46]

In short, if reasons exist for US policymakers to actively promote domestic manufacturing, jobs aren't one of them.

The Role of Increased Trade and Global Economic Integration

While numerous factors including productivity gains, changes in consumer preferences, and geographic shifts in manufacturing activity within the United States explain the lion's share of manufacturing's decline in employment, trade plays a role as well. Factories located in other countries have a comparative advantage over those in the United States for certain manufacturing activities. But this shouldn't provoke undue worry.

From a historical perspective, the dispersion of some manufacturing jobs to other countries since the 1950s was an inevitability. With much of Europe's and Japan's manufacturing reduced to rubble during World War II and much of the rest of the world forced into mistaken experiments with communism, the United States began the postwar era as the world's preeminent manufacturing power almost by default. From that point, the trend could only be in one direction as other countries rebuilt and reemerged as manufacturing powers.

Rather than undermining US prosperity, however, manufacturing's spread allowed for greater specialization and trade that undergirded the postwar economic boom and rise in living standards.[47] Outsourcing jobs abroad allowed for the creation of new and better compensated jobs within the United States. Driving down the cost of production through cheaper production overseas has allowed US firms to lower prices and increase sales of their products, which in turn increases demand for better-compensated jobs in areas such as design, market, and maintaining or servicing these products.

Although superficially worlds apart, there is little functional difference between manufacturing work being transferred to a worker in another country or to a robot or advanced machine on American soil. Both are properly understood as productivity drivers that lie at the root of prosperity. Through such productivity enhancements, the United States reduces the cost of producing goods and raises its standard of living.

The Value of Economic Diversity

Although US manufacturing's relatively reduced prominence and shift toward a more services-oriented economy has prompted worries, often overlooked are the benefits of such economic diversification. Germany, Taiwan, and South Korea, for example—all with economic fortunes significantly more tied to manufacturing output than the United States—have been hit hard in recent years amid supply chain problems and flagging demand for manufactured goods in overseas markets.[48] With far more of their economic eggs in a single basket, such downturns are more painful than in economies that rely on numerous industries and sectors to serve as growth drivers.

A country with too much manufacturing or high trade barriers can, perhaps contrary to perceptions of strength associated with industrial might, be less resilient and more prone to pronounced downturns or economic shocks.[49] Just as the United States should be wary of its manufacturing base disappearing (which has not happened!), it should also be cognizant of the downsides that come with an economy overly weighted toward factory output.

Dos and Don'ts for Boosting US Manufacturing

While manufacturing remains a vibrant part of the US economy, an optimized policy environment could help the sector retain its competitiveness and position it to meet current and future challenges. The following are policy recommendations to ensure that the United States remains an attractive location for manufacturing.

Don't engage in industrial policy: Politicians and myriad other commentators regularly call for new measures designed to promote the fortunes of selected industries, but such proposals should be greeted with extreme skepticism. Despite professed clairvoyance by some observers about which industries are destined to become key drivers of future growth, the future is often hazy, and such public-sector-backed bets rarely pay off. Businesses and investors, guided by price signals and market feedback—as well as incentivized by the profit motive—are far better positioned to assess and identify opportunities for growth than politicians and bureaucrats beholden to political pressures.

Don't impose new protectionist measures (and remove old ones): Protectionism seeks to bolster particular firms or industries by reducing or entirely removing competition by foreigners. Not only do such measures often fail to produce the desired effect—removing competition discourages the kind of innovation that helps keep firms competitive—but it also inflicts harm on the rest of the economy. Raising the price of steel through tariffs and quotas, for example, undermines the numerous domestic industries, such as automakers and construction, that rely on steel as an important input.[50] Thus, the many current tariffs on imports of manufacturing inputs—which constitute around half of all US imports—perversely harm most American manufacturers.[51]

Do expand immigration: An important determinant of manufacturers' success—as with all industries—is access to a talented and reliable workforce. Amid labor shortages, it is more important than ever that Congress reform the US immigration system to ensure that US manufacturing firms have access to the human capital needed to thrive. The National Association of Manufacturers has made this point in its advocacy for a streamlined immigration system.[52]

Do reform the US tax code: Manufacturing is a capital-intensive industry, but the US tax code forces deductions for such expenses to be spread out over a number of years.[53] By denying manufacturers the ability to fully recover their investments quickly, the tax code effectively raises the cost of capital investments due to inflation and the time value of money. To correct this, the tax code should be changed to allow for full, immediate expensing of capital investment.

Conclusion

Doom and gloom around the state of US manufacturing is deeply misplaced with a variety of metrics showing the United States as one of the foremost players in this important sector. Annual production and exports of manufactured goods reach into the hundreds of billions of dollars and include advanced products such as electrical machinery, aircraft, and medical equipment. That the sector employs fewer Americans and accounts for a lower percentage of economic activity than in years past is largely due to productivity gains and changes in consumer preferences in favor of services and fewer material goods. Rather than a harbinger of weakness, these shifts are consistent with those seen in other advanced economies. Furthermore, factory closures in some parts of the United States—including the so-called Rust Belt—reflect domestic rather than international shifts as production is transferred to US locations deemed more efficient centers of manufacturing.

Nevertheless, there is scope for policy reforms to further bolster the fortunes of US manufacturers, including the removal of tariffs and other impediments to the efficient sourcing of key inputs as well as expanded immigration to boost the human capital available to these firms. With such measures, the sector would be well positioned to remain a vital source of economic strength for many decades to come.

Chapter 13

The Dangers of Misunderstanding Economic Interdependence

Daniel W. Drezner

- Western scholars and policymakers used to think of economic interdependence as an unalloyed good; in recent years, however, it has been viewed as something that could be weaponized.
- Economic interdependence is hardly a cure-all for US national security concerns, but it also is not the acute national security threat that is commonly articulated in Washington, DC.
- Fears of malevolent interdependence can be self-fulfilling—if policymakers continue to view globalization as a threat, then the collective policy responses will increase the likelihood of great power conflict.

The liberal internationalism that guided American foreign policy throughout the post–Cold War era rested on multiple pillars: democracy promotion, expansion of human rights protections, bolstering global governance structures, and so forth. One of the most important elements, however, was making globalization truly global. By the mid-1980s, trade barriers and capital controls had been reduced within the first world. A central goal of the European Union was to bind France and Germany so closely together that the idea of going to war again seemed ludicrous. A key logic behind the North American Free Trade

Agreement was for the United States and Mexico to end centuries of enmity by expanding trade across the border.

The end of the Cold War discredited the development strategies of central planning as well as import substitution and industrialization. These failures buoyed advocates of the "Washington Consensus" to promote neoliberal policies as a template for transition economies as well as the Global South.[1] These ideas diffused through the rest of the world in the 1990s.[2] Neoliberalism was easier to advance as the United States encouraged developing and transition economies to join the Bretton Woods Institutions: the International Monetary Fund; World Bank; and World Trade Organization (WTO), the successor to the General Agreement on Tariffs and Trade (GATT). The GATT had fewer than 100 members as the Cold War was ending. By the end of 2000, an institutionally stronger WTO had added an additional 45 members, with China's 2001 entrance entering final negotiations.[3]

All of this was consistent with the tenets of liberal internationalism. Long before Adam Smith argued that free trade was economically beneficial, advocates for freer trade viewed international exchange as a means of reducing the risk of war.[4] As far back as Norman Angell's pre–World War I pamphlets, scholars had argued that the gains from trade far outweighed the gains of plunder. A more open economy would therefore reward productive entrepreneurship far more than destructive entrepreneurship.[5] The modern version of this argument came from political scientists Robert Keohane and Joseph Nye, who argued in *Power and Interdependence* that "networks of interdependence" would constrain the use of force across most issue areas.[6]

During the post–Cold War era, both scholars and policymakers embraced this view of interdependence. Since 2016, however, there has been a sea change in elite attitudes about the costs and benefits of economic interdependence. In 2019, Henry Farrell and Abraham Newman published a blockbuster paper in *International Security* pointing out that networked economic structures—such as global supply chains, energy pipelines, and capital markets—created interdependencies that state actors could weaponize.[7] Soon, everyone inside the Beltway had embraced the idea.[8] In *Chip War: The Fight for the World's Most Critical Technology*, Christopher Miller quoted one US official saying, "weaponized interdependence, it's a beautiful thing." The result has been widespread predictions of "deglobalization."[9]

The new security fears about interdependence meshed nicely with policymakers searching for a post-neoliberal worldview.[10] This search was rooted in part by an economic conviction that neoliberal economic policies had enriched China and the 1 percent on the backs of America's working class—a hypothesis that goes beyond the scope of this chapter and is addressed by others in this series. It was also rooted by the perception that multiple recent shocks had exposed the folly of excessive interdependence. The COVID-19 pandemic seemingly confirmed the risks of relying on other countries for vital supply chains. Russia's invasion of Ukraine and its weaponization of energy pipelines to Europe have highlighted the risk of weaponized interdependence.

This essay stands athwart this paranoia about malevolent forms of interdependence and yells, "stop!" Economic interdependence is hardly a cure-all for US national security concerns, but it also is not the acute national security threat that is commonly articulated inside the Beltway. Concerns have been greatly exaggerated, while the geopolitical benefits of interdependence have been underestimated. Even in 2023, China's interdependence with the Organisation for Economic Co-operation and Development economies has acted as a constraint on its foreign policy behavior. Indeed, the Biden administration seems belatedly aware that it has stigmatized trade with China a bit too much.[11] If current trends persist, however, the United States risks further geoeconomic fragmentation—and the loosening of those constraints. The worldview of malevolent interdependence is likely wrong, but those fears can be self-fulfilling. In other words, if policymakers continue to view globalization as a threat, then the combined policy responses are likely to increase the likelihood of great power conflict.

How Could Economic Interdependence Affect World Politics?

The liberal paradigm in international relations (not to be confused with how the word "liberal" is used in the left-right distinctions of American politics) rests on a "Kantian triad" of interlocking forces designed to prevent the anarchic nature of world politics from spilling over into violent conflict. It was believed that a world of democratic states, international organizations, and economic interdependence would lead to a pluralistic security community in which no state would have the incentive to start a war.[12] Within Kant's own writings, it is true that the economic interdependence plank was the weakest of the three.[13] Modern scholars, however, have argued that the logic of commercial peace is as strong or stronger than that of democratic peace.

Commercial peace between nations operates through multiple causal mechanisms. The simplest one is at the individual level: in trading states, ambitious individuals will flock to the commercial sector rather than the security sector, thereby taming man's passions and converting them into economic self-interest. At the domestic political level, the growth of trade between countries also creates interest groups on both sides with a vested interest in maintaining harmonious bilateral relations. At the level of the international system, commercial peace operates by a simple rational choice: state leaders will be wary of the loss of wealth that would come with a war against a trading partner. These logics are not mutually exclusive but rather reinforcing—and all of them contribute to the power of commercial peace.

Some liberal scholars have gone even further. Keohane and Nye argued that complex interdependence would drastically reduce the utility of force in world politics. Erik Gartzke argued that capitalist peace is so powerful that it is the primary driver behind democratic peace. Gartzke suggested that the spread of market forces reduces violence for multiple reasons, including that "the historic impetus to territorial expansion is tempered by the rising importance of intellectual and financial capital" and that "the rise of global capital markets creates a new mechanism for competition and communication for states that might otherwise be forced to fight."[14] He is hardly the only scholar to advance this argument.[15] More popular proponents, like Thomas L. Friedman, argued that globalization was so powerful that it flattened many power differentials that existed in the world.[16]

There have always been counterarguments to commercial peace within the scholarly literature. Even as the liberal paradigm was fleshing out the logic of commercial peace, scholars like Kenneth Waltz and Joanne Gowa were arguing that interdependence could actually *increase* the likelihood of conflict.[17] For one thing, high levels of trade can also increase frictions, triggering an interstate dispute. For another, as Waltz noted, increased interdependence implies a more specialized division of labor. As specialization increases dependency on others, according to Waltz, states react defensively: "like other organizations, states seek to control what they depend on or to lessen the extent of their dependency. This simple thought explains quite a bit of the behavior of states: their imperial thrusts to widen the scope of their control and their autarchic strivings toward self-sufficiency."[18] China's rapacious desire to lock down access to raw materials and critical minerals could be viewed as a modern-day manifestation of Waltz's prediction.

China's overall rise also posed a challenge to the liberal theory of interdependence. Critics highlight President Bill Clinton's March 2000 speech advocating for China's entry into the WTO.[19] In that speech, he promised, "the more China liberalizes its economy, the more fully it will liberate the potential of its people—their initiative, their imagination, their remarkable spirit of enterprise. And when individuals have the power not just to dream but to realize their dreams, they will demand a greater say." A generation later, that promise has clearly been unfulfilled (though Clinton's support for China's WTO accession had other, arguably more important, objectives beyond political liberalization). China's turn toward even more illiberal forms of autocracy in Hong Kong and Xinjiang are the most obvious manifestation of this broken promise.

Farrell and Newman's development of the weaponized interdependence concept added a new level of concern.[20] Scholars had long been aware that some states might be vulnerable to asymmetric dependence on larger economies. What Farrell and Newman proposed was that the globalized economy was dependent on networks and standards that were difficult for any actor to exit. Furthermore, these networks were not decentralized. Whether one looked at finance, the internet, or energy, central nodes emerged. As Farrell and Newman explained, "In contradistinction to liberal claims, [network structures] do not produce a flat or fragmented world of diffuse power relations and ready cooperation, nor do they tend to become less asymmetric over time. . . . Contrary to Keohane and Nye's predictions, key global economic networks have converged toward 'hub and spoke' systems, with important consequences for power relations."

Two events helped bolster the fear that weaponized interdependence had generated in the corridors of power. First, the COVID-19 pandemic convinced many observers that excessive dependence on international sourcing left their countries vulnerable to supply shocks. As Colin Kahl and Thomas Wright noted, China bought up all the personal protective equipment (PPE) in the first quarter of 2020, thereby leaving many countries high and dry when COVID-19 spread globally.[21] Canada's domestic procurement of PPE increased 250-fold after March 2020. The pandemic generated an entire discourse about how resiliency needed to be prioritized over efficiency. According to European Commission vice president Věra Jourová, COVID-19 "revealed our morbid dependency on China and India as regards pharmaceuticals." Japan launched a $2.2 billion fund to assist companies shifting production facilities out of China.[22]

Second, Russia's invasion of Ukraine has highlighted all the ways that Europe has been dependent on Russian energy. NATO secretary-general Jens Stoltenberg stated, "The war in Ukraine has . . . demonstrated our dangerous dependency on Russian gas. This should lead us to assess our dependencies on other authoritarian states, not least China."[23] The parallels between Russia's irridentist desire for Ukraine and China's ardent desire to absorb Taiwan are difficult to ignore. The return to great power competition has fed a belief that economic security must be prioritized over the efficiency gains from globalization.

How Economic Interdependence Has Actually Affected World Politics

While contemporary fears about excessive interdependence are real, that does not mean that these fears have been realized. Indeed, a quick perusal of the alleged downsides of interdependence reveal that much of what has been feared has not come to fruition.

For example, consider the allegations about how China gamed the liberal international order to serve its own revisionist ends. It is undeniably true that as China has grown economically stronger, it has also grown more repressive and more revisionist.[24] Neither of these facts, however, falsify the liberal theory of international politics. The liberal argument posits that interdependence constrains rising powers from pursuing more bellicose policies than they otherwise would have. It says next to nothing about interdependence triggering democratization. It is possible that China can repress domestically while still acting in a constrained manner on the global stage.[25] Most of China's alleged revisionist actions have been exaggerated. For example, neither the New Development Bank (formerly known as BRICS Bank) nor the Asian Infrastructure Investment Bank have challenged the Bretton Woods Institutions. Claims that the Belt and Road Initiative is an example of debt-trap diplomacy have also been wildly exaggerated; indeed, if anything, China's recent lending practices suggest that it will not weaponize debts from the Global South.[26] While China has built new institutions outside the purview of the United States, none of them contradict the principles of the liberal international order.

As for China's foreign policy more generally, the evidence that complex interdependence has failed is scant. By one metric, China's gross domestic product (GDP) surpassed the United States in recent years.[27] As Graham Allison has noted, over the past few centuries, such a great power transition caused a war 75 percent of the time.[28] While Sino-American relations have grown more fraught in recent years, war has not broken out—and that dog not barking might be the most important data point in favor of complex interdependence. Stacie Goddard argues that China's rise within the liberal international order has enabled it to engage in some revisionist actions, but its interdependence with the rest of the world has also constrained that revisionism.[29] The evidence that China seeks to upend this order wholesale remains scant. Iain Johnston concluded, "It is problematic to claim that China is less economically open to trade today than in 1997, or less supportive of the arms control regimes it has joined than in 1997, or less committed to global counterterrorism today than in 1997, or less committed to dealing with greenhouse gases today than in 1997."[30] My own research suggests that if China is intending to upend the global economic order, it is doing so in a radically suboptimal manner.[31]

China's autonomy has grown as its wealth has increased—but like every other actor in the international system, it remains constrained by its reliance on the global economy. Perhaps the best evidence for this is its constrained response to Russia's invasion of Ukraine. Russia is China's most important geopolitical partner on the global stage. Just a few weeks before the invasion, Russia and China publicly proclaimed a friendship without limits.[32] Despite this bonhomie and confluence of national interests, China's support of Russia since the start of the war has been decidedly meager. China has refrained from shipping weapons or other forms of materiel support to a Russia that badly needs it. That is due in no small part to the fact that China values its economic relationship with the West far more than it does its relationship with Russia.

Similarly, fears that the pandemic created vulnerabilities for economies dependent on global supply chains proved to be wildly misplaced. Ironically, most of the pandemic-induced stresses had to do with the private sector underestimating the robustness of government responses. As COVID-19 went global, firms responded by drastically scaling back production, anticipating a massive consumer slowdown. Instead, fiscal and monetary stimulus caused shifts in the composition of demand, mostly from services to manufactured goods. This caught many firms flatfooted, leaving them to scramble for newly scarce inputs. Furthermore, there was zero evidence that goods with more complex global supply chains suffered more severe disruptions than goods with regional supply chains.[33] Indeed, if anything, the evidence suggests the opposite: precisely because supply chains were globalized, they were more resilient to regional shocks.[34] This was because those firms who relied on global supply chains were more conscious about the possibility of disruption, thereby taking action to forestall it. By contrast, one of the most autarkic of US products—baby formula—suffered one of the period's deepest and longest shortages, which the federal government tried to alleviate by embracing imports.[35]

FIGURE 13.1

The number of active sanctions has significantly increased over the past few decades

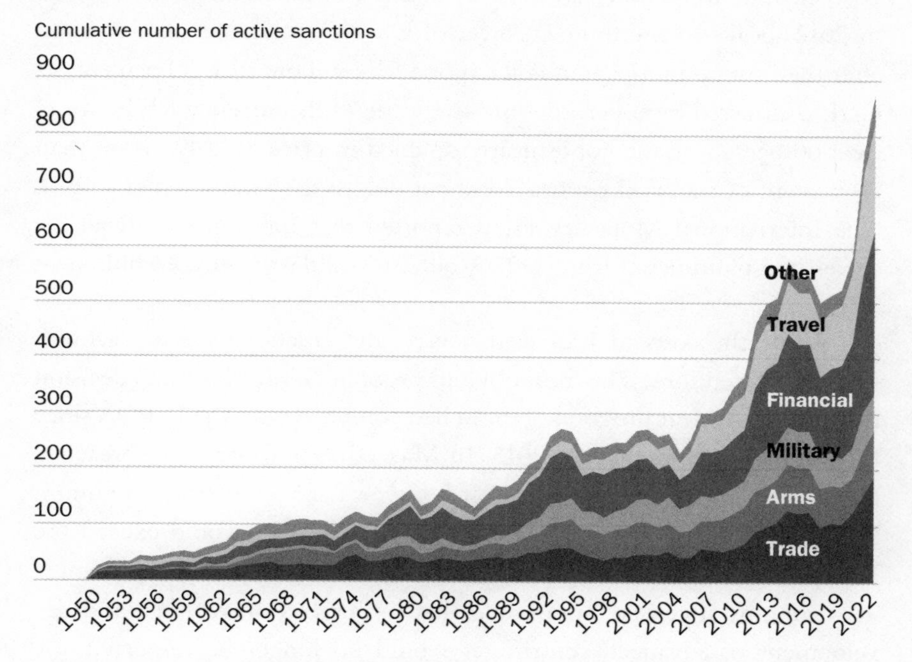

Source: Constantinos Syropoulos et al., "The Global Sanctions Data Base—Release 3: COVID-19, Russia, and Multilateral Sanctions," School of Economics Working Paper Series no. 2022-11, Lebow College of Business, Drexel University, November 13, 2022; Gabriel Felbermayr et al., "The Global Sanctions Data Base," *European Economic Review* 129 (October 2020): 103561; and Aleksandra Kirilakha et al., "The Global Sanctions Data Base (GSDB): An Update That Includes the Years of the Trump Presidency," in Peter A. G. van Bergeijk, ed., *Research Handbook on Economic Sanctions* (Northampton, MA: Edward Elgar Publishing, 2021).

As for fears about weaponized interdependence, the rate of sanctioning activity has increased considerably over the past few decades, as Figure 13.1 demonstrates.

The evidence to date suggests that while great powers have tried to exploit their network centrality to impose economic coercion, few of these events have been successful. The most prominent success was the joint US-EU sanctions against Iran that forced that country to sign the Joint Comprehensive Plan of Action (JCPOA). Interestingly, however, when the Trump administration exited the JCPOA and reimposed sanctions, the results were lackluster even though Iran suffered severe economic costs. As Esfandyar Batmanghelidj noted, "That the subsequent economic crisis in Iran was as severe as when multilateral sanctions were imposed in 2012 speaks to the unique power of US economic coercion."[36] Soon after their reimposition, Iran's oil exports fell by more than 50 percent, its GDP contracted by 6 percent, and the value of its currency fell by more than 60 percent. Basic goods nearly doubled in price in 2019. More than 80 percent of Iran's oil exports were cut due to the reimposed sanctions. The International Monetary Fund reported that Iran's gross official reserves had plummeted from $122.5 billion in 2018 to only $4 billion in 2020.

While the costs to Iran were severe, the sanctions did not achieve stated US intentions. The most obvious proof of failure was Iran's decision to restart its nuclear program. Tehran had complied with the JCPOA since its adoption on October 18, 2015. In May 2019, however, Iran breached the accords by exceeding limits on heavy water and enriched uranium stockpiles. Two months later, Iran announced that it would exceed the 3.67 percent uranium-235 enrichment limit and go up to 4.5 percent.[37] Two months after that, Iran stated that limitations on research and development of advanced centrifuges would no longer be respected. By January 2020, Iran announced that it would no longer be bound by any operational limitations of the JCPOA. Estimates for how long it would take for Iran to build a nuclear bomb fell from a year under the 2015 deal to a few weeks in 2021.[38] Simply put, Iran was willing to pay the price of sanctions to pursue its own national security policies.

Iran is a middle-range power. Attempts to weaponize interdependence against great powers have been even less successful. The sanctions imposed against Russia after the 2014 annexation of Crimea clearly failed to deter Russia from further aggression. The economic coercion implemented after the 2022 invasion was unprecedented, but the aggregate impact on Russia's economy was considerably less than analysts anticipated.[39] Russia's countersanctions also proved to be less than meets the eye, as Europe dealt with Russia's energy cutoff far better than expected.[40] It is possible that over time, the West's sanctions against Russia will degrade Russia's military capacities. Still, given all the fears about the power of weaponized interdependence, it is noteworthy that sanctions failed at both deterring and coercing Russia from invading Ukraine.

The unprecedented country-specific export controls put in place against China may have the desired effect of extending the United States' technological lead over its closest competitor. The more specific controls placed on access to Huawei seriously dented that firm's efforts in the smartphone market.[41] The broader export controls put in place in October 2022, however, are less likely to succeed. In 1999, concerned about leaks of satellite technology to China, the United States blocked American firms from providing US satellites to be launched on Chinese rockets. At the time, the United States dominated the satellite export market, controlling 73 percent. In response, China found alternative satellite suppliers—France, Russia, the United Kingdom, and even Ukraine.[42] Within six years, the export controls proved to be a complete failure, as the US share plummeted to 25 percent. On semiconductor chips, Washington has managed to attract more multilateral support, but China is also in a stronger position to compete.

Weaponized interdependence has whetted the appetite for economic coercion around the globe. The combined effect of recent measures and countermeasures, however, has been to create a global economy in which economic sanctions are frequently imposed but yield minimal concessions. Long-lasting sanctions will have knock-on effects on patterns of global investment. The result is a global political economy that more closely resembles older, less stable eras. Consider the interwar era, when sanctions helped destabilize the international system.[43] The League of Nations sanctions against Italy in response to its invasion of Ethiopia encouraged the Axis powers to pursue more autarkic policies; the US oil embargo of Japan led that country to bomb Pearl Harbor. Sanctions in this century will likely accelerate the trend toward geoeconomic fragmentation—economic and technological decoupling by attrition.[44]

Weaponized Interdependence and the Power of Self-Fulfilling Prophecies

Fears of excessive dependence are not unique to the 21st century. For much of the 20th century, there was concern that the great powers would be vulnerable to the cutoff of hydrocarbons. Fears of oil wars, however, turned out to be misplaced.[45] Nonetheless, the concern about the prospect of resource wars, or being vulnerable to weaponized interdependence, highlights a second-order concern: that the fears about malevolent interdependence prove to be self-fulfilling prophecies. Or, to put it another way: Angell was absolutely correct when he argued in *The Great Illusion* that war was a horribly inefficient way for countries to enrich themselves as compared to trade.[46] His error was in presuming that this fact would be so obvious to everyone that war would not happen. Writing just a few years before the start of World War I, Angell turned out to be badly mistaken.

Unfortunately, Angell's successors have made similar arguments about war being rendered obsolete.[47] If the wars of this century yield any lesson, it is that policymaker misconceptions can often turn into self-fulfilling prophecies. If the United States and China, for example, become convinced that they are targets to malevolent interdependence, they will take actions to decouple their economies from each other. In doing so, however, they would weaken the positive constraints that complex interdependence has placed on their foreign policies. While China and the United States continue to be each other's largest trading partner, that interdependence is lessening. As Figure 13.2 shows, in 2013, China was responsible for nearly 70 percent of US imports from Asia. In 2022, that figure had declined to 50 percent. The perceptions fostered by trade wars, the pandemic, and escalating geopolitical risk will cause that figure to decline even further. Just as the United States is talking about "de-risking" the West from China, Chinese officials stress the need for a "dual circulation" economy less dependent on export-led growth.

International relations scholarship has demonstrated the power of myths and misperceptions to trigger armed conflict.[48] While this essay has demonstrated that fears about excessive dependence have been exaggerated, a bipartisan elite consensus has calcified this fear into a stylized fact that is barely grounded in reality. Policymakers need to be more conscious about the tradeoffs between too much economic interdependence and too little economic interdependence before taking actions that increase the likelihood of a great power war.

FIGURE 13.2

While US imports from China have increased in absolute terms, China's share of total US imports from low-cost Asian countries is declining

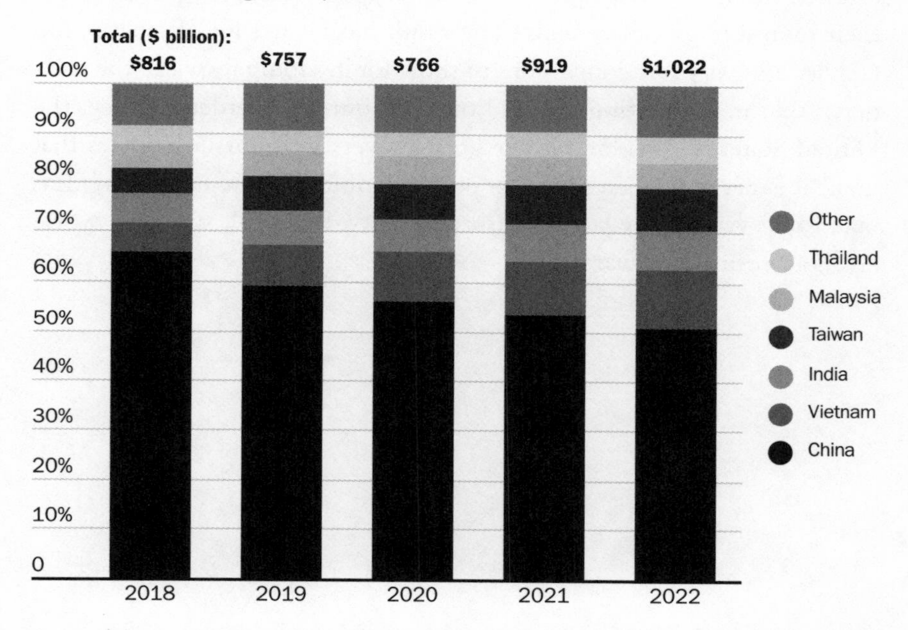

Source: Patrick Van den Bossche et al., "America Is Ready for Reshoring. Are You?: 2022 Reshoring Index," Kearney, 2023.

Note: "Other" includes Philippines, Indonesia, Pakistan, Sri Lanka, Bangladesh, Singapore, and Cambodia. Individual percentages do not add up to 100 due to rounding.

Conclusion

The neoliberal consensus about globalization is—rightly or wrongly—dead; the international relations consensus about the virtues of interdependence died along with it. Countries are erecting measures and countermeasures designed to reduce their dependency on the global economy. Some of this has been driven by the externalities allegedly created by globalization. Some of this has been driven by the desire for post-neoliberal ideas that encourage industrial policies and discourage untrammeled free trade. And some of it has been driven by the belief that the liberal theory of international politics has been falsified.

This essay has demonstrated that most of the fears about interdependence have been misplaced. Globalization is not responsible for Chinese bellicosity, and it is not responsible for the pandemic-fueled shortages. While weaponized interdependence is a real phenomenon, national governments have wildly exaggerated their capacity to exploit it to advance their own foreign policy ends. The result has been a lot of sanctioning activity and very few concessions to show for it. Going forward, the danger is that in attempting to ward off weaponized interdependence, the United States, China, and other great powers will pursue policies that make it easier to conceive of great power conflict. If post-neoliberal ideas take root even if they lack empirical validity, the result will be a world far more primed for war.

Chapter 14

Globalization: A Race to the Bottom—or to the Top?

Johan Norberg

- The idea that free trade would set off a race to the bottom is a myth. In the era of globalization, wages have increased, jobs have become safer, and child labor has declined.
- Companies and investors are not searching for the poorest places to do business but are investing mostly in relatively wealthy countries. When they do invest in poor countries, their main effect is to raise productivity and labor standards.
- There also is no environmental race to the bottom. The richer countries are, the more they protect their environment, and trade speeds up the transition to new and greener technologies around the world.

In 2002, Nobel laureate Joseph Stiglitz claimed that "globalization has become a race to the bottom, where corporations are the only winners and the rest of society, in both the developed and developing worlds, is the loser."[1]

Around the turn of the millennium, the fear of such a race to the bottom started haunting the debate about economic globalization. As capital and corporations became freer to move across borders, many worried that they would move to places with the lowest wages, worst working conditions, and least environmental protection. People believed that governments would be tempted to loosen standards to attract more investments and increase their participation in global supply chains.

But since then, the opposite has happened. The overall direction is one toward better jobs, higher wages, safer workplaces, and less child labor, and it has happened the fastest in the countries that have opened the most and are most integrated in global supply chains.

Astonishingly, these data are ignored by officials in the United States and elsewhere who—parroting Stiglitz two decades ago—still cling to the race-to-the-bottom narrative and decry a "colonial" and extractive economic model supposedly fueled by "traditional free trade agreements," as United States trade representative Katherine Tai put it in a speech on supply chain resilience. It's long past time for them and other globalization skeptics to update their script.[2]

What Has Happened to Work?

One typical op-ed in the *New York Times* asserted in 2015 that the race to the bottom encourages corporations to "relocate production to the lowest-cost country," employ children because they are paid less, and neglect safety measures, resulting in the deaths of more workers. This has always been a theoretical possibility, but empirical data have stubbornly refused to cooperate with it.[3]

The International Labour Organization considers the share of the labor force in elementary and lesser-skilled jobs as a proxy for low incomes and bad working conditions. This share has declined by more than 10 percentage points globally from 1994 to 2019. The decline was 6 percentage points in low-income countries and as much as 20 percentage points in upper-middle-income countries, the group of countries that have taken the greatest leaps to integrate with the global economy.[4]

The number of working poor has declined very fast. Between 1994 and 2022, the share of employed persons worldwide who live in extreme poverty (receiving an income below $1.90 adjusted for inflation and local purchasing power) declined by more than three-quarters, from 31.6 percent to 6.4 percent—a reduction of more than half a billion

FIGURE 14.1

The share of workers living in extreme poverty worldwide has significantly declined since 2000

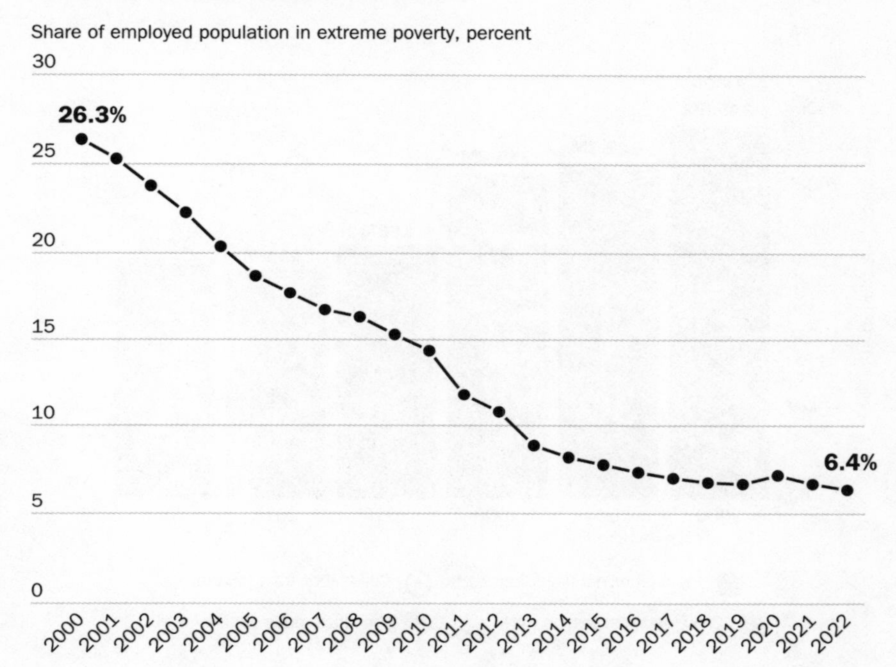

Source: Data for 2000–2010 are from *World Employment and Social Outlook: Trends 2020* (Geneva, Switzerland: International Labour Organization, 2020), p. 90; and data for 2011–2022 are from "SDG indicator 1.1.1—Working Poverty Rate (Percentage of Employed Living Below US$1.90 PPP) (%)—Annual," ILOSTAT, International Labour Organization, updated March 29, 2023.

Note: The International Labour Organization (ILO) defines extreme poverty as living below $1.90 a day, adjusted for purchasing power parity.

people despite setbacks during the pandemic (Figure 14.1). The share of workers in moderate poverty (earning between $1.90–$3.20) also declined, from more than 21 percent to around 12 percent. Poverty is strongly correlated with gross domestic product (GDP) per capita, and in upper-middle-income countries, the share of extreme working poor was less than 1 percent in 2022.

In East Asia, the developing region that has globalized the most, the share of workers in extreme poverty was just 0.5 percent in 2022. In

FIGURE 14.2

While much work remains, there has been significant progress in reducing child labor in the past two decades

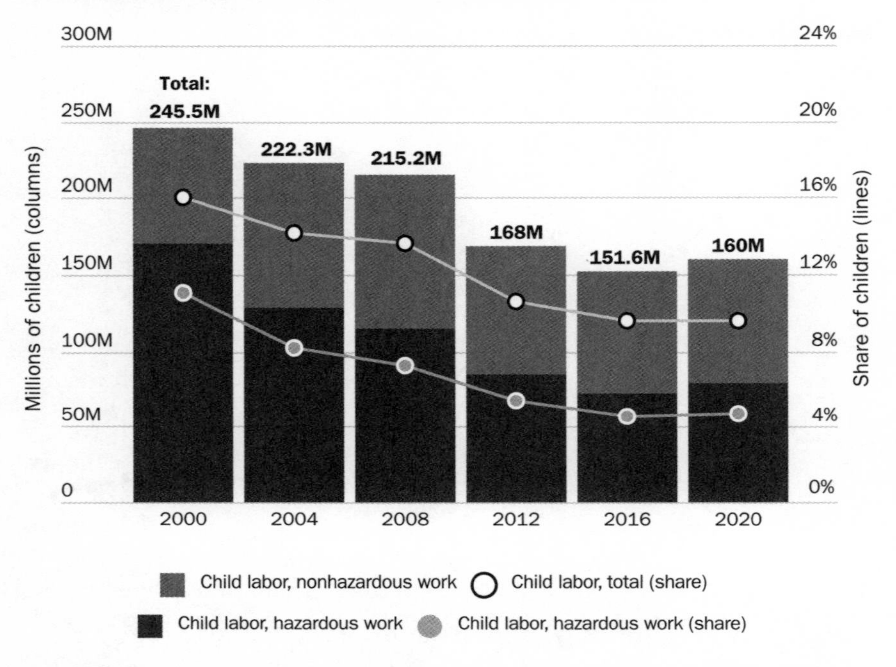

Source: *Child Labour: Global Estimates 2020, Trends and the Road Forward* (Geneva, Switzerland: International Labour Organization; and New York: United Nations Children's Fund, 2021), p. 23.
Note: Children ages 5–17 years.

contrast, the region with the least foreign investment and participation in supply chains, sub-Saharan Africa, had a rate of 38 percent.

It is more difficult to come up with comparable measures of labor standards, but the World Health Organization and the International Labour Organization have created a global set of estimates of work-related injuries and deaths between 2000 and 2016. Their data show a "substantial reduction in the total work-related burden of disease."[5] The loss of disability-adjusted life years attributable to occupational risk decreased by 12.9 percent between 2000 and 2016. The global rate of deaths related to work declined by 14.2 percent. The death rate from exposure to mechanical forces and fire or heat, two risks often associated with sweatshops in poor countries, declined by 18.3 percent and 26 percent, respectively.

Child labor declined fast over the same period.[6] Between 2000 and 2020, the share of children ages 5 to 17 years who were active in work that they were too young to perform or that was likely to harm their health or safety declined from 16 percent to 9.6 percent. The share of children performing hazardous work was reduced by more than half, from 11.1 percent to 4.7 percent (Figure 14.2). Children are three times more likely to work in rural areas than in urban areas and seven times more likely to work in agriculture than in industry.

On the whole and on average, jobs have become better paid and safer in the era of globalization, the complete opposite of what the race-to-the-bottom hypothesis predicted. The Organisation for Economic Co-operation and Development (OECD) concludes its review of the research:

> Indeed, the worst of fears about a race to the bottom do not appear to have materialized systematically in the real world, though examples do arise. A large empirical literature seems to point, if anything, to the opposite conclusion.[7]

Are We Racing to the Bottom on Labor Conditions?

This encouraging development did not happen despite globalization but to a large extent because of it. Using data from 114 countries, Andreas Bergh and Therese Nilsson found that increased globalization in a country, as measured by the KOF Globalisation Index, is associated with significantly faster poverty reduction.[8]

In his book *Globalization and Labor Conditions*, Robert Flanagan summarizes the evidence: "Countries that adopt open trade policies have higher wages, greater workplace safety, more civil liberties (including workplace freedom of association), and less child labor."[9] Flanagan and Niny Khor also document this relationship in "Trade and the Quality of Employment: Asian and Non-Asian Economies" in the OECD report *Policy Priorities for International Trade and Jobs*.[10]

This would be extremely surprising if companies always scoured the globe searching for the lowest-cost country. But they don't. If they did, 100 percent of foreign direct investment would go to the least developed countries, but in fact, no more than 2 percent of all foreign direct investment is heading in their direction. Most investment goes to relatively developed countries, and GDP per capita is the strongest influence on labor conditions. On average, richer countries have higher wages, safer jobs, shorter working hours, and stronger labor rights, such as freedom of association and less forced labor.

The race-to-the-bottom hypothesis got it wrong because it neglected half of the cost-benefit analysis. If labor compensation (in the broad sense, including working conditions) were just a gift generously bestowed on workers, it would make economic sense to reduce it as much as possible, but in a competitive labor market, it is compensation for the job that someone is doing, and therefore there is a tight link between pay and productivity. Some workers might be twice as well paid as others, but that does not make them uncompetitive if they are also twice as productive.

This is not the only flaw in the race-to-the-bottom hypothesis. Foreign trade and investment do indeed find their way to the poorest countries sometimes, especially in sectors where low capital investment means that labor costs are an important factor, such as the production of garments and footwear. But in those instances, their main effect is to raise the level of productivity and to improve wages and working conditions.

These jobs might look bad to journalists and activists in rich countries, who are used to much higher standards, but they usually offer something much better for people in poorer countries. Compared with the alternatives in agriculture, services, and domestic manufacturing, these factories offer better pay and working conditions. In fact, when the World Bank writes about how the Cambodian economy could improve the quality of jobs, it offers a recommendation that seems completely counterintuitive to the critics in rich countries: "Use the same labor standards applied in the garment factories to other industries and sectors."[11]

The emergence of international supply chains has meant that multinational companies now consider suppliers in a poor country an integral part of their own business. Therefore, it is in their own commercial interest to spread the latest technology and business processes that they need to produce better and cheaper. In this way, many poor countries, such as China, India, Indonesia, and Vietnam, as well as more developed ones, such as Poland and Romania, have been able to skip several stages of development and have managed to grow at a fast pace. And once you have built factories, roads, and ports to manufacture and transport clothes and shoes, you can also use them to produce and export high-tech components.

This enables workers to produce more value, and therefore they receive better compensation.[12] Research consistently shows that manufacturing firms pay better than other firms, export firms pay higher wages than producers for the domestic market, and foreign-owned companies pay higher wages than comparable local companies—between 16 and 40 percent more in Africa, Asia, and Latin America. There is also a positive effect on wages in local businesses that participate in international supply chains.

Bangladesh is an illustration of this globalization success story. After having acquired outside know-how and machinery in the 1980s, local entrepreneurs quickly turned the country into a global powerhouse for textile manufacturing. Before 1980, the desperately poor country did not have any factories that produced textiles and garments for exports; today, the sector contributes more than 13 percent of GDP and 80 percent of exports. This has created millions of jobs, especially for women. The economy has grown rapidly, and according to the World Bank, extreme poverty has been reduced from over 40 percent in 1991 to less than 14 percent in 2016 (Figure 14.3).

As new businesses attract workers, old ones have to improve their offers to workers. In 2003, a Vietnamese factory owner outside Ho Chi Minh City told me that competition from factories producing for Nike has changed his perspective on the importance of labor standards:

FIGURE 14.3

As Bangladesh has traded more with the world, a greater share of its population has escaped poverty

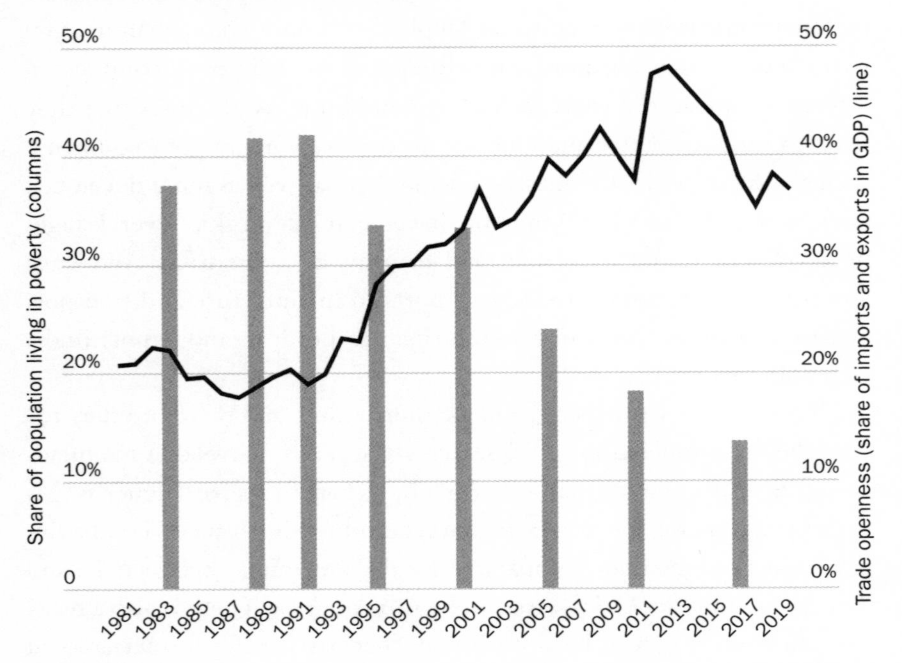

Source: "Trade Openness, 1959 to 2019," Our World in Data, November 28, 2022; and "Share of Population Living in Extreme Poverty, 1983 to 2016," Our World in Data, October 3, 2022.
Note: GDP = gross domestic product.

> The management of the Nike factory has understood how to make the employees satisfied. And I have seen that productivity comes not only from the machines, but also from the satisfaction of the workers. So when we now build a new factory, working conditions are one of the things we will concentrate on.

There are certainly instances of bad working standards even in companies producing for global markets, but there is "virtually no careful and systematic evidence demonstrating that, as a generality, multinational firms adversely affect their workers, provide incentives to worsen working conditions, pay lower wages than in alternative employment, or repress worker rights," according to Robert E. Baldwin and L. Alan Winters in the 2004 report *Challenges to Globalization: Analyzing the Economics*, who go on to say, "In fact, there is a very large body of empirical evidence indicating that the opposite is the case."[13]

As poor countries are integrated in international supply chains, there is also more pressure from Western consumers and watchdogs to root out abuse and bad working conditions. One example is the reaction after the deadly collapse in 2013 of Rana Plaza, an eight-story commercial building in Bangladesh that housed many garment factories producing for Western brands.[14] After the disaster, hundreds of American and European businesses signed two different initiatives that committed their local suppliers to safety inspections and improvements and provided funding for it. Safety committees were introduced as well as a mechanism whereby workers could raise concerns anonymously.

Since then, tens of thousands of factory inspections have taken place; electrical upgrades, fire alarm systems, fire doors, and sprinkler systems have been installed; and building foundations have been improved. Almost 200 factories that did not fulfill their commitments had lost their contracts by 2021.

In fact, even critics tend to agree that multinational companies have this effect. For example, in a book attacking global capitalism, Noreena Hertz admits that foreign corporations "usually pay higher wages and offer better working conditions than local corporations" and that they "often improve local conditions by exporting their own standards instead of adapting to local ones."[15]

Trade is also a remedy for child labor and helps to explain the declines shown in Figure 14.2. As parents get better jobs, they can afford to forgo their children's wages and instead invest in their education. One study found that a 10 percent increase in a country's economic openness is associated with a 7 percent decrease in child labor.[16] However, there is a surprising and important variation difference in effects depending on how regional trade agreements are designed. Agreements without social clauses that ban child labor increase school enrollment and reduce child labor, but perversely, trade agreements that ban child labor reduce school enrollment rates and *increase* child labor.[17] The explanation seems to be that a ban on child labor depresses child wages, so poor households who rely on their wages have to make up for it by putting more children to work more hours in the domestic and often informal economy. In other words, opening opportunities for lesser-skilled exports is a better way to combat child labor than bans.

Do We Trade Away the Planet?

At first look, the case for a possible race to the bottom when it comes to the environment is stronger. Competition forces businesses to compensate workers better when they get more productive opportunities, but there is no similar mechanism to increase the protection of a public good such as the environment, and if it entails costs for businesses, they might move elsewhere. Whether this is the case is an empirical question.

In an influential 2005 study, economists Jeffrey Frankel and Andrew Rose presented two important findings about trade and the environment.[18] One was the so-called Kuznets curve, which posits that many forms of environmental degradation look like an upside-down *U*. As countries urbanize and industrialize, the damage to nature and health increases rapidly, but at a certain point the curve reverses and increased incomes lead to environmental improvements. Therefore, because trade contributes to growth, it may initially harm the environment in low-income countries while improving it in middle- and high-income countries.

The idea of an environmental Kuznets curve is often dismissed in the debate because there is no automatic relationship between growth and the environment, and the relationship between economic growth and the environment differs depending on which environmental factor is considered, but the empirical relationship is now well established by researchers. After a certain point, richer populations start seeing the environment as more of a concern. They elect politicians who take the issue more seriously, and they acquire the economic resources and technological capabilities to develop and adopt greener technologies.

The Environmental Performance Index (EPI), by Yale University and partners, regularly ranks the ecological sustainability of 180

FIGURE 14.4
Wealthier countries tend to rank higher in ecological sustainability

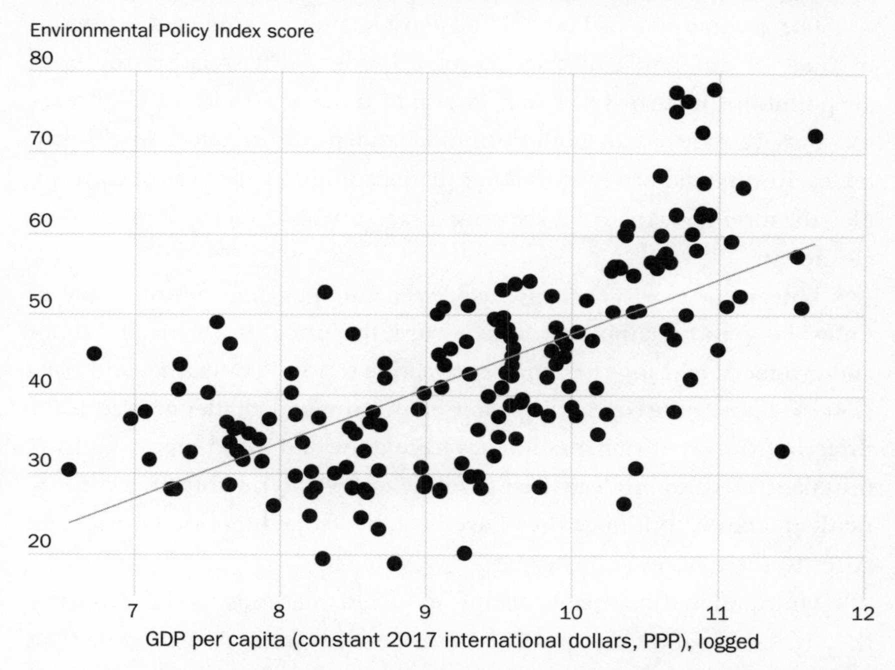

Source: "EPI 2022 Results," Environmental Performance Index, Yale Center for Environmental Law and Policy, 2022; and "GDP per Capita, PPP (Constant 2017 International $)," World Development Indicators, World Bank, updated May 10, 2023.
Note: GDP = gross domestic product; PPP = purchasing power parity.

countries.[19] It looks at 40 different performance indicators, including biological diversity and air pollution. The world's countries are very clearly grouped according to level of prosperity and region. High-income market-based democracies take all the top 30 places in the index, while the bottom is mainly made up of African countries and the poorest Asian countries.

The EPI's own conclusion is that "scores show a strong correlation with country wealth," although of course there are countries at every level of prosperity that perform better or worse (Figure 14.4).[20] The correlation is not automatic but has strong empirical support. Likewise, the OECD describes how its own measures of national environmental policy show "a significant positive correlation with GDP per capita, confirming that richer countries tend to have more stringent policies."[21]

The second part of Frankel and Rose's study looked at the amount of trade at different countries' income levels and its relationship with air pollution. It turned out that increased trade as a share of GDP correlates with reduced air pollution, independent of the effect wealth had on environmental progress. Rather than leading to a race to the bottom, globalization appears to be creating a race toward greener pastures and cleaner air.

This is primarily because trade encourages the transmission of know-how and technology. This lowers the price of greener methods and products, making them more attractive to local companies and consumers. Poor countries with greater environmental challenges can learn directly from what richer countries have done and avoid repeating their mistakes. Developing lead-free gasoline and catalytic converters is difficult and costly, but once they have been developed, poor countries can adapt to them faster and cheaper.

Multinational companies bring the latest methods to the countries they invest in, and these usually use less energy and raw materials than older ones. More trade can also create pressure to improve local environmental regulations, as consumers and organizations in rich countries demand responsibility throughout the supply chain.

The picture has been somewhat complicated by later studies of particular regulations. There are plenty of examples of rapidly increasing restrictions on emissions harming industries and benefiting competitors in poorer countries with less protection. The consequence is that wealthy countries import back some of that pollution from other countries. This means there is a certain leakage when we impose higher costs.

However, the notion that countries would dismantle their environmental protection to attract investors is not correct. On the contrary, national environmental measures are tightened globally as countries get richer, albeit at different rates. Remarkably, according to the OECD's measures, average environmental protection is now stronger in the BRIICS countries (Brazil, Russia, India, Indonesia, China, and South

Africa) than it was in Sweden, the United Kingdom, the United States, and almost all other rich countries in 1995.[22]

Is CO_2 an Exception?

Frankel and Rose's study did, however, show that one form of emissions had not decreased with increased prosperity; on the contrary, it continued to increase: carbon dioxide. Nor were the authors hopeful that it would decline, since these emissions mostly affected people in other places, giving less incentives to limit them. The major change since their results were published is that something is happening even in this case.

Since 2010, more than 40 countries have reduced their carbon dioxide emissions in absolute terms while also growing their economies (Figure 14.5). These are mostly the very richest countries, which indicates that there is a Kuznets curve even for CO_2 emissions, although with the characteristic that it turns downward at a significantly higher level than for other emissions. This curve begins to slope downward earlier in more economically free countries.[23]

As we get richer, we develop more energy-efficient products and processes and turn more goods into ones and zeros in digital systems.[24] In the world as a whole, the energy required to produce one unit of GDP fell by 36 percent between 1990 and 2020. Low- and middle-income countries have made an even faster journey because they have been able to move quickly from old, dirty technology to the very latest, which they imported. China's energy intensity fell by a whopping 72 percent during this period.

Furthermore, an ever-smaller part of this energy production requires fossil fuels when, for example, the price of solar power plummets.[25] From 2009 to 2019, the price of electricity from onshore wind fell by 70 percent and unsubsidized solar by an incredible 89 percent. This was made possible thanks to economies of scale. Innovation makes panels more efficient, large factories turn complicated processes into routine manufacturing, and more-efficient mining operations and processing of raw materials make inputs cheaper.

FIGURE 14.5

Many countries have decoupled economic growth from carbon dioxide (CO_2) emissions

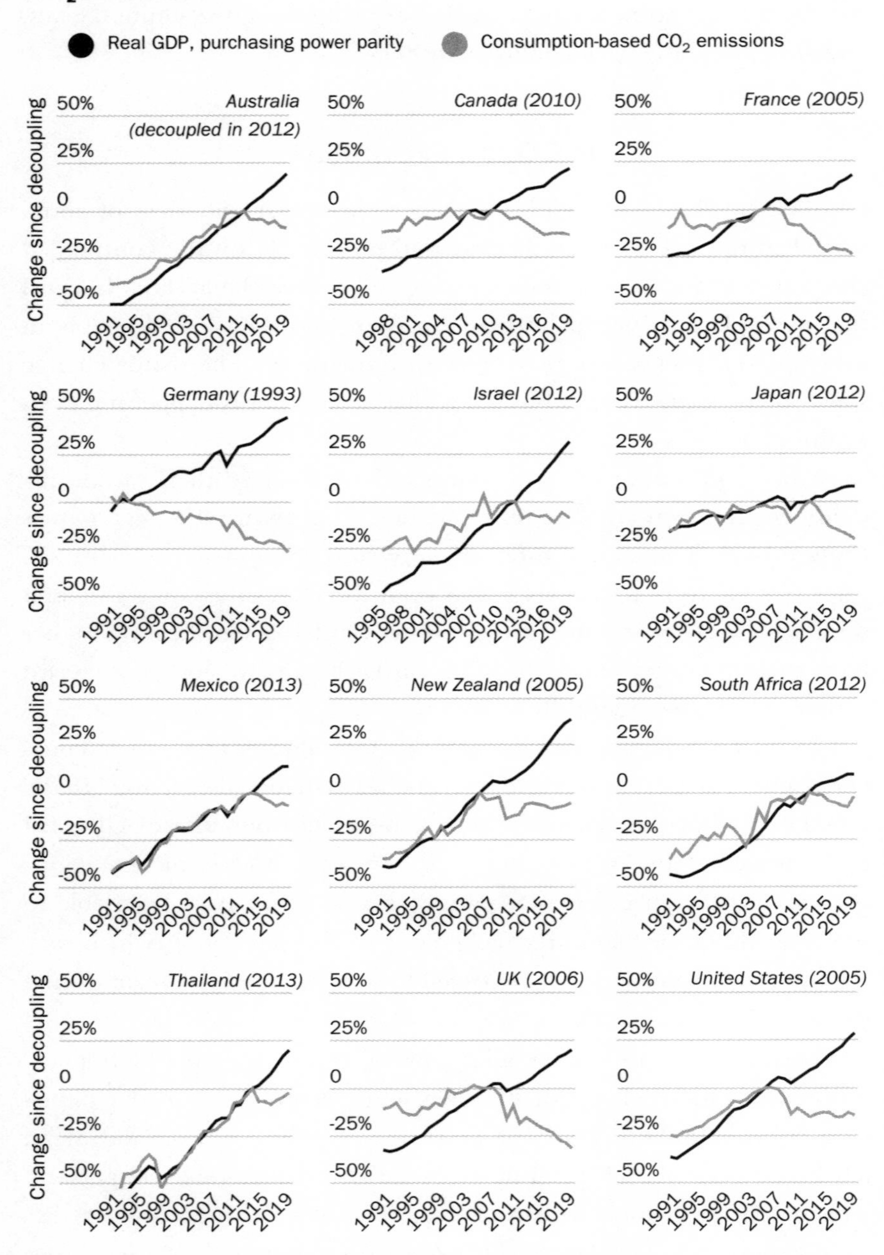

Source: "Change in CO_2 Emissions and GDP," Our World in Data, updated April 28, 2023.
Note: CO_2 = carbon dioxide; GDP = gross domestic product. CO_2 emissions adjusted to account for trade. The year of decoupling noted for each country in parentheses is the year from which a steady increase in GDP and a steady decline in CO_2 emissions are observed.

Such huge investments can only be profitable if the producers have access to the combined purchasing power of many foreign markets. It would, for example, be completely pointless to develop technologies for fossil-free steel in a country as small as Sweden, for 10 million consumers, if the end result could not be exported to the rest of the world.

The combination of increasing wealth, the spread of technology, and economies of scale clearly make open economies a force for higher environmental standards. In fact, the team behind the EPI explored how its results compared with broad measures of economic liberalism (including property rights, free enterprise, and free trade):

> We find that economic liberalism is positively associated with environmental performance. While our results do not give countries carte blanche to pursue laissez-faire economic strategies without regard for the environment, they do cast doubt on the implicit tension between economic development and environmental protection.[26]

Researchers disagree about why this is the case. Some think it can be explained exclusively by the fact that free markets increase GDP per capita, while others find an additional pro-environment effect of free markets independent of wealth.[27] However, the exact channel is not important for our purposes here. Each of these possibilities would be a decisive stroke against the race-to-the-bottom hypothesis, which posits market liberalization as the problem when in fact it is the solution.

Conclusion

The race to the bottom is a myth. Wages and working standards have not deteriorated in the era of globalization but improved, and they have done so the most in countries that have integrated the most into the global economy. Companies and investors are not searching for the poorest places to do business but instead invest mostly in relatively wealthy countries. More importantly, when they do invest in poor countries, their main effect is to raise productivity and compensation. If this is exploitation, the only thing that's worse than being exploited is not being exploited.

Also, there is no race to the bottom in environmental standards. Rich countries do not imitate the environmental standards of poor ones; instead, poor countries are catching up with rich ones in environmental sustainability. The richer countries are, the more they protect their environment; and free markets also speed up the transition to new and greener technologies around the world. As long as markets are open and trade is free, there is no race to the bottom; rather, there is an encouraging race to the top.

Chapter 15

Globalization and Growing Global Equality

Chelsea Follett

- There is a widespread but mistaken belief that global inequality is increasing, with the alleged increase often blamed on globalization, and this belief has potentially harmful policy consequences.
- The data on a variety of metrics—including income inequality, education inequality, and more—unambiguously show a decline in global inequality.
- Globalization and market liberalization over the past few decades have not only raised absolute living standards but have also reduced overall inequality.

An ascendant narrative claims that globalization-driven improvements in the standard of living have unfairly accrued to only a small elite, leaving much of the world's population no better or worse off in deteriorating circumstances. The facts say otherwise.

Indeed, recent decades have seen people around the world experience dramatic improvements in well-being across a broad range of indicators. Despite setbacks amid the disruptions of the COVID-19 pandemic, the long-term trends are positive across a host of key metrics, including average income, life expectancy, rates of educational attainment, and internet access. Data from respected scholars, academic institutions, and international organizations provide evidence of remarkable long-term improvements in living standards, especially over the past two centuries. Progress in the past few decades has been particularly pronounced in less developed countries.

Progress does not, of course, materialize at random and without a cause. Many economists attribute the extraordinary increase in human development, at least in part, to the revolution in international connectivity that has defined modern globalization. Indeed, the role of trade, and associated specialization, in creating economic growth and prosperity cannot be overemphasized. By liberalizing economic cooperation and exchange across borders, the expansion of global markets has helped produce the innovations and prosperity underlying many gains, as recorded on websites such as Our World in Data, Gapminder, and Human Progress.

But have those gains been widely shared? Have the benefits of globalization-driven economic growth reached people in different countries "equally"? Put simply, is the world becoming more equal?

As this essay will detail, the answer to these questions is an unequivocal "yes."

Misapprehensions of Inequality and Their Policy Consequences

Policy professionals, commentators, journalists, and the public have shown increasing interest in global inequality, the direction in which it is headed, and potential policy responses. According to Harvard University psychologist Steven Pinker, the share of *New York Times* articles mentioning "inequality" increased tenfold between 2009 and 2016.[1] In addition, Google Books' Ngram Viewer shows a clear rise in the frequency with which the word "inequality" appears in English-language print sources within Google's text corpora, starting around 1955 and continuing through 2019, the most recent year for which data are available (see Figure 15.1).[2]

Headlines in major publications spotlighting the topic of worldwide inequality abound; some representative examples are "It's an Unequal

FIGURE 15.1
Use of the word "inequality" in print sources has risen dramatically

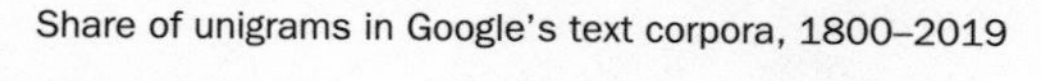

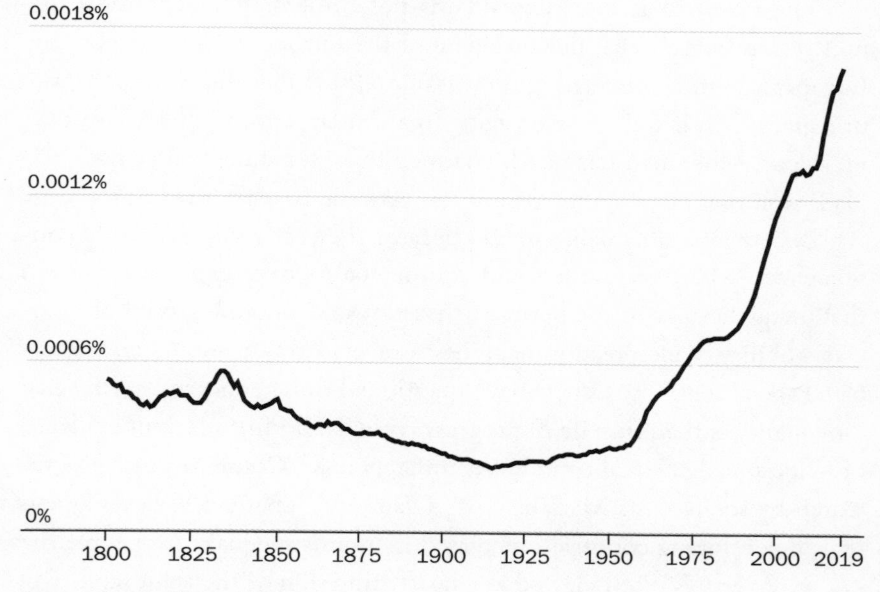

Source: Google Ngram Viewer.
Note: In this context, unigrams are single words. Print sources are in English within Google's text corpora.

World. It Doesn't Have to Be"; "Global Interpersonal Inequality through the Crisis Period"; "How Can We Bridge the Widening Global Inequality Gap?"; "Climate Change Has Already Increased Global Inequality. It Will Only Get Worse"; "The Deep Roots of Global Inequality"; "'Perfect Storm' of Crises Is Widening Global Inequality, Says UN Chief"; and "Global Inequality Is Rising Again."[3] These and other pieces in major publications feature diverse political perspectives on inequality but share a focus on global inequality as a timely topic of discussion.

The growing focus on inequality is surely connected to the spreading belief that inequality—among individuals in a single country or among people in different countries—itself is increasing. During his inauguration speech in 2020, US president Joe Biden mentioned "growing inequity," and US vice president Kamala Harris claimed at the 2021 Paris Peace Forum that the world has seen "a dramatic rise in inequality" and that leaders "must rise to meet this moment."[4]

The belief in rising inequality is not limited to US political figures. Josep Borrell, the vice president of the European Commission, the European Union's governing body, said in 2023 that the world is "more unequal" than it was 75 years ago.[5] In a similar vein, in 2022, Guyana's president, Mohamed Irfaan Ali, claimed that global inequality had "tripled" and that developing economies were the hardest hit.[6]

Beliefs about inequality matter because they can have real-world consequences. Many researchers and commentators have expressed concern that inequality may cause harms such as slower economic growth, less social mobility, widespread unhappiness, societal stratification, and exacerbated social tensions. Others have questioned those concerns, saying that "inequality is the midwife of progress" or even noting a lack of evidence of widespread inequality-induced unhappiness.[7] Counterintuitively, research by sociologists Mariah D. R. Evans and Jonathan Kelley suggests that in developing countries, increased economic inequality as people rise out of poverty is often viewed as a heartening sign of the achievability of upward mobility and thus often coincides with greater happiness.[8]

Regardless of whether—and to what extent—fears about inequality's potential harms are justified, such concerns, combined with the belief that worldwide inequality is on the rise, have inspired several policy proposals. Some of the more extreme proposals would entail unprecedented levels of mandated wealth redistribution.

A 2023 Oxfam report titled *Survival of the Richest*, addressing purported "rising global inequality," calls for a 5 percent tax on the world's multimillionaires.[9] Oxfam has also proposed government action "taking on monopoly power" and "boosting workers' rights," as well as major tax increases on income and wealth to fight what Nabil Ahmed, Oxfam America's director of economic justice, calls the world's "explosion of inequality."[10] "Taxing the richest will start to claw back their power and reduce not only economic inequality but racial, gender and colonial inequalities, too," opined Oxfam International's executive director Gabriela Bucher at the World Economic Forum's 2023 meeting in Davos.[11]

More than 200 millionaires, including entertainment-empire heiress Abigail Disney and actor Mark Ruffalo, similarly called on 2023's Davos attendees to "tackle extreme wealth" and "tax the ultra-rich" to promote the "common good" and counter "widening wealth inequality."[12]

The 2018 World Inequality Report, produced by French economist Thomas Piketty among others, claimed that "at the global level, inequality has risen sharply since 1980" and proposed various policies to remedy this supposed rise.[13] The suggested policy responses include higher taxes for the rich, implementation or increases in inheritance taxes (sometimes called "death taxes," although that term can also refer to estate taxes), and establishment of a global registry of financial asset ownership, eliminating financial privacy.[14]

All policies come with tradeoffs. Thus, many of the costly, far-reaching, and even unprecedented policies put forward to address the ostensible surge in global inequality will likely have countless unintended effects if enacted. Many of the proposed policies risk increasing bureaucracy, impeding economic growth, slowing poverty's global decline, decreasing the rate of innovation and technological progress, and infringing on privacy, among other deleterious effects. Moreover, a cool-headed assessment of gaps in global well-being shows that such policies would be based on a misapprehension. The popular narrative of rising inequality is mistaken. Rather than exacerbate inequality among the world's people, globalization has helped decrease gaps in well-being.

Beyond Income Inequality

While not as widely known as it should be, the fact that international income inequality has decreased since at least the mid-2000s has not gone unnoticed.[15] Branko Milanović, an inequality expert and former lead economist in the World Bank's research department, contends that population-weighted global intercountry income inequality has plummeted since 1980 (see Figure 15.2). Milanović's recent research has updated his popular but often misinterpreted "elephant chart"—which famously seemed to show the global poor, people in developing countries, and the wealthy reaping the benefits of globalization while the

FIGURE 15.2

Global intercountry income inequality declined significantly between 1952 and 2017

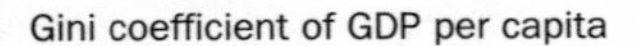

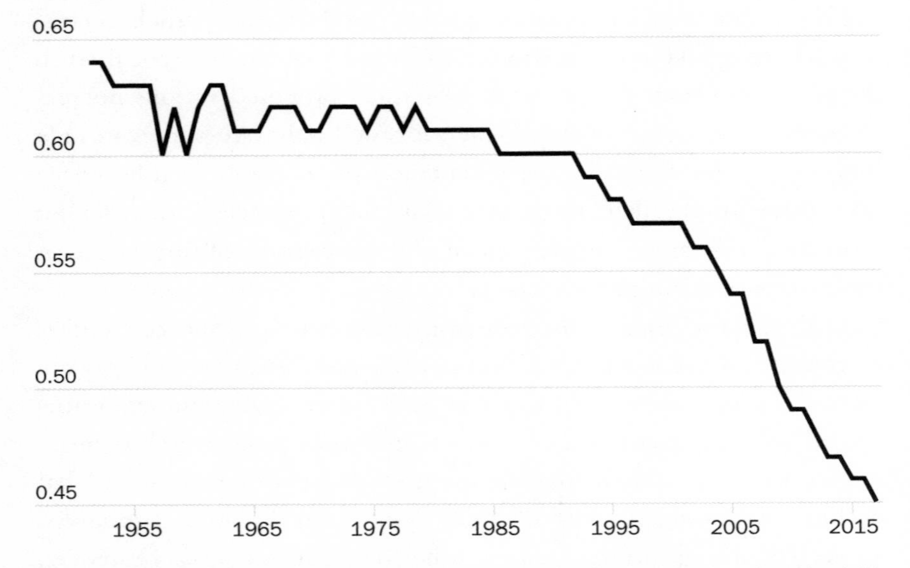

Source: Branko Milanović via Marian L. Tupy, personal communication with author, March 31, 2023.

Note: GDP = gross domestic product; Gini coefficient of GDP per capita among countries, weighted according to population.

middle class in rich countries lost out. His newer research suggests that the poor and middle class have made gains faster than the rich, revealing what the *Financial Times* economics editor Chris Giles calls a "link between trade integration and falling global inequality."[16] In fact, even Piketty's much-criticized calculations showed a decline in global income inequality over the long term.[17]

Domestic income inequality has similarly decreased. Economist John F. Early has found that income inequality in the United States has been falling for the past 70 years—yet official US statistics often do not fully account for the effects of important factors (such as transfer payments, income taxes, and inflation) and thus overstate the level of inequality by a factor of four, further distorting public perceptions.[18]

And while public opinion often blames domestic income inequality on globalization, even scholars who believe contra Early that US income inequality is increasing often question that simplistic causal narrative. Harvard University economist Elhanan Helpman contends that globalization cannot account for more than a small portion of US income inequality.[19]

Zooming out to a global view once again, *wealth* inequality has also fallen: the share of global wealth held by the top 10 percent decreased from 88.7 percent in 2000 to 81.8 percent in 2020, according to Credit Suisse.[20] Accordingly, the share of global wealth held by the bottom 90 percent has grown from 11.3 percent in 2000 to 18.2 percent in 2020.

Global gains in equality become even stronger when one considers how the distribution of well-being has changed across a broader array of indicators.[21] I explore these trends in a recent research paper, "Global Inequality in Well-Being Has Decreased across Many Dimensions," coauthored with George Mason University economist Vincent Geloso.[22] Our paper introduces the Inequality of Human Progress Index (IHPI) as a new way of measuring relative gaps in global development. The index was inspired by, and builds on, economist Leandro Prados de la Escosura's pioneering augmented human development index for assessing global inequality but captures a wider array of indicators.[23] In fact, the IHPI surveys worldwide inequality across more dimensions than any prior index of international development.

By analyzing inequality in a multidimensional way, the IHPI captures a fuller picture of international disparities and, in fact, takes the experience of inequality more seriously than do assessments based on income inequality alone.

As momentous as the global decline in income inequality is, measuring inequality beyond income differences is a more direct, comprehensive, and most important, accurate way to measure differences in well-being. As my coauthor and I point out:

> Inequality, in short, is multidimensional rather than purely monetary. It makes more sense to think about inequality in overall well-being rather than myopically focusing on income inequality, because income is only one (though admittedly very important) aspect of well-being. And as the economist P. T. Bauer famously noted, the death of a child

> raises a household's per capita income—a poignant reminder that income and well-being are not the same. Looking beyond the imperfect proxy of income to directly examine the constituent elements of well-being [that money often helps to purchase] avoids such contradictions. [Monetary income is ultimately an imperfect proxy for access to the things that add up to a high quality of life.[24]]

Moreover, as global development has raised incomes internationally and enlarged the share of humanity that can be classified as middle class or above, this enrichment has opened many paths to happiness beyond income maximization. In a subsistence society, income is a decent proxy for well-being because, in situations of dire poverty, income is often the difference between survival and starvation. However, in rich countries today, many people choose careers that do not maximize income potential but offer other benefits, such as the flexibility to spend more time with family and friends, a sense of purpose related to the mission of one's employing organization, one's prestige, or one's feeling of creative or intellectual fulfillment. Therefore, as Geloso and I note, "economic development foils the relevance of income as a proxy for well-being."[25] As global gross domestic product (GDP) grows and more people rise from subsistence-level poverty, it is less and less accurate to claim that income fully speaks to living standards, and it is increasingly urgent to emphasize a richer conception of living standards.

The IHPI thus considers material well-being, or income, and seven additional metrics: lifespan, infant mortality, adequate nutrition, environmental safety, access to opportunity (as approximated by education), access to information, and political freedom. Across all but two of these dimensions, the world has become more equal since 1990.

A New Way of Measuring Global Inequality

To understand the global distribution of well-being, my coauthor and I first needed to construct a measure of well-being. The result is the Human Progress Index (HPI). Like the United Nations (UN) Human Development Index (HDI), the HPI measures different aspects of human development on an easily understood scale, from 0 to 1, where higher values reflect greater well-being than lower values. As with the HDI, all index components in the HPI are given equal weight. The primary difference between the two indexes is that the HPI's view of well-being is more comprehensive.[26]

Generally, the HDI employs three components: life expectancy at birth (adjusted or unadjusted for disabilities), schooling (generally in mean years of schooling), and income. The HPI considers those components and adds political freedom, adequate nutrition, infant mortality, environmental quality, and internet access. All chosen indicators can be tracked continuously since 1990 across 142 countries.

Specifically, the HPI components are life expectancy at birth, in years (as measured by the World Bank); the infant mortality rate per 1,000 live births (as measured by the World Bank); food supply per person per day (as measured by the UN Food and Agriculture Organization); outdoor air pollution death rates (as measured by Our World in Data); mean years of schooling (based on data from Barro and Lee); internet users per 100 people (as measured by the UN and Our World in Data); GDP per person (as measured by the Maddison Project Database, 2020 edition); and democracy versus autocracy over time, on a scale of 0 to 40 (as measured by a rescaled version of the Polity5 database).[27]

The HPI confirms that over the past few decades, global human development has been significant. Figure 15.3 displays index measures with several different specifications: unweighted; weighted for global population; unweighted and excluding the internet access component; and weighted for population *and* excluding the internet access component. Including or excluding the internet component greatly changes the extent of progress that the index shows, given internet access's rarity in 1990 and its prevalence today. Excluding the internet access component, the improvement in HPI is between 35.9 percent (population weighted) and 41.8 percent (not weighted for population). With internet access included, the improvements in the HPI are between 415 and 509 percent. Put simply, this means that there has been an almost unfathomable improvement in equality of access to information, and in overall equality. While some may contend that including internet access skews the

FIGURE 15.3

Human Progress Index (HPI) shows improvements in global well-being since 1990, weighted for population, with and without internet

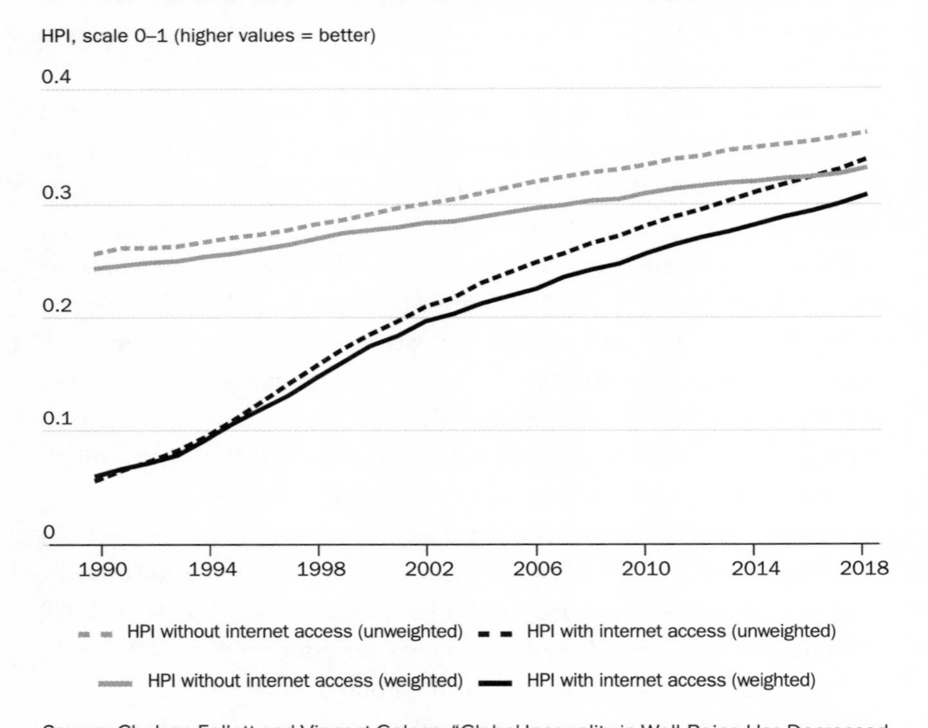

Source: Chelsea Follett and Vincent Geloso, "Global Inequality in Well-Being Has Decreased across Many Dimensions," Cato Institute Policy Analysis no. 949, June 8, 2023.
Note: The HPI measures different dimensions of human development on a scale from 0 to 1, where higher values are better than lower values. All index components are given equal weight.

results, the life-changing nature of the internet is worth capturing when measuring human progress.

Importantly, *all* variants of the HPI suggest larger improvements in human well-being than do either the UN's Human Development Reports, which report HDI, or the estimates from Prados de la Escosura's augmented index. But have those gains been widely shared, or have they accrued to a small elite as many globalization skeptics contend?

Calculating inequality within the HPI resulted in the IHPI. Because of a lack of detailed distribution data for many countries on key metrics, my coauthor and I examined global interpersonal inequality rather than within-country inequality.

To gauge the extent of inequality among people around the world, we applied two different measures of inequality to the HPI. Once again, we considered, for each measure, both an unweighted variant that treats each country equally (to capture intercountry inequality) and a variant weighted for each country's population (to approximate global interpersonal inequality). For each variant, we considered variations including internet access and excluding internet access, due to the large effect of that index component.

The two distinct measures that we have chosen are the mean log deviation (MLD) and the Gini coefficient. Both are ways to assess inequality among the values in a distribution, and both represent a situation of perfect equality as a value of zero (i.e., in a world where everyone has the same income, both the MLD and the Gini coefficient of income inequality are zero). The Gini coefficient represents maximal inequality as a value of one, whereas the MLD takes on larger positive values as incomes become more unequal. The measures are very similar and are commonly used by social scientists. The trends in inequality that we found were very similar for both measures.

Global Inequality Has Declined

Under a variety of specifications, the data unambiguously show a decline in global inequality. Irrespective of population weighting or the type of measure used (i.e., the Gini coefficient or the MLD), the data reveal an initial increase in inequality in the 1990s (driven by the rapid but unequal increase in internet access), followed by a significant overall global decline in inequality. When we excluded the internet access component, the index showed a continuous decline in inequality since 1990. These trends were almost exactly the same whether inequality was measured using the Gini coefficient, as in Figure 15.4, or the MLD, as in Figure 15.5.

An examination of the individual components of the index also reveals considerable progress toward worldwide equality in living standards, as

FIGURE 15.4

Global inequality declined in Human Progress Index, as measured by the Gini coefficient and without population weights

Gini coefficient, scale 0 (perfect equality) to 1 (maximal inequality), 1990–2018

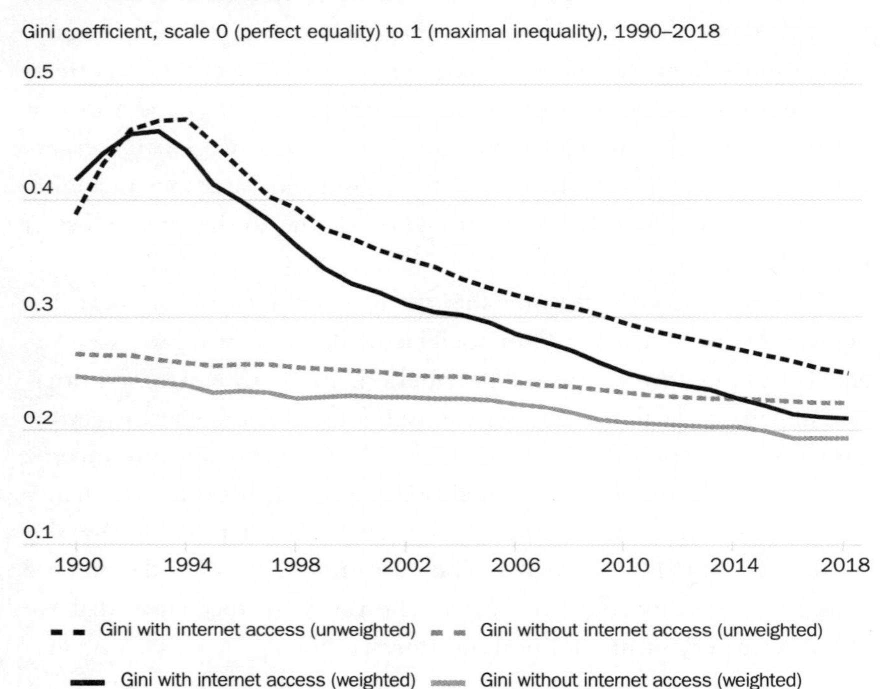

Source: Chelsea Follett and Vincent Geloso, "Global Inequality in Well-Being Has Decreased across Many Dimensions," Cato Institute Policy Analysis no. 949, June 8, 2023.

shown in Figure 15.6 and Figure 15.7. Global equality has continuously improved since 1990 for life expectancy, internet access, and education. Equality in enjoyment of political liberty has improved almost continuously since 1990, with a small decrease in equality in recent years. That recent slight reversal does not negate the long-term trend of increasingly widespread access to political liberty. Globally, incomes became more unequal until the mid-2000s, but income inequality has declined since then. For adequate nutrition, the trend line has been somewhat rocky, with a turn toward greater inequality in the early to mid-2000s. Nonetheless, the long-term trend has been one of considerable growth

FIGURE 15.5

Global inequality declined in Human Progress Index, as measured by the mean log deviation (MLD) and without population weights

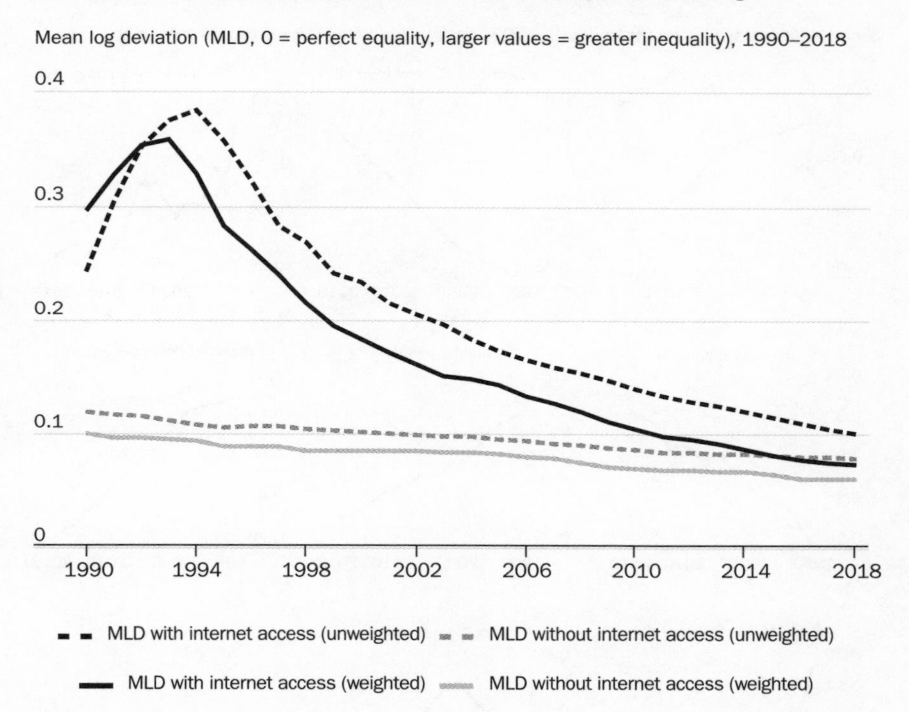

Source: Chelsea Follett and Vincent Geloso, "Global Inequality in Well-Being Has Decreased across Many Dimensions," Cato Institute Policy Analysis no. 949, June 8, 2023.

in nutritional equality, as access to an adequate diet becomes more common around the world.

There are, of course, exceptions to every rule. Thus, two indicators within the index display trends toward more inequality. As Geloso and I explain:

> This is the case for infant mortality and mortality from outdoor air pollution. With regards to the latter, this may be the result of the working of the environmental Kuznets Curve that stipulates that pollution increases with economic growth until a critical point is reached,

FIGURE 15.6

Inequality has declined in many areas, as measured by the Gini coefficient

Gini coefficient weighted for population (0 = perfect equality, 1 = maximum inequality)

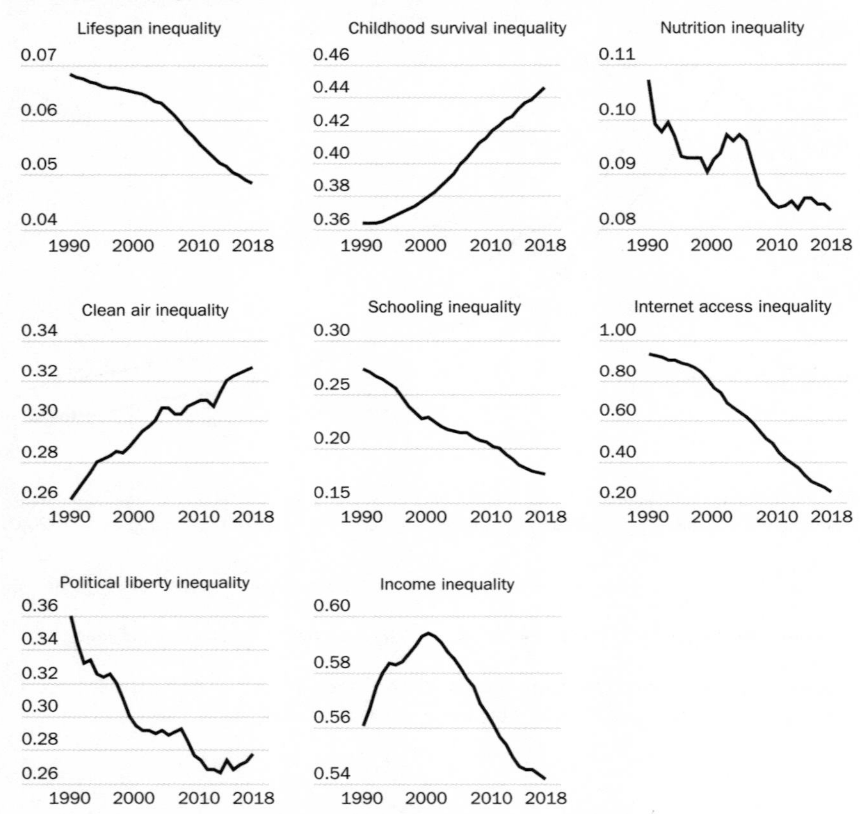

Source: Chelsea Follett and Vincent Geloso, "Global Inequality in Well-Being Has Decreased across Many Dimensions," Cato Institute Policy Analysis no. 949, June 8, 2023.

after which pollution starts to fall. In our case, the rising inequality in outdoor air pollution may reflect the fact that some countries are undergoing this transition. As for infant mortality, this may have to do with the fact that child mortality has not fallen faster (proportionally) in low-income countries than in high-income countries since 1990. To be sure, infant mortality has fallen globally in absolute terms. Improvements since 1990 seem to have simply happened proportionally faster in high-income countries. The latter have access to the latest medical

FIGURE 15.7

Inequality has declined in many areas, as measured by the mean log deviation

Mean log deviaton weighted for population (0 = perfect equality, larger values = greater inequality)

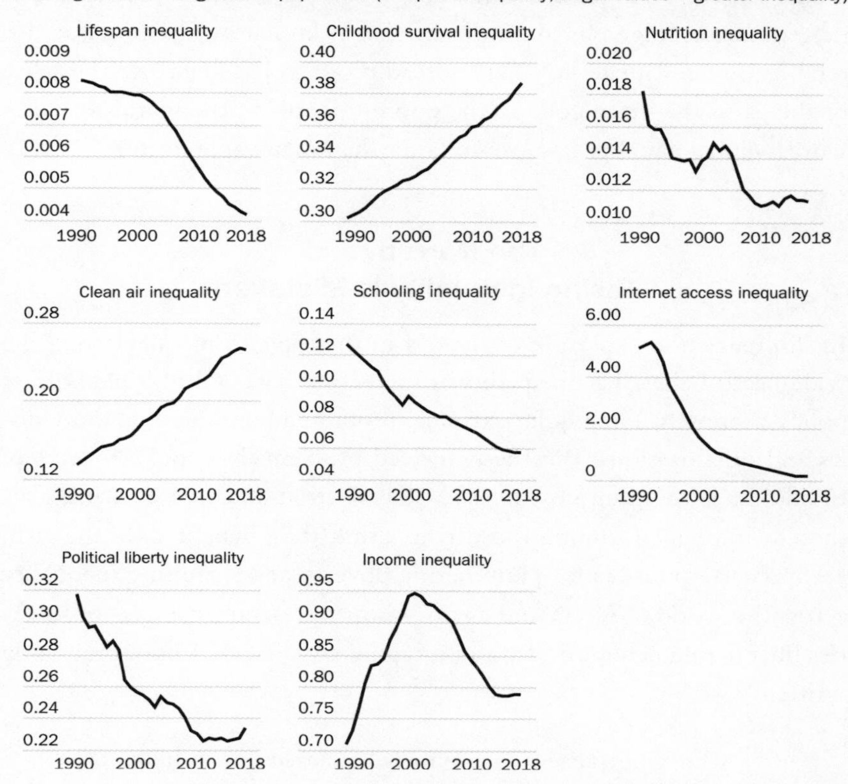

Source: Chelsea Follett and Vincent Geloso, "Global Inequality in Well-Being Has Decreased across Many Dimensions," Cato Institute Policy Analysis no. 949, June 8, 2023.

technology, such as state-of-the-art neonatal intensive care units that improve survival chances for premature infants, and thus global inequality may have failed to decline across this dimension post-1990.[28]

As explained more fully by Johan Norberg, developed countries' substantial improvements in environmental quality indicate that developing countries will very likely experience similar gains as they get richer (see Chapter 14, "Globalization: A Race to the Bottom—or to the Top?").

Just as importantly, *overall* inequality is down. In fact, when compared with inequality trends in the HDI and Prados de la Escosura's augmented index, the IHPI shows a greater degree of improvement toward global equality. This result suggests that the older indexes not only underestimate average global improvements in human well-being but also tend to underestimate how widespread progress has been and the share of the gains that have gone to the poorest people in the world. In other words, global equality has grown faster than many appreciate.

The Narrative of Rising Inequality Is Mistaken

In summary, the explosion of interest in the topic of inequality and the widespread belief that inequality is increasing have led to a plethora of policy proposals, some quite extreme, promoted by influential individuals and organizations. But the perceived problem these policies attempt to address is trending downward. Globalization and free exchange, although unpopular among those who think they benefit only the rich, are in fact responsible for plummeting poverty and shrinking inequality across the world.[29] Again and again, history presents examples of societies liberalizing economically and escaping poverty. As I have previously written:

> After China liberalized its economy, hundreds of millions of its people escaped extreme poverty. Once India moved toward economic freedom in the early 1990s, its population saw a remarkable decline in poverty as well . . . In contrast, no country has ever become rich through foreign aid, which is plagued by many problems.[30]

As the lives of people in distant countries become ever more linked through commerce, the benefits from globalization touch the lives of the poorest the most, because they have the most to gain. The economic growth and opportunities presented by international commerce have allowed countless individuals to break free from subsistence poverty, improve their lives, and move into the growing global middle class through mutually beneficial exchange.

There is an unfortunate, pervasive tendency to underestimate improvements in global well-being. For example, when polled, a majority of Americans and others living in advanced economies said that the share of the world population living in poverty was increasing, despite the dramatic, long-term, and well-documented trend of *declining* global poverty.[31] Since the polling occurred before the pandemic, one cannot attribute this response to the slight recent uptick in poverty due to pandemic-related disruptions. Not only are public perceptions often inaccurate when it comes to whether living standards are improving, but there is also a widespread tendency to underestimate how widely shared these global improvements are. The construction of the IHPI pushes back against such misperceptions and clarifies the impressive extent of the rise in global equality.

Because the IHPI comprises a larger number of dimensions than the HDI and uses an innovative methodology to properly capture improvements, it provides a richer measure of well-being—or human progress—than the HDI or, in fact, any prior development index. The IHPI shows that improvements have been both greater than is commonly appreciated and more dispersed—not accruing only to a small elite. Moreover, the IHPI's assessment of inequality in terms of human progress is a more meaningful gauge of well-being than are assessments based on inequality of income alone. The IHPI's greater number of dimensions directly measure many aspects of a good life that money may help to purchase. Furthermore, unlike examinations that focus on income alone, the IHPI is able to capture the many additional paths that individuals in rich societies can take to satisfaction, beyond single-minded income maximization. As a result, the IHPI takes the experience of inequality more seriously than do those that measure income inequality alone and provides a more meaningful understanding of the global distribution of well-being and progress.

It seems that globalization and market liberalization over the past few decades have both raised absolute living standards and reduced overall inequality. The IHPI adds to a growing body of knowledge that makes clear that the world is not only better off than many people realize but that the world is also becoming far more equal.

Chapter 16

The Conservative Case for Globalization

Jeb Hensarling

- Free trade is consistent with conservatism's historical and intellectual roots, including the writings of Edmund Burke, Adam Smith, and the Founding Fathers. American conservatism has long advocated economic freedom, of which free trade is a vital component.
- National security–based arguments for trade restrictions are almost always disguised protectionism. Conversely, open trade helps strengthen national security.
- Conservatives have long believed that families and communities are integral parts of a free and prosperous society. Free trade complements both.
- Free trade policies help the working class and domestic manufacturers. Protectionism empowers government bureaucrats and enriches well-connected lobbyists.
- Ultimately, free trade is merely an extension of human freedom more broadly.

A number of years ago *Saturday Night Live* featured a skit of a fictional game show asking contestants to compare two celebrities with this question: "¿Quién es más macho?," or "Who is the manliest?" The late Ricardo Montalbán fared well. Today within the Republican Party and the broader conservative movement, the popular question is now, "Who is the most conservative?"

Many self-styled conservative talking heads and members of Congress are calling for industrial policy, forms of wage and price controls, and new federal agencies to police free speech. Such positions have historically been anathema to the conservative movement and should remain so. Along with these issues, there is likely no other issue more timely or relevant to the question of just who is—and what is—a conservative than the issue of globalized free trade.

History

To settle the question of who may legitimately claim the title of "conservative" today, a quick reminder of the movement's origins and evolution and their relation to trade is helpful. Although admittedly there is no universally held definition of conservatism, there have been broadly recognized and accepted core principles, as well as a proud historical lineage. The English parliamentarian and philosopher Edmund Burke is generally recognized as the father of conservatism. Burke, throughout his career, advocated for freer trade. He understood that trade is not a zero-sum game between countries. In supporting reduced trade barriers between Britain and Ireland, Burke argued, "The prosperity which arises from an enlarged and liberal system improves all of its objects; and the participation of trade with flourishing Countries is much better than a monopoly of want and penury."[1]

His arguments included those based on economic utilitarian grounds. For example, he argued in Parliament that a free market without government interference is the best method to help the poor. As conservatives today continue to fight the rise of the social welfare state, they have historically recognized, as did Burke, that cost-increasing protectionism simply creates greater welfare dependency, not less.

Burke's more impassioned and important argument, however, rested upon a recognition and reliance on natural rights (conservatives should think, "We hold these truths to be self-evident"). Burke believed that these rights clearly entitled and protected an individual's right to both own property and trade it freely.

For decades, most conservatives have proudly viewed themselves as free-market conservatives, a moniker whose principled intellectual foundation rests upon Adam Smith's classic work *An Inquiry into the Nature and Causes of the Wealth of Nations*. Noteworthily, Smith was a friend and contemporary of Burke. Smith skewered the prevailing mercantilist and protectionist policies of the day and argued on utilitarian grounds that freedom of trade across international borders benefited the masses. He wrote, "Trade which, without force or constraint, is naturally and regularly carried on between any two places is always advantageous."[2] Some modern-day conservatives have now begun relying on the limited exceptions to the free trade rule (e.g., national defense) that Smith enumerated in his work to justify their protectionism. But any plausible reading of Smith indicates that these exceptions are just that—exceptions—which he further explained were rarely justified and often subject to abuse.[3]

Today, one of the greatest accolades within the conservative movement is that of "constitutional conservative," a term meant to convey fealty to the Founding principles contained within the Declaration of Independence and US Constitution. Any conservative would be well advised to carefully reread the Declaration's list of the repeated "injuries and usurpations" of the Crown, which evidenced its tyranny and justified American independence. The list includes "cutting off our Trade with all parts of the World." Thomas Paine, author of *Common Sense*, the most influential pamphlet of the Revolutionary era, wrote that to a trading country, freedom of trade was "of such importance, that the principal source of wealth depends on it; and it is impossible that any country can flourish . . . whose commerce is . . . fettered by laws of another. . . . A freedom from the restraints of the Acts of Navigation I foresee will produce . . . immense additions to the wealth of this country."[4]

In addition to Paine, most Founders believed in the goal of free trade and viewed it as necessary for the prosperity of the republic.[5] They believed the principal and proper use of tariffs should be limited to revenue raising, not protecting domestic industries. In fact, at the dawn of our republic and for more than a century thereafter, the bulk of tax revenues were derived from import duties, given their relative ease of collection, as Phil Magness lays out in his essay on the history of tariffs in the United States between 1787 and 1934 (see Chapter 2, "The Problem of the Tariff in American Economic History, 1787–1934"). The other recognized legitimate use of tariffs was to incentivize other nations to open their borders to our trade. These purposes are in distinct contrast to the purposes proposed by many today who seek to engage in industrial policy that benefits discrete economic sectors or industries or that promotes economic nationalism designed to severely limit or close off our international trade.

Article I, Section 8, of the Constitution unequivocally gives Congress the power to both "regulate Commerce with foreign Nations" and to "lay and collect Taxes, Duties."[6] Because of this section, some argue that conservatives stand on firm constitutional ground in favoring the imposition of tariffs. It should be noted that Section 8 also empowers Congress to borrow money. Given the magnitude and dangerous trajectory of the national debt, few conservatives believe the exercise of such power a wise one. The same is true for the imposition of tariffs.

Finally, the most conservative leader of the 20th century, President Ronald Reagan, confidently proclaimed that in America, "Our trade policy rests firmly on the foundation of free and open markets."[7] Although Reagan did implement some protectionist measures, they were part of his broader efforts to stave off even worse protectionism from Congress and to push for broader liberalization through the US-Canada Free Trade Agreement (the North American Free Trade Agreement's [NAFTA's] predecessor) and the US-Israel Free Trade Agreement, as well as launching negotiations that led to the creation of the World Trade Organization (WTO), the successor to the General Agreement on Tariffs and Trade (GATT).[8] Trade doubled on his watch.[9]

There has been debate over the use of tariffs ever since America became a constitutional republic. There have been times in our history when, regrettably, tariffs carried the day. And certainly, there have been tariffs enacted that have arguably fallen into Smith's enumerated and limited exceptions. What isn't debatable is that the conservative movement has always rested on a firm foundation of personal freedom, including economic freedom, based on natural rights, and at least in the post–World War II era, this has always included the freedom to trade.

Thirty-five years after Reagan, President Donald Trump tweeted, "The word TARIFF is a beautiful word indeed," as he proceeded to impose 10–50 percent tariffs on steel and aluminum and a wide array of Chinese goods.[10] He has now doubled down and called for a universal 20 percent tariff on all foreign-produced goods. Although conservatism has been the political movement supporting free trade for decades, a number of self-styled conservatives are now abandoning this long-held conservative principle and are finding common cause with both Trump and the majority of protectionist Democrats on the issue. They shouldn't, and their arguments in doing so are unpersuasive.

National Security and Protectionism

The number-one argument proffered to support protectionism is one based on national defense. After all, even Adam Smith admitted that national defense considerations were, of necessity, one of the exceptions to the free trade rule. However, from my personal experience of serving 16 years in Congress, I know firsthand how often bad policy is wrapped in the cloak of national defense.

When Trump unilaterally imposed his steel and aluminum tariffs in 2018, he did so under the authority of Section 232 of the misnamed Trade Expansion Act of 1962. To exercise that authority requires a finding that the imports in question threaten to impair national security. However, in the same year that the tariffs were imposed, James Mattis, then secretary of defense, noted that only 3 percent of US production of steel and aluminum was actually needed for our armed forces.[11] That begged the question of how, then, steel and aluminum tariffs were justified for everything from automobiles to beverage cans. Do some truly believe that a Toyota 4Runner or a can of Heineken beer threatens our national security?

Another example of the argument occurred during debate of the annual National Defense Authorization Act (NDAA). An amendment was offered to effectively force the military to buy only US-made running shoes for new recruits. Are running shoes critical to our national defense? Incidentally, the amendment would have had the effect of benefiting only one company: New Balance.[12] It was argued that many running shoes sold in America are manufactured in China. True, but they also continue to be manufactured in Taiwan, Indonesia, Finland, Italy, and Thailand as well. Should running shoes truly become critical to the defense of our nation? Could we not stockpile them when global prices are cheap? In a time of war, would we be unable to ramp up our own production of running shoes? After all, during World War II we showed that we could ramp up domestic production of aircraft from just over 2,000 in 1939 to 300,000 by 1945.[13] Hard to believe we're incapable of doing the same for running shoes or an array of other goods in the 21st century.

During debate on another NDAA bill, an amendment was offered to force the military to buy stainless steel flatware only from domestic sources.[14] In opposing the amendment during debate, House Armed Services Chairman Mac Thornberry (R-TX) remarked, "I just don't think that the knives and forks we use qualify as vital national security."[15] What does negatively impact national security, though, is the needless depletion of national wealth that occurs every time the government fails to buy the best product at the most economical price.

Washington undoubtedly has legitimate concerns over supply chain reliance on China for products with a clear national security nexus. But many companies are already in the process of, or have completed, a re-engineering or relocation of their supply chains, and with additional conservative tax and regulatory policies, even more would do so. Importantly, there remain a whole host of export controls, foreign direct investment approvals, and defense procurement requirements to help meet the threat that China poses. When it comes to our national defense, clearly the Trump administration's tariffs didn't mute China's saber rattling, its defense buildup, or its incursions into the South China Sea to threaten Taiwan.

As an aside, it needs to be noted that, in almost all respects, the tariffs imposed on Chinese goods by the Trump administration failed. The trade deficit, which remains a most misleading statistic but one favored by the former president, actually worsened during the Trump administration.[16] Furthermore, tariffs proved to be a two-way street—as they usually do. Just ask the Midwest farmers who suffered massive losses from retaliatory tariffs from China and had to be bailed out with $28 billion of subsidies from the US taxpayer.[17] Finally, it could not be clearer that the tariffs not only had no impact on weakening China's military, but also clearly had no impact on China's human rights abuses or its carbon footprint.

More often than not, the national defense argument for protectionism is unjustified and should never become a pretext for the abandonment of free trade in favor of industrial policy, corporate welfare, and protectionism. These all harm economic growth and innovation and consequently harm our national defense.

Additionally, although trade does not guarantee peace—Russia's gruesome invasion of Ukraine even though the two nations have a fair amount of two-way trade, for example—there is clear evidence that trade ties tend to reduce armed conflict between countries. This is consistent with what pro-market Enlightenment philosophers argued. Beginning in the aftermath of World War II, the United States used trade as a tool to enhance national security. It has been nearly 80 years since major world powers engaged one another in war—a period of relative peace that has coincided with the establishment of the US-led global trading system.

Likewise, trade can be an immense tool for American soft power. It helps spread American values and it enriches allies. In the early 1990s, Mexico was facing a policy choice: it could either continue down the path of protectionism and heavy government intervention, or it could move "toward decentralized, democratic capitalism."[18] The George H. W. Bush and Bill Clinton administrations understood that by better integrating the Mexican economy into the United States' economy, NAFTA could nudge Mexico away from the false allure of socialism. On top of the economic benefits of NAFTA, the agreement was a foreign policy success. Although certainly not perfect, and despite some recent backsliding, Mexico today is more committed to binding and predictable international trade and investment rules than it was in the 1980s and early 1990s.

Too often, trade is viewed as weakening America's national security when in fact it's usually the opposite.

Trade, the Working Class, and Domestic Manufacturing

Another prominent argument offered by self-styled conservatives is that free trade somehow hurts the working class. Conservatives undoubtedly consider the Tax Cuts and Jobs Act of 2017 (TCJA) to be the crowning achievement from when Republicans last governed. Yet many who heralded its pro-growth tax relief for working families turned around and supported tax increases on those very same families in the form of tariffs.

Countless studies have shown that almost all the costs of the tariffs initiated under the Trump administration were borne by consumers and businesses. At worst, these costs may have offset most of American households' average savings from the TCJA (Figure 16.1). For example, the cost of washing machines increased an average of $86 just months after tariffs were imposed on them.[19] According to the American Action Forum, all those tariffs combined have now increased consumer costs approximately $51 billion a year.[20] Some tax cut.[21] To make matters worse, the Tax Foundation calculates, based on current levels of imports, that Trump's universal 20 percent tariff proposal represents a whopping $320 billion tax increase. Just when did tax increases become popular among conservatives?

Today, most blue-collar workers work in services, not manufacturing, and their greatest concern is not the loss of their job due to foreign competition, it is the loss of buying power from a paycheck that has shrunk in the face of historic inflation. I doubt many so-called elites shop at Walmart, but many working people certainly do. If a customer buys a Zebco fishing rod there, it has been produced in China, and if they pick up a pair of Cowboy Cut Wrangler jeans, they'll likely have come from Bangladesh. Although Walmart doesn't like to advertise the fact, it remains the nation's largest importer, with its shelves stocked with tons of foreign-produced goods that help working families make ends meet.[22] Tariffs wouldn't bring back manufacturing jobs that produce fishing rods or blue jeans; they'd only make those products more expensive.

FIGURE 16.1

American households' average savings from the Tax Cuts and Jobs Act of 2017 were, at worst, almost completely offset by the costs of the Trump tariffs in 2018

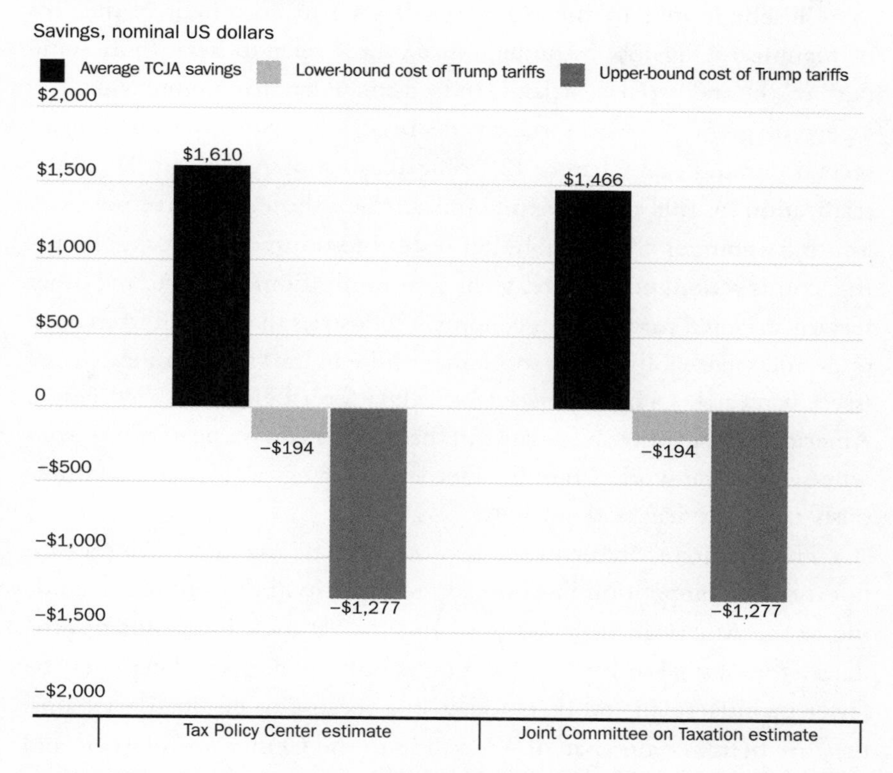

Source: Clark Packard and Scott Lincicome, "Course Correction: Charting a More Effective Approach to US-China Trade," Cato Institute Policy Analysis no. 946, May 8, 2023. The lower-bound estimate for the impact of Trump tariffs is from Pablo D. Fajgelbaum et al., "Updates to Fajgelbaum et al. (2020) with 2019 Tariff Waves," January 21, 2020. The upper-bound estimate for the impact of Trump tariffs is from "The Budget and Economic Outlook: 2020 to 2030," Congressional Budget Office, January 28, 2020, p. 33. Estimates for the impact of the Tax Cuts and Jobs Act of 2017 are from "Distributional Analysis of the Conference Agreement for the Tax Cuts and Jobs Act," Tax Policy Center, December 18, 2017; and "Distributional Effects of Public Law 115-97," JCX-10-19, Joint Committee on Taxation, Congress of the United States. Author's calculations are described in the note below.

Note: Estimates of the impact of Section 301 tariffs also include the effects of other tariffs imposed by the Trump administration from January 2018, but the Section 301 tariffs account for the largest share of the observed effect. The aggregate impact of Trump tariffs is divided by the number of US households in 2018 (approximately 127.6 million). The Tax Policy Center divides the aggregate impact of the Tax Cuts and Jobs Act of 2017 by "tax units," which are defined as an "individual, or a married couple, that files a tax return or would file a tax return if their income were high enough, along with all dependents of that individual or married couple." The Tax Policy Center estimates that the amount of tax units in a given year exceeds the number of households reported by other sources. The Joint Committee on Taxation reports the aggregate change in federal taxes and a distinct number of taxpayer units. Thus, aggregate savings from the Tax Cuts and Jobs Act of 2017, according to the Joint Committee on Taxation's estimates, are divided by the committee's number of taxpayer units (177 million) to obtain the average. TCJA = Tax Cuts and Jobs Act.

Closely related to the working-class harm argument is the loss of manufacturing jobs argument that others refer to as a "hollowing out" of the industrial heartland. Indeed, manufacturing employment as a percentage of the workforce has decreased dramatically over the past several decades (see Chapter 12, "The Reality of American 'Deindustrialization'"). But contrary to popular belief, those jobs have not been lost to hamburger-flipping jobs but instead to transportation, warehousing, construction, health care, tech, communications, finance, and other service-oriented parts of our economy—industries that benefit from open trade and whose jobs pay far more than those in low-skill manufacturing (see Chapter 11, "The Misplaced Nostalgia for a Less Globalized Past"). America's comparative advantage in these industries is one of the reasons why we are the world's number-one exporter of services and continuously run a services trade surplus.

The dominant factor in the loss of domestic manufacturing jobs is not foreign competition but instead productivity. For example, according to the American Iron and Steel Institute, it took 10.1 hours to produce a ton of steel in 1980; today it takes only 1.5 hours.[23] There may be fewer manufacturing workers today, but because of productivity gains, they are better compensated. According to the Center for Strategic and International Studies, the median income of the remaining US blue-collar manufacturing jobs has increased 50 percent in real inflation-adjusted terms between 1960 and 2019.[24]

The reality is that tariffs harm most manufacturing jobs. Relatively open trade is vital for manufacturing and our defense industrial base. As Scott Lincicome and Alfredo Carrillo Obregon document, around half of all goods imported are in fact intermediate goods, raw materials, and capital equipment used for domestic manufacturing.[25] For example, many pipeline manufacturing companies import specialty casing that is necessary for oil and gas pipelines. Taxing these imports hurts workers at these companies or, if the higher costs are passed on, their energy-producing customers. How ironic for any conservative to call for an "all of the above" energy policy (one that supports the development and deployment of every form of energy) yet support making hydrocarbons more difficult and expensive to produce.

We could strengthen domestic manufacturing, the defense industrial base, and our energy sector by unilaterally eliminating tariffs on intermediate inputs, raw materials, and capital equipment. Doing that would truly put America first.

Trade, Family, and Community

Trade makes the necessities of life cheaper and more abundant for families. Walking through a grocery store reveals that a lot of our everyday food items are imported from around the world (see Chapter 22, "Food Globalization Puts the World on Your Plate"). This raises real incomes for Americans by increasing their purchasing power. Indeed, according to recent research from the Peterson Institute for International Economics, reduced friction in international transactions since the end of World War II—from trade liberalization and improvements in transportation and technology—increased US gross domestic product by $2.6 trillion in 2022 dollars, or about $7,800 per person and $19,500 per household.[26] A 2016 study from two economists estimates that trade particularly benefited low-income consumers, who spend more of their income on items that were traded, including manufactured goods and food.[27]

Although the gains over the past 75 years have been significant, there is more work to be done. Consider a family outfitting their kids to go back to school in the fall. As Bryan Riley of the National Taxpayers Union recently noted, backpacks face a 17.6 percent tariff and rulers face a 13.6 percent tariff; meanwhile, blue jeans face an 8.4 percent tariff and shoes face an average tariff of 10.8 percent.[28] Eliminating these tariffs on basic family necessities would raise real incomes of American families.

Likewise, trade benefits communities and civil society. Because of relatively open trade, we can consume more for less and, as a result, we can work fewer hours, which means that it frees up time to participate in activities that build community, whether they're volunteering, going to church, or coaching tee-ball (see Chapter 20, "Trade Buys Goods, Services, and Time"). (The bats and tees are probably imported, too.)

Moreover, although the media focuses on midwestern cities that are hurt by import competition, there are countless stories about cities and towns that were once hurt by imports but that now thrive, in large part because of international trade.[29] Take the border areas in Texas. They once had large concentrations of low value-added manufacturing. But according to the Federal Reserve Bank of Dallas, "NAFTA, along with other market forces and technological change, created different jobs in Texas as low value-added manufacturing jobs were lost and as trade and investment increased. Border cities went on to gain far more employment than what they lost amid increased imports from Canada and Mexico and shifting production between the countries."[30] Indeed, economic integration has been enormously beneficial for Texas. The same Dallas Fed report notes, "A 10 percent increase in manufacturing on the Mexican side of the border increases employment 2.2 percent in Brownsville, 2.8 percent in El Paso, 4.6 percent in Laredo and 6.6 percent in McAllen."[31]

Conservatives have long argued that family and communities are the bedrocks of a free and prosperous society. Freer trade complements both. It's surely not a cure-all for what ails our culture, but it helps. And the things that actually have hollowed out many American families and communities go way beyond economics. The underlying causes lie more in the realm of cultural changes and bad public policies, especially in the area of welfare. Tariffs can't fix problems that trade didn't cause.

Protectionism, Bureaucracy, and Rent Seeking

One of the great rallying cries of many conservatives remains "Drain the swamp!" But after the previous administration imposed its tariffs, it immediately empowered hundreds of Washington bureaucrats at the Department of Commerce and the Office of the US Trade Representative to grant individual waivers from the very same tariffs under what can at best be described as an opaque process with discretionary standards. As one company officer of a small pipeline manufacturer put it, "[Applying for a waiver] is a nightmare, like dealing with a lawyer and the IRS at the same time."[32] A schedule of tariffs doesn't drain the swamp; it instead fills it with a cadre of well-connected lawyers, lobbyists, and special interests to work a system run by Washington bureaucrats.

It is difficult to comprehend how one can proudly wave the Gadsden flag, proclaiming "Don't Tread on Me," and then seemingly turn around and remark, "But go ahead 'swamp,' take away my freedom and choose for me which products I'm allowed to buy."

Others charge that global trade is inherently antithetical to American interests. Notwithstanding being polysyllabic, "globalization" is now treated as a four-letter word. Although "globalization" is not clearly defined, the word conveys to many not just a loss of American jobs but a loss of American interests, prestige, identity, and perhaps most importantly, a loss of American sovereignty. Undoubtedly what comes out of the vast array of international organizations and forums in which the United States participates has helped fuel these fears. Even if it is not harmful, US membership in many of these may be of dubious value to some conservatives. As one former congressman said in private conversation, "Why do we continue to pay the UN to insult us when they'd likely do it for free?" Conservatives legitimately question whether it is truly in America's interest to participate in global conferences and organizations such as the United Nations Climate Change Conference, the Inter-American Development Bank, and the International Trade Union Confederation.

What can't be questioned, though, is that Article I, Section 1, of the Constitution still reads, "All legislative Powers herein granted shall be vested in a Congress of the **United States** . . ." (emphasis added).[33] What can't be questioned, is that Article II, Section 2, still reads in part, "[The President] shall have Power, by and with the Advice and Consent of the Senate, to make Treaties, provided two thirds of the Senators present concur."[34] Whatever treaties we enter into, and whatever commitments we make to other countries or international organizations, are an exercise of US sovereignty, not the loss of such. And what we enter into, we can exit. The United States unilaterally terminated its first treaty in 1798 and has done so on many occasions since.

No nation-state or international body can compel us to do anything without our consent. Should we choose to walk away from an agreement or treaty, the other party or parties may, of course, then choose to treat us in ways in which we prefer to not be treated. But again, they simply cannot sanction us with fines or loss of property without our consent. Our elected officials may agree to be bound by certain international rules or obligations whenever they decide the mutual pledges of other nations are in our national interest. But whenever "We the People" disagree with those decisions, we have the opportunity to unbind ourselves by electing either a new president or a new Congress, or both.

When it comes to our trade relations, the WTO is singled out for usurping US sovereignty. It doesn't. It is simply a voluntary organization of trading nations attempting to come to consensus on accepted trade rules. Once rules are agreed upon, the organization attempts to arbitrate and it makes rulings by interpreting those rules. The WTO itself doesn't initiate action and has no ability to enforce dispute settlement rulings other than by authorizing a complaining (winning) member government to deny a responding (losing) member government some of the benefits of membership. The WTO is a most imperfect organization that is in constant need of reform. But it usurps no US sovereignty, and we have more global trade benefiting the United States because of it (see Chapter 7, "The World Trade Organization: Myths versus Reality").

Conclusion

In the final analysis, the most important reason conservatives should remain committed to trade has nothing to do with economics. Instead, it has everything to do with securing "the Blessings of Liberty to ourselves and our Posterity," something for which our Founders risked their lives, fortunes, and sacred honor. Trade should not be viewed as a matter of discretionary foreign policy or a lever to promote economic nationalism. And although the data and historic evidence are overwhelmingly convincing that trade leads to greater economic growth, ultimately trade remains an issue of personal freedom, specifically economic freedom and its relation to private property. To "Buy American" should not be a matter of where one buys. For conservatives, it should instead be a matter of how one buys, and that how is with freedom of choice. If the conservative movement is to still stand for freedom of speech, freedom of enterprise, and freedom to bear arms, as a matter of principle it must firmly and unequivocally stand for freedom of trade.

Chapter 17

The Progressive Case for Globalization

Inu Manak and Helena Kopans-Johnson

- Postwar trade liberalization has strong roots in the American progressive project.
- The driving force for the rules-based trading system strongly aligns with US efforts to promote shared values for a peaceful world based on the rule of law.
- Globalization has contributed to significant reductions in poverty while promoting shared prosperity at home and abroad—central components of the progressive policy agenda.

Globalization has transformed the world. Centuries ago, it brought exotic spices and wares to distant corners of the globe. More recently, it has allowed us to work, see our families, and live our lives despite the disruptions caused by a once-in-a-lifetime pandemic. Trade in particular is a major component of globalization, which has lifted over a billion people out of poverty, made us more productive, and contributed to peace. Despite this, globalization and trade are under attack.

US Trade Representative Katherine Tai argued that the traditional approach to trade, focused on economic efficiency, has contributed to "a race to the bottom."[1] Meanwhile, President Biden has been beating the drum for his Made in America approach, even if it harms ties with our allies.[2] Defending President Biden's "Invest in America" agenda, Heather Boushey, member of the president's Council of Economic Advisers, stated that "the global trading system has not always been fair, not always delivered the promised benefits to our citizens, [and] too often favored large corporate interests over workers' interests."[3] The administration has thus called for a "new Washington Consensus" but still has not answered the question posed by Jake Sullivan: "How does trade fit into our international economic policy, and what problems is it seeking to solve?"[4]

What is striking about these statements is how far removed they are from traditional progressive views on trade and globalization, namely, that domestic and international prosperity are interlinked, that trade institutions support the rule of law, and that globalization is a tool for advancing well-being among the poorest. Trade has thus been peripheral to the Biden administration's foreign economic policy. The shift in Washington toward favoring protectionist policies over trade openness is not only bad policy, but for progressives now calling for a new approach to trade, it also cuts against the very goals they are trying to achieve.

Tariff Liberalization as a Progressive Project

Economic turmoil and global conflict during the first half of the 20th century prompted a bold rethinking of the international order. President Franklin Delano Roosevelt led the charge, overcoming fractured views on trade within his own party. The pragmatic and strategic vision of his secretary of state, Cordell Hull, helped him recognize the necessity of international economic cooperation to generate peace and prosperity at home and abroad. Roosevelt saw firsthand the devastating economic and social consequences of the Great Depression and acknowledged the role of trade barriers in deepening the crisis.

In a 1936 speech in Buenos Aires, Roosevelt criticized countries for their "attempts to be self-sufficient," which "led to failing standards for their people and to ever-increasing loss of the democratic ideals in a mad race to pile armament on armament."[5] He called these policies "suicidal" and lamented that despite the suffering they caused, "many . . . people have come to believe with despair that the price of war seems less than the price of peace."[6]

The United States was no stranger to such policies. As post–World War I reconstruction was underway, European producers reemerged in the international market, fueling competition as they increased their exports. In the United States, amid a backdrop of economic uncertainty, many advocated for restrictive trade remedies that eventually culminated in the 1930 Smoot–Hawley Tariff Act, which led to an average tariff increase of 20 percent.[7]

Though originally intended to shield the agricultural sector from foreign competition through targeted tariffs, congressional logrolling greatly expanded the scope of the act to cover a broad range of products.[8]

Unsurprisingly, its implementation sparked retaliatory measures from US trading partners, which included tariffs and quotas on products primarily imported from American producers, as well as widespread boycotts of American goods.[9] While American exporters faced higher barriers to market access abroad, American consumers saw increases of between 4 and 6 percent in the relative price of imports, further reducing purchasing power and raising the cost of living. Though the tariffs did not bring about the Great Depression, economic historian Douglas Irwin notes that they contributed to both a "severe deterioration in trade relations in the early 1930s" and a global embrace of trade protectionism.[10]

On the campaign trail in 1933, Roosevelt lambasted President Herbert Hoover and Republican leaders for the Smoot–Hawley tariff, saying that "President Hoover probably should have known that this tariff would raise havoc with any plans that he might have had to stimulate foreign markets" and that the tariff was "the road to ruin, if we keep on it!" Retaliation from US trading partners was a major concern, making it difficult to sell products even to "logical customers, your neighbors across the border."[11] Roosevelt had another idea, which came from Hull, for "a tariff policy based on reason . . . a tariff policy based in large part upon the simple principle of profitable exchange, arrived at through negotiated tariff, with benefit to each Nation."[12] While Roosevelt was primarily concerned with economic stability in the United States, he was aware that this could not be achieved alone. In fact, he quickly recognized the symbiotic relationship between domestic recovery and the health of global trade.

The challenge, however, was that FDR lacked the authority to reduce trade barriers because the Constitution vests Congress with the power to regulate foreign commerce. Roosevelt and Hull thus jointly urged Congress to adopt the Reciprocal Trade Agreements Act of 1934 (RTAA), which, once passed, would empower the executive branch to negotiate tariff reduction agreements based on the principles of reciprocity and mutual benefit.[13] Roosevelt explained that "by reducing our own tariff in conjunction with the reduction by other countries of their trade barriers, we create jobs, get more for our money, and improve the standard of living of every American consumer."[14] Furthermore, by increasing the authority granted to the executive branch, the RTAA reduced the impact of parochial interests in trade policy, since the president represented a national constituency.

Though many sensitive domestic industries retained trade protections, the RTAA marked a turning point in US trade policy.[15] Not only did trade critics consider it to be fairly managed; it also found support among 71 percent of Americans. That did not mean its renewal did not face opposition in Congress, but as the United States entered the Second World War, sensible tariff policy became an instrument beyond domestic economic recovery and would serve as the foundation for a new international economic order guided by pragmatism, cooperation, and shared prosperity.

International Peace, Alliances, and the Rule of Law

Domestic economic recovery was not the only motivation for transforming the global economy defined by a liberalized trade regime. Rather, trade proponents strongly believed that deep economic integration would boost international peacebuilding and result in a freer, fairer world.

This idea is not new. In 1795, Immanuel Kant outlined how a constitution for civil law among nations could overcome the law of nature and create the conditions for perpetual peace. A key component of this was universal hospitality, which could make, among other things, "commerce with native inhabitants possible" so that "distant parts of the world can establish with one another peaceful relations that will eventually become matters of public law, and the human race can gradually be brought closer and closer to a cosmopolitan constitution."[16] The freedom to engage in commerce and avoid plunder was thus considered an important aspect of establishing a peaceful international community.

While the academic debate over the pacifying effects of international trade is ongoing, scholars agree that trade is an important variable that contributes to peace, though they place different weight on the explanatory power of liberal philosophy versus structural factors, such as liberal institutions, and the conditions under which the relationship is most salient.[17] Reflecting on his own experiences, Hull described his personal realization of the idea that trade could lead to peace:

> When the war came in 1914, I was very soon impressed with two points. The first was its terrific commercial impact on the United States. I saw that you could not separate the idea of commerce from the idea of war and peace. . . . And the second was that wars were often largely caused by economic rivalry conducted unfairly. I thereupon came to believe that if we could eliminate this bitter economic rivalry, if we could increase commercial exchanges among nations over lowered trade and tariff barriers and remove unnatural obstructions to trade, we would go a long way toward eliminating war itself.[18]

Hull's recounting provides further evidence for the argument that managing economic security concerns became a central issue for the architects of the postwar international order.[19] One such way to address these concerns was through a framework of rules that would lower barriers to trade and provide for the peaceful settlement of disputes. The first step to achieve this was the General Agreement on Tariffs and Trade (GATT), which helped facilitate open trade relations based on the principles of reciprocity, nondiscrimination, transparency, and enforceability. At the launch of the GATT negotiations, Roosevelt made the case before Congress for why US participation was so important, noting that "the purpose of the whole effort is to eliminate economic warfare, to make practical international cooperation effective on as many fronts as possible, and so to lay the economic basis for the secure and peaceful world we all desire."[20]

By establishing a rules-based system, the GATT prioritized a predictable trade environment that would prevent the resurgence of the protectionist policies that worsened the economic instability and political conflicts of the first half of the 20th century. However, the GATT needed to be updated and expanded through successive rounds of negotiations that moved beyond simple tariff barriers. Another Democratic president was responsible for one of the most important rounds of GATT negotiations, which was eventually named after him—the Kennedy Round.

Prior to starting those talks, John F. Kennedy had secured authorization from Congress for additional tariff cuts up to 50 percent under the Trade Expansion Act of 1962. Upon signing the legislation, Kennedy remarked that "this act recognizes, fully and completely, that we cannot protect our economy by stagnating behind tariff walls, but that the best protection possible is a mutual lowering of tariff barriers among friendly nations so that all may benefit from a free flow of goods."[21] Kennedy argued that expanding trade would not only strengthen the US economic position but also bolster US alliances and, in doing so, help counter the threat posed by communism. He thus called the Trade Expansion Act "an important new weapon to advance the cause of freedom."[22]

International institutions were central to advancing these goals and supported a strong belief in the centrality of the rule of law and fairness that undergirds the progressivism movement. In a 1942 radio address, Hull explained why Americans should support US involvement in the war, stating that "liberty under law is an essential requirement of progress." Liberty, to Hull, was "more than a matter of political rights." In fact, he argued that the United States had "learned from bitter experience that to be truly free, men must have, as well, economic freedom and economic security." Extending that internationally, Hull argued for "cooperative action under common agreement," which "will enable each to increase the effectiveness of its own national effort."[23] Fifty-two years later, to mark the signing of the Uruguay Round Agreements

Act that established the World Trade Organization (WTO), President Bill Clinton also made the case for "a fair and increasingly open world trading system that allows the free market to work and rewards the most productive people in the world," as a means to "restore stability to the lives of the working people of our country."[24] Economic security at home, it was understood, required international institutions based on the principle of fair competition, which would facilitate access to economic opportunities.

An important way to ensure fairness is to have a system of rules that applies equally to all and a means of recourse when those rules are violated. At the WTO, that has been the dispute settlement system, which allows countries to peacefully resolve trade disputes among themselves. What is truly amazing about this system is that even the smallest countries have access to it, and throughout most of the organization's history, no country has seen itself as above the law.

A rules-based trading system was therefore always a precondition for economic interdependence that would be fair and accessible to all. Today, economic interdependence is still a core principle of liberal internationalism, though in Washington policy circles it has become less valued over time (see Chapter 13, "The Dangers of Misunderstanding Economic Interdependence"). Part of this stems from a loss of confidence in the rules-based order. President Biden's national security adviser, Jake Sullivan, questioned "the premise that economic integration would make nations more responsible and open, and that the global order would be more peaceful and cooperative," arguing that "Russia's invasion of Ukraine underscored the risks of overdependence."[25] Tai shares this view, when in response to a question about how Russia's invasion of Ukraine had upended the accepted wisdom of trade promoting peace, she said, "Peace is probably more necessary for prosperity than prosperity is for peace."[26]

Each of these arguments veers far from the progressive views toward trade and interdependence held by Roosevelt (whose portrait hangs above the fireplace in President Biden's Oval Office), as well as other progressives. They also fail to understand the nuance in the trade-promotes-peace literature by arguing that the presence of *any conflict* disproves the theory that economic integration *reduces* the frequency and scope of conflict.

Furthermore, as political scientist Daniel Drezner points out, complex interdependence made it difficult for Russia's closest geopolitical ally, China, to provide strong public support for the war in Ukraine. In fact, he argues that China's links to the global economy and Western countries in particular curbed its behavior by tipping the cost-benefit analysis to favor adopting a less prominent role in the war (see Chapter 13, "The Dangers of Misunderstanding Economic Interdependence"). The Russia-Ukraine war thus reveals that while interdependence does not eliminate all security concerns, the liberal international order still effectively constrains aggressive foreign policy behavior and fosters collective responses. This is precisely why, in his famous address at American University in 1963, Kennedy remarked that "even the most hostile nations can be relied upon to accept and keep those treaty obligations, and only those treaty obligations, which are in their own interests."[27] A material interest in accessing markets can thus moderate a country's behavior.

The loss of faith in the power of interdependence as a restraint and the benefits of a system based on rules appears to be the new consensus in Washington, perhaps best executed by former president Donald Trump. Under his administration, the United States launched a series of trade wars that not only resulted in significant economic harm at home and retaliation that soured relations with our closest trading partners but also undermined the rules-based trading system.[28] Though President Biden has made important strides in improving relations with our allies, on trade, he has largely preserved, and defended, some of Trump's most controversial policy actions.

For example, when the metals tariffs that were applied for alleged national security concerns were found to violate international trade rules, Adam Hodge, who was then a spokesperson for the US Trade Representative, denounced the ruling, saying that "the United States strongly rejects the flawed interpretation" of the rules and that "issues of national security cannot be reviewed in WTO dispute settlement."[29] To make the US objection clear, he went on to say, "We do not intend to remove the Section 232 duties as a result of these disputes."[30] What is interesting about the Biden administration's position is that in saying its actions are above the law, the United States has now established a slippery slope whereby other countries can claim national security interests as cover for trade protectionism.

The US approach to trade has shifted far from its progressive roots in another important way as well. The spirit of cooperation and need for predictability that underscored the postwar institution-building efforts are also under threat, not just with adversaries but with allies too. Discussing the sunset review of the United States-Canada-Mexico Agreement, Tai stated that "the whole point" of the negotiations "is to maintain a certain level of discomfort, which may involve a certain level of uncertainty."[31] During the Trump administration, uncertainty was a driving strategy of trade policy.[32]

The problem with uncertainty, however, is that it breeds confusion, economic disruption, loss of trust, and hesitancy over making commitments. This is the direct opposite of what motivated the architects of the modern international trading system and its most steadfast champion, the United States. The last expression of those progressive ideals was shared by former US trade representative Michael Froman in his exit memo, where he wrote: "Through our trade policy, we bolster our partners and allies, lead efforts to write the rules of the road for fair trade among partners, and promote broad-based development. Trade done right is essential for our economy here at home and for America's position in the world."[33] In contrast, US policymakers today have increasingly embraced a more zero-sum logic and thus failed to appreciate the importance of leading by example on trade and other foreign economic policies.

Tackling Poverty and Promoting Shared Prosperity

Though many advocates of trade protectionism today often point to levels of global inequality, stalled development, and middle-class stagnation as justifications for deglobalization, the evidence paints a more positive picture of globalization. In fact, looking at indicators such as life expectancy, infant mortality, literacy, and living standards, the story of the era of globalization is one of considerable progress and declining inequality.

From 1990 to 2019, the share of the global population living below the poverty line—set at $2.15 per day based on 2017 prices—decreased

FIGURE 17.1

The share of the global population living below the poverty line decreased by nearly 30 percentage points from 1990 to 2019

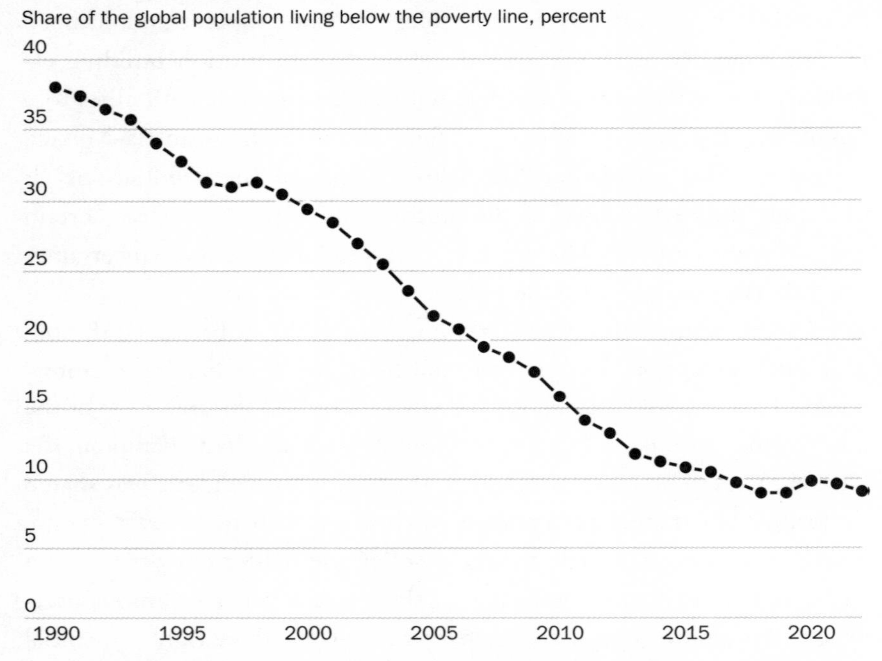

Source: "Share of Population Living in Extreme Poverty: 2011 vs. 2017 Prices, World, 1990 to 2022," Our World in Data, updated March 27, 2024.
Note: The international poverty line is set at $2.15 a day based on 2017 prices, adjusted for purchasing power parity.

from 38.01 percent to 8.98 percent (Figure 17.1).[34] Economist Kimberly Clausing explains that within China alone, "the share of the population living in poverty fell from 88 percent of the population to 2 percent of the population between 1980 and 2012," suggesting that a billion people were lifted out of extreme poverty by China's economic opening.[35] The negative correlation between trade openness and poverty levels is difficult to dispute, especially considering that regions with the most stagnant economic growth are those that maintain high tariff barriers and have therefore seen slow trade growth, such as sub-Saharan Africa. In addition to reducing poverty, expanded trade led to increased gross domestic product (GDP) growth.[36] Economists Gary Hufbauer and Megan

FIGURE 17.2
Inequality has declined in many areas

Gini coefficient weighted for population (0 = perfect equality, 1 = maximum inequality)

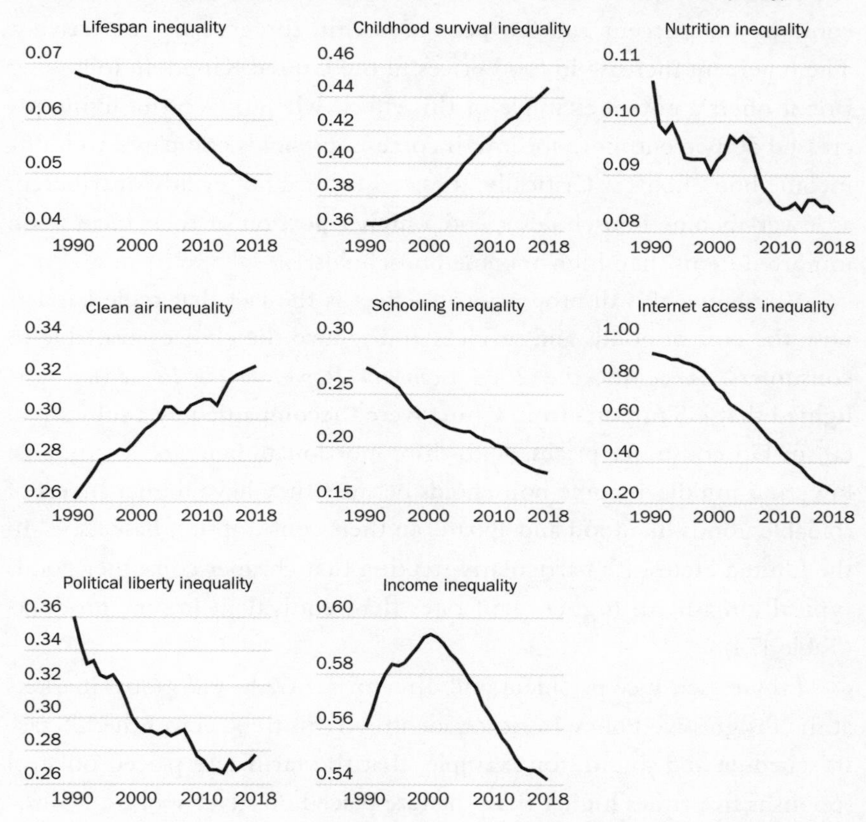

Source: Chelsea Follett and Vincent Geloso, "Global Inequality in Well-Being Has Decreased across Many Dimensions," Cato Institute Policy Analysis no. 949, June 8, 2023.

Hogan estimate that without post–World War II trade liberalization, US GDP would have been $2.6 trillion lower in 2022, at $22.9 trillion instead of $25.5 trillion, averaging to welfare gains of $19,500 per household in 2022.[37] These gains from trade have broadly benefited consumers and reduced inequality. As Chelsea Follett explains in Chapter 15, "Globalization and Growing Global Equality," this time period has also witnessed considerable progress toward raising living standards worldwide (Figure 17.2).

While small changes to tariff rates may appear inconsequential, the WTO estimates that universal withdrawals from free trade agreements and increases in most-favored-nation tariff rates would decrease real income by 0.3 percent and 0.8 percent within three years, respectively. The 6 percent increase in food prices in the United Kingdom following Brexit offers a potent example of this effect, when the cost of living increased 50 percent more for low-income households compared to high-income households.[38] Critically, these costs were not evenly distributed, as lower-income households spend a higher portion of their income on imported items than high-income households.

Worsening this disproportionate effect is the fact that trade barriers raise the cost of goods and services and reduce the choices available to consumers. Recently, the *2024 Economic Report to the President* highlighted that US imports from China were "accompanied by a substantial fall in US consumer prices, with disproportionate benefits accruing to low- and middle-income households because they have higher shares of tradable goods like food and apparel in their consumption baskets."[39] In the United States, it's particularly striking that cheaper consumer goods typically maintain higher tariff rates than equivalent luxury products (Table 17.1).

Ed Gresser, vice president and director for trade and global markets at the Progressive Policy Institute, identified this trend across the US tariff schedule and found, for example, that the tariff rate placed on steel spoons is five times higher than the rate placed on silver spoons.[40] Similarly, while a cashmere sweater has a 4 percent tariff rate, wool sweaters have a 17 percent rate, and acrylic sweaters have a 32 percent tariff rate.[41] This makes the US tariff schedule a regressive tax whereby low-income households are not only spending a higher portion of their income on imported items, but they are also paying a higher average tariff rate on those purchased goods. A growth in protectionist measures would exacerbate these inequities.

However, since the gains from trade are often diffused throughout the economy, they can often go unnoticed and are given less attention than trade costs, which are often concentrated. As a case in point, the "China Shock" serves as a common talking point for critics of globalization, even

TABLE 17.1

Tariffs are higher on mass-market products than equivalent luxury goods

Product	Luxury good	Medium-end good	Mass-market good
Shoes	8.5% (men's leather dress shoes)	20.0% (running shoes)	48.0% (valued at $3 or less)
Sweaters	4.0% (cashmere)	16.0% (wool)	32.0% (acrylic)
Men's shirts	0.9% (silk)	19.7% (cotton)	32.0% (polyester)
Handbags	5.3% (snakeskin)	10.0% (leather valued at $20 or less)	16.0% (canvas)
Pillowcases	4.5% (silk)	11.9% (cotton)	14.9% (polyester)
Necklaces	5.0% (gold)	6.3% (silver)	13.5% (silver jewelry valued at $1.50 or less)
Scarves	1.5% (silk)	9.6% (wool)	11.3% (polyester)
Blankets	0.0% (wool)	8.4% (cotton)	8.5% (polyester)

Source: US International Trade Commission Tariff Database, https://dataweb.usitc.gov/tariff/database.

Note: The tariff codes for these products are 64035960, 64029142, 64029160, 61101210, 61101100, 61103030, 61059040, 61051000, 61052020, 42022130, 42022160, 42022215, 63022900, 63022130, 63022210, 71131921, 71131110, 71131120, 61171040, 61171010, 61171020, 63012000, 63013000, and 63014000.

though the findings of the famous study that coined the term have been strongly contested.[42]

In placing so much emphasis on concentrated and marginal direct employment losses, globalization's critics also fail to see the widespread economic benefits of trade through greater competition with foreign producers, which results in lower prices for consumers and limits domestic firms' ability to pursue monopolies, as Clausing explains in her book, *Open: The Progressive Case for Free Trade, Immigration, and Global Capital.*[43] On the other hand, Clausing also calculates that "protectionist measures cost consumers as a group, on average, over $500,000 per job saved" through added taxes caused by higher tariffs.[44] In some industries this cost is more extreme; according to economist Anne Krueger, "it is estimated that the annual cost of one job 'saved' in the steel industry is about $900,000."[45]

These unemployment-based evaluations also ignore that lower tariff rates reduce the costs of intermediate goods for domestic manufacturers, which in turn leads to greater production capacity and hiring ability. Final made-in-America products are thus cheaper because of these foreign intermediate inputs, increasing their market competitiveness.

Clausing thus analogizes the trade shock to technology shocks: while advances in technology can reduce the demand for some jobs, they simultaneously increase productivity and efficiency, create many new job opportunities, and benefit everyday users.[46] It would be unusual to come across someone who would argue that the internet should not have been broadly adopted for the sake of conserving a small portion of jobs. This is not to suggest that these shocks are not serious policy concerns; rather, it is intended to demonstrate that imposing protectionist measures to save jobs will fail to achieve the desired effect and instead will reduce economic growth and impose widespread costs. Broadly speaking, these negative externalities should be remedied through more robust public policy instead of trade restrictions to assist Americans in adjusting to economic disruptions.[47]

As one of the report's authors, Gordon Hanson, later remarked in *Foreign Affairs*, though the China Shock "hurt many US workers and their communities . . . so, too, have automation, the Great Recession, and the COVID-19 pandemic. And because the scarring effects of job losses are the same whether imports, robots, or a virus is responsible, responses to the damage should not depend on the identity of the culprit."[48] He therefore argued that protectionist measures "will do little to help workers who are already hurting or to help others avoid a similar fate" and that instead, the president "should establish targeted domestic programs that protect workers from the downsides of globalization."[49]

Though trade generally acts as a positive force, challenges persist. The economic disruptions and global health crisis caused by the COVID-19 pandemic drove many countries, including the United States, to grow wary of globalization, leaning away from international trade cooperation in favor of a more protectionist and, at times, fragmented system. However, the presumption that the optimal solution to these global challenges lies solely in unilateral or regional action is flawed. As WTO director-general Ngozi Okonjo-Iweala noted in the *World Trade Report 2023*, "a retreat from economic integration would roll back recent development gains, make it harder for countries to grow their way out of poverty, and harm future economic prospects for the poorest people the most."[50] In other words, fragmentation would only exacerbate existing challenges.

The *World Trade Report* instead advocated for addressing the world's most pressing challenges through greater global openness, integration, and cooperation, contingent on the reform of the international trading system. This approach, termed "re-globalization," aims to integrate more economies into the global trading system and to promote a more equitable, transparent, and reliable trading framework. As President Barack Obama once stated, "globalization is a fact," and while the United States can't "build a wall" around globalization, he said, "what we can do is to shape how that process of global integration proceeds so that it's increasing opportunity for ordinary people."[51]

The United States has long shaped that process. In fact, it was American leadership in the global economy that established the WTO, which President Clinton described as "a victory for a couple of simple ideas." Essentially, "the idea that America can lead in the 21st century, that we need not fear competition, that we want our neighbors to do better than they have been doing, and when they do better, we will do better."[52] Though the belief that a rising tide can lift all boats is no longer in vogue in Washington, it has been a driving force for US engagement in the world economy and has contributed to a healthier, wealthier, and more stable world.

Conclusion

US leadership in the global economy is needed now more than ever, yet there is no need to rethink the entire trading system. The blueprint is well known, and as this essay shows, the driving force behind the modern trading system is deeply rooted in American values. Many progressives have called this system unfair. No institution is perfect, and it is true that the WTO and US trade agreements as we have known them would benefit from reform. However, their critics have lost sight of the very real benefits globalization and trade have provided and have also forgotten the progressive ideas that helped shape the international trading system after the Second World War. That system has not only reduced poverty but has also promoted shared prosperity, at home and abroad. Progressives would do well to remember these achievements and their important part in securing them.

Chapter 18

The Moral Case for Globalization

Tom G. Palmer

- Globalization has had tremendous net benefits for humanity, and the freedom to move, trade, accept influences from far away, and incorporate those influences into your experience and identity is central to being human. Every person should enjoy the equal presumption of liberty to travel and of liberty to exchange, just as there is a presumption of the liberty to think, speak, and live.
- Consequentialist condemnations of globalization only have force if they are based on evidence. The evidence shows that the world has improved during, or more strongly, *because of* globalization, so consequentialism should lead us to embrace globalization rather than condemn it.
- Wealthier populations can afford to invest more in maintenance of cherished traditions than can poorer populations. The human experience and appreciation of diversity has grown enormously because of globalization. Attempts to maintain "pure cultures," free of "pollution" from others, are doomed to fail. Cultural purity is a myth; it has never existed.
- There is a causal relationship between globalization and war, but not in the way the critics think. The greater the globalization of commerce, the lower the likelihood of armed conflict. The causes of freedom of trade and of peace have long been closely entwined. Those who prefer peace over war should embrace globalization.

It's common for debaters to define their terms in ways that are inherently "moralized" (i.e., ways that signal to the audience that the speaker embraces or rejects whatever is denoted by the term). If a debater refers to globalization in terms of "rising living standards," people might be more likely to embrace it. If referring to globalization in terms of "declining living standards," people might reject it. The term typically used to denote advocates of globalization is "globalists," which has emerged primarily as a term of abuse, especially on the far right.

According to the far-right French politician Marine Le Pen, "There is no more left and right. The real cleavage is between the patriots and the globalists."[1] Kevin Roberts, president of the Heritage Foundation, maintains that "conservatives everywhere need to define the choice as what it is—US vs THEM, everyday people vs globalist elites, who've shown they hate us."[2] Thus globalists are alleged to be anti-patriotic and enemies of "US," that is, of "everyday people," whom globalists allegedly hate. Another polemical use of the term has been advanced by the left-wing writer Quinn Slobodian, who defines "globalism" as "a coherent ideology" and "a project to restore class power" in *Globalists: The End of Empire and the Birth of Neoliberalism*. Donald Trump was more direct, "You know what a globalist is, right? You know what a globalist is? A globalist is a person that wants the globe to do well, frankly, not caring about our country so much."[3]

To seriously consider globalization, it's best to avoid definitions that contain the conclusions of complex arguments. A fruitful discussion of globalization requires a nonmoralized and operational use of the term. The definition is nonmoralized if it does not signal whether we should embrace or reject the term defined and is operational if it identifies uncontested, or at least verifiable, features of the world that people of different moral traditions and ideologies can agree are features of the world. So, this essay's definition of globalization is the relatively free movement of people, things, money, and ideas across natural or political borders. Thus, increasing globalization means reducing or eliminating state-enforced restrictions on voluntary exchanges or interactions across political borders that would be permitted if the private (nonstate) parties were on the same side of a border. A consequence of increasing globalization is an increasingly integrated and complex global system of production and exchange.

Some critics of globalization include in their definition the existence of certain international organizations, such as the World Trade Organization (WTO), the International Monetary Fund, the International Labour Organization, the World Bank, and the World Health Organization. While there are arguments for and against those organizations, none of the organizations are essential to globalization, and some have hindered it. Moreover, none of them are world governments, and none have enforcement powers, armies, and so forth. They are created by treaties among sovereign states. James Bacchus addresses many myths about the WTO in Chapter 7 of this volume (see "The World Trade Organization: Myths versus Reality").

The Equal Presumption of Liberty to Travel and Exchange

Are rights inherent, and thus, do they constitute a presumption of how others should treat individuals, or are rights mere permissions from those with power, dispensations that may be given or withheld by those holding power? Free societies require *the equal presumption of liberty*, which requires that any prohibitions imposed on the exercise of liberty be justified, whereas the exercise of liberty does not require justification. Just as in a court of law those accused of crimes (and thus liable to loss of liberty) are not required to prove their innocence and the prosecutor must prove that the accused is guilty, restricting someone's liberty requires justification, whereas its exercise (whether to pray as one chooses or to buy or sell as one wishes) does not. You need not explain to and then request permission from the authorities to realize your choice to wear blue sneakers or brown loafers, to eat potatoes fried or baked, or to listen to classical music, country and western, or Lady Gaga.

The American abolitionist and political thinker Frederick Douglass, in his 1867 "Composite Nation" speech, stated,

> There are such things in the world as human rights. They rest upon no conventional foundation, but are eternal, universal and indestructible.
>
> Among these is the right of locomotion; the right of migration; the right which belongs to no particular race, but belongs to all and to all alike. It is the right you assert by staying here, and your fathers asserted by coming here.[4]

The presumption of liberty is embedded in America's Founding documents. The rights of individuals are, as those documents make clear, unenumerated and thus presumed, whereas the powers of government are expressly stated (i.e., enumerated) and thus limited. The Bill of Rights enumerates certain familiar rights, while the Ninth Amendment makes it clear that those enumerated rights are not all we have, as it would be impossible to "enumerate all the rights of the people":

> The enumeration in the Constitution, of certain rights, shall not be construed to deny or disparage others retained by the people.[5]

In contrast, the Constitution states that all laws must be both "necessary and proper," and the 10th Amendment states that the powers of government are delegated, enumerated, and as such, the only powers they have:

> The powers not delegated to the United States by the Constitution, nor prohibited by it to the States, are reserved to the States respectively, or to the people.[6]

The right to come and go, to converse with whom we wish, to exchange with others on mutually agreeable terms, and more are presumed rights of human beings. Any who would restrict a person from interacting voluntarily with people of another religion, language, county, or country, must bear the burden of justifying such restrictions. Some restrictions are readily justified, such as restricting divulging or trading in defense secrets that would put all at risk of invasion or prohibiting the exchange of stolen goods or the products of forced labor. But protecting the interests of established producers of children's socks is not a sufficient justification to restrict people from buying socks for their children's feet from producers in other cities or countries.[7]

The principles of exchange for mutual advantage do not vary when one party speaks English and another Spanish, or when one is Christian and the other Buddhist, or when one lives in Missouri and the other in Manitoba. They are global. About the year 420 BCE the philosopher Democritus of Abdera wrote, "To a wise man, the whole earth is open; for the native land of a good soul is the whole earth."[8] The people of Hangzhou, the capital of the Southern Song dynasty of China, had a famous saying: "Vegetables from the east, water from the west, wood from the south, and rice from the north."[9] People can be attached to places, as most of us are, and still purchase goods and services from outside their localities, as we all do. Some may choose to stay rooted in one place and find happiness there, whereas others choose to travel or to relocate, sometimes to avoid oppression, sometimes to seek new opportunities. Whether one stays or moves from Boston to Los Angeles or from Los Angeles to Tokyo is a decision for the person doing the staying or moving. People can trade goods, services, or ideas with their next-door neighbors or with people who live far away.

Restricting the liberty of people to travel or exchange information, ideas, goods, or services requires justification. The burden of proof lies with the party that would restrict the liberty of another, just as the burden of proof in a criminal case lies with the one making the charge (the prosecutor). In contrast, the *immorality* of arrogating to oneself the power to restrict the choices of others is more evident: it violates the presumption of equal liberty that is foundational to free, harmonious, and prosperous societies by presuming instead that some people be required to ask permission to act from some privileged class. At the very least, such assertions require more justification than is generally offered by advocates of restrictions on trade, travel, or the exchange of goods, services, and ideas.

There is evidence that our commonly accepted norms of morality emerge from trade, which established the importance of legitimate expectations and reputations, both of which are necessary for the emergence of law and morality.[10] Morality itself is a product of exchange, and the more trade, generally the more humane a society is.

Consequences: Human Flourishing, Poverty, Health, Inequality

There is a vast amount of evidence that documents the impact of reducing barriers to trade, travel, and other forms of exchange across borders. Much of it is presented in other chapters in this book, such as Johan Norberg's "Globalization: A Race to the Bottom—or to the Top?" (see Chapter 14). Contrary to some critics of globalization, the results have been spectacularly positive for the world's poor, as wages have increased, jobs have become safer, and the use of children for labor has plummeted. Increasing wealth, in turn, is strongly connected to improving health, and the global spread of improvements in medicines and technologies has improved health outcomes even in regions that have not participated as much in the exchange of goods.

It is sometimes difficult for people living in already wealthy societies to understand economic growth, because the prosperous often take prosperity for granted. I wrote a book with my colleague Matt Warner, *Development with Dignity: Self-Determination, Localization, and the End to Poverty*, in which we tried to make the matter clearer via a thought experiment:

> Imagine a very poor country. The average life expectancy is 44 years, sixteen years fewer than in the Democratic Republic of the Congo. Indoor plumbing is considered a luxury. More than one out of four children (28%) die before the age of five. Forty three percent of "gainful workers 10 years and older" work just to grow food, and that doesn't count the almost universal use of the labor of children younger than 10 years of age on farms, also known as "chores." Nearly ten percent of the working population 10 years or older provide domestic and personal services for those considered wealthy by the standards of that society. No one has a cell phone, not even a radio or a television.[11]

What country would that be? It would be a good candidate for the very poorest country in the world. In fact, it was the United States of

America when my grandparents were born. The growth of incomes and the corresponding improvements in every empirical measure of well-being in just two generations has been astonishing. And if we do not screw things up—by, among other things, reversing globalization—two generations from now, people will look on all of us as desperately poor.

The positive benefits of globalization were felt not only in wealthier countries, such as the United Kingdom, Sweden, the United States, and Japan, but even more in the poorest. In fact, the uplift of the lives of poor people in poor nations has been, if anything, more astonishing. The historically marginalized and downtrodden Dalit people of India, for example, have seen more dramatic improvements in their lives and in their social status since the opening of the Indian economy and India's embrace of globalization than over the preceding thousand years.[12] Measurement of inequality of income, wealth, and consumption (and they are different) is a complicated matter, but the evidence is that rising incomes in increasingly globalized economies, such as China after 1978 and India after 1991, has led to a dramatic fall since the 1990s in global inequality, that is, inequality between countries.[13]

People agree to exchange because they expect to be better off by exchanging than by not exchanging. Making it possible to exchange with more people is beneficial to those whose range of potential exchange partners has increased. Adam Smith titled the third chapter of his *An Inquiry into the Nature and Causes of the Wealth of Nations* "That the Division of Labour is Limited by the Extent of the Market," a thesis that he illustrated by demonstrating the greater prosperity and progress in the ancient world for those nations with proximity to the sea and to navigable rivers.[14] Due to the lower friction of transportation over water compared to land, that proximity facilitated exchange with much larger areas and with many, many more people. To the extent that policies of governments erect barriers to exchange, it is analogous to making transportation deliberately more difficult, which would generally be understood to be harmful to the vast majority of people. Barriers to trade, of course, are generally imposed to benefit those who wish to charge higher prices for their goods by blocking competitors (i.e., by limiting the extent of the market). A legal monopoly is the extreme case of such limitation of the market, by allowing only one party to provide a good or service to others. Common misconceptions governing trade are readily refuted, and the principles of trade are not difficult to master.[15]

Some note that there may be a downside to reducing barriers to travel, as it may make some infectious diseases spread faster. Examples include influenza and COVID-19. On the other hand, the far greater wealth made possible by the expansion of the market also makes such illnesses easier to combat. Globalization is not limited to the exchange of goods and services across borders; it also encompasses the exchange of ideas, as well as scientific, economic, artistic, and other forms of cooperation. In the case of COVID-19, Hungarian-born biochemist Dr. Katalin Karikó and American-born immunologist Dr. Drew Weissman jointly received the recognition of the Nobel Prize in Physiology or Medicine for their research that led to the development of the mRNA vaccines.[16] And two German scientists of Turkish origins, oncologist and immunologist Dr. Uğur Şahin and physician Dr. Özlem Türeci (founders of BioNTech), and a Greek veterinarian, Dr. Albert Bourla (CEO of US-based Pfizer), developed and brought to the market the Pfizer-BioNtech COVID-19 vaccine.[17] The benefits of the medical cooperation entailed by increasing "the extent of the market" deserve to be more widely known.[18]

Among readily justified exclusions from permissible cross-border transfers are stolen goods and products of forced labor, such as goods manufactured by Uyghur people who are forced into concentration camps organized by the Chinese Communist Party.[19] Free countries do not establish concentration camps for the forced production of textiles. Forced labor should be forbidden, and the products of forced labor should not enter the stream of commerce, just as stolen goods may not be legally exchanged.[20] There is no human right to traffic in stolen products or compelled labor. That some stolen goods and products of involuntary labor manage to evade legal restrictions is no argument in favor of imposing restrictions on the exchange of products of voluntary labor and cooperation, any more than people committing fraud is an argument in favor of forbidding honest exchange. The overwhelming bulk of goods and services exchanged across political borders are products of voluntary labor and cooperation and should be permitted. Those that are the products of forced labor (or of theft) should be prohibited from entering the stream of commerce, whether domestically or internationally.

For the same reasons, organized raids of plunder and conquest (e.g., Russian troops plundering Ukrainian homes for washing machines) are contrary to the globalization defended here. Merely happening on the globe is not sufficient to be "globalization." As Adam Smith noted, imperialism, conquest, and the mercantilistic restrictions on freedom of exchange that followed were both immoral and harmful: "Folly and injustice seem to have been the principles which presided over and directed the first project of establishing those colonies; the folly of hunting after gold and silver mines, and the injustice of coveting the possession of a country whose harmless natives, far from having ever injured the people of Europe, had received the first adventurers with every mark of kindness and hospitality."[21]

Diversity of Human Experience

The same medicines can be found in hundreds of countries. Familiar names of hotel companies can be seen around the world. Italy, a country with its own rich culinary traditions, is also the location of Ethiopian, Thai, Ukrainian, and Korean restaurants, while Italian restaurants can be found in those countries. Credit cards and debit cards affiliated with Visa and Mastercard and American Express can be used in most countries. Do longer lives, greater convenience, and more opportunities for choice mean a loss of diversity? If so, would that be a diversity worth preserving?

In a deglobalized world in which only privileged people were free to travel and trade, those few privileged people would experience tremendous diversity every time they traveled from one country to another. Most people, however, would experience far less diversity. In a world in which people are free to trade and travel, though, most of us experience far more diversity than we would in a world without such freedom. Wealthy visitors to poorer countries often identify the culture of those countries with their poverty and "quaintness." That is a mistake. Icelanders, to take an example of a small nation with a distinct culture, maintain their language and way of life not by being isolated but by trading with foreigners and using their resulting wealth to sustain publishing houses, film production, education, and much more in their own language.[22] Economist Tyler Cowen described the forms of variety in his book *Creative Destruction: How Globalization Is Changing the World's Cultures*:

> When one society trades a new artwork to another society, diversity within society goes up (consumers have greater choice), but diversity across the two societies goes down (the two societies become more alike). The question is not about more or less diversity per se, but rather what kind of diversity globalization will bring. Cross-cultural exchange tends to favor diversity within society, but to disfavor diversity across societies.[23]

Cultural Identity and Purity

Moral opposition to change—to the erosion of cultural monotony—induced by the processes of globalization has deep roots. Plato's, and his student Aristotle's, praise of self-sufficiency (*autarkia*) is at the root of their general hostility to trade, their insistence on the distinction between Greeks and non-Greeks (i.e., barbarians, so-called because instead of speaking Greek, their words seemed to sound like "bar bar bar"), and their suspicion of *chrematistic*, or money-making. Thus, in Book IV of Plato's dialogue *The Republic*, it is agreed that a polis (or city-state) should be of a size and so structured as to be "sufficient and one."[24] Aristotle argued in Book VII, Chapter 4 of *The Politics* that a state (the translator's term for *polis*), "when composed of too few, is not, as a state ought to be, self-sufficient; when of too many, though self-sufficient in all mere necessaries, as a nation [*ethnos* in Greek] may be, it is not a state, being almost incapable of constitutional government. For who can be the general of such a vast multitude, or who the herald, unless he have the voice of a Stentor?"[25] Interdependence beyond the small embrace of the polis was considered perilous to unity and to autarkia; the extraordinary experience of Greek commerce in the ancient world was upending established moral orders and entrenched ruling classes by introducing new ideas, among them democracy and liberty, even to the point of questioning and undermining slavery, as Karl Popper documents in *The Open Society and Its Enemies*.[26] Plato and his students sought to preserve static social relations—analogous to his theory of unchanging forms—that were being overturned by globalization.

Ever since Plato's assault on the open society, critics of globalization have tended to view cultural innovation and exchange as a pure loss rather than as the emergence of new forms of human life that increase the available store of possible human understandings and experiences.

The modern form of that yearning for "unity" and the attendant criticism of globalization focuses on "identity." According to journalist Nadav Eyal in *Revolt: The Worldwide Uprising against Globalization*, "Economic globalization poses a significant threat to identity. It inevitably injects universal values into the local discourse, because of its need for supranational relations. Prosperity cannot be achieved alone, and the need for the economy to interact globally does not coexist easily with exclusive national power structures and community."[27] Setting aside the reification of globalization as an "it" that "needs" things, Eyal overlooks the fact that globalization is and always has been constitutive of identity. There are no "pure identities," just as there are no "pure races" or "pure cultures." Identities are constituted by the interplay of many influences, the intersections of ideas, trends, customs, practices, and experiences. As Jeremy Waldron asks, "What if there has been nothing but mélange all the way down? What if cultures have always been implicated with one another, through trade, war, curiosity, and other forms of intercommunal relation? What if the mingling of cultures is as immemorial as cultural roots themselves? What if purity and homogeneity have always been myths?"[28]

The anti-liberal writer Patrick Deneen enthusiastically embraces the illiberal ideas of Plato, whom he curiously refers to as "the Greeks," as if Plato represented them all, including those Plato lambastes in his writings.[29] Deneen blames globalization for the creation of identities that are "globally homogeneous, the precondition for a fungible global elite who readily identify other members capable of living in a culture-less and placeless world defined above all by liberal norms of globalized indifference toward shared fates of actual neighbors and communities. This in turn induces the globalized irresponsibility that was reflected in the economic interactions that precipitated the 2008 economic crisis but which is assuaged by calls for 'social justice,' generally to be handled through the depersonalized levers of the state."

Besides the sweeping economic claims (which notably ignore irresponsible domestic governmental policies in the United States that were ostensibly intended to secure ownership of homes for all Americans regardless of financial capability but instead created a massive real estate bubble, financial contagion, and global crisis), Deneen misunderstands what economic interdependence entails.[30] Trade tends to make people more connected to others and more interested in their welfare, precisely because their prosperity is entwined more when they trade than when they don't. Indeed, the prosperity of one community is beneficial to that of those with whom they trade, contrary to the zero-sum, beggar-thy-neighbor view embraced by anti-globalization advocates. Deneen identifies as the beneficiaries of globalization not the low-income people who have seen their real incomes rise as prices of goods, telecommunication, travel, and previously unimaginable things have plummeted but instead a shadowy "fungible global elite," which is an old trope in the repertoire of illiberalism, that of the "rootless cosmopolitans." As the economist Jean-Baptiste Say noted,

> A good harvest is favourable, not only to the agriculturist, but likewise to the dealers in all commodities generally. The greater the crop, the larger are the purchases of the growers. A bad harvest, on the contrary, hurts the sale of commodities at large. And so it is also with the products of manufacture and commerce. The success of one branch of commerce supplies more ample means of purchase, and consequently opens a market for the products of all the other branches; on the other hand, the stagnation of one channel of manufacture, or of commerce, is felt in all the rest.[31]

The same is true of nations across whose borders goods and services are freely traded. Peace and harmony are consequences of trade.[32]

Cultural exchange is foundational to living cultures. Pasta, for which Italian cuisine is famous, has origins in Asia, whether it was brought to Italy by Marco Polo, as folklore tells, or earlier, and the tomatoes that form the base of many Italian sauces are cultivated from plants brought from Mesoamerica by Spaniards. Food has been globalized for millennia, but somehow that has not stopped it from developing an amazing diversity of identifiable cuisines, styles, and dishes with many distinctive characteristics (see Chapter 22, "Food Globalization Puts the World on Your Plate"). The same can be said of architecture, traditions, mores, religions, and every other element of human culture.

Some local customs have dwindled or disappeared. Consider the virtual disappearance of human sacrifice and slavery, both of which had long traditions in many cultures. In that respect, all cultures have become more similar over time—and a good thing too. As a political example, if all the countries of the world were to adopt democracy and to throw off autocracies, tyrannies, colonial masters, and so on, there would be less diversity among systems of government, although a wide variety of forms (Westminster parliamentarism, federalism, presidential systems, constitutional monarchies, etc.) would remain. If genocide, ethnic cleansing, and colonialism were to be eliminated and replaced by some form of live-and-let-live mentality, another kind of diversity would be reduced.

But are such reductions of diversity morally objectionable? Some people, such as the influential legal theorist of the Third Reich Carl Schmitt, who posited the distinction of friend and enemy as the foundation of "the concept of the political," consider the replacement of tyrannies and dictatorships an unacceptable form of political homogenization.[33] However, people who wish to defend such political heterogeneity need to offer justification for their preference for dictatorship and violence and not merely assume that variety is preferable—just as someone advocating disease and suffering should not assume that it's better for some to be ill and some to be healthy on the grounds of variety. It matters what kind of variety is protected.

Globalization and Peace

In 1901, the first Nobel Peace Prize was awarded to Frédéric Passy "for his lifelong work for international peace conferences, diplomacy and arbitration."[34] Passy worked tirelessly for globalization because of its role in making war less likely and peace more likely.[35] As he wrote in *Leçons d'économie politique faites à Montpellier, 1860–1861*:

> Despite too many sad exceptions, the prevailing tendency is the rule of harmony and of universal agreement, which is so well expressed by the sublime idea of the unity and of the fraternity of the human race. The spring of that movement is exchange. Without exchange, human beings and whole peoples are lost brothers and become enemies. Through exchange, they learn to understand and to love one another. Their interests reconcile them and that reconciliation enlightens them. Without exchange, each stays in his corner, estranged from the whole universe, fallen in some way from the bulk of creation. . . . The doctrine of prohibition and of restriction not only preaches isolation and desolation but it condemns mankind to enmity and hatred.[36]

Passy's appreciation of the role of exchange in reconciling people and reducing war has been amply borne out by empirical research. Political scientist Erik Gartzke found that the well-known "democratic peace" is composed not only of the democratic practices of government by discussion, free elections, and freedom of the press (valuable and important as they are) but by the trade and development entwined with such democratic practices.[37] As he found, "Economic development, free markets, and similar interstate interests all anticipate a lessening of militarized disputes or wars. This 'capitalist peace' also accounts for the effect commonly attributed to regime type in standard statistical tests of the democratic peace." In other words, nations that embrace free exchange are more likely to enjoy peace than those that do not.

The key to such peace is not merely the movement of goods and services across borders but *voluntary exchange*. The study of interstate military conflict by political scientist Patrick J. McDonald came to two primary conclusions, which he notes in *The Invisible Hand of Peace: Capitalism, the War Machine, and International Relations Theory*: "First, liberal economic institutions promote peace. Second, these economic institutions have historically played a stronger role in promoting peace than democracy."[38] Trade among private parties—rather than between governments, such as characterized by the Communist trade bloc COMECON or today the export of state-owned oil and gas from Russia, which is, in effect, owned by the dictator Vladimir Putin—is essential to peace. Freedom to trade refers to the voluntary transfers of goods and services and not to state trafficking in tanks and missiles, the sale of products of forced labor (such as the products of Uyghur laborers imprisoned by the Chinese Communist Party), or the sale of nationalized products (such as the oil and gas resources that were confiscated by Putin). Exchange and transfers organized by conquest are mutually impoverishing, as Adam Smith demonstrated of the British Empire in the second volume of *The Wealth of Nations*:

> In the system of laws which has been established for the management of our American and West Indian colonies, the interest of the home-consumer has been sacrificed to that of the producer with a more extravagant profusion than in all our other commercial regulations. A great empire has been established for the sole purpose of raising up a nation of customers who should be obliged to buy from the shops of our different producers, all the goods with which these could supply them. For the sake of that little enhancement of price which this monopoly might afford our producers, the home-consumers have been burdened with the whole expence of maintaining and defending that empire. For this purpose, and for this purpose only, in the two last wars, more than two hundred millions have been spent, and a new debt of more than a hundred and seventy millions has been contracted over and above all that had been expended for the same purpose in former wars. The interest of this debt alone is not only greater than the whole extraordinary profit, which, it ever could be pretended, was made by the monopoly of the colony trade, but than the whole value of that trade or than that whole value of the goods, which at an average have been annually exported to the colonies.[39]

Mercantilistic policies impoverish.

Some people, of course, consider the achievement of peace insignificant and focus instead on the moral character of the motives of traders.

Although trade reduces war, if it stems from the pursuit of self-interest, they believe, trade should be condemned. Prominent among such critics was the businessman Friedrich Engels, the coauthor with Karl Marx of *The German Ideology*, *The Communist Manifesto*, and other works, who attacked the liberal case for peace and free trade in no uncertain terms:

> You have brought about the fraternization of the peoples—but the fraternity is the fraternity of thieves. You have reduced the number of wars—to earn all the bigger profits in peace, to intensify to the utmost the enmity between individuals, the ignominious war of competition! When have you done anything "out of pure humanity," from consciousness of the futility of the opposition between the general and the individual interest? When have you been moral without being interested, without harboring at the back of your mind immoral, egoistical motives?[40]

In other words, liberalism and free trade may have "reduced the number of wars," but it was done only "to earn all the bigger profits in peace." The point deserves emphasis: Engels found bigger profits, which he abhorred (unless they were his), of far greater concern than reducing the number of wars.

Contrast the bitter disdain for peace of Engels with the liberal and humanitarian approach of Voltaire, who dismissed the pretentions of self-styled superior people and embraced the benefits of trade:

> In France anybody who wants to can be a marquis; and whoever arrives in Paris from the remotest part of some province with money to spend and an ac or an ille at the end of his name, may indulge in such phrases as "a man of my sort," "a man of my rank and quality," and with sovereign eye look down upon a wholesaler. The merchant himself so often hears his profession spoken of disdainfully that he is fool enough to blush. Yet I don't know which is the more useful to a state, a well-powdered lord who knows precisely what time the king gets up in the morning and what time he goes to bed, and who gives himself airs of grandeur while playing the role of slave in a minister's antechamber, or a great merchant who enriches his country, sends orders from his office to Surat and to Cairo, and contributes to the wellbeing of the world.[41]

Reasonable concerns about "weaponized interdependence" (e.g., the Putin dictatorship's use of oil and gas exports to control neighboring countries) have not seriously dented the case for globalization. Tailored responses, principally those initiated by market participants, but also including by governments, may be justified without undermining the general case for globalization and the benefits of increasing the extent of the market. As Daniel Drezner concluded in Chapter 13 of this book, "The Dangers of Misunderstanding Economic Interdependence,"

> While weaponized interdependence is a real phenomenon, national governments have wildly exaggerated their capacity to exploit it to advance their own foreign policy ends. The result has been a lot of sanctioning activity and very few concessions to show for it. Going forward, the danger is that in attempting to ward off weaponized interdependence, the United States, China, and other great powers will pursue policies that make it easier to conceive of great power conflict.

Increasing globalization makes war less likely and peace more likely. Obviously globalization does not make violence impossible, but it makes violence less likely, and that certainly should count as a strong reason to embrace globalization.

Conclusion

Since the days of Plato, people have denounced globalization as immoral. They have claimed that globalization leads to changes in culture and identity, without grasping that cultures and identities are not ideal forms to be preserved eternally but changing and evolving practices. Since Plato's time, opponents of globalization have sought to protect established orders from the voluntary choices of those who live in them. Increasing the opportunities for exchange, cooperation, communication, and travel is enriching for the majority, although it may threaten the hold on power of the rulers. Some prefer war over peace, because "making bigger profits in peace" is worse than war. Reasonable people should think before embracing such attacks on globalization, even if they are attributed to "the Greeks," or at least to some of them.

Rigorous thinking and empirical research refute, one by one, attacks on globalization in the name of morality. The world is better when barriers to free and voluntary cooperation are reduced. The world is better because of globalization.

SECTION THREE

Globalization in Our Lives

Chapter 19

The More Resources We Consume, the More We Have

Marian L. Tupy

- It is conventional wisdom that adding billions of people to the global economy must result in increased use and therefore greater scarcity of resources, but that is wrong.
- Resources have become significantly cheaper since 1980 relative to wages, thereby becoming much more abundant.
- Humans, especially those living in countries on the frontier of innovation, create new knowledge that allows us to grow our resources well beyond our consumption.
- Globalization allows this new knowledge to flow from the countries on the frontier of innovation to the "catch-up" nations, leading to improved economic and environmental outcomes worldwide.

Common sense dictates that adding billions of people to the global economy—and the subsequent rise in production and consumption—must result in increased use and, therefore, greater scarcity of resources.[1] Many of the academic and nonacademic opinions agree on that point, but they are all mistaken. Relative to wages, resources have grown significantly cheaper since 1980, thereby becoming much more abundant. We thus face a seeming contradiction: the more resources we use, the more we end up with. Resolving that requires us to understand the key role played by the creation of knowledge.

Knowledge possesses a peculiar characteristic: the more knowledge we consume, the more knowledge we have. Furthermore, generation of new knowledge is the exclusive domain of the human mind. So, the more people who inhabit the planet and partake in global exchange, the more knowledge is created. This new knowledge, in turn, expands our resource base. Globalization—or the process of interaction and integration between people and companies worldwide—supercharges the process of knowledge creation and knowledge dissemination, thereby leading to greater resource abundance.

Empirical Evidence for Falling Resource Prices

The Simon Abundance Index, which I coauthored with Gale L. Pooley, is an annual measure of the relationship between population growth and the abundance of 50 basic commodities, including food, energy, materials, minerals, and metals.[2] The base year of the index is 1980, and the base value of the index is 100 percent. In 2020, the index reached 708.4 percent. In other words, the index rose by 608.4 percentage points over the preceding four decades, implying a compound annual growth rate in resource abundance of around 5 percent and a doubling of global resource abundance every 14 years or so (Figure 19.1).

The Simon Abundance Index is measured in time prices, or the number of hours that the average worker must work to earn enough money to buy something. To calculate a commodity's time price, the nominal price of a commodity is divided by the global average nominal wage per hour worked. Between 1980 and 2020, the average nominal price of the 50 commodities rose by 51.9 percent and the global average nominal hourly wage rose by 412.4 percent. So the average time price of the 50 commodities fell by 75.2 percent.

The personal resource abundance multiplier is calculated by dividing the average time price of the 50 commodities in 1980 by the average time price of the 50 commodities in 2020. The multiplier tells us how

FIGURE 19.1

The Simon Abundance Index rose by over 600 percentage points over the past 40 years

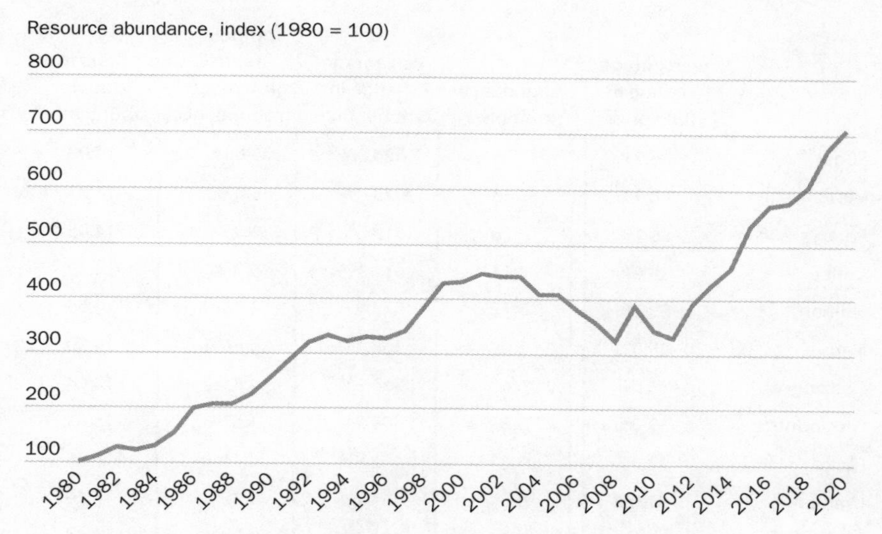

Source: Gale Pooley and Marian Tupy, "The Simon Abundance Index 2021," Human Progress, April 22, 2021.

much more of a resource a person can buy for the same hours of work between two points in time. Pooley and I found that the same hours of work bought one unit in the basket of 50 commodities in 1980 and 4.03 units in the same basket in 2020.

The average worker's personal resource abundance rose by 303 percent. The compound annual growth rate in personal resource abundance amounted to 3.55 percent, implying that personal resource abundance doubled every 20 years.

Between 1980 and 2020, the average time price of the 50 commodities fell by 75.2 percent and the world's population increased by 75.8 percent. So, for every 1 percent increase in the world's population, the average time price of the 50 commodities decreased by almost 1 percent (i.e., −75.2 percent ÷ 75.8 percent = −0.992 percent).

Note that the personal resource abundance analysis looks at resource abundance from the perspective of an individual human being. The

FIGURE 19.2

The time prices and abundance of 50 basic commodities over time (1980–2018)

	Percentage change in time price	Abundance multiplier	Percentage change in abundance	Compound annual growth rate in abundance	Years to double abundance
Sugar	−86.2%	7.25	624.9%	5.08%	14.00
Hides	−86.2%	7.23	623.4%	5.07%	14.01
Pork	−86.1%	7.20	619.6%	5.06%	14.05
Coffee	−85.9%	7.11	611.1%	5.03%	14.13
Salmon	−85.1%	6.72	572.4%	4.88%	14.55
Natural gas, EU	−85.0%	6.68	568.1%	4.86%	14.60
Cotton	−85.0%	6.65	564.6%	4.85%	14.64
Groundnuts	−83.0%	5.89	489.2%	4.53%	15.63
Cocoa	−82.2%	5.63	462.8%	4.41%	16.05
Uranium	−82.0%	5.54	454.1%	4.37%	16.19
Aluminum	−81.3%	5.34	434.3%	4.28%	16.54
Lamb	−81.1%	5.30	429.8%	4.26%	16.63
Silver	−80.7%	5.19	419.5%	4.21%	16.83
Tin	−80.1%	5.03	402.5%	4.12%	17.17
Crude oil	−78.2%	4.58	358.4%	3.88%	18.21
Rice	−76.4%	4.24	324.2%	3.68%	19.19
Rubber	−76.3%	4.21	321.1%	3.66%	19.29
Wheat	−76.1%	4.18	317.9%	3.64%	19.39
Barley	−75.7%	4.11	311.2%	3.60%	19.61
Shrimp	−75.6%	4.11	310.5%	3.59%	19.63
Natural gas, US	−75.2%	4.04	303.8%	3.55%	19.87
Average	−75.2%	4.03	303.0%	3.55%	19.89
Palm oil	−74.8%	3.97	297.2%	3.51%	20.10
Platinum	−74.6%	3.94	294.3%	3.49%	20.21
Corn	−74.5%	3.93	292.6%	3.48%	20.27

FIGURE 19.2 (*continued*)

The time prices and abundance of 50 basic commodities over time (1980–2018)

	Percentage change in time price	Abundance multiplier	Percentage change in abundance	Compound annual growth rate in abundance	Years to double abundance
Sorghum	−74.0%	3.85	285.3%	3.43%	20.56
Soybeans	−72.4%	3.62	261.9%	3.27%	21.56
LNG, Japan	−71.6%	3.52	251.6%	3.19%	22.05
Fertilizer	−71.6%	3.52	251.6%	3.19%	22.05
Coconut oil	−70.8%	3.42	242.4%	3.12%	22.53
Orange	−70.8%	3.42	242.0%	3.12%	22.55
Coal	−70.5%	3.39	238.7%	3.10%	22.73
Logs	−70.4%	3.38	238.1%	3.09%	22.76
Rapeseed	−69.9%	3.32	232.3%	3.05%	23.09
Wool	−69.7%	3.30	230.4%	3.03%	23.20
Tea	−68.3%	3.15	215.4%	2.91%	24.14
Sawnwood	−67.6%	3.09	209.1%	2.86%	24.57
Beef	−67.0%	3.03	203.2%	2.81%	25.00
Plywood	−63.6%	2.75	174.5%	2.56%	27.46
Sunflower oil	−63.0%	2.70	170.0%	2.51%	27.92
Tobacco	−62.5%	2.67	166.6%	2.48%	28.27
Lead	−60.7%	2.55	154.6%	2.36%	29.67
Nickel	−58.8%	2.43	142.5%	2.24%	31.29
Chicken	−58.2%	2.39	139.2%	2.20%	31.79
Copper	−44.8%	1.81	81.3%	1.50%	46.60
Fish meal	−44.6%	1.81	80.6%	1.49%	46.92
Gold	−43.2%	1.76	76.1%	1.43%	48.97
Zinc	−42.0%	1.72	72.3%	1.37%	50.97
Banana	−37.5%	1.60	59.9%	1.18%	59.04
Iron ore	−24.4%	1.32	32.3%	0.70%	99.07

Source: Author's calculations.

Note: EU = European Union; LNG = liquefied natural gas.

question we aim to answer is: How much more abundant have resources become for the average worker?

Population resource abundance analysis, in contrast, allows us to quantify the relationship between global resource abundance and global population growth. You can think of the difference between the two levels of analysis by using a pizza analogy. Personal resource abundance measures the size of a slice of pizza per person. Population resource abundance measures the size of the entire pizza pie.

The population resource abundance multiplier is calculated by multiplying the change in personal resource abundance with the change in global population (i.e., 4.03×1.758). The multiplier of 7.08 corresponds to the 708.4 percent increase in the Simon Abundance Index. It indicates an increase in the global resource abundance of 608.4 percent at a compound annual growth rate of around 5 percent. As such, Pooley and I estimate that global resource abundance doubled every 14 years or so.

Finally, let us look at the resource abundance elasticity of population. In economics, elasticity measures one variable's sensitivity to a change in another variable. If variable x changes by 10 percent, while variable y, because of the change in x, changes by 5 percent, then the elasticity coefficient of x relative to y is 2.0 (i.e., 10÷5). A coefficient of 2.0 can be interpreted as a 2 percent change in x corresponding to a 1 percent change in y.

Pooley and I found that every 1 percent increase in population corresponded to an increase in personal resource abundance (i.e., the size of the slice of pizza) of 4 percent (i.e., 303÷75.8). We also found that every 1 percent increase in population corresponded to an increase in population resource abundance (i.e., the size of the pizza pie) of 8.03 percent (608.5÷75.8).

Knowledge Creation and Resource Expansion

There are several ways in which humans can make resources more abundant. To start, consider the increase of supply. When the price of a commodity increases, people have a monetary incentive to start searching for new sources of that commodity. For example, when the price of petroleum increases, people will look for more oil deposits. Thus, after a century of petroleum use, we have more known reserves of oil than ever before. Moreover, much of Earth's crust, not to mention the ocean floor, remains unexplored. The potential for finding much more petroleum when the price of oil is high enough to induce us to dig deeper and explore more exotic locations is very high. The supply of petroleum can also be increased through technological change. Many of the oil fields that were previously deemed exhausted still contain a great deal of oil trapped in underground shale rock. Replacing conventional oil drilling with hydraulic fracturing allows us to get at that oil in an economical way.

Increased efficiency is also important. Efficiency can increase in relative and absolute ways. For example, when the Coca-Cola can first appeared on the market in the late 1950s, it contained three ounces of aluminum. Today, it contains half an ounce. Of course, it is possible to decrease the amount of aluminum in each soda can while producing so many cans that the absolute amount of aluminum used increases. Remarkably, Andrew McAfee from the Massachusetts Institute of Technology found that the total amount of resources used by the US economy peaked in the first decade of the new millennium and then started to decline. To be precise, 66 out of 72 resources tracked by the US Geological Survey were "post-peak" when McAfee wrote his book *More from Less* in 2019.[3] In the meantime, the US economy continued to expand. Similar trends could be observed in the United Kingdom and some other advanced economies.

Dematerialization helps to explain why economic growth and resource use reduction can go hand in hand. Most readers will be familiar with thick blue copper cables that ran from the walls of most hotel rooms in the United States until recently. That cable enabled hotel guests to access the internet—a task that can now be accomplished via Wi-Fi. No cables are necessary, and all that saved copper can be used somewhere else. The iPhone is another example of dematerialization, for it replaces (or substantially decreases the need for) calculators, satellite navigation, watches, torches, radios, compasses, cameras, postal mail, telephones, voice recorders, stereos, alarm clocks, and many other things. In addition to the materials not used in the process of making an iPhone, we must also add the energy not used in the mining of the resources that are no longer needed and in the running of all the separate devices that the iPhone replaces.

New knowledge can also help us create ever more value from the same resource. Around 5,000 years ago, someone in Mesopotamia noticed that when sand is heated to 3,090 degrees Fahrenheit, it melts and turns to glass. Our distant ancestors' first use of glass was for decorative purposes, such as glass beads. Sometime later, they started to use sand to make glass jars, cups, and, later still, windows. Today, we use glass in fiberoptic cables and microchips. With every step of the way, the value we derived from a grain of sand increased, and no one knows what marvelous innovations will rely on sand in the future. The US economist Thomas Sowell is thus surely correct to observe that "the cavemen had the same natural resources at their disposal as we have today, and the difference between their standard of living and ours is a difference between the knowledge they could bring to bear on those resources and the knowledge used today."[4]

Consider also our ability to turn a previously useless or even harmful resource to our benefit. In the early 20th century, when oil was the primary target of drilling operations, natural gas was often seen as a byproduct with little or no economic value. As such, gas was frequently vented into the atmosphere or flared (burned off), which was wasteful and environmentally harmful. Moreover, natural gas leaks were a significant hazard, particularly in oil fields, where accidental ignitions could lead to explosions. Today in advanced economies, we have the technology to capture, transport, sell, and use gas in great volumes, thereby increasing our resource base and reducing our carbon dioxide emissions into the atmosphere.

Substitution is a crucial economic concept that's much underappreciated by the public. Generally, we don't care how we obtain a good or a service, so long as we get it at an acceptable cost. Thus, humans felled forests to get the wood they needed to heat their homes and slaughtered whales to get lamp oil for illumination. Today, many of us heat and light our homes using electricity derived from a variety of sources, including mostly carbon dioxide–free nuclear fission, with the added benefit that both forests and whales have rebounded. Those concerned about resources that are currently in high demand (such as lithium, which is needed to make batteries for electric vehicles) should take substitution into account. No one knows what resources will be needed to make batteries in 50—let alone 100—years' time. But new technology-driven surprises are almost guaranteed.

We can also recycle and reuse our resources. The aforementioned copper internet cables, for example, were almost certainly recycled and turned into something else—perhaps copper pipes used in residential plumbing. The 14,000 tons of US government silver, which was used in electromagnets needed by the Manhattan Project to make atomic bombs, was similarly recovered after the end of World War II and added to the stock of precious metals that propped up the value of the US dollar. The point is that atoms of copper, silver, zinc, and much else are only temporarily assigned to perform a certain task. If necessary, they can be extracted and reassigned to make or do something else.

While humans have explored only a tiny fraction of our planet, it is theoretically possible that at some point in the distant future we could encounter an acute shortage of a resource, such as the very rare rhodium, which is currently used in catalytic converters. Let us further assume that the limits on the natural supply of that metal cannot be overcome via increased efficiency, dematerialization, substitution, recycling, or anything else.

In such a case, our descendants could turn to transmutation. Transmutation, which was once a province of alchemy, became real in 1919 when scientists turned nitrogen into oxygen. According to an article I coauthored with University of Oxford physicist David Deutsch, today, transmutation is everywhere. The smoke detectors in our homes, for example, contain americium—a synthetic radioactive metal produced by plutonium's absorption of neutrons in nuclear reactors. Specialists transmuted lead into gold many years ago—though the process is currently uneconomical, for it requires far too much energy to replace mining.[5]

The key to transmutation, then, is plentiful, reliable, supercheap energy, which could be provided by, for example, future fusion reactors. Lest we forget, it was via fusion (nucleosynthesis, to be precise) that many of the elements we use on Earth were created in the first place. Incredibly high temperatures and pressures inside different stars transformed lighter elements into heavier ones, and the heavier elements dispersed throughout the universe after supernovae. Some of those elements eventually helped to form our planet and can be mined from Earth's crust.

By the time humanity needs to resort to such sophisticated measures to increase our resource base, we may well be a spacefaring civilization, mining the asteroid belt between Mars and Jupiter by ourselves or with the help of AI robots. The belt is rich in resources, including water. Water, which covers 71 percent of our planet, is key, for it contains hydrogen, which also happens to be the most common element in the universe. The Big Bang created only the lightest elements, primarily hydrogen. All other elements are derived from those. A combination of hydrogen and fusion, therefore, could allow us to create everything else we need de novo—indefinitely.

Globalization, the Spread of Knowledge, and Resource Creation

In the 2021 edition of the Simon Abundance Index, Pooley and I found that the time price of wheat fell by 76.1 percent between 1980 and 2020. That means that for the same number of hours of work that would have bought our worker a pound of wheat in 1980, he or she could have bought 4.18 pounds of wheat in 2020. Resource abundance of the worker rose by 318 percent, growing at a compounded annual rate of 3.64 percent, thereby doubling every 19.4 years. (The COVID-19 pandemic and the Russian war on Ukraine affected these numbers negatively, yet Pooley and I found that the trend still holds in the 2024 edition of the index.[6])

Over the same period (1980–2020), the world's population rose from 4.44 billion to 7.82 billion, or by 76 percent. Put differently, for every 1 percent increase in global population, the time price of wheat fell by 1 percent. In addition to population growth, the latest round of globalization, which is generally taken to have started in 1980, added billions of new workers to the global economic exchange. These factors contributed to a massive increase in resource consumption and output not only in the countries on the frontier of innovation, such as the United States and those in Western Europe, but also in the "catch-up" countries, such as Bangladesh, Brazil, China, India, Vietnam, and the nations of the former Eastern Bloc. Personal incomes and consumption rose.

Yet wheat, a staple eaten all over the world, became much more abundant. Here the salutary effects of globalization are easily discernible because several Western companies have been at the forefront of the agricultural revolution that provided technologies, seeds, and farming practices that enhanced wheat productivity in the catch-up countries. Consider some real-life examples:

- **Syngenta's disease-resistant wheat varieties.** Syngenta, a global agribusiness company headquartered in Switzerland, has developed wheat varieties that are resistant to common diseases and pests. For instance, in parts of Africa and Asia, Syngenta's disease-resistant wheat varieties have helped farmers combat issues such as wheat rust, a major threat to wheat crops. These varieties have not only increased yields per acre of land but also ensured more stable wheat production.
- **John Deere's advanced agricultural machinery.** American company John Deere is known for its advanced agricultural machinery. The adoption of this machinery in countries such as India and Ethiopia has revolutionized wheat farming. Mechanized tractors, planters, and harvesters have increased the efficiency of planting and harvesting wheat, leading to higher yields and reduced labor costs.
- **BASF's agronomic solutions.** German chemical company BASF provides various agronomic solutions, including fertilizers and pesticides, which are crucial in wheat cultivation. For example, in countries such as Mexico and Pakistan, the use of BASF's fertilizers and pesticides has resulted in better wheat crop health and increased yields by controlling pests and enhancing soil fertility.

- **Bayer's crop science innovations.** Bayer, following its acquisition of Monsanto, has become a key player in agricultural technologies. The company's development of integrated crop solutions, including advanced seed treatments and chemical products, has improved wheat yields. For example, in Brazil and parts of Africa, Bayer's products have helped farmers grow wheat more efficiently, even under challenging climatic conditions.
- **DuPont's hybrid wheat seeds.** DuPont (now part of Corteva Agriscience after a merger with the Dow Chemical Company) has developed hybrid wheat seeds that are tailored to specific climatic and soil conditions. These seeds have been particularly effective in Eastern Europe and parts of Asia, where they have helped boost wheat yields through improved disease resistance and stress tolerance.
- **CIMMYT's collaboration with Western companies.** The International Maize and Wheat Improvement Center (CIMMYT), though not a commercial entity, collaborates with Western companies to develop high-yielding wheat varieties. CIMMYT's work in countries such as Kenya and India, often in partnership with Western agricultural companies, has led to the introduction of wheat varieties that are well suited to local conditions, resulting in significant yield improvements.

The results of the spread of information and technologies from the countries on the frontier of innovation to the catch-up countries are readily discernible. In 1980, wheat productivity measured in 100 grams per hectare was lower, sometimes substantially, in the catch-up countries relative to the United States and Western Europe.[7] By 2020, some had overtaken the United States, while all of them, including the United States, remained less productive relative to Western Europe. Still, all the selected catch-up countries experienced greater productivity gains than the United States and Western Europe between 1980 and 2020 (see Table 19.1).

TABLE 19.1

"Catch-up" countries experienced greater wheat productivity gains than the United States and countries in Western Europe between 1980 and 2020

Country/region	Output in 1980 (100 grams per hectare)	Output in 2020 (100 grams per hectare)	Percent increase
Western Europe	46,726	65,421	40
United States	22,513	33,417	48
Brazil	8,653	26,073	201
China	18,914	57,421	204
India	14,356	34,398	140
Northern Africa	12,749	22,784	79
Eastern Europe	29,395 (1992)	48,913	66
World	20,395	33,737	65

Source: "Production / Crops and Livestock Products—Metadata," Food and Agriculture Organization of the United Nations, June 22, 2023.

Environmental Benefits

The period of globalization saw absolute poverty (the threshold of which is considered to be earning wages of $2.15 or less per day) measured in 2017 dollars adjusted for purchasing power parity decline from 43.8 percent in 1981 to 8.9 percent in 2019.[8] Concomitantly, the calorie supply per person rose from 2,497 in 1981 to 2,928 in 2018, or by 17 percent.[9] In Africa, the world's poorest continent, the calorie supply per person rose from 2,238 to 2,604, or by 16 percent, over the same period.[10] That's higher than the Portuguese calorie supply in the early 1960s. This trend is likely going to improve in the future, raising the obvious question: What will happen to the animal and plant habitats as humans strive to produce more food and other resources? The answer is once again counterintuitive.

Writing about US corn production in 2015, Jesse H. Ausubel, an environmental scientist at the Rockefeller University, said: "The average yield of American farmers is nowhere near a ceiling. In 2013, David Hula, a farmer in Virginia, grew a US and probably world record: 454 bushels of corn per acre—three times the average yield in Iowa. . . . In 2014, Hula's harvest rose 5 percent higher to 476 bushels, while Randy Dowdy, who farms near Valdosta, Georgia, busted the 500-bushel wall with a yield of 503 bushels per acre and won the National Corn Growers Contest."[11] And, Ausubel continued, "if we keep lifting average yields toward the demonstrated levels of David Hula and Randy Dowdy . . . then an area the size of India or of the United States east of the Mississippi could be released globally from agriculture over the next 50 years or so."

A similar story can also be told of wheat, rice, barley, potatoes, cassava, beans, and other crops. There is no obvious limit on our ability to produce ever more staples per hectare, thus returning ever larger chunks of the planet back to nature, except for the generation of knowledge and its dissemination to (and acceptance in) the least developed corners of the world. Whether lab-grown meat can alleviate the environmental footprint of cattle, chicken, and pig farming is still an open question. At present, the knowledge to make lab-grown meat economical does not exist.[12] But knowledge is not stagnant. It grows, and those who are betting against lab-grown meats may yet lose their shirts. Finally, the exploitation of raw materials has grown much cleaner in recent decades, a trend that's likely to continue as nations develop and, per the environmental Kuznets curve, place greater emphasis on environmental quality.[13]

Conclusion

Humans, especially those living in the countries on the frontier of innovation, create knowledge that allows us to grow our resources well in excess of the resources that we consume. Consequently, resources have grown much cheaper relative to wages and, therefore, more abundant. In terms of overall human well-being, however, it is globalization that allows the new knowledge to flow from the countries on the frontier of innovation to the catch-up nations. Finally, the planet and its biosphere benefit as catch-up nations adopt best practices and begin to approximate the care for the environment that's characteristic of innovative societies.

Chapter 20

Trade Buys Goods, Services, and Time

Gabriella Beaumont-Smith

- Trade provides many benefits to consumers beyond "cheap T-shirts."
- Liberalizing trade increases product variety, boosts companies' competitiveness, promotes innovation, and increases disposable incomes.
- Trade also provides nonfinancial benefits for people and their communities: by helping us consume more for less, we have more time for hobbies, charity work, or other forms of social interaction.
- While global trade has liberalized extensively since the 18th century, there is still work to be done to reduce tariffs and other trade restrictions and thus further enhance trade's important consumer benefits.

International trade is an important part of globalization, and consumers are one of trade's biggest beneficiaries. Most obviously, trade provides consumers—both people and companies—with lower prices and expanded variety, but it does much more than that. Trade gives people the autonomy to specialize in activities they're good at, earn income from that activity, and then buy goods and services from others who excel at producing those things. As a result, people have more resources, bigger paychecks, and more time to invest in other activities. Overall, they're better off—much better off—than they'd be in a world with less trade.

While trade has liberalized, especially in the last 75 years, much work remains. The most basic trade restriction—a tariff (a tax on imports)—is ever present and needlessly raises the prices of goods and services. Today, although tariffs are a far cry from the prohibitive rates of the 19th century, policymakers instead craft complicated rules that people must navigate to buy and sell across borders. Domestic regulations can further stifle trade, far beyond what may be necessary to protect health, safety, or the environment.

Nonetheless, how trade raises peoples' standards of living is unquestionable; in order to continue pulling people out of poverty, promoting innovation, and raising living standards for all, further liberalizing trade is imperative.

Why Do People Trade?

Before modern-day currency, people traded by bartering—or exchanging goods and services for other goods and services. However, this required people to have an array of things to offer as some goods and services were worth more than others, thus a "diversity" in "currency" was necessary. By 3000 BC, bartering developed into long-distance trade as people needed different materials for the development of civilization.[1] Through this process, people began to discover what they could do and make well and began to exchange with one another, driving specialized production and laying the bedrock for today's supply chains.

Adam Smith explores this phenomenon in *An Inquiry into the Nature and Causes of the Wealth of Nations*. Smith observes that "every man thus lives by exchanging, or becomes in some measure a merchant, and the society itself grows to be what is properly a commercial society."[2] Simply put, a developed society and economy is borne of people specializing in what they are good at and exchanging with others.

The example of how we moved from growing our own food and making our own clothes to buying these products illustrates specialization's benefits. Purchasing food and clothes from those better suited to make these goods (i.e., they have a comparative advantage) allows buyers to hone their skills in other sectors (see Chapter 3, "Comparative Advantage"). Specialization also saves resources such as time and money. Fewer wasted resources means people can consume more leisure or invest in themselves so that they can better compete in their industry, contributing to entrepreneurialism and innovation, and overall economic growth.

How Was Multilateral Trade Liberalization Established?

Specialization also applies internationally: countries (like people) are better off producing the goods and services in which they have a comparative advantage and trading for everything else. Trade barriers make it more difficult for people to do this; thus, lowering trade restrictions helps to maximize national welfare.

Governments have long entered into international agreements to achieve this trade liberalization (see Chapter 6, "Why Do We Need Trade Agreements at All?"). In 1860, two significant world powers, Great Britain and France, signed the Cobden-Chevalier Treaty, which liberalized trade and is considered the first significant bilateral preferential trade agreement. It stipulated preferential tariffs (lower taxes on imports) for important traded goods between the two nations and included most-favored nation treatment—nondiscriminatory treatment for all other goods traded between the two countries.[3] The Cobden-Chevalier Treaty was followed by 56 similar bilateral trade agreements in Europe, laying the foundation for multilateral trade liberalization. Though the network created by these agreements resembled multilateralism, the liberalization was not uniform and not convened by all parties. For example, Britain and France could freely trade, and France and Belgium could freely trade, but Britain did not have an agreement with Belgium. For Britain to receive preferential treatment for Belgian products, those goods would need to be traded through France, whereas in a multilateral system, Britain would be able to freely trade with Belgium because France, Belgium, and Britain would grant equal treatment to one another.

On the contrary, the United States teetered between increasing and decreasing tariffs from 1790 to the 1930s. The newly independent United States used tariffs to raise government revenue. US tariffs ranged from around 12 percent to over 60 percent between 1790 and 1830.[4] As illustrated in Figure 20.1, tariffs fell to around 19 percent by 1861. From 1862 to 1932, the average US tariff on dutiable imports reached almost 60 percent and remained high for several decades. However, as France and the United Kingdom liberalized trade through the Cobden-Chevalier Treaty, the United States returned to a protectionist agenda.

FIGURE 20.1

The average US tariff has declined substantially over the past 200 years

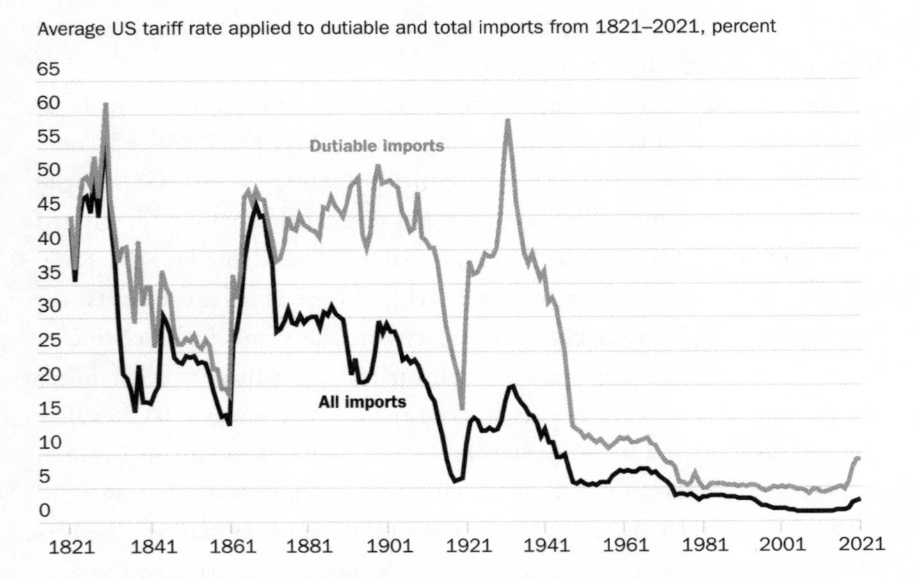

Source: Bureau of the Census, "Series U 207–212. Value of Merchandise Imports and Duties: 1821 to 1970," in *Historical Statistics of the United States: Colonial Times to 1970, Part II* (Washington: Department of Commerce, 1975), p. 288; and "Table 1. US Imports for Consumption, Duties Collected, and Ratio of Duties Collected to Value, 1891–2021 (Thousand $)," US International Trade Commission.

Note: Only covers goods imports. Dutiable imports are imports that are subject to tariffs (i.e., did not enter duty-free).

FIGURE 20.2

While the United Kingdom and France lowered tariffs in the 1860s, the United States radically increased them

Average tariff rate on all imports, 7-year moving average, percent

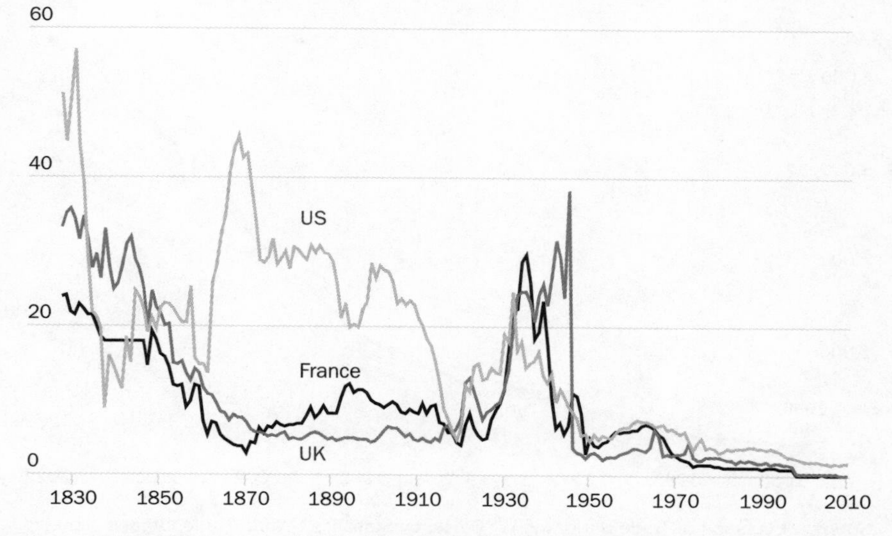

Source: Michael Fouquin and Jules Hugot, "Back to the Future: International Trade Costs and the Two Globalizations," Centre d'Etudes Prospectives et d'Informations Internationales Working Paper no. 2016-13, May 2016, p. 35.

As illustrated in Figure 20.2, while the United Kingdom and France lowered tariffs in the 1860s, the United States radically increased them. In fact, during this period, US tariffs were among the highest in the world.

However, after World War II, trade liberalization was recognized as the pathway to peace and prosperity and expanded by multiple rounds of multilateral trade negotiations. In 1948, the General Agreement on Tariffs and Trade (the GATT) entered into force. The agreement was founded by 23 countries that agreed to reduce tariffs and create rules against members implementing other restrictive trade measures. Between 1948 and 1994, the GATT attracted 128 members and completed seven rounds of negotiations to increase tariff concessions and establish global trading rules.[5] In 1995, the GATT was absorbed into the World Trade Organization (WTO), which continues negotiations to establish

FIGURE 20.3

World trade volume grew nearly 45-fold between 1950 and 2022

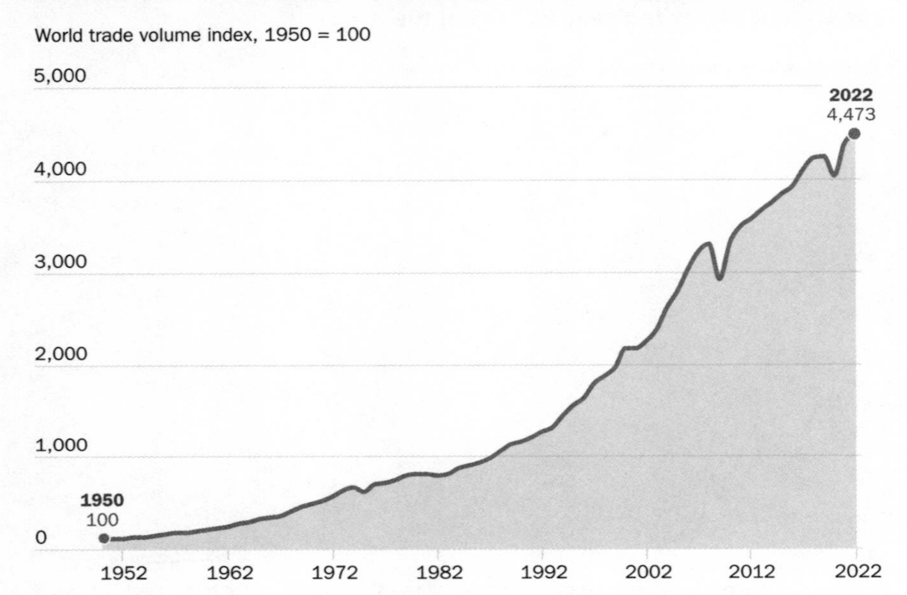

Source: "Evolution of Trade under the WTO: Handy Statistics," World Trade Organization.

new trade rules and attract new members.[6] Today, the WTO comprises 166 members, and the average tariff rate between member countries is 9 percent.[7] As a result of the GATT and the WTO, world trade grew exponentially. From 1950 to 2022, trade volumes increased by almost 45 times, as shown in Figure 20.3.

How Has Trade Improved Living Standards?

Liberalizing trade on a multilateral level brought immense benefits to global welfare, particularly those living in extreme poverty (defined today as living on less than $2.15 per day).[8] According to the Organisation for Economic Co-operation and Development, in 1820, more than half of the world lived in extremely impoverished conditions.[9] In 1995, after the establishment of the WTO, 32.8 percent of the global population lived in poverty, but by 2019, that share dropped to 8.5 percent (Figure 20.4).

FIGURE 20.4

Poverty has declined in the last 40 years, in part due to multilateral trade liberalization

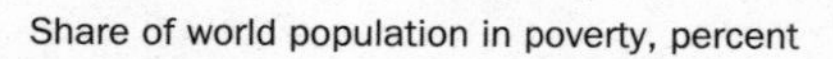

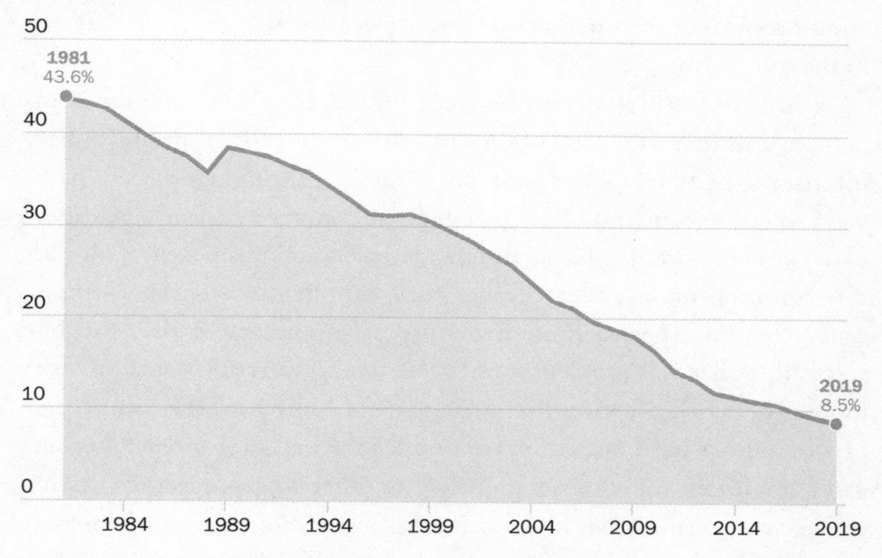

Source: "Poverty Headcount Ratio at $2.15 a Day (2017 PPP) (% of Population)," World Development Indicators, World Bank.
Note: Poverty is defined as living on $2.15 or less a day, in 2017 purchasing power parity terms.

Much of this decline came from China's shift toward a market economy in the 1980s and entrance into the global trading system. Almost 585 million or so Chinese people escaped extreme poverty between 1995 and 2021, but about 640 million other people worldwide did too.

The freedom to trade directly contributed to these improvements. When trade barriers are lowered, for example by reducing tariffs, imports become cheaper. Lower import prices provide multiple avenues to raise real incomes. Removing tariffs eliminates the tax burden imposed on those that consume imported products, and all taxes are regressive, which means that they disproportionately impact the poorest people. Thus, those in the lowest income brackets benefit most from the removal of tariffs.

It is not always the case that reducing or removing tariffs makes imports cheaper than domestic products that compete with imports. Rather, the benefit is that the market sees more price variety offered by both foreign and domestic sellers when trade barriers are lowered. The cheaper varieties—whether domestic or foreign—create price competition. This is when companies strive to provide lower prices to lure customers, creating pressure on competitors to lower prices so that prices overall fall in the long term.

Price competition occurs between both domestic and foreign competitors and increases accessibility to substitutes. Not all products have substitutes, particularly not good ones, but liberalizing trade opens pathways to individuals and businesses in other countries that produce alternatives. Therefore, people at all income levels and businesses of all sizes can consume more either because they can choose a cheaper option, thus extending the reach of their financial resources, or they can buy something that was previously not accessible. As a result, trade provides more product choice as well as price variety. Moreover, the competitive process pushes businesses to strive to offer the best of *something*; in some cases, it is prices, for others, it is quality, or other nonprice factors. During this process, firms often make strides in innovation. These opportunities help businesses grow and workers benefit from higher incomes, thus allowing all to increase consumption. The following examples illustrate how liberalized trade spurred the innovation of once unimaginable products that many of us take for granted but that undeniably contribute to improved living standards.

Televisions

The television was invented in 1927 in the United States, but those TVs did not have remotes, the displays were black and white, and they were big, heavy, clunky pieces of furniture with small screens. Technological improvements made TVs more accessible to consumers by the 1950s, with prices ranging from $189 ($1,573 in 2022 dollars) for a 17-inch black-and-white tabletop TV to $1,000 ($8,325 in 2022 dollars) for a 15-inch color console in 1954, but they were a far cry from the sleek, detailed displays we have today. As discussed earlier, countries have comparative advantages, and Japan has a comparative advantage in producing televisions. By 1997, Sharp and Sony had introduced the first 42-inch flat-screen TVs, which cost $15,000 each. These companies capitalized on demand for televisions and continued innovating, and now, a 43-inch liquid-crystal-display TV can be purchased for under $200.

As outlined in *Superabundance*, a book by Marian Tupy and Gale Pooley, these price improvements, along with higher wages, mean that workers do not have to work as long in order to afford a television.[10] The authors calculate that in 1997, a worker making $18.12 per hour would need to work 828 hours to afford the $15,000 flat-screen.[11] That same worker made $32.36 an hour in 2019 and could buy a television for $148, meaning only 4.6 hours of work was needed to afford a flat-screen television.[12]

Fruits and Vegetables

Another example of the benefits of trade is evident in the produce section of the grocery store. The US Department of Agriculture (USDA) emphasizes the importance of trade not only for ensuring fresh produce year-round but for a wider range of consumers to be able to consume fresh produce:

> With their warmer climates and alternate growing seasons, imported produce from these countries, together with domestic production, assure a year-round supply of many types of fresh produce. US grocery shelves and restaurant kitchens are stocked with types of fruit that used to be consumed mainly during part of the year or by a smaller portion of consumers.[13]

As people became wealthier, demand for year-round fresh produce increased.[14] In turn, companies invested in improvements in containerized shipping and storage. These technological advancements helped US produce imports soar starting in the 1980s. Now, people can purchase fruits and vegetables year-round instead of being limited by seasonal availability. In fact, one study from the USDA estimates that during the winter months, US imports of Chilean berries contributed to falling berry prices between 49 percent and 69 percent.[15]

For the first time, in 1995, fresh fruit became the United States' top agricultural import. This is an unsurprising change given the North American Free Trade Agreement (NAFTA) entered into force in 1994. Canada already had duty-free treatment through the US-Canada free trade agreement, but Mexico did not. However, even before NAFTA, Mexico was a top trading partner for the United States for fresh produce because its climate provides a better environment for quality produce year-round. After NAFTA entered into force and Mexican fruits and vegetables were no longer subject to high tariffs (e.g., Mexican asparagus was subject to a tariff between 5 percent and 25 percent depending on the time of year it was imported in 1993), fresh fruit and vegetable imports from Mexico soared, as shown in Figure 20.5.[16]

More Means More

Trade contributes to higher wages not only because we import lower-priced goods from trading partners but also because we then boost production in the industries in which US workers and companies have a comparative advantage (and thus specialize). The jobs in these industries tend to be better paying than the ones eliminated by competition. As a result, the time price of certain goods and services (e.g., the television) is even lower than the inflation-adjusted list price.

Looking at the changes in time price is significant, particularly for necessities such as food. A reduction in the time price of food means that an individual does not need to work a lot of hours simply to get food on the table, freeing resources for other things. According to *Superabundance*, the average time price of 42 common food items fell by an average of 91.2 percent for blue-collar workers and 87.8 percent for unskilled workers between 1919 and 2019.[17] The average personal resource abundance multiplier (the quantity of items that one can buy for the same amount of labor at different points in time) for food increased by 1,032 percent and 722 percent for blue-collar and unskilled workers, respectively.

Once again, the benefits of import liberalization in the declining time price of food tells an important story for how living standards are

FIGURE 20.5

After NAFTA entered into force, US imports of fruits and vegetables from Mexico rose

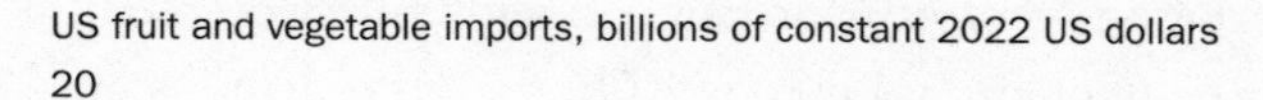

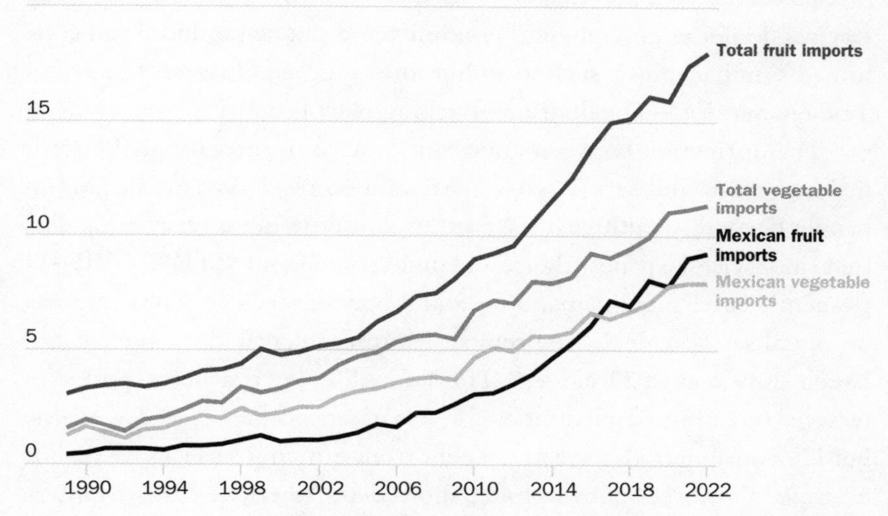

Source: US Department of Agriculture, "Global Agricultural Trade System," updated August 8, 2023; and author's calculations.

improved, especially for those in the lowest income brackets. In fact, as trade increases the availability of other resources, like time, people are returning to growing food not for necessity but for fun.[18] Overall, people can consume more financial and nonfinancial resources to live a more prosperous life.

How Are Services Important for Trade and Improved Living Standards?

Trade traditionally focuses on goods, but services trade—transportation, travel, insurance, finance, and so forth—underpins globalization. Services are intangible and often embodied in products as intermediate inputs, for example in the design and engineering of a product, through trade facilitation such as transportation and logistics, or bundled with goods such as installation. Some services require physical proximity, such as transportation; without transportation, very little production and trade would exist as it physically connects suppliers and markets. On the other hand, some services do not require physical proximity and can be produced and consumed simultaneously, such as online tutoring (see Chapter 9, "Digital Trade in Services: Globalization's Exciting New Frontier").

The distinction between goods and services is increasingly blurred, making goods and services two parts of a whole.[19] As a result, and as people become wealthier, they tend to consume more services, and as trade in services expands, choice and innovation boom.[20] The COVID-19 pandemic accelerated demand for and supply of services: global exports of digital services, including remote learning, increased 37 percent between 2019 and 2022 alone.[21] The United States is a net exporter of services, creating opportunities for American businesses and workers, but US consumers also greatly benefit from growing services trade. For example, Upwork, a jobs website, allowed an American father to interview and hire a PhD mathematician to tutor his son.[22] This mathematician is based in Pakistan and asked for $4 an hour—a steal compared to the average $24 an hour for an American tutor but a well-paid opportunity for the mathematician as this rate far exceeds Pakistan's less than $1 an hour minimum wage.

The pandemic demonstrated how much services-based work can be performed remotely. The benefits that remote work provides increase living standards and can even help with job retention. In fact, new data illustrate that US labor force participation for women with children under the age of five leapfrogged its pre-pandemic rate, and the flexibility that remote work offers, particularly to caregivers, is a compelling factor behind the trend.[23] Moreover, the flexibility has pro-social benefits by making it easier to become parents or have more children.[24]

However, remote work would not be possible without cheaper electronics. In 1996, the WTO signed the Information Technology Agreement that eliminated tariffs on hundreds of information and communications technology products.[25] Such liberalized trade encouraged global supply chains that significantly contributed to the rise of accessible electronics.[26] Not only can people carry mini computers in their pockets in the form of smartphones, but home offices are made more affordable. Indeed, as documented by Pooley, in 1991, Apple introduced its PowerBook 1000 priced at $2,500.[27] At the same time, the average blue-collar worker made $14.93 an hour, so it took 168 hours to earn one of these laptops. Today, Apple's 13-inch MacBook Air costs $999, and the average blue-collar worker makes $36.50 an hour, so it only takes a little over 27 hours to earn a laptop. Put differently, today the average blue-collar worker can buy six MacBook Airs for the time price of one PowerBook 1000 in 1991.

Further, cheaper electronic equipment combined with the invention of cloud services created more location options for starting a business.[28] As these entrepreneurs take advantage of remote work and hire workers from anywhere in the world, a feedback loop is created of improved living standards, increased innovation, and higher economic growth—not only domestically but globally.

Insurance is a less considered service but is vital for trade facilitation and comprises a significant part of trade cost by itself (included in the import, cost, insurance, and freight price). Doing business comes with risks, and those risks can be heightened when using suppliers in different countries with different legal systems. Insurance enables businesses to mitigate risk and thus operate more cost-effectively. For example, importers benefit from product liability insurance; importers are responsible for ensuring that the products they import are compliant with domestic law, but product liability insurance protects them if a foreign supplier provides an inadequate product that requires legal action or if the foreign supplier does not have insurance coverage with protection in the importer's jurisdiction.[29] On the other side, exporters benefit from cargo (or freight) insurance, which protects shipments from loss, damage, or theft during transportation.[30]

More broadly, global insurance protects companies with global operations from a variety of claims, such as property damage, cyber hacks, data breaches, or even personal injury.[31] This risk mitigation streamlines the trading process by ensuring businesses are protected from unforeseen complications while providing resources for navigating what United-Healthcare Global calls "a complicated maze of red tape due to language barriers, local laws, customs, and norms that differ from country to country."[32] Finally, companies based in foreign countries also help communities by providing opportunities for local workers, facilitating trade, enabling foreign direct investment, reinforcing integration, and contributing to global economic growth.

For consumers, services trade further improves living standards by providing more choice. For example, streaming services (bundled in many televisions nowadays) have a breadth of options available that is largely a result of increased digital trade. In fact, 45 percent of Netflix's library is made up of foreign-language titles.[33] The Korean television show *Squid Game* became Netflix's most watched show in 2021 and maintains that record—a testament to not only Americans' enjoyment of the show but also the benefits of services trade.[34]

As consumers become familiar with foreign services, they often crave more of them. And South Korean services, which have gained popularity around the world starting in the 1990s, are again a good example.[35] After the US-South Korea trade agreement went into effect in 2012, South Korean media exports to the United States surged.[36] The COVID-19 pandemic particularly vitalized US demand for Korean media exports.[37] Moreover, the popularity of Korean media products spills over to other Korean products. In fact, one study of Korean cultural good exports from 2001 to 2007 found "that the export creation of cultural goods led to the export of consumer goods, the trade creation effect that the export of cultural goods drives the export of consumer goods was significantly found."[38] The authors found that a 1 percent increase in South Korean cultural exports led to a 0.136 percent increase in exports of consumer goods, including information technology products, cosmetics, clothing, and processed foods. Put differently, a $100 increase in Korean cultural goods exports created an average $2,244 increase in Korean exports of other consumer goods. Therefore, the benefits of US-South Korea trade multiply, allowing Americans to consume more varieties of Korean products. The same goes for services from other countries (and, of course, for foreigners' consumption of American services).

Measuring the Benefits of Trade

Quantifying the effects of trade on consumers is difficult, and thus few studies have tried. However, one study by James Langenfeld and James Nieberding finds that US households gained around $2,500 in 2002 ($3,806 adjusted for inflation in 2022; however, this is an unsophisticated estimate and likely conservative compared to the results of an updated analysis) as a result of increased trade.[39] Specifically, the expanded availability of imports from trade liberalization and increased trade is estimated to have had a cumulative total benefit of around $2.3 trillion between 1992 and 2002 (around $3.5 trillion in 2022 dollars). More importantly, it is estimated that the real disposable income per US household increased by $10,387 each year between 1992 and 2002. Put differently, increased trade during this period accounted for 12–20 percent of the increase in US real disposable household income.

More recent estimates from the Peterson Institute for International Economics show even greater gains from trade liberalization and improvements in transportation and communications technology.[40] The authors estimate that between 1950 and 2016, the payoff to the United States was roughly $2.1 trillion (in 2016 dollars), amounting to around $18,131 per household with disproportionate gains probably accruing to poorer households. Meanwhile, several other studies have found that US trade with just China saved American consumers hundreds of dollars per year, with disproportionate benefits for middle- and low-income households that shop at "big-box" retailers like Walmart.[41]

In the United States, disposable income has generally increased as a result of improved tax, regulatory, and trade policy, helping offset increases in particular consumer expenditure categories, thus translating into higher overall living standards.[42] Yet, policymakers often resort to income-based approaches such as transfers, minimum wage laws, and subsidies to financially assist poor households. However, prices for highly government-controlled services, such as health care, have increased.[43] On the contrary, largely as a result of trade liberalization, prices of highly traded products, such as clothing, have fallen.[44] This demonstrates that a cost-based approach to reform existing government interventions—including trade barriers—that artificially raise the prices of essential goods is much more effective.[45]

Opportunities for Trade Liberalization Remain

Contrary to the conventional wisdom, neither the United States nor the rest of the world embraced "neoliberal free trade" or "market fundamentalism" in recent decades. The average global tariff rate is still quite high at 9 percent, and many tariff schedules, particularly the US tariff schedule, are regressive. This means that the poor are disproportionately affected as tax burdens are higher on those in lower income brackets. However, many tariff schedules are also regressive in that cheap, mass-market goods tend to be taxed at a much higher rate. For example, in the United States, men's leather dress shoes are subject to an 8.5 percent tariff whereas a pair of shoes valued at under $3 are subject to a 48 percent tariff.[46] Therefore, policymakers would be remiss not to consider amending the tariff schedule at the very least by removing tariffs on these mass-market products that are mostly consumed by those in the lowest income brackets.

The costs of continued protectionism are disproportionately borne by families. Families in the lowest quintiles spend a greater share of their income on necessities, so lower prices provided by trade liberalization and import competition benefit those groups most. For example, in 2019, single-parent households devoted almost 5 percent of their annual spending to clothes, shoes, linens, and other miscellaneous houseware, totaling about $2,400 per family.[47] However, the recent 2022 US infant formula crisis demonstrates the risks of protectionism.[48] High tariffs and nontariff barriers prevented the necessary flexibility during a crisis. As domestic supplies dried up, imports could not fill the gap, and parents faced empty shelves and short supply for almost a year.

Further, as illustrated in Table 20.1, tariffs are highest on the baby products that parents need to buy most frequently—clothes and diapers—increasing the tax burden on parents. This regressive pattern is found throughout the US tariff schedule but hurts those in the lowest income brackets the most.[49]

Moreover, as trade liberalization reduced or removed tariffs, many countries employed nontariff barriers—quotas, local content requirements, labeling regulations, assessment and conformity standards, and

TABLE 20.1

Tariffs on the baby products parents need to buy more frequently are high

Product	Tariff rate
Baby carriage	4.4%
Baby bottle	3.4%
Washcloth (cotton)	9.2%
Diapers*	0–16%
Pacifier	3.1%
Crib	0.0%
Breast pump	0.0%
Baby monitor (with video)	0.0%
Blanket (cotton)	8.4%
Baby garments*	0–32%

Source: "Harmonized Tariff Schedule," US International Trade Commission.
* = Depending on material.

so forth—to maintain some semblance of protectionism.[50] The proliferation of nontariff barriers makes trading more complex. For example, paying a 17.5 percent tariff per kilogram of product is much simpler than a quota, which is often calculated based on some percentage of a previous year's trade volume and may have time restrictions or be divided into units.[51] A tariff is simpler still than an antidumping duty, which is essentially a tariff on goods allegedly sold at "less than fair value."[52] However, navigating the antidumping duty process is extremely complex, burdensome, and costly, and duties may be imposed retroactively. Indeed, a tariff is simpler to manage than complex regulatory schemes. Businesses and individuals must therefore spend unnecessary amounts of time navigating nontariff barriers or pay hefty attorneys' fees to ensure compliance with the law.

These costs are not limited to incumbents but can hinder new entrants. These hindrances delay or even prevent future opportunities, growth, and price and choice variety. That is not to say that rules are unnecessary. Rules and enforcement mechanisms are vital for a well-functioning trading system; however, policymakers should be wary of the rise of nontariff barriers, particularly when lobbied for by special interests to protect specific industries or products.

Finally, services trade is in desperate need of liberalization. The Uruguay Round at the WTO is considered the largest trade negotiation to ever take place.[53] However, efforts to liberalize services trade were lackluster. Since services are "invisible," they are mostly subject to nontariff barriers (although new proposals such as digital services taxes increasingly threaten services).[54] For example, domestic regulations such as certification requirements hinder financial services trade.

Regulatory barriers to services are complex to measure even more than measuring regulatory barriers to trade in goods. However, economists have estimated that the tariff equivalents (essentially turning a regulation into a tax rate) of barriers to services trade are high and significantly exceed tariff equivalents of barriers to trade in goods.[55] For example, restrictions in transport are particularly important for trade performance. One study looks at time as a trade barrier by looking at transit and finds that each day in transit is equivalent to an ad valorem tariff of 0.6 percent to 2.1 percent.[56]

Given that services are traded directly and indirectly through other services and goods, they are paramount to international trade. In fact, there is strong evidence that open services markets positively impact manufacturing productivity, particularly manufacturing sectors that intensely use services inputs.[57] Overall, the relationship between goods trade and services is strongly interlinked, and therefore, restrictions on services trade—particularly barriers to transport, logistics, distribution, and computer services—negatively impact goods trade.

Conclusion

Policymakers continue to debate the benefits of trade liberalization, but the benefits are so dispersed that people often take them for granted. As Smith notes in *The Wealth of Nations*, "Consumption is the sole end and purpose of all production; and the interest of the producer ought to be attended to only so far as it may be necessary for promoting that of the consumer."[58] However, firms are also consumers, and the increasingly problematic barriers to both goods and services trade impact their ability to provide products that people desire to improve their lives.

There is no doubt that trade liberalization is key to raising living standards and to increasing peoples' ability to consume more—more time, more goods, more services. Freer trade promotes channels for specialization through comparative advantage, increased business sales through access to new and larger markets, technological spillovers that spread innovation, and competition that helps increase variety to consumers and shift resources to more productive uses. These four channels expand trade flows and increase income. Centuries of evidence establish that trade improves peoples' lives—providing us with not only more stuff to consume but with more free time to spend on family, friends, and the other things we most enjoy in life.

Chapter 21

Fast Fashion, Global Trade, and Sustainable Abundance

Joy Buchanan

- Historically clothes have been very expensive. Thanks to globalization, almost everyone in the world now has abundant clothing in many styles.
- A globalized apparel industry raises wages and supplies low-income families with affordable clothes.
- Clothing abundance may have environmental impacts, but new technology was the solution to clothing scarcity, and it will continue to help us mitigate the downsides.

Plentiful cheap clothes are a triumph of innovation and markets. Most of human history has been characterized by privation and low-productivity toil. As one American sharecropper exclaimed in John Steinbeck's Depression-era novel *The Grapes of Wrath*, "We got no clothes, torn an' ragged. If all the neighbors weren't the same, we'd be ashamed to go to meeting."

Today, things are different. People in wealthy countries can order a new outfit for less than a day's wages. We enjoy new styles and trends that were once reserved for the ultra-rich. Even our poorest are rarely lacking sufficient clothes and shoes.

Much of this abundance is owed to globalization. Clothing is so plentiful that unwanted new garments are piling up on the beaches of Ghana.[1]

African consumers can no longer absorb the quantities shipped to them by rich ones, so they choose the styles they love and discard the rest.

There are, however, critics of these trends, especially the recent phenomenon labeled "fast fashion," the rapid production of inexpensive, trendy clothing that is quickly made available to consumers, often resulting in short product life cycles. The United Nations Economic Commission for Europe called the fashion industry an "environmental and social emergency" because clothing production has roughly doubled since the year 2000.[2] Their main concerns are fast fashion's environmental impact and working conditions. As Figure 21.1 shows, Americans are indeed consuming more clothing.

FIGURE 21.1

Americans are consuming more clothes than ever

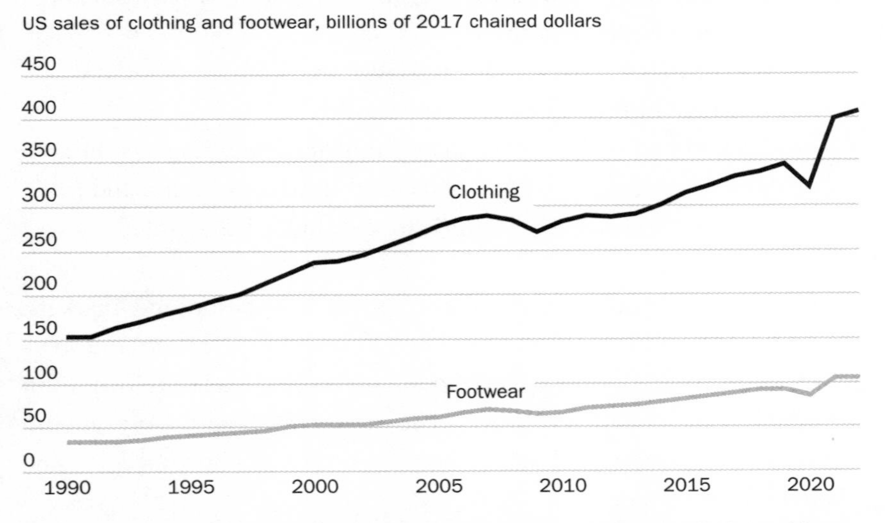

Source: "Table 2.5.5. Personal Consumption Expenditures by Function," National Income and Product Accounts, National Data, US Bureau of Economic Analysis, updated September 29, 2023; converted to real values using "Table 2.5.3. Real Personal Consumption Expenditures by Function, Quantity Indexes," National Income and Product Accounts, National Data, US Bureau of Economic Analysis, updated September 29, 2023.

Note: "Chained dollars" is a method for adjusting nominal dollar amounts for inflation that better accounts for price-induced changes in consumption and production patterns over time.

Is apparel a menace? In short, no. Globalization of the clothing industry has been good for the United States and the world.

Clothing Abundance and Globalized Fashion Provide Myriad Benefits

From the runways of Paris and Milan to the shops on Savile Row and the streets of Brooklyn, fashion has long been global and one of the ways people around the world can learn from one another. It used to be, however, that most fashion was reserved for the elite while common folk got by on a few well-worn staples. The recent explosion of cheap mass-produced clothes is a testament to the power of specialization and exchange on a global scale. Elizabeth Cline wrote, "If you ever wonder how we went from living in a world of relative clothing scarcity to feeling like we're swimming in the stuff, ponder no further than China."[3] One city in China produces most of the world's socks, over 20 billion pairs a year. This works because of an integrated international supply chain. It was only with the expiration of the Multifiber Arrangement in 2005 that the global textile and apparel trade was fully opened, following decades of gradual liberalization efforts through agreements such as the Agreement on Textiles and Clothing negotiated as part of the Uruguay Round of the General Agreement on Tariffs and Trade (the GATT).

Critics sometimes ignore the social benefits of cheaper clothes that weigh against its costs. Globalization has increased the variety of clothes we can choose from, and we can express ourselves in almost any way imaginable. What *The Economist* calls "mass customization" is fun.[4] A fashion influencer summarizes the attitude of fans of low-budget brands like Shein: "People deserve to have nice things. . . . A lot of us that work regular 9-to-5 jobs can't afford $2,000 shoes."[5]

But having plenty of textiles is about more than just people looking good or buying new dresses. Abundance means that children have winter hats and burn victims have bandages. And the global nature of fast fashion fosters economic integration and understanding. The exchange of fashion ideas creates a merging of cultures as designers draw inspiration from different traditions and consumers embrace trends from around the world. Fast fashion has the potential to democratize new trends and ideas, making them accessible to a broader demographic.

There are also other ways that cultural exchanges happen. Global supply chains bring people together to solve problems and foster an exchange of businesspeople to run these supply chains. For-profit clothing businesses achieve the goals of cultural nonprofits such as the Rhodes Trust and the Olympic Foundation for Culture and Heritage. And thanks to the internet, any person in any country can share what they love with a global audience of fans. This is what a rich globalized world looks like.

Textiles Trade Supports Better Jobs—Here and Abroad

Critics also misunderstand that what might be considered a sweatshop in the United States is an improvement over the real-world alternatives available in poorer countries—a step that Americans themselves took a century ago.

Dana Thomas sums up the sentiment toward trade and technology among fast-fashion critics in her book *Fashionopolis*:

> Since the invention of the mechanical loom nearly two and a half centuries ago, fashion has been a dirty, unscrupulous business that has exploited humans and Earth alike to harvest bountiful profits. Slavery, child labor, and prison labor have all been integral parts of the supply chain at one time or another—including today. On occasion, society righted the wrongs, through legislation or labor union pressure. But trade deals, globalization, and greed have undercut those good works.[6]

The implication that child labor is the result of mechanized manufacturing is backward. Children today have been largely freed from production jobs because of the wealth created by machines and globalization. It is not primarily legislation that creates safer jobs but rather economic growth.[7]

Preindustrial women spent much of their lives spinning thread.[8] In the United States today, it would be illegal to pay as little as these

FIGURE 21.2
Americans are producing less clothing

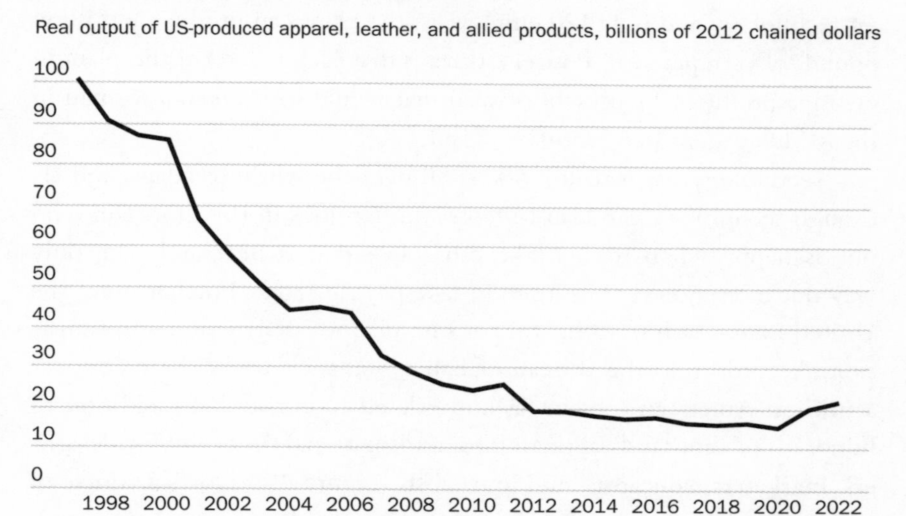

Source: "Gross Domestic Product by Industry and Input-Output Statistics," Previously Published Estimates, US Bureau of Economic Analysis, June 29, 2023.
Note: "Chained dollars" is a method for adjusting nominal dollar amounts for inflation that better accounts for price-induced changes in consumption and production patterns over time.

women earned for their labor. The reality was that these women were not very productive because they were working with poor technology, and yet they did the work because it was their best option. Machines and synthetics allow us to produce more textiles with less labor.

Another common complaint is that Western corporations outsource manufacturing to low-wage Asian countries and reduce the number of jobs in rich countries. But this story is incomplete. Multinational corporations have moved some manufacturing operations abroad. Figure 21.2 indicates that fewer clothes are made in the United States, meaning most of the clothes represented in Figure 25.1 were imported. Thus, some manufacturing jobs in fashion have moved from domestic producers to lower-cost factories in Asia. However, these jobs might have been offshored even earlier if regulations had allowed, because the United States currently specializes in high-tech and high-skill production.

In *The Fabric of Civilization*, Virginia Postrel reports on one of the few plants in the United States today that manufactures thread. With the latest technology and only 120 employees, the plant can produce 9 million pounds of yarn per year. Postrel estimates that each worker at this plant in Georgia produces an amount of yarn that would have taken a woman in the Middle Ages three centuries to spin.[9]

Technology has forced workers all over the world to adapt, and although technology can lead to fewer human jobs in the short run—no one is happy when robots take our jobs—that is ultimately the only way out of *everyone* being stuck in low-paying work. Furthermore, the United States' fashion-jobs story is one of both destruction and transition. According to the Bureau of Labor Statistics, today there are over a million American jobs in fashion-related industries.[10] In addition to hundreds of thousands of retail jobs, multinational firms employ designers, marketers, educators, and journalists. Figure 21.3 shows a sample of remaining fashion-related jobs in America. As shown in new research by Teresa Fort and others,American multinational firms with offshore manufacturing operations, such as Oregon-based Nike, tend to have more of these "knowledge jobs" here in the United States.[11] Many also have domestic manufacturing operations.

Factories dubbed sweatshops are best understood from a historical perspective. Whether speaking of England in 1830 or Vietnam today, garment manufacturing has typically been characterized by long hours and intensive manual labor. Sweatshops are problematic for Westerners because, in addition to concerns about unpleasant conditions, the wages are low. And sometimes cheaply constructed factories lead to injury or even death. In 2013, the Rana Plaza garment factory collapsed in Bangladesh, killing over 1,100 people; *Fashionopolis* contains interviews with survivors who saw coworkers die. In response to this tragedy, new safety guidelines were instituted, and fortunately, there have been no mass-casualty events since then.[12] The tradeoff is that the stricter standards resulted in fewer jobs in garment factories in Bangladesh.[13]

In 1998, the year that American students founded United Students Against Sweatshops (USAS), per capita gross domestic product (GDP) in Bangladesh was estimated to be under $500. Most of the population

FIGURE 21.3
There are many fashion-related jobs in the United States today

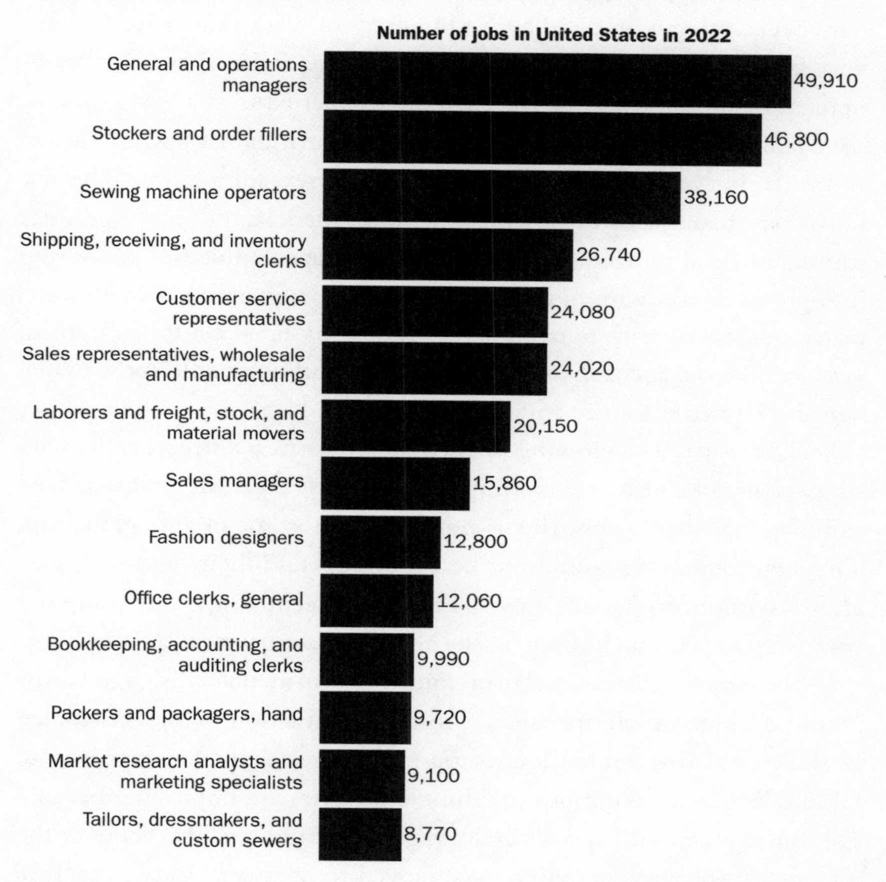

Source: "Occupational Employment and Wages—May 2022," news release, Bureau of Labor Statistics, April 25, 2023.

lives in poverty, experiencing health crises and premature deaths that go with material lack. Yet recently the nation has undergone what some might call a development miracle, with per capita GDP rising to $2,500. This rapid economic growth in Bangladesh is closely linked to garment exports, a main source of income for the country. To protect this source of revenue, the government has created rules that support garment manufacturers.[14] From the perspective of people inside the country, this is a link to the world economy that employs millions of people (see Chapter 14, "Globalization: A Race to the Bottom—or to the Top?"). Humans have been voting with their feet for hundreds of years, indicating a preference for factories over subsistence farming and rural life. Economic development requires moving up the chain in productivity.

Dana Thomas celebrates the opening (reshoring) of a sewing shop in Alabama, but most Americans do not want to sew for a living. The few businesses manufacturing clothes in the United States employ mostly immigrants and refugees who have few other opportunities.[15] Reshoring low-productivity work in rich countries is not a guaranteed way to improve outcomes. If the goal is to generate a living wage for billions of people, then our focus should be on making stuff more efficiently, which can also be better for the environment.

Thomas paints a glowing picture of new British entrepreneurs who process thread and weave cloth near the sites of the early industrialized mills in Manchester, but this is not really a portrait of anti-globalism. These entrepreneurs would not be able to operate their high-tech machines without importing raw material and technology and computer parts. There is no such thing as "local" manufacturing.

One reason multinational firms initially set up manufacturing in China was that labor was cheap. It is not through legislation (which is avoided by subcontracting with illegal shops) that sweatshops are receding in China. Working conditions in Chinese factories are improving because of economic growth, and Chinese wages are rising quickly. Many of the jobs that were once in China have moved to Vietnam; today, the *Wall Street Journal* reports, those factories can't find enough workers because young people would prefer to work in service industries.

This is a separate topic from sweatshops, but it is important to acknowledge that there is still slavery in the world. Walk Free estimates that there are tens of millions of enslaved people in the Asian and Pacific regions today.[16] Although I would not advocate sanctioning manufacturers over low wages, I and other free traders support private boycotts and laws, such as Section 307 of the Tariff Act of 1930, targeting goods made from forced labor. For example, the US government is scrutinizing the Chinese fashion firm Shein over the issue of forced labor. To trade in the global economy, companies should have to follow such laws. But forced labor is different from the issue of poverty and low wages.

Indeed, activists for raising wages must be passionate advocates of sustaining and accelerating economic growth. That is the only way to generate enough income for tens of millions of garment workers in Asia and elsewhere. Elizabeth Cline defines a living wage as one that affords "food and water, housing and energy, clothing, health care, transportation, education, and child care, as well as modest funds for savings and discretionary spending."[17] This is not a mandate to return to nature or retreat from globalization. Because trade increases wealth, in fact, this is a mandate for more globalization in the years ahead.

Can Global Fashion Become More Sustainable?

The desire to see poorer nations catch up to Western living standards may or may not conflict with the other concern about fast fashion: its impact on the natural environment. Producing and disposing of clothes affects the Earth. Well-meaning folks donate their used clothes instead of throwing them away. The good news is that clothing that cannot be resold as garments can find a second use as industrial rags. However, there are so many clothes that some donated garments end up in the trash, even if they're transported to Africa to be looked at one last time. (Adam Minter provides a more optimistic view of the global trade in secondhand goods.)[18] Most cheap clothes are made of plastic, which does not biodegrade like cotton.

Recycling entrepreneur Kerem Saral explained to me, "We are eating the stuff now that we took to Goodwill." Americans' unwanted clothes contain synthetic materials that enter the food chain as microplastics.[19] At a global level, discarded garments do not all make it into lined landfills that corral garbage.

Scientists are studying microplastics and trying to determine whether they pose a health threat.[20] Today we know that lead is toxic and that no amount is safe for humans. In the future, we might discover microplastics are so bad that we need to change our way of life, which for many people often includes disposable forks and shirts. It is difficult to determine the optimal level of textile production without clear facts about the effects of disintegrating polyester on human health. In recognition of the negative externality for the disposal of clothes, European governments are considering a new tax per garment.[21]

For those concerned about discarded clothes, I propose three reasons for optimism about the future: information, innovation, and economic growth.

Information

Individuals, clothing brands, and governments are starting to react to new information on an unintended, unforeseen consequence of a recent increase in production: polyester littering the ocean. Minter's practical suggestion is that clothes should be labeled by durability to combat the race to the bottom on quality. It can be hard for consumers to know in advance how quickly a pair of shoes will wear out, so this data would nudge people away from buying disposable fast fashion. In addition to more data, we need more intelligence to help get optimal clothes to consumers. Artificial intelligence (AI) tools are already helping brands produce only what will sell and helping sellers find buyers in secondhand markets. When people live close enough to make travel costs negligible, with the help of Facebook for coordination, they can exchange goods in a Buy Nothing group.[22] Websites such as Poshmark .com make it easier to sell unwanted clothes and give people an incentive to recirculate.

Innovation

A pathway to cleaner fashion is technology, and we are already seeing innovations along several dimensions:

- **Materials.** Like lab-grown meat, lab-grown fibers are in the early stages but could generate cloth in ways less polluting than cotton farming or leather tanning. With continued advances in chemistry and biology, we might move away from harvesting raw materials on farms and shipping them for large-volume production runs in low-income countries.

- **Production.** The introduction of sewing-capable robots could disrupt the current model that created millions of manufacturing jobs in Asia. The International Labour Organization reports, "Prominent occupations in certain countries face extreme risks of automation. For example, in Cambodia, where garment production dominates the manufacturing sector, close to half a million sewing machine operators face a high automation risk."[23] The future might look like print-on-demand clothes made by highly paid technicians.
- **Recycling.** All garments eventually become unwanted, but clothes do not have to become garbage. Clothes are already recycled for use as industrial rags or insulation; a goal among fast fashion activists is to see more clothes recycled into raw fibers that could make new clothes. If it works, we could achieve what is known as "circularity."
- **Matching.** Fabric is not scarce in America today, but attention is. AI can fill the attention gap and become a personal assistant for obtaining clothes, with the option of finding sustainable products. At the same time, technology could help or replace workers at organizations like Goodwill who are tasked with separating donated goods into piles for resale or recycling—a costly and time-intensive process. Smart robots powered by AI could scan donated clothes and direct them to a new buyer or an appropriate recycling plant. The gains from cheap decision-making would be high and the potential for harm through AI errors is limited.[24] If AI-powered sorting is the future, then it could become efficient enough for people to sell their unwanted clothes to sorters, which would increase circularity compared to the donation model.

Economic Growth

The world is getting richer, and rich countries have more capacity to protect the environment—whether through information, innovation, or regulation.[25] Already, some clothing brands are taking steps toward cleaner clothes. For example, financial backers for the Better Cotton Initiative are not consumers but rather multinational brands like Adidas and Walmart. Patagonia is one of the leading brands known for trying to avoid the fast fashion race to the bottom on quality. They use mostly recycled materials and organically grown cotton, and they accept certain returned Patagonia gear in exchange for store credit. Leveraging their data and scale, funded by wealthy consumers who can afford to be more conscientious, brands can make changes to reduce waste.

Thanks to these three factors, much of the world is becoming cleaner and greener, even as we consume more stuff. Just as cars today have cleaner emissions, we can expect improvements for fashion too—to get more clothes from fewer natural resources. And globalization will play an important role, fueling the growth needed to afford better conditions and develop better technologies while fostering information-sharing and collaboration among the best minds in the world. Since globalization lowers the cost of producing any good, we would need it to maintain an abundant supply of clothes in the face of new and costly environmental regulation (similar to the regulation of plastic bottles).

Conclusion

For millennia, clothing ourselves was a struggle that consumed much of our time. Today an American teenager with a minimum-wage job can summon a new outfit from an app.

To describe modern fashion as a disaster fails to recognize the improvement in well-being from cheap, globalized textiles. After Alden Wicker conducted an exhaustive survey on the cutting edge of recycling and green tech for apparel, his conclusion was, “We need to make and buy less stuff. Does anyone have an innovation for that?” Someone from the past would never believe that we are struggling to have *fewer* clothes.[26] Be happy that these are our new problems.

Globalization is part of the solution to environmental concerns and poverty wages rather than the primary cause of those problems, as some fast fashion critics have claimed. The mass production of the world’s socks all in one place might actually be better for the environment than individual plants in multiple cities, and reshoring could deny some of the world's poorest people an established avenue out of abject poverty. Achieving higher wages for workers and a cleaner Earth requires highly efficient manufacturing, and globalization enables not only cheaper production but also the proliferation of ideas to solve real problems. In certain cases, to alleviate the dumping of plastic in places other than landfills, new regulations might be enacted; however, it will take a rich world to enforce them.

We innovated our way to making clothes plentiful and cheap. Now we can get smarter about reusing fibers and sorting the garments we have. AI might help us achieve more circularity and less waste in the apparel industry, where the primary constraint seems to be human time and attention.

Part of the upset over fast fashion is symptomatic of a false doomer eschatology in which the world cannot get better. In the good future, clothes can be plentiful and cheap and green.

Chapter 22

Food Globalization Puts the World on Your Plate

Scott Lincicome and Sophia Bagley

- Though "globalization" usually conjures images of container ships and geopolitics, there may be no better symbol of it than the food we eat.
- Globalization has revolutionized cuisine and restaurants here and abroad, offering consumers a wide and ever-changing variety of flavors and styles.
- Grocery stores are another testament to globalization, with aisles increasingly stuffed with international products and low-cost produce that was once available only a few months a year (if at all).
- Food is an important way for immigrants to find employment and share their cultural traditions and experiences, and it can promote liberty and mutual understanding through peaceful (and tasty) international exchange.

When you hear the word "globalization," you probably think of giant container ships, wonky economic terms like "offshoring" and "trade deficit," or geopolitical tensions or agreements. But there may be no better symbol of *real globalization* than the restaurant down the street. There, you'll almost certainly find something on the menu that didn't originate in the United States. If you're at an ethnic restaurant, it'll be almost everything listed, but even the classic American bar and grill serves nachos or egg rolls or French fries (that probably originated in Belgium). The food you'll eat, meanwhile, will contain numerous imported ingredients—spices, sauces, or produce that don't grow locally this time of year (if ever)—and likely imported plates, glasses, and flatware. Maybe you also enjoy imported beer or Australian wine (though even your Miller Lite comes from Czech hops and German yeast).[1] And it's a good bet that at least one person in the kitchen—and often a waiter or even the owner—was born outside the country.

You might *think* you're having a good ol' American cheeseburger, but you *really* have the whole world on your plate.

Food globalization isn't new—as long as chefs have been cooking, they've been looking abroad for ideas and ingredients—but it's surely accelerated in recent decades as global trade, migration, and wealth have increased. In just the authors' lifetimes, the variety of flavors and availability of ingredients have exploded. This essay will explain how globalization has revolutionized our palates, our groceries, and the people connected to it all.

Globalization Has Radically Changed Our Restaurants and Cuisines

Imagining a supermarket without ready-made sushi seems almost impossible, especially for younger generations who have never known a world without it. Much of the American population had never tried (or even heard of) sushi two generations ago. Although the first sushi restaurant opened in the United States in the 1960s, sushi wasn't popular in big cities until the 1980s and became ubiquitous a decade after that.[2] Today it's found in children's lunchboxes. In just the past year, Americans purchased 43.7 million servings of sushi at grocery stores—an increase of more than 50 percent in volume and 72 percent in value since 2019—and another 238.6 million sushi servings from US restaurants.[3] Kroger alone sells more than 40 million pieces of sushi a year, generating between $400 million and $600 million in sales and boosting sales of related items like poke bowls (2.5 million servings) and dumplings (1.4 million).

Over those same decades, the American restaurant scene has gone from hosting only a handful of foreign cuisines (mainly Italian, French, and Chinese) to one with almost every food from every major country on the planet—and plenty of smaller countries and "fusion" styles to boot. This variety is evident on the popular restaurant review app Yelp, which, in May 2023, boasted about 311 cuisine categories for US restaurants—almost double the number of categories that were listed in January 2018 (157), as Figures 22.1 and 22.2 show. From Eritrea to Peru, Andalusia to Mongolia, the ever-expanding list shows the evolving influence of global flavors on our local dining scenes.

Unsurprisingly, this diversity is widest in America's largest cities, but smaller places also have plenty to choose from. A Yelp search in

FIGURE 22.1

In 2023, Yelp listed 311 cuisine categories for US restaurants

Source: "The Complete Yelp Business Category List," Yelp, May 4, 2023.

FIGURE 22.2

In 2018, Yelp listed 157 cuisine categories for US restaurants

Source: John Carroll, "The Complete Yelp Business Category List," Yelp via the Wayback Machine, January 31, 2018.

Cleveland, Ohio, for example, shows around 200 local restaurants serving more than 50 different cuisines (Figure 22.3).

At the same time, American restaurants are common sights abroad. Fast-food staples like McDonald's, Hardees, Five Guys, and KFC dot streets in Riyadh. Outback Steakhouse, a US-based chain serving "Australian" food, just opened its 150th location in Brazil and has been voted Rio de Janeiro's most popular restaurant for five years running.[4] And Chili's—which serves burgers, ribs, and Tex-Mex—has 364 international locations spread across 28 countries and four continents.[5] If you don't like those choices, don't worry: thousands of other American restaurants are available abroad too.

FIGURE 22.3

Yelp lists around 200 restaurants serving more than 50 cuisines in Cleveland, Ohio

American (Traditional)
Tapas/Small Plates
Korean
Pizza Szechuan Tiki Bar Dim Sum
Brewpubs Chinese African
Soul Food Indian
Vietnamese Dominican
French
Cantonese Portuguese
Thai Kebab Brazilian Italian Caribbean
Beer Bar Spanish Tacos
Gastropub Ramen German Falafel
Lebanese Irish
Noodles Pub
Middle Eastern Cajun/Creole Mexican
Brasseries Halal
Breweries Seafood Barbeque
Wine Bar
Salvadoran American (New) Ethiopian
Japanese Asian Fusion Burgers
Pan Asian Mediterranean Colombian
Latin American Chicken Wings Cocktail Bar
Shanghainese Smokehouse
New Mexican Cuisine

Source: "All Results in Cleveland, Ohio," Yelp.

Globalization has similarly affected what many consider to be comfort foods. Instant ramen, takeout Chinese, burritos, and pizza are staples for American college students. Halfway around the world, those same college students can follow up a late night in Thailand at any number of places serving "American breakfast" or brunch.[6] Back in the United States (and in Canada), many Asians grew up with a steady supply of Sara Lee frozen pound cake—an "Asian culinary icon" that was so ubiquitous in their households that it appeared on the Netflix comedy *Beef*, which tracks the lives of several Asian Americans living in Los Angeles.[7] At one time, Sara Lee operated in 40-plus countries and sold ready-made baked goods in more than 180.

Consumers' takeout preferences—both here and abroad—are further testament to the globalization of our palates, as Figure 22.4 shows.

FIGURE 22.4

Consumers' top takeout preferences in the United States and abroad are further testament to the globalization of our palates

Pizza

Albania
Argentina
Armenia
Austria
Barbuda
Belgium
Belize
Bhutan
Botswana
Bulgaria
Croatia
El Salvador
England
Finland
France
Georgia
Germany
Iceland
India
Indonesia
Italy
Jamaica
Madagascar
Mali
Monaco
Montenegro
Morocco
Namibia
Norway
Peru
Poland
Qatar
Rwanda
Saudi Arabia
Slovenia
South Korea
Spain
Switzerland
Tunisia
United Arab Emirates
Zambia

Chinese

Australia
Bahamas
Bolivia
Chile
China
Colombia
Costa Rica
Cyprus
Ecuador
Egypt
Ghana
Greece
Hong Kong
Hungary
Ireland
Kenya
Mauritania
Mexico
Nepal
New Zealand
Nigeria
Panama
Philippines
Sri Lanka
Taiwan
Tanzania
United Kingdom
United States
Zimbabwe

Sushi

Azerbaijan
Brazil
Japan
Mozambique
Portugal
Romania
Sweden
Ukraine
Vietnam
Zanzibar

Fried Chicken

Bangladesh
Cambodia
Gambia
Lao PDR
Myanmar

Fish & Chips

Canada
Fiji
Grenada
Saint Lucia
South Africa

Indian

Israel
Netherlands
Pakistan

Korean

Jordan
Lebanon
Oman

Fish & Chips

Saint Vincent and the Grenadines
Singapore

Pasta

Turkey

Malaysian

Malaysia

Tacos

Cabo Verde

Burrito

Thailand

Tapas

Djibouti

Kebab

Russia

Source: "Top Takeouts: What Are the Most Popular Takeaway Choices around the World?," MoneyBeach, last modified January 11, 2021.

Chinese food remains a popular option for Americans (though delivery apps have put almost any type of food on our doorsteps), while countries such as South Korea, Indonesia, Saudi Arabia, and India all prefer pizza.[8] Thailand—for some reason—reaches for burritos, and Cambodia wants fried chicken.

Indians' pizza cravings also show how globalized cuisine encompasses not only the transfer of dishes across continents but also the regional availability of ingredients, cultural norms, and consumer preferences. When India opened its economy to the world in the 1990s,[9] Domino's was one of the first players to enter the market and has dominated ever since.[10] Because of religious food restrictions and local tastes, however, you won't find a pepperoni pie on the menu. Instead, pizzas there are topped with chicken tikka or tandoori paneer. And, as India's economy and people have become more globalized, pizzas topped with Indian ingredients have become relatively common in the West (including Domino's original home in Michigan).

A similar phenomenon has occurred in Pakistan, where one of the most popular cuisines in the city of Lahore is the Philly cheesesteak. In fact, multiple Pakistani restaurants have featured the classic American sandwich on their menus since 1995, coinciding with a surge in Pakistani emigration to the United States. Post-9/11, stronger Pakistan-US ties and the spread of American pop culture further familiarized Pakistanis with the cheesesteak, leading many to learn how to make it themselves. Meanwhile, the general manager of the Philly's Steak Sandwich restaurant in Lahore, which opened after a Philadelphia traveler showed a video of a cheesesteak to a local chef, draws inspiration from Charleys Philly Steaks, a renowned US chain that has become popular in Dubai, a favorite tourist destination for Pakistanis.[11] And once again, the trend has come full circle: cheesesteaks with ingredients and flavors from Pakistani cuisine have started popping up in the United States.

This culinary cross-pollination not only makes life tastier but also can create *new foods* that introduce eaters to *very old* ones. Traditional Japanese nigiri, for example, didn't originally captivate American sushi consumers, who were skeptical of raw fish and seaweed. Presented with this challenge in 1971, Vancouver-based sushi chef Hidekazu Tojo filled sushi rolls with cooked crab and concealed the seaweed by putting the rice on the outside, thus creating the iconic California roll.[12] Although highly unorthodox in Japanese cuisine, Tojo's creation helped spur the proliferation of sushi in the West and earned him the title of "goodwill ambassador for Japanese cuisine" from the Japanese government in 2016.[13]

Often, chefs and restauranteurs go one step further and produce not only fusion dishes but entire fusion cuisines. This trend has roots dating back to the Silk Road when pasta likely made its way from China to Italy, but modern-day globalization—trade, travel, information, and so forth—has surely accelerated the proliferation of fusion cuisines in recent years.[14] Today's fusion trends are believed to have originated in the 1980s, with chefs like Wolfgang Puck combining his European heritage and enjoyment of Asian flavors on the menu at his now-world-famous Spago restaurant in Los Angeles.[15] Since then, fusion cuisines have popped up all over the world, and chefs continue to blend traditional cuisines in new and exciting ways.

National culture and history—not always good—can often do the same. Vietnam blends indigenous and regional influences with those from France because of the latter's colonization. Next door Thailand, however, was never colonized by a European power, yet its cuisine blends local flavors with numerous foreign influences, thanks to the expansion of global commerce starting in the 1500s. An essential ingredient in Thai cuisine—the chili pepper—comes from the Americas via Portuguese and Spanish traders.[16] Further south, Australia has gone from a meat-and-potatoes country to one with a local cuisine that harnesses the culinary talents of Italian and Greek migrants, as well as closer neighbors from China, Japan, Vietnam, Thailand, and Malaysia.[17] And halfway around the world, Guyanese cuisine includes African, Amerindian, Chinese, Creole, East Indian, European, and Portuguese influences. Many other Caribbean cuisines have similar fusions.[18]

The globalization of food has even affected our languages. Numerous English cooking terms—"à la carte," "sauté," "sommelier," and even "cuisine"—are originally French, and English is littered with loanwords like "deli" (from the German "Delikatessen") and "ketchup" (from the Cantonese 茄汁 [qié zhī], which means "tomato sauce"). But the linguistic links extend well beyond those common terms and to other countries. The word "Kentucky," for example, has developed into a Farsi verb meaning "to bread and fry a chicken," while KFC is called "肯德基 (kěn dé jī)" in China, even though the characters individually translate to "to consent," "virtue," and "foundation," respectively.[19] And how could we forget the iconic scene in *Pulp Fiction* about the metric system pushing the French to call the Quarter Pounder a "Royale with Cheese"?

Trade and Travel Have Globalized Our Grocery Stores

The globalization of our palates has undoubtedly been influenced by our grocery stores, which have expanded dramatically in recent years—thanks in no small part to that same globalization. Indeed, the number of products in an average US supermarket increased between 1975 and 2022 more than threefold, from 8,948 products to 31,530.

Much of this growth is owed to the continuous expansion of the "ethnic" or "international" food aisle, which originated after World War II when US soldiers returned home with palates accustomed to foods from places like Germany, Japan, and Italy.[20] Back then, imported items satisfying these new cravings were all placed in one aisle for easy access. Today, however, putting all such items in one aisle is not nearly so simple: according to the *New York Times*, cramming countless cultures into a single small enclave is both difficult and nonsensical, especially in a country with large and growing foreign-born and nonwhite populations. Thus, major grocery chains have increased efforts to move products from the "ethnic" or "international" aisle into other parts of the store (though many consumers and producers still prefer them all in one place). At the same time, local grocers like Food Bazaar in New York have innovated and dedicated sections to specific countries rather than a single aisle, and Asian supermarkets, such as H Mart and Patel Brothers, have exploded in popularity.[21] All of this is a testament to how globalization has vastly transformed our eating patterns in the decades since the ethnic aisle first appeared.

Today's produce section has undergone a similar transformation. According to *The Packer*, supermarkets in 1980 carried an average of 100 different produce items, and by 1993, the number approached 250. Even then, however, certain fruits and vegetables were limited to North American growing seasons, and no one had ever even heard of products like rambutans, lychee, or jackfruit. A casual stroll through the same aisles today, by contrast, contains an incredible variety—thanks in large part to global trade. As shown in Figures 22.5 and 22.6, for example, imports of essentially every type of food have increased since the 1990s, often substantially.

FIGURE 22.5

US imports of virtually every type of food have increased since the 1990s, measured by value

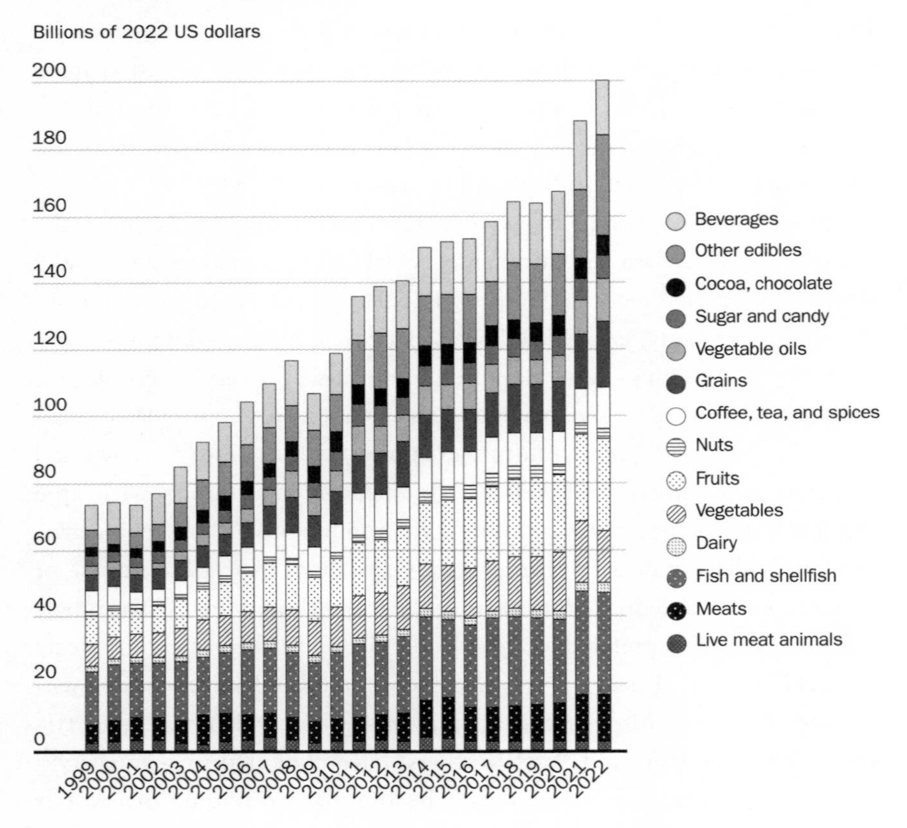

Source: "Summary Data on Annual Food Imports, Values and Volume by Food Category and Source Country, 1999–2022," US Food Imports, Economic Research Service, Department of Agriculture, updated March 23, 2023.

Agricultural imports are particularly noteworthy (see Figure 22.7). According to the US Food and Drug Administration, for example, 55 percent of fresh fruits and 32 percent of fresh vegetables today are sourced from abroad. The US Department of Agriculture adds that the combination of imported produce and domestic production ensures a year-round supply of fresh, healthy foods for consumers. Fresh fruit has

FIGURE 22.6

US imports of virtually every type of food have increased since the 1990s, measured by volume

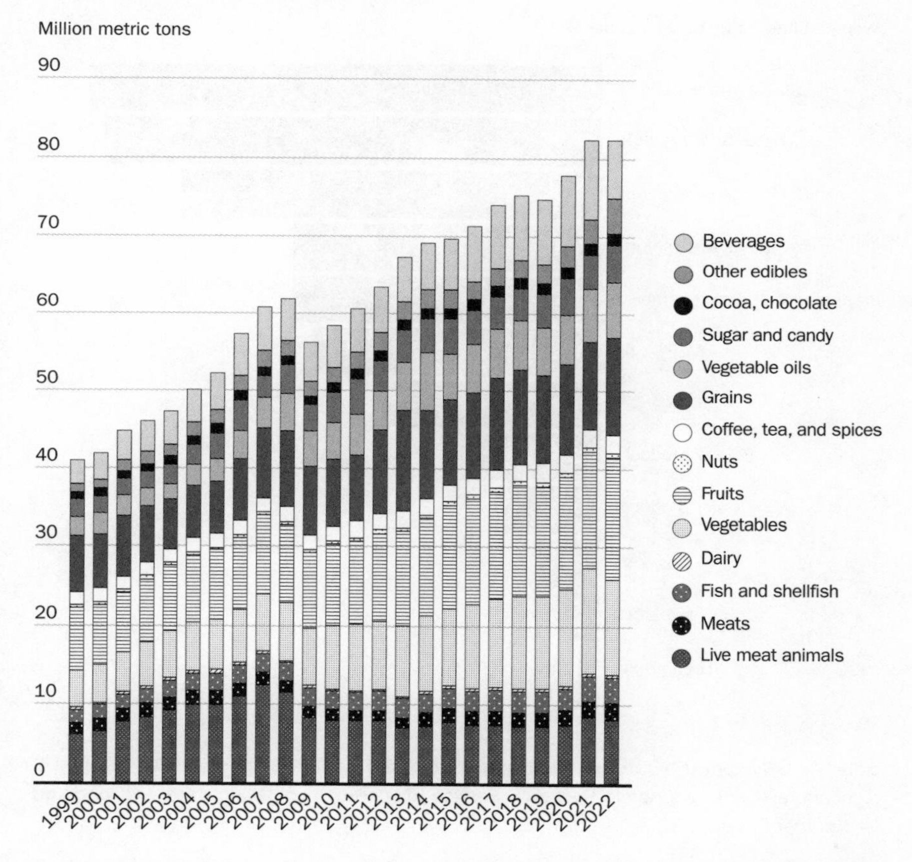

Source: "Summary Data on Annual Food Imports, Values and Volume by Food Category and Source Country, 1999–2022," US Food Imports, Economic Research Service, Department of Agriculture, updated March 23, 2023.

emerged as a significant driver of agricultural imports, growing faster than any other horticultural import in the last decade.

Much of the expansion in international trade in food is owed to trade agreements completed in the 1990s. In the United States, the 1994 North American Free Trade Agreement improved Americans' access to

FIGURE 22.7
Imports make up a significant share of US food consumption, particularly sweeteners, fruits, and vegetables

Average share in 2011–2021, percent

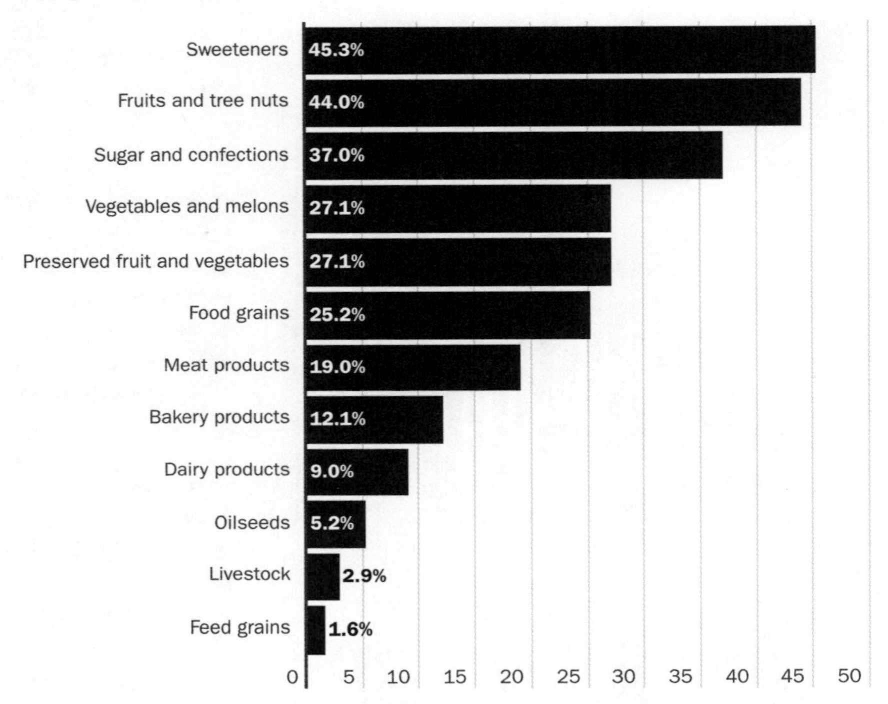

Source: "US Export Share of Production, Import Share of Consumption (2008–2021)," US Agricultural Trade, Economic Research Service, Department of Agriculture, last updated September 5, 2023.

warm-weather produce grown in Mexico and foods in which Canada specialized (and not just maple syrup). As a result, the volume of fresh vegetables imported into the United States, primarily from Mexico and Canada, has almost doubled since the late 1990s.[22] Perhaps the best example is the avocado, about 90 percent of which ($3.1 billion annually) is imported—almost all from Mexico. Our southern neighbor also supplied more than half of all US berry imports (excluding strawberries) in 2022.[23]

Globally, the 1995 World Trade Organization agreements, especially the Agreement on Agriculture, dramatically reduced global food and

FIGURE 22.8

Connectivity between countries in global food and agricultural trade has increased significantly between 1995 and 2019

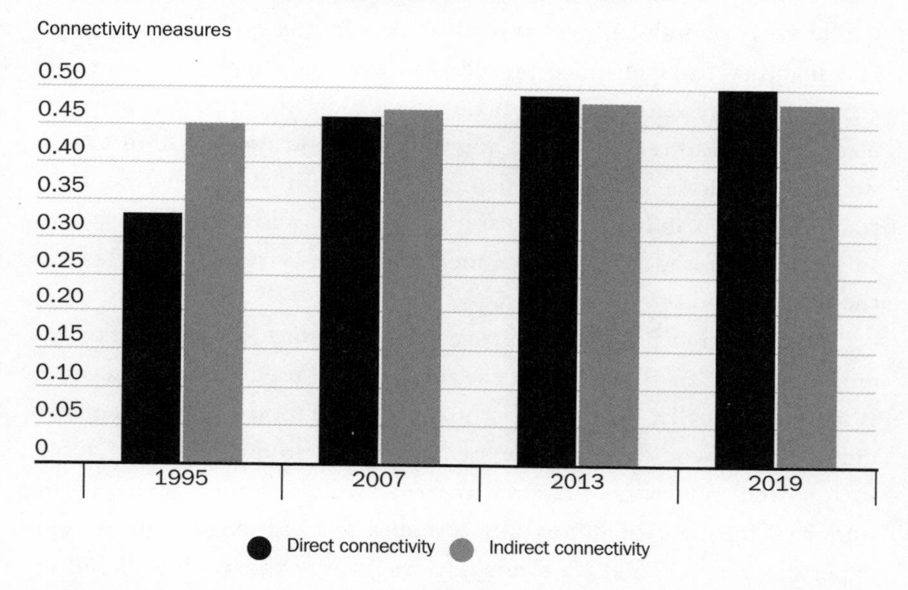

Yaghoob Jafari, Helena Engemann, and Andrea Zimmermann, "The Evolution of the Global Structure of Food and Agricultural Trade: Evidence from Nerwork Analysis," Food and Agriculture Organization of the United Nations, 2023.

related trade barriers.[24] Since then, agricultural trade connectivity has increased significantly (Figure 22.8) and agricultural trade has doubled in volume and calories. By 2019, countries were 50 percent more likely to form a direct global food trade link with another country than in 1995.

Over the same period, global agricultural trade flows between countries have increased from around 11,000 to more than 17,000. And, contrary to the conventional wisdom that trade openness increases a nation's economic fragility, it was these very trade connections that, as the *Financial Times* reported in mid-2023, helped *prevent* the global food crises that many warned would occur during the pandemic and ongoing Russia-Ukraine conflict.[25]

Even these data, however, understate the remarkable effects of globalization on our daily diets (and grocery expectations) over the long term. Consider, for example, the pineapple: native to South and Central America, the fruit first made its way to Europe around the time of the 15th-century Columbian exchange, when many crops and cuisines began to be traded globally. Due to their demanding growing conditions and inability to ripen once picked, however, pineapples for centuries remained a rare status symbol in Europe. Often, the fruit was not even eaten but instead rented by the hour—at rates hitting $8,000 in today's dollars—for those seeking to flaunt their wealth. Today, by contrast, trade expansion and technological improvements allow for the easy consumption of fresh, dried, and canned pineapples virtually anywhere in the world—and for cheap!

Globalization has even improved our *domestic* food supply. For example, more than 40 percent of the tinplate steel used for canning goods is sourced globally, meaning that many canned foods, although grown domestically, would be more expensive if US producers lacked access to imported materials.[26] American farmers, meanwhile, often rely on imported fertilizer or use export revenues to fund expansions or crop experimentation. Total US food and agriculture exports hit $196 billion in 2022, almost half of which ($88 billion) went to Asia.[27]

Our Food Reflects the Immigrant Experience

Food has also been a critical part of the American immigrant experience. As immigrants settle in unfamiliar places, their cuisines become conduits for cultural exchange—something most people born in the United States have experienced firsthand via, for example, a friendly chat with a new restaurant's immigrant owner or employee. In 2014, the Americas Society/Council of the Americas reported that immigrants accounted for 37 percent of small restaurant owners.[28] Moreover, according to the Bureau of Labor Statistics, immigrants comprised 30 percent of food service workers in 2022,[29] despite making up only 13.8 percent of the US population.[30] Including undocumented individuals would likely push these numbers even higher.[31]

Immigrants flock to restaurants for many reasons. Ones that specialize in their home country's cuisines, for example, can be comforting and feel like home. After arriving in a new country, being able to work and socialize with people who share your culture—and perhaps your language—is invaluable. Restaurants can also help immigrants become accustomed to the cultural norms of their new country of residence—often with the help of other immigrants who also work there. Immigrants also gravitate toward living in urban areas, which happen to be where most eateries are concentrated.

Restaurants also provide jobs and economic mobility for people with little formal education. According to the Brookings Institution,[32] for example, the US food service industry has long been both a major entry point for noncollege workers *and* among the industries in which "people gain the skills that enable them to climb the ladder in those sectors." Food service is also commonly cited as among the handful of industries with "great potential" for upward mobility,[33] and the National Restaurant Association estimates that about 90 percent of restaurant managers and 80 percent of owners started out in entry-level positions.[34] Not all of these people are immigrants, of course, but many of them are.

Indeed, stories abound of immigrants making a life in the restaurant business and greatly improving their communities in the process. Many people know Los Angeles as the "donut capital" of America,[35] but what they may not know is that Cambodian immigrants, fleeing the Khmer Rouge in the 1970s and 1980s, are largely responsible for the pastry's regional success. One such immigrant, Ted Ngoy,[36] arrived in California with his family in 1975 facing financial struggles and working multiple service jobs. A coworker introduced Ngoy to donuts, and the taste flooded him with memories of the Cambodian round cakes he had as a boy. Intrigued, Ngoy dove into the donut industry, honed his management skills, and within a year owned his own donut shop and gained fame for using fresh ingredients and a made-to-order approach. As his success grew, he sponsored hundreds of visas for fellow Cambodians fleeing the Communist regime back home, playing a major role in establishing LA's donut empire and improving the lives of both his employees and his many customers.

Around the same time, Argentinian immigrant Lorena Cantarovici moved to Denver and, even though she had a background in finance, pursued a job in the food service industry because she couldn't speak English.[37] She went from dishwasher to busser to server to the owner of several empanada restaurants that won the US Small Business Administration's 2017 Business Person of the Year for Colorado.[38] Miles away in Texas, Atour Eyvazian went from being smuggled out of Iran in the 1980s to working as a Jack in the Box janitor and today co-owning 106 Jack in the Boxes and 8 El Pollo Locos.[39] He considers restaurants to be the "only industry that opens the doors and opens the arms and accepts people like me when we come to this country."

Ngoy, Cantarovici, and Eyvazian are living the American Dream, and they certainly aren't alone.[40]

Food Provides a Taste of Western Values

Food also provides ample opportunities for outbound cultural exchange, giving people in "hostile" nations a *taste* of the West without all the tense and often messy geopolitics. As noted, KFC dominates the fast-food market in China and today boasts more than 9,000 restaurants there.[41] The establishment opened in 1987 and was the first American fast-food chain to operate in China, rendering it a long-standing symbol of the country's newfound openness and partial embrace of Western capitalism (even as KFC workers near Tiananmen Square served chicken in traditional "Mao" suits).[42] In Iran, meanwhile, McDonald's has been banned since the 1979 revolution, yet the Golden Arches, Ronald McDonald, and Big Macs remain in the country via the knockoff Mash Donald's in multiple Iranian cities. The chain's owner Hassan explained in 2015 that government officials and hard-liners have threatened the restaurant because they see it as still "too Western," yet Mash Donald's remains open and popular because Iranians equate Western chains with cleanliness and profitability. "McDonald's means quality," Hassan said, adding that "people in Iran know this too."[43]

The proliferation of American restaurant chains in these and other authoritarian nations (see, for example, the 602 Starbucks in Turkey) won't solve all their internal and geopolitical problems. Yet, like film and music, American restaurant chains can nevertheless introduce capitalism and Western values to millions of people taught or told to be skeptical (at best) of the United States and its people. When managers first attempted to train KFC employees in China, for example, they quickly realized that Western perceptions of customer service were unfamiliar to Chinese citizens due to decades of communism. Managers also found that one-child families and the proliferation of home computers were cloistering Chinese children, making them more difficult to train. So to account for these differing norms, they curated training programs that were wildly successful and "difficult for any competitor to emulate."[44]

Like KFC in China, McDonald's was the first American fast-food restaurant to enter the Soviet Union.[45] Russians waited in an hours-long line not only for a meal but also for the opportunity to experience a sliver of the utopia they imagined the West to be after enduring tyranny and food insecurity for decades. Years later, one exchange student recalls how puzzling it was that while Russia was enduring widespread food shortages, McDonald's "never ran out of anything." The chain's Soviet debut was so revolutionary that it gave rise to the "Golden Arches Theory," which posited that nations hosting McDonald's would never engage in war due to their interdependence.[46]

Add to these types of interactions the simple pleasures of the food itself, and it's easy to see why KFC, McDonald's, and other restaurant chains have long been considered a pillar of American "soft power" abroad.[47]

Food can also teach the benefits of free market abundance to people from countries that lack such privileges. Before the Berlin Wall fell, East Germans revered bananas as a luxury good and would wait in winding lines for a chance to purchase the fruit, often to no avail. West Germans, by contrast, had easy access to bundles of the cheap fruit and took such abundance for granted. After German reunification, bananas became a symbol of socialist economic failure: when Germans in the east today see a long line, they jokingly ask whether the store is selling bananas.[48]

Western grocery abundance may have even contributed to the fall of Soviet Communism. Boris Yeltsin, the first freely elected leader of Russia, admitted that an impromptu visit to a grocery store in Houston two years before his election had catalyzed his exit from the Communist

Source: Houston Chronicle Publishing Co. Reprinted with permission.

Party.[49] As those close to him reported, Yeltsin was astonished with the variety and affordability of products and thus concluded that Russia had "committed a crime against our people by making their standard of living so incomparably lower than that of the Americans."[50] It was after this visit that the "last vestige of Bolshevism collapsed" inside of Yeltsin, who then spearheaded Russia's attempt at a democratic, capitalist society.

Given the hope that Western enterprises evoked in Russia, the 2022 suspension of McDonald's, KFC, Pizza Hut, Starbucks, and other firms because of the Russia-Ukraine war evokes a melancholy sentiment.[51] The closures signify more than just business shutdowns; they portend a potential era of isolationism and abuses of power—a stark contrast to the peace, hope, and happiness these establishments once embodied.

Conclusion

Globalization expands our palates, fosters the sharing of diverse culinary traditions, and enables year-round access to fresh and healthy foods—

championing free markets and transcending countries' often-stark geopolitical, cultural, and ideological divides. Yet, while these results are to be cheered, perhaps the greatest benefit of all is simply the joy that this variety and abundance brings to each of us—alone, at home, or out with family and friends. *That* globalization is a lot more fun than a container ship.

Chapter 23

The Democratic Promise of Globalized Film and Television

Paul Matzko

- Globalization mitigates the "nobody knows anything" problem—the inability of Hollywood to consistently predict hits and misses—by increasing the likelihood that a film or show will find success somewhere in the world.
- Advances in digital technology have radically democratized film and television production, enabling artists worldwide to create high-quality content without the need for massive budgets or studio support.
- The invention of the internet and the advent of streaming platforms has made it possible for films and TV shows to frictionlessly reach global audiences, bolstering Hollywood's bottom line while spurring beneficial competition from foreign filmmakers.
- The number of movies and shows being released has exploded without reducing the quality of that content. The typical consumer enjoys a wider, more diverse array of high-quality film and television than ever before.

Bluey is an Australian children's show featuring a family of anthropomorphized cattle dogs. It is also a global phenomenon. Since the show was added to Disney+, Americans have spent a collective 32.82 billion minutes watching the Heeler family's gentle parenting. That is several billion more minutes than the total viewing time for the record-breaking 2024 Super Bowl.[1] The show, meant for preschoolers, is currently ranked 14 on the Internet Movie Database's (IMDB) list of the top 250 shows ever made, with an average user score as high as feted shows like *Band of Brothers* and *The Wire*.[2]

This would have been unlikely in a pre-digital era, when an aspiring animator would have had to relocate to Hollywood and punch the clock for an American studio that could afford to produce expensive, animated shows. But the creator of *Bluey*, Joe Brumm, worked out of a small studio in Brisbane, Australia. In global film and television industry terms, this was a backwater of a backwater. Yet the Down Under success of *Bluey* attracted Disney, which acquired its global streaming rights—worth an estimated $2 billion.[3] Disney was merely attempting to keep pace with Netflix, which, as of 2024, spends more on foreign-made movies and TV shows than it does on all North American productions combined.[4]

Bluey's surprising success is emblematic of the ongoing transformation of the film and television industry. New digital technologies have radically globalized and democratized TV production and distribution. Informational goods, like entertainment, are particularly amenable to rapid globalization, which is, simply put, the free movement across political borders of people, ideas, capital, goods, and services. The World Wide Web is fundamentally globalist, a (mostly) borderless and (mostly) untaxed network that facilitates spontaneous cultural exchange at an unprecedented scale. As a result, it has never been easier or cheaper to make, share, and watch high-quality film and TV, launching an era of ever-increasing global exchange and visual innovation.

Nobody Knows Anything

The fundamental problem with making film and television is that, in the words of screenwriter William Goldman, "Nobody knows anything."[5] He meant that predicting box office success is a crapshoot, neither science nor art. The most well-regarded work often fails, while surprise hits crop up out of nowhere. Thus, the acclaimed *Citizen Kane* (1941) flopped at the box office yet micro-budget flick *Paranormal Activity* (2007) returned nearly 200 times its investment. Even knowing what has worked in the past is no guarantee. As an executive at the Australian Broadcasting Corporation put it, "If we set out to make half a billion dollars by creating a new *Bluey* then we'd fail. For all [the show's] success, it's lightning in a bottle."[6]

Goldman's aphorism—the "*nobody knows* property"—is a problem because of the high stakes involved in the film industry.[7] The expense of financing, distributing, and promoting a movie or TV series can be immense. While it was true, to quote a former chairman of Walt Disney Studios, that "very few entities in this world can afford to spend $200 million on a movie," a bad enough flop could still sink a studio.[8] Historically, that created an incentive structure that led to the consolidation of the studios into a handful of major companies.[9] The studio system mitigated the dangers inherent to producing uncertain products with high sunk costs through economies of scale and by pooling risk. Only about 10 percent of movie releases ever made a significant profit, as economist Harold Vogel once noted, but that was sufficient to finance the 70 percent that failed outright and the 20 percent that broke even; it was a viable strategy for an organization with enough capital to survive the lean spells.[10]

It also propelled vertical integration in which the studios acquired movie theaters, giving them significant control over film distribution (especially until antitrust action in 1948). In addition, the big six studios operated as a semi-monopsony regarding creative talent. Aspiring actors, filmmakers, and showrunners had vanishingly few other options for selling their labor; thus, restrictive contracts and broken promises of box office backend were routine.

Gradually, over the back half of the 20th century, the centralized Hollywood model slowly broke down under increased competitive pressures. That included the rise of the indie film festival circuit, which gave non-studio filmmakers a market to showcase and sell their films and to attract top acting talent. Likewise, government deregulation in the late 1970s enabled the proliferation of cable channels in the 1980s, which offered an alternative distribution mechanism for films and TV shows; the theater box office now had to compete with the likes of the Home Box Office (HBO).[11]

These new venues for creators and new channels for distribution to consumers sparked a Golden Age of Television. HBO, for example, was an innovation engine even in its early years. It experimented with shows that would have been considered either too niche or too obscene for primetime broadcasting, such as *Tales from the Crypt* and the pioneering news satire show *Not Necessarily the News*. By the turn of the century, television—once considered a second-run proposition for aging movie stars—increasingly competed with film studios for talent and financing.

"Prestige" TV shows such as *The Sopranos* and *Mad Men*—a single season of which could cost as much as a movie to produce—also fueled rising consumer demand for boxed VHS or DVD sets, a highly lucrative revenue stream for an industry no longer solely reliant on box office receipts. Every new movie or TV show became an opportunity to quadruple dip on revenue: a theatrical release, VHS/DVD sales, broadcast syndication, and eventually, streaming rights. While "US population grew by 41 percent," as economist Joel Waldfogel notes, "movie revenue grew by almost 400 percent" by the turn of the 21st century.[12]

Still, these changes to the movie industry were fairly incremental, albeit a useful reminder that expanded market competition promotes innovation and consumer welfare. But what has happened since the turn of the 21st century is anything but incremental. The rise of the internet and the advent of new digital technologies have accelerated the transformation of film and TV.

Hacking the Film Lottery

To borrow a concept from Waldfogel, it is helpful to think of making a movie or show as buying an "expensive lottery ticket."[13] The odds that any particular ticket will win are small, but if you pool resources and buy enough tickets, it may be possible to guarantee a hit. This is not only the plot of the 2022 movie *Jerry & Marge Go Large*—starring Bryan Cranston—but an apt description of how Old Hollywood increased its odds of winning at the box office by concentrating capital investment in a handful of studios.

But now consider what would happen if one could lower the price of lottery tickets while simultaneously increasing the number of winning tickets. More people would buy more tickets! As a result, the necessity of a capital concentration strategy would wane. That is what the digitization of production and the rise of globalized distribution channels have done for the film and television industry. Cheaper camera and editing technologies—which are themselves products of globalization—have allowed many more films and shows to be produced. And new distribution channels increase the odds that any given project will succeed in at least one regional audience in the global marketplace. Globalization has meant more movies and TV shows produced more cheaply than ever before.

Until the 2000s, most movies and shows were shot using expensive film cameras, each of which could cost at least $250,000. Even the film stock was expensive and required a significant number of crew to handle; a 90-minute movie required perhaps 9,000 feet of film, translating into nine film reels that weighed in total about 60 pounds.[14] And thousands of copies of the film had to be sent to movie theaters across the country. Even setting aside salaries and other expenses, the cost of the cameras and film alone could be exorbitant.

Digital cameras have exponentially reduced that cost. While there are still expensive cameras—such as those used to film for IMAX—there are now consumer-grade cameras that can capture picture quality as high as even the highest-grade film cameras of a generation ago. The 2014 Academy Award–winning documentary *The Lady in Number 6* was shot with a Canon 5D Mark III, which retails for about $1,500. For comparison, that is little more than what it once cost to rent a film camera for a single day of shooting.[15] The cost of editing has followed suit. A cutting-edge Ediflex nonlinear editing system in the 1980s cost $150,000 (about $429,000 in 2024 dollars).[16] Today, movies and shows edited with software like Final Cut Pro—which retails for $300—routinely win major cinema awards.

The result is that any relationship between big budget and high quality has blurred. Director Edward Burns made the 2011 indie darling *Newlyweds* on a total budget of $9,000 using a Canon 5D Mark II and free iMovie software. As Burns puts it, "If you can scrounge together a few thousand dollars, you can make the kind of film you want to make without having to worry about making your money back." Given the proliferation of smartphones with quality cameras, Burns further imagined, "If you're a kid who wants to go out and shoot a movie as a one-man band, it's great." It is a sentiment echoed by directing legend Francis Ford Coppola: "One day, some little fat girl in Ohio is gonna be the new Mozart and make a beautiful film with her little father's camcorder, and for once the so-called professionalism about movies will be destroyed forever."[17]

It is telling that the limits of Coppola's imagination extended only as far as Ohio (which, to be fair, might as well be Timbuktu in the Hollywood mind). The reality is that cheaper tools have expanded the pool of creators to include people from all over the world. It is hard to exaggerate just how much more global our televisual diets are today. It used to be hard to find foreign content, often requiring visiting an arthouse cinema or a niche movie rental store. But today, one can open an app and watch a bewildering array of high-quality content on demand, from *Trollhunter*, a Norwegian mockumentary-style creature feature, to South Korea's *Parasite*, the first non-English film to win Best Picture at the Academy Awards.

From Phnom Penh to Pagosa Springs

Digitization has not only globalized the creation of film and television; it has also widened its distribution. High-speed internet enabled the creation of streaming video platforms that have global audiences and a voracious appetite for content. This has decentered Hollywood and given a particular boost to "smaller-market repertoires" from Scandinavia, East Asia, and Latin America.[18]

This is practicable because the marginal cost of distribution for informational goods—whether newspapers or movies and TV shows—has fallen to near zero. In a pre-digital era, every additional copy of a book, CD, or tape that was made and sold carried additional costs. That was a function of both its material inputs and the expense required to move the object from the site of production through the point of sale to the moment of consumption (expenses that grew with global distance). But the 1,000th copy of a digital good costs no more than the 10th copy. And that holds true regardless of location and distance. The marginal cost to stream a movie in Phnom Penh, Cambodia, is the same as in Pagosa Springs, Colorado.

Furthermore, globalization and digitization have allowed studios and streamers to develop a "digital farm system," a way of discovering local hits that they can either redistribute or remake for other regional markets.[19] For example, Netflix used data generated by its tens of millions of subscribers to identify a promising intersection of trends: their subscribers 1) were fans of films made by David Fincher, 2) liked actor Kevin Spacey, and 3) disproportionately borrowed copies of a critically well-regarded but obscure 1990 British political thriller titled *House of Cards*.[20]

Based on that data, Netflix acquired the rights to the show and greenlighted an American remake with Fincher and Spacey. It became the first original streaming show to win an Emmy and helped Netflix triple its subscriber base.[21] Globalization is no panacea, but it appears capable of improving upon the old gut intuition approach to predicting the future success of film and television. We might have to soften Goldman's principle from "nobody knows anything" to "sometimes, somewhere somebody knows something."

Raising All Boats, Junks Included

The globalization of film and television distribution has been a rising tide raising all boats. American movie studios now earn as much as three-quarters of total box office receipts from international markets.[22] That revenue has papered over a steady decline in domestic ticket sales, which, even before the pandemic, had fallen by 25 percent between 2002 and 2019.[23] Studios have been able to compensate for their losses to cable, streaming, and user-created competitors by pitching their content to international audiences. Globalization has been a lifeline for Hollywood.

Movies that underperform expectations in the domestic box office can sometimes make up the difference by overperforming in foreign markets. That even applies to the highest-grossing movies of all time, such as James Cameron's *Avatar.* Given its high production and marketing expenses (about $500 million), *Avatar* would have been only a moderate success based on domestic receipts alone (about $785 million).[24]

But a movie that North Americans saw as a "standard, perhaps preachy, allegory about racism and environmental destruction" struck Chinese audiences as a timely message about the "forced appropriation of property" by government-sanctioned developers demolishing homes to throw up high-rises and highways.[25] International receipts passed $2.138 billion, turning a moderate success into a historic triumph.[26] Nobody in Hollywood can reliably predict these specific cultural resonances, but a wider global audience increases the odds that any given movie or show will be a hit somewhere in the world, whether in theaters or on streaming services.

This also cuts against a popular narrative about the relationship between Hollywood and China that goes something like this: The American film industry was once capable of producing innovative, novel, mid-budget films. But then China entered the picture, with its massive filmgoing audience gatekept by censorial Communist Party officials. As a result, Hollywood became more risk-averse and more reliant on safe sequels with broad global appeal.

The problem with this story is that by the time China entered the picture, the Hollywood studio model was already unsustainable. As one distribution executive put it, "When studios greenlight a movie, it used to be about, 'What are the DVD sales going to be?'" But competition from streaming platforms had choked off the addicted studios' access to so uncut a form of revenue. Instead, executives now cared about one question: "How's the movie going to do in China?" The result, as entertainment journalist Ben Fritz put it in 2016, was that "China is now the wallet. And Hollywood is the factory."[27]

Understanding that reality flips the story of China and Hollywood on its head. The global expansion of the film industry to China was not the cause of Old Hollywood's decline but rather a consequence. Indeed, pivoting to blockbusters and sequels with an appeal to a Chinese audience was a life raft for American studios—but one that only temporarily masked the ongoing decline of an already failing industry. If China had not been an option, it would have merely advanced the eschaton, as it were; the conversations about the end of Hollywood that we are having in the 2020s might simply have taken place in the 2010s instead.

Democratizing Film and Television

Globalization has fueled a radical democratization of the film and television industry. The Old Hollywood pipelines for funneling (and controlling) creative talent and capital financing have burst wide open. "Until now, those of us in the television and film business had been able to wait for the talent to find us," said Spacey in 2013, because "we had the keys to the kingdom, and folks needed to bring us their stories if they wanted to find a route to an audience."[28] Hollywood, as an enterprise, had profited from its gatekeeping power; whether that system benefited either customers or creative talent is another matter entirely.

But now, because of digitization and globalization, an unprecedented number of people worldwide can bypass the big studios and make and distribute films and television on their own. This is upsetting to former cultural tastemakers, such as *New York Times* film critic Manohla Dargis, who once complained about the excessive number of indie films being sold to distributors at indie film festivals because "dumping 'product' into theaters . . . damages an already fragile ecosystem" (and creates unwelcome additional work for film critics). It is not hard to understand why organizations and individuals who benefited from the older, less competitive era of the film and TV industry would be dismayed that today "the impulse to make a film has far outrun the impulse to go out and watch in a theater."[29] Their livelihoods are at stake.

Sometimes, the cultural gatekeepers are backed by the power of the state. During trade negotiations involving the United States and the European Union in 1993—which ultimately led to the creation of the World Trade Organization—the French minister of culture, Jacques

Toubon, worried that unrestricted access of Hollywood studios to European audiences would destroy their local film and television industries. "We must not let our souls be asphyxiated, our eyes blinded, our businesses enslaved," Toubon fulminated, and to which French President Francois Mitterand added, "A society that relinquishes to others its means of representation, is an enslaved society."[30] This species of cultural obscurantism propels domestic film quotas, industry subsidies, and other attempts to protect from foreign cultural influence.

Their fears came true, to an extent. France's protectionist film industry "mega subsidies" failed to "stop [the] US content onslaught," to quote one breathless headline. By 2014, US-produced programming owned a 66.4 percent market share in Europe.[31] But that was a shortsighted complaint; even as European audiences were watching more *American* content, it was simultaneously the case that American—and global audiences—were watching more *European* content. That had a net positive financial effect on European film and television industries, especially in smaller countries.[32]

Quality and/or Quantity

Gatekeepers and protectionists have reason to fear the democratization of film and TV; it leads to a loss of state and professional control of the industry, even if it is an overwhelming net positive for consumers and independent producers. But it is worth considering whether they have a point when they worry that televisual democratization reduces the quality of what is being produced. Perhaps the new movies and shows are just the lowest common denominator schlock, a degraded mockery of what was once art. One can gesture at the box office popularity of movie franchises, sequels, and remakes—from superheroes to space fantasies—and lament the decline of originality and artistry.[33]

No one can dispute that a globalized industry produces films and TV in much greater quantity than before. The number of movies released each year in the United States nearly tripled between 2000 and 2016 (Figure 23.1). And as television distribution grew from just three networks in 1980 to more than 100 platforms by the 2010s, the number of new TV

FIGURE 23.1

The number of movies released each year in the United States nearly tripled between 2000 and 2016

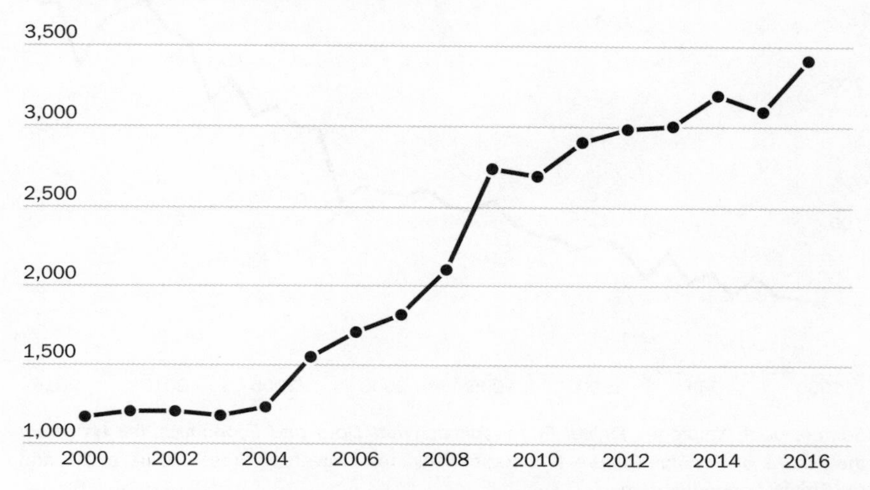

Source: Joel Waldfogel, *Digital Renaissance: What Data and Economics Tell Us about the Future of Popular Culture* (Princeton: Princeton University Press, 2018), p. 93.

shows introduced each year more than quadrupled (Figure 23.2).[34] We are swimming in an ocean of content.

Those are impressive quantities, but are the critics right about the degraded quality of the content? When Waldfogel tracked a popular measure of quality—the number of movies with a critic score of at least 90 percent "fresh" according to Rotten Tomatoes—he found that the number of well-regarded films released each year had exploded from 12 to 83 between 1998 and 2016 (Figure 23.3). User-generated IMDB scores followed suit, as did the number of Emmy awards given to streaming platforms and cable channels (Figure 23.4).[35] Thus, by every metric—other than the personal taste of crotchety gatekeepers—increasing quantity also meant increasing the number of quality shows.

This makes sense on an intuitive level. After all, competition between studios and streaming platforms increases their willingness to take risks. When, for example, the remake of *House of Cards* became a sensation for Netflix, former Disney head Michael Eisner noted that if he had attempted

FIGURE 23.2

The number of TV shows introduced each year in the United States more than quadrupled between 1980 and 2016

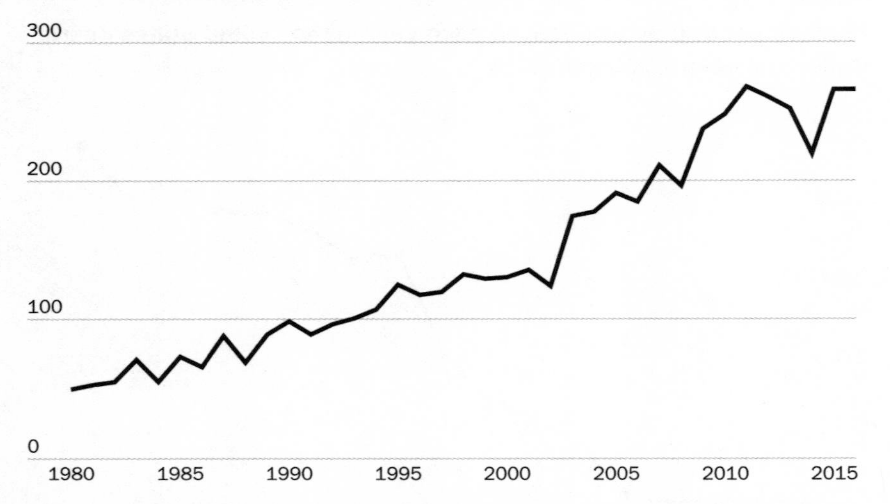

Source: Joel Waldfogel, *Digital Renaissance: What Data and Economics Tell Us about the Future of Popular Culture* (Princeton: Princeton University Press, 2018), p. 111; and "All Shows," epguides.com.

FIGURE 23.3

The number of movies earning a critics' rating of 90 or above on Rotten Tomatoes increased almost sevenfold from 1998 to 2016

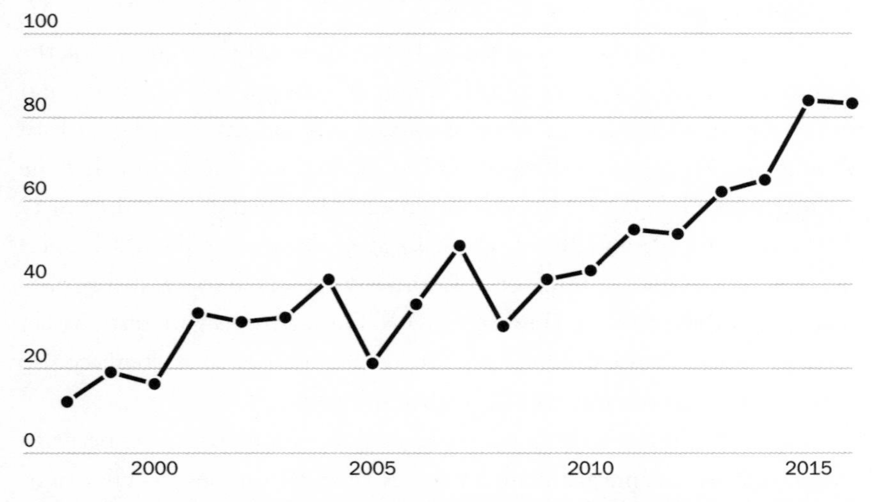

Source: Joel Waldfogel, *Digital Renaissance: What Data and Economics Tell Us about the Future of Popular Culture* (Princeton: Princeton University Press, 2018), pp. 100–101; and Joel Waldfogel, personal communication with the author.

FIGURE 23.4
The Internet Movie Database (IMDB) rating of the top-ranked TV shows released each year also increased from 1998 to 2015

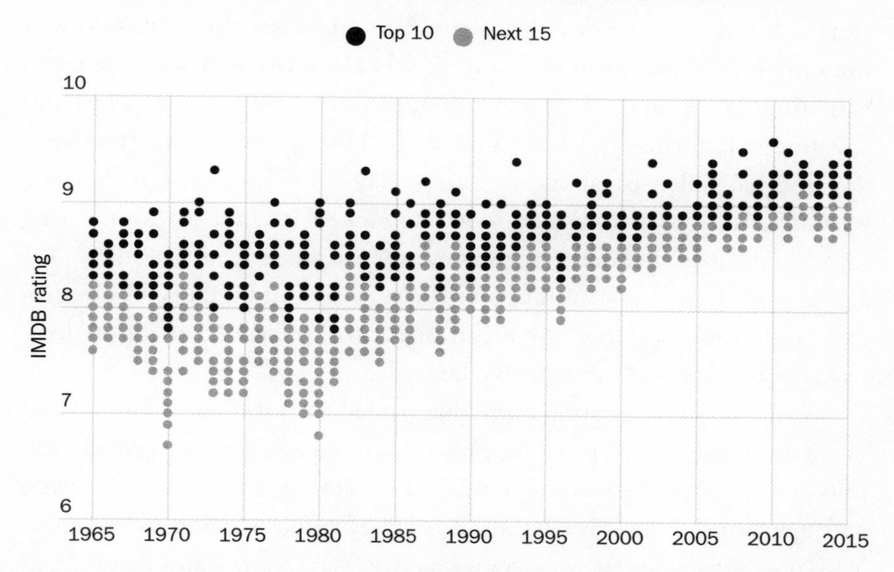

Source: Joel Waldfogel, "The Random Long Tail and the Golden Age of Television," Innovation Policy and the Economy 17 (2017): 14; and Joel Waldfogel, personal communication with the author.
Note: The data displays only TV shows that received 25 or more ratings on IMDB.

to start a broadcast TV show in like fashion—with the anti-hero killing a neighbor's dog—then he would have been fired within 10 minutes.[36] As entertainment journalist Ben Fritz put it, "Shifting economic and technological factors have fueled an explosion of originality and risk taking."[37]

The biggest movies or splashiest shows aren't the only winners. An academic study found that the shift from renting at physical stores to streaming and mail delivery—with their much larger catalogs of titles—made consumers "significantly more likely to rent niche titles relative to blockbusters." Previously, almost half of all physical rentals were dedicated to the top 10 movies by revenue; afterward, that number fell to 11 percent.[38] There is strong evidence that globalization and digitization simultaneously improved the quantity, quality, and breadth of consumption of the typical film and television consumer.

Apocalypse or Apotheosis: User-Created Video

Consumers are enjoying an embarrassment of riches, but there are storm clouds on the horizon for the film and television industry, and not only for the lingering remnants of Old Hollywood. Total time spent watching movies and TV shows at home—including both broadcast and streaming platforms—peaked in the early 2010s at nearly nine hours per day and has fallen by about an hour a day since.[39] What has replaced television time is user-created video content. After all, streaming platforms and cable channels once stole audience share from broadcast TV and movie theaters by multiplying the quantity and quality of alternative programming. Now it is streaming's turn to face a new set of alternative platforms and substitutable content.

And whereas streaming and cable tripled the number of movies and quadrupled the number of TV shows released each year, it is small peanuts compared to the volume of televisual content that users are creating and uploading daily. Five hundred *hours* of video is being uploaded to YouTube per *minute*! If the average person were to try and drink from that firehose—even dedicating every waking minute to the task—they would only make it through 832 minutes, or about half a day's worth of upload in one lifetime.[40] And that does not include other platforms that host video content, from TikTok to Twitch.

Critics of social media, such as jazz reviewer Ted Gioia, dismiss user-created video as mere "distraction" that has replaced true "entertainment." We are locked into a mindless, addictive, ceaseless cycle of swiping such that "even the dumbest [legacy] entertainment looks like Shakespeare" by comparison.[41] Likewise, technologist Ted Keen calls social media a "dictatorship of idiots" over a system in which "ignorance meets egoism meets bad taste meets mob rule."[42]

Yet however discombobulating a fact it is for an older generation of elite cultural gatekeepers, the reality is that talent, knowledge, and insight are widely distributed. This conforms with the observation of economist F. A. Hayek about the distribution of expertise, although he applied his "Knowledge Problem" to the political economy rather than to the entertainment industry. Yet if it is true that, to quote Hayek, "the utilization of knowledge . . . is not given to anyone in its totality" and instead many individuals possess "dispersed bits of incomplete and frequently contradictory knowledge," then the democratization of art and entertainment is a thrilling opportunity.[43] Or, to use vernacular popular among YouTube compilation videos, "Humans Are Awesome." To quote author Neal Stephenson, "The results of the creative frenzy of millions of people are always more interesting than what a single person can think of," no matter how brilliant the individual.[44]

Consider, for example, how short-form video is transforming comedy into a more diverse artistic space featuring comedians from all over the globe. The most-followed TikTok account currently belongs to Khaby Lame, a Senegalese-Italian and former factory worker with over 162 million followers on TikTok who is known for his humorous expressions that have cross-cultural appeal.[45] Humor is not the exclusive preserve of any one nationality or identity; comedic talent is widely distributed, and the democratization of cultural production allows more of that humor to find a global audience.

But this is not just a matter of the comedy industry transitioning between older and newer generations of professional comedians. Whether old school or new school, a comedian can spend months honing a tight five-minute set capable of bringing down the house but still not out-joke the aggregated humor of a globe's worth of user-created content. An ordinary person might have come up with only a single joke or truly funny experience in their lifetime, but if even a fraction of billions of users come up with one such bon mot and then upload it to a platform where it can be algorithmically distributed, it is more than enough to create a continuous stream of crowd-sourced hilarity that surpasses the focused efforts of even the funniest professional comedian. Call it the humor of the crowd.

Blurred Lines

Increasingly, the distinctions between terms like "streaming," "traditional TV," and "user-created video" are blurring. The different platforms, once relatively distinct from each other in terms of the content they peddled, have been merging. Disney movies are now released on its streaming platform, Disney+. YouTube is now the largest provider of "broadcast" television programs, beating out streaming platform Hulu.[46] As Ben Fritz notes, "The terminology we use for visual content is already antiquated, given how often we watch TV shows on devices other than TVs and view films without any cellophane in sight."[47]

But that blurring also has to do with the nature of the content itself. Communications theorist Michael Strangelove has described the rise of user-created, short-form video as a transition into a "post-television era."[48] But that framing assumes that there is a meaningful difference between film and television and the forms of video replacing them. Bear in mind that the development of these categories was rooted in historical circumstances. Early television was primarily financed by commercials and gradually optimized into 22 minutes of serialized "villain of the week" content with 8 minutes of ads. But that does not make those norms a universal or ahistorical constant.

This is why Netflix and other streaming platforms have found success in releasing entire seasons of a show all at once. This blurred the previously rigid differences between medium-length serialized content and longer, unitary movies. To quote Fritz again, a "Marvel 'movie' is . . . best understood as a two-hour episode of an ongoing television show, while one season of *Fargo* or *American Crime Story* is, essentially, an eight- or ten-hour film." Similarly, there are often marginal differences between older genres of film and television and their online substitutes. What, in the end, is the great distinction between the old TV variety shows, like *The Ed Sullivan Show*, and daily YouTube channels like *Good Mythical Morning*, which features celebrity appearances, oddball games, and audience interaction? Ultimately, "the lines that divide these types of content will blur to non-existence."[49]

Yet as dramatic as the transformation of film and television has been over the past several decades, even greater changes may be in the works. Filmmaking tools using artificial intelligence (AI) promise not only to blur but to erase the line between creator and consumer. If the ultimate end of AI filmmaking is generating entire movies with a series of written prompts, then, in the words of Neal Stephenson, we are still in the "transistor-radio stage of AI."[50]

But filmmakers are already using AI tools to de-age actors, dub films into foreign languages, and quickly render visual effects. It is not hard to imagine a future in which, as actor and director Donald Glover put it in an advertisement for Google's prompt-based video tools, "Everyone's going to become a director. And everybody should be a director."[51] Of course, that is hyperbole in service of advertisement, but it is logical that further decreasing the costs of video creation would increase the number of people creating videos. It is a lesson that has been proven time and again by the advent of camcorders, editing software, and short-form video apps.

Conclusion

Regardless, the rise of streaming video and user-created content platforms has already decentered Hollywood studios and even the American film industry. Fully 80 percent of YouTube traffic comes from abroad. That has created a much more diverse televisual landscape while enabling "marginal, alternative, subcultural, and subaltern voices" to flourish.[52] And despite the concerns of reactionary critics, the effect of this globalization has not been cultural homogeneity. Rather, in the words of anthropologist Richard Wilk, "We are not all becoming the same, but are portraying, dramatizing, and communicating our differences to each other in ways that are more widely intelligible."[53]

Thus, a show like *Bluey*, despite being intentionally Australian in orientation, has resonated with global audiences. One might object that the cultural distance between Australia and other former English colonies is not all that wide. But consider the success of *Squid Game*, a 2021 Korean-language drama—inspired by Japanese manga—about a fictional game-show in which desperate contestants compete to the death to win a cash prize.

It is not an unchallenging show. The title is a reference to a traditional Korean children's game, although the show was rated for mature audiences. Thematically, it critiques Korea's state capitalist political economy over the past half-century.[54] It is not the kind of content one would intuitively expect to perform well internationally. And yet, when

Netflix released *Squid Game*, 111 million households watched it in its first month.[55]

Then it caught the attention of Jimmy Donaldson, a YouTuber better known as "MrBeast," who has over a quarter of a billion subscribers (the most in the world as of 2024 after surpassing the Hindi-language music video channel T-Series). MrBeast is known for his lavish video productions—such as playing Battleship with real boats or spending 50 hours buried alive—that are created at Hollywood scale but from his small hometown of Greenville, North Carolina. Nothing about his biography—a college dropout with no formal film training—suggests mogul material. Yet, his expertise in gaming the YouTube algorithm has created an enterprise worth more than a billion dollars.[56]

But MrBeast surpassed himself when he remade *Squid Game* in real life, featuring 456 contestants competing for a $456,000 prize. The 25-minute YouTube video has garnered 617 million views; for comparison, that is *three times* the number of people who bought tickets for *Gone with the Wind*, the highest-grossing movie of all time.[57] MrBeast's version of *Squid Game* stripped the story of its anti-capitalist messaging and thus encapsulated precisely the social behavior of which the Netflix show was a critique.[58]

The story of *Squid Game*'s creation and re-creation is reminiscent of something Web 2.0 critic Andrew Keen wrote dismissively of those who believed in the democratizing power of the internet. These optimists, Keen wrote, promise "an infinite market in which we cycle and recycle our cultural production to our hearts' content." Keen dismisses such pie-in-the-sky promises because he believes there is a "scarcity of talent, expertise, experience, and mastery in any given field."[59] But the success of *Squid Game*—a story repeatedly mixed and remixed, that hopped from Japanese manga to Korean show to North Carolina YouTube sensation, and that has perhaps been viewed by more than a billion people across all its iterations—offers a rebuke to the limited imaginations of those who are nostalgic for the days of a smaller film and TV industry, a smaller circle of creators and gatekeepers, and, ultimately, a smaller world.

Chapter 24

The Globalization of Popular Music: A Case Study on the Beatles

Clark Packard

- Thanks to advancements in technology and the internet in particular, music today is more globalized and easily accessible than ever before. In particular, Latin American music continues to make significant inroads into both the United States and other markets worldwide.
- Today's global artists are largely following a path laid out by the Beatles, who were the first truly global musical sensation. No musical artist did more to globalize popular music than the Beatles. They were influenced by cultural globalization, including early American rock and roll, French philosophy, and Indian religious practices.
- The Beatles influenced subsequent rock and roll and popular musical artists around the world, including modern artists like Taylor Swift, and brought Western attention to Eastern religious and cultural practices.

A good shorthand definition of globalization is the movement of people, ideas, capital, goods, and services across borders. Whether it's the Ethiopian restaurant in an American suburb, the development of the COVID-19 vaccine, or a cargo ship brimming with containers transporting goods between Chinese and Latin American ports, globalization comes in many forms. It is ubiquitous. Even if protectionist politicians "succeed" in stemming the inflow of certain foreign products, other forms of globalization march on.

Take music. Today, American pop star Taylor Swift is arguably the most famous person in the world, partly due to the advancement in technology and streaming music services. Demand for Taylor Swift concert tickets in France was so large that it crashed Ticketmaster France's website in the summer of 2023.[1] "Swifties," as her fans are known, would be rioting in the streets of Paris if the Macron government prohibited French fans from streaming Swift's music on Spotify or banned her from performing concerts in the country.

In early 2024, an international diplomatic spat erupted among governments over the American pop star's services. The *Wall Street Journal* reported that the Singapore government offered significant financial incentives for the American pop star to perform exclusively in the city-state instead of in other Southeast Asian countries. Thailand and other regional governments made clear their unhappiness over the arrangement.[2] Singapore defended the exclusive arrangement by claiming that the additional tourism and spending generated by Swift's concerts outweighed the cost of the financial incentives. In other words, a foreign government subsidized a very wealthy American to provide services in its country—much to the chagrin of neighboring countries. Yet the Taylor Swift global phenomenon is not new. It follows a playbook similar to that of the Beatles, who supercharged the globalization of popular music in the 1960s. In short, the cultural globalization genie, particularly music, has long been out of the bottle.

At its best, music has always been a blend of cultures and influences. Blues and jazz, for example, were genres largely created by black musicians who fused musical elements from the Americas, Europe, and Africa, including traditions brought to the United States by enslaved people. Yet a truly comprehensive analysis of the globalization of music—from German classical composers to the creation of the phonograph to migration to the rise of the internet—is beyond the scope of this essay. Instead, it will trace how popular music became globalized, with particular attention paid to the Beatles. No musical artist or group has embodied and defined the globalization of popular music like the iconic British band.

The Beatles: Globalization Trailblazers

Early History

Following World War II, the United States was the world's dominant economic and military power. During the late 1940s and into the 1950s, during the formative years of what eventually became the Beatles, American art was also ascending. American visual artists like Jackson Pollock were globally recognized, Hollywood was becoming what we think of it as today, and—most importantly for this essay—rock and roll was born, which originated from African American music like rhythm and blues, jazz, gospel, and country music.[3] By the late 1940s, more than half the records in the world were made and sold in the United States.[4]

John Lennon, Paul McCartney, George Harrison, and Richard Starkey—better known as Ringo Starr—were all born during the early 1940s, the height of World War II, in the port city of Liverpool, England.[5] They grew up in working-class neighborhoods in the aftermath of the war.[6] As Europe began its postwar recovery, record sales started to explode in the region. Like many British kids at the time, the Fab Four all gained their first exposure to American rock and roll via the radio, which was broadcast into Liverpool from across the channel on Radio Luxembourg. Most influential were American artists Chuck Berry, Little Richard, Elvis Presley, and Buddy Holly. In fact, Lennon and McCartney, the band's two primary songwriters, first bonded over their shared love of American country music and early rock and roll.[7]

The Beatles evolved from a band called the Quarrymen, which Lennon formed in 1956.[8] In 1960, the band that would become the Beatles was offered an opportunity to travel abroad and play professionally in Hamburg, Germany. During this early period, with greased-back hair and leather motorcycle jackets, the Beatles' aesthetic borrowed heavily from Marlon Brando's character in *The Wild One*, a popular American film at the time.[9]

In Hamburg, another port city, they became the house band in a strip club and played at various other bars and music halls in the city. Around this time, the Beatles were introduced to French existentialist philosophers like Cocteau and Camus, and their aesthetic changed—replacing greased-back hair with the early mop-top, a "French cut . . . that was worn in German art schools and universities."[10] About this period, Lennon once said, "I grew up in Hamburg, not Liverpool."[11] By 1962, the band had returned to England and signed a record contract with a British label, EMI Parlophone, in March of that year.

It was a tale of cultural globalization and migration: British teens heavily influenced by American rock and roll and Hollywood fashion and then French philosophy and fashion honing their skills in Germany and returning to remake music back in England—and eventually conquering the musical world.

Success around the World

In March 1963, the Beatles released their debut album *Please Please Me.* The album remained in the British top 10 for over a year. By the fall of 1963, the group was starting to achieve success outside of the United Kingdom. They had topped the charts in Australia, France, the Netherlands, Ireland, New Zealand, Norway, and Hong Kong and grossed more than $17,500,000 internationally (or nearly $180,000,000 adjusted for inflation).[12]

Yet the United States was something of a relative laggard in its enthusiasm for the Beatles. Much of this was driven by a pervasive nationalist assumption in the American record industry that foreign acts couldn't sell in the United States. They would soon learn how wrong they were. Capitol Records, an American subsidiary of EMI Parlophone, had the option to release the Beatles music but initially passed. Transglobal Inc., a clearinghouse, purchased the rights to several Beatles songs and then leased them to a small independent label out of Chicago called Vee Jay, which failed to gain traction with those songs. Other labels, including Swan and Tollie, had the rights to the Beatles songs in the United States, and eventually, Capitol exercised the right to release some of the material.[13] It was a confusing legal mess but ultimately proved fortuitous for the Beatles.

On February 1, 1964, the Beatles scored their first number-one hit—"I Want to Hold Your Hand"—in the United States. Six days later, the band arrived in New York City from London and were greeted by thousands of screaming fans. Two days after that, the Beatles performed on the *Ed Sullivan Show* and reached an audience of an estimated 73 million

Americans—or about 40 percent of all Americans at the time.[14] Watching that night from Gainesville, Florida, was a young boy named Tom Petty, who later said that the Beatles' performance on the show "changed everything."[15]

By early April, the Beatles had 12 songs on the Billboard chart, including the top five songs.[16] Usually a label won't release multiple singles at the same time, but because multiple record labels held the rights to the Beatles music, the result was something of a free-for-all when the Beatles began to break. As Sam Lebovic notes in his 2017 *Journal of American Studies* essay, "Here, There and Everywhere": The Beatles, America, and Cultural Globalization, 1964–1968":

> When the Beatles had their greatest success on the Billboard chart on 4 April 1964, Capitol held positions one and four with "Can't Buy Me Love" and "I Want to Hold Your Hand," Tollie had the number two record with "Twist and Shout," Swan had the third most popular disk with "She Loves You" and Vee Jay held number five with "Please Please Me."[17]

Demand for Beatles records was so great that Capitol Records had to subcontract record pressing to its primary rivals, RCA and MGM. In other words, the Beatles were a tremendous financial success for the American recording industry, as well as record stores. This perhaps helps explain why there was no protectionist response to the Fab Four's success.

About $50 million (or about $500 million adjusted for inflation) worth of Beatles merchandise was sold to American fans in the immediate aftermath.[18] *Life* magazine declared, "In '76 England lost her American colonies, [but] last week the Beatles took them back."[19] *Variety*, an entertainment publication, noted in February that the Beatles, "fundamentally shook up and globalized the music biz."[20] By August 1964, it is estimated that the band had sold 80 million albums worldwide, and by February 1965, they had sold more than 100 million albums worldwide.[21]

Over the next several years, Beatlemania hit overdrive. The band continued to record new commercially successful albums and play to adoring fans all over the world. At the same time, they were pushing the envelope for the delivery of music. Shortly after the Beatles released arguably their masterpiece *Sgt. Pepper's Lonely Hearts Club Band* in the summer of 1967, they played live on the BBC and European Broadcasting Union, which was the first international satellite broadcast of a television show. The performance of "All You Need is Love" featured a chorus consisting of Eric Clapton, the Rolling Stones, Keith Moon of the Who, and Marianne Faithful and was broadcast to 24 countries simultaneously—a tremendous feat given technical limitations at the time.[22]

Not only influenced by the globalization of music, fashion, and ideas, the Beatles helped expand the globalization of those very things.

Global Travelers

More than virtually every musical act at the time, the Beatles were truly a global phenomenon. They toured all over the world in a way that few acts did, which was driven by—and further cemented—their global reach (Figure 24.1).

Following their appearance on the *Ed Sullivan Show*, the Beatles performed a few more East Coast dates and then toured heavily around the UK in the spring and summer of 1964. Later that summer, they played in Hong Kong as well as Australia before heading back to the United States for West Coast dates. They finished the year back playing in the UK.[23]

In 1965, the Beatles played all over Europe in the early part of the year and then came to North America in the late summer. The Beatles finished the year touring across the United Kingdom.[24]

In 1966, the Beatles embarked on their final tour. The initial leg included 13 dates in Germany, Japan, and the Philippines, followed by 18 concerts in North America (16 in the United States and two in Canada).[25] In Tokyo, about 200,000 fans applied for 30,000 tickets. Meanwhile, in the Philippines, the Beatles played for 80,000 fans in one day—a truly staggering figure at the time.[26]

The tour was marred by controversies. In the United States, there was a backlash to John Lennon's March 1966 quip that the Beatles were "more popular than Jesus."[27] In Japan, there was intense debate about whether the culturally conservative nation should welcome the British band to an esteemed venue like Nippon Budokan, which is situated

FIGURE 24.1
The Beatles played over 1,000 concerts in over 200 locations around the globe

Source: Wikipedia, "List of the Beatles' Live Performances," last edited August 31, 2024.

between the Yasukuni Shrine and the Imperial Palace. Fearing massive protests from conservatives, the government had to deploy approximately 35,000 police officers, and eventually, Prime Minister Eisaku Satō called for the shows to be canceled. The shows, however, went on since the contract had already been signed.[28]

In the Philippines, the Beatles refused an invitation to the Malacañang Palace and the opportunity to meet the president and first lady of the country, which was in keeping with the band's policy of refusing official government visits during tours. The snub was viewed poorly in the press, and the Beatles faced significant backlash, including death threats.

After the 1966 tour and the various controversies that ensued, the Beatles quit touring—preferring instead to make studio albums and begin experimenting sonically, which is widely considered their most innovative period. But their international traveling days and global influence were far from over.

Today, Taylor Swift travels all over the world performing for adoring crowds and, like the Beatles, occasionally creates international controversies. Meanwhile, foreign artists find massive demand in the United States. Indeed, successful musicians tour all over the world, but that wasn't always the case. In fact, the Beatles were very much at the forefront of global travel by popular musical acts. Facilitated by the spread of their music across borders and the relative ease of international travel made possible by technological advancements, the Beatles were in demand all over the world. In other words, the triumph of the Beatles was at least in part a triumph of globalization.

India

As Lebovic notes, "The international success of the Beatles had become self-reproducing—the scale of their market allowed them to borrow from an ever-expanding cultural palette, which in turn helped to expand the scale of their market."[29] And by 1965, the Beatles were increasingly interested in India—and Eastern practices.

In 1965, the Beatles released *Rubber Soul*, which included a John Lennon–composed song called "Norwegian Wood." It was the first pop song to feature a sitar—a stringed instrument popular in India, Pakistan, and Bangladesh—played by George Harrison on the recording.[30] The follow-up album, 1965's *Revolver*, began a string of Harrison-composed songs that were heavily influenced by Indian music. The first track was "Love You To," which Harrison composed entirely on a sitar. Modeling its arrangement on North Indian classical music, the recording "features Indian musicians playing the tanpura (plucked string instrument) and the table (percussion instrument)."[31] David Reck, a former professor at Amherst College, wrote of the song, "One cannot emphasize how absolutely unprecedented this piece is in the history of popular music. For the first time Asian music was not parodied utilizing familiar stereotypes and misconceptions, but rather transferred in toto into its new environment with sympathy and rare understanding."[32] (Table 24.1 below lists some instruments from the Indian subcontinent that the Beatles used in their recordings.)

A year later, on *Sgt. Pepper's Lonely Hearts Club Band*, the Beatles released a Harrison-composed song called "Within You Without You," which "features Indian instruments played by Indian musician and a

TABLE 24.1
The Beatles used an assortment of instruments of Indian origin in their music

Instrument	Type
Sitar	String
Tambura	String
Tabla	Percussion
Dilruba	String
Swarmandal	String
Shehnai	Wind
Sarod	String
Pakhavaj	Drum

Source: "The Beatles' Albums in Order—Complete List!," Beatles Bible, personnel listing of the albums *Rubber Soul, Revolver, Sgt. Pepper's Lonely Hearts Club Band*, and *Let It Be*, and of the single "The Inner Light."

Western string ensemble playing in conversational texture (call and response interaction among instruments," and uses several Indian musical genres, rhythmic patterns, and time signatures. Scholars point out that a number of the Beatles' other compositions frequently contain subtle and unnoticed Indian aspects, including "Tomorrow Never Knows," "Strawberry Fields Forever," which "features a swarmandal (a string instrument in Hindustani music similar to a harp)," "Lucy in the Sky With Diamonds," and "Across the Universe," which includes Lennon using an Indian mantra "Jai guru deva om," which roughly translates to "Hail to the devine guru" in the pre-chorus.[33]

Though the Beatles had experimented with Indian influences in their own music, they had not spent much time in India. In August 1967, Harrison and his wife attended a lecture in London to hear the Maharishi speak about Transcendental Meditation. Harrison then convinced the other members of the Beatles that they should decamp from London to the Maharishi's ashram in Rishikesh, India, to study the mantra-based meditation in early 1968. Here the Beatles were—in the prime of their careers and arguably the most famous people in the world at the time—leaving their home in London to study meditation with a guru in a small town in the foothills of the Himalayas. The Beatles spent about two months in India, meditating daily and listening to the Maharishi "lecture about reincarnation and consciousness." The trip was widely covered in the press, and *Life* magazine declared 1968 to be "'The Year of the Guru,' and featured the Maharishi on the cover with groovy, hallucinogenic spirals framing his face.'"[34]

Given the Beatles' massive fame and genuine curiosity, interest in Indian music and traditions was clearly on the rise. Within a few years, the Beatles' contemporaries were making Indian-inspired music, including the Rolling Stones with "Paint It Black,"[35] which features a sitar, Donovan's "Hurdy Gurdy Man," and the Moody Blues released an entire Indian-inspired album called *In Search of the Last Chord*.[36] Likewise, Ravi Shankar, the famous Indian sitar player, played at Woodstock in 1969.

And it wasn't just music. It is estimated that by the mid-1970s, the Transcendental Meditation movement was estimated to have 600,000 devotees, with the Maharishi's techniques and vision promoted by celebrities such as Shirley MacLaine and football star Joe Namath.[37] Indeed, scholars point to the Beatles' absorption and promotion of Indian practices and traditions as a partial explanation for the explosion of yoga and meditation centers in Western countries.[38]

Author Philip Goldberg wrote in his book *American Veda: From Emerson and the Beatles to Yoga and Medication—How Indian Spirituality Changed the West* that the trip to study under the Maharishi "may have been the most momentous spiritual retreat since Jesus spent those forty days in the wilderness."[39] Though perhaps a bit hyperbolic, it is clear that the Beatles did help spread Indian spiritual practices to a wider Western audience. In his book on how the year 1965 changed music history, Andrew Grant Jackson wrote, "It was George Harrison's songs espousing Hindu philosophy and featuring Indian musicians, and the Beatles' study of Transcendental Meditation . . . [that] helped expand the freedom of religion the United States was founded on to encompass options outside the Judeo-Christian tradition."[40]

The Beatles were influenced by Indian spiritual practices and musical techniques, which they used to write experimental songs that were popular worldwide. They used their fame to help globalize interest in

Indian culture, Hindu spiritual traditions, and other Eastern practices that are still popular today.

Musical Influence

It is hard to overstate how influential the Beatles were on subsequent music artists around the world, particularly in North America and the United Kingdom. The shape and fabric of popular music today would not exist in its current form without the Beatles. Even artists who sound nothing like the Beatles are nevertheless influenced by the musical world the band created.

In the United States and Canada, the list of musical artists that cite the Beatles as influences is extremely long and includes globally successful artists such as the Byrds, the Beach Boys, the Grateful Dead, Creedence Clearwater Revival, The Eagles, Bruce Springsteen, Tom Petty, Jackson Browne, Billy Joel, Michael Jackson (who co-wrote three songs with Paul McCartney in the early 1980s and then subsequently purchased the publishing rights to the majority of the Beatles catalog), Nirvana (the Beatles song "In My Life" was played at Kurt Cobain's funeral), Neil Young, and Joni Mitchell.[41] Indeed, Taylor Swift has cited McCartney as one of her greatest influences.[42]

As Beatlemania spread around the world, London quickly displaced the United States as the epicenter for pop and rock and roll music. By the late 1960s and into the 1970s, based on the success of the Beatles, London-based artists, including the Rolling Stones, Led Zeppelin, Pink Floyd, Eric Clapton, Badfinger, David Bowie, and Black Sabbath—all of whom were influenced by the Beatles—achieved significant worldwide commercial and critical success.[43]

Popular Music Today

Owing to advances in technology and the internet in particular, music today is more popular and more accessible than ever before. Streaming services such as Spotify, Apple Music, and YouTube—not to mention social media platforms such as Instagram, Facebook, Twitter, and TikTok—have largely displaced purchasing physical copies of vinyl records,

FIGURE 24.2
Streaming accounted for the overwhelming majority of the music industry's revenue in 2023

Net revenue, millions of US dollars

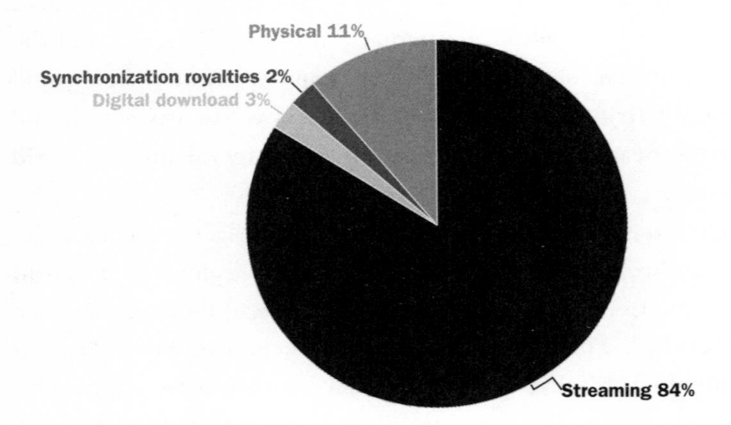

Source: Matthew Bass, "Year-End 2023 RIAA Revenue Statistics," Recording Industry Association of America, 2024.
Note: Synchronization royalties include fees and royalties from synchronization of sound recordings with other media.

eight tracks, cassettes, and compact discs. In fact, according to the Recording Industry Association of America (RIAA), streaming made up 84 percent of recorded music revenue in the United States in 2023 (Figure 24.2). As of March 2024, more than 600 songs have more than a billion streams on Spotify. The Weeknd's song "Blinding Lights" is the most streamed song of all time on the platform with over 4.1 billion plays.[44] In 2023, there were 4.1 trillion streamed songs worldwide, which represented a 22.3 percent increase from 2022.[45]

Nearly anyone in the world with an internet connection can hear any music they want at any time facilitated by technology. Take the app Shazam, which was founded by two American-born Cal Berkeley MBA students: a Stanford electrical engineering PhD graduate and a London-based, Indian-born internet consultant. The company was founded in London and is still headquartered in London, though it was purchased by Apple in 2018 for $400 million.[46] When a person connected to the internet via a smartphone hears a song they like but do not recognize, they can turn on Shazam, which listens to a very short snippet of the song, identifies it using an algorithm, and then pulls up the song automatically on Apple Music. Gone are the days when a person had to remember the lyrics, type them into a search engine, and hope it led them to the right song.

And it's not just songs in English that are exported around the world. Plenty of songs sung in foreign languages have become major hits in the American music market. Driven by a music video that has received over five billion views since its 2012 release, South Korean singer Psy's smash "Gangnam Style" hit number one on the iTunes charts in 31 countries. Since then, numerous other "K-Pop" bands singing in Korean have become popular in the United States and around the world.[47] In 2017, "Despacito," a song sung in Spanish by Puerto Rican singer Luis Fonsi and Puerto Rican rapper Yankee Daddy topped Billboard's charts for 16 weeks.

Puerto Rican artist Bad Bunny is a massive global artist. In fact, in 2020, 2021, and 2022, he was the most-streamed artist in the world on Spotify.[48] Bad Bunny was slightly eclipsed by Taylor Swift in 2023.[49] He was the first non-English language artist to hold that title. In 2022, his songs were streamed 18.5 billion times on Spotify, and his album *Un Verano Sin Ti* is the single most-streamed album on Spotify, with over 15 billion streams as of December 2023.[50] Bad Bunny was one of six Spanish language artists with over a billion streams in 2023.[51] Nearly half of Spotify's top 10 most-streamed artists of 2023 were of Hispanic origin (Table 24.2).

In April 2024, the Latin American Music Awards (AMA) was presented in both English and Spanish, which is the first time a major US awards show was shown on a bilingual broadcast.[52] As *Axios* noted, "Unlike most awards shows, winners for the Latin AMAs are selected by popular vote, not fellow artists" and the "Latin AMAs have attracted more US viewers than the American Music Awards" demonstrates the growing demand for Spanish and Latino music in the United States. The RIAA reported in April 2024 that Latin music revenues in the United States hit an all-time high in 2023 of $1.4 billion—up from $1.1 billion in 2022.[53]

TABLE 24.2

Nearly half of Spotify's top 10 most-streamed artists of 2023 were of Hispanic origin

Rank	Artist	Country/region of origin
1	Taylor Swift	United States
2	**Bad Bunny**	**Puerto Rico**
3	The Weeknd	Canada
4	Drake	Canada
5	**Peso Pluma**	**Mexico**
6	**Feid**	**Colombia**
7	Travis Scott	United States
8	SZA	United States
9	**Karol G**	**Colombia**
10	Lana del Rey	United States

Source: "The Top Songs, Artists, Podcasts, and Listening Trends of 2023 Revealed," Spotify, November 29, 2023.

Today, the growth of Latin music outpaces the growth of overall recorded music sales in the United States. The RIAA estimates that Latin music represents about 8 percent total share of music in the United States, up substantially from 5.9 percent in 2021.[54] As *CBS News* recently reported, "US listeners are streaming more non-English music . . . [and] the fastest growing audio streaming genres were world and Latin, which saw increases of 26 percent and 24 percent respectively compared to 2022."[55]

There are plenty of other examples of non-English songs becoming globally popular, and many more are sure to follow. In short, music today both is wholly dependent on globalization and helps fuel cultural globalization on a massive scale.

Conclusion

In both style and delivery, much has changed since the days of tribal or classical music performed in Africa or Europe in the 1700s and 1800s.

Thanks to the internet, it is now possible to instantly hear obscure music from all over the world. Musicians continue to tour globally and use new methods to distribute their music but largely follow the Beatles' groundbreaking work.

Indeed, it's hard to overstate the band's importance in terms of the spread of popular music around the world. As Dr. Michael Weis, a history professor at Illinois Wesleyan University, noted, "The Beatles, in a lot of ways, were the first truly globalized entertainment act."[56] They are arguably the most successful musical act of all time. In 2012, it was estimated that the Beatles had sold more than 600 million records, cassette tapes, and compact discs.[57] In *Rolling Stone*'s 2021 ranking of the 500 greatest songs, the Beatles had 12—the most by far. Likewise, the Beatles had 9 of the top 500 albums of all time according to *Rolling Stone*'s 2023 edition of the ranking—the most of any artist.[58]

The kids from Liverpool were influenced by early American rock and roll, took early fashion cues from American cinema and then French philosophers, honed their skills in German strip clubs, became a global phenomenon performing to adoring crowds all over the world, studied Eastern meditation in India, incorporated Indian music into their own, and in the process, influenced everything from music to yoga. The band helped shape the globalized world in which we live today.

Today, music is more accessible than ever before—and it is increasing in popularity. At its best, music—and cultural globalization more broadly—helps break down barriers while building bridges among people worldwide. Music is both a product of globalization and an important contributor to it.

Chapter 25

How Global Markets Helped the Video Game Industry

Juan Londoño

- The global expansion of the gaming market has kick-started a virtuous cycle in which more people are interested in gaming-related media and products, investors are more eager to invest in the industry, and gamers have access to more and better games.
- The transition to digital marketplaces has catalyzed the growth of the gaming industry, benefiting both gamers and developers. Developers now have a global, frictionless distribution platform, while gamers have easier and faster access to their favorite titles.
- Gaming is a prime example of how globalization has torn down physical and cultural barriers to human interaction. Online gaming experiences have become a medium in which gamers from different cities, countries, or continents can interact, with complete disregard to language barriers.
- As gaming-related media can now tap into audiences of millions of users worldwide, creative and entrepreneurial gamers can now monetize their gaming habits either by going pro or through gaming-related content creation.

Few industries have benefited from streamlining global trade and e-commerce as the video game industry has. If you were a kid in the 1970s and 1980s, your experience with video games was often mainly through an arcade machine, a piece of hardware that allowed you to play only a single game on any one machine. Today, gamers around the world can use gaming consoles, high-end personal computers (PCs), handheld devices, virtual reality headsets, or even their phones to play a variety of games from an ever-expanding library provided by digital software marketplaces.

Some of these advances can be attributed to technological progress and advances in computing power, but they are also attributed to an increasingly efficient supply chain that makes these components affordable and accessible. Once gamers have a device, they can acquire games from developers worldwide thanks to global distribution platforms or online software marketplaces. When they boot up their games, they can join online multiplayer experiences with players from different cities, countries, or even continents. Globalization has made video games more abundant and accessible and has opened avenues for gamers to monetize their hobby.

A Globalized Gaming Market Means More Games and More Ways to Play Them

The increase in foreign trade and streamlining of global commerce had one very noticeable benefit for the gaming industry: the user base is bigger than ever. This expanded market made gaming the most lucrative entertainment industry, with higher revenue than the music and film industries combined (Figure 25.1).[1] The rapid expansion of the gaming market has caused revenue for the industry to nearly triple in the span of 50 years, going from an average of $27 billion in the 1980s to over $184 billion by the end of 2022.

The increase in revenue and market size has also benefited gamers. A more robust gaming market has translated into increased funding opportunities for independent studios and developers.[2] Traditional investors and venture capitalists are more eager to fund gaming projects because of higher revenue opportunities. Studios also can leverage their worldwide audiences by relying on crowdfunding platforms like Kickstarter, Patreon, or IndieGoGo. And as video game development has become more lucrative, more passionate individuals have had the chance to venture into game development. Indie developers' passionate, risk-taking approach to video game development drives innovation and evolution in the gaming market, often pushing the frontier of available genres.

FIGURE 25.1

Gaming has become the most lucrative entertainment industry largely because of globalization

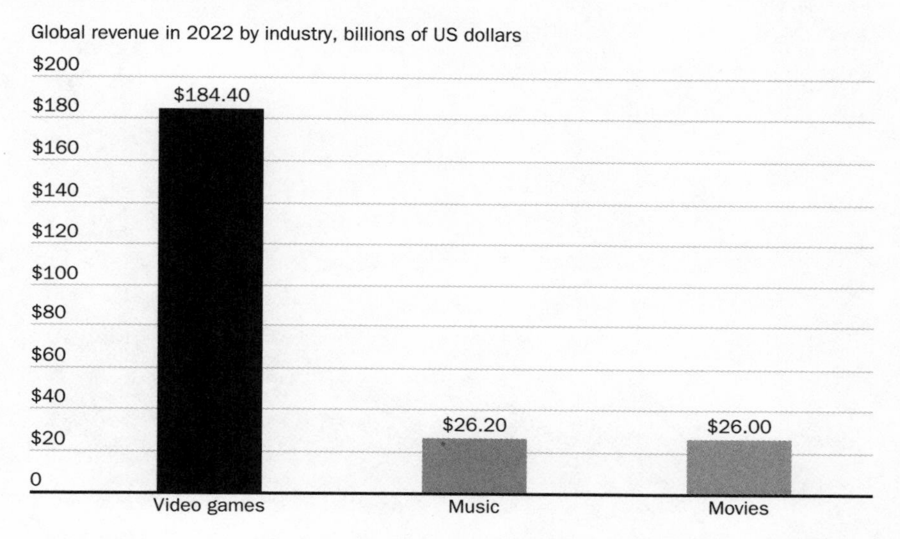

Source: Krishan Arora, "The Gaming Industry: A Behemoth with Unprecedented Global Reach," Forbes, November 17, 2023.

One example is the rise of the battle royale genre. One of the genre's most popular games, *PlayerUnknown's Battlegrounds*, also known as *PUBG*, was created under the direction of Brendan Greene, an avid player of the military simulation game *Arma 2*.[3] While playing *Arma 2* under the "PlayerUnknown" alias, Greene developed a "mod," a term used by gamers for unofficial modifications of a game, for the existing mod *DayZ* that helped give rise to the battle royale genre. Greene's mod eventually led Sony to pay him to consult in creating *H1Z1*, the first major standalone battle royale game ever released. In 2016, South Korean indie developer Bluehole asked Green to help develop a battle royale concept, which became *PUBG*. The game was an instant success, disrupting the gaming market and inspiring the creation of games like *Fortnite* and *Call of Duty: Warzone*, two of the most popular and lucrative games on the market.[4] Massive market expansion, investor trust, and broad community support thanks to globalization and global e-commerce quickly scaled the battle royale genre from

FIGURE 25.2
The gaming industry's revenue tripled in 50 years

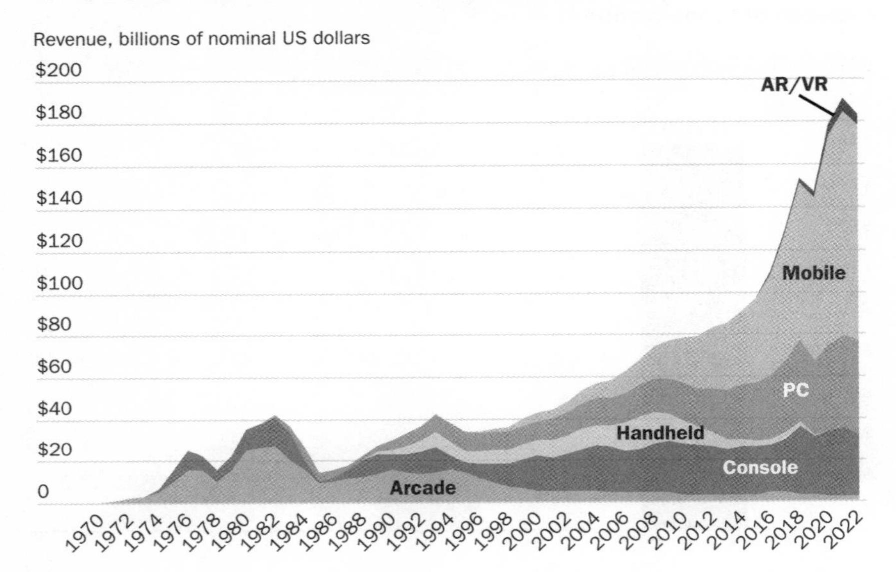

Source: Pallavi Rao, "50 Years of Video Game Industry Revenues, by Platform," Visual Capitalist, December 31, 2023.
Note: AR = augmented reality; VR = virtual reality.

passion project mods into multimillion-dollar trendsetting standalone games.

As with software, the increased profitability of video games has led to higher investment into hardware developments and the integration of gaming-capable hardware in nongaming-specific devices. As Figure 25.2 highlights, in the past 50 years, options have expanded from arcade machines to home consoles, high-end PCs, smartphones, virtual reality headsets, and cloud computing.

The explosion of the gaming industry has been tremendously beneficial for the United States. According to revenue estimates from Statista, the US gaming industry brought in approximately $68.3 billion in revenue in 2023.[5] According to the Entertainment Software Association, the US gaming industry directly employs 104,080 people and sustains a workforce of 350,015 people when accounting for indirect jobs and other economic impacts.[6]

TABLE 25.1

Since 2014, video game studios from 12 countries have been nominated for or won the Game of the Year award

Country	Nominations	Winners
United States	19	4
Japan	21	3
Canada	3	1
Poland	1	1
Sweden	1	1
Belgium	1	1
France	3	0
Netherlands	2	0
Finland	2	0
Denmark	1	0
South Korea	1	0
Spain	1	0

Source: Jose, "Every Game of the Year Winner in Chronological Order," HackerNoon, February 17, 2023.

Video Games Are More Culturally Diverse than Ever

The expansion of the gaming market to new regions has also led to a higher degree of cultural diversity in terms of where games are produced and where they are played. For most of the late 20th century, the industry was dominated mostly by Japanese and American firms like Atari, Sega, Sony, and Nintendo. However, the market has seen an increase in studios being founded in other countries and regions. And these studios can keep up and effectively compete with established ones, as reflected in the lineup of games that have either been nominated for or won the Game of the Year award since the launch of the Game Awards in 2014. While the United States and Japan continue to assert themselves as game development powerhouses, Canadian, South Korean, and European studios have emerged as contenders and winners for the award (Table 25.1).

Gamers are also likely to connect with people from different cultures when playing online multiplayer games. Spending metrics indicate that more countries are spending more on gaming. Global gaming spending is

FIGURE 25.3
Spending on gaming is growing quickly in Africa, South America, and Asia (excluding Japan and China)

Average year-over-year revenue growth from 2017 to 2023, percent

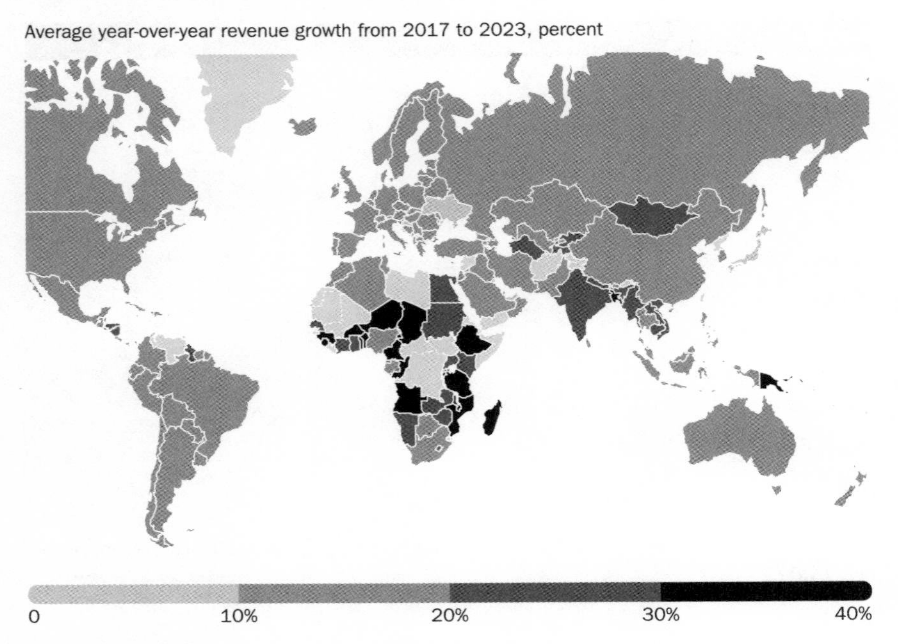

Source: "Video Games—Worldwide," Statista, updated November 2023.

increasing beyond the three highest-spending countries—China, Japan, and the United States—with regions like Africa, Latin America, and Southeast Asia seeing the highest rates of growth (Figure 25.3). According to revenue estimates, from 2017 to 2023, 16 of the 20 countries with the highest average year-over-year increases in gaming revenue were in Africa.[7] The continent tripled its gaming spending during that time. South America and North America (excluding the United States) also saw significant increases in revenue in this same period, with increases of nearly 150 percent and 130 percent, respectively. Asia (excluding Japan and China) also had similar growth rates, with gaming revenue increasing by nearly 130 percent in this period.

User penetration rate estimates, which measure the proportion of potential customers that have made at least one purchase, confirm this

FIGURE 25.4

User penetration rate estimates confirm the growth of the gaming industry in regions like Africa, South America, and Asia (excluding Japan)

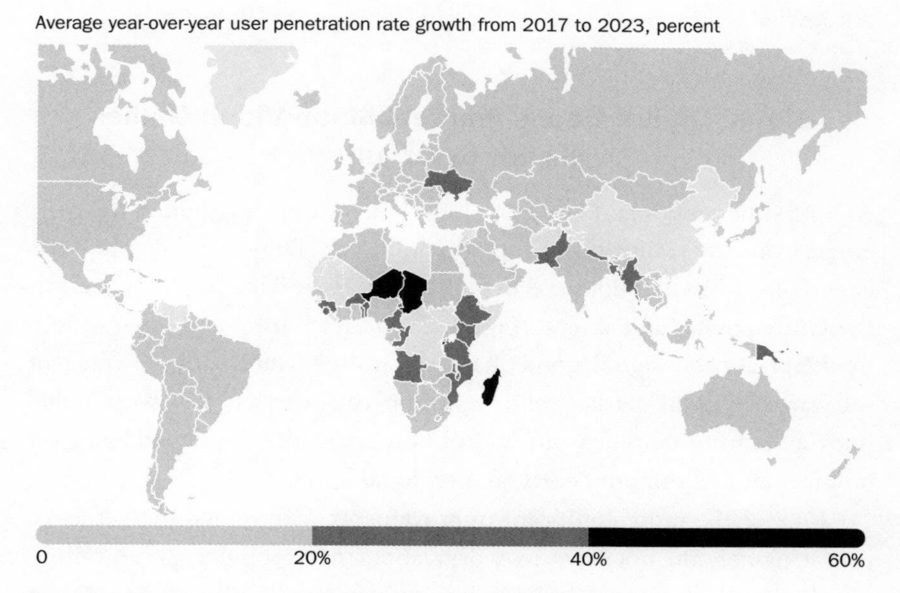

Source: "Video Games—Worldwide," Statista, updated November 2023.

tendency as well (Figure 25.4).[8] Africa continues to establish itself as the fastest-growing market in gaming, with increases of nearly 130 percent of its gaming population in the past six years. North America (excluding the United States), Asia (excluding Japan), and South America also have seen significant increases in their gaming populations, with all of them presenting increases in user penetration rates of 50 percent or more in the same six-year period.

Ultimately, what these statistics show is that video games have become a prime example of how globalization has removed physical and cultural barriers, connecting individuals worldwide. When gamers go online to play multiplayer games, they are likely to run into players from other cities, states, countries, or even continents. In the physical world, it is likely that some of these players would not be able to converse due to language differences. They could also be in various age brackets. However, these things do not matter in the gaming world. In-game communications systems and other types of in-game expression allow players to coordinate and play together. Age and cultural differences are not often acknowledged or are put aside to complete the team's objective.

Global Digital Goods Markets Made Video Games Easier to Acquire

As with other goods and services, global video game distribution has benefited from the transition to digital commerce. Digital goods trade has experienced a tremendous rise in global markets and has helped gamers in the United States and abroad (Figure 25.5).[9] App stores and other online marketplaces for digital goods have streamlined international trade of software.[10] Digital markets removed numerous barriers that were holding the gaming market from its full potential, like the dependence on physical media, shipping costs, and regional locks.

One of the most significant improvements with digital marketplaces is that gamers do not have to worry about new popular games selling out. Before the move to digital stores, gamers would have to line up for hours to acquire a recently launched game.[11] Today, gamers worldwide can rest assured that the game they want will be available for purchase on their preferred digital store, often with the option to pre-download the game so that they can start playing it as soon as it is launched. Digital stores have been particularly beneficial for gamers in developing markets. Often, gamers in these markets would struggle to find physical copies of new games, as the costs of shipping physical media worldwide made these games prohibitively expensive. Additionally, if retail stores in developing countries miscalculated how well a game would sell, gamers had to wait weeks, even months, before they could buy newly released games.

Digital commerce has also benefited small and indie developers, as their sales no longer depend on finding a manufacturer and the number of physical copies sold. Instead, they can pocket more profit and focus on how they sell online. In the physical media era, if a new release was to become suddenly popular, there could be a significant lag between the moment a game would sell out and when stores could restock the shelves

FIGURE 25.5

Exports of digitally delivered services have grown faster than other exports in recent years

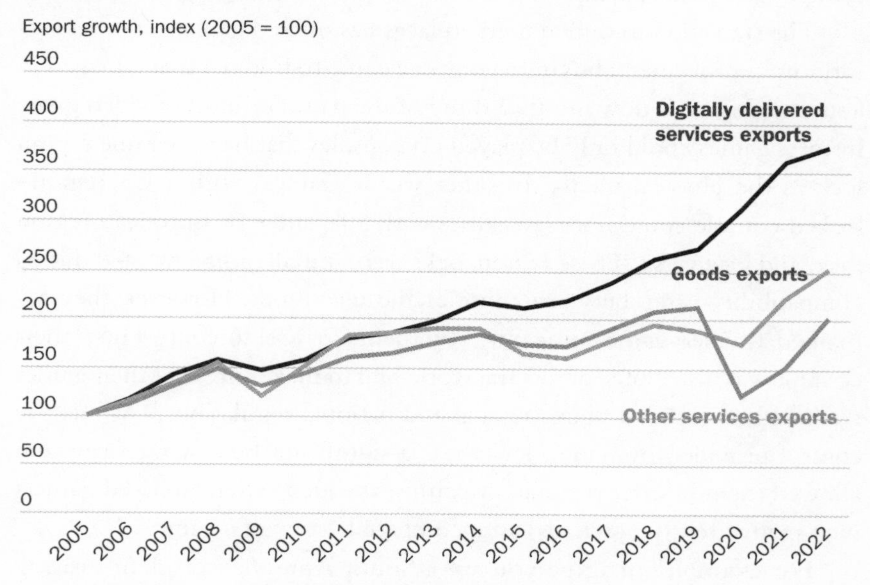

Source: "Global Trade Outlook and Statistics," World Trade Organization, April 5, 2023.

with new copies. Retailers abroad would also add to this backlog, as they would have to place massive orders to compensate for an unexpected rise in demand. This wait could kill momentum for a game, slowing potential new sales. Nowadays, if a game suddenly becomes popular, developers can fully capitalize on that virality by selling as many copies in as many countries as possible, as was the case with games like the pandemic-era hits *Among Us* and *Fall Guys*.[12]

Having a worldwide and largely frictionless user base has also allowed developers and publishers to experiment with different business models that have made gaming more affordable. Ad-supported games let players download and play the games for free, tapping into a user base of millions of potential gamers. Developers can leverage these user bases to sell ad space that brings revenue that matches or even surpasses what they would have made under a traditional sales model.[13] The "freemium" model is another type of business model in which games are available to download and play for free but offer optional in-app purchases. Freemium games have been particularly effective in developing countries, as they provide a significantly more affordable option for gamers in countries where exchange rates make paying for a full-priced game financially prohibitive.

The transition to digital marketplaces has offered gamers another significant improvement: buying a copy of a game to find out that it locked to a specific region is now mostly a thing of the past. For most of video game history, games could only be played on consoles that had the same region lock as the physical media. In other words, gamers with a US region–locked console could not play games with a Japanese or European region lock, and vice versa. These region locks were initially implemented due to compatibility issues between consoles and televisions. However, they remained as video game companies saw them as a tool to control how their content was distributed across the world and to make sure that their games complied with the various regional and national regulations.[14] While the control provided by region locks was a significant benefit for firms and allowed them to offer regional discounts, the locks often annoyed gamers who inadvertently purchased an incompatible copy of a game.

For example, imagine you are a South American resident visiting a European or Asian country and you discover that retail stores have a better video game offering than in your home country. If you were to acquire a copy of a video game while on your trip, it is likely that said copy would be incompatible with your console, as the console you own would probably have an Americas—NTSC-U—region lock, while the game would have an NTSC-J/C or PAL region lock. Additionally, as it is unlikely that anyone in your city has a Europe- or Asia-compatible console, there is no option to resell this game in a secondary market. Customers who made this mistake usually ended up with an expensive and disappointing paperweight.

With the digitalization of video game marketplaces, the days of worrying whether a purchased game is locked to a region are largely over. While digital stores still have region- and even country-specific content and pricing, if a game is available for purchase in the store shown on a device, the game is compatible with that device. Importing a game nowadays is much simpler than in the days of physical media since publishers can now simply submit their game to a digital store, which vets the game to determine if it complies with any regional and country regulations and then places it in the virtual storefront.

The streamlining of video game sales has also impacted sales of physical media. To stay competitive with digital marketplaces, console makers and video game publishers realized that regional locks on physical copies of games could no longer be implemented. The latest game consoles, including the PlayStation 5, Xbox Series X, and Nintendo Switch, are all region-free, and the companies have mostly discouraged game developers from applying region locks to their games.[15] Gamers who enjoy collecting and preserving physical copies of games now have the benefit of being able to buy any copy of a game in any part of the world and have peace of mind that it will be compatible with their console.

Thanks to the Global Gaming User Base, Gamers Can Now Monetize Their Hobby

As gaming is now a hobby for more people in more countries, global interest in gaming-related content has increased as well, with a rise of gaming-focused content creators, livestreamers, journalists, TV shows, movies, and, most notably, e-sports.[16] Games like *Fortnite*, *Call of Duty*, *Rocket League*, *Apex Legends*, *Valorant*, *League of Legends*, *Counter Strike*, and *Mobile Legends: Bang Bang* have amassed passionate fan bases that not only enjoy playing the game but also enjoy watching high-performance gamers pitted against each other. The last *League of Legends* world championship set the record for the most watched e-sports event in history, with a peak viewership of 6.4 million viewers.[17] The event also sold out a 16,000-seat venue in South Korea in a matter of minutes.[18]

Widely attended events and popular broadcasts usually translate into high revenues from sponsorships, ad sales, ticket sales, and image rights. This has given place to the concept of e-sports, where high-performing gamers can now live as full-time professional gamers. With cumulative prize pools of up to $30 million per year, professional gaming has become lucrative for those who can make it to a team in a league. E-sports players can thank the globalized, streamlined gaming market for creating that virtuous cycle that funds their careers.

The global nature of e-sports is strongly represented by the team rosters in the various professional video game tournaments. Teams in the major tournaments of games like *Apex Legends*, *League of Legends*, *Counter Strike*, *Mobile Legends: Bang Bang*, and *Fortnite* had representatives of over 20 countries in their rosters; in the case of *Counter Strike*, it was 34.[19] While teams are usually headquartered in a specific country, a team's roster is not necessarily composed of players of a single nationality. For example, Team Vitality, the current champions of the *Counter Strike* tournament, is a French team, but its roster was composed of French, Danish, and Israeli players. Tournaments also offer livestreams in multiple languages, ensuring that gamers across the world can tune in and listen to real-time analysis and commentary.

However, the monetization of gaming does not stop at professional competitive leagues. When global gaming audiences are paired with globalized content distribution platforms like YouTube, Twitch, Kick, or Discord, charismatic and social media–savvy gamers can also make a living as content creators. Livestreamers like Ninja, Ibai, and Shroud are the best examples of this synergy.[20] The three of them participated in professional gaming leagues before making the jump to content creation. Ibai started as a commentator/analyst of the *League of Legends* competitive league, while Ninja and Shroud were professional e-sports players. All signed multimillion-dollar contracts with different streaming platforms, and it is estimated that Ibai is currently the highest-paid streamer on Twitch.[21]

Platforms can offer these lucrative contracts thanks to the existence of a global gaming-centered audience, as these content creators have become an important source of revenue for platforms that can sell highly targeted—and therefore efficient—ads and profit from subscription fees. Aside from these contracts, these content creators can bring in more revenue through sponsorship deals or live events like Ibai's amateur boxing event *La Velada del Año*, which has continued to shatter livestreaming viewership records every year.[22] The global, diversified audience of the gaming world is also well represented by the most-watched streamers of 2023 (Table 30.2). By looking at the 25 most-watched streaming channels of the year on Twitch, one could draw two main conclusions:

TABLE 25.2

The most-watched streamers in 2023 show the gaming world's diversity

Position	Channel	Watch time (hours)	Average viewers	Followers	Country	Language
1	KaiCenat	116,742,633	61,965	8,701,353	United States	English
2	Gaules	111,266,323	12,812	4,047,243	Brazil	Portuguese
3	ibai	104,035,527	74,444	15,406,559	Spain	Spanish
4	xQc	91,487,992	50,840	11,974,242	Canada	English
5	fps_shaka	85,123,894	24,277	1,347,350	Japan	Japanese
6	Kingsleague*	74,966,044	128,476	3,015,231	Spain	Spanish
7	tarik	71,892,548	31,210	2,947,836	United States	English
8	eliasn97	63,688,397	23,575	1,757,065	Germany	German
9	HasanAbi	62,346,872	25,028	2,560,878	United States	English
10	IlloJuan	61,560,645	37,807	3,918,951	Spain	Spanish
11	한동숙 (handongsuk)	56,488,217	18,473	657,390	South Korea	Korean
12	loud_coringa	54,531,060	29,921	4,928,681	Brazil	Portuguese
13	summit1g	52,911,505	13,589	6,236,744	United States	English
14	加藤純一です (kato_junichi0817)	51,624,896	21,659	866,947	Japan	Japanese
15	ESLCS**	50,640,910	6,282	6,208,634	Germany	English
16	zackrawrr	50,614,814	20,956	1,671,782	United States	English
17	Papaplatte	48,646,944	18,138	2,105,655	Germany	German
18	PaulinhoLOKObr	47,252,786	59,719	2,737,376	Brazil	Portuguese
19	otplol_	46,819,006	5,540	698,535	France	French
20	Cellbit	45,985,752	22,135	3,285,174	Brazil	English
21	auronplay	44,102,609	50,059	15,984,080	Spain	Spanish
22	Fextralife***	42,896,008	17,670	1,600,214	United States	English
23	Jynxzi	42,056,332	18,722	3,843,322	United States	English
24	shroud	39,654,602	15,849	10,742,205	United States	English
25	우왁굳 (woowakgood)	38,698,855	18,540	1,042,086	South Korea	Korean

Source: "Most Watched Twitch Channels—Stats and Analytics," SullyGnome, updated March 27, 2023.

*Kingsleague is the streaming channel of the Kings League, a pro-am soccer league organized by Ibai and Gerard Piqué, a former soccer player.

**ESLCS is the streaming channel of the ESL, a competitive e-sports league.

***Fextralife is the streaming channel of a specialized gaming news source and hub.

gaming-focused channels are the most popular on the platform, and those channels are made up of a very culturally diverse group, both in terms of nationality and languages spoken.[23]

Conclusion

The streamlining of international trade and e-commerce has made gaming more accessible for more people all over the world. Gamers have access to more games than ever, have more ways to play them, and play them with more people worldwide. What used to be a niche hobby exclusive to a handful of countries is now a global entertainment machine with a global presence. The expansion of the industry has also provided gamers with avenues to monetize their passion, like professional gaming leagues or content creation. Globalization was the ultimate power-up that took gaming from the arcade to living rooms to practically anywhere.

Notes

INTRODUCTION

1. Andrew Ross Sorkin et al., "Wall Street Warns about the End of Globalization," *New York Times*, March 24, 2022.

2. Anne Kim, "Toilet Paper: A Uniquely American Obsession," *Global Trade*, April 6, 2020.

3. "Manufacturing, Value Added (% of GDP)," World Development Indicators, World Bank, 2024; and "Agriculture, Forestry, and Fishing, Value Added (% of GDP)," World Development Indicators, World Bank, 2024.

4. "Real Data (Chained 2017 Dollar)," US Census Bureau, 2024.

5. Steven A. Altman and Caroline R. Bastain, *DHL Global Connectedness Index 2022* (Bonn, Germany: Deutsche Post DHL Group, 2023).

6. Steven A. Altman and Caroline R. Bastain, *DHL Global Connectedness Report 2024* (Bonn, Germany: DHL Group, Headquarters, 2024).

7. "Trade in Services (% of GDP)," World Development Indicators, World Bank, 2024.

8. World Trade Organization, *World Trade Statistical Review 2022* (Geneva, Switzerland: World Trade Organization, 2022).

9. World Trade Organization, *World Trade Statistical Review 2021* (Geneva, Switzerland: World Trade Organization, 2022), p. 9.

10. Richard Baldwin, "Globotics and Macroeconomics: Globalisation and Automation of the Service Sector," in *ECB Forum on Central Banking: Challenges for Monetary Policy in a Rapidly Changing World, Conference Proceedings,* June 27–29, 2022.

11. World Bank and World Trade Organization, *Trade in Services for Development: Fostering Sustainable Growth and Economic Diversification* (Geneva, Switzerland: World Trade Organization, 2023).

12. Brendan Murray, "WTO's Forecasts for Global Trade Are Clouded by Political Uncertainty," Bloomberg, April 11, 2024.

13. James Manyika et al., *Digital Globalization: The New Era of Global Flows* (McKinsey Global Institute, February 24, 2016), p. 1.

14. Marie McAuliffe and Linda Adhiambo Oucho, *World Migration Report 2024* (Geneva, Switzerland: International Organization for Migration, 2024).

15. *2024 World Investment Report* (New York: United Nations Publications, 2024).

16. Altman and Bastain, *DHL Global Connectedness Report 2024.*

17. Altman and Bastain, *DHL Global Connectedness Report 2024*, p. 5.

18. Althea Legaspi, "Bad Bunny Is the Most Streamed Artist on Spotify for Third Consecutive Year," *Rolling Stone*, November 30, 2022; and "Most Streamed Male Group on Spotify," Guinness World Records, March 3, 2023.

19. Priya Krishna, "Why Do American Grocery Stores Still Have an Ethnic Aisle*?," New York Times*, August 10, 2021.

20. Sam Cook, "Netflix Statistics: How Many Movies and TV Shows Do They Have? 2024," Comparitech, January 9, 2024.

21. Joan E. Solsman, "Netflix's Biggest Hit Movies and Shows, Ranked (According to Netflix)," CNET, February 28, 2023.

22. Lucas Shaw and Yasufumi Saito, "These Are Netflix's Most Popular Shows (According to Netflix)," Bloomberg, March 13, 2022.

23. Lucas Shaw, "Netflix's Foreign-Language Shows See Popularity Soar in the US, " Bloomberg, December 10, 2020.

24. Jeffrey J. Schott, "Which Countries Are in the CPTPP and RCEP Trade Agreements and Which Want In?," Peterson Institute for International Economics, July 27, 2023; and Cathleen D. Cimino-Isaacs, Ben Dolven, and Michael D. Sutherland, "Regional Comprehensive Economic Partnership (RCEP)," Congressional Research Service In Focus IF11891, updated October 17, 2022.

25. "Operational Phase of the African Continental Free Trade Area Launched," African Union, July 2, 2024.

26. "Negotiations and Agreements," European Union, 2024.

27. Lucian Cernat, "On the Importance of Trade Openness," European Centre for International Political Economy, March 2024.

28. "India-Australia Comprehensive Trade Deal Negotiations from February 20," *Business Standard*, February 14, 2023; and Manoj Kumar, "Key Details of India's Pact with Four-Nation European Trade Bloc," Reuters, March 10, 2024.

29. Hannah Feng, "China's Free Trade Agreements Framework," China Briefing, July 2024; Ismael Lopez, "Free Trade Agreement between Nicaragua

and China Begins," Reuters, January 1, 2024; "Ecuador Reaches Trade Deal with China, Aims to Increase Exports, Lasso Says," Reuters, January 3, 2023; and "Serbian Trade Minister Hails China-Serbia FTA," The State Council of the People's Republic of China, July 2, 2024.

30. Clark Packard, "Correcting the Record on the Trans-Pacific Partnership," *Cato at Liberty* (blog), Cato Institute, April 1, 2022; Inu Manak and Simon Lester, "Evaluating the New USMCA," *Cato at Liberty* (blog), Cato Institute, December 11, 2019; and "Japan Trade Agreement," US Customs and Border Protection, January 12, 2023.

31. "The UK and the Comprehensive and Progressive Agreement for Trans-Pacific Partnership (CPTPP)," GOV.UK, May 20, 2024.

32. "RTAs Currently in Force (by Year of Entry into Force), 1948–2024," World Trade Organization, updated July 29. 2024.

33. Kevin Varley, "US Reshoring of Supply Chain to Be Limited by Costs, Studies Say," Bloomberg, January 13, 2023.

34. Ellesheva Kissin, "Logistics Turns to Tech to Meet New Demand," *Financial Times*, April 5, 2023.

35. Brooke Sutherland, "Supply Chains Aren't Fixed, but They're Getting There," Bloomberg, February 24, 2023.

36. Scott Lincicome, "The Baltimore Accident and Other 'Supply Chain Crises' That Keep Not Happening," *The Dispatch*, April 24, 2024.

37. Pinelopi Goldberg and Tristan Reed, "Is the Global Economy Deglobalizing? And if So, Why? And What Is Next?," *Brookings Paper on Economic Activity* (Spring 2023), p. 33. Emphasis in original.

38. Scott Lincicome, "The Suez Canal Debacle Reveals Less–and More–about 'Globalization' Than You Think," *The Dispatch*, March 31, 2021.

39. Adam Smith, *An Inquiry into the Nature and Causes of the Wealth of Nations*, ed. Edwin Cannan, vol. 1 (London: Methuen, 1904), pp. 15–17.

40. Marian L. Tupy and Gale L. Pooley, *Superabundance: The Story of Population Growth, Innovation, and Human Flourishing on an Infinitely Bountiful Planet* (Washington: Cato Institute, 2022).

41. International Labour Organization and United Nations Children's Fund, *Child Labor: Global Estimates 2020, Trends and the Road Forward* (New York: International Labour Organization and United Nations Children's Fund, 2021); Chelsea Follett and Vincent Geloso, "Global Inequality in Well-Being Has Decreased across Many Dimensions," Cato Institute Policy Analysis no. 949, June 8, 2023; and Scott Lincicome, "Celebrating the World's 8 Billionth Person with . . . Lots and Lots of Charts," *The Dispatch,* November 24, 2022.

CHAPTER 1

1. Shelby Simon and Corinne Tynan, "Everything You Need to Know about American Solar Panel Manufacturers," *Forbes*, July 31, 2023.

2. Marian L. Tupy and Gale L. Pooley, *Superabundance: The Story of Population Growth, Innovation, and Human Flourishing on an Infinitely Bountiful Planet* (Washington: Cato Institute, 2022).

3. John B. Clark, "The Society of the Future," *The Independent*, July 18, 1901, p. 1,651.

4. Israel Kirzner, *The Foundation of Modern Austrian Economics* (Kansas City, MO: Sheed & Ward, Inc., 1976), p. 84.

CHAPTER 2

1. Michael Lind, *Land of Promise: An Economic History of the United States* (New York: HarperCollins, 2012).

2. Robert Lighthizer, *No Trade Is Free: Changing Course, Taking On China, and Helping America's Workers* (New York: HarperCollins, 2023).

3. A. P. Lerner, "The Symmetry between Import and Export Taxes," *Economica* 3, no. 11 (1936): 306–13.

4. "Jay to the President of Congress," in *The Revolutionary Diplomatic Correspondence of the United States*, ed. Francis Wharton, vol. 3, *A Century of Lawmaking for a New Nation: US Congressional Documents and Debates 1774–1875* (Washington: Government Printing Office, 1889), p. 718.

5. James Madison, "Preface to Debates in the Convention of 1787," in *The Founder's Constitution*, ed. Philip B. Kurland and Ralph Lerner, Article 1, Section 8, Clause 1 (Chicago: University of Chicago Press).

6. "Records of the Federal Convention," in *The Founder's Constitution*, ed. Philip B. Kurland and Ralph Lerner, Article 1, Section 9, Clause 5 (Chicago: University of Chicago Press).

7. *The Debates and Proceedings in the Congress of the United States*, comp. Joseph Gales, vol. 1, 1789–1791 (Washington: Gales and Seaton, 1834), p. 107.

8. *The Debates and Proceedings in the Congress of the United States*, comp. Joseph Gales, vol. 1, 1789–1791 (Washington: Gales and Seaton, 1834), p. 111.

9. James Madison, *Letters and Other Writings of James Madison*, vol. 1 (Philadelphia: J. B. Lippincott & Company, 1865).

10. Phillip W. Magness, "Constitutional Tariffs, Incidental Protection, and the Laffer Relationship in the Early United States," *Constitutional Political Economy* 20, no. 2 (2009).

11. "A Full Vindication of the Measures of the Congress, &C., [15 December] 1774," Founders Online, National Archives.

12. *The Works of Alexander Hamilton*, ed. Henry Cabot Lodge (Federal Edition) (New York: G.P. Putnam's Sons, 1904).

13. Douglas A. Irwin, "The Aftermath of Hamilton's 'Report on Manufactures,'" *Journal of Economic History* 64, no. 3 (2004): 800–21.

14. Phillip W. Magness, "Alexander Hamilton as Immigrant: Musical Mythology Meets Federalist Reality," in *Independent Review* 21, no. 4 (Spring 2017): 497–508.

15. James Madison, "To Henry Clay, April 24, 1824," Founders Online, National Archives.

16. James Madison, "To Thomas Jefferson, December 24, 1825," Founders Online, National Archives.

17. Gordon Tullock, "The Welfare Costs of Tariffs, Monopolies, and Theft," *Economic Inquiry* 5, no. 3 (June 1967): 224–32.

18. Daniel Peart, *Lobbyists and the Making of US Tariff Policy, 1816–1861* (Baltimore: Johns Hopkins University Press, 2018).

19. Douglas A. Irwin, "Antebellum Tariff Politics: Regional Coalitions and Shifting Economic Interests," *Journal of Law & Economics* 51, no. 4 (2008): 715–41.

20. Phillip W. Magness, "The American System and the Political Economy of Black Colonization," *Journal of the History of Economic Thought* 37, no. 2 (2015): 187–202.

21. Scott C. James and David A. Lake, "The Second Face of Hegemony: Britain's Repeal of the Corn Laws and the American Walker Tariff of 1846," *International Organization* 43, no. 1 (1989): 1–29.

22. Phillip W. Magness, "Tariffs and the American Civil War," Essential Civil War Curriculum, April 2017.

23. William Stanley Jevons, *The Coal Question: An Inquiry Concerning the Progress of the Nation, and the Probable Exhaustion of Our Coalmines* (London: Macmillan and Co., 1865), p. 326.

24. Phillip W. Magness, "Morrill and the Missing Industries: Strategic Lobbying Behavior and the Tariff, 1858–1861," *Journal of the Early Republic* 29, no. 2 (2009): 287–329.

25. Douglas A. Irwin, "Tariffs and Growth in Late Nineteenth Century America," National Bureau of Economic Research Working Paper no. 7639, April 2000.

26. J. Bradford De Long, "Trade Policy and America's Standard of Living: An Historical Perspective," working paper, University of California at Berkeley, 1995.

27. Frank Chodorov, *Income Tax: Root of All Evil* (New York: Devin-Adair Company, 1954), p. 40.

28. Proceedings of Congress and General Congressional Publications, Volume 71, Part 2 (May 13, 1929 to June 3, 1929), *Congressional Record* (bound ed.), 71st Cong., 1st sess., June 3, 1929, pp. 1167–2304.

29. Elmer Eric Schattschneider, *Politics, Pressures, and the Tariff: A Study of Free Private Enterprise in Pressure Politics, as Shown in the 1929–1930 Revision of the Tariff* (Englewood Cliffs, NJ: Prentice-Hall, 1980), p. 238.

CHAPTER 3

1. Charles L. Schultze, "Industrial Policy: A Dissent," *Brookings Review* (Fall 1983): 3–12; Don Lavoie, *National Economic Planning: What Is Left?* (Washington: Cato Institute, 1985); Deirdre McCloskey and Alberto Mingardi, *The Myth of the Entrepreneurial State* (Great Barrington, MA: American Institute for Economic Research, 2020); Scott Lincicome, "Manufactured Crisis: 'Deindustrialization,' Free Markets, and National Security," Cato Institute Policy Analysis no. 907, January 27, 2021; Scott Lincicome and Huan Zhu, "Questioning Industrial Policy," Cato Institute White Paper, September 28, 2021; Samuel Gregg, *The Next American Economy: Nation, State, and Markets in an Uncertain World* (New York: Encounter Books, 2022); and Linda R. Cohen and Roger G. Noll, *The Technology Pork Barrel* (Washington: Brookings Institution, 1991).

2. Donald J. Boudreaux, "Do Subsidies Justify Retaliatory Protectionism?," *Economic Affairs* 31, no. 3 (October 2011).

CHAPTER 4

1. Perfect correlation would receive a score of 1.0. Moving in precisely the opposite directions would get a score of –1.0. Zero would suggest they don't move together.

2. An accounting identity is a statement or equation that is true by definition or construction. It does not make any bold assertions about how the world works; it simply classifies elements in a way that ensures they add up. It's similar to saying that the number of people in a group who are less than six feet tall plus the number who are six feet or taller adds up to the total number of people in the group. In this example, we're not making a claim about the determinants of stature; we're only tallying the number of people in a group.

3. Scott Lincicome and Daniel Griswold, "On Today's Bad GDP Number, Please Remember: Imports Aren't a 'Drag on Growth,'" *Cato at Liberty* (blog), Cato Institute, April 28, 2022.

4. See, for example, John Tschetter, "Exports Support American Jobs," International Trade Research Report no. 1, International Trade Administration, US Department of Commerce, April 10, 2010. Similar arguments, though, went back at least into the mid-1990s.

5. Lest one think: "Wait, don't those input orders need additional workers?" The answer is not necessarily. Suppose the inputs are imported—a reasonably common scenario. Here, we are only counting US workers.

6. See Andreas Freytag, "Should Europe Really Worry about Its Trade Deficit with China?," *VoxEU*, May 19, 2008.

7. Since this relationship always holds and has—ex ante—no theoretical implication, economists call it an identity. Causal relationships between the variables are context driven and will be discussed below.

8. Intranational transactions are taken out as they add to zero. Thus, only international transactions are counted.

9. Any individual who wants to spend more than he or she has earned needs a credit approved before the real transaction takes place.

10. The distinction between foreign direct investment (FDI) and portfolio investment is rather arbitrarily drawn by the Organisation for Economic Co-operation and Development. The purchase of 10 percent of the equity or more defines an FDI; less is a portfolio investment. It is easily possible that an investor purchases 11 percent of a company for speculation purposes, whereas another buys 7 percent of another company with a long-term plan behind this transaction.

11. Because of the comprehensive nature of the current account, to document the full counterpart of the capital account, we refer to the current account here.

12. To be sure, these transitions and their costs for individuals, companies, and regions are policy issues to be addressed by economic, social, or education policy. Our argument is that the trade balance is not the field to mitigate the costs; rather, they would increase if the trade balance were disrupted.

13. The following simple example may illustrate this point: American mobile telephones are mainly assembled in China, but their innovative content is mostly produced in the United States. This particularly holds for research and development and intellectual property, which capture a high share of the value-added in American mobile phones.

14. See Daniel Griswold and Andreas Freytag, "Balance of Trade, Balance of Power: How the Trade Deficit Reflects US Influence in the World," Cato Institute Policy Analysis no. 944, April 25, 2023.

15. See, for instance, Maurice Obstfeld, "Eine Bedrohung der Globalen Finanzstabilität," *Die Welt*, August 6, 2018.

CHAPTER 5

1. Elizabeth Gehrman, "A Ringing Defense of Trump on Trade," *Harvard Gazette*, April 26, 2019.

2. "Budget and Economic Data," Congressional Budget Office.

3. Douglas A. Irwin, "Does Trade Reform Promote Economic Growth? A Review of Recent Evidence," National Bureau of Economic Research Working Paper no. 25927, June 2019.

4. Scott Lincicome, "Doomed to Repeat It: The Long History of America's Protectionist Failures," Cato Institute Policy Analysis no. 819, August 22, 2017.

5. James M. Lindsay, "TWE Remembers: Herbert Hoover Signs the Smoot–Hawley Tariff into Law," Council on Foreign Relations, June 17, 2013.

6. Andrew Chatzky and Anshu Siripurapu, "The Truth about Tariffs," Council on Foreign Relations, October 8, 2021.

7. Adam S. Posen, "The Price of Nostalgia: America's Self-Defeating Economic Retreat," *Foreign Affairs*, April 20, 2021.

8. Erica York, "Tracking the Economic Impact of US Tariffs and Retaliatory Actions," Tax Foundation, July 7, 2023.

9. "Automakers Warn Trump Metal Tariffs Will Drive Up Car Prices," Reuters, March 2, 2018; and Michael Schultz et al., *US Consumer & Economic Impacts of US Automotive Trade Policies* (Ann Arbor, MI: Center for Automotive Research, 2019).

10. Mary Amiti, Stephen J. Redding, and David Weinstein, "The Impact of the 2018 Trade War on US Prices and Welfare," National Bureau of Economic Research Working Paper no. 25672, March 2019.

11. Aaron Flaaen, Ali Hortaçsu, and Felix Tintelnot, "The Production, Relocation, and Price Effects of US Trade Policy: The Case of Washing Machines," Becker Friedman Institute for Economics Working Paper no. 2019-61, April 2019.

12. Pablo D. Fajgelbaum et al., "The Return to Protectionism," National Bureau of Economic Research Working Paper no. 25638, March 2019, revised October 2019.

13. Alberto Cavallo et al., "Tariff Passthrough at the Border and at the Store: Evidence from US Trade Policy," National Bureau of Economic Research Working Paper no. 26396, October 2019.

14. US International Trade Commission, *Economic Impact of Section 232 and 301 Tariffs on US Industries*, USITC Publication 5405, Investigation No. 332-591 (Washington: USITC, March 2023, corrected May 2023).

15. Katheryn Russ, "Tariffs on Chinese Imports Have Only Marginally Contributed to US Inflation," Peterson Institute for International Economics, January 13, 2022.

16. Douglas A. Irwin, *Three Simple Principles of Trade Policy* (Washington: AEI Press, 1996).

17. Kyle Handley, Fariha Kamal, and Ryan Monarch, "Rising Imports Tariffs, Falling Export Growth: When Modern Supply Chains Meet Old-Style Protectionism," International Finance Discussion Papers no. 1270, Board of Governors of the Federal Reserve System, February 2020.

18. David Autor et al., "Help for the Heartland? The Employment and Electoral Effects of the Trump Tariffs in the United States," National Bureau of Economic Research Working Paper no. 32082, January 2024.

19. Lincicome, "Doomed to Repeat It."

20. Gary Clyde Hufbauer and Sean Lowry, "US Tire Tariffs: Saving Few Jobs at High Cost," Peterson Institute for International Economics Policy Brief 12-9, April 2012; and Heather Long, "Trump's Steel Tariffs Cost US Consumers $900,000 for Every Job Created, Experts Say," *Washington Post*, May 7, 2019.

21. Erica York, "The Economic and Distributional Impact of the Trump Administration's Tariff Actions," Tax Foundation, December 5, 2018.

22. Katheryn N. Russ, Jay Shambaugh, and Jason Furman, "US Tariffs Are an Arbitrary and Regressive Tax," Centre for Economic Policy Research, January 12, 2017.

23. Miguel Acosta and Lydia Cox, "The Regressive Nature of the US Tariff Code: Origins and Implications," working paper, February 4, 2024.

24. Pablo Fajgelbaum and Amit Khandelwal, "The Economic Impacts of the US-China Trade War," National Bureau of Economic Research Working Paper no. 29315, revised December 2021.

25. Mark J. Perry, "The Economists' Tariff Protest of 1930," American Enterprise Institute, March 5, 2018; and "Steel and Aluminum Tariffs," Kent A. Clark Center for Global Markets, University of Chicago Booth School of Business, March 12, 2018.

26. Aaron Flaaen and Justin Pierce, "Disentangling the Effects of the 2018–2019 Tariffs on a Globally Connected US Manufacturing Sector," Finance and Economics Discussion Series 2019-086, Board of Governors of the Federal Reserve System, December 2019.

27. "World Economic Outlook, April 2019: Growth Slowdown, Precarious Recovery," International Monetary Fund, April 2019.

28. Peter Dixon and Maureen Rimmer, "USAGE-ITC: Theoretical Structure," Global Trade Analysis Project Resource no. 1034, 2002; and US International Trade Commission, *The Economic Effects of Significant US Import Restraints*, 9th update, 2017, Investigation no. 332-325, Publication 4726 (Washington: USITC, September 2017).

29. Erica York, "Trump's $300 Billion Tax Hike Would Threaten US Businesses and Consumers," Tax Foundation, August 25, 2023.

30. Davide Furceri et al., "Macroeconomic Consequences of Tariffs," International Monetary Fund working paper no. 2019/009, January 15, 2019.

31. Jeff Ferry, "How Steel Tariffs Are Helping US Workers," Coalition for a Prosperous America, July 22, 2022; Jeff Ferry, "Tariffs and Tax Credits Driving a New Manufacturing Boom," Coalition for a Prosperous America, April 25, 2023;

and "Section 232 Investigation on the Effect of Imports of Steel on US National Security," US Department of Commerce.

32. Lincicome, "Doomed to Repeat It."

33. "ADCVD Proceedings," International Trade Administration.

34. David G. Tarr and Morris E. Morkre, *Aggregate Costs to the United States of Tariffs and Quotas on Imports: General Tariff Cuts and Removal of Quotas on Automobiles, Steel, Sugar, and Textiles* (Washington: Federal Trade Commission, December 1984).

35. Aaron Tornell, "Rational Atrophy: The US Steel Industry," National Bureau of Economic Research Working Paper no. 6084, July 1997.

36. Stefanie Lenway, Randall Mork, and Bernard Yeung, "Rent Seeking, Protectionism and Innovation in the American Steel Industry," *Economic Journal* 106, no. 435 (March 1996).

37. James Lake and Ding Liu, "Local Labor Market Effects of the 2002 Bush Steel Tariffs," Cato Institute Research Briefs in Economic Policy no. 332, May 17, 2023.

38. Kadee Russ and Lydia Cox, "Will Steel Tariffs Put US Jobs at Risk?" EconoFact, February 26, 2018.

39. Joseph Francois and Laura M. Baughman, "The Unintended Consequences of US Steel Import Tariffs: A Quantification of the Impact during 2002," Trade Partnership Worldwide, Februrary 4, 2003.

40. US International Trade Commission, *Economic Impact of Section 232 and 301 Tariffs on US Industries.*

41. Gary Clyde Hufbauer and Euijin Jung, "Steel Profits Gain, but Steel Users Pay, under Trump's Protectionism," Peterson Institute for International Economics, December 20, 2018.

42. "Nippon Steel Corporation (NSC) to Acquire US Steel, Moving Forward Together as the 'Best Steelmaker with World-Leading Capabilities,'" press release, United States Steel Corporation, December 18, 2023.

43. Scott Lincicome, "Some Welcome Trade Facts from White House Economists," *Cato at Liberty* (blog), Cato Institute, March 22, 2024.

44. Mary Amiti et al., "Do Import Tariffs Help Reduce Trade Deficits?," *Liberty Street Economics* (blog), Federal Reserve Bank of New York, August 13, 2018.

45. Steve H. Hanke, "A Message for Trump on Trade: Get Real," Cato Institute, March 6, 2019; and Jim Tankersley, "Trump Hates the Trade Deficit. Most Economists Don't," *New York Times*, March 5, 2018.

46. Daniel Griswold and Andreas Freytag, "Balance of Trade, Balance of Power: How the Trade Deficit Reflects US Influence in the World," Cato Institute Policy Analysis no. 944, April 25, 2023.

47. Sunghyun Henry Kim and Serge Shikher, "Can Protectionism Improve Trade Balance?," US International Trade Commission Economics Working Paper 2017–10–B, October 2017.

48. Lukas Boer and Malte Rieth, "The Macroeconomic Consequences of Import Tariffs and Trade Policy Uncertainty," International Monetary Fund Working Paper WP/24/13, January 2024.

49. Boer and Rieth, "The Macroeconomic Consequences of Import Tariffs."

50. Johannes Eugster et al., "Economic Forces, Not Tariffs, Drive Changes in Trade Balances," International Monetary Fund, April 3, 2019.

51. Furceri et al., "Macroeconomic Consequences of Tariffs."

52. Lincicome, "Doomed to Repeat It."

53. Matilde Bombardini, Olimpia Cutinelli Rendina, and Francesco Trebbi, "Lobbying behind the Frontier," National Bureau of Economic Research Working Paper no. 29120, August 2021.

54. Thiemo Fetzer and Carlo Schwarz, "Tariffs and Politics: Evidence from Trump's Trade Wars," *Economic Journal* 131, no. 636, May 2021: 1717–41.

55. Alberto Cavallo et al., "Tariff Passthrough at the Border and at the Store: Evidence from US Trade Policy," National Bureau of Economic Research Working Paper no. 26396, October 2019.

56. Stephen Morgan et al., *The Economic Impacts of Retaliatory Tariffs on US Agriculture*, Economic Research Report no. ERR-304 (Washington: US Department of Agriculture, January 2022).

57. Randy Schnepf, "Farm Policy: Comparison of 2018 and 2019 MFP Programs," Congressional Research Service In Focus IF11289, August 12, 2019.

58. Alex Gangitano, "Business Pulling Out All Stops against Trump Tariffs," *The Hill*, June 23, 2019, 8:30 a.m.

59. Andres B. Schwarzenberg, "Section 301 Tariff Exclusions on US Imports from China," Congressional Research Service In Focus IF11582, January 29, 2024.

60. Scott Lincicome and Inu Manak, "Protectionism or National Security? The Use and Abuse of Section 232," Cato Institute Policy Analysis no. 912, March 9, 2021.

61. "Proclamation on Adjusting Imports of Derivative Aluminum Articles and Derivative Steel Articles into the United States," Economy & Jobs, Trump White House Archives, January 24, 2020.

62. Scott Lincicome, "A(nother) Case Study of Terrible US Tariff Policy," *The Dispatch*, July 19, 2023.

63. Jorge Uquillas, "Health Care, Trade Defy Downward Trend in First Quarter Lobbying," Bloomberg Law, April 25, 2019, 9:50 a.m. EDT.

64. Lincicome, "Doomed to Repeat It."

CHAPTER 6

1. Utah's Libertarians! (@libertarianutah), "A Libertarian free trade agreement would be one page long," X post, July 18, 2021, 1:13 p.m.

2. Paul Krugman, "What Should Trade Negotiators Negotiate About?," *Journal of Economic Literature* 35, no. 1 (1997): 113–20.

3. "Chile—Country Commercial Guide, Import Tariffs," International Trade Administration, December 7, 2023.

4. "General Agreement on Tariffs and Trade," *Encyclopaedia Britannica*, last updated March 14, 2024; Douglas Irwin and Chad Brown, "The Urban Legend: Pre-GATT Tariffs of 40%," Centre for Economic Policy Research, December 19, 2015.

5. Brink Lindsey and Daniel J. Ikenson, *Antidumping Exposed: The Devilish Details of Unfair Trade Laws* (Washington: Cato Institute, 2003).

6. Ian F. Fergusson and Brock R. Williams, "The Trans-Pacific Partnership (TPP): Key Provisions and Issues for Congress," Congressional Research Service Report R44489, June 14, 2016.

7. United States-Mexico-Canada Agreement (USMCA), art. 23, July 1, 2020.

8. Ryan M. Abman et al., "Child Labor Standards in Regional Trade Agreements: Theory and Evidence," National Bureau of Economic Research Working Paper no. 30908, February 2023.

CHAPTER 7

1. Simon Lester, "Congressman DeFazio's Misinformed Arguments for Leaving the WTO," *Cato at Liberty* (blog), Cato Institute, June 29, 2020; and Lester, "Congressman DeFazio's Misinformed Arguments."

2. "WTO Accessions," World Trade Organization.

3. "Who We Are," World Trade Organization.

4. James Bacchus, "On Policy Space and Post-Paris Climate Action" in *The Willing World: Shaping and Sharing a Sustainable Global Prosperity* (Cambridge: Cambridge University Press, 2018).

5. James Bacchus, "On the Indivisibility of Our Economic and Environmental Future" in *The Willing World: Shaping and Sharing a Sustainable Global Prosperity* (Cambridge: Cambridge University Press, 2018).

6. Jagdish N. Bhagwati, "The Case for Free Trade," *Scientific American* 269, no. 5 (1993): 42–49; and Leslie Paul Thiele, *Sustainability (Key Concepts)*, 2nd ed. (Cambridge, UK: Polity, 2016).

7. David Collins, *An Introduction to International Investment Law* (Cambridge: Cambridge University Press, 2016).

8. Bacchus, "On the Indivisibility of Our Economic and Environmental Future" in *The Willing World*.

9. Daniel W. Drezner, "Bottom Feeders," *Foreign Policy*, November 19, 2009.

10. "WTO Secretariat Budget for 2022," World Trade Organization.

11. "Congressional Budget Justification: Department of State, Foreign Operations, and Related Programs," US Department of State, 2024.

12. Gabriel Felbermayr et al., *The World Trade Organization at 25: Assessing the Economic Value of the Rules Based Global Trading System* (Gutersloh, Germany: Bertelsmann Stiftung, 2019).

13. Laura M. Baughman and Joseph Francois, *Trade and American Jobs: The Impact of Trade on US and State-Level Employment: 2022 Update* (Washington: Business Roundtable, 2022).

14. Galina Hale et al., "How Much Do We Spend on Imports?," Federal Reserve Bank of San Francisco Economic Letter 2019–01, January 7, 2019.

15. Gary Clyde Hufbauer and Zhiyao (Lucy) Lu, "Policy Brief 17-16: The Payoff to America from Globalization: A Fresh Look with a Focus on Cost to Workers," Peterson Institute for International Economics, updated May 2017.

16. Donald J. Trump (@realDonaldTrump), "The WTO is BROKEN when the world's RICHEST countries," X post, July 26, 2019, 2:29 p.m.

17. James Bacchus and Inu Manak, *The Development Dimension: Special and Differential Treatment in Trade* (Abingdon, UK: Routledge, 2023).

18. Emmanuel Ornelas, "Special and Differential Treatment for Developing Countries Reconsidered," Centre for Economic Policy Research, May 14, 2016.

19. Bacchus and Manak, *The Development Dimension*.

20. James Bacchus, Simon Lester, and Huan Zhu, "Disciplining China's Trade Practices at the WTO: How WTO Complaints Can Help Make China More Market-Oriented," Cato Institute Policy Analysis no. 856, November 15, 2018.

21. Robert Farley, "Trump Wrong about WTO Record," FactCheck, October 27, 2017.

22. "US Keeps Winning WTO Cases, Despite Claim of Anti-US Bias," Bloomberg Law, March 7, 2019; and Jeffrey J. Schott and Euijin Jung, "In US-China Trade Disputes, the WTO Usually Sides with the United States," Peterson Institute for International Economics, March 12, 2019.

23. "Rules of Conduct for the Understanding on Rules and Procedures Governing the Settlement of Disputes," World Trade Organization, WT/DSB/RC/1 (96-5267), December 11, 1996.

24. Vienna Convention on the Law of Treaties, May 23, 1969, *United Nations Treaty Series*, vol. 1155, at p. 331.

CHAPTER 8

1. Mukhisa Kituyi, "The Costs of Trade War," United Nations Conference on Trade and Development, June 20, 2018.

2. "Trade (% of GDP)," World Development Indicators, World Bank.

3. Sharat Ganapati and Woan Foong Wong, "How Far Goods Travel: Global Transport and Supply Chains from 1965–2020," National Bureau of Economic Research Working Paper no. 31167, April 2023.

4. *Review of Maritime Transport 2021*, United Nations Conference on Trade and Development; and Joseph Connors, James D. Gwartney, and Hugo M. Montesinos, "The Transportation-Communication Revolution: 50 Years of Dramatic Change in Economic Development," *Cato Journal* 40, no. 1 (Winter 2020).

5. Richard Martin Humphreys, "Why Ports Matter for the Global Economy," *Transport for Development* (blog), World Bank, May 17, 2023.

6. "The History of Container Shipping," *Container News,* November 9, 2022.

7. "The Power of an Empty Metal Box," *Unsung Science* (podcast), CBS News, May 26, 2023; and "FreightWaves Classics/Pioneers: Malcolm McLean Changed the Freight World with Intermodal Containers," Naegeli Transportation Inc., May 27, 2023.

8. "Potrero Hills," Auke Visser.

9. "The World in a Box," *The Economist*, March 16, 2006.

10. Brian J. Cudahy, *Box Boats: How Container Ships Changed the World* (New York: Fordham University Press, 2006).

11. "Liverpool Bay—IMO 7126762," ShipSpotting; and "Priam," Nautilus International.

12. Christopher Buckley, *Steaming to Bamboola: The World of a Tramp Freighter* (Guilford, CT: Lyons Press, 1982); and Daniel M. Bernhofen, Zouheir El-Sahli, and Richard Kneller, "Estimating the Effects of the Container Revolution on World Trade," *Journal of International Economics* 98 (2016): 36–50.

13. Jasmina Ovcina Mandra, "MSC Shatters Records with Delivery of 24,346 TEU MSC Irina," Offshore Energy, March 13, 2023.

14. "Meet MSC Oscar, the World's Largest Container Ship at 19,224 TEU," Mediterranean Shipping Company, December 16, 2024; and Joseph Stromberg, "The MSC Oscar Just Became the World's Biggest Container Ship," *Vox*, January 8, 2015.

15. "Container Ships: Is Bigger Always Better?," *Hellenic Shipping News*, January 21, 2020; and Chris Baraniuk, "Why Container Ships Probably Won't Get Bigger," BBC, July 4, 2022.

16. "Energy, IMO 5055062" Baltic Shipping; and "Ship Launched, Ways Set for 'Sister' in Half Hour," *New York Times*, September 26, 1948.

17. "Biggest Vessel Tested in Japan; 104,520-Ton Tanker Built There Expected to Cut Oil Freight Cost," *New York Times*, February 14, 1959; and "Construction of Mammoth Tankers," Idemitsu.

18. "Universe Ireland," Auke Visser.

19. *Comparison of US and Foreign-Flag Operating Costs* (Washington: US Department of Transportation Maritime Administration, 2011).

20. "Economies of Scale Made Steel: The Economics of Very Big Ships," *The Economist*, November 12, 2011.

21. Wikipedia, "Slow Steaming," last edited August 15, 2024.

22. Francisco Piniella, Juan Ignacio Alcaide, and Emilio Rodriguez Diaz, "The Panama Ship Registry: 1917–2017," *Marine Policy* 77 (2017).

23. "White, Grey and Black List," Paris MoU.

24. "Japan's First Pure Car Carrier 'Toyota Maru No. 10' Awarded 'Ship Heritage' Recognition," *Hellenic Shipping News*, July 23, 2019.

25. Shamseer Mambra, "Carlos Fischer: The Fruit Juice Carrier," Marine Insight, May 18, 2019.

26. Wikipedia, "MV *Blue Marlin*," last edited March 11, 2024; and MachinePix, (@MachinePix), "VEKA / Dockwise Blue Marlin semisubmersible heavy-life ship," X post, July 19, 2022, 5:01 p.m.

27. Ganapati and Wong, "How Far Goods Travel."

28. Richard Milne, "Nils Andersen, CEO, AP Møller-Maersk," *Financial Times*, October 6, 2013.

29. Anastasia Kharina and Daniel Rutherford, "Fuel Efficiency Trends for New Commercial Jet Aircraft: 1960 to 2014," White Paper, The International Council on Clean Transportation, September 3, 2015.

30. David Hummels, "Transportation Costs and International Trade in the Second Era of Globalization," *Journal of Economic Perspectives* 21, no. 3 (2007): 131–54.

31. Adam Satariano, "The IPhone's Secret Flights from China to Your Local Apple Store," *Bloomberg Businessweek*, September 11, 2013.

32. Emil Protalinksi, "iPhone Prices from the Original to iPhone X," *VentureBeat*, September 12, 2017.

33. Ben Glickman, "Air Freight Demand Grows Even as Supply Bottlenecks Ease," *Financial Times*, July 26, 2022.

34. "World Air Passenger Traffic Evolution, 1980–2020," International Energy Agency, last updated December 3, 2020.

35. "Rates on Overseas Phone Calls Decline," *New York Times*, May 19, 1982.

36. "Marc Levinson," Marc Levinson.

37. Geoffrey Garrett, "The Causes of Globalization," *Comparative Political Studies* 33, no. 6/7 (2000): 941–91.

38. Martin Stopford, "The Shipping Supercycle Saga," Maritime Lectures website, April 13, 2022.

39. Martin Stopford, *Maritime Economics*, 3rd ed. (Abingdon, UK: Routledge, 2009).

40. Rachel F. Fefer, "International Trade and E-commerce," Congressional Research Service In Focus IF11194, March 14, 2022.

41. "Supplier List," Apple, 2023.

42. Boeing, "Diverse Suppliers Bring Big Value to Boeing and Their Communities," July 2, 2020.

43. *Modernization of the North American Free Trade Agreement (NAFTA), Statement of the Alliance of Automobile Manufacturers, Before the Senate Comm. on Finance Subcommittee on International Trade, Customs, and Global Competitiveness*, 115th Cong. (2017) (statement of Mitch Bainwol, President and CEO of the Alliance of Automobile Manufacturers).

44. Timothy S. Simcoe and Emek Basker, "Upstream, Downstream: Diffusion and Economic Impacts of the Universal Product Code," Centre for Economic Policy Research, January 18, 2018.

45. Scott Lincicome, (@scottlincicome), "'Globalization, the jobs ladder and economic mobility,'" Twitter post, July 10, 2023, 9:26 a.m.

46. Scott L. Baier and Jeffrey H. Bergstrand, "The Growth of World Trade: Tariffs, Transport Costs, and Income Similarity," *Journal of International Economics* 53, no. 1 (2001): 1–27.

47. Andrew B. Bernard et al., "Global Firms," National Bureau of Economic Research Working Paper no. 22727, October 2016.

48. Nicolas Rivero, "Japan Is Home to the World's First Autonomous Container Ships," *Quartz*, February 12, 2022; Adrienne Murray, "Crewless Container Ships Appear on the Horizon," BBC, March 23, 2023; "New $2.15bn Automated Terminal Opened in China's Yangshan Port," Ship Technology, January 5, 2018; Ann Koh, "Singapore Pursues Goal of a Fully Automated Port amid Cargo Chaos," *Bloomberg Businessweek*, June 29, 2022; and "Our Terminal," APM Terminals.

49. Marilyn J. Field, ed., *Telemedicine: A Guide to Accessing Telecommunications in Healthcare* (Washington: National Academies Press, 1996).

50. "Project on Jones Act Reform," Cato Institute; Scott Lincicome, "How US Air Travel Can Get (a Little of) Its Groove Back," *The Dispatch*, June 29, 2022; and *Rethinking Maritime Cabotage for Improved Connectivity*, Transport and Trade Facilitation Series, no. 9 (Geneva: United Nations Conference on Trade and Development, 2017).

CHAPTER 9

1. Chris Koerner, (@mhp_guy), "Last night my 12 year old was struggling with Algebra," X post, March 21, 2023, 10:15 a.m.

2. Gary Winslett, "LP #32: Promoting Peloton Globalization," *The Libertarian-Progressive Papers* (blog), Substack, March 25, 2022.

3. Joseph Francois and Bernard Hoekman, "Services Trade and Policy," *Journal of Economic Literature* 48, no. 3 (2020): 642–92.

4. Alan Beattie, "The Case of the Missing Services" in *World Trade Report 2019: The Future of Services Trade* (Geneva: World Trade Organization, 2019).

5. Scott Lincicome, "Globalization Isn't Going Anywhere," Defending Globalization, Cato Institute, September 12, 2023.

6. Shawn Donnan, "*Fortnite*'s Digital Goods Are Key to the Future of Global Trade," Bloomberg, January 11, 2019.

7. Sherry Stephenson and Jimena Sotelo, "Trade in Digital Services Is Booming. Here's How We Can Unleash Its Full Potential," World Economic Forum, June 8, 2020.

8. Kennedy O'Dell, *Redefining Rural: Towards a Better Understanding of Geography, Demography, and Economy in America's Rural Places* (Washington: Economic Innovation Group, 2021).

9. David J. Bier, "US Immigration Policy Lags behind a Globalizing World," Defending Globalization, Cato Institute, September 4, 2023.

10. Richard Baldwin, "The Globotics Upheaval: Globalisation, Robotics, and the Future of Work," Organisation for Economic Co-operation and Development: The Forum Network, April 2019.

11. "It's Not Just a Fiscal Fiasco: Greying Economies Also Innovate Less," *The Economist*, May 30, 2023.

12. Leila Erfannia and Jahanpour Alipour, "How Does Cloud Computing Improve Cancer Information Management? A Systematic Review," *Informatics in Medicine Unlocked* 33 (2022).

13. Satish Nambisan and Yadong Luo, "Think Globally, Innovate Locally," *MIT Sloan Management Review* 63, no. 3 (February 2022).

14. "Global Digital Trade Barriers," Trade, Computer and Communications Industry Association.

15. Rachel F. Fefer, Shayerah I. Akhtar, and Michael D. Sutherland, "Digital Trade and US Trade Policy," Congressional Research Service Report R44565, updated December 9, 2021.

16. "Services, Value Added (% of GDP)," World Development Indicators, World Bank.

17. "The Multiplier Effect of Innovation Jobs," *MIT Sloan Management Review*, June 6, 2012.

18. Scott Lincicome (@scottlincicome), "Better detail here," X post, July 10, 2023, 4:23 p.m.

19. Fefer, Akhtar, and Sutherland, "Digital Trade and U.S. Trade Policy."

20. Archana Sristy, "Blockchain in the Food Supply Chain: What Does the Future Look Like?," Walmart Global Tech.

21. "US Service Exports: Michigan," Coalition of Services Industries, 2023; "US Services Exports: Missouri," Coalition of Services Industries, 2023; "US Services Exports: Kentucky," Coalition of Services Industries, 2023; "US Services Exports: Utah," Coalition of Services Industries, 2023; and "US Services Exports: Ohio," Coalition of Services Industries, 2023.

22. "US Services Exports: United States of America," Coalition of Services Industries, 2023.

23. Francis Agustin, "After a Near Record-Run at the Top of Netflix's US Top 10 List, Pop Culture Smash 'Squid Game' Has Been Bumped by Another Show," *Business Insider*, October 16, 2021.

24. "Global Digital Trade Barriers," Trade, Computer and Communications Industry Association.

25. "Fact Sheet: United States and European Commission Announce Trans-Atlantic Data Privacy Framework," White House, March 25, 2022.

26. Jianli Yang and Lianchao Han, "US-China Trade Talks Prioritize Opening Up China's Internet," *Foreign Policy*, November 16, 2021.

27. International Chamber of Commerce and International Trade Centre "The WTO Moratorium on Customs Duties on Electronic Transmissions: What Is Really at Stake?," Joint Policy Brief, April 2023.

28. United States-Mexico-Canada Agreement, art. 19, July 1, 2020.

29. Angelique Chrisafis, "France Hits Back at US over Tax on Digital Giants," *The Guardian*, July 11, 2019.

30. Text of the Comprehensive Economic and Trade Agreement, Government of Canada, April 19, 2018.

CHAPTER 10

1. Lingling Wei, "Xi Jinping Aims to Rein in Chinese Capitalism, Hew to Mao's Socialist Vision," *Wall Street Journal*, September 20, 2021.

2. Adam Hayes, "What Is Comparative Advantage?," Investopedia, updated June 26, 2024.

3. Scott Lincicome and Arjun Anand, "The 'China Shock' Demystified: Its Origins, Effects, and Lessons for Today," Defending Globalization, Cato Institute, December 12, 2023.

4. Premier Li Keqiang, press conference, Third Session of the 12th National People's Congress, The State Council of the People's Republic of China, March 15, 2015.

5. Jasper Becker, *The Chinese* (New York: The Free Press, 2000), p. 157.

6. Cyril Zhiren Lin, "Open-Ended Economic Reform in China," in *Remaking the Economic Institutions of Socialism: China and Eastern Europe*, ed. Victor Nee and David Stark (Stanford, CA: Stanford University Press, 1989), p. 100.

7. Kate Xiao Zhou, *How the Farmers Changed China: Power of the People* (Boulder, CO: Westview Press, 1996), pp. 3–4.

8. Zhou, *How the Farmers Changed China*, p. 4.

9. Yasheng Huang, "How Did China Take Off?," *Journal of Economic Perspectives* 26, no. 4 (Fall 2012): 147–49, 154, and 158.

10. Deng Xiaoping, *Fundamental Issues in Present-Day China* (Beijing, China: Foreign Languages Press, 1987), p. 189.

11. Wu Jinglian et al., "The Role of the 'Dual Track' System and Its Consequences," in Wu Jinglian and Ma Guochuan, eds., *Whither China? Restarting the Reform Agenda* (New York: Oxford University Press, 2016), pp. 120–34.

12. Weiying Zhang, "The Power of Ideas and Leadership in China's Transition to a Liberal Society," *Cato Journal* 35, no. 1 (Winter 2015): 17.

13. Barry Naughton, *Growing out of the Plan: Chinese Economic Reform 1978–1993* (New York: Cambridge University Press, 1995), pp. 8–9.

14. Nicholas Lardy, "Private Sector Development," in Ross Garnaut, Ligang Song, and Cai Fang, eds., *China's 40 Years of Reform and Development: 1978–2018* (Acton, Australia: ANU Press, 2018), p. 333.

15. Zhao Ziyang, *Prisoner of the State: The Secret Journal of Premier Zhao Ziyang*, trans and ed. Bao Pu, Renee Chiang, and Adi Ignatius (New York: Simon and Schuster, 2009), pp. 270–71.

16. Deng Xiaoping, "Excerpts from Talks Given in Wuchang, Shenzhen, Zhuhai and Shanghai," January 18–February 21, 1992.

17. Barry Naughton, *The Chinese Economy: Transitions and Growth* (Cambridge, MA: MIT Press, 2007), p. 99.

18. Milton Friedman, "Using the Market for Social Development," *Cato Journal* 8, no. 3 (Winter 1989): 569.

19. Deng, "Excerpts from Talks Given in Wuchang, Shenzhen, Zhuhai and Shanghai."

20. "Decision of the Central Committee of the Communist Party of China on Some Major Issues Concerning Comprehensively Deepening the Reform," USC US-China Institute, University of Southern California Annenberg, November 12, 2013.

21. See Nicholas R. Lardy, *The State Strikes Back: The End of Economic Reform in China?* (Washington: Peterson Institute for International Economics, 2019).

22. Constitution of the People's Republic of China, ch. 1, arts. 1 and 7; ch. 3, art. 51, March 14, 2004.

23. James A. Dorn, "China's Challenge: Expanding the Market, Limiting the State," *Man and the Economy* 3, no. 1 (June 2016): 27.

24. Nicholas R. Lardy, *Integrating China into the Global Economy* (Washington: Brookings Institution Press, 2002), pp. 24–25.

25. Xiaolu Wang, Gang Fan, and Hengpeng Zhu, "Marketisation in China: Progress and Contribution to Growth," in Ross Garnaut and Ligang Song, eds., *China: Linking Markets for Growth* (Acton, Australia: ANU Press, 2007), pp. 30–44.

26. Fan Gang, Guangrong Ma, and Xiaolu Wang, "Marketisation in China from 1997 to 2014: Achievements and Contribution to Growth," in Ross Garnaut, Ligang Song, and Cai Fang, eds., *China's 40 Years of Reform and Development: 1978–2018* (Acton, Australia: ANU Press, 2018), pp. 257–70.

27. Martin Ravallion, "Poverty in China since 1950: A Counterfactual Perspective," National Bureau of Economic Research Working Paper no. 28370, January 2021.

28. Lardy, *Integrating China into the Global Economy*, p. 41.

29. Wang, Fan, and Zhu, "Marketisation in China: Progress and Contribution to Growth," p. 35.

30. Peter Drysdale and Samuel Hardwick, "China and the Global Trading System: Then and Now," in Ross Garnaut, Ligang Song, and Cai Fang, eds., *China's 40 Years of Reform and Development: 1978–2018* (Acton, Australia: ANU Press, 2018), p. 552.

31. See Justin Yifu Lin, "The Current State of China's Economic Reforms," in James A. Dorn, ed., *China in the New Millenium: Market Reforms and Social Development* (Washington: Cato Institute, 1998), pp. 39–74.

32. Zhao Ziyang, *Prisoner of the State*, p. 137.

33. Lincicome, "The 'China Shock' Demystified."

34. Lardy, "Private Sector Development," pp. 335–36.

35. Zhang Zhenjiang, "China's Globalization and Its Policies: Focusing on Sino-American Relations," *Journal of Ritsumeikan Social Sciences and Humanities* 1 (2009): 100.

36. Lardy, *Integrating China into the Global Economy*, p. 24.

37. "People's Republic of China: 2021 Article IV Consultation-Press Release; Staff Report; and Statement by the Executive Director for the People's Republic of China," International Monetary Fund Country Report no. 2022/021, January 28, 2022.

38. Wei, "Xi Jinping Aims to Rein in Chinese Capitalism."

39. "China's Young Want to Work. For the Government," *The Economist*, May 31, 2023.

40. "China Mortgage Boycott Widens as Homebuyers Demand Construction, Environment Quality," Bloomberg, September 23, 2022.

41. Alexandra Stevenson and Cao Li, "China Evergrande Defaults on Its Debt. Now What?," *New York Times*, December 9, 2021.

42. Stella Yifan Xie and Jason Douglas, "China's Fading Recovery Reveals Deeper Economic Struggles," *Wall Street Journal*, May 30, 2023.

43. Rebecca Feng and Cao Li, "A Poor Province in China Splurged on Bridges and Roads. Now It's Facing a Debt Reckoning.," *Wall Street Journal*, updated May 21, 2023.

44. Feng and Li, "A Poor Province in China Splurged on Bridges and Roads."

45. Stella Yifan Xie, Yoko Kubota, and Cao Li, "China's Cities Struggle under Trillions of Dollars of Debt," *Wall Street Journal*, March 6, 2023.

46. "Xi's Latest Crackdown Snares Experts Hired by Hedge Funds, CEOs," Bloomberg, May 10, 2023.

47. Jianli Yang, "China-Australia Trade War Shows No Sign of Abating," *The Diplomat*, February 2023.

48. Cheng Leng, "Foreign Direct Investment in China Falls to Lowest Levels in Decades," *Financial Times*, February 19, 2024.

49. Cheng Leng, "Foreign Direct Investment in China Falls to Lowest Levels in Decades," *Financial Times*, February 19, 2024.

50. Y. P. Rajesh, "India's Population to Overtake China by Mid-2023, UN Estimates," Reuters, April 20, 2023.

51. Carl Minzner, "China's Doomed Fight against Demographic Decline," *Foreign Affairs*, May 3, 2022.

52. Minzner, "China's Doomed Fight against Demographic Decline."

53. Roland Rajah and Alyssa Leng, "Revising down the Rise of China," Lowy Institute, March 14, 2022.

54. Dennis Normile, "China's Population May Start to Shrink This Year, New Birth Data Suggest," *Science*, January 18, 2022.

55. Normile, "China's Population May Start to Shrink This Year."

56. Niall Ferguson, "China's Demographics Spell Decline Not Domination," Bloomberg, August 14, 2022.

57. Xiujian Peng, "Could China's Population Start Falling?," BBC, June 5, 2022.

58. Liyan Qi, "China's Economic Slump Bodes Ill for Birth Numbers," *Wall Street Journal*, September 4, 2022.

59. Qi, "China's Economic Slump Bodes Ill for Birth Numbers."

60. Qi, "China's Economic Slump Bodes Ill for Birth Numbers."

61. Greg Ip, "How the West Can Win a Global Power Struggle," *Wall Street Journal*, March 18, 2022.

62. Remco Zwetsloot and Dahlia Peterson, "The US-China Tech Wars: China's Immigration Disadvantage," *The Diplomat*, December 31, 2019.

63. Ishan Banerjee and Matt Sheehan, "America's Got AI Talent: US' Big Lead in AI Research Is Built on Importing Researchers," MacroPolo, June 9, 2020.

64. Banerjee and Sheehan, "America's Got AI Talent."

65. Michael G. Finn and Leigh Ann Pennington, "Stay Rates of Foreign Doctorate Recipients from US Universities, 2013," National Center for Science and Engineering Statistics, National Science Foundation by the Oak Ridge Institute for Science and Education, January 2018.

66. Remco Zwetsloot, "Winning the Tech Talent Competition," Center for Strategic and International Studies, October 28, 2021.

67. Zwetsloot and Peterson, "The US-China Tech Wars: China's Immigration Disadvantage."

68. "Archive: US-China Strategic Competition in Technology: Analysis and Prospects (Chinese Language)," US-China Perception Monitor, February 6, 2022.

69. Richard Van Noorden, "Global Mobility: Science on the Move," *Nature* 490 (2012): 326–29; and Zwetsloot and Peterson, "The US-China Tech Wars: China's Immigration Disadvantage."

70. Pak Yiu, "China to See Biggest Millionaire Exodus in 2024 as Many Head to US," *Nikkei*, June 18, 2024.

71. Seth G. Benzell et al., "The Future of Global Economic Power," National Bureau of Economic Research Working Paper no. 30556, October 2022.

72. Rajah and Leng, "Revising down the Rise of China."

73. Loren Brandt et al., "China's Productivity Slowdown and Future Growth Potential," World Bank Policy Research Working Paper no. 9298, June 2020.

74. Diego A. Cerdeiro and Cian Ruane, "China's Declining Business Dynamism," International Monetary Fund Working Paper WP/2022/032, February 18, 2022.

75. Lardy, *The State Strikes Back*, pp. 50–52; 139–41.

76. Lee G. Branstetter, Guangwei Li, and Mengjia Ren, "Picking Winners? Government Subsidies and Firm Productivity in China," National Bureau of Economic Research Working Paper no. 30699, December 2022.

77. Lee G. Branstetter and Guangwei Li, "Does 'Made in China 2025' Work for China? Evidence from Chinese Listed Firms," National Bureau of Economic Research Working Paper no. 30676, November 2022.

78. Shang-Jin Wei et al., "Mild Government Failure," National Bureau of Economic Research Working Paper no. 31178, April 2023.

79. "People's Republic of China: 2022 Article IV Consultation-Press Release; Staff Report; and Statement by the Executive Director for the People's Republic of China," International Monetary Fund Country Reports 2023, no. 67, February 3, 2023.

80. Xie and Douglas, "China's Fading Recovery Reveals Deeper Economic Struggles."

81. "2023 World Press Freedom Index: Journalism Threatened by Fake Content Industry," Reporters Without Borders, 2024.

82. Eswar S. Prasad, *Gaining Currency: The Rise of the Renminbi* (New York: Oxford University Press, 2016), p. 156.

83. Ronald Coase and Ning Wang, *How China Became Capitalist* (New York: Palgrave Macmillan, 2012), p. 207.

84. See Nicholas R. Lardy, *Markets over Mao: The Rise of Private Business in China* (Washington: Peterson Institute for International Economics, 2014); and James A. Dorn, "The Genesis and Evolution of China's Economic Liberalization," in Benjamin Powell, ed., *Economic Freedom and Prosperity: The Origins and Maintenance of Liberalization* (Abingdon, VA: Routledge, 2020), chap. 10.

CHAPTER 11

1. Ro Khanna, "America Should Once Again Become a Manufacturing Superpower," *Foreign Affairs*, December 20, 2022; and Josh Hawley, "The GOP Is Dead. A New GOP Must Listen to Working People," *Washington Post*, November 18, 2022.

2. "Table 1.1. US International Transactions," International Data, US Bureau of Economic Analysis, March 23, 2023.

3. "Table 1.2. US Net International Investment Position at the End of the Period, Expanded Detail," International Data, US Bureau of Economic Analysis, March 29, 2023.

4. "America's Foreign Born in the Last 50 Years," US Census Bureau, last revised October 8, 2021.

5. Brink Lindsey, "Paul Krugman's Nostalgianomics: Economic Policies, Social Norms, and Income Inequality," Cato Institute White Paper, February 9, 2009, p. 15.

6. Scott Lincicome, "Manufactured Crisis: 'Deindustrialization,' Free Markets, and National Security," Cato Institute Policy Analysis no. 907, January 27, 2021.

7. The Advisory Commission to Study the Consumer Price Index, *Toward a More Accurate Measure of the Cost of Living: Final Report to the Senate Finance Committee* (Washington: Senate Finance Committee, December 4, 1996).

8. Phil Gramm, Robert Ekelund, and John Early, *The Myth of American Inequality: How Government Biases Policy Debate* (Lanham, MD: Rowman and Littlefield Publishers, 2022), p. 93.

9. US Bureau of Labor Statistics, "Nonfarm Business Sector: Real Hourly Compensation for All Workers," Federal Reserve Economic Data, Federal Reserve Bank of St. Louis, updated June 1, 2024.

10. William R. Cline, "US Median Household Income Has Risen More Than You Think," *Cato Journal*, Winter 2019; and *Income in the United States: 2021*, Report no. P60-276, "Table A-2: Households by Total Money Income, Race, and Hispanic Origin of Householder: 1967 to 2021," US Census Bureau, September 13, 2022.

11. Gramm, Ekelund, and Early, *The Myth of American Inequality*, p. 90.

12. US Census, *Income in the United States: 2021*, Table A-2.

13. Marian L. Tupy and Gale L. Pooley, *Superabundance: The Story of Population Growth, Innovation, and Human Flourishing on an Infinitely Bountiful Planet* (Washington: Cato Institute, 2022).

14. Tupy and Pooley, *Superabundance*, p. 171.

15. Tupy and Pooley, *Superabundance*, appendix 16, pp. 454–56.

16. W. Michael Cox and Richard Alm, *Onward and Upward! Bet on Capitalism—It Works* (Dallas: William J. O'Neil Center for Global Markets and Freedom, SMU Cox School of Business, 2016), p. 13.

17. "Characteristics of New Housing," US Census Bureau.

18. "Historical Census of Housing Tables: Homeownership by Selected Demographic and Housing Characteristics," US Census Bureau, last revised October 8, 2021; and "Homeownership Rate in the United States," Federal Reserve Economic Data, Federal Reserve Bank of St. Louis, updated April 30, 2024.

19. Gramm, Ekelund, and Early, *The Myth of American Inequality*, pp. 3–6.

20. Gramm, Ekelund, and Early, *The Myth of American Inequality*, p. 36.

21. Bruce Sacerdote, "Fifty Years of Growth in American Consumption, Income, and Wages," National Bureau of Economic Research Working Paper no. 23292, 2017, pp. 5–8, 12–13.

22. Gramm, Ekelund, and Early, *The Myth of American Inequality*, p. 47.

23. Gramm, Ekelund, and Early, *The Myth of American Inequality*, p. 50.

24. "Real Value Added by Industry," Industry Data, US Bureau of Economic Analysis, last revised March 28, 2024.

25. Lincicome, "Manufactured Crisis," pp. 4–5.

26. Lincicome, "Manufactured Crisis," p. 3.

27. Lincicome, "Manufactured Crisis," pp. 7–10.

28. Scott Lincicome, introduction to *Empowering the New American Worker: Market-Based Solutions for Today's Workforce* (Washington: Cato Institute, 2022), p. 6.

29. Daniel Griswold, "Fail or Flourish: American Workers, Globalization, and Automation," Research Paper, Mercatus Center at George Mason University, January 30, 2020, table 1, p. 13.

30. Lincicome, introduction to *Empowering the New American Worker*, p. 5.

31. "Industry Injury and Illness Data," US Bureau of Labor Statistics; and "Census of Fatal Occupational Injuries—Archived Data ," US Bureau of Labor Statistics.

32. "Poverty Status of People by Family Relationship, Race, and Hispanic Origin: 1959 to 2021," US Census Bureau, 2022.

33. "Households by Total Money Income, Race, and Hispanic Origin of Householder: 1967 to 2021," US Census Bureau, updated January 30, 2022.

34. "US Approval of Interracial Marriage," Human Progress, September 10, 2021.

35. "Your Life in Numbers," Human Progress.

36. "Your Life in Numbers," Human Progress.

37. "US Cancer Death Rate Drops by 30% Since 1991," BBC, January 12, 2023.

38. "Emissions of Air Pollutants, United States, 1970 to 2016," Our World in Data, updated February 18, 2018; and "EPA at 50: Progress in Providing Safe Drinking Water," Environmental Protection Agency news release, February 18, 2020.

39. Gramm, Ekelund, and Early, *The Myth of American Inequality*, p. 85.

CHAPTER 12

1. Charles F. McElwee III, "The 'Rust Belt' Echoes American Loss, but It's No Cliche," *The American Conservative*, May 30, 2018.

2. Donald Trump, "Declaring America's Economic Independence," June 28, 2016, *Politico*, June 28, 2016; "President Trump: 'We Have Rejected Globalism and Embraced Patriotism,'" Trump White House Archives, August 7, 2020; and Eduardo Porter, "Trump, Biden and 'Made in U.S.A.': Same Refrain, Varying Notes," *New York Times*, September 28, 2020.

3. US Bureau of Labor Statistics "All Employees, Manufacturing," Federal Reserve Economic Data, Federal Reserve Bank of St. Louis, last updated May 3, 2024.

4. Scott Lincicome, "Manufactured Crisis: "Deindustrialization," Free Markets, and National Security," Cato Institute Policy Analysis no. 907, January 27, 2021.

5. "Industries at a Glance: Manufacturing: NAICS 31–33," US Bureau of Labor Statistics.

6. Nike, *2022 Form 10-K* (Beaverton, OR: Nike, 2022), p. 1.

7. Wallace Witkowski, "Nvidia CEO Feels 'Perfectly Safe' Sourcing from Taiwan's TSMC amid China Tensions," Market Watch, June 1, 2023.

8. Marc Levinson, "Job Creation in the Manufacturing Revival," Congressional Research Service Report R41898, updated May 15, 2018.

9. "GDP/Breakdown at Current Prices in US Dollars (All Countries)," United Nations Department of Economic and Social Affairs; and Felix Richter, "These Are the Top Ten Manufacturing Countries in the World," World Economic Forum, February 25, 2020.

10. "World Steel in Figures 2021 Now Available," World Steel Association press release, June 3, 2021; "2021 Production Statistics," International Organization of Motor Vehicle Manufacturers; and "Leading Countries with the Highest Aerospace Exports in 2022," Statista, 2023.

11. "Manufacturing Sector: Real Sectoral Output for All Workers," Federal Reserve Economic Data, Federal Reserve Bank of St. Louis, last updated May 2, 2024.

12. "Real Value Added by Industry: Manufacturing," Federal Reserve Economic Data, Federal Reserve Bank of St. Louis, last updated March 28, 2024.

13. "Inward FDI Stocks by Industry," Organization for Economic Cooperation and Development; "New Foreign Direct Investment in the United States, 2021," US Bureau of Economic Analysis news release, July 6, 2022.

14. Scott Lincicome, "Manufactured Crisis: 'Deindustrialization,' Free Markets, and National Security," Cato Institute Policy Analysis no. 907, January 27, 2021.

15. "United States Manufacturing Facts," National Association of Manufacturers; and "United States," Observatory of Economic Complexity.

16. "High-Technology Exports (% of Manufactured Exports)—United States," World Development Indicators, World Bank; and "High-Technology Exports (Current US$)—United States," World Development Indicators, World Bank.

17. "The People's Republic of China," Office of the US Trade Representative; "Japan," Office of the US Trade Representative; and Office of Technology Evaluation, "US Trade with Germany Overall Trends," Bureau of Industry and Security, 2020, p. 1.

18. "European Union," Office of the US Trade Representative.

19. "United States," Observatory of Economic Complexity.

20. "Manufacturing Sector: Labor Productivity," Federal Reserve Economic Data, Federal Reserve Bank of St. Louis, last updated April 1, 2024.

21. Levinson, "Job Creation in the Manufacturing Revival," p. 2.

22. Michael J. Hicks and Srikant Devaraj, *The Myth and the Reality of Manufacturing in America* (Muncie, IN: Ball State University Center for Business and Economic Research, April 2017), p. 6.

23. Katharine G. Abraham and Melissa S. Kearney, "Explaining the Decline in the US Employment-to-Population Ratio: A Review of the Evidence," National Bureau of Economic Research Working Paper no. 24333, 2018, pp. 9–16.

24. Robert Rowthorn and Ramana Ramaswamy, "Deindustrialization—Its Causes and Implications," International Monetary Fund, *Economic Issues* no. 10 (1997): 5.

25. "Real Median Household Income in the United States," Federal Reserve Economic Data, Federal Reserve Bank of St. Louis, last updated September 12, 2023; and "The Changing American Consumer," *The Economist*, May 29, 2022.

26. Kristen Tauber and Willem van Zandweghe, "Why Has Durable Goods Spending Been So Strong during the COVID-19 Pandemic?," Economic Commentary 2021–16, Federal Reserve Bank of Cleveland.

27. Robert Lawrence and Lawrence Edwards, "US Employment Deindustrialization: Insights from History and the International Experience," Peterson Institute for International Economics Policy Brief no. PB13–27, October 2013; and "Manufacturing Share of Gross Domestic Product in Selected Advanced Economies," United Nations.

28. Andrew Witherspoon and Courtenay Brown, "Southern States Won the Most Auto Manufacturing Jobs," *Axios*, December 16, 2018.

29. Christopher D. Watson, "Domestic Steel Manufacturing: Overview and Prospects," Congressional Research Service Report R47107, May 17, 2022. p. 11.

30. Paul Holmes, "Governor, US Steel Executives Break Ground on $3 Billion Steel Mill in Osceola," *Talk Business and Politics*, February 8, 2022; and Andrea Bossi and Joe Deaux, "Steel Plant Trump 'Saved' Slated to End Steelmaking Forever," Bloomberg, June 28, 2022.

31. Jaison R. Abel and Richard Deitz, "Where Are Manufacturing Jobs Coming Back?," *Liberty Street Economics* (blog), Federal Reserve Bank of New York, February 6, 2019.

32. Katherine Eriksson et al., "Trade Shocks and the Shifting Landscape of US. Manufacturing," *Journal of International Money and Finance* 3 (2021): 102254.

33. John F. Kennedy, "New England and the South," *The Atlantic*, January 1954.

34. Marsha Mercer, "Textile Industry Comes Back to Life, Especially in South," *USA Today*, February 5, 2014.

35. John Mullin, "The Rise and Sudden Decline of North Carolina Furniture Making," Econ Focus, Federal Reserve Bank of Richmond, Fourth Quarter 2020.

36. "The World Is in the Grip of a Manufacturing Delusion," *The Economist*, July 13, 2023.

37. Marc Levinson, "US Manufacturing in International Persepective," Congressional Research Service Report R42135, February 21, 2018, p. 12.

38. "Average Hourly Earnings of All Employees, Total Private," Federal Reserve Economic Data, Federal Reserve Bank of St. Louis, last updated May 3, 2024.

39. Levinson, "Job Creation in the Manufacturing Revival," p. 8.

40. Charles S. Gascon, "Labor Constraints Remain Greatest Challenge for Resurgent Manufacturing Sector," Federal Reserve Bank of St. Louis, July 13, 2022.

41. "The Relative Weakness of Earnings in Production Workers in Manufacturing, 1990–2018," US Bureau of Labor Statistics, December 2019.

42. Kimberly Bayard et al., "Are Manufacturing Jobs Still 'Good' Jobs? An Exploration of the Manufacturing Wage Premium," Finance and Economics Discussion Series 2022–011, Board of Governors of the Federal Reserve System, 2022, p. 1.

43. Gascon, "Labor Constraints Remain Greatest Challenge."

44. Chris Giles, "IMF Raps Politicians' Obsession with Manufacturing Jobs," *Financial Times*, April 9, 2018.

45. Scott Lincicome and Alfredo Carrillo Obregon, "It's World Trade Week . . . and (Apparently) the Start of the 'Silly Season' in Washington," *Cato at Liberty* (blog), Cato Institute, May 25, 2023.

46. Giles, "IMF Raps Politicians' Obsessions."

47. Gary Clyde Hufbauer and Zhiyao (Lucy) Lu, "The Payoff to America from Globalization: A Fresh Look with a Focus on Costs to Workers," Peterson Institute for International Economics Policy Briefs 17–16, May 2017, p. 21.

48. Scott Lincicome, "When 'Success' Breeds (Even Bigger) Failure," *The Dispatch*, March 29, 2023.

49. Scott Lincicome, Gabriella Beaumont-Smith, and Alfredo Carrillo Obregon, "Formula for a Crisis," Cato Institute Briefing Paper no. 146, January 11, 2023.

50. Scott Lincicome, "This (Steel) Deal Is Getting Worse All the Time," *Cato at Liberty* (blog), Cato Institute, February 8, 2022.

51. Daniel J. Ikenson, "Tariffs by Fiat: The Widening Chasm between US Antidumping Policy and the Rule of Law," Cato Institute Policy Analysis no. 896, July 16, 2020; and Scott Lincicome and Inu Manak, "Protectionism or National Security? The Use and Abuse of Section 232," Cato Institute Policy Analysis no. 912, March 9, 2021.

52. "What Manufacturers Want Out of an Immigration System," National Association of Manufacturers, October 26, 2022.

53. Adam N. Michel, "Expensing and the Taxation of Capital Investment," Cato Institute Briefing Paper no. 159, June 7, 2023.

CHAPTER 13

1. Douglas A. Irwin and Oliver Ward, "What is the 'Washington Consensus?,'" Peterson Institute for International Economics, September 8, 2021; and Daniel Yergin and Joseph Stanislaw, *The Commanding Heights: The Battle for the World Economy* (Washington: Free Press, 2002).

2. Jeffrey Chwieroth, "Neoliberal Economists and Capital Account Liberalization in Emerging Markets," *International Organization* 61, no. 2 (2007): 443–63.

3. "GATT Members," World Trade Organization; and "Understanding the WTO: The Organization," World Trade Organization.

4. Albert O. Hirschman and Jeremy Adelman, *The Passions and the Interests: Political Arguments for Capitalism before Its Triumph*, rev. ed. (Princeton, NJ: Princeton University Press, 2013).

5. William J. Baumol, "Entrepreneurship: Productive, Unproductive, and Destructive," *Journal of Political Economy* 98, no. 5 (1990): 893–921.

6. Robert Keohane and Joseph Nye Jr., *Power & Interdependence*, 4th ed. (New York: Pearson, 2011).

7. Henry Farrell and Abraham L. Newman, "Weaponized Interdependence: How Global Economic Networks Shape State Coercion," *International Security* 44, no. 1 (2019): 42–79.

8. Gavin Bade, "Biden Trade Team: RIP Globalization," *Politico*, May 8, 2022.

9. Chris Miller, *Chip War: The Fight for the World's Most Critical Technology* (New York: Scribner, 2022), p. 317.

10. Rana Foroohar, "After Neoliberalism All Economics Is Local," *Foreign Affairs*, October 28, 2022.

11. Daniel W. Drezner, "The Risks of De-risking," *Drezner's World* (blog), Substack, May 1, 2023.

12. John R. Oneal, Bruce Russett, and Michael L. Berbaum, "Causes of Peace: Democracy, Interdependence, and International Organizations, 1885–1992," *International Studies Quarterly* 47, no. 3 (September 2003): 371–93.

13. Immanuel Kant, *Perpetual Peace: A Philosophical Essay*, trans. M. Campbell Smith (New York: The Macmillan Company, 1917).

14. Erik Gartzke, "The Capitalist Peace," *American Journal of Political Science* 51, no. 1 (January 2007): 166–91.

15. Patrick J. McDonald, *The Invisible Hand of Peace: Capitalism, the War Machine, and International Relations Theory* (New York: Cambridge University Press, 2009); and Michael Mousseau, "The Democratic Peace Unraveled: It's the Economy," *International Studies Quarterly* 57, no. 1 (March 2013): 186–97.

16. Thomas L. Friedman, *The World Is Flat: A Brief History of the Twenty-First Century* (New York: Farrar, Straus and Giroux, 2005).

17. Kenneth N. Waltz, *Theory of International Politics* (Long Grove, IL: Waveland Press, 2010); and Joanne Gowa, *Allies, Adversaries, and International Trade*, rev. ed. (1994; repr., Princeton, NJ: Princeton University Press, 1995).

18. Kenneth N. Waltz, *Theory of International Politics* (Long Grove, IL: Waveland Press, 2010), p. 106.

19. "Text of President Clinton's News Conference in China," *New York Times*, March 9, 2000.

20. Henry Farrell and Abraham L. Newman, "Weaponized Interdependence: How Global Economic Networks Shape State Coercion," *International Security* 44, no. 1 (2019): 42–79.

21. Colin Kahl and Thomas Wright, *Aftershocks: Pandemic Politics and the End of the Old International Order* (New York: St. Martin's Press, 2021).

22. "Jourova Slams Europe's 'Morbid Dependency' on China," *Euractiv*, April 20, 2020; and Isabel Reynolds and Emi Urabe, "Japan to Fund Firms to Shift Production Out of China," *Bloomberg Businessweek*, April 8, 2020.

23. Rachel More, "NATO's Stoltenberg Cautions against Economic Dependency on China," Reuters, December 1, 2022.

24. Nate Schenkkan, "Best Antidote to Beijing's Authoritarian Influence Campaign: Democracy Itself," Freedom House, September 8, 2022; and Bonnie Glaser, "China as a Selective Revisionist Power in the International Order," (report of a seminar presentation at the ISEAS—Yusof Ishak Institute, January 2019).

25. Ketian Zhang, "Cautious Bully: Reputation, Resolve, and Beijing's Use of Coercion in the South China Sea," *International Security* 44, no. 1 (2019): 117–59.

26. Deborah Brautigam, "A Critical Look at Chinese 'Debt-Trap Diplomacy': The Rise of a Meme," *Area Development and Policy* 5, no. 1 (2020): 1–14; and S. Horn et al., "China as an International Lender of Last Resort Dataset," National Bureau of Economic Research Working Paper no. 31105, March 2023.

27. Graham Allison, "China Now the World's Largest Economy; We Shouldn't Be Shocked," Belfer Center for Science and International Affairs, Harvard University Kennedy School, October 15, 2020.

28. Graham Allison, "The Thucydides Trap: Are the US and China Headed for War?," *The Atlantic*, September 24, 2015.

29. Stacie E. Goddard, "Embedded Revisionism: Networks, Institutions, and Challenges to World Order," *International Organization* 72, no. 4 (2018): 763–97.

30. Alastair Iain Johnston, "China in a World of Orders: Rethinking Compliance and Challenge in Beijing's International Relations," *International Security* 44, no. 2 (2019): 9–60.

31. Daniel W. Drezner, "Counter-Hegemonic Strategies in the Global Economy," *Security Studies* 28, no. 3 (2019): 505–31.

32. "Russia-China Joint Statement on International Relations," USC US-China Institute, University of Southern California, February 4, 2022.

33. Gaurav Khanna, Nicolas Morales, and Nitya Pandalai-Nayar, "Supply Chain Resilience: Evidence from Indian Firms," National Bureau of Economic Research Working Paper no. 30689, November 2022.

34. Barthélémy Bonadio et al., "Global Supply Chains in the Pandemic," *Journal of International Economics* 133 (2021).

35. Scott Lincicome, Gabriella Beaumont-Smith, and Alfredo Carrillo Obregon, "The Formula for a Crisis," Cato Institute Briefing Paper no. 146, January 11, 2023.

36. Esfandyar Batmanghelidj, "The Inflation Weapon: How American Sanctions Harm Iranian Households," Sanctions & Security Research Program, 2022.

37. "The Joint Comprehensive Plan of Action (JCPOA) at a Glance," Arms Control Association, last reviewed March 2022.

38. Nahal Toosi and Stephanie Liechtenstein, "Maximum Fissures: Iran Nuclear Deal Talks Head toward Oblivion," *Politico*, November 27, 2021.

39. Maria Snegovaya et al., "Russia Sanctions at One Year," Center for Strategic & International Studies, February 23, 2023.

40. David Frum, "Why Putin's Secret Weapon Failed," *The Atlantic*, June 2, 2023.

41. Arjun Kharpal, "Huawei Pivots to Software with Google-Like Ambitions as US Sanctions Hit Hardware Business," CNBC, April 25, 2021.

42. David Lague, "Special Report: In Satellite Tech Race, China Hitched a Ride from Europe," Reuters, December 22, 2013.

43. Nicholas Mulder, *The Economic Weapon: The Rise of Sanctions as a Tool of Modern War* (New Haven, CT: Yale University Press, 2022).

44. Shekhar Aiyar et al., "Geoeconomic Fragmentation and the Future of Multilateralism," International Monetary Fund Staff Discussion Note 2023/001, January 15, 2023.

45. Emily Meierding, "Dismantling the Oil Wars Myth," *Security Studies* 25, no. 2 (2016): 258–88.

46. Norman Angell, *The Great Illusion* (Toronto: McClelland and Goodchild, 1910).

47. Michael Mousseau, "The End of War: How a Robust Marketplace and Liberal Hegemony Are Leading to Perpetual World Peace," *International Security* 44, no. 1 (2019): 160–96; and John Mueller, "War Has Almost Ceased to Exist: An Assessment," *Political Science Quarterly* 124, no. 2 (2009): 297–321.

48. Robert Jervis, *Perception and Misperception in International* Politics (Princeton, NJ: Princeton University Press, 2017); and Stephen Van Evera, "The Cult of the Offensive and the Origins of the First World War," *International Security* 9, no. 1 (1984): 58–107.

CHAPTER 14

1. Joseph E. Stiglitz, *Globalization and Its Discontents* (New York: W. W. Norton, 2003).

2. Katherine Tai, "Ambassador Katherine Tai's Remarks at the National Press Club on Supply Chain Resilience" (speech, National Press Club, Washington, June 15, 2023).

3. Mark Weisbrot, "To End Child Labor, Washington Must Press Companies to Act," *New York Times*, June 30, 2015.

4. International Labour Office, *World Employment and Social Outlook: Trends 2020* (Geneva, Switzerland: ILO, 2020).

5. World Health Organization and International Labour Organization, *WHO/ILO Joint Estimates of the Work-related Burden of Disease and Injury, 2000–2016: Global Monitoring Report* (Geneva, Switzerland: World Health Organization, 2021).

6. International Labour Office and United Nations Children's Fund, *Child Labour: Global Estimates 2020, Trends and the Road Forward* (New York: ILO and UNICEF, 2021).

7. Organisation for Economic Co-operation and Development, *Policy Priorities for International Trade and Jobs* (Paris: OECD Publishing, 2012).

8. Andreas Bergh and Therese Nilsson, "Is Globalization Reducing Absolute Poverty?," *World Development* 62 (2014): 42–61.

9. Robert J. Flanagan, *Globalization and Labor Conditions: Working Conditions and Worker Rights in a Global Economy* (New York: Oxford University Press, 2006).

10. Robert J. Flanagan and Niny Khor, "Trade and the Quality of Employment: Asian and Non-Asian Economies," in *Policy Priorities for International Trade and Jobs* (Paris: OECD Publishing, 2012), 259–80; and Organisation for Economic Co-operation and Development, *Policy Priorities for International Trade and Jobs* (Paris: OECD Publishing, 2012).

11. World Bank, *Where Have All the Poor Gone? Cambodia Poverty Assessment 2013* (Washington: World Bank, 2014).

12. Abhishek Saurav, Yan Liu, and Aarushi Sinha, *Foreign Direct Investment and Employment Outcomes in Developing Countries: A Literature Review of the Effects of FDI on Job Creation and Wages* (Washington: World Bank, 2020).

13. Robert E. Baldwin and L. Alan Winters, eds., *Challenges to Globalization: Analyzing the Economics* (Chicago: University of Chicago Press, 2004).

14. Oscar Holland, "10 years after Rana Plaza, Is Bangladesh's Garment Industry Any Safer?," CNN, April 23, 2023.

15. Noreena Hertz, *The Silent Takeover: Global Capitalism and the Death of Democracy* (New York: Harper Business, 2003).

16. Eric Edmonds and Nina Pavcnik, "International Trade and Child Labor: Cross-Country Evidence," National Bureau of Economic Research Working Paper no. 10317, February 2004.

17. Prashant Bharadwaj, Leah K. Lakdawala, and Nicholas Li, 2020, "Perverse Consequences of Well-Intentioned Regulation: Evidence from India's Child Labor Ban," *Journal of the European Economic Association* 18, no. 3 (2020): 1158–195.

18. Jeffrey A. Frankel and Andrew K. Rose, "Is Trade Good or Bad for the Environment? Sorting Out the Causality," *The Review of Economics and Statistics* 87, no. 1 (2005): 85–91.

19. M. J. Wolf et al., *2022 Environmental Performance Index* (New Haven, CT: Yale University, 2022).

20. M. J. Wolf et al., *2022 Environmental Performance Index* (New Haven, CT: Yale University, 2022).

21. Tomasz Koźluk and Gregoire Garsous, "How Stringent Are Environmental Policies?," *OECD Policy Perspectives* (February 2016).

22. Organisation for Economic Co-operation and Development, "Environmental Policy Stringency Index."

23. Christian Bjørnskov, "Economic Freedom and the CO_2 Kuznets Curve" (IFN working paper no. 1331, Research Institute of Industrial Economics, Stockholm, Sweden, 2020).

24. International Energy Agency, "Energy End-uses and Efficiency Indicators Data Explorer," last updated December 18, 2023.

25. Max Roser, "Why Did Renewables Become So Cheap So Fast?," Our World in Data, December 1, 2020.

26. "Environmental Performance Index, 2020 Release (1950–2020)," Socioeconomic Data and Applications Center, Columbia University, City of New York.

27. Robert Y. Shum, "Can Attitudes Predict Outcomes? Public Opinion, Democratic Institutions and Environmental Policy," *Environmental Policy and Governance* 19, no. 5 (September/October 2009): 281–95; and Amaryllis Mavragani, Ioannis E. Nikolaou, and Konstantinos P. Tsagarakis, "Open Economy, Institutional Quality, and Environmental Performance: A Macroeconomic Approach," *Sustainability* 8, no. 7 (2016): 601.

CHAPTER 15

1. Steven Pinker, *Enlightenment Now: The Case for Reason, Science, Humanism, and Progress* (New York: Viking, 2018), p. 97.

2. "Google Ngram Viewer," Google Books.

3. Eduardo Porter and Karl Russell, "It's an Unequal World. It Doesn't Have to Be," *New York Times*, December 14, 2017; Cardiff Garcia, "Global Interpersonal Inequality through the Crisis Period," *Financial Times*, August 15, 2017; Winnie Byanyima, "How Can We Bridge the Widening Inequality Gap?," *Al Jazeera*, January 23, 2018; Justin Worland, "Climate Change Has Already Increased Global Inequality. It Will Only Get Worse," *Time*, April 22, 2019; Jay Elwes, "The Deep Roots of Global Inequality," *The Spectator*, June 11, 2022; Karen McVeigh, "'Perfect Storm' of Crises Is Widening Global Inequality, Says UN Chief," *The Guardian*, July 2, 2022; and "Global Inequality Is Rising Again," *The Economist*, August 2, 2022.

4. Brian Naylor, "VP Harris, in Paris, Says Infrastructure and Spending Bills Will Help Cut Poverty," NPR, November 11, 2021; and Chelsea Follett, "What Kamala Harris Gets Wrong about Inequality," *National Review*, November 19, 2021.

5. Josep Borrell, "Let's Make 2023 a Year of Turning the Tide on Human Rights," European Union External Action, January 7, 2023.

6. "World Leaders Must Address Disparities among Countries in Climate Change Fight—President Ali," High Commission of the Cooperative Republic of Guyana in the Republic of South Africa, June 5, 2022.

7. Others have questioned these views, describing inequality as "the midwife of progress." See, for example, Marian L. Tupy, "'Space Barons' and Advantages of a Free Economy," *National Review*, August 16, 2021.

8. Jonathan Kelley and Mariah D. R. Evans, "Societal Inequality and Individual Subjective Well-Being: Results from 68 Societies and Over 200,000 Individuals, 1981–2008," *Social Science Research* 62 (2017): 1–23; and Krzysztof Zagorski, Jonathan Kelley, and Mariah D. R. Evans, "Economic Development and Happiness: Evidence from 32 Nations," *Polish Sociological Review* 169 (2010): 3–19.

9. Martin-Brehm Christensen et al., *Survival of the Richest* (Nairobi: Oxfam, 2023), pp. 40–42.

10. Nabil Ahmed, "New Oxfam Report on Rising Global Inequality Calls for 5% Tax on Super-Rich," interview by Scott Harris, *Between the Lines*, January 25, 2023.

11. Gabriela Bucher, "Global Inequality Is a Failure of Imagination. Here's Why," World Economic Forum, January 16, 2023.

12. "End the Age of Extreme Wealth. Tax the Ultra Rich," The Cost of Extreme Wealth.

13. Facundo Alvaredo et al., *World Inequality Report, 2018* (Paris: World Inequality Lab, 2017).

14. Facundo Alvaredo et al., *World Inequality Report, 2018.*

15. Marian L. Tupy, "Stop Obsessing about Inequality. It's Actually Decreasing around the World," *Washington Post*, January 8, 2015.

16. Chris Giles, "The Globalisation Elephant Has Left the Room," *Financial Times*, November 24, 2022.

17. Lucas Chancel and Thomas Piketty, "Global Income Inequality, 1820–2020: The Persistence and Mutation of Extreme Inequality," World Inequality Lab Working Paper no. 2021/19, July 2021; and Mads Lundby Hansen, "Global Inequality at Lowest Level for 140 Years," European Policy Information Center, September 16, 2021.

18. John F. Early, "The Myth of American Income Inequality," Cato Institute, September 20, 2022.

19. Elhanan Helpman, Globalization and Inequality (Cambridge, MA: Harvard University Press, 2018).

20. Credit Suisse, "Global Wealth Report 2021," June 2021, p. 25.

21. Chelsea Follett, "Globalisation Is Slashing Inequality—Here's How," CapX, March 30, 2017.

22. Chelsea Follett and Vincent Geloso, "Global Inequality in Well-Being Has Decreased across Many Dimensions: Introducing the Inequality of Human Progress Index," Cato Institute Policy Analysis no. 949, June 8, 2023.

23. Follett and Geloso, "Global Inequality in Well-Being Has Decreased across Many Dimensions," p. 3.

24. Leandro Prados de la Escosura, *Human Development and the Path to Freedom* (Cambridge: Cambridge University Press, 2022).

25. Follett and Geloso, "Global Inequality in Well-Being Has Decreased across Many Dimensions," p. 4.

26. For a full discussion of the development of this alternative to the HDI, see Follett and Geloso, "Global Inequality in Well-Being Has Decreased across Many Dimensions."

27. "Life Expectancy at Birth, Total (Years)," World Development Indicators, World Bank; "Mortality Rate, Infant (per 1,000 Live Births)," World Development Indicators, World Bank; "Death Rate from Air Pollution, World," Our World in Data; "Barro-Lee Educational Attainment Dataset," GitHub, last updated September 2021; Adoption of Communication Technologies per 100 People, World," Our World in Data; Jutta Bolt and Jan Luiten van Zanden, "Maddison Project Database, 2020," University of Groningen, updated May 22, 2022; note that the eighth component, "democracy versus autocracy over time, on a scale from 0 to 40," is rescaled from the Polity5 Database, Center for Systemic Peace.

28. Follett and Geloso, "Global Inequality in Well-Being Has Decreased across Many Dimensions," p. 8.

29. Martin Wolf, "Waging War on Trade Will Be Costly," *Financial Times*, April 4, 2023.

30. Chelsea Follett, "No Discernible Rise in Well-Being? Look at the Data . . . ," Human Progress, December 16, 2016.

31. "Public Perceptions of the Change in Global Extreme Poverty," Our World in Data, September 2017.

CHAPTER 16

1. Edmund Burke, *The Correspondence of Edmund Burke,* vol. III, ed. G. H. Guttridge (Chicago: University of Chicago Press, 1961), p. 426.

2. Adam Smith, *An Inquiry into the Nature and Causes of the Wealth of Nations* (London: Methuen & Co., Ltd., 1776; now available online at Marxists Internet Archive), bk. 4, chap. 3, part 2.

3. Scott Lincicome, "Manufactured Crisis: 'Deindustrialization,' Free Markets, and National Security," Cato Institute Policy Analysis no. 907, January 27, 2021.

4. Thomas Paine, *Common Sense* (Philadelphia: R. Bell, 1776; now available online at the Online Library of Liberty); and Thomas Paine, *The Crisis* (Philadelphia: *The Philadelphia Journal*, 1777; now available online at The Independence Hall Association).

5. Douglas A. Irwin, "Trade Policy for the New Nation, 1789–1815," in *Clashing over Commerce: A History of US Trade Policy* (Chicago: University of Chicago Press, 2017).

6. US Const. art. I, § 8, cl. 3 and cl. 2.

7. Ronald Reagan, "Remarks at a White House Meeting with Business and Trade Leaders," (speech, White House, Washington, September 23, 1985).

8. Colin Grabow and Scott Lincicome, "The Many Myths of Reaganite Protectionism," National Review Online, November 30, 2017.

9. Daniel Griswold, "Reagan Embraced Free Trade and Immigration," Cato Institute, June 24, 2004.

10. Donald J. Trump (@realDonaldTrump), "When you are the 'Piggy Bank' Nation . . .," X post, June 1, 2019, 6:20 p.m.

11. "Memorandum for Secretary of Commerce," Secretary of Defense.

12. Michael A. Needham, "New Balance's Cronyism Invades Defense Bill," RealClearPolitics, May 17, 2016.

13. Dana T. Parker, *Building Victory: Aircraft Manufacturing in the Los Angeles Area in World War II* (self-pub., Amazon, 2013), Kindle edition, p. 2.

14. Colin Grabow, "The Self-Imposed Blockade," Cato Institute Policy Analysis no. 933, August 16, 2022.

15. *Hearing on National Defense Authorization Act for Fiscal Year 2018*, 115th Cong. (2017) (statement of Marc Thornberry, House Armed Services Chairman), July 14, 2017, C-SPAN video, 5:01:48.

16. Daniel Griswold and Andreas Freytag, "Balance of Trade, Balance of Power," Cato Institute Policy Analysis no. 944, April 25, 2023.

17. Dan Charles, "Farmers Got Billions from Taxpayers in 2019, and Hardly Anyone Objected," *The Salt* (blog), NPR, December 31, 2019.

18. Daniel Griswold, "NAFTA at 10: An Economic and Foreign Policy Success," Cato Institute Free Trade Bulletin no. 1, December 17, 2002.

19. Aaron Flaaen, Ali Hortaçsu, and Felix Tintelnot, "The Production Relocation and Price Effects of US Trade Policy: The Case of Washing Machines," *American Economic Review* 110, no. 7 (2020): 2105–06.

20. Tom Lee and Jacqueline Varas, "The Total Cost of US Tariffs," American Action Forum, May 10, 2022.

21. Clark Packard and Scott Lincicome, "Course Correction," Cato Institute Policy Analysis no. 946, May 9, 2023.

22. JOC Staff, "JOC Top 100 US Importer and Exporter Rankings 2020," *Journal of Commerce*, May 25, 2021.

23. *Profile 2015: American Iron and Steel Institute* (Washington: American Iron and Steel Institute, 2023), p. 9.

24. Stephen J. Rose, "Do Not Blame Trade for the Decline in Manufacturing Jobs," Center for Strategic and International Studies, October 4, 2021, p. 11.

25. Scott Lincicome and Alfredo Carrillo Obregon, "The (Updated) Case for Free Trade," Cato Institute Policy Analysis no. 925, April 19, 2022, p. 4.

26. Gary Clyde Hufbauer and Megan Hogan, "America's Payoff from Engaging in World Markets since 1950 Was Almost $2.6 Trillion in 2022," Peterson Institute for International Economics Policy Brief no. 23–17, December 2023, p. 2.

27. Pablo D. Fajgelbaum and Amit K. Khandelwal, "Measuring the Unequal Gains from Trade," *Quarterly Journal of Economics* 131, no. 3 (2016).

28. Bryan Riley, "Import Taxes Inflate Back-to-School Prices," National Taxpayers Union, August 10, 2023.

29. Scott Lincicome, "A Tale of Two Cities," *The Dispatch*, June 23, 2021.

30. Jesus Cañas, "Texas Border Cities Illustrate Benefits and Challenges of Trade," Southwest Economy, Federal Reserve Bank of Dallas, Fourth Quarter 2016, p. 17.

31. Cañas, "Texas Border Cities Illustrate Benefits and Challenges of Trade," p. 18.

32. Scott Horsley, "Tariff Waivers Let US Government Pick Winners and Losers," NPR, May 15, 2019.

33. US Const. art. I, § 1.

34. US Const. art. II, § 2.

CHAPTER 17

1. Katherine Tai, "Ambassador Katherine Tai's Remarks at the National Press Club on Supply Chain Resilience" (remarks, National Press Club, Washington, June 15, 2023).

2. Joseph Biden, "Statement from President Biden on US Steel," The White House, March 14, 2024.

3. Heather Boushey, "Remarks by Heather Boushey on How President Biden's Invest in America Agenda Has Laid the Foundation for Decades of Strong, Stable, and Sustained, Equitable Growth," The White House, May 31, 2023.

4. Jake Sullivan, "Remarks by National Security Advisor Jake Sullivan on Renewing American Economic Leadership at the Brookings Institution," The White House, April 27, 2023.

5. Franklin D. Roosevelt, "Address before the Inter-American Conference for the Maintenance of Peace, Buenos Aires, Argentina" (address, Buenos Aires, Argentina, December 1, 1936), The American Presidency Project.

6. Roosevelt, "Address before the Inter-American Conference for the Maintenance of Peace."

7. Douglas A. Irwin, "The Smoot–Hawley Tariff: A Quantitative Assessment," *Review of Economics and Statistics* 80, no. 2 (May 1998): 326–34.

8. Douglas A. Irwin and Randall S. Kroszner, "Logrolling and Economic Interests in the Passage of the Smoot–Hawley Tariff," National Bureau of Economic Research Working Paper no. 5510, March 1996.

9. Kris James Mitchener, Kirsten Wandschneider, and Kevin Hjortshøj O'Rourke, "The Smoot–Hawley Trade War," National Bureau of Economic Research Working Paper no. 28616, March 2021.

10. Douglas A. Irwin, "The Hawley-Smoot Tariff and the Great Depression, 1928–1932," in *Clashing over Commerce: A History of US Trade Policy* (Chicago: University of Chicago Press, 2017), pp. 371–410.

11. Franklin D. Roosevelt, "Campaign Address in Seattle, Washington on Reciprocal Tariff Negotiations (Excerpts)" (address, Seattle, September 20, 1932), The American Presidency Project.

12. Roosevelt, "Campaign Address in Seattle, Washington on Reciprocal Tariff Negotiations (Excerpts)."

13. "Eighty Years After the Reciprocal Trade Agreements Act," Office of the US Trade Representative, June 2014.

14. Franklin D. Roosevelt, "Message to Congress on the Trade Agreements Act" (speech, Congress, Washington, March 26, 1945), The American Presidency Project.

15. Douglas A. Irwin, "The New Deal and Reciprocal Trade Agreements, 1932–1943," in *Clashing over Commerce: A History of US Trade Policy* (Chicago: University of Chicago Press, 2017), pp. 413–54.

16. Immanuel Kant, *Perpetual Peace and Other Essays*, trans. Ted Humphrey (Cambridge: Hackett Publishing Company, 1983).

17. Håvard Hegre, John R Oneal, and Bruce Russett, "Trade Does Promote Peace: New Simultaneous Estimates of the Reciprocal Effects of Trade and Conflict," *Journal of Peace Research* 47 no. 6 (November 2010): 763–74; and Erik Gartzke and Oliver Westerwinter, "The Complex Structure of Commercial Peace Contrasting Trade Interdependence, Asymmetry, and Multipolarity," *Journal of Peace Research* 53, no. 3 (May 2016): 325–43.

18. Cordell Hull, *The Memoirs of Cordell Hull*, vol. 1 (New York: Macmillan Publishers, 1948).

19. Mona Paulsen, "The Past, Present, and Potential of Economic Security," *Yale Journal of International Law* 50 (forthcoming).

20. Roosevelt, "Message to Congress on the Trade Agreements Act."

21. John F. Kennedy, "Remarks upon Signing the Trade Expansion Act" (remarks, White House, Washington, October 11, 1962), The American Presidency Project.

22. Kennedy, "Remarks upon Signing the Trade Expansion Act."

23. Cordell Hull, "What America Is Fighting For" (speech, president's press conference, Washington, July 23,1942), General Records of the Department of State, Record Group 59, radio audio, National Archives at College Park, College Park, MD.

24. Bill Clinton, "Remarks on Signing the Uruguay Round Agreements Act December 8, 1994," in *Public Papers of the Presidents of the United States: William J. Clinton*, book 2 (Washington: Government Printing Office, 1994), pp. 2160–61.

25. Jake Sullivan, "Remarks by National Security Advisor Jake Sullivan on Renewing American Economic Leadership at the Brookings Institution" (remarks, Brookings Institution, Washington, April 27, 2023), The White House.

26. Katherine Tai, "Free Trade in the Balance: A Discussion with US Trade Representative Katherine Tai," University of Chicago Institute of Politics, streamed live on February 6, 2024, YouTube video, 41:39.

27. John F. Kennedy, "Commencement Address at American University, Washington D.C., June 10, 1963" (speech, American University, Washington, June 10, 1963), John F. Kennedy Presidential Library and Museum.

28. Mary Amiti, Sang Hoon Kong, and David Weinstein, "The Effect of the US-China Trade War on US Investment," National Bureau of Economic Research Working Paper no. 27114, May 2020; Brock R. Williams and Keigh E. Hammond, "Escalating US Tariffs: Affected Trade," Congressional Research Service Insight IN10971, January 29, 2020; and Scott Lincicome, Inu Manak, and Alfredo Carrillo Obregon, "Unfair Trade or Unfair Protection? The Evolution and Abuse of Section 301," Cato Institute Policy Analysis no. 930, June 14, 2022.

29. Adam Hodge, "Statement from USTR Spokesperson Adam Hodge," Office of the US Trade Representative, press release, December 9, 2022.

30. "Statement from USTR Spokesperson Adam Hodge."

31. Katherine Tai, "Some 'Discomfort' Will Be Key to Successful USMCA Review," *World Trade Online*, June 6, 2024.

32. Lydia DePillis, "Robert Lighthizer Blew up 60 Years of Trade Policy. Nobody Knows What Happens Next," *ProPublica*, October 13, 2020.

33. Michael Froman, "Trade, Growth, and Jobs: US Trade Policy in the Obama Administration," The White House: President Obama, January 5, 2017.

34. Joe Hasell, "From $1.90 to $2.15 a Day: the Updated International Poverty Line," Our World in Data, October 26, 2022.

35. Kimberly Clausing, *Open: The Progressive Case for Free Trade, Immigration, and Global Capital* (Cambridge, MA: Harvard University Press, 2019).

36. World Trade Organization, *World Trade Report 2023: Re-globalization for a Secure, Inclusive and Sustainable Future* (Geneva: World Trade Organization, 2023).

37. Gary Hufbauer and Megan Hogan, "America's Payoff from Engaging in World Markets since 1950 Was Almost $2.6 Trillion in 2022," Peterson Institute for International Economics Policy Brief no. 23–17, December 2023.

38. Jan David Bakker et al., *Post-Brexit Imports, Supply Chains, and the Effect on Consumer Prices* (London: UK in a Changing Europe, April 2022).

39. Council of Economic Advisers, *Economic Report of the President* (Washington: Council of Economic Advisers, March 2024).

40. Ed Gresser, "PPI'S Trade Fact of the Week: US Tariffs on Cheap Stainless Steel Spoons Are 5 Times Higher than on Sterling Silver Spoons," Progressive Policy Institute, April 12, 2023.

41. Miguel Acosta and Lydia Cox, "The Regressive Nature of the US Tariff Code: Origins and Implications," University of Wisconsin, Madison Working Paper, February 2024.

42. Scott Lincicome, "Testing the 'China Shock': Was Normalizing Trade with China a Mistake?," Cato Institute Policy Analysis no. 895, July 8, 2020.

43. Clausing, *Open*.

44. Clausing, *Open*.

45. Anne O. Krueger, *International Trade: What Everyone Needs to Know* (New York: Oxford University Press, 2020).

46. Krueger, *International Trade*.

47. Edward Alden, *Failure to Adjust: How Americans Got Left Behind in the Global Economy* (Lanham, MD: Rowman & Littlefield, 2016).

48. Gordon H. Hanson, "Can Trade Work for Workers? The Right Way to Redress Harms and Redistribute Gains," *Foreign Affairs*, April 20, 2021.

49. Hanson, "Can Trade Work for Workers?"

50. World Trade Organization, *World Trade Report 2023*.

51. Barack Obama, "Remarks by President Obama and President Pena Nieto of Mexico in Joint Press Conference" (remarks, White House, Washington, July 22, 2016), The White House: President Obama.

52. Clinton, "Remarks on Signing the Uruguay Round Agreements Act," pp. 2160–61.

CHAPTER 18

1. Gideon Rachman, "Patriots vs Globalists Replaces the Left-Right Divide," *Financial Times*, April 18, 2022.

2. Kevin Roberts, (@KevinRobertsTX), "If exit polls are right, then conservatives will come to power in Italy," X post, September 25, 2022, 6:26 p.m.

3. Donald Trump, "Donald Trump Holds a Political Rally in Houston, Texas—October 22, 2018," Roll Call, Factbase, Houston, TX, October 22, 2018.

4. Frederick Douglass, "Composite Nation," (speech, Parker Fraternity Course, Boston, MA, 1867), Frederick Douglass Papers at the Library of Congress, Manuscript Division.

5. Max Farrand, ed., *The Records of the Federal Convention of 1787,* vol. 3 (New Haven, CT: Yale University Press, 1911).

6. US Const., amend. 10.

7. Jean F. Maguire, "Customs Ruling NY 890276" (Customs Mobile, New York, 1993).

8. Kathleen Freeman, "Dêmocritus of Abdêra" in *Ancilla to Pre-Socratic Philosophers: A Complete Translation of the Fragments in Diels, Fragmente der Vorsokratiker* (Cambridge, MA: Harvard University Press, 1983), p. 114.

9. Louise Levathes, "Confucians and Curiosities" in *When China Ruled the Seas: The Treasure Fleet of the Dragon Throne, 1405–1433* (New York: Oxford University Press, 1996), p. 42.

10. David Schmidtz, *Living Together: Inventing Moral Science* (Oxford: Oxford University Press, 2023).

11. Tom G. Palmer and Matt Warner, *Development with Dignity: Self-Determination, Localization, and the End to Poverty* (London: Routledge, 2022).

12. Swaminathan S. Anklesaria Aiyar, "Capitalism's Assault on the Indian Caste System: How Economic Liberalization Spawned Low-Caste Dalit Millionaires," Cato Institute Policy Analysis no. 776, July 21, 2015; and Swaminathan S. Anklesaria Aiyar, "Globalization Has Propelled India to Prosperity," Defending Globalization, Cato Institute, October 24, 2023.

13. World Bank, *Poverty and Shared Prosperity 2016: Taking On Inequality* (Washington: World Bank, 2016).

14. Adam Smith, "That the Division of Labour Is Limited by the Extent of the Market," in *An Inquiry into the Nature and Causes of the Wealth of Nations*, ed. Edwin Cannan, 5th ed. (Carmel, IN: Library of Economics and Liberty, 2000).

15. Paul R. Krugman, "What Do Undergraduates Need to Know about Trade?," *American Economic Review* 83, no. 2 (1993): 23–26; Douglas A. Irwin, *Three Simple Principles of Trade Policy* (Washington: American Enterprise Institute Press, 1996).

16. "The Nobel Prize in Physiology or Medicine 2023: Katalin Karikó and Drew Weissman," The Nobel Assembly at Karolinska Institutet, press release, October 2, 2023.

17. David Gelles, "The Husband-and-Wife Team behind the Leading Vaccine to Solve Covid-19," *New York Times*, November 10, 2020.

18. Scott Lincicome, "The COVID Vaccines Are a Triumph of Globalization," *The Dispatch*, December 8, 2020.

19. "Against Their Will: The Situation in Xinjiang," US Department of Labor Bureau of International Labor Affairs.

20. "Human Trafficking: Forced Labor for Global Supply Chains," US International Trade Administration.

21. Smith, "Of the Motives for Establishing New Colonies," in *An Inquiry into the Nature and Causes of the Wealth of Nations*.

22. "Iceland Trade Statistics," World Integrated Trade Solution.

23. Tyler Cowen, *Creative Destruction: How Globalization Is Changing the World's Cultures* (Princeton, NJ: Princeton University Press, 2004), p. 15.

24. Plato, *The Republic of Plato*, trans. Allan Bloom, 2nd ed. (New York: Basic Books, 1968).

25. Aristotle, *Aristotle: The Politics and Constitution of Athens*, ed. Stephen Everson, rev. student edition, Cambridge Texts in History of Political Thought (Cambridge: Cambridge University Press, 1996).

26. Karl Raimund Popper, *The Open Society and Its Enemies: The Spell of Plato* (Princeton, NJ: Princeton University Press, 1971).

27. Nadav Eyal, *Revolt: The Worldwide Uprising against Globalization* (New York: Ecco, 2021).

28. Jeremy Waldron, "Multiculturalism and Mélange," in *Public Education in a Multicultural Society: Policy, Theory, Critique*, ed. Robert K. Fullinwider (Cambridge: Cambridge University Press, 1996).

29. Patrick J. Deneen, *Why Liberalism Failed* (New Haven, CT: Yale University Press, 2019).

30. Johan Norberg, *Financial Fiasco: How America's Infatuation with Home Ownership and Easy Money Created the Economic Crisis* (Washington: Cato Institute,

2009); Lemar Wooley, "Bush Administration Announces New HUD 'Zero Down Payment' Mortgage," US Department of Housing and Urban Development, news release no. 04-006, January 19, 2004; and Jeffrey Friedman, "A Perfect Storm of Ignorance," Cato Institute Policy Report, January/February 2010.

31. Jean-Baptiste Say, "Of the Demand or Market for Products" in *A Treatise on Political Economy* (Carmel, IN: The Library of Economics and Liberty, 2018).

32. Tom G. Palmer, ed., *Peace, Love, and Liberty: War Is Not Inevitable* (Ottawa, IL: Jameson Books, 2014).

33. Lars Vinx, "Carl Schmitt," Stanford Encyclopedia of Philosophy, August 7, 2010, rev. August 29, 2019; and Tom G. Palmer, "The Re-Emergence of Central Themes of the 'Conservative Revolution.'" *Isonomia Quarterly* 2.1 (Spring 2024), 49–50n11.

34. "Frédéric Passy—Speed Read," Nobel Prize Outreach AB 2024.

35. Frédéric Passy, *Leçons d'économie politique faites à Montpellier, 1860–1861: Recueillies par MM.* Émile Bertin et Paul Glaize (Brookline, MA: Adamant Media Corporation, 2003).

36. Passy, *Leçons d' économie politique.*

37. Erik Gartzke, "The Capitalist Peace," *American Journal of Political Science* 51 no. 1 (2007): 166–91.

38. Patrick J. McDonald, *The Invisible Hand of Peace: Capitalism, the War Machine, and International Relations Theory* (Cambridge: Cambridge University Press, 2009).

39. Adam Smith, *An Inquiry into the Nature of the Causes of the Wealth of Nations*, ed. Edwin Cannan, vol. 2 (London: Methuen, 1904).

40. Frederick Engels, "Outlines of a Critique of Political Economy," *Deutsch-Französische Jahrbücher*, February 1844, trans. Martin Milligan, Marxists.org.

41. Voltaire, *The Works of Voltaire: A Contemporary Version,* trans. William F. Fleming, vol. 19 (New York: E. R. DuMont, 1901).

CHAPTER 19

1. Ian Schwartz, "Maher: 'Falling Birth Rates Are a Good Thing'; World Is 'Too Crowded,'" RealClearPolitics, April 13, 2019; and Paul R. Ehrlich, *The Population Bomb* (New York: Ballantine Books, 1968).

2. Gale Pooley and Marian L. Tupy, "The Simon Abundance Index 2021," Human Progress, April 22, 2021.

3. Andrew McAfee, *More from Less: The Surprising Story of How We Learned to Prosper Using Fewer Resources—and What Happens Next* (New York: Scribner, 2019).

4. Thomas Sowell, *Knowledge and Decisions* (New York: Basic Books, 1996).

5. Marian L. Tupy and David Deutsch, "We Will Never Run Out of Resources," *Wall Street Journal,* July 20, 2023.

6. Marian L. Tupy and Gale Pooley, "The Simon Abundance Index 2024," Human Progress, April 22, 2024.

7. "Wheat Yields," Human Progress.

8. "Poverty Headcount Ratio at $2.15 a Day (2017 PPP) (% of Population)," World Development Indicators, World Bank.

9. "Daily Supply of Calories per Person, 1981 to 2018," Our World in Data.

10. "Daily Supply of Calories per Person, 1981 to 2018," Our World in Data.

11. Jesse H. Ausubel, "The Return of Nature: How Technology Liberates the Environment," The Breakthrough Institute, May 12, 2015.

12. "Will Lab-Grown Meat Ever Make it onto Supermarket Shelves?," *The Economist,* December 12, 2023.

13. M. J. Wolf et al., *Environmental Performance Index 2022: Ranking Country Performance on Sustainability Issues* (New Haven, CT: Yale Center for Environmental Law and Policy, 2022).

CHAPTER 20

1. Heather Whipps, "How Ancient Trade Changed the World," *Live Science,* February 17, 2008.

2. Adam Smith, "Of the Origin and Use of Money" in *An Inquiry into the Nature and Causes of the Wealth of Nations* (London: Methuen, 1904), p. 37.

3. Markus Lampe, "Effects of Bilateralism and the MFN Clause on International Trade: Evidence for the Cobden-Chevalier Network, 1860-1875," *Journal of Economic History* 69, no. 4 (2009): 1014–1018.

4. Douglas A. Irwin, "US Trade Policy in Historical Perspective," National Bureau of Economic Research Working Paper no. 26256, 2019, p. 5.

5. "The 128 Countries That Had Signed GATT by 1994," World Trade Organization.

6. "Trade Negotiations," in "The WTO in Brief," World Trade Organization.

7. "Members and Observers" World Trade Organization; and "Evolution of Trade under the WTO: Handy Statistics," World Trade Organization.

8. "Measuring Poverty," World Bank.

9. Michail Moatsos, "Global Extreme Poverty: Present and Past since 1820," in *How Was Life?*, vol. 2 (Paris: OECD, 2021).

10. Marian L. Tupy and Gale L. Pooley, *Superabundance: The Story of Population Growth, Innovation, and Human Flourishing on an Infinitely Bountiful Planet* (Washington: Cato Institute, 2022), pp. 370–372.

11. Tupy and Pooley, *Superabundance*, p. 371.

12. Tupy and Pooley, *Superabundance*, p. 370.

13. Biing-Hwan Lin and Rosanna Mentzer Morrison, "A Closer Look at Declining Fruit and Vegetable Consumption Using Linked Data Sources," US Department of Agriculture Economic Research Service, July 5, 2016.

14. Joanne Guthrie et al., "Understanding Economic and Behavioral Influences on Fruit and Vegetable Choices," US Department of Agriculture Economic Research Service, April 1, 2005; Lin and Morrison, "A Closer Look at Declining Fruit and Vegetable Consumption Using Linked Data Sources"; Victoria Miller et al., "Availability, Affordability, and Consumption of Fruits and Vegetables in 18 Countries across Income Levels: Findings from the Prospective Urban Rural Epidemiology (PURE) Study," *Lancet Global Health* 4 (2016): 700–701.

15. Carlos Arnade and Fred Kuchler, *Measuring the Impacts of Off-Season Berry Imports*, ERR-197 (Washington: US Department of Agriculture, Economic Research Service, 2015), pp. 18–19.

16. US International Trade Commission, "Chapter 7: Edible Vegetables and Certain Roots and Tubes," in *Harmonized Tariff Schedule of the United States* (Washington: US International Trade Commission, 1993), p. 7-4.

17. Tupy and Pooley, *Superabundance*, p. 167.

18. Scott Lincicome, "The Joy and Luxury of Growing Food for Fun," *The Dispatch*, June 9, 2021.

19. Scott Lincicome, "Globalization Isn't Going Anywhere," Defending Globalization, Cato Institute, September 12, 2023.

20. Lincicome, "Globalization Isn't Going Anywhere."

21. Harriet Tory, "Where to Find a $4-an-Hour Math Tutor with a Ph.D.? Overseas," *Wall Street Journal*, August 6, 2023.

22. Chris Koerner (@mhp_guy), "Last night my 12 year old was struggling with Algebra," X post, March 21, 2023, 10:15 a.m.

23. Stephanie H. Murray, "The Other Work Remote Workers Get Done," *The Atlantic*, September 1, 2023.

24. Derek Thompson, "The Surprising Effects of Remote Work," *The Atlantic*, March 7, 2023.

25. "Information Technology Agreement," World Trade Organization; and Stephen Ezell and Trelysa Long, *How Expanding the Information Technology Agreement to an 'ITA-3' Would Bolster Nations' Economic Growth* (Washington: Information Technology and Innovation Foundation, 2023).

26. Jason Dedrick and Kenneth L. Kraemer, "Intangible Assets and Value Capture in Global Value Chains: The Smartphone Industry," World Intellectual Property Organization Working Paper no. 41, 2017, pp. 1–9; and Jason Dedrick, Greg Linden, and Kenneth L. Kraemer, "We Estimate China Only Makes $8.46

from an iPhone—and That's Why Trump's Trade War Is Futile," *The Conversation*, July 6, 2018; and Jason Dedrick, Greg Linden, and Kenneth L. Kraemer, "We Estimate China Only Makes $8.46 from an iPhone—and That's Why Trump's Trade War Is Futile," *The Conversation*, July 6, 2018..

27. Gale Pooley, "Laptops Galore," *Gale Winds* (blog), Substack, November 7, 2023.

28. Christopher Mims, "How the Pandemic Broke Silicon Valley's Stranglehold on Tech Jobs," *Wall Street Journal*, March 12, 2022.

29. "What Many Importers Don't Know about Liability Insurance," Sadler Insurance.

30. "Cargo Insurance," UPS.

31. "Multinational Business Coverage," The Hartford.

32. "Welcome: Explore the Ways Your International Benefit Plan Can Help You Thrive," UnitedHealthcare Global, 2022, p. 8.

33. Kasey Moore, "Does Netflix Have Too Much Foreign Content?" What's on Netflix, August 5, 2020.

34. Todd Spangler, "'Squid Game' Is Decisively Netflix No. 1 Show of All Time with 1.65 Billion Hours Streamed in First Four Weeks, Company Says," *Variety*, November 16, 2021.

35. Jin Dal Yong, *New Korean Wave: Transnational Cultural Power in the Age of Social Media* (Champaign, IL: University of Illinois Press, 2016), pp. 3–39.

36. August Brown, "K-Pop Enters American Pop Consciousness," *Los Angeles Times*, April 29, 2012.

37. Kai Curry, "The Korean Wave Brings All Things Korean to the US," *Northwest Asian Weekly*, May 2, 2023.

38. Hun Kim et al., "The Impact of Korean Wave on the Distribution of Consumer Good Exports," *Journal of Distribution Science* 19, no. 4 (2021): 49.

39. James Langenfeld and James F. Nieberding, "The Benefits of Free Trade to US Consumers," *Business Economics* (2005): 41.

40. Gary Clyde Hufbauer and Zhiyao (Lucy) Lu, "The Payoff to America from Globalization: A Fresh Look with a Focus on Costs to Workers," Peterson Institute for International Economics Policy Brief, updated May 2017, p. 18.

41. Lawrence J. Lau and Junjie Tang, "The Impact of US Imports from China on US Consumer Prices and Expenditures," Institute of Global Economics and Finance Working Paper no. 66, 2018, pp. 10–27; and Scott Lincicome, "Testing the 'China Shock': Was Normalizing Trade with China a Mistake?," Cato Institute Policy Analysis no. 895, July 8, 2020.

42. Scott Winship and Jeremy Horpedahl, "The Cost of Thriving Has Fallen: Correcting and Rejecting the American Compass Cost-of-Thriving Index," American Enterprise Institute, June 22, 2023.

43. Mark J. Perry, "Chart of the Day . . . or Century?," American Enterprise Institute, July 23, 2022.

44. Gabriella Beaumont-Smith, "Essential Goods," in *Empowering the New American Worker: Market-Based Solutions for Today's Workforce* (Washington: Cato Institute, 2022).

45. Ryan Bourne, "Government and the Cost of Living: Income-Based vs. Cost-Based Approaches to Alleviating Poverty," Cato Institute Policy Analysis no. 847, September 4, 2018.

46. Gabriella Beaumont-Smith, "Trade in Real Life: Why You Should Oppose Shoe Tariffs with Your Heart and Sole," *Cato at Liberty* (blog), Cato Institute, March 20, 2023.

47. Ed Gresser, *Trade Policy, Equity, and the Working Poor: United States MFN Tariffs Are Regressive Taxes Which Help Few Workers and Harm Many* (Washington: Progressive Policy Institute, 2022), p. 6.

48. Scott Lincicome, Gabriella Beaumont-Smith, and Alfredo Carillo Obregon, "Formula for a Crisis: Protectionism and Supply Chain Resiliency—the Infant Formula Case Study," Cato Institute Briefing Paper no. 146, January 11, 2023.

49. Miguel Acosta and Lydia Cox, "The Regressive Nature of the US Tariff Code: Origins and Implications," working paper, 2024.

50. J. Gourdon, "CEPII NTM-MAP: A Tool for Assessing the Economic Impact of Non-Tariff Measures," Centre for Prospective Studies and International Information Working Paper no. 2014–24, 2014, pp. 3–4.

51. Gabriella Beaumont-Smith, "Do No Harm: Tariffs and Quotas Hurt the Homeland," Heritage Foundation Backgrounder no. 3413, May 30, 2019, pp. 5–6.

52. Catherine DeFilippo, *Antidumping and Countervailing Duty Handbook*, 14th ed. (Washington: US International Trade Commission, 2015), p. A-4.

53. "The Uruguay Round," World Trade Organization.

54. Gary Clyde Hufbauer and Megan Hogan, "How Do Digital Services Taxes Work?," Peterson Institute for International Economics, March 8, 2022.

55. Lionel Gerard Fontagne, Amelie Guillin, and Cristina Mitaritonna, "Estimations of Tariff Equivalents for the Services Sectors," Centre for Prospective Studies and International Information Working Paper no. 2011-24, 2012, p. 9.

56. David L. Hummels and Georg Schaur, "Time as Trade Barrier," *American Economic Review* 103, no. 7 (2013): 2935–39.

57. Polina Ustyuzhanina, "In Goods We Trust: Trade Barriers in Services—Should We Care?" (master's thesis, Orebro University, 2017), pp. 3–4.

58. Adam Smith, *An Inquiry into the Nature and Causes of the Wealth of Nations* (Edinburgh: Adam and Charles Black, 1863), p. 298.

CHAPTER 21

1. Liam James, "Mountains of Clothes Washed Up on Ghana Beach Show Cost of Fast Fashion," *The Independent*, July 27, 2022.

2. "UN Alliance Aims to Put Fashion on Path to Sustainability," United Nations Economic Commission for Europe, July 12, 2018.

3. Elizabeth L. Cline, *Overdressed: The Shockingly High Cost of Cheap Fashion* (New York: Penguin Group, 2013).

4. Luke Leitch, "Jiggery-bespokery," *The Economist*, October 28, 2016.

5. Jessica Testa, "The People's Republic of Shein," *New York Times*, September 1, 2022, updated June 21, 2023.

6. Dana Thomas, *Fashionopolis: The Price of Fast Fashion and the Future of Clothes* (New York: Penguin, 2019), p. 4.

7. Paul Krugman, "Reckonings; Hearts and Heads," *New York Times*, April 22, 2001.

8. Virginia Postrel, *The Fabric of Civilization: How Textiles Made the World* (New York: Basic Books, 2021).

9. Postrel, *The Fabric of Civilization*.

10. "Occupational Employment and Wages—May 2023," US Bureau of Labor Statistics, news release, April 3, 2024.

11. Teresa C. Fort, "The Changing Firm and Country Boundaries of US Manufacturers in Global Value Chains," National Bureau of Economic Research Working Paper no. 31319, June 2023; and Pol Antràs et al., "Exporting, Global Sourcing, and Multinational Activity: Theory and Evidence from the United States," National Bureau of Economic Research Working Paper no. w31488, July 2023.

12. Johan Norberg, "Globalization's Race to the Top: A Case Study from Bangladesh," *Cato at Liberty* (blog), Cato Institute, November 9, 2023.

13. Kevin Grier, Towhid Mahmood, and Benjamin Powell, "Anti-sweatshop Activism and the Safety-Employment Tradeoff: Evidence from Bangladesh's Rana Plaza Disaster," *Journal of Economic Behavior & Organization* 208 (2023): 174–90.

14. Sanjay Kathuria, "Bangladesh Is Clothes-Minded," *Foreign Policy*, October 7, 2021.

15. Thomas, *Fashionopolis*, p. 125.

16. "Modern Slavery in Asia and the Pacific," Global Slavery Index, Walk Free, accessed April 16, 2024.

17. Elizabeth L. Cline, *Overdressed: The Shockingly High Cost of Cheap Fashion* (New York: Penguin Group, 2013).

18. Adam Minter, *Secondhand: Travels in the New Global Garage Sale* (New York: Bloomsbury Publishing, 2019).

19. Isabelle Gerretsen, "How Microplastics Are Infiltrating the Food You Eat," BBC, January 3, 2023.

20. XiaoZhi Lim, "Microplastics Are Everywhere—but Are They Harmful?," *Nature*, May 4, 2021.

21. Corina Pons and Helen Reid, "Fast Fashion Firms Prepare for EU Crackdown on Waste Mountain," Reuters, September 1, 2023.

22. Joy Buchanan, "Buy Nothing Groups," *Economist Writing Every Day* (blog), March 6, 2021.

23. Jae-Hee Chang, Gary Rynhart, and Phu Huynh, "ASEAN in Transformation: The Future of Jobs at Risk of Automation," International Labour Organization, Bureau for Employers' Activities Working Paper no. 9, 2016, p. 1.

24. Joy Buchanan, Stephen Hill, and Olga Shapoval, "ChatGPT Hallucinates Nonexistent Citations: Evidence from Economics," SSRN, November 14, 2023.

25. Soumyananda Dinda, "Environmental Kuznets Curve Hypothesis: A Survey," *Ecological Economics* 49, no. 4 (2004): 431–55.

26. Alden Wicker, "How Can Companies Recycle Clothes Back into Clothes?," *Wired*, May 18, 2023.

CHAPTER 22

1. "Miller Ingredient," Miller Lite.

2. Leah Bhabha, "The History of Sushi in the US," Food52, November 29, 2013.

3. Jaewon Kang, "How Kroger Became the Biggest Sushi Seller in America," *Wall Street Journal*, August 21, 2023.

4. Terrence McCoy, "Why Beef-Loving Brazil Is So Obsessed with an American Steakhouse Chain," *Washington Post*, June 20, 2023.

5. Brinker International, "Annual Report 2022," 2022, p.1.

6. "15 Best Places for American Breakfast in Bangkok," Bangkok Nightlife.

7. Charmaine Mok, "How Did Frozen Sara Lee Pound Cake, Seen on Netflix's Beef, Become an Asian Culinary Icon and Loved the World Over?," *South China Morning Post*, April 23, 2023.

8. "Top Takeouts: What Are the Most Popular Takeaway Choices around the World?," MoneyBeach, last modified January 11, 2021.

9. Swaminathan S. Anklesaria Aiyar, "Globalization Has Propelled India to Prosperity," Defending Globalization, Cato Institute, October 24, 2023.

10. Darren Geeter, "How Domino's Beat Papa John's and Pizza Hut in India's Pizza War," CNBC, April 28, 2020.

11. Kunwar Khuldune Shahid, "The Amazing Story of How Philly Cheesesteaks Became Huge in Lahore, Pakistan," *Philadelphia Magazine*, April 8, 2023.

12. Sara Harowitz, "Vancouver's Legendary Sushi Chef Hidekazu Tojo Invented Far More than the California Roll," *Montecristo Magazine*, December 11, 2017.

13. Alec Jordan, "Inventor of the California Roll Named 'Culinary Ambassador' by the Japanese Government," *Tokyo Weekender*, June 17, 2016, updated July 12, 2017.

14. Anna Haensch, "From Ramen to Rotini: Following the Noodles of the Silk Road," NPR, July 20, 2013.

15. Hayley Helmstetler, "The Fusion Revolution: The Evolution of Fusion Cuisine," *P Magazine*, PreGel America, Issue 8, December 19, 2016.

16. Suthon Sukphisit, "Chilli's Complicated History," *Bangkok Post*, *B*, May 5, 2019.

17. Susan Gough Henly, "Australian Cuisine Is a Delicious Mix: A Worldly Flavor Fusion," *New York Times*, September 15, 2000.

18. "Guyana—Food and Drink," Goway Travel.

19. Tahmineh Dehbozorgi (@DeTahmineh), "Fun Fact: did you know that 'Kentucky' has turned into a verb in Farsi, meaning 'to bread and fry a chicken'?," X post, April 15, 2024, 10:15 a.m.

20. Lauren Shamo, "Hidden Racism in Your Supermarket's Ethnic Food Aisle," *Business Insider*, October 30, 2020.

21. Cathy Erway, "All Hail the Asian Supermarket: An American Institution," *TASTE*, October 15, 2018.

22. Wilma V. Davis and Gary Lucier, "US Fresh Vegetable Imports from Mexico and Canada Continue to Surge," *Amber Waves* (blog), US Department of Agriculture, November 8, 2021.

23. Tom Karst, "Mexico's Dominance in Imports Is Revealed in USDA Statistics," The Packer, January 30, 2023.

24. *The State of Agricultural Commodity Markets 2022: Global and Regional Trade Networks, Part 1: Global and Regional Trade Networks* (Rome: Food and Agriculture Organization of the United Nations, 2022).

25. Alan Beattie, "Global Food Crisis That Resolutely Fails to Happen," *Financial Times*, July 24, 2023.

26. Scott Lincicome, "A(nother) Case Study of Terrible US Tariff Policy," *The Dispatch*, July 19, 2023.

27. "US Agricultural Trade at a Glance," US Department of Agriculture.

28. "Get the Facts: Five Ways Immigrants Drive the Essential Economy," Americas Society/Council of the Americas, June 26, 2014.

29. "Table 4. Employed Foreign-Born and Native-Born Persons 16 Years and Over by Occupation and Sex, 2022 Annual Averages," news release, US Bureau of Labor Statistics, last modified May 18, 2023.

30. "Selected Social Characteristics in the United States," 2022, American Community Survey, ACS 1-Year Estimates Data Profiles, Table DP02, US Census Bureau.

31. Esther Tseng, "Undocumented Workers Hold the Restaurant Industry Together. Now, They Stand to Lose the Most," Eater, May 29, 2020.

32. Alan Berube, "Three Things That Matter for Upward Mobility in the Labor Market," Brookings Institution, January 15, 2019.

33. Molly Peck, "Careers with Upward Mobility," SelectOne, December 30, 2019.

34. "National Statistics," National Restaurant Association.

35. Kyle Almond, "What It's Like in America's 'Doughnut Capital,'" CNN June 2019.

36. Greg Nichols, "Dunkin' and the Doughnut King," *California Sunday.*

37. Dennis Huspeni, "The Story, and the Woman, behind Denver's Maria Empanada," *Denver Gazette*, February 19, 2022, updated February 23, 2022.

38. "Lorena Cantarovici, Owner of Maria Empanada Named Colorado's 2017 Small Business Person of the Year Winner," US Small Business Administration, accessed April 18, 2024.

39. Jonathan Maze, "For Many Immigrants, Restaurants Are the American Dream," *Nation's Restaurant News*, March 29, 2017.

40. Bao Ong, "Polo Becerra, Who Fulfilled His American Dream as Post Oak Grill's Chef and Owner, Dies," *Houston Chronicle*, updated January 19, 2023.

41. "Our Brands," Yum China.

42. Harrison Jacobs, "KFC Is by Far the Most Popular Fast Food Chain in China and It's Nothing Like the US Brand—Here's What It's Like," *Business Insider*, March 8, 2019.

43. Thomas Erdbrink, "Iran Capitalizing on a Taste for America's Biggest Brands," *New York Times*, August 2, 2015.

44. David Bell and Mary L. Shelman, "KFC's Radical Approach to China," *Harvard Business Review*, November 2011.

45. Dee-Ann Durbin, "Once a Powerful Symbol in Russia, McDonald's Withdraws," Associated Press, March 14, 2022.

46. Jonathon Haeber, "What Is the Golden Arches Theory of Conflict Prevention?," CBS News, January 28, 2008.

47. Christian Reynolds, "The Soft Power of Food: A Diplomacy of Hamburgers and Sushi?," *Food Studies: An Interdisciplinary Journal* 1 (2012).

48. Romina Boccia, "What Bananas Tell Us about Socialism and the Fall of the Berlin Wall," Fox News, November 9, 2019.

49. Craig Hlavaty, "When Boris Yeltsin Went Grocery Shopping in Clear Lake," *Houston Chronicle*, April 7, 2014.

50. Marilyn Berger, "Boris Yeltsin, Russia's First Post-Soviet Leader, Is Dead," *New York Times*, April 23, 2007.

51. Julia Kollewe, "KFC and Pizza Hut Owner and Heineken Pause Business in Russia," *The Guardian*, March 9, 2022.

CHAPTER 23

1. Rick Porter, "'Tracker,' 'Bluey' and a Big Scripted Deficit: Hidden Numbers of the 2023–24 TV Season," *Hollywood Reporter*, May 29, 2024.

2. "Top 250 TV Shows," IMDb.

3. Jessica Beck, Thomas Lu, and David Gura, "*Bluey*: A Blue Heeler Worth $2 Billion," Bloomberg, April 12, 2014.

4. Neil Anderson, "More than Half of Netflix's Content Spending Now Outside of North America," *Ampere Analysis*, March 11, 2024.

5. William Goldman, *Adventures in the Screen Trade: A Personal View of Hollywood and Screenwriting* (New York: Grand Central Publishing, 1983).

6. Nic Fildes, "How Australia's 'Bluey' Conquered Children's Entertainment," *Financial Times,* December 31, 2023.

7. Richard Caves, *Creative Industries: Contracts between Art and Commerce*, rev. ed. (Cambridge, MA: Harvard University Press, 2002), p. 3.

8. Alan Horn quoted by Kelefa Sanneh, "Blockbluster," *New Yorker*, November 24, 2013.

9. Edward Jay Epstein, *The Big Picture: Money and Power in Hollywood*, rev. ed. (New York: Random House, 2006).

10. Hardol L. Vogel, *Entertainment Industry Economics: A Guide for Financial Analysis*, 9th ed. (Cambridge: Cambridge University Press, 2014), p. 163.

11. Paul Matzko, "Jimmy Carter vs. the Fairness Doctrine," *Matzko Minute* (blog), March 13, 2023.

12. Joel Waldfogel, *Digital Renaissance: What Data and Economics Tell Us about the Future of Popular Culture* (Princeton: Princeton University Press, 2018), pp. 80–82.

13. Joel Waldfogel, *Digital Renaissance: What Data and Economics Tell Us about the Future of Popular Culture* (Princeton: Princeton University Press, 2018), p. 13.

14. Christian Roemer, "Fun Facts about Film Reels," *Analog: A Legacybox Blog.*

15. Michael D. Smith and Rahul Telang, *Streaming, Sharing, Stealing: Big Data and the Future of Entertainment* (Cambridge, MA: MIT Press, 2017), p. 103; and

Joel Waldfogel, *Digital Renaissance: What Data and Economics Tell Us about the Future of Popular Culture* (Princeton, NJ: Princeton University Press, 2018), p. 84.

16. Sherry Sontag, "Film Editing Goes Electronic," *New York Times*, October 19, 1986.

17. Jefferson Graham, "Talking Your Tech: Edward Burns Delivers Small Films Straight to You," *USA Today*, December 18, 2012; and Kevin EG Perry, "Francis Ford Coppola: 'Apocalypse Now is Not an Anti-War Film,'" *The Guardian*, August 9, 2019.

18. Joel Waldfogel, *Digital Renaissance: What Data and Economics Tell Us about the Future of Popular Culture* (Princeton, NJ: Princeton University Press, 2018), p. 242.

19. Joel Waldfogel, *Digital Renaissance: What Data and Economics Tell Us about the Future of Popular Culture* (Princeton, NJ: Princeton University Press, 2018), p. 178.

20. Michael D. Smith and Rahul Telang, *Streaming, Sharing, Stealing: Big Data and the Future of Entertainment* (Cambridge, MA: MIT Press, 2017), p. 5.

21. Paul R. La Monica, "'House of Cards' Made Netflix a Powerhouse. What Now?," *CNN Business*, November 1, 2017.

22. Antonios Vlassis, "Soft Power, Global Governance of Cultural Industries and Rising Powers: The Case of China," *International Journal of Cultural Policy* 22, no. 4 (January 2015): 8.

23. Laura Carollo, "Number of Movie Tickets Sold in the United States and Canada from 2001 to 2023," *Statista*, May 28, 2024.

24. "Avatar (2009)," Box Office Mojo.

25. Ben Fritz, *The Big Picture: The Fight for the Future of Movies* (Boston: Houghton Mifflin Harcourt, 2018), p. 209.

26. Production and marketing costs are contested. See Josh Dickey, "'Avatar's' True Cost—and Consequences," *The Wrap*, December 3, 2009.

27. Ben Fritz, *The Big Picture: The Fight for the Future of Movies* (Boston: Houghton Mifflin Harcourt, 2018), pp. 204–205.

28. John Plunkett and Jason Deans, "Kevin Spacey: Television Has Entered a New Golden Age," *The Guardian*, August 22, 2013.

29. Manohla Dargis, "As Indies Explode, an Appeal for Sanity," *New York Times*, January 9, 2014.

30. Douglas Fraser, "Upbeat about Le Download," *BBC News*, June 14, 2013; and Darrin McMahon, "Echoes of a Recent Past: Contemporary French Anti-Americanism in Cultural and Historical Perspective," Historical Roots of Contemporary International and Regional Issues Occasional Paper Series, no. 6. International Security Studies, Yale University, cited in Fernando Ferreira and Joel Waldfogel, "Pop Internationalism: Has A Half Century of World Music Trade Displaced Local Culture?," *Economic Journal* 123, no. 569 (June 2013): 634–64

31. Faultline, "There's Nothing on TV in Europe—American Video Dominates," *The Register,* July 21, 2014.

32. Joel Waldfogel, *Digital Renaissance: What Data and Economics Tell Us about the Future of Popular Culture* (Princeton, NJ: Princeton University Press, 2018), p. 245.

33. Adam Mastroianni, "Pop Culture Has Become an Oligopoly," *Experimental History* (blog), May 2, 2022.

34. Joel Waldfogel, *Digital Renaissance: What Data and Economics Tell Us about the Future of Popular Culture* (Princeton, NJ: Princeton University Press, 2018), pp. 92–93, 110–111.

35. Joel Waldfogel, *Digital Renaissance: What Data and Economics Tell Us about the Future of Popular Culture* (Princeton, NJ: Princeton University Press, 2018), pp. 100–101, 112, 116.

36. Michael D. Smith and Rahul Telang, *Streaming, Sharing, Stealing: Big Data and the Future of Entertainment* (Cambridge, MA: MIT Press, 2017), p. 7.

37. Ben Fritz, *The Big Picture: The Fight for the Future of Movies* (Boston: Houghton Mifflin Harcourt, 2018), p. xviii.

38. Alejandro Zentner, Michael Smith, and Cuneyd Kaya, "How Video Rental Patterns Change as Consumers Move Online," *Management Science* 59, no.11 (November 2013): 2622–34.

39. Alexis C. Madrigal, "When Did TV Watching Peak?," *The Atlantic*, May 30, 2018.

40. Laura Ceci, "Hours of Video Uploaded to YouTube Every Minute as of February 2022," *Statista*, June 2022. Estimated time spent based on US average of 912 waking minutes a day multiplied times the average US lifespan of 27,375 days divided by 30,000 minutes of YouTube content a minute. See Esteban Ortiz-Ospina, Charlie Giattino, and Max Roser, "Time Use," *Our World in Data*, revised in February 2024.

41. Ted Gioia, "The State of the Culture, 2024," *Honest Broker* (blog), February 18, 2024.

42. Andrew Keen, *The Cult of the Amateur: How Blogs, MySpace, YouTube, and the Rest of Today's User-Generated Media are Destroying Our Economy, Our Culture, and Our Values* (New York: Doubleday, 2007), pp. 2–3, 9, 14, 35.

43. F. A. Hayek, "The Use of Knowledge in Society," *American Economic Review* 35, no. 4 (September 1945): 519–30.

44. Matteo Wong, "Neal Stephenson's Most Stunning Prediction," *The Atlantic*, February 6, 2024.

45. Jason Horowitz and Taylor Lorenz, "Khaby Lame, the Everyman of the Internet," *New York Times*, June 2, 2021.

46. Kayla Cobb and Lucas Manfredi, "YouTube TV Is Thriving in the Cable Replacement Space as a 'One-Stop Shop' for Consumers," *Wrap Pro*, March 12, 2024.

47. Ben Fritz, *The Big Picture: The Fight for the Future of Movies* (Boston: Houghton Mifflin Harcourt, 2018), p. 240.

48. Michael Strangelove, *Watching YouTube: Extraordinary Videos by Ordinary People* (Toronto: University of Toronto Press, 2010), p. 4.

49. Ben Fritz, *The Big Picture: The Fight for the Future of Movies* (Boston: Houghton Mifflin Harcourt, 2018), pp. xxiv–xxv.

50. Matteo Wong, "Neal Stephenson's Most Stunning Prediction," *The Atlantic*, February 6, 2024.

51. Google, "Filmmaking with Donald Glover and His Creative Studio, Gilga | Veo," video, YouTube, 1 min., 37 sec., May 14, 2024.

52. Stuart Cunningham and David Craig, *Social Media Entertainment: The New Intersection of Hollywood and Silicon Valley* (New York: NYU Press, 2019), p. 223

53. Richard Wilk, "Learning to Be Local in Belize: Global Systems of Common Difference," in Daniel Miller, ed. *Worlds Apart: Modernity through the Prism of the Local* (New York: Routledge, 1995), p. 118.

54. Jin-Wook Shin, "The Reality behind Squid Game," *International Politics and Society*, August 12, 2021.

55. Alexander Ross, *The Evolution of Hollywood's Calculated Blockbuster Films: Blockbusted* (Lanham, MD: Lexington Books, 2023), loc. 4775, Kindle.

56. Amanda Silberling, "Is MrBeast Actually Worth $1.5 Billion?," *TechCrunch*, October 25, 2022.

57. MrBeast, "$456,000 Squid Game in Real Life," video, YouTube, 25 min., 41 sec., November 24, 2021; and "Top Lifetime Adjusted Grosses," Box Office Mojo, data as of August 28, 2024.

58. Abigail Ong-Pizarro, "Squid Game Creator Gives His Thoughts on MrBeast's YouTube Version," *ScreenRant*, December 4, 2021.

59. Andrew Keen, *The Cult of the Amateur: How Blogs, MySpace, YouTube, and the Rest of Today's User-Generated Media are Destroying Our Economy, Our Culture, and Our Values* (New York: Doubleday, 2007), pp. 29–30.

CHAPTER 24

1. Larisha Paul, "Ticketmaster France Couldn't Handle Taylor Swift Demand Either," *Rolling Stone*, July 11, 2023.

2. Jon Emont, "Taylor Swift's Asia Tour Stirs Some Bad Blood," *Wall Street Journal*, March 1, 2024.

3. *Encyclopaedia Britannica*, "Rock and Roll," by Greg Kot, updated August 1, 2024.

4. Sam Lebovic, "'Here, There and Everywhere': The Beatles, America, and Cultural Globalization, 1964–1968," *Journal of American Studies* 51, no. 1 (February 2017): 50–51.

5. *Encyclopaedia Britannica*, "The Beatles," by James E. Miller, updated August 25, 2024.

6. "History of the Beatles' Childhood Homes," National Trust; and John Boughton, "A Housing History of the Beatles: Three 'Working-Class Heroes' and John," *Municipal Dreams* (blog), August 30, 2016.

7. Sam Lebovic, "'Here, There and Everywhere': The Beatles, America, and Cultural Globalization, 1964–1968," *Journal of American Studies* 51, no. 1 (February 2017): 48, 50–51.

8. Alice Broome, "65 Years: The Quarrymen, Who Later Became the Beatles, Record Their First Demo in Liverpool," British Online Archives, July 12, 2023.

9. Sam Lebovic, "'Here, There and Everywhere': The Beatles, America, and Cultural Globalization, 1964–1968," *Journal of American Studies* 51, no. 1 (February 2017): 49.

10. Sam Lebovic, "'Here, There and Everywhere': The Beatles, America, and Cultural Globalization, 1964–1968," *Journal of American Studies* 51, no. 1 (February 2017): 50.

11. John Lennon et al., *The Beatles Anthology* (San Francisco: Chronicle Books, 2000), p. 45.

12. Sam Lebovic, "'Here, There and Everywhere': The Beatles, America, and Cultural Globalization, 1964–1968," *Journal of American Studies* 51, no. 1 (February 2017): 51.

13. Sam Lebovic, "'Here, There and Everywhere': The Beatles, America, and Cultural Globalization, 1964–1968," *Journal of American Studies* 51, no. 1 (February 2017): 51.

14. "The Beatles Arrive in New York," This Day In History, History, updated February 5, 2024.

15. Tom Petty, "Tom Petty: The Beatles on Ed Sullivan 'Changed Everything,'" Grammy, Recording Academy, February 8, 2014.

16. Sam Lebovic, "'Here, There and Everywhere': The Beatles, America, and Cultural Globalization, 1964–1968," *Journal of American Studies* 51, no. 1 (February 2017): 43.

17. Sam Lebovic, "'Here, There and Everywhere': The Beatles, America. and Cultural Globalization, 1964–1968," *Journal of American Studies* 51, no. 1 (February 2017): 52.

18. Sam Lebovic, "'Here, There and Everywhere': The Beatles, America. and Cultural Globalization, 1964–1968," *Journal of American Studies* 51, no. 1 (February 2017): 52.

19. Gail Cameron, "Yeah-Yeah-Yeah! Beatlemania Becomes a Part of US History," *Life*, February 21, 1964, pp. 34A–34B.

20. Herm Schoenfeld, "Britannia Rules Airwaves: Beatles Stir Home Carbons," *Variety*, February 12, 1964. p. 63.

21. "Beatles Record Sales around the World," BeatlesRadio.com.

22. Sam Lebovic, "'Here, There and Everywhere': The Beatles, America, and Cultural Globalization, 1964–1968," *Journal of American Studies* 51, no. 1 (February 2017): 55.

23. Wikipedia, "List of the Beatles' Live Performances," updated August 1, 2024.

24. Wikipedia, "List of the Beatles' Live Performances," updated August 1, 2024.

25. Wikipedia, "List of the Beatles' Live Performances," updated August 1, 2024.

26. Sam Lebovic, "'Here, There and Everywhere': The Beatles, America, and Cultural Globalization, 1964–1968," *Journal of American Studies* 51, no. 1 (February 2017): 51.

27. Jordan Runtagh, "When John Lennon's 'More Popular than Jesus' Controversy Turned Ugly," *Rolling Stone*, July 29, 2016.

28. Matthew Hernon, "The Fab Four, 50 Years Back: Looking Back on the Beatles Historic Show at the Budokan," *Tokyo Weekender*, updated July 12, 2017.

29. Sam Lebovic, "'Here, There and Everywhere': The Beatles, America, and Cultural Globalization, 1964–1968," *Journal of American Studies* 51, no. 1 (February 2017): 55.

30. Rodrigo Guerrero, "The Role of the Beatles in Popularizing Indian Music and Culture in the West," *The Owl* 5, no. 1 (Spring 2015): 33.

31. Rodrigo Guerrero, "The Role of the Beatles in Popularizing Indian Music and Culture in the West," *The Owl* 5, no. 1 (Spring 2015): 33.

32. David R. Reck, "Beatles Orientalis: Influences from Asia in a Popular Song Tradition," *Asian Music* 16, no. 1 (1985): 102.

33. Rodrigo Guerrero, "The Role of the Beatles in Popularizing Indian Music and Culture in the West," *The Owl* 5, no. 1 (Spring 2015): 34–35.

34. Claire Hoffman, "How the Beatles in India Changed America," *Rolling Stone*, February 16, 2018.

35. Tina Benitez-Eves, "Behind the Song Meaning: How Brian Jones' Sitar Transformed 'Paint It Black' by the Rolling Stones," *American Songwriter*, updated March 24, 2022.

36. Rodrigo Guerrero, "The Role of the Beatles in Popularizing Indian Music and Culture in the West," *The Owl* 5, no. 1 (Spring 2015): 37.

37. Claire Hoffman, "How the Beatles in India Changed America," *Rolling Stone*, February 16, 2018.

38. Gary Tillery, *Working Class Mystic: A Spiritual Biography of George Harrison* (Wheaton, IL: Quest Books, 2011), p. 151.

39. Philip Goldberg, *American Veda: From Emerson and the Beatles to Yoga and Meditation; How Indian Spirituality Changed the West* (New York: Harmony Books, 2010), p. 7.

40. Andrew Grant Jackson, *1965: The Most Revolutionary Year in Music* (New York: Thomas Dunne Books, 2015), p. 282.

41. Rob Hughes, "Ten Bands Who Owe It All to the Beatles," *Louder*, August 15, 2019; Holden McNeely, "Making Masterpieces: The Beach Boys and the Beatles Inspired Each Other," *CultureSonar*, August 26, 2017; Blair Jackson, *Garcia: An American Life* (New York: Penguin Books, 1999), p. 67; André Millard, *Beatlemania: Technology, Business, and Teen Culture in Cold War America* (Baltimore: Johns Hopkins University Press, 2012), p. 36; "The Sad Passing of Glenn Frey: The Beatles Inspired Him to Be a Rock Musician," BeatlesHistorian.com, January 20, 2016; Joe Taysom, "The 'Raucous' Beatles Song That Changed Bruce Springsteen's Life," *Far Out*, September 20, 2022; Tom Petty, "Tom Petty: The Beatles on Ed Sullivan 'Changed Everything,'" Grammys, February 8, 2014; Larry Widen, "7 Questions for Singer-Songwriter Jackson Browne," *OnMilwaukee*, November 10, 2015; Frank Mastropolo, "Top 11 Musicians Influenced by the Beatles," *Rock Cellar*, February 4, 2014; Callum Crumlish, "Michael Jackson Honoured John Lennon by Singing a Beatles Song Years after His Death," *Express*, December 10, 2020; Jacob Uitti, "The Story behind Michael Jackson Buying the Beatles' Catalog and Angering Friend Paul McCartney," *American Songwriter*, updated September 30, 2022; Alexandre G., "Kurt Cobain's and the Beatles Influence: From 'About a Girl' to 'All Apologies,'" Musiclipse.com, January 24, 2024; Tom Taylor, "The Song Played at Kurt Cobain's Funeral," *Far Out*, May 9, 2022; and Tyler Golsen, "The Two Artists Neil Young Said Were 'Way Beyond' Everybody Else," *Far Out*, August 28, 2024.

42. Dana Rose Falcone, "Taylor Swift Names Her Top 3 Influences—and Yes, Her Two Cats Make the List," *People*, April 25, 2019.

43. Liberty Dunworth, "Keith Richards on How the Rolling Stones Were 'Envious' of the Beatles during Their Early Days: 'They Were Doing What We Wanted,'" *Guitar.com*, July 15, 2022; Tim Coffman, "The Beatles Trick That Inspired an Iconic Led Zeppelin Song," *Far Out*, December 15, 2023; Drew Wardle, "The Day Pink Floyd Met the Beatles," *Far Out*, February 22, 2022; Arun Starkey, "When Eric Clapton Called the Beatles 'Inspiring,'" *Far Out*, April 20, 2022; Rob

Hughes, "Ten Bands Who Owe It All to the Beatles," *Louder*, August 15, 2019; and Kieran McGovern, "From Fan Boy to Fame," *The Beatles FAQ* (blog), December 2, 2019.

44. Wikipedia, "List of Spotify Streaming Records," updated August 29, 2024.

45. Simrin Singh, "Taylor Swift, Bad Bunny Helped Drive over 4 Trillion Global Music Streams in 2023, Report Finds," *CBS News*, January 10, 2024.

46. Ingrid Lunden, "Apple Closes Its $400M Shazam Acquisition and Says the Music Recognition App Will Soon Become Ad Free," *TechCrunch*, September 24, 2018.

47. Psy, "Gangnam Style," video, YouTube, July 15, 2012; and Raisa Bruner, "BTS Explains Why They're Not Going to Start Singing in English," *Time*, March 28, 2019.

48. Jem Aswad, "Bad Bunny, the Weeknd Top Spotify's Year-End 'Wrapped' Lists," *Variety*, November 30, 2020; Mark Savage, "Apple and Spotify Reveal 2021's Most-Streamed Songs," BBC, December 1, 2021; and Todd Spangler "Spotify Launches Wrapped 2022: Bad Bunny, Taylor Swift Are Most-Streamed Artists of the Year," *Variety*, November 30, 2022.

49. "The Top Songs, Artists, Podcasts, and Listening Trends of 2023 Revealed," Spotify, November 29, 2023.

50. Daniela Avila, "Bad Bunny, Taylor Swift and Drake Are the Most-Streamed Artists on Spotify Globally," *People*, November 30, 2022; and Vicki Newman, "Spotify Wrapped 2023: Bad Bunny Claims Most Streamed Album with Un Verano Sin Ti," Guiness World Records, December 19, 2023.

51. Simrin Singh, "Taylor Swift, Bad Bunny Helped Drive over 4 Trillion Global Music Streams in 2023, Report Finds," *CBS News*, January 10, 2024.

52. Sara Fischer, "Exclusive: TelevisaUnivision Will Air First-Ever US Bilingual Award Show," *Axios*, April 23, 2024.

53. Matthew Bass, "Year-End 2023 Latin RIAA Revenue Statistics," Recording Industry Association of America, April 2024.

54. Matthew Bass, "Year-End 2023 Latin RIAA Revenue Statistics," Recording Industry Association of America, April 2024.

55. Simrin Singh, "Taylor Swift, Bad Bunny Helped Drive over 4 Trillion Global Music Streams in 2023, Report Finds," *CBS News*, January 10, 2024.

56. Amy Young, "The Beatles Were First Example of Modern Globalization," News and Events paper no. 2330, Illinois Wesleyan University, 2014.

57. Russell Hotten, "The Beatles at 50: From Fab Four to Fabulously Wealthy," *BBC News*, October 4, 2012.

58. "The 500 Greatest Albums of All Time," *Rolling Stone*, December 31, 2023.

CHAPTER 25

1. Patrick McGee, "Is It Over for the Console?," *Financial Times*, September 25, 2020; and Krishan Arora, "The Gaming Industry: A Behemoth with Unprecedented Global Reach," *Forbes*, November 17, 2023.

2. Jules Herd, "The Global Surge of Independent Games Development Studios," *Forbes*, August 21, 2023.

3. Joakim Henningson, "The History of PlayerUnknown's Battlegrounds," Red Bull, August 27, 2020.

4. Evgeny Obedkov, "Fortnite Generated Over $20 Billion in Lifetime Revenue, According to Its Co-Creator Donald Mustard," Game World Observer, November 21, 2023.

5. "Video Games—Worldwide: Revenue," Statista.

6. Martin Grueber and Dylan Yetter, *Video Games in the 21st Century: The 2024 Economic Impact Report* (Washington: Entertainment Software Association, 2024), p. 15.

7. "Video Games—Worldwide: Revenue," Statista.

8. "Video Games—Worldwide: Users," Statista.

9. Scott Lanman and Stephanie Flanders, "What Fortnite Teaches Us about Globalization," Bloomberg, April 4, 2019.

10. Shirin Ghaffary, "OpenAI's Secret Weapon Is Sam Altman's 33-Year-Old Lieutenant," Bloomberg, February 9, 2024.

11. "'Halo 3' Hits Stores Prompting All-Night Lines," ABC, September 25, 2007.

12. Wes Fenlon, "How Among Us Became So Wildly Popular," PC Gamer, September 24, 2020; and Ryan Browne, "How Fall Guys, a Battle Royale Game with Jelly Beans, Became This Summer's Mega Hit," CNBC, September 7, 2020.

13. "Supercharge Your Game Globally: Read the 2020 Mobile Games Advertising Report," Meta Audience Network, July 28, 2020.

14. Evan Elkins, "Console Games: How Regional Lockout Shaped the Video Game Industry," in *Locked Out: Regional Restrictions in Digital Entertainment Culture* (New York: NYU Press, 2019).

15. Rafly G., "PS5 Games Will No Longer Be Region-Locked, Sony Confirms," *iTechPost*, November 9, 2020; and Kern Campbell, "Is the Xbox Series X Region-Locked?," The Gadget Buyer, August 18, 2023.

16. "The Growth of Gaming and the Role of Influencers in the Gaming Industry," Influencer Marketing Hub, June 2, 2022; "The Witcher," IMDB; and "52 Video Game Movies Ranked by Tomatometer," Rotten Tomatoes.

17. Tom Daniels, "The Most Viewed Esports Events of 2023," Esports Insider, December 20, 2023.

18. Hyun Young Yi and Hyunsu Yim, "Thousands Attend League of Legends World Finals in South Korea," Reuters, November 20, 2023.

19. "Apex Legends Global Series: 2023 Championship," Liquipedia; "2023 World Championship," Liquipedia; "Blast.tv Paris Major 2023," Liquipedia; "M5 World Championship," Liquipedia; and "Fortnite Championship Series 2023—Global Championship," Liquipedia.

20. Matt Gardner, "The Top 10 Twitch Streamers and Games of 2021 So Far," *Forbes*, July 17, 2021.

21. Alex Tsiaoussidis, "Most Lucrative Streamer Deals: Biggest Streaming Contracts Signed by xQc, Amouranth, More," Dot Esports, June 22, 2023; and Adam Straker, "Ibai Reveals Where He Will Continue Streaming after the Million-Dollar Contracts to Switch to Kick," www.gearrice.com, June 20, 2023.

22. Carver Fisher, "Ibai Llanos Breaks Twitch Viewers Record with La Velada del Año 3," Dexerto, July 1, 2023.

23. "Most Watched Twitch Channels—Stats and Analytics," SullyGnome.

About the Contributors

JAMES BACCHUS is Distinguished University Professor of Global Affairs and director of the Center for Global Economic and Environmental Opportunity at the University of Central Florida. He was a founding judge and was twice the chairman of the Appellate Body of the World Trade Organization in Geneva, Switzerland. He is also the author of several books, including *Trade Links: New Rules for a New World* (2022) and *Truth about Trade: Reflections on International Trade and Law* (2023).

SOPHIA BAGLEY is a research associate for economic policy at the Cato Institute. Prior to her time at Cato, she worked in the US Senate on transportation and technology policy. Bagley received her BS in quantitative analysis of markets and organizations at the University of Utah in 2021.

GABRIELLA BEAUMONT-SMITH was a policy analyst at the Cato Institute's Herbert A. Stiefel Center for Trade Policy Studies, where her research focused on the economics of US trade policy. Previously, Beaumont-Smith was a senior policy analyst in trade and macroeconomics at the Heritage Foundation, where she developed trade models to analyze extant trade policies such as tariffs.

DONALD J. BOUDREAUX is a professor of economics at George Mason University in Fairfax, Virginia and senior fellow at George

Mason's Mercatus Center. He is the author of *Globalization* (2008) and is published in the *Wall Street Journal*, the *New York Times*, *Regulation*, and *Reason*, as well as scholarly journals including the *Supreme Court Economic Review*, *Southern Economic Journal*, *Antitrust Bulletin*, the *Cato Journal*, and the *Journal of Money, Credit, and Banking*. He blogs at CafeHayek.com.

JOY BUCHANAN is an associate professor of quantitative analysis and economics at Samford University's Brock School of Business. Her research is in behavioral economics with a focus on applying experimental methods to issues in the labor market. Her articles have appeared in peer-reviewed journals, including *Labour Economics* and *Experimental Economics*.

JAMES A. DORN is senior fellow emeritus at the Cato Institute and served as editor of the *Cato Journal* from 1982 to 2022. He has written widely on Federal Reserve policy and monetary reform and has edited more than 10 books, including *The Search for Stable Money: Essays on Monetary Reform* (with Anna J. Schwartz, 1987); *China in the New Millennium: Market Reforms and Social Development* (1998); *The Future of Money in the Information Age* (2012); *Monetary Alternatives: Rethinking Government Fiat Money* (2017); *Monetary Policy in an Uncertain World: Ten Years after the Crisis* (2018); and *Populism and the Future of the Fed* (2022).

DANIEL W. DREZNER is Distinguished Professor of International Politics at the Fletcher School of Law and Diplomacy at Tufts University. He is the author of several books, including *All Politics Is Global: Explaining International Regulatory Regimes* (2007) and *Theories of International Politics and Zombies* (2011). He has received fellowships from the German Marshall Fund of the United States, the Council on Foreign Relations, and Harvard University's Olin Center for Strategic Studies.

CHELSEA FOLLETT is a policy analyst at the Cato Institute's Center for Global Liberty and Prosperity, and the managing editor of HumanProgress.org, a project of the Cato Institute that seeks to educate the public on global improvements in well-being by providing free empirical data on long-term developments. She is the author of *Centers of Progress: 40 Cities That Changed the World* (2023).

ANDREAS FREYTAG is a professor of economics at the Friedrich Schiller University Jena, an honorary professor at the University of Stellenbosch, and a visiting professor at the Institute of International Trade at the University of Adelaide. He obtained his diploma from the University of Kiel and his doctorate from the University of Cologne. He is also the director of Tutwa Europe consulting group, a member of the CESifo research network, a Stellenbosch Institute for Advanced Study fellow, a senior research fellow at the European Centre for International Political Economy, and a senior research associate at the South African Institute of International Affairs.

COLIN GRABOW is the associate director of the Cato Institute's Herbert A. Stiefel Center for Trade Policy Studies, where his research focuses on domestic forms of trade protectionism, such as the Jones Act and the US sugar program. He is the coeditor of *The Case against the Jones Act* (2020).

DANIEL GRISWOLD is an adjunct scholar at the Cato Institute specializing in trade and immigration policy. He is a former director of the Center for Trade Policy Studies at Cato and former codirector of the trade and immigration project at the Mercatus Center at George Mason University. Griswold is also the author of *Mad about Trade: Why Main Street America Should Embrace Globalization* (2009).

JEB HENSARLING represented the Fifth District of Texas in the US Congress for eight terms, which included serving three terms as chairman of the House Financial Services Committee. Hensarling was previously managing director and executive vice chairman of UBS Americas and currently serves on the board of directors of Cox Media Group and Aero Design Labs.

HELENA KOPANS-JOHNSON is a trade policy research associate at the Council on Foreign Relations. Kopans-Johnson is a graduate of Colby College, where she received a BA in political science and government.

SIMON LESTER is a nonresident fellow for the Baker Institute International Economics Program and the cofounder of the trade law and policy websites WorldTradeLaw.net and *China Trade Monitor*. Previously, he served as the associate director of Cato's Herbert A. Stiefel Center for Trade Policy Studies. His articles have appeared in such publications as the *Stanford Journal of International Law*, the *George Washington International Law Review*, and the *Journal of World Trade*.

PHIL LEVY is a lead trade economist at the World Bank. He has taught economics at Yale University, the Kellogg School of Management at Northwestern University, University of Virginia Darden School of Business, Georgetown University, and Columbia University's School of International and Public Affairs. He has served as senior economist for trade for the President's Council of Economic Advisers and as a member of the Secretary of State's Policy Planning Staff.

SCOTT LINCICOME is the vice president of general economics and the Herbert A. Stiefel Center for Trade Policy Studies at the Cato Institute. He is also a senior visiting lecturer at Duke University Law School, where he has taught a course on international trade law and previously taught international trade policy as a visiting lecturer. Lincicome has written on numerous economic issues, including international trade; subsidies and industrial policy; manufacturing and global supply chains; economic dynamism; and regulation. Prior to joining Cato, Lincicome spent two decades practicing international trade law. He is the editor of *Empowering the New American Worker: Market-Based Solutions for Today's Workforce* (2022).

JUAN LONDOÑO is a senior policy analyst at the Taxpayers Protection Alliance. Before joining TPA, he was a policy analyst at the Information Technology and Innovation Foundation, where his research focused on immersive technologies. Due to his work in this field, Londoño was selected by the Organisation for Economic Co-operation and Development to participate at the Global Forum on Technology's focus group on immersive technologies. Prior to that, he worked as a technology and innovation policy analyst at the American Action Forum.

PHILLIP W. MAGNESS is a senior fellow and the David J. Theroux Chair in Political Economy at the Independent Institute. He is the author of several books, including *Cracks in the Ivory Tower: The Moral Mess of*

Higher Education, coauthored with Jason Brennan (2019), and most recently *The 1619 Project: A Critique* (2020).

INU MANAK is a fellow for trade policy at the Council on Foreign Relations. She studies issues relevant to US trade policy, such as trade politics and institutions, trade negotiations, and dispute settlement. Her recent book, *The Development Dimension: Special and Differential Treatment in Trade* (2021), was coauthored with James Bacchus. She was previously a research fellow at the Cato Institute's Herbert A. Stiefel Center for Trade Policy Studies and a junior visiting fellow at the Centre for Trade and Economic Integration at the Graduate Institute in Geneva.

PAUL MATZKO is a historian and adjunct fellow at the Cato Insitute. Matzko's research focuses on mass media in all its forms, from the abuse of the Fairness Doctrine in the 1960s to radical proposals to impose link taxes on the internet. His book, *The Radio Right: How a Band of Broadcasters Took on the Federal Government and Built the Modern Conservative Movement* (2020), was on the *Wall Street Journal*'s list of best books of 2020.

DEIRDRE N. McCLOSKEY is the Isaiah Berlin Chair in Liberal Thought at the Cato Institute and distinguished professor emerita of economics and of history and professor emerita of English and of communication at the University of Illinois at Chicago. She has written 24 books, including *The Bourgeois Virtues: Ethics for an Age of Capitalism* (2006), *Bourgeois Dignity: Why Economics Can't Explain the Modern World* (2010), *Bourgeois Equality: How Ideas, Not Capital or Institutions, Enriched the World* (2016), and *Leave Me Alone and I'll Make You Rich: How the Bourgeois Deal Enriched the World*, coauthored with Art Carden (2020).

JOHAN NORBERG is a senior fellow at the Cato Institute, a historian of ideas, and a writer who focuses on globalization, human progress, and intellectual history. Some of the more than 20 books he has authored or edited include *In Defense of Global Capitalism* (2003), *Progress: Ten Reasons to Look Forward to the Future* (2016), *Open: The Story of Human Progress* (2020), and *The Capitalist Manifesto: Why the Global Free Market Will Save the World* (2023). Norberg has received several awards, including the Sir Antony Fisher Memorial Award from Atlas Network, the Walter Judd Freedom Award, the Julian L. Simon Memorial Award, and the gold medal from the German Hayek Stiftung.

CLARK PACKARD is a research fellow in the Herbert A. Stiefel Center for Trade Policy Studies at the Cato Institute. He was previously a resident fellow at the R Street Institute focusing on international trade policy. Packard is a contributor to *Foreign Policy* and has written for *National Review*, *Lawfare*, *The Bulwark*, *Business Insider*, the *National Interest*, and other publications.

TOM G. PALMER is the George M. Yeager Chair for Advancing Liberty and executive vice president for international programs at Atlas Network. He is also a senior fellow at the Cato Institute. The many books he has authored or edited include *Realizing Freedom: Libertarian Theory, History, and Practice* (expanded edition, 2014), *The Morality of Capitalism: What Your Professors Won't Tell You* (2011), *After the Welfare State: Politicians Stole Your Future . . . You Can Get It Back* (2012), *Why Liberty: Your Life, Your Choices, Your Future* (2013), and *Peace, Love, and Liberty* (2014).

MARIAN L. TUPY is the founder and editor of HumanProgress.org and a senior fellow at the Cato Institute's Center for Global Liberty and Prosperity. He is the coauthor of *Superabundance: The Story of Population Growth, Innovation, and Human Flourishing on an Infinitely Bountiful Planet* (2022) and *Ten Global Trends Every Smart Person Should Know: And Many Others You Will Find Interesting* (2020).

GARY WINSLETT is an associate professor of political science and the director of the International Politics and Economics program at Middlebury College. He was a postdoctoral fellow at the European University Institute in Florence from 2016 to 2017. His current research examines the relationship between large technology companies and the US government.

ERICA YORK is a senior economist and research director with the Tax Foundation's Center for Federal Tax Policy. Her analysis has been featured in the *Wall Street Journal*, the *Washington Post*, *Politico*, and other national and international media outlets.

About the Cato Institute

Founded in 1977, the Cato Institute is a public policy research foundation dedicated to broadening the parameters of policy debate to allow consideration of more options that are consistent with the traditional American principles of limited government, individual liberty, and peace. To that end, the Institute strives to achieve greater involvement of the intelligent, concerned lay public in questions of policy and the proper role of government.

The Institute is named for *Cato's Letters*, libertarian pamphlets that were widely read in the American Colonies in the early 18th century and that played a major role in laying the philosophical foundation for the American Revolution.

Despite the achievement of the nation's Founders, today virtually no aspect of life is free from government encroachment. A pervasive intolerance for individual rights is shown by government's arbitrary intrusions into private economic transactions and its disregard for civil liberties.

To counter that trend, the Cato Institute undertakes an extensive publications program that addresses the complete spectrum of policy issues. Books, monographs, and shorter studies are commissioned to examine the federal budget, Social Security, regulation, military spending, international trade, and myriad other issues.

In order to maintain its independence, the Cato Institute accepts no government funding. Contributions are received from foundations, corporations, and individuals, and other revenue is generated from the sale of publications. The Institute is a nonprofit, tax-exempt, educational foundation under Section 501(c)3 of the Internal Revenue Code.

CATO INSTITUTE
1000 Massachusetts Ave. NW
Washington, D.C. 20001
www.cato.org